Anthology of Magazine Verse

&

Yearbook of American Poetry
1984 Edition

YEARBOOK RESEARCH & COMPILATION:

JASON R. PATER

ANTHOLOGY OF MAGAZINE VERSE

AND YEARBOOK OF AMERICAN POETRY

1984 EDITION

Edited by

ALAN F. PATER

Introduction by
EMERY GEORGE

BEVERLY HILLS
MONITOR BOOK COMPANY, INC.

COPYRIGHT © 1984 BY MONITOR BOOK COMPANY, INC.,

Printed in the United States of America

ISBN number: 0-917734-10-6

ISSN number: 0196-2221

The Anthology of Magazine Verse & Yearbook of American Poetry
is published annually by Monitor Book Company, Inc.,
mailing address: P.O. Box 3668, Beverly Hills, CA 90212.

Preface

Much of the world's finest and most prolific poetry has first appeared in periodical literature: poetry monthlies and quarterlies, general literary magazines, college journals, etc.

Regrettably, most of those publications have limited circulations, and once an issue has been read—and the next one arrives—it is filed away and rarely opened again. But the wealth of excellent work contained in their pages—by both talented, promising new poets and well-known, established writers—should be kept alive, distributed more widely and be readily available. That is the *raison d'etre* of the *Anthology of Magazine Verse*.

After William Stanley Braithwaite ended his much respected annual surveys of magazine poetry in 1929, there was a lamentable gap in the important business of selecting and preserving in book form the verse of the day. That pause was temporarily filled with the re-emergence of the *Anthology of Magazine Verse* in the mid-1930's through the early 1940's by the editor of this current volume, but World War II then interrupted the continuation of the series.

Now, this new series of annual collections is aimed at re-establishing the purpose and spirit of the Braithwaite books on a continuing basis, and thereby providing a yearly barometer of the trends of poetry in the United States and Canada.

An effort has been made to include poems of various lengths, forms and styles, as well as a multiplicity of subjects and geographical originations. And the spread of magazine sources chosen reflects these criteria.

It should be noted that the sources included in any given volume of the Anthology constitute only a portion of the total number of periodicals regularly received by the editor and considered for suitable material. Since the quality of the individual poem is the main criterion for acceptance, the specific magazines represented in each edition of the Anthology will necessarily vary from year to year.

Magazine poetry best represents the era in which it is written—it is current, abundant, as varied in style and content as the numberless journals in which it is published. Its topics are today's issues and events, as well as the perennial ones. New poets, who, because of the current realities of the book world, find it difficult to have their work published in hardcover, fortunately have an outlet in the increasing volume of magazines that print new and original poetry. It is from their ranks that the future major poets will emerge.

Also part of this volume is the *Yearbook of American Poetry*—the first and only annual gathering of factual material in this burgeoning field. The *Yearbook*'s directories, bibliographies and listings (to be updated with each succeeding edition) will provide a yearly record of information and reference material for the world of poetry—an area heretofore lacking a comprehensive information sourcebook of its own.

Together, the *Anthology of Magazine Verse and Yearbook of American Poetry* will, hopefully, be inspiring, stimulating, informative, and an accurate reflection of the state of the poetic form today.

Beverly Hills,
California   A.F.P.

Table of Contents

PART ONE

Anthology
of Magazine Verse

Introduction

MIRACLES—AND OUR COMMON VOICE

by
Emery George

Professor of Comparative Literature,
*The University of Michigan, Ann Arbor**

I have just finished judging, at the University of Michigan, Avery Hopwood contest entries in the division of Major Poetry—the work of young men and women coming out of our creative writing courses, seeking advice, some of them beginning to unfold. They are asking, in these manuscripts, how they can become themselves, whether they should be writing like Olson or like Hecht, like strident Allen Ginsberg or like fastidious Richard Wilbur, or like any one of a thousand poets on the finely calibrated scale between these two extremes. They have, I am certain, read their magazine verse, wondered over and over again about the secret of acceptance in places like *The Hudson Review* or *Poetry*. Wishing the best among them well, I go out for coffee; returning, I find two magnificent anthologies on my desk, brought to me by the morning mail—answers, as it were, to these young people's questions. Recorded in these two volumes—the *Anthology of Magazine Verse for 1938–1942* and that for 1984 (the latter in galley proof)—are testimonials, in verse, to the artistic being of individual poets, and also to communication; to the possibility of miracles in poetry, as well as to our community in song.

The two anthologies, both of them edited by Alan F. Pater, embrace almost half a century in the making of American verse. Here is lyrical bread made with the yeast of Yeats, of the warmth of Frost, and of the lightness of Pound. And not only is it true that, indeed, Avery Hopwood winners are present in both volumes—John Ciardi ("Museum") in the earlier, Dorothy Donnelly ("The Small Brown Bat") in the later—it is compellingly true that some of the best poets writing during these four decades and a half are participants in either of these two works. Among distinguished contributors to the earlier volume are such poets as Robert Frost, Langston Hughes, Josephine Johnson, Archibald MacLeish, Vladimir Nabokov, Theodore Roethke, Winfield Townley Scott, Karl Shapiro, Wallace Stevens, and William Carlos Williams; in the 1984 selection we are delighted to see the work of Robert Bly, Philip Booth, Richard Eberhart, David Ignatow, Philip Levine, Howard Nemerov, Grace Schulman, Harvey Shapiro, Dave Smith, John Updike, Robert Penn Warren, Richard Wilbur, and Marya Zaturenska. Immediately "below" these members of what might be called the club of our top fifty (Dave Smith, I understand, was a recent runner-up for the Pulitzer Prize), I perceive the work of top-quality younger poets, just beginning to be recognized (poets "to watch"), some of them winners of prestigious prizes: in the 1984 volume, Amy Clampitt, Sandra Gilbert, Lisel Mueller, Bin Ramke, Philip Schultz. Clampitt's work has recently been published by Knopf, Schultz's, by Viking/Penguin; Ramke is a Yale Younger Poets Competition winner.

The phrase "poets to watch" is, of course, synonymous with our future hopes for the art and for its best practitioners; where the past and the future join hands is in the strong suggestion that there are many more fine poets "out there" than can ever receive one or more of our national prizes, and many more fine poems than meet any but the most searching and discriminating eye. For, yes, that is what the critical eye is here to do—to search, to seek out the excellent and the very good, to give credit where it is due, regardless of the name attached to the poem, as well as to discriminate, to tell the

---

*Mr. George's official appointment at Michigan is in Germanic Languages and Literatures. However, he has taught numerous courses in English and American poetry, as well as in Comparative Literature. He considers himself a Comparatist.

gold from the rest of the ore. Anthologies are bouquets of flowers (that is precisely what the Greek word *anthologia* denotes), but I am thinking of another, perhaps even more revealing, metaphor— they are angels, messengers of the important truth that in poetry it is the poems that should matter, and not their authors. Pound's view that it is extremely important that good writing take place while it matters not a whit who does the writing, and I. A. Richards's classroom experiments in "practical criticism," in which students are asked to comment on poems unidentified as to author, drive home precisely such a point. And here are the two volumes I am looking at—at least one fine poet who is nevertheless not a star, Brewster Ghiselin, contributes to both. In the 1938–1942 anthology he has a modified sonnet ("Waking"); in the 1984 offering, a splendid sestina ("Flame"), making me ask about formal discipline, control, brevity. Embodiments of the principle that it is poems rather than poets that matter, make their epiphanies in surprising ways. In the 1938–1942 volume, for example, there is a sonnet by Edna St. Vincent Millay which, I am sorry, I do not particularly care for—too many *thee*'s and *thou*'s, among other features that seem to date the poem (e.g., line 6 "anear"); in the anthology for this year, we have the splendid sonnet "Commemorative," by Virginia E. Smith, subtitled "(*Edna St. Vincent Millay, American Poet*)." Let me quote its opening lines:

> Within an oval frame, inside a square,
> Her profile and her red-gold hair outshine
> The postage stamp, too delicate, too fine
> To risk to commerce, to her name unfair.
> Yet poets must go public now to share
> Her lyric voice along its classic line.
> She leads us upward to a towering pine
> Revealing transient youth, its fresh despair.

Experiencing that fresh despair, sharing in the music of the lyric voice, are exactly what seem to matter to the great majority of the truly fine poems by our unjustly neglected unknowns, printed in both anthologies. Among the harvest of the late thirties and early forties, there are such serendipitous finds as "Grey" by Fray Angelico Chavez:

> I think of grey and gray
> As different words.
> Gray are the sides of battleships,
> And grey are birds.

and "Excellence" by Robert Francis, a miniature *ars poetica;* here is the whole text:

> Excellence is millimeters and not miles.
> From poor to good is great. From good to best is small.
> From almost best to best sometimes not measurable.
> The man who leaps the highest leaps perhaps an inch
> Above the runner-up. How glorious that inch
> And that split-second longer in the air before the fall.

The physics of color and of excelling; the metaphysics of transience and of endurance—are they really opposed? Here are two tiny poems, parts of poems, the latter from the 1984 harvest, that provide very different, yet equally suggestive answers. Marcella Hartman's "Rejection Slip" (*1938– 1942,* p. 202) is witty; I do think that all of us who work with poetry should have a copy of this one pinned above our beds:

> Your soul, so kindly submitted for our consideration,
>   Is here returned to you with deep appreciation.
> No criticism of its merit is implied,
>   But Heaven is at present very well supplied.

Bin Ramke's "Syllogism" (*1984,* p. 400), one of the finest poems in this year's *Anthology,* is fraught with wisdom; listen first to what the Bible says, then feel that reminder of our mortality transformed into joy:

> Sing something, solemn boy, and press your head deeply
> into the flank of the cow while the music of milk
> deepens in the bucket. All flesh is grass.

Side-by-side with brevity, wit and the sudden insight are the tall poems, in either volume, poems that occupy a page or more, the great, discursive utterances in the tradition of Robert Frost. Frost himself contributes one poem to the earlier volume ("A Considerable Speck"); Frost-like there, without damage to the singing voice, are Valentine Ackland's "Night Driving," as well as Glenn Ward Dresbach's "Late for Chores." In the poem by Ackland, the concluding three lines strike me particularly as sharing in Frost's voice and manner; we are keeping in mind that this poem depicts a positive attitude toward the subject of its title:

> Sometimes I've wondered what we have to give
> That shadows want—watching them as they strive
> Mothily to the lights for the brief time they live.

Compare and contrast this gesture with those in Catharine Savage Brosman's poem "Cleaning the Shed" (*1984,* pp. 57–58), like Dresbach's piece, also a work about chores, but, like Ackland's, also wonderfully informed by wonder, and the desire to give. This cleaning-out job is, as the voice claims, "no domestic rage, / no charade to please the neighbors, / but a gesture to myself"; the "liens," the day's, the hours' demands on us being "less possessing / than possessed." And how not? Are these moments, in Brosman's lyrical language, "the gift outright"? And is the emotion Frost's, rather than this poet's? These are not easy questions; for the time being I would vote that a latterday modern who carries on a classical tradition can still be very much herself. Brosman achieves this moment of selfhood, as does also Peter Davison in "Fawn" (*1984,* pp. 100–01). And as I go on in the anthology, reading and savoring, I am grateful for the juxtaposition of Davison's poem with "The Dark Is a Door" by Susan Strayer Deal, crafter, out of a Frostian vision and subject, of a pronouncedly non-Frostian artifact: "We open a door of the dark / to enter a history, a memory."

It is Robert Frost who, in "The Figure a Poem Makes," the famous preface to his *Collected Poems* of 1949, spoke of the one great requirement for a poem, namely, of a subject that shall be fulfilled. Here, if anywhere in these two generous collections, these articulate lyrical symposia, we have that reaching out of hands, one anthology to the other, that sense of community, while at the same time sensing what the necessary differences shall and must be between two fathomings of the national poetry scene standing more than four decades apart. Among major subjects that the two volumes share are parents and children, family, the body, eros and love. As almost always, there are poems on farm life, on the city, on definitions of being American. One notable difference between the two anthologies is the high incidence in the earlier volume of poems about war, oppression, fugitives: on Hitler's machine, whether it wreak its havoc in Spain or Poland, Norway or Greece. In very few instances do we encounter open rhetoric, the kind of stridency that endangers the integrity of the poem as a work of art; very often we encounter energetic and moving lyricism, as in Joy Davidman's "Jews of No Man's Land" (*1938–1942,* pp. 114–16), or in Rosalie Moore's "Wandering Woman" (ibid., pp. 339–41), a thoughtful and sensitively image-laden lyric statement in free verse. Then we come to a classic: Langston Hughes's "Air Raid: Barcelona"; surrounded by poems that operate with exclamation points, this slender piece is interested in the power of words alone:

> Black smoke of sound
> Curls against the midnight sky.
> Deeper than a whistle,
> Louder than a cry,

> Worse than a scream
> Tangled in the wail
> Of a nightmare dream,
>   The siren
> Of the air raid sounds.
>   . . .
> In what was a courtyard
> A child weeps alone.

But loneliness and weeping are not limited to war; the two anthologies are not unmindful of our mortality, and of images of memory, of family members, especially dying fathers, and of grandparents long gone. Here one of the most moving realizations comes in the 1984 anthology, toward the end, in "Some Other Body" by Jeanne Murray Walker, a poem on the theme of the dead father. In it a young girl, attending a school dance, is asked by a schoolmate what her father does:

> "My father plays the harp," I said,
> hoping no one remembered the week
> in seventh grade I left to bury him.

We try to think of a man who plays the harp for a living; then in a split-second the awful truth comes even before we have reached the words "to bury him." The metaphor of the poem, the dance, fulfills the subject, and itself:

> But death is a dance we all finally learn
> practicing small desertions the dead teach us.
> I write this down to keep it straight.
> My father turned to face the wall the way
> a harpist bends fretfully to touch the strings.
> His arpeggio still shivers on my backbone . . .

But subject itself resides in an arpeggio, an iridescence, of suggestions, and this insight intensifies our sense of what an embarrassment of riches we are here confronting. Inevitably, too, it leads us back to a view of the present two treasuries of lyric poetry as having more in common than what may at first seem to separate them. In the above passage we have intimations of mortality, of love of daughter for father, images of dance and music, of shuddering and premonition—and above all, a sense of America, a land of school proms and of memories of menfolk departed all too early. These resonances make us ask whether that refractory beast, the lyric poem, does not live lordliest, and does not best fulfill its subject, when in the company of other poems whose counterpoint is clear reminder, across many miles of the land, pages of an anthology, even when the subjects seem distant, one from the other. It may seem strange to claim that Archibald MacLeish's poem "Colloquy for the States" (*1938–1942*, pp. 295–300) reverberates with suggestive emotional and sound values in Lucie McKee's "Brahms on the Woodpile" (*1984*, p. 318)—how distant from each other can two poems get? Surely "Colloquy" keeps its own eminently believable company with all the fife-and-drum-corps poems in the 1938–1942 volume, an anthology compiled, among other occasions, at a time when poems with overt patriotic sentiment were acceptable? And is it not also true that the Brahms poem has other poems with musical subjects with which to form audible chamber groups? Yet, strangely—or perhaps not so strangely—"Brahms on the Woodpile" and "Colloquy for the States" whisper a very similar music. It is the rustling of corn and wheat, the low, humming tones of the land and of animate nature, less the nocturnal cricketdin than muted voices under, let us say, a Midwestern summer sun. And then we remember: it was not unlike a composer like Brahms to listen for his music in the music of nature to begin with. And then, a propos of the music of the land,.and of quotation and song within the poem, there is such a miracle as "Ol' Bill," by Josephine Johnson (*1938–42*, pp. 240–41), a wonderful composite lyric reading like an ethnographic transcript. I must not resist the temptation of quoting the footnote at its end: "I learned these rhymes from a mountaineer who could neither read nor write, and regret so much that I did not take down more of them.—J. J."

One large difference between the two anthologies is bound to be a formal one; we see, in the earlier volume, few of the villanelles and sestinas that remain in fashion in the eighties (in the 1984 anthology, see the fine villanelles by Rebecca N. Bailey-Tyner and by Ricardo Pau-Llosa), and there is pronouncedly less rhyming in the later volume than in the earlier. Somewhat ironically—and with audible ambiguity—F. C. Rosenberger offers his "The State of the Art" (*1984,* pp. 422-23):

> In my youth, that far-off time,
> Strict was meter, sure was rhyme.
> In this, a more permissive day,
> Every doggerel has its say.

Perhaps. The poem represents a statement that—old truism—in contemporary writing, as in all the arts, we get the bad with the good; time is the great sifter. But viable poetics in our time, which encourages off-rhyming and suggestive irregularity in meter, constitutes the very countervention of doggerel. And in the earlier anthology, on the track of free-verse offerings and past all the "sure" rhymes (e.g., *desire/fire, night/light, fountain/mountain,* and the like), we come upon such a diamond in the rough as "The Swamp" by Ritchie Lovejoy. In the poem a Filipino boy draws a knife on three black boys and is killed; two of the Negroes escape:

> The killer stayed.
> After awhile he rose, walking slowly. Down the street
>   two blocks
> He dived into another alley; in sudden panic he ran to a garbage can,
> Stepped up on it, stretched to grab a brace in the fire escape,
> Pulled himself up to a window and entered a building.

This is heady stuff, good, strong lyricism in a narrative mode. We are reminded that William Carlos Williams, too, contributed to the wartime anthology; his vision may be different but his voice is not ("A Vision of Labor"):

> The girl lying there
> supine in an old rowboat reading an
> adventure magazine and the two guys
> —six foot three each of them
> if they were an inch—washing their
> hip-boots off in the stream jerking
> from the pump at the finished manhole,
> washing their hands, . . .

What wonder, then, that even William Butler Yeats, perhaps our greatest creator of pure song, counterpoints the occasion for song with the image of dreary reality, politics and war with thoughts of youth and love, as in "Politics" (*1938–1942,* p. 528), headed by a quotation from the political writings of Thomas Mann. One senses that this must surely be one of Yeats's very last poems:

> How can I, that girl standing there,
> My attention fix
> On Roman or on Russian
> Or on Spanish politics,
> . . .
> And maybe what they say is true
> Of war and war's alarms,
> But O that I were young again
> And held her in my arms.

And despite all, this seems excellent doggerel indeed. As always in Yeats, the aim is song.

II

Grandparent and grandchild our two anthologies may be, yet the child leaves home; this year's harvest is, if anything, a fresh and independent offering. One of the surest signs of its independence, in spirit and tone, from the earlier gathering (and, most probably, others of its vintage), is the vigorous interest it evidences in poetry in translation; *Anthology of Magazine Verse, 1984 Edition,* is surely a memorable international congress of poets. Whereas the 1938–1942 volume contains only one example of work by a European poet ("Psaume sur une voix" by Paul Valéry), here we have poetry translated from a Babel of languages: Bengali, Bulgarian, Catalan, Chinese, Dutch, French, Gaelic, German, Greek (both classical and modern), Gujarti, modern Hebrew, Hindi, Italian, Japanese, Latin (both classical and mediaeval), Norwegian, Persian, Polish, Romanian, Russian, Serbo-Croatian, Spanish, Swedish, Tamil, Turkish, and Yiddish do not even exhaust the list. One of the palpable rewards of an innocent reading of these pages, straight through from beginning to end, is that, as early as page 3, one encounters a poem by Anna Akhmatova and that, expecting other work by the Russian moderns, we are not disappointed; Akhmatova is joined by Bella Akhmadulina and by Boris Pasternak. The classics of twentieth-century German lyric poetry are well represented by Gottfried Benn, Bertolt Brecht, Stefan George, Georg Heym, Friedrich Georg Jünger, Karl Krolow, Rainer Maria Rilke, Ernst Stadler, and Georg Trakl. And here are some of tha great poets from a number of the Spanish-speaking countries: Rafael Alberti, Vicente Aleixandre, Jorge Luis Borges, Luis Cernuda, Carlos Drummond de Andrade, Pablo Neruda and Ernesto Cardenal are, again, only some of the important names. Then there are individual representatives of their respective literatures who stand out: for Polish letters, Tadeusz Borowski; for Romanian, Nina Cassian; for Yiddish, Jacob Glatstein and Itzik Manger; for Swedish, Edith Södergran. It is surely one of the delights of the anthology that it listens to voices that sang before our century. I am delighted to see represented that great early modern of the Italian nineteenth century, Giacomo Leopardi; and a Latin love poem of the twelfth century, "A Touch of Impatience" by Peter of Blois (in the skillful translation by Fleur Adcock) asks to be quoted. Here is its concluding stanza:

> Grapes are luscious things to squeeze;
> sucking honey's nice for bees,
> What's my meaning? Darling, please
>   accept a full translation:
> not in language; what you'll see's
>   a graphic demonstration.

And that is what these poems are—translations, graphic demonstrations, miracles. I am looking for the miracles, and am led back to an early translation in the volume, a poem by Gottfried Benn entitled "Appendix." Benn, perhaps our most important physician-poet after Chekhov and Williams, has not hesitated to depict the anatomical details of operating room and morgue with merciless clarity; at times the voice seems to mourn not the victim of, say, cancer or a fatal car accident, but some flowers left on the victim's body. Here, as in "Appendix" (p. 35), such seemingly desperate bravado successfully masks a surgeon of our feelings; mortality and death cannot be countered by tears. I pause to wonder at what an incredible emotional gap separates John Donne's holy sonnet, "Death Be Not Proud," from such lines by Benn as these: *"Ether, ether! Keep him under. / Who the hell can operate / On a man out walking with his gut!"* And, as if even this were not enough, this poem waves an ever so faintly visible greeting to one of ever darker humor, "Necessity" by Rhea Tregebov, a Canadian colleague of Benn's:

> As a physician, I can understand
> the passion for money.
> I myself, after four
> or five hours in the operating room,
> prefer an object that won't bleed,
> that is durable.

> The human heart
> is more than a muscle.
> . . .
> I keep my wallet in my breast pocket.
> Sometimes I hear it beating.

And yet, of course, it is not the end; the poem brings us back to life. Leopardi sings the heart in that other sense, and the poems themselves, for the most part in translations that are carefully sensitive to the tones of the originals, lead us back to our own hearts of darkness and light. The original texts could not be supplied; most of us could not read them even if they had been. But what attentive listener to period styles in verse can fail to hear, or overhear, the very clear differences, in this regard, between a translation of a poem by the symbolist Stefan George ("After the Gleaning," p. 167) and one of a work by the expressionist Georg Heym ("The Demons of the Cities," pp. 218–19)? This particular juxtaposition is of special interest, for two reasons: both poems are written in iambic pentameters, arranged in quatrains rhymed *abab,* and the translator of both is the same person—Peter Viereck, distinguished playwright, poet and translator. We thus have what we might call two control samples of the language that translators of verse use. In the poem by Stefan George a turn-of-the-century, almost secessionist, cadence is clearly audible, despite Viereck's practice of skillful off-rhyme, as in the opening stanza:

> We're striding up and down the lane of beeches,
> Their leaves aglitter, almost to the portal,
> And see across the field beyond the hedges
> The almond tree a second time in petal.

Now let us take a stanza from the Heym poem, one that also includes a reference to trees, albeit a passing one. The "she" of the first word refers to a mother in the pangs of childbirth; here the rhyme scheme happens to be *abba:*

> She's tossed yet anchored. Overhead, her bed's
> Whole ceiling shakes with howlings of the tortured.
> Red furrow—redder, longer. Now the orchard
> Brings forth the fruit. It rips her womb to shreds.

Are the differences between the two voices subtle? The difference in vision, in the use to which Heym and George put language and imagery, is not. George's peaceful landscapes are depicted in the imagery of withdrawn peace and tranquility and almost aristocratic privilege; Heym's city demons symbolize the anxieties of civilization caught in the thicket of the two great social evils, crime and war. But Georg Trakl, too, was an expressionist, and we have every right to ask whether his vision, alluding to nature, like George's initially peaceful, does not in the end-product of the poem stretch out kindly nature on the strident expressionist canvas. Does Trakl's oeuvre, in a sense, mediate between the achievements of a George and a Heym? Let us listen to a short, eight-line, poem, entitled "Landscape" (p. 501):

> September evening. The dark shouts of shepherds sound sadly
> Through the dusky village. Fire spurts at the blacksmith's.
> A black horse rears powerfully; the girl's chestnut hair
> Strains for the warmth of his red nostrils.
> The cry of the doe freezes at the edge of the forest
> And the yellow autumn flowers bend speechless
> Over the blue face of the pond.
> A tree burns in red flame; the dark faces of bats fly up.

And there is always gentle but sharply perceptive Rilke, with his finely attuned, controlled free verse ("Childhood"; "Dear Neighbor God"; "Like Water").

Here, then, are some of the great Germans of our century; but what about resemblances, friendly reachings-out, across cultures? If we go both backwards from Rilke, to Eugenio Montale, and forward a bit, to Yannis Ritsos, we will find examples for an existential (and post-existential) subgenre of lyric self-consciousness, each with its own distinct lexicon, but couched in disturbingly similar free-verse language. In Montale's "Two in Twilight," here in the translation by William Arrowsmith, there are clear lyric dissonances: the language of distortion, of the sense of being overwhelmed "by the power weighing around us," bewilderment. Rapidly now, at poem's end, the light sinks:

> . . . the words fall lightly
> between us. I look at you in a soft
> quivering. I don't know
> whether I know you; I know that never have I
> been so divided from you as in this late
> returning.

In the miniature inner world of Ritsos's "At Least," translated by Edmund Keeley (pp. 413–14)—a world that strongly suggests the lonely townscapes of Giorgio di Chirico—we encounter statues, which "too die if you don't look after them," and many mirrors, "hung on the walls" of the shops; "they mirror / one another among themselves," and here is the end of day:

> Late in the evening, around eight, when the stores close, the
> mirrors
> empty all at once. Everyone—clerk or owner or customer—
> takes a mirror and shuts himself up in his room,
> while in the streets outside the stillness of insomnia already begins
> to jell.

Surrealistic visions both; the light descends and goes out; here is depicted the sorrow, the tragedy, of separateness; there is no handclasping. Within the poem, this seems to hold sway; yet by virtue of such similarities—of the common task of depicting what deeply matters to all of us—the poems, and perhaps the poets themselves, achieve a measure of victory over isolation and loneness.

Examples are all we can single out here; the poems, of course, shine in their typographically and visually articulated singularity, in their truly splendid isolation, in the anthology itself. The search for the miracles, among poets known and unknown, goes on, and it deserves to be said that both eye and mind go back and forth between the traditional and the innovative, the bound and the relatively free, eminently between good translations (and almost all of them in this gathering are very good indeed) and original poems by American artists. I am looking for the miracles, for the fresh handhold on control in the voice, for the new twist, the sudden enlivening of a dead metaphor, as, for example, in Martha Hollander's "Venetian Blinds." The insistence that the scene the poem portrays is not Venice makes it Venice; the girl stands, "Renaissance-naked" and half-hidden behind the slats of the blinds: "It isn't Titian / Approaching the royal nymph to paint her // But a shabby man who sketches, a friend . . . ." And here are some of my other favorites: E. G. Burrows, "Anthology"; Lawrence Dugan, "In Memory of Eight Firemen"; Dave Etter, "Leonard Massingail: Fatherly Advice"; Ruth Lake, "Long Island Spring"; Philip Levine, "The Conductor of Nothing"; Laurence Lieberman, "The Mensch"; going on to the second half of the Greek alphabet: Peter Makuck, "Players"; Rennie McQuilkin, "Mark's Used Parts"; Philip Miller, "Blood Brothers" (no doubt one of the best cat poems since Eliot); G. E. Murray, "Winter Sermon: Northside Chicago"; Linda Pastan, "The Printer" (mistaking "Garamond" for the name of a dance I find especially suggestive); Philip Schultz, "Pumpernickel"; Dave Smith, "Bats"; Gerald Stern, "The Red Coal"; Robert Swanson, "Looking at a Painting of Constantinople by Paul Signac"; finally, Miller Williams, "Normandy Beach." And these are only poems that one individual singles out, without wishing to slight, and thereby do injustice to, a good deal of other deserving work on these pages.

Criticism is in good measure the exercise of taste, and, just as in the 1938–42 anthology we looked for, and continue to examine, outstanding poems (e.g., William Rose Benét, "God of the Young";

Lois Arnold Bolton, "The Farmer's Wife"), so in this year's selection, too, all of us will, I hope, find not only "our favorites" but a very considerable selection of poems whose selection and preservation we can remain grateful for. We are reminded, of course, that, just as this anthology is already the result of careful sifting among the spate of distinguished journals whose poets and poems it features (*American Poetry Review, Antaeus, The Atlantic Monthly, The Classical Outlook, College English, The Georgia Review, The Hudson Review, The Kenyon Review, The New Yorker, Poetry,* and *The Southern Review* are only some of the sources), the magazines have already accomplished the most important job: selecting and bringing to our attention what seems to be the most deserving work in poetry during any one year. At both the magazine and anthology levels, surely the discovery of new talent is an editor's most rewarding experience. The principle, however, that a major national anthology such as the present one keeps in view is that the "newcomers" are busily engaged in the process of arriving, and are eagerly joining their voices to the voices of those who are already there. Distinction, then, is only one-half the issue in the work of compiling and perceiving the riches of anthologies such as this. Distinction implies separateness, and the ancient idea of distinction in the arts is, of course, buried in the ethical values of our Occidental, Judaeo-Christian culture, which on a theological plane teaches that each and every one of us is a responsible mind-soul with a destiny of its own. In our distinction-oriented society, we are not in a position to quarrel with that fundamentally. But a great anthology such as the one that I here have the privilege of introducing drives home yet another important point, one that is neither opposed to nor in complete agreement with our unspoken assumptions about excelling. And that is that we are tied in a bond of community, that we share not only language but also critical concepts and notions concerning poetic language, and that one of the unignorable tasks of artists is communication and the achievement of resonance. As Hölderlin formulates it in his late Pindaric hymn "Celebration of Peace" (my translation):

> Much, since morning
> (since we are a conversation, and hear, one from the other),
> man has experienced; soon, however, we shall be song.

Anthology of Magazine Verse for 1938–1942 and *Anthology of Magazine Verse, 1984 Edition,* speak to each other, both through the similarities and through the important differences that would only seem logical in two national gatherings separated, as are these two, by two generations of aspiring—and in a number of instances regrettably forgotten—poets. But this is one reason why I would like to stress, in conclusion, that it is the poems that matter as much as the poets; the spirit of a great anthology is that the preservation of excellent texts in very realistic abundance should help offset the sad but necessary fates, "in the after time," as one poet puts it, of the poetic reputations themselves. And, in the midst of our search for the miracles among these already very good poems, we come upon the greatest miracle of all—perhaps the greatest, the more miraculous if unintended (as it must needs be). And that is that, just as the 1938–1942 volume opens (all but opens) on W. H. Auden's great dirge, "In Memory of W. B. Yeats," so the 1984 volume closes (or all but closes) on Stephen Spender's equally monumental and deeply-felt "Auden's Funeral." Indeed this has been a double festival of poetry, with the volumes, and the poets, reaching out hands, clasping, hoping to grasp, to understand. In tribute to the man who has the wealth—the true humility and love—to make the festival a reality, let me quote stanza 2 of David Citino's "Telling the Bees," a poem that pursues a metaphor of relevance, and beauty:

> Bees never sleep, knowing how much
> beauty would be lost to the world each night
> without their diligent love, how much
> sweetness to themselves, to those they serve.

Index of Poets *(Dates in parentheses indicate year of birth)*

Index of Translators

(Poems for this edition of the Anthology were selected from magazines with cover dates of January 1 through December 31, 1983. In addition, some poetry from magazines with cover dates of 1981 and 1982 have also been included, since the Anthology missed two volumes of publication due to the illness of the editor.)

WINTER IN MARYLAND

All winter, the snow shining,
I walked to school in a long green
Overcoat, hands deep
In my pockets, with sense enough
To know this phase of my life
Would soon be over; and while school
And teachers were useless,
It was an evil necessary to please
My parents and the truant officer.
                    Well,
I've changed my opinion
Not one whit since, and while
The pleading and beatings have stopped,
And my father's belt is not so easy now
For him to take off, I would rather
Have remained the child
Weighing the risks of skipping
To the drudgery of the classroom,
Than to grow up,
                    Armed with math and history,
In a world where the only true path
To wisdom is the one
We haven't yet taken ourselves.

The Sun   WILLIAM ABERG

SALOME

I scissor the stem of the red carnation
and set it in a bowl of water.
It floats the way your head would
if I cut it off.
But what if I tore you apart
for those afternoons
when I was fifteen
and so like a bird of paradise
slaughtered for its feathers.
Even my name suggested wings,
wicker cages, flight.
Come, sit in my lap, you said.
I felt as if I had flown there;
I was weightless.
You were forty and married.
That she was my mother never mattered.
She was a door that opened onto me.
The three of us blended into a kind of somnolence
and musk, the musk of Sundays, Sweat and sweetness.
That dried plum and licorice taste
always back of my tongue
and your tongue against my teeth,
then touching mine. How many times?—
I counted, but could never remember.
And when I thought we'd go on forever,
that nothing could stop us
as we fell endlessly from consciousness,
orders came: War in the north.
Your sword, the gold epaulettes,
the uniform so brightly colored,
so unlike war, I thought.
And your horse; how you rode out the gate.
No, how that horse danced beneath you
toward the sound of cannon fire.
I could hear it, so many leagues away.
I could see you fall, your face scarlet,
the horse dancing on without you.
And at the same moment,
Mother sighed and turned clumsily in the hammock,
the Madeira in the thin-stemmed glass
spilled into the grass,
and I felt myself hardening to a brandy-colored wood,
my skin, a thousand strings drawn so taut
that when I walked to the house
I could hear music
tumbling like a waterfall of China Silk
behind me.
I took your letter from my bodice.
Salome, I heard your voice,
little bird, fly. But I did not.
I untied the lilac ribbon at my breasts

and lay down on your bed.
After a while, I heard Mother's footsteps,
watched her walk to the window.
I closed my eyes
and when I opened them
the shadow of a sword passed through my throat
and Mother, dressed like a grenadier,
bent and kissed me on the lips.

Antaeus   AI

CHRISTMAS MORNING WITHOUT PRESENTS:
THE DEPRESSION, GRANITE CITY, ILLINOIS

It is 1929. The moon falls on the floor,
the pantry is empty, beans hardening like rocks in the cans.
No, you did not expect this.
The same cracked wall with its stains,
odor of your mother's cleaning fluid,
curtains with their clean hems,
blowing in and out.
You touch the bones and lumps of the chair,
the broken wireless with its dial, you pick up a spoon,
and it's cold. A clock ticks. The chipped plates
fill up with the moon.
You look back at the window,
tubes and vats of the factories
quiet for once.
The garbage truck rolls up the alley,
the bristles of the streetcleaner's brush rasp on the pavement.
Your hand closes on the doorknob, quietly.
You begin to carry the stone of your childhood:
The moon. The empty room.

Ploughshares   ELLERY AKERS

THEY DIDN'T BRING ME A LETTER TODAY

They didn't bring me a letter today.
He forgot to write, or he's gone.
Spring like a trill of silver laughter,
Boats are rocking in the bay.
They didn't bring me a letter today . . .

He was still with me so recently,
So much in love, so tender and mine.
But that was white wintertime.
Now it is spring, and spring's sadness is poisonous.
He was still with me so recently . . .

I listen: the bow of a violin vibrates.
Like the pain before death it beats, it beats.

How terrible that my heart will break
Before I finish these tender lines.

Poetry Now   ANNA AKHMATOVA
                                —Translated from the Russian
                                by Judith Hemschemeyer and
                                        Anne Wilkinson

FOR US TO LOSE FRESHNESS

For us to lose freshness of words and simplicity of feeling—
Isn't it the same as for a painter to lose his sight?
Or an actor, his voice and the use of his body?
Or a beautiful woman, her beauty?

But it's useless to try to save
This heaven-sent gift for yourself.
We are condemned—and we know this ourselves—
Not to hoard it, but to give it away.

Walk alone and heal the blind
That you may know in the heavy hour of doubt
The gloating mockery of your disciples,
The indifference of the crowd.

The Hudson Review   ANNA AKHMATOVA
                                —Translated from the Russian
                        by Judith Hemschemeyer and Anne Wilkinson

BURY ME, BURY ME, WIND!

Bury me, bury me, wind!
My family will not come.
The earth breathes quietly over me,
The evening roams.

Like you I was free,
But I wanted too much to live.
Here is my cold corpse, you see?
And no one to fold my palms.

Wind, shroud this black wound
In evening gloom
And tell the blue mist
To say psalms over me.

And help me, who am all alone,
Gently to my final rest
By rustling through the sedge
With news of spring, my spring.

Prism International   ANNA AKHMATOVA
                                —Translated from the Russian
                        by Judith Hemschemeyer and Anne Wilkinson

ONE HEART ISN'T CHAINED TO ANOTHER

One heart isn't chained to another.
If you want to—leave!
There's lots of happiness in store
For one who's free.

I'm not weeping or complaining;
Happiness was not for me.
Don't kiss me, I'm so weary—
Death will kiss me.

Days of gnawing tedium endured
The winter snows.
Why, oh why should you be better
Than the one I chose?

Poetry Now   ANNA AKHMATOVA
                                —Translated from the Russian
                        by Judith Hemschemeyer and Anne Wilkinson

FROM "NORTHERN ELEGY"

The grim age turned me like a river,
turned my life into another channel,
and drifting in it I do not recognize
my shore. What visions of things
I let get away! The curtain rises
without me and falls. So many friends
I've never met even once. So many faces
of cities might have moved me, yet in this world
I know only one city and discover it in dream.
So many poems I haven't written
whose secret chorus rambles near by
and one day will choke me.
I am forced to know the beginnings and ends
and life after the end, and something
I don't have to remember.
An indistinct woman occupied my natural place
with my legal name, and has left me a nickname.
I did what I could with it, thank you.
I won't lie in my own grave.
But sometimes a mad spring wind
or the combination of words in a chance book
or someone's smile suddenly pulls me
into an unrealized life.
Back then, something might have happened:
I could have traveled, seen and thought things,
recalled my past or gone into a new affair
as into a mirror, with a blunted awareness
of betrayal. But yesterday I wasn't
so wrinkled . . .
But if I looked from there

at my present life
I'd finally acknowledge envy.

The Massachusetts Review   ANNA AKHMATOVA
                              —Translated from the Russian
                                     by Mary Maddock

IN INTIMACY THERE'S A SECRET PLACE

(for N. V. N.)

In intimacy there's a secret place
even passion cannot penetrate,
even when lips touch in horrible silence
and love rips the heart like paper.

There, friendship, there, years of fury
are meaningless.
There, slow sensuality
leaves the soul alone.

Those who want intimacy go mad,
and those finding it are ravaged.
do you understand—why my heart stops
under your hand?

Chicago Review   ANNA AKHMATOVA
                              —Translated from the Russian
                                     by Mary Maddock

IN THE HIGH STARS

In the high stars: all the souls
of those close to me. How good
there's no one left to lose. And I'm free
to cry. The air of heaven was made
for repeating songs. A silver willow tree
touches September-clear waters.
My shadow rising out of the past
comes soundlessly. There are many harps
hanging in the branches, but one spot
is for mine. The rain is sunny and rare
and heals like good news.

New Letters   ANNA AKHMATOVA
                              —Translated from the Russian
                       by Mary Maddock and Willis Barnstone

PRISONER

Trees are the prisoners of their roots
Which jail them to the ground.
Birds in the morning, seeming-free,

Flit wilfully around
But evening brings them back to nest.

So, too, with humankind.

Though, on the surface, heart and soul
Seem free and unconfined,
We wake, get up and go to rest
As though to prison bred
In the same parish,
                    street,
                    house-number:
Even the same bed.

Denver Quarterly   YOSANO AKIKO
                    —*Translated from the Japanese*
                    by Graeme Wilson

YOU'RE MY ENEMY

I thought: you're my enemy,
you're my oppression and catastrophe.
But it's like this: you're simply a liar
and all your games are cheap.

On Manezhnaya Square
you threw money into the snow
and used it to guess
whether I loved you or not.

And you looped your neckerchief around my legs
there in the Aleksandrovsky Garden
and warmed my hands, but all along
deceived me: you thought I was lying, too.

Your lies circled over me
like crows.

Here, for the last time you say goodbye.
In eyes neither blue nor black.

But for me there's nothing at all.

How futile everything is, how absurd!
For you to drift off to the right,
for me to drift off to the left.

International Poetry Review   BELLA AKMADULINA
                    —*Translated from the Russian*
                    by Mary Maddock

DO NOT DUMP RUBBISH HERE

Rinds, rags, stalks, eggshells,
cans, wires, bits of glass, chamber-pots,
hulks of cars and motorbikes,
bottles, boots, paper, boxes.

Rats that make light meals of mice,
cats with all kinds of table manners,
filth on the patios, cracks in the walls,
clothing drooping on balconies.

Singing fountains, shouts of vendors,
arches, columns, gates emblazoning
famous names, brilliant centuries.

And among so much glory and so many rags,
as night falls, a hand that draws
on the walls hammers and sickles.

Poetry Now   RAFAEL ALBERTI
                                        —Translated from the Spanish
                                                   by Brian Swann

IN THE PLAZA

It's beautiful, beautifully humble and confident, invigorating
     and profound,
to feel yourself under the sun, among the others, stimulated,
lifted, carried, absorbed by the crowd, scandalously dragged along.

It isn't good
to remain on the margin
like a jetty or a mollusk that tries, in its chalky way, to imitate
     the crag.
But it's pure and serene to dissolve in the rapture
of flowing and sinking under,
surfacing in the commotion that pounds in the great, spacious
     heart of humanity.

Like the man who lives over there—I don't know on which floor,
but I've seen him climb down some stairway
and shoulder valiantly into the multitude and vanish.
The great throng was passing by. Yet his little poured-out heart
     was recognized.
There—who recognized it? There with his hope, with resolution
     or faith, with timorous courage,
with mute humility, there he also
passed on by.

It was a great open plaza, and it had the smell of existence.
The smell of a great unveiled sun, of wind rippling it,
a great wind that swept its hand over the heads,
its great hand that caressed the massed brows and refreshed them.

And it was a serpentine undulation that moved the crowd
like a singular being, whether helpless or mighty I don't know,
but existent and perceptible, spawned by the earth.

There everyone can regard himself and rejoice and understand.
On some sweltering afternoon—alone in your study,

with eyes wide in wonder and the question on your lips—
when you may want to ask your reflection something,

don't look for yourself in the mirror,
in a long dead dialogue where you can't hear yourself.
Climb, climb down leisurely and seek yourself among the others.
They're all there, and you among them.
Oh, strip down and ground yourself, and know yourself.

Enter lazily, like the swimmer who—timidly, with such cautious
    love of the water—
at first dips only his feet in the surf,
and feels the water rising, then ventures forward, and finally
    almost decides.
And now with the water at his waist he's still unsure.
But he extends his arms, opens his two arms at last and gives in
    completely.
And there forcibly knows himself, and grows and lets loose,
and pushes forward and kicks up foam, and frisks and trusts it,
and cleaves and throbs in the living water, and sings, and is young.

So step in with bare feet. Enter into the maelstrom in the plaza.
Enter the torrent that reclaims you and know yourself there.
Oh small, diminished heart! Heart that so wants to beat
and be, as well as itelf, the unanimous heart that carries it off!

Pendragon　　　　　　　　　　　　　　　　VICENTE ALEIXANDRE
　　　　　　　　—*Translated from the Spanish by Joseph Hutchison*

LOVE'S CUTTING EDGE

When I look at you, mountain or tiny rose,
When I hold you, blue mountain pressed to my heart,
butterfly that comes as lightly as love,
like two royal lips spread out in the sky . . .

When I look at your soft form stretched out,
your faithful dream where even the smiles are true,
body that seems to me a heap of ripened wheat,
golden harvest that sleeps on the ground like happiness . . .

I see your young face smiling without fear
while thin clouds pass before it,
and your skin feels the high-flying birds
like feathers that brush you gently and smile.

Yes, lying down, you never imitate a held-back river,
nor a lake with the sky finally resting in its depths.
Nor are you a sweet hill that comes to life
whenever the moon makes the earth's softness shine.

Your arm that lies resting on the grass
could be, yes, it could be something warm, inviting,
a sweet light that blends with moons
or cool stars as the night comes on.

Who are you calling?
The earth turning like a slow head
leaves its wake or long, silver hair,
leaves a murmur of voices or beloved words
that the stars hear, like a water flowing out.

All of your crystal, or love,
all the mystery that rolls on unaware of you,
all the joy that comes of speaking gently in your ear
while your mouth surrenders like a half-open sea . . .

Tell me: Who kisses like the stars?
Who feels a steely moon at the back of the neck?
Who understands that light is a shiny blade
that slices in two whenever earthly lovers kiss?

Poetry Now   VICENTE ALEIXANDRE
                                          —Translated from the Spanish
                                          by Lewis Hyde and David Unger

EVENING

Coming to a small town, alone,
five o'clock of a late-winter day,
I find every store I stop at
closed. Someone's sweeping, someone's
counting change. It's warm, a false
spring, whose lie I don't question
too closely, as I mightn't a lover
I was trying to keep. The sky,
deep blue, deepens, as lights go on
in old buildings. Lamplight funnels
up a wall, over a bed. A woman works
in a kitchen; who will come home?

Two lovers walk ahead of me, slowly,
as if they've found their destination;
but for everyone else, hurrying
around them, it seems anything can
happen before the settling of night.
The passing faces are bright, as I imagine
my own face at thirteen, someone kindly
telling me I'd be beautiful, be famous.
I think how people must live in rooms
smaller than they dreamed of, how
their faces gradually dim.

Eating alone, I watch the river
surge through town, high with run-off.
Dark and sleek, it moves under
the hands of light that stroke it,
like a wild horse, like whatever
makes me get up each morning, what

brought me here. Sensing the approaching
evening of my life, I carry only
questions, as lights in a darkening
world: Where am I? Where can I go?
How long do I have until night?

Tendril   JOAN ALESHIRE

GÖTTERDÄMMERUNG

One day you wake up thirty-one years old
wearing your hair like Margaret O'Brien.
Your face gets older while the rest of you goes
backwards, younger and younger each day.
Regret—something you never knew before—
sets in. Regret for not going to Kenya
in '69, regret for selling the Jeep,
regret that your father never taught you
to shoot, regret for all the hours wasted
explaining.

You start wearing cheap black nylon shorts
and lace-up shoes that hide your feet.
You crave peanut butter sandwiches,
french fries and cherry colas, so you eat them
and get pimples. The thirty-second birthday
hangs over the end of the summer like a tropical storm.
The prim suits and clipped hair
that gave structure to your twenties
suffocate you. You want to change, don't know how.

But that's okay. Change comes by itself.
One morning you find the coffee sickening.
One afternoon, you're hanging laundry and singing.
Insomnia is the only constant now.
One night you sit in the dark bathroom
brooding. Gypsy moths flutter at the screens.
In the moonlight you can see the freckles of age
rising on the backs of your hands
and you imagine that the tapping at the window
is your past, saying come out, it's time,
bury me.

Southern Humanities Review   BONNIE L. ALEXANDER

COMPOSITION AFTER LI PO

Me and the flowers,
the one and the many,
yet I am drinking alone;
so I lift the glass, invite Moon,

and now we are three: Moon, me and Shadow.
And though Moon cannot drink
and Shadow can only pretend—
still, they're company for the moment—
and it is spring, a time to be carefree.

I sing, Moon lingers.
I dance, Shadow scatters.
Still sober, we share our joy,
drunk with wine; we say good-bye.

O let us always be friends like this—
free, without passion,
expect to meet again later,
in the distant Cloud River Sky.

The Malahat Review   MARTA ALINE

ATLANTA

Arrivals—here in the hub
they cross and cross,
wirewalking the great lines drawn
on the world maps of airlines—
Northwest Orient, Aer Lingus, Qantas, El Al—
jumping-off sounds.
I am ticketed home
but pause, teeter for balance,
one concourse, another,
trembling with presences under my feet,
all my unknown kin
signaling, my baggage checked through.
It is a powerful drug to be
alone at the hub, choosing
the milesquare grid of Ohio
or clouds at thirty thousand feet over the Rockies,
shuttled blindboxed in rain into Manhattan,
warehoused in Soho, or headed north to the Sault.
There are men of powerful voice ploughing the hillsides
in Kentucky and West Virginia, poets
in the tidewater, on oil rigs in the Gulf.
I have counted my travellers checks,
written down four untraceable jobs,
settled on names to assume, before
I remember you, and choose
to follow my baggage home.

Chiaroscuro   LINDA ALLARDT

FINALE

The music was thrilling. But when we left the concert
gullies of rain washed down between those buildings
lining the dark street up to the subway station,
and pockmarked your naked shoulders as we walked
slowly, resigned. For a moment, I thought
of doing a bright Gene Kelly on the pavement,
but you looked so drowned, so unhappy
I bullied slightly ahead—the rainstorm too loud
even for yelling. There is a tiny passage
in "Tender Is the Night" where the hero, Dick Diver,
knows everything's over. Everything. And it's so simple:
a brief streak of sky, a storefront boarded up,
strands of wet hair plastering our skulls,
a thousand rainy windows to Far Rockaway.

The New Yorker   DICK ALLEN

ON THE BRINK

I come awake slowly
        In the blue room
                of my grandfather's
House. The cows are
Complaining now, lolling
        Heavily over their udders.
                The dog is barking at
Falling apples. It is
Five a.m. Autumn is
        Smoking in the leaves,
                Old shadows lean out
Of the trees and fall
Heavily against the barn.
        Color builds fast in the
                Fields, golds and yellows
Flaming in the wheat, the
Apples and pears shining in
        Their new light. I can feel
                The harvest moving in the
Trees, in the slow stirring
of my wife's sleep. She has
        Pulled a blanket of leaves
                Over us, piled them high
Against the winter. She is
Dreaming of her first child,
        And the brink of her harvest
                Lights the dark hours awake.

Passages North   JAMES B. ALLEN

DRIVING TO THE HOT SPRINGS

The buses show destination signs
that flash by like a friendly greeting,
and I want to honk my horn, blink
my lights, but that could be mistaken
for a warning instead of the spirit
of spring. I'm on my way to soak out
the aches of a winter's shoveling snow
in water heated by the planet's core.
If a little April snow from the hill
has slid down by the pool, I'll be tempted
to roll around in it, then take the plunge.
I was warned once that the shock could bring on
cardiac arrest, but everything I see
along the road stops me between beats,
like that cow wading right into the slough
to drink followed gingerly by her calf.

Dalhousie Review   BERT ALMON

FREEZE

Across the tall sky,
ragged and swift
an exodus of dream stuff:
shadows, white peaks, blossoms, wisps,
and rare islands of blue
where the stranded early-morning moon
will flare for a moment
before it dissolves into wild smoke.

I stand in the blowing dawn,
breathless, cold,
unable to turn away.
It comes on like a spell
of misery. Mist
swarming the houses and bare trees.

By noon, branches rattle
their glass antlers at the sun.
There's a glittering skin
on the statues, the streets
are varnished, the government
buildings locked in a bright daze.

This morning, I was lazy.
Now I walk for miles, thinking
To whom do we owe the favor of such armor?
Even the churches wear stiff coats and glare.

The New Yorker   GEORGE AMABILE

OBLIVION IS BIRDS

How quickly we forgot the flimsy world
insects put together from the rubbish.
Rain was falling on an old lily.
The moon went on and on in the wrinkled sky
it had painted a short while ago.
It left to grow again, pledged by day,
the archway laid waste.

How quickly we forgot the morning—
ancient writing undeciphered
either from left to right with butterflies,
or from bottom to top with a quill
and erased with amazing speed.
Maybe it is the name of a sleepless flower
in its untouchability.

On the field of the old roofs
how quickly we forgot the morning.
To immortality, oblivion is birds,
and the scarecrow with tattered pants.
Everything is so old old old.
And morning, the saint who wakes the birds,
turns to his gods.

Webster Review   MELIH CEVDET ANDAY
                              —Translated from the Turkish by
                              Brian Swann and Talat S. Halman

SUNLIGHT/1944

(for Jack Ladd)

In a yard near Brooks' Pond
In the lattice of turning shadows
Cast below apple branches
My grandfather stands. I am
Almost three, witless,
Yet will remember his attitude,
Its ease. Also sunlight,
The delicate ponderous movement
Of the tree above him,
Remember because he then stood
At the exact center
Of everything that matters.

Amateur painter; amateur
Photographer. For thirty years
I have not seen those
Tiny gray-white sunsets which
Were set to color by
His hand. A man of patience,
So those photographs,

Lavish minute windows, flicker
Their little intensities
    Past me yet, as if particular
        Landscapes seen speeding
From my Lionel electric train.

    Everything that matters:
Patience, the green-gold light
        Off apple branches. Now
He laughs, bows lightly to lift
        & clip a bit of ash-
Blond hair from behind my ear.

    This he will tape to
A wooden match & make a faerie
        Brush. That the clouds
May have color, the tree bear
        Its intricate lattice
Of sunlight, the child remember.

Antaeus   JON ANDERSON

AS CLOSE

I could stay awake for years driving the nighttime
streets of this West Virginia city in a rusted VW
that doesn't belong to me. I am alive in October, ready
to record the rise in the wind. It's because of the leaves.
How they shine from the inside with that bright light,
how they shift their colors from hour to hour, how they
traipse around the bends of the Kanawha like scrip
pulsing down to the coal towns. I don't want anyone
I've ever loved to leave me now. I want all my friends
and old lovers and the children I know to stand beside me
and push their heels with mine down into the damp ground
if it rains. I want us all to stand together in our red boots
in the early morning fog, watching the wet webs on the weeds
and connecting our strong eyes to their fragility.
If we should begin to cry, I want us to know it's because of the way
our shirt sleeves brush against our own arms and each other's,
as close as the coming snow will be to the stark trees
and the black branches it will pack up into.

Quarterly West   MAGGIE ANDERSON

FOR ANNA AKHMATOVA

(1888-1966)

Not being one who left the land,
You built nests of patience
        for three generations,

Decades you held at bay with grief
"That made the mountains stoop."

Through the 30's, 40's, 50's
You lit fires in millions of lamps;
  Scent of pine rose
  above scent of blood
As strangers clutched your hands.

Daily, beneath Kremlin walls,
You howled storms of prophecies
  As war bled from your pen;
But never did you masquerade your heart
In Requiem for Mandelstam and Blok.

The skyline of your poems remained "The Tower,"
A high gray house above the Neva
  Where poets gathered at Sunday dusk
  and read, shivering in shabby clothes,
Until light pulled itself across red roof tops.

 In timid hands, words are shadows,
  But yours, cast in iron,
   Repeatedly echo
    and strike the clock
     of our century.

event   MARIANNE ANDREA

ELEGY FOR DYLAN THOMAS

You did not disappear in the dead of winter,
But in that instant when you slipped
Into a void where something rests
That never reached oblivion;
Your mind held the last scar
And thrust your heart into all
Fragments of the dream
Your flesh had shattered.

On the edge of many loves
Against which other flesh hammered,
You left us with a guilt:
Where did we fail you?
Or fail to see that you
Were not merely one—
But all of us in one.

  The sports, the satyrs, the incorrigibles—
  Also born into a world of alien strangers—
  Was not the point to mollify or console.

And though it is a distant call to silence,
You are the heron and the rook above the waves.

           MARIANNE ANDREA

HOME POEM

The night sends another wave of breeze
up the curve of our necks, down the streets
into places already darkened. Assured, in fashionable wraps,
we can feel it this time and know from somewhere
the firmness of crosswalks, traffic going
that way, parti-colored shops and huge buildings
jammed to the grid of the city. At 11th
& Santa Monica we call it stylish, though
we're not the more inventive for saying so.
Beneath the marquee we are suddenly beige
in the beige light, a little dumpier, close together.
With this quiet, how our faces grow louder
and vague. Here, nobody shudders;
we don't take the risk, or it passes like tickets
through a hole in a window. At whatever distance
we are the easy invitation, a steadiness in line,
strengthening our avoidance and the other times.
We chatter, comb our hair, puff a cigarette, involved
in the movement, yet we can almost sense
the damp, echoing parking lot, the reach for our keys
around a quarter past midnight, as if we have no need
to be here. And somehow the river
is no longer too wet, or too slow, each member of
the expedition has already fallen
into depths of an unfamiliar reflection,
and we are sitting on a cold seat, *en route,* in our cars.

The American Poetry Review   RALPH ANGEL

TO MUSIC

Finesse of flute, richness of clarinet,
profundity of cello, give me these
your instruments, give me a string quartet
sure as an archway in its symmetries,
and I would move with your sonorities.
If I could answer to a metronome
and measure my effects like harmonies,
I too could close my structures like a dome.
But here I make you, music, in a poem
with words as common as a newsboy's cry
and as disputed as the legal code.
I'm like a child who whistles through a comb.
I have no tuning fork. These words erode
as rapidly as boys and statesmen lie.

The Arizona Quarterly   JOHN S. ANSON

THE BROKEN LAMP

The broken lamp was lighted by the sun.
The rays had so collected in the glass
that an electric current seemed to run
up through the hollow pedestal of brass.
It seemed a miracle had come to pass
until I recognized how it was done.
A shadow fell on the surrounding grass.
The broken lamp was lighted by the sun.

The Threepenny Review   JOHN ANSON

JONQUILS

At the ruined homestead in spring,
Where armatures of honeysuckle,
Baskets of weed-wire sprawl over
Old rows, twine up fruit trees,
Where poison oak thicker than adders chokes about
Stones of a hearth—a broken altar—
The jonquils have risen. Their yellows gather
On sea-colored stems. The frilled bells
Face in all directions, with a scattering of general
Attention toward the sun: now gone, yet source
Of their butter, their gold, this lidded day—
As if sunlight broken in pieces were
Rising from the earth. Like
Bright women abandoned in the wilderness.

Southern Humanities Review   JAMES APPLEWHITE

BRAILLE FOR LEFT HAND

(To My Translator)

1

The world does not close in your eyes; there
you are born, with the weight of one lip on another.
There everything fits, as in a room that grows emptier
and emptier.

You are not in your eyes. You are here,
hinting at presence. Irresistible. As if
trapped in a statue.

Someone buries you, forgets you behind
awkwardness.

2

Yes, the shadow is astute. The statue
knows a lot. But once again you touch walls,
faces; and the warmth of a cup creates
order.

3

Beside you, brewing words. Braising them.
Since you have not stayed on your eyelid. You are
here, in palms no gypsy will
read.

Touch them. Tunnel between these
lines, mole; make your little space; read.

New Orleans Review   OCTAVIO ARMAND
—Translated from the Spanish by Carol Maier

DESTINATION

With crime in streets and riots, looting,
With arson, hostages, and shooting,
And things on Earth not going well,
There ought to be a boom in Hell.
Down there, all over, there must be
Signs that proclaim "No Vacancy."
And those of us who thought we knew
Where we were going (quite a few)
Now wonder whether lack of space
In Hell, will mean the other place.

Pulpsmith   RICHARD ARMOUR

GRAND CENTRAL STATION

Odors from Hell's Kitchen & the Bowery
mingle with Park Avenue perfume.
That's America, boy: Equality.
Freedom to be down & out, stinking of booze & dope,
nodding on the hard benches
one eye peeled for the cops with their nightsticks.
The cops melt like butter against the Mafia
but watch their smoke against these bums.

Freedom to be rich, uptight,
furs flying heels clacking on the concourse,
tickets to Paradise, Connecticut, clutched in dainty hands.
Or in summer, dressed in almost nothing
to give dirty old men a thrill
as they ascend from the men's room
in urine-stained trousers
to ogle a pair of tits here a pair of thighs there,
grubby & quite content in their misery.

Downstairs they still have the showers,
fifty cents for thirty minutes;
but the old shoeshine stand lives on memories
attended by gum-chewing rag-popping wise-cracking ghosts.
Other invisible ones haunt the waiting room
where a plaque commemorates their sacrifice
in World War II which freed the world
except for a few million Blacks, Indians & Puerto Ricans.
But no war is perfect.

Beige wall lockers bang open & shut
incessantly, harried travelers hustle off to nowhere.
Underground, Amtraks & New Havens come & go,
giant snakes with luminous intestines.
One guy sleeps, another stares into the dark,
a third pops *The News World* out with snaps
of the wrists to find out who did what to whom:
That's America, boy—dreams, stares, curiosity, aching backs,
cigarette smoke, a long ride home.

Black American Literature Forum   ASA PASCHAL ASHANTI

THE CITY

I am not a nonpolitical person.
I have an opinion on how the grind stones
should be handled in this country.
I consider peace our most important concern.
But I don't want to cut the web of the smaller dream
with the scissors of the larger dream.
It is the time of day
when the tug boat Rex leaves for the archipelago
in order to fetch the sunrise.
It is the time of year
when the giant in Skinnarviks mountain
has bunches of lilacs in his hair.
Soon he will open his jaw and spit
a flock of seagulls out over the city.
I think it's beautiful, that's all.
I think it is human, somehow.

Poetry Now   WERNER ASPENSTRÖM
                              —*Translated from the Swedish by Siv Cedering*

HAMLET OUGHT TO DIE IN THE FIRST ACT

Say something, silent mountains,
to me, or to each other.
Talk with each other, simply,
like the women in the milking shed,
about the weather, about the wind,
about your frost bumps.

Every monologue consumes itself,
is choked and becomes rotten like the fish
that drank all the water from his lake.
Hamlet ought to die in the first act.
Say something!
Say something to me
or to each other!

The Nantucket Review   WERNER ASPENSTRÖM
                              —Translated from the Swedish by D. L. Emblen

ONE DAUGHTER SHORT IN VERMONT

How peaceful it is here without you.
Wind swims the trees
And down the deep rim of the valley
The night sky is a clarity of clouds.
The loudest sound I cannot hear is you
As if somewhere in all these miles
You were an infant just about to cry.

When you were small
I would have wrapped you
For a night like this:
A jersey sacque, a flannel sheet, a quilt.
Now, far away, you may not even be
Encased in sleep.

I dream you here
A stilted water bird,
Your eyes full of the pond
But even in my dream
You are recalcitrant,
Kicking at the fish that
Flow obediently toward you,
Biting at each placid aspect
Of the moon.

Soon we will leave Vermont
The way we found it.
Your sister will bring back
A piece of marble which will
Not seem so remarkable at home.
Your father will bring back
Three dozen photographs in which
No matter how he tries
You will never develop.

Years from now these pictures
Of the trip you did not take
Will bring back vividly
Exactly what you did not say
And did not do.

Poet Lore   SUSAN ASTOR

HORACE CARMINA 1.5

Pyrrha, what blade bedewed with sweet perfume
'Neath cooling cavern on a rosy bed
    Woos you today?
For whom do you bind back your locks
    In simple way?

Too soon the storm will rage; black clouds arise;
The sea grow rough beneath his failing oar.
    Ah, woe to him
Who thinks you his, pure gold and fancy-free.
    His feeble whim!

Ah, wretched they on whom you beam untried!
But courage, lads! I, too, put forth my barque
    (Ill-omened ship!)—
My garments hang as off'rings on the wall,
    And there they drip!

The Classical Outlook   GEORGIA C. ATWOOD

THE WORDS CONTINUE THEIR JOURNEY

Do poets really suffer more
than other people? Isn't it only
that they get their pictures taken
and are seen to do it?
The loony bins are full of those
who never wrote a poem.
Most suicides are not
poets: a good statistic.

Some days though I want, still,
to be like other people;
But then I go and talk with them,
these people who are supposed to be
other, and they are much like us,
except that they lack the sort of thing
we think of as a voice.
We tell ourselves they are fainter
than we are, less defined,
that they are what we are defining,
that we are doing them a favour,
which makes us feel better.
They are less elegant about pain than we are.

But look, I said *us*. Though I may hate your guts
individually, and want never to see you,
though I prefer to spend my time
with dentists because I learn more.

I spoke of us as *we*, I gathered us
like the members of some doomed caravan

which is how I see us, travelling together:
the women veiled and singly, with that inturned
sight and the eyes averted,
the men in groups, with their moustaches
and passwords and bravado

in the place we're stuck in, the place we've chosen,
a pilgrimage that took a wrong turn
somewhere far back and ended
here, in the full glare
of the sun, and the hard red-black shadows
cast by each stone, each dead tree lurid
in its particulars, its doubled gravity, but floating
too in the aureole of *stone,* of *tree;*

and we're no more doomed really than anyone, as we go
together, my loved ones, through this moon terrain
where everything is dry and perishing and so
vivid, into the dunes, vanishing out of sight,
vanishing out of the sight of each other,
vanishing even out of our own sight,
looking for water.

The American Poetry Review   MARGARET ATWOOD

NIGHT VISIT

When you live alone in a house in a canyon
Among dark forested mountain walls,
You do not expect to be awakened at 3 A.M.
By an arm around your body just under your breasts
With a hand seeking your hand.
You do not move, you hold your breath in terror.
Then, for sanity, for desperate confirmation
That this is a dream,
Your hand touches. *Real!*

If this is my destiny, cruel in the guise of love,
I must see its stranger's face,
Be sudden in lesser strength
And use my cunning to escape.
I turn: the arm, as alone as I, lifts tenderly.
Your hand as familiar to me as my own
Smooths away my fear.
This was as much as your uncaged spirit
could manifest this time, as much perhaps
As my mortal heart could bear.
If you can come to me again from that far place
(Or is it here pulsing too fine a beat
For our bound senses to understand?),
If you should come to me again saying your love,

Come to me in a dream and speak my name.
I will open an ancient door in my mind
And walk into that dream.

The Southern Review   SANORA BABB

THE VIOLINIST SINGS JULY

No words will do, unless the sound can sing.
The jasmine hums alive with honeybees;
I bow by dancing on the thinnest string.

Some think July too hot, prefer the spring—
But summer rain is best on dusty leaves.
No words will do unless the sound can sing.

All day, the melons ripen on the vine.
I wear no watch but feel the time through heat,
And bow by dancing on the thinnest string.

The sun has split the brown and swollen figs
And still we've more preserves than we can eat.
No words will do, unless the sound can sing.

At dusk I seem to hear swift, distant wings:
Only swirl of summer dresses in the street.
I bow by dancing on the thinnest string.

Who'd trade the summer's gold for winter's silver?
When petals only stir, we bless that breeze.
No words will do, unless the sound can sing.
I bow by dancing on the thinnest string.

The Southern Review   REBECCA N. BAILEY-TYNER

TWO POETS TALK OF DYING

Well, we all have devised methods of dying.
We fantasize our death,
theorize the startled second
when blood bursts, breath is arrested,
heart rests.
I say I'll die like Shelley,
drowning, since I rarely make
two lengths of the pool,
taste terror in salt spray,
flounder like a fool when waves break at the Cape.

But my ample friend Mac swims laps every day,
star-gazes the hospitable sky,
shies away from Thruways.
He says one day he's bound to be hit
slam-bang

by a Hostess Twinkie Cup Cake truck.
Upside down in a ditch,
his black beard frosted with synthetic cream,
licking his sweet lips he waits
for the sirens,
the arrival of angels.

Poetry Now   ANSIE BAIRD

YARDSALE

The state was new to me.
I let my car lose speed on its long climbs,
braked on descending slopes—

so I was not moving fast when on my right
I passed four men and women on chairs near the road,
the ends of forty years strewn about them

in crumpled boxes, rusting barrels, a pair of stained sinks.
I stopped, walked back among spokeless wheels,
corroded locks, playpens, an unpainted baby carriage,

old tables and books, wrinkled trousers and jackets,
balled-up scarves, a carton of unsorted lipsticks, perfumes,
face powders, rouge—and, amidst all, three large containers

of dolls' heads—no bodies anywhere, only stained faces,
lidless eyes, the great vents of severed necks.
I wondered who had committed these beheadings, and why—

who would sit in broad day with three boxes of heads
for sale, sun fading their plastics, and who could hope
for a sale, and who would want to buy?

Piedmont Literary Review   MARY BALAZS

SOUTH

It's true what you've heard: the first cattlemen
here ordered brides out of catalogues
the way they might leather saddles or hinges.
Light-boned Dutch girls, their necks ringed
with lace, or the fourth daughter of an Oslo butcher
who never managed to lose her faint odor of roast.
Sharing the dock with the rest of the new arrivals,

the silver and oolong and lashed otter pelts,
they must have squinted overhead at the
sound of those small oiled wheels that turned out
to be gulls after all, and tightened
their fists around the scraps of envelopes and
the smeared ink of impossible instructions.
Next came the inventing of faces,

cheeks coppered beneath shapeless hats,
faces they would have to learn to trim beards on
and kiss. A prayer in the old language and braids
tied over again. Then, too soon, the ride south:
the taking of the coast route out of San Francisco
just like we've done, the sea quilted on our right
all morning and no end to the

threat of rain. How much of travel is just this:
the sealing of prior arrangement, a movement
towards beds that have been made ours. It's true
what you've heard. In the dream I plan to have, I'm not
the name on the envelope but the one delivering you;
the one watching two horses swaying upslope between
shocks of lupine and yours not stopping once.

Poetry Northwest   DAVE BARBER

MASSASOIT

I share my kingdom in this golden land
with warriors of the world, no stranger here
among the great, the wise, the young and old.
How well do I recall the constant wars,
the misery, the stings of hate among
the people of this land, diverse in race
and creed. I yearned for love and peace and signed
a treaty, pledging trust I never broke.

O, brothers, too much blood at Gettysburg,
Verdun, and too much hate at Austerlitz;
and, oh, the haunting wounds of Viet Nam!
Deplorable, that Nature's richest gems,
its people, nurslings of the earth, drain blood
for peace that never comes. The ugly scars
degrade the stature of a nation. The sun
can only make the rainbow dreams come true
if hearts enlarge to circle earth and ease
the hunger pains of all humanity.

O, people, your words are best unspoken, vows
and statutes best unwritten if a trust
is broken. Betrayal stains this shining land,
magnificent in wealth of granite hills
and verdant meadows, a radiant land
of contrasts . . . Freedom fighting Tyranny.

O, world, the deed of trust is noble quest
of peace, and granted to all signers who
can learn through wisdom's eye that only this
will let this world of yours and mine exist.

North American Mentor Magazine   MARY JANE BARNES

RED LIGHT

Seeing you sitting there in the next car, I am violated,
assassinated by your style. Surely we have paused here,
not for the light, but for me to gaze

rudely through your tinted glass,
over the mounds of your barely visible
tires, above the fenders nearly kissing asphalt

to your black polished nails on their tiny chain wheel,
to the smoke from your cigarette curling about you
like my eyes, white on black.

I can't help but check my hair, and the informal
exhibit of my chest crowding the vee of my shirt.
I can see from your blouse you are well

to do with strangers. It doesn't matter.
Because every motion is charged: your gangster
lean, the studied study of every nail,

the blossoming smoke from your combustible
lips. Dear lady, I am candy, I want to melt in your mouth.
Your hand, even now, touching your nose, endears you to me

and I love you
as the light that held us changes, and you evaporate with your fog,
leaving me, as you always did,

with the wealth of your neglect.

Poetry   RICHARD BARNES

THE CASTLE MEADOWS

Late September and the grass is drenched in cold
Dew; last martins skip and twitter over the water.
The sky is stretched and seamless, and hills about the town
Are great cathedral bells somber with shadow. It's
Early morning. Soon the earth will be beaten down,
Last sparks of flowers and leaf stamped out
In the hedgerows, as the soil congeals, and frost
Crisps the brambles and grass, white oxide on the living
Metal. Berries will glow like dying suns, and birds flock
Like a shower of seeds flung to waste over the ploughland's
Barren ribs. But now in these late days, I quarter
The fields, searching the bright grass for the cautious
Domes of mushrooms, the brilliant tender white
That snaps off clean when I close its coolness in my palms.

Kayak   JOHN BARNIE

THE GREAT THEATER OF THE WORLD

Time is always losing itself. The past
is loss, the future never found. And yet
I circle ancient sites with an old cast
of grubby actors who invent places and time.
My time had come. Against the cold sunset
I gulp hot milk, ride back along a road
dark, my headlights gone, and begin to mime
flying Hell's angels. The bike flips. The load
of steel and plastic lands on me. My God!
What a farcical exit! Bloody death is not
choosy or decorous. Without a nod
from hell or heaven, I get up, an actor
inventing actors, comically doomed, caught
in time, a slob on stage with no director.

The Southern Review   WILLIS BARNSTONE

NOTHING

Until our birth we are our mother's age.
Then zero. Time begins. But I am back
to zero now. Not time, for I've a page
stained with 600 glasses of cognac
I've drunk to sleep. My start is solitude,
the strange divorce from history of a life
and family. Even pills don't calm a brooding
storm of memory. What is a wife
and child to solitude? I hold my breath
to act (I can't look back), and mutely walk
into illusion. From an unclean bed
I think of whiteness. Serifos. Good smoke
of seafish. Peace. A friend. The death of death
for I can dream. Only my heart is dead.

The Arizona Quarterly   WILLIS BARNSTONE

GOD

My act of faith does not lead to your sky,
to your sly world inside my world, to shade,
light, or wherever you hang out. You made
the others and yourself perhaps. Not my
mistake of birth. My faith is vague and dark
like a small coin that may, or may not, be
in my pants pocket. It buys me vague hope
of knowing who I am. So I can cope
with time, it buys me time. For ordinary
failure, gloom, half love, I wander a park

at night, squeezing it for a glimpse of the Jew
you sent down, the white Christ you murdered or
(if he was you) who killed himself. I want more
than our lone dust. I need another you.

The Literary Review   WILLIS BARNSTONE

A LEAVE-TAKING: TO SUSAN

("Distance, and no space was seen"—Shakespeare)

The bus slides over plains.
I saw a small creek bed
Furious with quick rains.
The desert is ahead.

Yesterday, when we parted,
The last hour was too brief;
And when the motor started,
Our only speech was grief.

But distance can't deceive,
Unless grief misconstrues
The mere fact that I leave
And measures what we lose.

Nostalgia is untrue,
An imaginary form
That, though it promise to,
Can never keep us warm.

Although I can't assuage
Your fears by speaking of
Ourselves on the cold page,
Words may embody love

Until absence recedes,
In time, and we retrace
Identities and needs,
Quietly, face to face.

The Southern Review   R. L. BARTH

FROM VIETNAM LETTERS

A LETTER TO THE DEAD

The outpost trench is deep with mud tonight.
Cold with the mountain winds and two-weeks' rain,
I watch the concertina. The starlight—
Scope hums, and rats assault the bunkers again.

You watch with me, Owen, Blunden, Sassoon.
Through sentry duty, everything you meant
Thickens to fear of nights without a moon.
War's war. We are, my friends, no different.

NIGHT-PIECE

In night when colors all to black are cast,
Distinction lost, or gone down with the light—
    —*Fulke Greville*

No moon, no stars, only the leech-black sky,
Until Puff rends the darkness, spewing out
His thin red flames; and then the quick reply
Of blue-green tracers climbing all about.
My God, such lovely ways to kill, to die.

Southern Humanities Review   R. L. BARTH

THE SOWER

Sixty seasons I have sowed, man and boy,
and I tell you, Matthew, that a seed
can not grow in the heart. No, one may
as well throw it away or feed
the chickens with it. For a fact, love
is something that only the devil
understands. I'd rather put my trust
in stones and reap a quick crop, for ill
or good. That way, you have no roots and
get what you can in a few short suns.
Or take cactus plants—at least a man
sees the thorns and expects to be stuck,
unless he's a fool (some choke on wool).
As for good ground, Matthew, that's just luck.
I've seen other fellows' orchards full
year after year, where no one's lifted
a hand or a hoe except to pull
the ripe fruits down. Some men are gifted.

Prism International   ELIZABETH BARTLETT

MARCONI STATION, SOUTH WELLFLEET

From this height and in this calm
we can see almost to Europe and the waves
come toward us like open parentheses, cupped fire
in their uncompleted curves. If ocean
is a word like *month* or *year* we use

to measure time, its slow erosion
of this cliff took longer
than the average life. Marconi built
four towers to send his invisible words
and what remains crumbles back to sand.

All the ways I had of trying to talk.
I set fires on the dark plain, clouds

ascended in a vacuum the sky built. Tongue
twisted with dashes and dots, arms
like semaphores. Some days I was a ship

in distress, the wireless stuttered
Mayday and the ocean drowned the call.
This need to speak out of myself
does nothing for the sun's dazzle
and spark, a rawness the season breeds.

North toward Truro, two boats
troll the quiet water. Whatever we think
the wind steals away from us. But the waves
flash back, electromagnetic, a measured silence
where words are unnecessary, and the heart goes on.

The Massachusetts Review   STEVEN BAUER

RING-NECKED PHEASANT

He appeared this afternoon, an apparition
waddling down the hill behind my house, an outsized
belly of a bird, lifting one scrawny leg,
and then the other. I went outside

to watch his feathers magnify the light.
At first he was oblivious, his brilliant head
jerking at the barberry, and then he turned
a mournful wall-eyed stare at me. I took a step
and stopped, and then another, as in a game of Freeze
until I could have reached and stroked him,
I was that close.

Instead, I bullied him, I admit it, waving my arms.
He stumbled into air and sailed over the ridge,
hitting the ground a hundred yards away,
the air he gracelessly abandoned ringing with cries
so strident and betrayed I felt ashamed.
He might never be back, I'd lost him

through my bluster, or perhaps he'd come tomorrow—
who could tell?—hesitant as a child
who learns the others hate him for no reason
and can do nothing but leave, or try again.

Poetry Now   STEVEN BAUER

NIGHTPOEM IV

If it is true that we are as we should be,
then why do we conceal our thoughts and yield
them up with such remorse; and why should we
be so shy about this rare give and take,

like the sea with its reluctance to give up
gold and rubies from its lime-blue deeps.
Why in your hands do you take my clay cup,
filling it with wine, as if it should make
us speak the things we have so long concealed.
And why, without exchange, do we fall to sleep
with ritual words and worn ceremony,
leaving our oak and pine rockers to keep
the secret of our unspoken harmony.

Kansas Quarterly   RICHARD BEHM

OLD DOG

What am I to do with you, then?
Half blind, nearly toothless, bony paws waggling in dream-chase,
you lie there, who cannot even walk
some days, when the arthritis swells your joints.
And on those days, on those cold gray November afternoons,
those premature, mizzling March evenings
when I carry you nearer the fire,
your eyes, your deep hazel eyes,
speak something that is not pain; your tail moves slowly.
We grow old, my friend;
you my companion, my fore-shadow.

Is it misery to be so, to be stiff, and still to dream:
to run breathless miles now only in sleep;
to be carried, carefully, like a full cup of tea,
merely to feel the fire's warmth on your trembling flanks?
Would you be out of this, then;
would you be away, dead, gone who knows where,
but leaving my stove-side vacant, incomplete,
your pillow put into the trash, as though you never lived,
as though our eyes had never met, before yours clouded blue,
our needs never converged these empty winter nights?
Do I love you, somehow, or you me,
or have we merely shared a time and space,
a cabin with a fire, some little food?

You have earned your warm place, your meals
softened in my kitchen, spooned when you cannot lift your head.
They are yours, and I should carry you always,
burn this house to warm you.
Do I owe you, at last, death? Is that dignity, finally?
I am your tormentor, then, withholding what I might give,
outside, with my knife, my gun.
I shall try to make you easy in your grief
for I am selfish
both for myself now, watching you sleep,
and for myself someday, some deep day, only remembering.
Sleep, old friend: I shall not be your death
though we share a thousand winters at this fire,

I gazing at your dark side, watching you breathe,
losing you at every moment,
grieving for us both, indistinguishable,
while outside the soft snow falls in silence.

The Texas Review   STEPHEN C. BEHRENDT

SOME PICTURES FROM THE WARSAW GHETTO

Pinned against the wall,
standing like a scarecrow
holding up the sky, he stood
the two rocks of justice in
each hand, his *teffilin* target
practice for the young Wehrmacht
hero, his beard falling down until
finally, in mercy, a crow pecked his
eyes out and they had to shovel his
body back to the earth.

Midstream   RUTH BEKER

JANE WAS WITH ME

Jane was with me
the day the rain dropped a squirrel *like that.*
An upside-down embrace,
a conical explosion from the sky,
a thick flowering of sudden water—
whatever it was,
the way it happened is
that first the trees grew a little,
and then they played music
and breathed songs and applauded themselves,
and that made the squirrel
surrender to nothing but the beauty
of a wet tree
about to shake its upper body like the devil.
And of course, of course,
he went out on that tree just as far as he could
when things were not so beautiful
and that was it: hard onto the roof of our car
before he could set his toes.

The flat whack of the body.
He lay in the street breathing and bleeding
until I could get back,
and then he looked me in the eye exactly.
Pasted to the concrete by his guts,
he couldn't lift, or leave, or live.
And so I brought the car and put its right tire

across his head. If in between
the life part and the death part,
there is another part,
a time of near-death,
we have come to know its length and its look
exactly—in this life always near death.
But there's something else.
Jane was with me.
After the rain, the trees were prettier yet.
And if I were a small animal with a wide tail,
I would trust them too. Especially
if Jane were with me.

The Atlantic Monthly   MARVIN BELL

APPENDIX

Everything, white and ready, waits;
Waits for the cut. Knives steam. Below
Its sterile paint the belly bulges.
Tiny throe on tiny throe,
The body's white cloth-covers shudder.

Well, Sir Alderman, here we go.

Like slicing bread, the first incision.
Clips. Bright blood, a scarlet jet.
Deeper. The muscles, unbelievably
Fresh and sparkling. *Deeper yet.*
You'd think it was a bunch of roses
Dumped on the table, glistening-wet.

Was that pus which squirted there?
Check the intestine. Still all right?
Nothing's nicked it? Dammit, doctor,
Don't just stand there in the light.
Non-clairvoyant, I can't see
Stomach-walls by second sight!

Ether, ether! Keep him under.
Who the hell can operate
On a man out walking with his gut!

Western Humanities Review   GOTTFRIED BENN
                    —*Translated from the German*
                    by Graeme Wilson

COME, LET US TALK TOGETHER

Come, let us talk together,
Who talks is not yet dead.
Ominous flames are rising
From our hearth of dread.

Come, let us say: this blue one,
Let us say: this red.
We listen, look, know one
Another. Who talks is not yet dead.

Alone amid desert dust
In this Gobi of ill omen,
With no kit-kat, no bust,
No dialogue, no women

And so close to the reefs
In your frail frigate:
Come, open your lips, tell your griefs.
Who talks is not dead yet.

Poetry Now   GOTTFRIED BENN
—Translated from the German by Francis Golffing

THE WILD HORSES OF ASSEATEAGUE ISLAND

Although the sign says
Do not feed the horses,

my husband cannot help but admire
their docile looks, the delicate size

of their bodies, and the ease
with which they nibble

the crackers from his hands.
He says: *Why waste stale crackers*

*when the least we can do
is make friends?*

They lean across the picnic table
and stretch their lips.

Losing its fear, a small herd
drifts across the road toward us.

From behind the dunes
a string of ten or twelve

breaks into a run.
The car, he says, *run for it*!

The home movie later shows
tongues licking the windows,

lips and teeth caressing
the hood. My husband's mouth opens.

He is saying: *Sign? What sign?*
Under the perspective

of wild brown eyes peering in.

Poetry   JOHN BENSKO

A YOUNG DOCTOR IN THE GARDNER MUSEUM

(for Elizabeth)

You sit down in the cloisters.
Moss speckles the marble basin,
the stone fish glide into your heart.
The fountain diffuses its cool smells.
Light polishes a turned hip, grey patina
on a vault of shoulder; the marbles
are clothed in flawless presence,
and the fountaintop sustains its kiss
while your hands remember

patching bones and bloody tatters.
In the vinegar light of the clinic,
you've done too little, just to do it all:
sent the sewn arm back to the needle
and mended legs to prison. The drained knees
are back on the job, mopping water
off the hallway floor; you smiled at her.

Their lives are thin floss jerked
again and again to breaking;
sometimes you long to handle
only the mottled organs spilling their histories.
Will you delegate, finally, someone else to pound
a drunk's tenth life into his stale lungs?

From the galleries' pierced arches
Saint Lucy looks down on you, her body
a garden of enamel, gown and flowers.
Surely it was for this
singing helplessness, music in the water,
in the marble souls and the tenacious moss,
that you first set to work
uncovering a robe of blood, a living ruby hidden
in the toad's forehead of our stricken race.

The Yale Review   S. BEN-TOV

A CHILD'S POEM FOR LUCRETIUS

Come, quickly bring the honeyed cup
That we might drink the other up.
Our time is clear. We cannot stay.
The bitters help us know our way.

Since love and warmth deny us room,
We touch the cold embrace of doom.
Diffusion, rife with void, beguiles
With wondrous nonexistent wiles.

We trust not what we cannot see,
For in distrust is surety.

The Southern Review   THOMAS BERESFORD

EVERY MORNING

(And a voice like Lazarus waits
to be told: rise and walk.)
—*G. A. Becquer*

Every morning
When I wake up
I raise a corpse
Lying in my bed.

From the empty grave
of dream I draw
a live Lazarus
from a dead Lazarus.

And with what tedious,
useless effort
I help to his feet the ghost
in me that flees from time!

Denver Quarterly   JOSÉ BERGAMÍN
—*Translated from the Spanish*
by David Garrison

AUNT IDA'S LAST EVASION

Home for Christmas, I
visit my great aunt
Ida in the hospital.
I had grown that fall
a large scholarly beard
that stretched
like a dark smile
from ear to ear.
My mother goes in first
to set the stage, shakes
my aunt's arm grown
thin as a spider
in a web of tubing
and whispers, "Look
who's here to see you."
And turning to the door,
my aunt screams, "MY GOD,
IT'S THE ANGEL OF DEATH,"
but in Yiddish, "MEIN GOTT,
MEIN GOTT," over and over
no matter how hard
we explain. A week later,
she's dead; by her own orders
attended by only clean
shaven men, a final ruse
to trick the demon
of the *shtetl*.

Foolish really, to think
he'd give up so easily
after coming all the way
to Worcester, Massachusetts
to get her. It takes
a *dubbyk*, how long?
maybe a week or two at most
to grow his whiskers back.

The American Scholar   DAVID BERGMAN

WITH MY DAUGHTER, AGE 3, AT THE FAIR

The wheel took us higher than she'd ever been,
higher than Daddy's shoulders, or the balloons
down the midway she almost touched. Higher even
than the back of a pony in a tiny corral
near the livestock pavilion, where her pure smile
also lifted her father. And faster, too:
we let the wheel take us, like pebbles in a sling
waiting for some perfect and final expulsion,
and clung to each other and the rocking car
as if we might follow the cow past the moon.
Her little buttocks tensed and quivered
on my lap, and through a stratosphere of delight
she looked up at me like a girl in love,
as if nothing mattered but trajectory,
faster and higher, never an end,
and holding someone holding on.

Kansas Quarterly   ROGER BERGMAN

PICASSO'S WOMEN

Yes, a clown in the tub
or riding my metal goat.
But the paintings were different.
They were mostly women.
Again and again
women.
Here my first wife, Olga,
in her correct colors
sniffing at us.
Or perhaps at Marie-Thérèse—
my poor goddess—spilling
out of the canvas.
These twisted limbs, splintered
features
are all Dora. That one.
Of the blood years.
Of the brilliant,

the terrible, eyes.
Here is Françoise, my flower woman.
You see the stalk.
Petal face with its edges . . .
And the clay vases.
Notice the waists, the delicate
elbows, the lips?
Even the photos of light
weren't a trick.
Look. You may see the flash
of a woman—Jacqueline
who was all
the shapes.
As if lightning had formed
her cheekbones.
As if the night sky lived
in her hair.
Her body—all full moons
and streams.
And such earths!
Where a man could put down
his brushes
and sleep.

Kansas Quarterly   JUDITH BERKE

THE DAY NOBODY DIED

The day nobody died was in other respects
exactly like any other. In fact, it passed
completely without notice. The sun rose, people
went about their ordinary pursuits, of love
and eating and conducting business, of trying
to be a little better or a little worse
—in short, all those activities that Auden was
so fond of reminding us constitute our lives.
The editors of obituary columns
must have been merely grateful for an easy day,
and some few readers of *The New York Times* the next
morning must have cocked briefly a bemused eyebrow
before turning to the sports or financial pages.

Yet something extraordinary was happening.
It was happening in Africa and China,
in all the prisons and hospitals of the world,
in the torture chambers and concentration camps,
on the battlefields and highways and home ladders,
in the metabolisms of a million people.
Many cases, no doubt, were pure luck: a stock split-
ing instead of a cancer cell, a pistol mis-
firing, a general altering his plans, a
lover thinking, well, I'll give her just one more chance.

Yet there it was, and it happened so quietly
and beyond belief that there were no instruments
designed to record it, and therefore no one knew
that the most astonishing event in the whole
history of mankind had occurred. There were no
celebrations, no poems written, the churches
pursued their customary pieties, no one
to raise the cry of joy, the cry of victory.
On the following day, things were back to normal.

Poetry Now   BRUCE BERLIND

HANDS

(to a First Love)

No longer child, yet socially naive,
I smiled at you who nodded gravely, then
Came close and laid your hand upon my sleeve;
We flirted, played a game as old as sin.
At length my hand in yours was cool and dry,
I did not know nor even could have guessed
The primal pattern surely triggered by
Your hands that pulled me tight against your chest.
I did not move away at once, instead,
I floundered in my careful stilted role;
Aware that blood kept rushing to my head,
I loved the kiss you gave, the kiss you stole.
    My hands pushed you away, you spoke my name,
    And afterward I never was the same.

Blue Unicorn   ILA BERRY

KINGMAN, KANSAS

I grew up in and out of Kansas,
out of the wheat
and the white heat of August
that bleached the cottonwoods bare.
After thirty years, it's hard to remember
which houses sang, which ones blinded
themselves to the sun.

Something forgotten remembered:
three silos and a railroad track,
the helium plant where my father worked.
The names of small towns
repeating themselves in the wheat—
Kingman, Wichita, Hutchinson.

My father sits at the kitchen table,
leans into the flicker and buzz of the radio.
A fan churns the air. My mother brushes her hair.

A fly treads oil from the butter dish.
Another town whispers its name.

Something remembered is not enough—
a bolted cellar door unlocked,
a black dog leaping in mad dance,
my father watching the green sky, waiting.
And everywhere, the wheat listening.

Southern Poetry Review   OLIVIA BERTAGNOLLI

WORKING AT HOME

1 NEWLY RENTED HOUSE

They hardly know we live here yet. The sound
Of wheels on gravel would be harsh enough
To prick the cat's ears up, to send him round
The house to where he suns on logs and bluffs
The birds with mottled breasts and those with rust
For whom he has no name but appetite—
It drives him to the useless hunt. (And toast
I threw to them is ground to dust.) The white
And listing mailbox we set up, the blue
and white rack for the *Daily Sun* both wait.
They hardly know we live here yet. The view
Lets in the pines and clouds in equal weight.
Deposits were too high. We have no phone.
Grateful, we move in silence not our own.

2 THE FIGHT

I went to find myself some peace beneath
A tree. The needles pierced my socks and bark
Caught in my hair, but then the sun streamed
Down to turn the wildness into a park
And warmed me where I sat. Cones all about
Began to drop like bits of thoughts and words
That I had meant to lose by walking out.
Deluge of sticks and bracts and chips, I heard
A squirrel nagging as he aimed the chaff.
To punctuate, he'd beat the tree and bend
A branch. Mock anger, how it made me laugh
The first time on that day. Until he ran,
I thought his furious interest was in me,
But I was blocking paths to distant trees.

3 WORKING AT HOME

Each morning I rise early whether nights
Were late. Before I write, I sit and watch
The hummingbirds that ravish in mid-flight
The stalks of pale orange flowers and the arch
Squirrels who bait the cat. Light comes in kitchen
Windows first and fills the house with clarity

I rarely reproduce. I give attention
To thunder mixed with freeway drone, offkey
And threatening. The sky dumps summer rain
On roads: bad drivers skid, accelerate.
Drops fall in patterns on my window panes.
At home and safe, I want to celebrate.
I move from task to task, a petty clerk,
Finding the cloud-filled skies the masterwork.

The Threepenny Review   W. BISHOP

WAVING GOOD-BYE TO MY FATHER

(Fleischmanns, N.Y., 31 August 1981)

My father, folding towards the earth again, plays
his harmonica and waves his white handkerchief
as I drive off over the hills to reclaim my life.

Each time, I am sure it's the last, but it's been
this way now for twenty-five years: my father
waving and playing "Auf Wiedersehn," growing
thin and blue as a late summer iris, while I,
who have the heart for love but not the voice for it,
disappear into the day, wiping the salt from my cheeks
and thinking of women. There is no frenzy
like the frenzy of his happiness, and frenzy, I know now,
is never happiness: only the loud, belated cacophony
of a lost soul having its last dance before it sleeps forever.

The truth, which always hurts, hurts now:
I have always wanted another father—one
who would sit quietly beneath the moonlight, and in
the clean, quiet emanations of some essential manhood,
speak to me of what, now a kind of man myself,
I wanted to hear.

But this is not a poem about self-pity.

As I drive off, some deep, masculine quiet rises,
of its own accord, from beneath my shoes. I turn
to watch my father's white handkerchief flutter,
like an old Hasid's worn prayer shawl, among
the dark clouds and the trees. I drive out
into the clean, quiet resonance of my own life.
To live, dear father, *is to forgive*. And I forgive.

The American Scholar   MICHAEL BLUMENTHAL

THERE ARE FIERY DAYS . . .

But I love you also in slow, dim-witted ways; we pass
the slow afternoon hibernating together . . .
one or two words spoken, and tears run down.

The quivering wings of the winter ant
wait so for winter to end; and there are tidal creatures
who know whether the other is there or not
restless all night on the Carolina marshes
under the quiet moon, almost no sound at all.

Ploughshares   ROBERT BLY

FARMLAND AFTER RAIN

These fields are ready now,
rain-runneled, brown-black in the evening air,
          and waiting for
the long clean cut-lines of the coming plough
          to make them look less bare.
          Somehow before

the single first seed sinks
into this acreage, its future shoots
          tickle the sense,
thrusting their nascent tips through mud that drinks
          the rain, as do their roots.
          What is as dense

as what cannot be seen?
Here a potential thicket is more lush
          than a real plain
is flat, and an expectancy of green
          suffuses the brown rush
          of April rain.

Just so, away from you,
I sense a presence absence can't erase.
          Think of it thus:
it is the gold-green dust of something new
          spread on the fields' brown face,
          eluding us.

Poem   BRUCE BOEHRER

EAVESDROPPING

It was Mrs. Garvin, the doctor's wife,
who told my mother, Well, if you're that broke,
put the kids up for adoption.
Out under the porch light that summer,
we slapped at mosquitoes and invented
our brave escape—luminous sheets
knotted out the window
were the lines of a highway down the house.
We would know the way,
like ingenious animals, to go
quietly toward the river,

but we could imagine no further
than the shacks on stilts
shivering the water,
the Kentucky hills on the other side.
Denise, the youngest, took to sleepwalking,
wading room to room for the place
one of us—curled up in a bed's corner—
might have left her. I'd wake
to her face pressed against my back,
her hands reining the edges of my nightgown.
I didn't tuck her into my shoulder
but loosened her fingers and led her
back to her own bed, her fear
already seeping into me like water
or like the light spilling
from the milk truck
as it backfired down the street.

The Georgia Review   MICHELLE BOISSEAU

FIREFLIES

Tonight, crossing the street,
I saw them as I had not for years
Here-and-gone for all the world
Like a madrigal, or the camera's
Quick click, these delicate ornaments
Of lawns up the hill.

I had read *Pale Fire*, knew
Indian Lore, but thought
Only of Cousin Royce, tutor in cruelty
Through my primary years, and how he taught
That their light could be separate, could hang
from ears and ring our throats
Not pale at all: how, disembodied, they
could disembody till we hung apart,
Faces only, floating in the dark.

The Threepenny Review   CHARLES E. BOLTON

PLAIN SPEECH

There are two great things: in the day, work;
in the night, heartbeats. Against these is the grave.
Not the sensory qualities of its earth lining,
but the isolation of the hole itself, the non-place.
In the day, love is as unseen as the sun;
it simply illumines with a general light.
In the dark, like the stars, it draws attention as it
    becomes particular.
Work is as unnoticed in the night as sleep;

the shadows which made the day's forms distinct
have come to a fullness, one that love rides.
The earth turns as imperceptibly as the sonnet
used to do; it's come about now.
Mouths touch and separate, feet feel the floor.
From the center, gravity holds everything down.

Southern Poetry Review   PAULA BONNELL

PROCESSION

A white-throat flicked into the sunset window.
How small a thing to bury: his short neck limp,
eye perfectly blank, the feathers warm in my hand.

Nothing left now to whistle *Old Sam Peabody,*
Peabody, Peabody . . . The rest in their thickets,
knowing to go. The winter stars coming. Out early

this morning I see Orion, the first time this fall,
Aldebaran brilliant in Taurus, the Dipper's
handle tipped down toward daybreak. As sun-up

dims Venus, I walk the first frost out into ground fog,
as it happens. Slowly, it comes to me: today
would be father's 85th birthday. I hear

today's birds in the cedars, woken, knowing to go.
I think of a boy years beyond me, back in Council Bluffs,
a boy with father's name, out on a third-floor porch

after midnight, without knowing why, watching (he must
have told me hundreds of times) against his own horizon
these same winter stars beginning to show.

The Hudson Review   PHILIP BOOTH

TO THINK

Suppose the astronomers right:
the original bang, the cosmos

expanding: a fraction less
expansion, the universe would

have collapsed; a fraction more,
gravity wouldn't have held its

stars. But luck, if it was,
made possible biota. We began

to evolve toward wonder: man
on earth. But what if we alone

are conscious, if outside us
there is no measure of our

complexity? Who else could
believe the ways we invent

to see ourselves across time,
to hear across distance, to fire

ourselves into unbreathable sky?
Fire stations, curtainrods,

dogs, zoos, the traffic
down school steps to recess,

the beds we make kids in, the streams
we dam; who, in a cosmos

empty of us, could account for
twi-night baseball or why

we bid Two No Trump or name
a trout fly Blue Cupsuptic?

If only we diagram stars,
and dream them into daylight

as signs of our meaning, as
proof of intent, or hope of

reason beyond our own, what
reason have we to imagine

that anyone might imagine us?
Who, for Christ's sake?

Until we invented God,
who could believe? We love

to believe, we have to believe
we love. But to think:

after we go, in the last
millisecond when boats,

Chicago, tulip beds,
wolves caged in Stuttgart,

incubators, and condoms
all blow, that the planet

will be beyond wonder, without
wonder what we were ever about.

The American Scholar   PHILIP BOOTH

THE NIGHTINGALE

In what secret night out of England
Or from the constant incalculable Rhine,
Lost among the nights of my nights,
Could your voice charged with mythologies
Have reached my unknowing ear,
Nightingale of Virgil or the Persians?

Perhaps I never heard you, but your life
And mine are joined inseparably.
Your symbol was a wandering spirit
In a book of riddles. The Sea
Nicknamed you siren of the forests
And you sing in Juliet's evening
And on the intricate Latin page
And from the pine groves of the other
Nightingale of Judea and Germany,
Heine joking, on fire, sad.
Keats heard you for everyone, forever.
Among the bright names the peoples
Of the earth have given you,
Not one is unworthy of your music,
Nightingale of the Darkness. The Moslem
Dreamed you in a rage of ecstacy,
His chest pierced by the thorn
Of the rose sun that reddens
With your deepest blood. Assiduously
In the evening I scheme this exercise,
Nightingale of the sand and of the seas.
In memory, in exaltation, in fable,
You burn with love and die melodiously.

Denver Quarterly   JORGE LUIS BORGES
                                —Translated from the Spanish by Willis Barnstone

AUSCHWITZ SUN

You remember the Auschwitz sun
and the far green of fields lightly
lifted by birds into the clouds
but not green yet and in the clouds
a whitish aquamarine. Together,
we stood looking into the distance, feeling
the far green of fields and the clouds'
white aquamarine, as if looking into ourselves,
as if the color of distant fields
were our blood or the pulse
beating in us, as if the world
existed only through us and could never
fail, while we were. I remember
your smile, slippery
as a shade, the color of the wind
that shakes a leaf on the verge
of sun and shadow, but continually
changes and remains. So are you today
for me: through the aquamarine
of the sky, through green and a wind
shaking a leaf. You are
my blood and my pulse. I can feel
you in each shadow, in each movement,
and so you surround me with the world

as if with your arms, so I feel the world
like your body. With the whole world
you look in my face, you call me.

Webster Review   Tadeusz Borowski
                              —Translated from the Polish by Addison Bross

PHOENIX RAIN

At last, the rain. I wonder if its wings
will green the city dump, that open grave
of leftovers and old unwanted things
too tough to shred or burn, too spent to save.
What if a sudden fuse of rainfed grass
like cool green fire ran zigzag down a mound
of rags and bottles, and lit the broken glass
and broken bits of lives and barren ground
itself with flares of wild unpatterned hue—
nasturtium bronze and yellow, poppy gold,
hot pink of fireweed, lupine's purple-blue—
and a million green flamboyant leaves unrolled?
What if all that melancholy plain
should blaze to life, a phoenix of the rain?

Blue Unicorn   Martha Bosworth

TURNING THE DOUBLE PLAY

(for Doug Fowler)

In the noon-swelter, dust
hanging over the infield like red fog, we stand at the edge
of the grass and watch the ball draw white arcs
toward home, the umpire easing back on his heels,
a coach behind the backstop
second-guessing.

In the oak shade behind third base, our wives
sit in lawn chairs and guard our cooler of Gatorade.
They wonder why we never win,
and why we seem content to stand out here at the edge
of middle age and watch the hits line into the outfield.
They say, the teams you play are so young.

Yes, they are. And some runner's always on first,
the heat rising in waves off the cracked dirt, the bat
a blur and a white shot toward short. And yet
when the double play is finally turned, the way we both
turned it years ago on different teams in different leagues,
something is won back for a moment,
no matter what the score.

The Virginia Quarterly Review   David Bottoms

HANDS

Hands don't go blind. It's where
we begin. They know
that what fits in the palm, say a stone

or a shell, becomes vast as a city.
Hands are what we need for a journey,
fresh water springs

for the thirsty,
tents to shield the head from weather.
Without words, they tell us

what we want to hear. When they flow
around a table they are a river
rising above its banks.

Poised in mid-air, the hands
want to believe,
hold a bird or a feather.

While we sleep, they stretch out into
the towns of our childhood,
gather an odor of leaves and rain.

The Literary Review   MARGUERITE G. BOUVARD

MY FATHER'S BEST PICTURE

My mother and brother and I stand
perfectly still, holding our breath
and everything for the shutter.
Our smiles say it is all right
to wear 1950's styles forever
on this black and white lawn
where the bird never sings,
never flies from his tree.
We are looking at my father
as he slowly frames and focuses.

If you could look deep into our eyes
you would see him reflected there,
his head bowed over the black box camera,
trying hard to get it right.

Look deeper and you'll see him laugh,
taking another step backward,
almost trampling the brilliant irises.
The wind that makes his cheeks blush
blows his tie across his shoulder
like a blue scarf, rocks
the limbs of the budding maple.
From somewhere a chickadee calls.

On his side the world is all
sound and color; everything's in motion,
and he keeps saying over and over again
that we should "Hold it!"—"Hold it!"
as he moves across the lawn
making infinite adjustments,
saved forever from our small extinction.

Great River Review   NEAL BOWERS

VOYEUR

All day long I watch the women walk:
Their brown legs disappear beneath their skirts.
          Rain is in the air.
Their hair slants thickly, like grass after rain.

Beneath their loose clothes I feel the brush
Of skin and cloth, the soft molded palate
          Of ribs ascending
With each breath they take, like sand under water.

Everywhere the air is heavy with their smell,
Like air loaded with rain. Far away, lightning
          Dances on a dry hill.
I am waiting for rain where the rain never falls.

Southern Humanities Review   P. C. BOWMAN

DEPARTURES

1
After you left,
I stood in the yard, drank a beer,
watched the banks of lilacs burn
through the hot afternoon. Bees sang
in the vanishing blossoms.

Later, I walked to Green Lake;
sunlight spread like gold
leaf across the water. Then
it was evening. And then it was night.

Where my lamp burns now in the window, wings
tick against the glass. I sit here listening
in the stillness of summer.

2
Five years ago I stood beside my father's bed,
watched him dying in his heart. He said:
Come closer, closer, and slipped back
into his final dream. I still do not believe
he spoke to me, but to some vision

of life that had escaped him. As he lay there
sleeping, I kissed his eyes. I tell you
because we die.

3
Sometimes, on my way to the lake or the garden,
I pass through the deep shade
beneath the oak and pine beside the barn.
Sometimes I pause,
there where the air is cooler, and imagine
this is how my ghost will see the world,
staring out of the shadow in which he must live forever
into the light that livens every blade of grass
and makes the dusty road seem golden.
I think he will weep and shake his head and yearn
to feel that warmth, forgetting,
even as I do now,
the sorrows that lead us into darkness.

Passages North   NICK BOZANIC

THE BURNING OF BOOKS

When the Regime decreed that books with dangerous thoughts
Should be burned at the stake, and everywhere oxen were yoked
To draw cartsful of books to the pyre, an exile poet
—One of the best—saw with rage, when he studied the list
Of the burnt, that his books had been missed.

                             He roared to his desk
And he wrote to those in power:
"Burn me," he splashed with his pen, "burn me!
"Don't treat me this way! Don't leave me out. Haven't I always
"Told the truth in my books? And now you
"Treat me like a liar.
                 I order you:
"BURN ME!"

Poetry Now   BERTOLT BRECHT
                               —Translated from the German by John Pauker

CALLING MY GRANDMOTHER FROM NEW YORK

The thin wire of her voice
shivers and fails, and between her words
she is a steady wishing, a sound
the white froth of water makes, tossed
back over a line of rocks,
a quiet insistence that keeps on going.

She says her feet hurt her
and she cannot hear me, two thousand
miles away, calling her from a place
she cannot imagine, lifting her from a sleep

that carries her each night
closer to something she fears beyond all else.

Today she has done mostly
the small few needful things that keep
her buoyant against the long waves
of silence swelling beneath her, moving her
with a dizzying and final intensity.
But what can I say to make it any easier?

She has become a strange fish,
lucid and small in the cool river of her body,
schooled here for so long she remembers,
without knowing, where the undercurrents
draw her, eddied for a moment now,
listening to a voice at the other end of her life.

Poetry   JOHN BREHM

IN MEMORY OF MY GRANDFATHER

(1883-1972)

I have a photograph Dad took in 1957
of Pop and me sharing an armchair and showing
the same complacent, incipient smile—
as if he knew some secret and, without a single
syllable or motion, had impressed it on my mind.

I've never remembered posing for that picture,
parting my lips to inhale the breath he just sighed—
but engraved in time, like Dürer woodcuts,
are the stories he'd tell in Forest Park
where afternoon light would hit his face and hold,
for an instant, the gleam that gave his eyes their look:

Like the time, installing spotlights in the dark dome
of the Arena ceiling, he lost footing and fell
off the scaffold, but having, that morning, shunned
suspenders for a thick cowhide belt, he was
caught by the buckle by his partner's free hand;

Or the time he boarded the train bound for Topeka
and got off to sleep in Booneville before moving on—
but feeling sick and restless checked out
and rode all the way home, where he read the next day
the hotel had burned down, everything reduced to ashes
so no one could tell one corpse from another.

On that Thanksgiving, my first visit in two months,
he wore the same gay smile, lying
shriveled in the bedsheets like a leprechaun:
I see myself bending for the last press of his lips—
but I never saw him again, never
asked how to charge this etching with ink.

Webster Review   MATTHEW BRENNAN

HOMAGE TO WEBERN

Your music lasts three hours—a lifework pent
inside one Mozart opera. Each note leans
into the next with a panicked urgency
that would have seemed, to Mozart's audience,
surrender to the unredeemed condition
music heals by giving every moment,
through relation to the rest, a sweetness
it had lacked alone. But here, relation
means anticipating when the brutal
interval, the interrupting silence
comes, as someone in the woods at night
might trip and, knowing he had lost the path,
guess from his accident where it must be.
Yours was the modern genius that knows the heart
not as a rhythm deep inside the body
urging us outward to our loves and wars,
but as mind's object, "Here Be Monsters" scrawled
across the very center of the map.
Your music ends as we're afraid we'll end:
the pattern secretly completes itself
before we understand it, leaving us
to ask whose will we did, if not our own.

The American Scholar   PAUL BRESLIN

PERPETUAL CONFINEMENT

Where to awake from corrupting sleep?
Life is violent as space impossible.
Time, it was, time opened my eyes
and now stops my ears, erases my lips.
Who can really either close or open time? There is no destiny.

It was night, and there were stars,
useless and lovely, giving light. After loving
bodies both ardent and false, I grew up, perhaps I grew old.
Music attended my soul in a dark room
reeking with the odor of jasmines. Now words
work paper, soundless and cold.
Days and years I endured the earth:
to endure is to love whatever ruins us.
Even the images of childhood
are lost: it was for them I lived
everlasting spring, the light of day.
I doubt it all ever really existed.
Nothing is left of whatever happened:
neither melancholy nor even pleasure.

Who, then, congeals my heart?
Sleep and dreams corrupt the flesh,

disintegrate the easy decency of looking
at the world with slighted love and even pardon.
There are no answers left. And any possible
truth is beside the point when life lacks sense.
Only perhaps a simple question without imagination
or any knowing: why awake,
why come to in any place so dark?

Denver Quarterly   FRANCISCO BRINES
                                    —Translated by Anthony Kerrigan

A DAY IN THE LIFE OF WILLY SYPHER

No Huckleberry Findelbaum am I,
But Willy Sypher,
Peddler to the mid-Western territory
Serviced by Acme-Zenith Clothing,
Lighting out again this lonely morning,
Not even hoping to open new accounts,
Just hold my own
Against competition and a limp economy.

The road has come to own me,
Dreams and soul, body, spirit, volition,
(Synonyms line up at my heart's gate
To gain audience with my popish tongue):
I've known so many homes
These past twenty-five centuries;
Bedouin tents, nomadic oases, posadas,
Hostels, motels, boarding houses.

Gas station attendants, reservationists,
Waitresses, union musicians,
Bartenders are the ephemerae
In my unchanging equation of transience.
Uprootedness is crucial to erosion;
The topsoil in the cradle
Through which I commute is constantly removed,
Replaced by newer sediments.

Yet, I alone remain untouched
By each upheaval
As I hustle overstocks and "thirds,"
Garments not-quite-perfect
For mill flaws, manufacturing defects,
And hawk merchandise from swatch books,
Samples locked in my trunk,
Pushing worsteds and corduroy in July,

Cotton tropicals and whisper flannels in February.
Unphased by such paradoxes,
I've grown accustomed to existence
Lived upside-down, inside-out;
Despite marrying a Midianite wife

Who raised two kids in my hiatus,
My entire life
Has been a night shift bereft of family ties.

Just now, I press westward,
Hurrying to arrive in time for lunch
With the buyer for Quicksilver's in Tipton,
A mama and papa shop
I've called on for thirty-five years.
As I approach and park,
Signs splayed on the plate glass curse me:
GONE OUT OF BUSINESS—PERMANENTLY!

The Southern Review   LOUIS DANIEL BRODSKY

REDBUDS

My excited eyes take me by the hand,
Lead me through a pure fuchsia net
Of redbuds yawning and stretching into bloom:
We awaken each other with our subtle touching

As I pass from one room to another
Within this open-air greenhouse.
Apple trees and dogwoods arouse me
To taste their lacy white fragrance; I linger,

Stop long enough to memorize their scent,
Then continue along the labyrinthian path
My eyes cut through winter's debris.

Everywhere in April's aquamarine sea
Along whose lee shore I leisurely loaf,
Clipper ships, frigates and whaling packets
Rolling in irons this early springtide,

Begin lifting green sails up masts,
Prepare to raise anchor for summer oceans.
I wave to invisible crews active as bees
Aboard the mind's fleet and secretly contrive

A means of stowing away, securing release
From the land-locked harbor where my spirit
Has lain in dry dock too long.

No escape outlines its design on my irises;
Yet, as I retreat from daydreams,
My feet going towards the new season,
I realize that freedom requires little more

Than rediscovering life-cycles
That connect us to each other, and each
To original Creation; survival depends on eyes
Apprehending future and past in the universal Now;

They alone can sow the seeds, plant the soul
In fertile earth, fuse bones with air:
Mine is the blood of the redbud tree.

The Cape Rock   LOUIS DANIEL BRODSKY

GREAT GRANDMOTHER

(for "Mamo"; Mrs. Harry Hofmann, Sr.)

Not her palsied fingers and hands,
But eight decades and a solitary year
Memorized to their craft, fashion a nosegay
That our child, Trilogy, watches materialize
From paraphernalia scattered within the shadow
Named Mamo that covers the table like dust.

The slow metamorphosis of a wedding bouquet
From individually clipped miniature carnations,
Unopened Joanna Hill roses
And baby's breath sprigs enraptures her;
The magical appearance of a perfect bunch
From nothingness frustrates her imagination.

Unable to ascertain the nature of creation
Or fathom the tricks of mundane conditioning,
Our baby imitates her great grandmother:
Silently she unwinds yards of floratape,
Scatters velvet leaves from their cellophane,
Drains green plastic waterpicks,

Then bends the slender wires
Used for supporting scissored stems
Into shapes resembling nesting snakes.
Through the myopia of triple-thick years
The white-haired maker of corsages
Peers at her tiny apprentice and concentrates,

As if recognizing for the first time in ages,
In the silk-fine gold hair
And delicate face of her great grandchild,
The godly design of her tedious arrangement.
Smiling, she hands our infant a bloom
With which to begin her own bouquet of years.

St. Andrews Review   LOUIS DANIEL BRODSKY

CLEANING THE SHED

Something should be done to show out
the old year; inside, work aplenty
waits, or one could celebrate with

an early cheer the sense of change;
but I must look in at what remains
of the year's promises to myself.
Newspapers overflow that old crock,
better fit for moonshine; half-filled
with dirt, pots and jars line a rack;
webby marks on the single pane trace
last summer's spiders. For weeks
I have walked in a net of broken toys,
fallen rakes and brooms, and watched
the sun's motions grow short; now
in the declining afternoon, little time
is left. This is no domestic rage,
no charade to please the neighbors,
but a gesture to myself, reminding me
of the liens on us, less possessing
than possessed, unless we learn how
to jettison what is outworn. Around
the door, the wind stirs, scattering
twigs from the cedar; birds sort through
the rest of fall. I will pour out
the soil for new worms, cart the trash
for burning, discard the impediments
to plain steps, and clear a few shelves
in my mind—needing to deny Mammon
in at least one way before its trap
consumes me, and make a spot for new
growth, waking in the earth's bones.

The Sewanee Review   CATHARINE SAVAGE BROSMAN

A DREAM BEFORE SLEEP

Do you know how some houses
where you've spent years as a child
have shapes you keep on seeing?
So many of my dreams still happen there.
In the big attic we would lie on cots.
Miss Staples read *Kidnapped* again and again,
but I didn't mind because I never heard it all.
When rain fell on the slates,
dripping onto windowsills, I'd doze.
She had a steady, quiet voice
I think of sometimes when I'm trying to sleep.

There was a boy named Nicky, hulking in his walk
and always poking a cheek with his tongue
or chewing on it when he worked at math.
We never knew how old he was.
He'd hurt himself when young,
fell off a bike, and he wasn't dumb,
but his head worked poorly in some ways.
He loved recess and being *it* and showing

how fast and far he could run.
He'd take the small ones and make them all join hands
around the maple stump, and then he'd dance.
Oh, it was beautiful, though I didn't know it then,
like the house before it burned.

He was much bigger than us all,
bent double with one of our hands in each of his,
singing as we circled
then fell down.

New England Review & Bread Loaf Quarterly   T. ALAN BROUGHTON

BESSIE

Bessie and her invalid husband
lived here fifty years
without plumbing or a well,
put down the pine floors
upstairs and the cement walk,
raised two children,
drained the wash water onto the road.
The back room served as summer kitchen
for her kerosene stove. She put in
the vegetables and years of care.
She's still alive, in town
across from the park in a modern house.
I use her curtains in the kids' room,
find little wads of rags in drafty crannies.
Before she left she showed me how
to draw cistern water,
to wash the house front with a broom.
Her linoleum stays on the outhouse floor,
and the movement of her heart stirs
in the iris tucked around the big maple,
and in the columbine blooming in May
gently nodding its bright head
like an old woman unused to compliments.

Passages North   CRYSTAL BROWN

BAPTISMS

Believing that people
were or became
what they were named,
they rose with the Sun,
called themselves Eagle,
Fox, Otter, Hawk, Wolf,
Bear and Deer.

Then new ones came,
those who named

themselves for forgotten memories,
great-grandfathers seeking
hard dominion over rock and stream,
ownership of forest and plain,
with names of Farmer, Smith and Weaver,
Joiner, Carpenter, Stoner, Wright.

Then they gave
the first people new names.
Government men and preachers smiled
as they christened Washingtons,
Wilsons, Garcias, Smiths—
and waited for them to change.

Yet even today,
when the newest names,
Citizen Band, Breeder Reactor,
Missile Range, Strip Mine and Pipe Line
have begun to move in,
residing where Bark Lodge, Wigwam
and Tipi, Wickiup and Hogan stood,
things have not ended as they should.

Somewhere, it is whispered,
at some ragged edge
of the unfinished land
the Sun is rising, breathing again
names which we have not yet heard,
names about to be spoken.

The Chariton Review   JOSEPH BRUCHAC

CANTON

(for Grace)

He is in every face I met on Main
smiling at me, telling a joke
of Franklin McGee, forecasting rain
for the end of the week. Lighting a smoke

in a pick-up, he waves for me
to come over, rolls down the window,
passes on some gossip about Old Lady
Miller. He says he's got to go

out to the big pasture to fix fence.
He is in the face of every old man
who sits and chats on the bench
in front of Roe's holding a can

of Seven-Up in a gnarled fist,
taking in the cool morning blue
sky, guessing that he wished
there was something else to do.

He is in every window up the street
staring back at me in the moment I pass,
in the broken sidewalk under my feet,
in the cracks, in each blade of grass.

He is there in the American flag
decal on the window in the door
half off a hinge, and in the nag-
ging grate of it on the floor

when it's opened, and he's there
in each face that rises to stare
like a fish coming out of water.
Sometimes he's more than I can bear

to see in the cheap porcelain cup,
the hand that holds it out to my
hand, the arm I follow up
to look in an old woman's brown eye.

I know him buried but not yet dead.
He is in every word his friends have said,
in every breath these people take,
and I listen and look for his memory's sake.

The Midwest Quarterly   J. V. Brummels

DOORS

(for my father)

When you died I dreamed of snow
And the white field of your chest
Stiff with cold, your eyes sealed with frost
And silence, the dull coins of ice. I watched them drag you in
On a door torn from some cabin made of birch and moss,
Under a sky sagging from the weight of the moon.
I remember the air holding on and the wind
Rising in my throat, the shadows
Of your face that waited
For the warm room to wake you
To something better
Than the poor light of dreams.
        But you died years ago,
And there was no door, no dream,
Just the watery grave of a nurse's voice,
Small and far away, lighting my way home.
        And still your breath
Rises with the dawn coming up from the lake
Until it brushes my face, and when I reach
The door it could open to anything—
Even your heart selling its old song
Once more.

Tendril   Thomas Brush

VIEWING THE BODY

I hate that phrase, says my ex-
quisitely private mother, embarrassed
for those who can't return

our gaze. Once we might have watched
for stirrings, as of water before a diver
breaks the surface. What is the body

to us now, all its fluidity
gone absolutely, false to the life
it carried until the articulate

bones appear? An antonym, a place
to begin, the deliberate fire
that drives memory

into the open, toward the hunters.

The Atlantic Monthly   SHARON BRYAN

WAITING FOR THE HANGMAN

I see strangers I dreamed
when ten years old
waiting on the couch
when my parents were gone,
folded under my bunkbed
where they rustled like
alligators,
or hiding to knife me,
behind the refrigerator.
I hear the buzzing I only
dreamed then, growing loud—
and snail shells cracking
under a small child's thumb.
And once I dreamed
I pushed at a dead carp's
eye with a stick,
in the back yard, taking out
the garbage.
The eye turned half over,
on hinges. Now I see the other
side. Now I remember the truth—
I never dreamed any of that.
And I am not dreaming now.

Kansas Quarterly   CARL BUCHANAN

TO A COLD EAST

Today, you would see postcards of royal palms sway,
banana palms roll gold as cigars in Beverly Hills.
January, and we are tanning in our shirt sleeves;
the sailboats flock like pigeons off Marina del Rey.
Even the poor rowing skiffs in Echo Park can turn
and see the modest snow peaked on close resorts.
You would say we have the best of both worlds
as if there were only two sides of this life,
as if there were not questions to be asked.
But off 101 the Castle Argyle and Hollywood Tower
are slack under their last whitewash, and dreaming—
they forget themselves like an aging actress, over-
powdered and spreading in an afternoon swoon of martinis.
The yellow grease of 50 years dims the windows and poses:
Who can live for long on the inconstant light of stars?

And though this winter of even heat fooled blossoms
and brought the tourist trade, it took our rain away—
it's all you can do to get a glass of water in a cafe,
all you can do to ignore the rank signs in a dire year.
The West died long ago, collapsed like a lung when
the gold bled out; bankers pumped in iron and rivers,
and lettuce shined like coins; the oil produced two wars.
And now the hot Santa Ana winds have the call of creditors.

Our Utilities study the upper desert floor.
They puzzle at half this state's over-bite on the other,
at the salt-steam thrust they might harness from
a 10-mile bulge in the crust near Palmdale—better
they study the sand-white lizard slipping through
the bones of a horse, the asters pushing out the eyes.
We have built on a primary split down a length of land
like the line in your hand saying when your life will end.
The Indians on this western shelf said the quaking
was the dead fighting among themselves and that will
finally mean as much to us as anything. This evening
private planes sparkle with the spray of Christmas lights;
screen doors swing open to cool. The air is dry,
still as paint or unread roman numerals in the stars.
East and West, we hold down equal portions of this earth
against the steady suck of space—the imponderable
weight of nothing that pulls our atmospheres apart—
but we have all the people, the slippage of the plates
heading our way and down, and no reason to take heart.

The Threepenny Review   CHRISTOPHER BUCKLEY

EROS

Warm, on the shopping center, the night air hangs,
warm about the laundromat's doorway open.

It is bright white inside, and only a couple
of people are there, save for the old man
hunched over the table with the change.
From the center of the shopping plaza it shines;
the Grand Union is the only other thing open—
otherwise it is the summer country dark.

Now to walk past those machines and movie magazines
and the scattered women in curlers reading them and smoking
    their long
filter cigarettes, which they butt disconsolately out, belipsticked,
in the imitation copper ashtrays in that tedium—
to lounge outside watching
the roadway hanging with the summer air where it stretches
one way into town, past the clock at the bank, the other
out into the open road with cornfields, thickening underneath a
    harvest moon—
to wander about there is but to prolong
and heighten the night's midsummer dream,
the strange madness that is on everyone.

Come to the window, sweet is the night air!
—almost too sweet for me, drifting along the sidewalk, and
also for those sleeping along the lonely highways,
where distant individual cars
thunder by with an urgency that grows
as the dream of indulgence richens.

For how large that dream of indulgence is:
how it has waxed full and strong, until it has taken everyone in,
into its great sensual gladness and unrestrictive permission,
no matter how complicated we consider ourselves
or, with a rare and touching humility, how unprepossessing.

For desire levels, and is our common dream.

For listen: the streets are calm tonight, the
bars are full,
and the moon lies deep upon the fields;
and out amidst plumes
of dusty gravel, a car races, and is gone,
boiling up the road with several couples inside,
hooting as they pass a darkened cowbarn;
out there, tonight is doubly enchanting,
as, in all that gorgeous, radical novelty, some
to the appointment with the god are hastening.

Poetry   FREDERICK BUELL

OF ELLIPSES AND DEVIATIONS

How to get back to the careless caring,
The hopeless hope, the useless cry that
Does not consider utility worth a praise—

How to feel again, so that the saying of it
May come with the grace of the chickadees'
Alighting in the spare feast of the January lilac,

How to feel again that the puffy flurry
Of small birds in winter's snow-bright risk
Is worth an ablation moraine of praise.

I am, at least, midway on the journey
Of this life, and I have gone out into
The big woods and the small woods,

The high woods and the low woods: I have
Seen the scattered feathers left of the grouse
After the horned owl's night-roaming, rib-bones

In the forest duff lighted by the cleanliness
Of fate. Nobody cares about this stuff:
Nothing's redeemed by poetry, and that's enough.

Poetry   JERALD BULLIS

THE GIVEN

There is a poem in here
somewhere. It displaces
doorbell and telephone
and the voices
of strangers asking for light,
neighbors at the door
offering persimmons.
Enemies and scholars
have been locked out;
the room is emptied
of dissertations and numbers.
Far away, horns argue
in the streets. Nothing
comes closer than the memory
of hands.
What is absent is not
the poem, nor is it
a synonym for silence.
The poem is what a spider
weaves out of the emptiness
in the last light.
I undo the spider's web,
then slowly, strand by hair,
reinvent
its secret threads. That
is the poem.

New Jersey Poetry Journal   JEAN BURDEN

WINTER APPLES

All summer, and today, the white sun
Warmed our breakfast apples, crisp as frost.
My knife flicks slices, so thin that green
Light shines through. The point twirls
Out spots, the sweet brown pulp that tastes
Like honey, and earth after a rain. All winter,
I'll eat sharp apples, tasting you,
while at breakfast, across a thousand miles
Of orchards and apple-roads, you remember
How my hands tasted of apple, how
The green fruit you ate before we slept
Sweetened our mouths all night.
When you kissed my breasts, or woke with my hair
Coiled on your tongue, you'd taste salt, and apple.
Now at the damp end of summer, we eat
This stubborn fruit, tasting snow
In the sharp green skin
And cider swelling under the light bruise.

The Literary Review   DEBORAH BURNHAM

MOVING FROM CLEAR CREEK

First frost. The walnut has started to strip,
and brittle twigs, some of their leaves still green,
drop in the morning sun as if by signal.
Out my kitchen window, their solemn beauty
is only like the soft disrobing of a woman
when her gown spills to her feet
and leaves her ugly,
like these naked limbs, this stark fruit.

I will move away from here this fall.
Let someone else come next year to lie down
to sleep in a high wind, while branches scrape
and blow, and listen in this dark as the hard
green balls of the walnut drop,
rumble down the roof to waste in the yard.

The Midwest Quarterly   MICHAEL BURNS

FIREFLIES

Above corn, in June, in order
to find one another, fireflies
nudge Indiana air
like cinders in love. Absently
we spend a day turning a soil
that isn't ours while blackbirds roll

way up high, pinpoints,
the opposite of fireflies.

Two beliefs like that, or one,
in a flickering time of night,
lead easily to this life,
to slopes, to flat nights of gentle
towns, to clear nights of neighbors
in love, and whatever is lost
does not matter; it will rise
and dip and curve and go on

above corn, under the silk ear
of the half moon, next to barns,
next to cows and shadows of cows.

Quarterly West   RALPH BURNS

ANTHOLOGY

Calcified sheets flake
like scalp crust, scar
tissue where the spine cracks,
a paperback, discard
of the Fifties, juvenilia
or a poetry of decline.
As I skim, pages
come unmoored and drift
as deuce or trey
from a spilled pack, a shuffle
of wild cards, fifty
of the more bearded kind.
Kings without suit, knaves
with a one-eyed tic
crying to the Pacific,
the bull's-eye of an ace
strafed like a pop sign,
riddled by 22's,
a slam, a trick for the grate.
Nails grow on the dead,
a gutter of diamonds
under paper lids.
The final poetry says:
if you are cold, burn this.

Michigan Quarterly Review   E. G. BURROWS

AN OLIVE TREE IN KORFU

In Korfu (I was not there)
a friend once bought for me,
without sign and seal,
only on good faith,

an olive tree.
It stands on the shore of a bay
and has since become my most prized possession,
mine like nothing else
because I place no demands.

I cannot care for it,
will never in my life see it,
but it is there.
I know it looks after the ships,
gives lodging to wind and light,
and with my soft olives
it entertains strangers.
To no one need I refuse its shadow,
I can without worry
grant hospice to anyone,
and my treeless and sealess window
is by day and by night
full of departure and arrival.

My olive tree becomes more beautiful each year.
Secretly I am already looking for
an heir to it.
One needs no testament
to obtain my Korfu.

The Literary Review   CHRISTINE BUSTA
—Translated from the German
by Beth Bjorklund

GRASSHOPPER

When I was ten,
I sneaked a hypodermic needle
from my mother's nursing bag,
filled it with red food coloring.

I went out on the back porch,
got the mayonnaise jar,
unscrewed the lid, slowly,
so I could get my hand in
to grab the grasshopper.

I injected him.

His straw color turned
the color of a tangerine
and every bit as radiant.
I ached for something
to inject myself with
to make *me* shine.

I took the grasshopper to the meadow
back behind the house,
and watched him hop away,
robbed of natural protection.

Same way lipstick and high heels
later did me in.

The Ohio Journal   MARSHA CADDELL

THE STRAND THEATRE

Lovesick girls, old men in foul underwear
inhabit this movie theatre
in Trenton, New Jersey, in the fifties,
before the riots, before debutantes
are murdered in their townhouses.
The most beautiful man we have ever seen
is making love to a woman we envy.
She lifts her thigh, we are breathless.
When they are not making love,
she cries, he drives his Ferrari
to an empty beach where he paces
the cliffs, imagining how he will leave
his wife. She waits in a back room,
as if she would wait there her whole life,
until one night coming to see her,
he crashes the Ferrari into a parked truck,
dies in her arms. We sob, lurching
in our seats. Old men yell at us
from the balcony, only I can't stop,
neither can you. You make syncopated snorts,
I hiccup as if on a megaphone.
Then you whisper *we sound like toads,*
and we are laughing, bleating like little goats
through the funeral all the way to the cemetery;
and God knows what has happened to the woman
whose man just died, because we are ushered
from the theatre, returned to the street,
where on the littered sidewalk
we stand astonished and thirteen.

Tendril   TERESA CADER

RESEARCH AND SCHOLARSHIP

First you need *Sitzfleish*
For sitting on your ass
All day long,
With, *naturlich*, brief recesses
To piddle and also poo,
Auch to ingest, digest, and eject.
And you need eyes, if not strong,
Then with good glasses,
To peer and pore and make out
What the scraggly lines black-on-white

Say that's of any slightest import
To man and the world, and, praise God,
The advancement of learning (*loud cheers*).

Most of all, you need courage,
The unvanquishable hope and faith
That out of this mind-deadening
Pick-and-shovel work
Something alive and glistening
Will come to term,
Birthing after long labor,
Out of these piles of 3 by 5's
And 4 by 6's and God knows
What other entry forms
A building, order, a world will come:

That marvelous miracle
Where something new-formed stands
Where nothing was before,
And dead stones live and speak
To listening ears.

Midstream   SEYMOUR CAIN

WAKING HERE

(for Kathleen and Zap)

This night, one of those clouded
nights that glue the sheets
to your legs and drain the hope
of sleep from you, so that even the woman
tossing beside you becomes nothing more
than an irritation. So, the two of you
grow slowly stupid in the dark,
being for the most part awake but
numbed by heat and darkness. At such a time,
you might believe you'll go on like this
forever; but the night
above you clears, and your borrowed room
cools by slow degrees, and the moment
arrives when you startle to the fact
of having slept.
If, at this moment, you would lift
yourself to one elbow and witness
the moonlit room, you would know
that there is waking
in this house a word
simple as blood, whose sound spoken
clearly enough might make things right,
a word like *water* or *light,* a word
clean and honest as *dirt,* or a woman
you wake to clear autumn nights, the odd light

of the moon on her, a quiet word that tells you
all you're in the world to learn.

Quarterly West   SCOTT C. CAIRNS

ORLEANS REVISITED

The night is called
Desire.
In the warmth
We walked the cobblestone
Streets.
We lived
In the Quarter
Where Jazz is soft
As blue.
Old ladies sat
Fanning and scowling,
Drunken tourists
Hopping the dives, and whores
Who counted
Their silver glistening
In the moonlight.

Ball State University Forum   VINCE CANIZARO

MAGPIES

I have two memories of this place
besides the magpies.
First, our fort—my friend's and mine—
up in the pines. It was Indian country,
so we each had a tree, close branches touching and wide
worn crotches where we'd sit and look out
high up, the brown needles soft below
when we'd jump down on them.

Years later, when I came
leaping the sage with a laughing girl
(I have her eyes by heart), surprised
to find the trees so small
and that favorite branch not in the clouds
(though the tree had grown ten rings),
the needles were still soft below
when we lay and loved on them.

The hill now has its loneliness.
That best friend of my youth is dead—
shot by his own hand one black day
when his marriage died.
Also gone is the silken girl,
away white thighs with another man.

And I seldom come here any more
except to see the magpies.

I worshipped them, sunblazed watchers of the wood,
brothers of the tailflicked treetop,
and guarded the ungainly nest
growing each year where Indian horses died.
They still slide in the sky there
down the sandhills to the river
brashly beautiful, ambivalent birds
lavishing black and white life on the pinetrees and me.

The Malahat Review   ROBERT A. CANNINGS

LETTER TO DYLAN

How else but "gentle into that good night"?
What other way but gentle when the strength
To rage has died, killed slowly by the rite
Of strangers, ministering, and by the length,
The terrifying length, of hours that creep,
Clock-faced, toward dusk and dinner-trays, toward pills
And geriatric jokes and fitful sleep.
Who hears a whimpering? Upon the sills
The dusty leaves of philodendron lie,
Reproachful. In the gaudy light of day
The curtains are too bright. Who hears a cry,
Or stops to wonder if the glib cliché
Offends, or if it's heard, or why the hands,
Palms upward, lie so still? Who understand
The shape of fear, what waiting is? How might
They go? How else but gentle into night?

The Lyric   MAUREEN CANNON

STAY AS SIMPLE . . .

"Stay as simple as this glass of water
where the bleuets are soaking," my mother'd say.
I'm remembering that, as I sit near my window
in front of this glass of water filled with light.

And I used to laugh, thinking it was easy
to stay like that quite simply
near my window, quiet and serene,
in this room where the pulse of time is beating.

Through the pane, I see folk rushing
by. Then I watch the sun
        creating a gleam like a bee
in my glass, and I smile, grown still,

at the bleuets which are my mother's eyes
smiling at me in the light.

Poetry Now   MAURICE CAREME
                                    —Translated from the French (Belgium)
                                                    by Ruth Farber

THE THING ABOUT FARMING

The thing about farming is there is nothing
between you and the world. Everything
you touch either wounds or responds.
Everything you love touches back
with food or with poison.

The thing about farming is nothing lasts
for more than one season. For the rest
of your life you plant and cuddle and encourage,
still, every Winter, all your children have gone.

The thing about farming is you work
most of your life alone,
for better or for worse—
no god but the seasons, no lover but the earth,
no enemy but the weather and the wind, the wind, the wind.

The thing about farming is you tend a small portion of the planet.
You keep it or you lose it and it changes
no matter what according to your efforts.
But what's important is
when you wake and pick blueberries,
not only are they good—they're yours.

The thing about farming is it's so easy,
half of it is learning to kill. The earth turns green
each Spring, regardless of your attentions.
For every seedling you nourish
the rest of creation is weeds.

The thing about farming is it's not all food and abundance.
Sometimes it's drought. Sometimes you get eaten
by your own machinery. The banks don't give you that loan,
and you go under. Sometimes you find a deer
snagged on a fence and along with an underworld of stealth
you are drawn to the spot—curious about the carcass—
its death and your own.

Sou'wester   MICHAEL A. CAREY

ANCESTOR

My father was an ancestor well before he died.
By eight, his real eyes, too blind to see the stars,
Knew what lay around the next bend in the river,

Listening to his father,
Pontifical master of misinformation,
Running on about the crows and their sagacity,
"They know immediately if you have a gun."
Statement of fact. The crows cawed smugly above their heads.
The boy took a firm grip on the pistol in his pocket
And, on his own counsel,
He never let it go.
An ancestor is, by definition, deaf,
No matter how he smiles in his brocade,
Bows deeply to his wife, feeds his goldfish,
Cares for his water lilies, strolls with his reverent Pekingese.
He is soundproofed in another time zone,
Secure in his kimono.
Gliding, at last, downstream, gathering speed,
He left us all, outdistanced on the bank,
Dumbfounded to see his frantic waving,
Watching as the whole thing capsized into earshot.

The American Scholar   ANNE NICODEMUS CARPENTER

A PICTURE OF THE REVEREND'S FAMILY
WITH THE CHILD OF ONE

Particularly at the left side of his face,
As you face him, the line is so distinct
You might suppose the negative was inked
To heighten contrasts. I am in my place,
But all my shadows blend into his clothes
Where hardly a button shows, they are so black.
My father's right hand rests on Mother's neck.
The parted curtains at the left disclose
A sunlit bowl with fruit and gourds—perhaps
Real ones. The fluid drape of Mother's dress
Softens the chaste and angular plainness
Of this memorial scene, where in their laps
I reach up past my boyish-girlish curls
To his priest's collar and her string of pearls.

Poetry   THOMAS CARPER

WORDS IN A CERTAIN APPROPRIATE MODE

It is not music, though one has tried music.
It is not nature, though one has tried
The rose, the bluebird, and the bear.
It is not death, though one has often died.

None of these things is there.

In the everywhere that is nowhere
Neither the inside nor the outside
Neither east nor west nor down nor up

Where the loving smile vanishes, vanishes
In the evanescence from a coffee cup
Where the song crumbles in monotone
Neither harmonious nor inharmonious
Where one is neither alone
Nor not alone, where cognition seeps
Jactatively away like the falling tide
If there were a tide, and what is left
Is nothing, or is the everything that keeps
Its undifferentiated unreality, all
Being neither given nor bereft
Where there is neither breath nor air
The place without locality, the locality
With neither extension nor intention
But there in the weightless fall
Between all opposites to the ground
That is not a ground, surrounding
All unities, without grief, without care
Without leaf or star or water or stone
Without light, without sound
                  anywhere, anywhere. . .

Ploughshares   HAYDEN CARRUTH

THE PURPOSE OF POETRY

This old man grazed thirty head of cattle
In a valley just north of the covered bridge
On the Mississinewa, where the reservoir
Stands today. Had a black border collie
And a halfbreed sheepdog with one eye.
The dogs took the cows to pasture each morning
And brought them home again at night
And herded them into the barn. The old man
Would slip a wooden bar across both doors.
One dog slept on the front porch, one on the back.

He was waiting there one evening
Listening to the animals coming home
When a man from the courthouse stopped
To tell him how the new reservoir
Was going to flood all his land.
They both knew he was too far up in years
To farm anywhere else. He had a daughter
Who lived in Florida, in a trailer park.
He should sell now and go live with her.
The man helped bar the doors before he left.

He had only known dirt under his fingernails
And trips to town on Saturday morning
Since he was a boy. Always he had been around
Cattle, and trees, and land near the river.
Evenings by the barn he could hear the dogs

Talking to each other as they brought in
The herd; and the cows answering them.
It was the clearest thing he knew. That night
He shot both dogs and then himself.
The purpose of poetry is to tell us about life.

Images   JARED CARTER

DEATH IN THE WELL

Surprised at how easy it is
to dive into the deep
and then, again, amazed
at the roundness of sky
that can be reached no more,
the bird,
who flew in open space,
beholds a bordered world
it learns too late,
at the last second—
crushed against the wall.

Chelsea   NINA CASSIAN
                              —Translated from the Romanian
                                            by Eva Feiler

SEAGULLS IN THE PARKS

Mistress of sweatshops, factories, barrooms,
All of them dark stones under an overcast sky,
Quiet at night, pious on Sundays, this is
The devout city that denies her sins.

The muddy green of the grass and trees breaks up
The sameness of the buildings with its parks,
And in this dull landscape, in the rain,
It suddenly sees gulls with their wild feathers flying.

Having wings, why are they spending time in the smoke,
The filthy creeks, the wooden bridges in these parks?
An unwelcomed gust of wind or a thoughtless hand
Brought them inland away from their native harbors.

Their nest at sea, rocked by winter storms, radiantly
Calm in the summer, is far from here.
Now their lament shoots up like the cry of souls in exile.
Whoever gave them wings doesn't give them room to fly.

Poetry Now   LUIS CERNUDA
             —Translated from the Spanish by David Unger

FORECAST

The bombs are not falling yet—
Only snow, wet snow, thick snow. Storybook snow.
Yet like most of us, I keep waiting for the bombs.
We know that one day the weatherman will say,
Good morning, America! Dress warmly.
Stay indoors if you can. Try not to drive.
And now for the outlook. Observe
Our wonderful satellite photograph:
In this area, we expect a high pressure area
Of MX missles, and over here, to this side
Of the Rockies, something is brewing,
Something radioactive. But cheer up.
This is only the outlook. Weather is wonderful;
It can always change. For today,
Your typical air masses are cold but stable,
And the SAC umbrella remains furled
In the closet of its silos, underground bases,
And twenty-four-hour sky-watches. Today
We have snow, wet snow, thick snow. Storybook snow.
Today we are all going to live happily ever after.

Open Places   KELLY CHERRY

SUNDAY

Innocent girl, once Sunday comes I'll give you
Everything. Marvelous flowers, like eyes,
And a drop of blood pure as a flower: I'll give you
Everything. I'll steal the unmindful, weary sunset
From the Bazaar in my town; from my mother,
The years she has to live; from my little sister,
Her sinless hands (without her knowledge).
Darling, I will fill your belly.

The flowers, the blood, the sun: all these
I'll steal for you, innocent girl, once Sunday comes.
But Sunday will never come. Not until you arrive
Shod in your torn shoes; not until the hard-working god of time
Falls asleep. Sunday
Will never, never come 'til you commit
The world's most innocent sin, beside me,
Naked, in a closed room.

New Letters   DEVDAS CHHOTRAY
                            —Translated from the Oriya by Jayanta Mahapatra

THE BROWN HOUSE

There is a house
on a hill,
tuxedoed in brown shingles,
the people brown inside it,
and all its studies brown.
There is Mr. Brown,
a good man and true,
and Mrs. Brown, lovely in mahogany,
and that tall young man Brown
with his rustbrown mustache
and the beautiful Brown girl
with long bronze hair,
whose eyes open like morning
under an amber sky.
Oh, brown is my color,
the color of love,
and I love the Browns
in their chocolate house.
May the gods visit sweetness
on the Brown tree,
and on all its branches,
mocha, amber, mahogany, rust.

Poetry Now   WILLIAM CHILDRESS

I HAVE HEARD THE IMMPASSIONED
WEEPING OF A RACHEL . . .

I have heard the impassioned weeping
of a Rachel standing in the dawn
over the bodies of her slaughtered sons.
I have seen rise up, from crematories,
from chimneys over tranquil roofs,
the theories of men, of women, children,
turned into smoke and floating up to heaven—
tranquilly killed by gas
that so might come the cleansing of your sewers,
my German brothers!
It is the blood, the blood, that preys upon my mind;
so many throats cut open,
so many skulls laid bare,
so many butchered bodies,
such horrors and such agonies,
the hungers unappeased, the tears,
the thirst unquenched,
and those that died
that so might come the saving of my lambs.

Midstream   ANDRÉ CHOURAQUI
—Translated from the French
by Kenton Kilmer

SISTER MARY APPASSIONATA LECTURES
THE PRE-MED CLASS

Chemistry informs us, quickens even
the dead. Four fluids God gave Adam
combine and recombine, gurgle
and roar, simmer and cool even as we
do, in the body's labyrinthine tubes.

Blood. Dark as midnight when it
pools, deep enough to drown us all.
A race's history smeared thin as dust
over the pathologist's slide, life
inscribed, unfathomable as the tide.

Milk. Blood purified by the loveliness
of breasts, kiss of nipples stiff
and soft as lips, one of love's recurring
wounds, smooth as the belly rounded
and taut. In a world of ice, it's fire.

Tears. Blood conducted through canals
of sense: touch, sight, scents, speech
and feel. Juice squeezed from fruit
of generation. How we pronounce
our sentence, mourn our receding sea.

Semen. Blood boiled, concentrated
in love's retort. Man's acrid dew.
God's manna brightening our fields as we
sleep and love. Yeast by which we rise.
Puddles of the sea that spawned us.

San Jose Studies   DAVID CITINO

TELLING THE BEES

The Greeks built tombs to resemble
beehives, a prayer that in the other world
they'd find design, endless fields of
vivid blooms and, after labor, sweet reward.

Bees never sleep, knowing how much
beauty would be lost to the world each night
without their diligent love, how much
sweetness to themselves, to those they serve.

Tell the bees for three straight days
the dead one's name, and in their ceaseless dance
and toil they'll lament, and in his name
labor to bring the gray world to brilliant life.

Pluck one from the air with your bare hand,
and make a sudden fist. The awful pain means
you've closed your heart and hand to love,
you've sinned against what's sweet and light.

The Literary Review   DAVID CITINO

LUST

Lust,
You creeping nocturnal pest,
I've come to know your cruising gray coat
and scurf-like tail—
but will I set the traps?

This night you come albino;
pink and white, tender pure amor.
Shall we both pretend?

Hot breath sniffs my cornerstone,
a monogamous rock that hardly hides its cracks.
Insistent paws scratch at windows
opaque with promises I etched inside.
These rodent teeth gnaw at loins
of proud oak and sweet pine
that needn't be reduced to ordinary sawdust.

Come 'round to my back door, ole Lust,
I'll let you in this time.

Washington Review   MAXINE CLAIR

LETTERS FROM JERUSALEM

Engines of burning took him there
and brought back the first postcard,
a view of Jerusalem. The high air
swam with domes, their drowned gilding
glimmering like live fish scales.
The sky at night was an aquarium
of light years whose distances
at noon, converging, turned the desert
        to burning glass.

The kibbutzim aren't quite, he admits,
what he'd expected. The Talmud
couldn't care less about anybody's
happiness. But is that (he writes)
even important? Perhaps the true
arrival is always inward? He walks
the hills, the clogged bazaars,
everywhere. He is learning Hebrew.
        Immerse, immerse—

inward but also downward. He sees
time impend, the weather changing.
Clouds mass on the horizon; daylight
shrinks backward to the Maccabees'
last reckoning. In secret, from
the squalid rigor of the Yeshiva
and his unheated room, he flees
with St. Exupéry into regions
        of wind, sand and stars.

Immersion, thirst for roots, the passion
of expecting less: he asks now (he writes)
no more than to be here as a witness.
He begins even to dream in Hebrew:
locutions bend as though half in,
half out of water. But the watershed
that waits is made of fire: a cherub
in the doorway poses the blazing
     conundrum of the Jews

whose Biblical injunction is: if he stays
he must go into the army. The 'sixties
subversive pacifist he was must unadopt
that arrogance or lose Jerusalem.
A bush burned once; volcanoes
tutored the patriarchs; Elijah
was taken up in rafts of flame.
From Moscow, rumors arrive of new
     pogroms. He stays.

The latest letter, with no date, begins
Shalom! Tomorrow his leave ends,
then back to the desert. Tanks are less
accommodating even than the Talmud
to a divided mind. The promised land
increasingly is dense with engines.
Converging overhead in skies that swam,
the distances, grown predatory, swarm
     with burning seraphim.

The Yale Review   AMY CLAMPITT

BEECH HILL AFRICAN BAPTIST CHURCH

these corpsed years promise
not an olive branch, but a fasces;
not the messiah, but sure doom.
yet, we maintain our faith,
strengthened by memories of black-clothed
Father Preston erecting a church of pines
and wan sunlight sifting through web-branches years ago,
without assurance that walls and belief would sprout,
one from the other.
for we have survived this hard graveland,
once of shackle and sagging shack,
now of ragged folk and rat poison poverty.
for firmfaith flourishes not in the gilded
temples of moneychangers,
but in the wresting of a potato crop
from the boulder-barren, stone-strewn soil
of Beechville, Nova Scotia.

The Fiddlehead   GEORGE ELLIOTT CLARKE

A CERTAIN SQUINT

*("You can even make something not a
poem become a poem . . . by a certain
squint or a certain way of leaning our ears,
we find them."—W.S.)*

If I could only squint like Bill Stafford,
then I would be in that country
where men and women speak poetry,
unsurprised, as trees speak in a mild wind,
naturally as leaves come to them

not years ago when wild men dragged
ecstatic women by the hair
but here in America where Walt Whitman
husbanded his words and reaped
the wind that is still soughing.

Now Bill Stafford is old enough to be me.
One squint and the "snarl of a map"
becomes a world he gives his word to,
a little wood we can survive in.
It's a pretty good trick, Bill.

I lean my ears against a tree
that has been patient for a century,
knowing it to be inhabited
by more than grubs and birds.
I squint into the sweet silence.

Ploughshares   CHARLES H. CLIFTON

"NUMBS"

Grandmother lay sick, slowly dying of
Something called a stroke, which meant she often
Switched the words on things and asked for a comb
When she wanted a book or a blanket.
She told my mother while I was downstairs
Practicing scales with a six-year-old's
I'm-never-getting-married dedication,
"That child makes points." Mother said this almost
Ungarbled statement was a good sign for
Both of us. Yet a few days later,
Grandmother was dead in her sunny room whose
Long windowsill boasted an enormous
Red geranium in a small clay pot . . .
When grandmother finally died, mother was out
Shopping, the nurse was nowhere to be found—
That left me. Grandmother began to ask for
What sounded like "Numbs," a word the dentist used,
In ways that scared me. I tried bringing her

Things that had worked in the past—magazines,
Books, a comb, a brush, cold cream, another
Blanket, though it was sunny and warm. But
Grandmother kept saying "Numbs . . . Numbs . . ." in her
Insective voice. As soon as she was quiet,
I knew she was dead . . . At the funeral, I
Found time to wonder where grandmother had gone, by dying,
And if she'd found there whatever it was
She wanted . . . Such questions disappeared with
My seventh birthday and second grade, but still—
I've hated the smell of geraniums for
Seventy-seven years, and it only
Occurred to me today, when I was buying
White crysanthemums for my great-grandaughter's
Room, that perhaps what grandmother wanted
Was to smell that red geranium—Perhaps
That was the reason the geranium was
The one portable thing I didn't try.

The Hollins Critic   LYN COFFIN

WHAT MAKES THINGS TICK

*(". . . All week long I tinkered with it
and it still wouldn't get going. Fi-
nally I just grabbed the damn thing
and threw it clear across the room.
And wouldja believe it?—there it
was, ticking away . . .")*

Even machines need anger.
Even machines need a good shaking up now
    and then.
Even machines get kinks and short-circuits
    and air pockets.
Even machines have a few microscopic bones
    here and there, bones so small that no
    man, woman or doctor can detect them,
    and the bones of even machines can become
    dislocated.
Without anger, clocks clear their throats and
    furnaces moan and grumble and refrigera-
    tors develop a ringing in their ears.
Why, even the universe—the biggest and
    most important machine of all—even the
    universe needed an explosion to get start-
    ed, needed particles out of place, some-
    thing irregular—even the universe need-
    ed that big bang, complete with noise,
    chaos, and probably somebody's anger.

Sojourner   MARION COHEN

MORE ABOUT THE BEAR

This winter I live in a small house at the edge
of the tall woods. Brown trim. Latticed windows.
Rosy curtains that glow, late in the day,
when I'm inside. Outside's snow, and black bears,
who like honey, like all bears, and seeds
and berries, and sleep in black caves.

I never met a bear in the woods, but when
I was ten it was bear instead of doll, instead
of story. I'd mix up stories, end them wrong,
but when I went to school I'd send my Bear
off to Bearland. Later, thinking I knew
so much, I'd swear I loved that bear.

Later still, lulling a child, I told
about the bold girl who went to live
with the bears. Then I slept on her small bed,
a bear above my head, and dreamed of golden yarn
to mend the ravelled story of my life.
Was I the rose-red wife with the golden hair?

When I woke, I thought of the good gray wolf, and today
at the edge of the woods I dreamed Persephone's story
and got the beginning wrong: she needed a father,
and maybe there's a longer story there.
I worked in the dark myself sometimes and, after
the dream, numb with sleep, I saw through trees

to the house where love sings, and mends old clothes.
I don't know how this story ends, but this
is where I rub my eyes. Hi-ho, my father, I
am the bear, and here, in Bearland's rosy air,
where work is play and play is dare,
I eat red seeds, and you are the papa bear.

The Virginia Quarterly Review   MARTHA COLLINS

THE CENSUS TAKER
ON THE NAVAJO RESERVATION

Down a dirt road, eight miles off the state highway,
Past goat herds, gullies, chaparral, the census taker
Arrives in a truck. No one is home. Two tricycles
In the front of a house built by the U.S. Government.
No landscaping. Close by, a hogan, old, with mud roof,
Known to be cool during summer months, warm in
The winter. A door facing east, always toward
The first light. Black-gray ashes in the open fire pit.
Around back, gaping chicken wire between tree posts.
Slight rectangular outline of tarweed. An open gate,
Hinges rusted brown. Piles of fire wood, split oak

And cedar. The maul left leaning against a chain-saw
Out of gas. Corral to the north, alongside a canyon
Wall. An appaloosa watches, motionless. Raised faucet
From the well leaks, and the white propane tank
Disconnected. After a short wait, the census taker
Drives off, having made up some figures of his own.

The Threepenny Review   BRAD COMANN

A THOUSAND STRINGS OF WATER

I

mountains, white-tipped and blue
with winter light, close around
my throat. in their shadows,
on bare green grass, we create
distances: come and go;
retreat, advance. you look the same
over breakfast as you will
three thousand miles away,
or will you. don't expect much,
I told you. closeness can burn.

what can I offer with so much air
between us; a barrier of mountains,
miles of snowed-in prairies.
a few letters & calls. hardly
substantial.

II

I didn't intend to get close
to you. I was still and motionless
as a rock polished by a thousand
strings of water; content to be alone.
you saw love glow on my eyelids,
turned over a stone.
look where it got you.

III

how easy it is to love
from a distance. no pain,
no intrusions. perhaps also
less joy. I would rather
go on like a tree watered daily
and rarely struck by lightning.
I'm not constant. I don't
shine like you.

event   JAN E. CONN

IN THE PARK

Dogs snap at air beside ball-
wielding children who yammer to one another
over batting orders and whether or not
a kid sister should play shortstop
with a brother's ratty glove.

In the park,
I walk across deep center careful
of territory and watch a woman wind up
for a lofty underhand on the pitcher's mound
as her own kids
and their friends scramble
and scream around the bases while she pitches
equally for both teams. The egalitarian.

The judge. No rules to fistfight over,
particularly when her legs are lithe
and her lungs full of sharp spring air.

She can bring down the game
or keep it going: I stop in right field;

leaves, newly exposed
from the snow strata now gone of last week,
shuffle on the ground like
nervous girls waiting a turn on the wind.

She is still young enough to play,
young enough to glide to her daughter's pop-up,
hogging the easy out. No tears shed,

none allowed. All sides
change with the precision of the seasons.

Quarterly West   PAUL COOK

LEAVES AMONG THE SNOW

Waste paper in the gutter
And dead leaves in the snow
Obey the wind: they wander
Where the lost and lonely go.

The destitute, the outcast,
All whom the world brings low
Are driven like the paper
Or the leaves among the snow.

The Malahat Review   R. L. COOK

FROG HUNTING

Almost always ahead of us,
hippety, in the night,
their sixth sense
radar to pick us up
& give them, hippety,
one jump on us,
the frogs dot the sidewalk
of summer after rain.
They are pursued, hop,
by two little girls,
barefoot, hair loose
in their faces, their hands
hippety, clasped in mine,
tugging this tired father.
Through sidestreets, the puddles
like black marshes, the concrete
buckled & split, hip-
pity, I'm pulled, hop.
But should a tired frog,
hippety, a lazy one,
a dreamer, one fat
with too many flies
or a frogleg-watching stud,
hippety, happen to pause
& feet of a demoiselle or two
land on his clamminess,
then, hippety, hippety, up
the father's legs they jump
to be carried, shrieking,
one in each arm, wriggling
home to their mother, hop,

The Yale Review   PETER COOLEY

THE OTHER SIDE

After lunch you leave the clouds behind.
You drive west and the sun gains ground.
By the time you stop for gas,
where a strong boy mans the pump
and slowly counts your change,
you must look into the sun
to see the road. This lasts for hours.

Thirty years ago a road was cut
through these small hills by men
who carried rakes and shovels.
They laid a good road down,
a road that runs west straight as the equator.
The sun follows it all afternoon,
making the summer grass shine,

making you squint, making a shadow
behind your car. And if you're walking
like the men who made this road,
with a rake and a shovel, you get
your own shadow, one that grows
with every step, one that looks
just like you, only taller, one

that looks the way you want to look,
next week or next year, tomorrow
or in thirty years, tall and sure-footed,
swinging your arms, twirling your rake,
bouncing on the balls of your feet,
thinking of the other side
of the next small hill.

Quarterly West   WYN COOPER

THE RETIRED PHANTOM JETS
OF LOWRY AIR FORCE BASE

They were not created as works of art,
merely mass-produced to bomb given targets,
support ground fire and infantry,
and machine-gun enemy aircraft
into a flash of burning steel.
Yet they are beautiful in the manner
of yawning tigers or well fed sharks.
With their swept back wings
and gray, tapering noses
they were the sharks of the sky.

Now they are monuments, statuary
to line the avenues of this air force base.
They are operable only as symbols
of what they once were.
Thus, in repose they have edged closer
to art; no longer the object,
only the perfect imitation.

They have subsided into beauty,
having become by disuse
what sculptors have struggled
so long, so hopelessly, to carve
from perfect slabs of Parian marble.

The Ohio Journal   ROBERT COOPERMAN

WORK

Maybe it was the way our bodies worked too hard
at pleasure, or simply that morning's windy romanticism.

Whatever, you asleep, your breasts fluttering unevenly
to a dream where you'd gone without me, I left.
Outside, taken by wind, no time for split decisions,
two swallows moved in and out of the barn windows
like children young enough to walk out of their clothes.
It was what we imagined, and still hoped for,
though hoping was hard work, work a kind of loss.
There are some things we should not imagine.
It is true two swallows piercing windows
only resembled two lovers, and the windows,
without panes of glass, only resembled the window
which you appeared at, but . . . . How we waited,
each of us in our strange human body, for some sign:
would you come out, would I be coming in.

Quarterly West   ROBERT CORDING

DIVORCE

When you die in a northern town
our two graying daughters call me home.
Driving in, I find the strange
countryside and town the same
as places where we met: endless
hills of maple, pine, corn and cattle,
red-brick streets, high wood-frame houses.
I arrive with my second wife,
my thirty years with her
twice what I had with you.
Only my daughters know me—
our friends different, parents dead,
other relations afraid to come.
Nothing I've known prepared me
for this moment at your grave.
Your second husband four years dead,
I feel, for the first time,
I must be yours again.
Never mind our thirties,
when youth unravelled
to its opposites—selfishness and fear.
Once, you talked and kissed
only that I might remember, and I do.
By the stone you share with him
my arms encircle our daughters.
Their heads press my chest
in the vice I have avoided
for so long: difficult love.
The rows of stones radiate from yours.
The sun shone for your burial.
The maples here look healthy,
yet the tips of many branches
hang snapped, as if a storm
had passed through yesterday.

As ever, I don't know how to leave—
which last word to blurt across this mound,
which woman to clutch as I turn,
which wrong choice to make once more.

California Quarterly   STEPHEN COREY

THE WATER HOLE

The force that drives the sun up drives the sun
To batter the red earth flat, crack its skin
And bake it. Not a bird is flying. Zebras
Gather herd by herd in dust. And stand.
Lions loll about the water hole.
A lion drinks. A lion sits in water.
Zebras gather and stand in herds and watch.
Male and female. Young. Their hides are parched
And red with dust. Some tremble. The smallest totter.
The stallions see all this. But the zebras do not approach.
They do not gather together to attack.
They are afraid of lions. Scorched earth congeals
To four horizons. They endure. They stand and wait
For lions in their time to feed upon.

Dandelion   TONY COSIER

SUNBATHERS ON THE CHARLES

Many are not pretty.
Seen from above, these banks
might look like panels of a tapestry,
a colorful, logical drama
halved by water. But you
and I have often walked among them,
since the river is not far,
and we take walks as others take
vacations: to find a place so odd
in its confusing streets, currency,
and in compact, egg-shaped cars,
we recognize ourselves more easily.
The women braid, unbraid their hair,
spread aromatic oils on their men
grown quarrelsome in the heat.
Somewhere along this route
we've turned away from each other.
Discouraging—the river casting back
its thousand useless coins.
When we paused by the water,
what delayed us there—
the music from the boats, their songs
of someone rescued or spared?

Such a reassuring fiction—
we might draw it over us,
as now this woman slips her tunic on,
her peasant skirt, moves to a bench in shade.
Is she tired of these bodies sleeping
as if sewn into the banks, or the water
that attracts, reflects, but never clarifies?

The Boston Review   STEVEN CRAMER

SOUTHERN TIER

I give you hardwood hills of orange and flame,
hardrock living in the hollows, where houses
are tar paper, tin roofed, cinder blocks; where the
shallow Chemung valleys the hillsides, and the
names are lost in their Indian past: Painted
Post, Big Flats, Horseheads, Elmira, Cohocton.
I give you finger lakes of glacial water,
long hard winters and brief sweet springs; where it is
overcast most of the year and the factory
smoke of Corning Glass Works clouds the crowned ridges,
the far hills to the north. Hilled in, houses flock
and crowd, nestled in hedgerows, braced for the snow.
Snow and flood are constants, but there are moments:
coined orange leaves, the gilded corn, jeweled crocus
braving the thin northern air. I give to you
Ithaca, Cayuga, Canandaigua, grape
vines, old schools, thin soil, rusty cars clumped in yards,
marigolds sunk in bathtubs, pinwheels in grass,
and always the hills, the gathering hills, and
the silver river ribboning the valley.

Plains Poetry Journal   BARBARA CROOKER

THE REFUGEES

From my kitchen I see
large white birds sailing
in the distance,
a familiar crook of wing.
I grab my glasses in disbelief:
seagulls in March? And so far inland?
The wind washes like surf;
the corners of my mouth taste salt.

Later, I read in the paper
of this annual flight,
see a grainy print of an Amish farmer
warding off their wheeling wings—
"They'll steal my worms," he cries.

Later, I am at a table
trying to teach English
to a family from Vietnam.
They have lived three years in camps;
they have come with nothing but their names.
My letters are bird tracks in the sand;
their words fly back and forth between them,
bird songs on the tongue.

Oh, this long slow flight through language—
years before we will talk together.
Seagulls, this far inland,
seagulls, in Pennsylvania—
working their wings for the long flight home.

South Dakota Review   BARBARA CROOKER

IN SPITE OF ALL

I'm whiffing the sweet manure of the meadows,
Cattle, shocks of grain, the ingathered gleams
Of that world of horizons where the wing
Of a magpie traces in black on the gold sky.

Startlingly, here comes just what I want,
A girl who knows nothing of what I want of her,
Perfection's perfection, essence of the season,
A goddess with clearest of sky-mirroring eyes.

Of course her armpits are rank and dank with work,
But I'm far from the sea, the kempt lawns and towns,
And I want to have her, I want to forget

In her sweated thick hair my crazed craziness.
I'll speak straight: Girl, I want to drown in you,
Then die criminally insane forever and ever!

The Chariton Review   CHARLES CROS
                            —*Translated from the French by Karl Patten*

OH LOVE

(for Oahira)

Oh love,
where do you go with your silonce?
I am moving into
the infinite walls of your skin
in search of our being.
Only this oneness knows
eternity's secret to prayer,
or the music of spheres
which I have seen whirling in your eyes.

From a sacred rock
together we saw the ancient dance of stone.
How the mist reveals the mountains
and the mountains move!

Somewhere through the non-existent doors of my heart,
an eagle will fly,
and this race of wind in my mind
will cease.
And there again we will meet.
God looking God in the eye.
On the first full moon of fall.

You have come to me
like the very first beat of my heart.
The first breath.
Or happiness
showing itself in tears
or smiles that will forever glow!

Oh love,
as I move deep into the gardens of your dreams,
you are still asleep in me.
Every miracle that a man with a woman can be.
You are everything!
Sight. Sound. Touch.
And the Ancient One
walking in silence from the sea—
You are everything:
The silence.
The song.
And the one inside that is me!

The Sun   THOMAS RAIN CROWE

SPRING FED

the stone basin
fills and fills
from the swivel tap's
trickle.

The hills have shed
so much snow
and now,
the first brown grasses
clear of it,
the heifers push
up into the fields
to take the early shoots.

And it comes
again—
the whole slow
turning of the season—

the softer touch of air,
the shine on the bucket,
the unclenching of things,
the lapping of the water
in the stone basin
up to the rim,
and the very first,
this
delicious overspilling
onto our boots.

Kayak   TONY CURTIS

A SHORT HISTORY OF THE MIDDLE WEST

Under this corn,
these beans,
these acres of tamed grasses,

the prairie still rolls,

heave and trough,
breaker and green curl,

an ocean of dirt tilting and tipping.

Its towns
toss up on the distance, your distance,
like the wink

of islands.

And the sky
is a blue voice
you cannot answer for.

The forked and burning wildflowers
that madden
the ditches

nod without vocabulary.

Your neighbor
is out early this morning—the air
already humid as a diamond.

Drunk or lonely,
he's scattering large scraps of white
bread for the birds,

as if it were winter.

He'd give you the sour undershirt off
his back—
sweet, bad man.

Does he remember
rain salting down from that flat, far shore
of clouds

slowly changing
its story?

On this shore,
the trees all babbling with their hands?

The New Yorker   ROBERT DANA

MY FATHER WORKED LATE

Some nights we were still awake,
my brother and I, our faces smearing the window,
watching the headlights bounce up the driveway
like wild pitches of light
thrown by a tired moon.
We breathed in the huge silence
after the engine died,
then ran to the door, grabbing his legs
as if we could hold him there
through night, morning, forever.

Some nights when he wasn't too tired
he'd take off his shirt
and sit in the middle of the floor.
We would wrestle, trying to pin
back his arms, sitting on his chest,
digging our heads into the yellow stains
under the arms of his t-shirt.
Each time we thought we had him:
"Do you give, huh, do you give?"
he'd sit up, straddling us both in headlocks
in the closest thing to an embrace
that I remember, and carry us to bed.

Other nights, he looked right through us
mechanically eating his late dinner,
yelling at anything that moved.
Some mornings we woke to find him
asleep on the couch, his foreman's tie twisted
into words we couldn't spell.
We ate our cereal as carefully as communion
until our mother shook him ready for another day.

*

My father carries no wallet full of lost years,
carries no stubs, no guarantees,
no promises.
We could drive toward each other all night
and never cross the distance of those missing years.

Today, home for a visit, I pull up to the house.
My father walks down the steps
limping from his stroke;
he is coming toward me

both of us pinned to the wind;
he is looking at me as if to say,
"give, give, I give"—
as if either of us
had anything more to give.

Passages North   JIM DANIELS

THE SEA SHORE

On some evenings I drive past the cremation ground
And seem to hear the crunch of bones in those vulgar
Mouths of fire, or at times I see the smoke, in strands,
Slowly stretch and rise, like serpents, satiated,
Slow, content and, the only face I remember
Then is yours, my darling, and the only words your
Oft-repeated plea, give me time, more time and I
Shall learn to love. How often I wish, while you rest
In my arms, that I could give you time, that this great,
All enveloping thng I offer you, calling
It meekly, love, can take us to worlds where life is
Evergreen, and you, just at those moments, raise your
Red eyes at me and smile, perhaps at the folly
Of my thoughts. Shall I forgive the days, that speeding,
Shed as footmarks, the wrinkles beneath your eyes, or
Forgive the crowds who come to you to talk, to plead,
To argue, and the gay brittle ones who flash such
Fake smiles at you and ask you for drinks or are asked
For drinks . . . all those destroying ones who leave you by
Night, to lie so ravaged, so spent, like a sea shore
In empty hours under moon . . . ? Not knowing what
Else to do, I kiss your eyes, dear one, your lips, like
Petals drying at the edges, the burnt cheeks and
The dry grass of your hair and, in stillness, I sense
The tug of time, I see you go away from me
And feel the loss of love I never once received.

New Letters   KAMALA DAS

A POEM SMUGGLED OUT OF PRISON

Jail handicrafts are no longer what they used to be!
We do not cut diamonds nor polish rubies.
The silk woven in Ward Thirteen
Was fit for even a Chinese queen.
Indeed, for the wedding of Princess Alexandra, Bengal's gift
Was a durbar scene done in gold by a blind convict.

It is but natural that the most seductive wedding veils
Shall be the produce of the midnight looms of repressed males.

The loveliest roses of the Governor's annual flower show
Always came from the condemned prisoners' row.
Perhaps that is one of the reasons
The only cheerful poems these days come out of prisons.

New Letters   JYOTIRMONY DATTA
                              —Translated from the Bengali by the author

A TAKE OFF ON A PASSING REMARK

Tall buildings impress me,
    the ones which cut off half the sky.
I like tall stories, even though false;
    not the half-truth sleeping with the half lie.
I want things on a large scale:
    amplitudes, a sense of space and light,
the great yellow eye of the train
    lighting up the distances of the night.
Urchins, furred caterpillars, moles
    and fern-beds are all right.
But I want flowering trees, long
    streamers of moss, flaming parasites.

But when you ask, still squirrel-young
    short as twilight
    short as a shadow at noon
why I love you, what can I answer?

New Letters   KEKI N. DARUWALLA

IN SEARCH OF WARM SHADOWS

I am growing a need of sun,
like spring snake or ripening fruit,
old bones and just-washed clothes.

Today hawks cruise high as jets.
They are out in squadrons,
bodies light and black against the sunless air.
Centered in a field of winter rye
a bronze cat sits, her forehead blessed in white,
waiting;
still waiting
though I watch her with accusing eyes.

We are all of us awaiting something:
some need, some want, some danger.
Some around-the-corner magic.
No sounds come but that cow aching with milk,
a distant tractor,
the rustle of brittle leaves without shadow.

My own waiting wears a restless foot,
down toward the valley
where above the mists one patch of blue mountain
is circled wistfully
in remnants of elusive sun.

Poem   ANNE DAVIDSON

THROUGH BIFOCALS

This you have heard before;
Have heard to the point where it serves
Only to numb, of the insult
Historical markers invite
With such inconsequence: Battle
Of Murfreesboro, of Franklin . . .

Two hours ago a boom
And a brief billow of pink
Dust was how a small
Recalcitrant bluff was cleared for
"A Planned Community in
The Williamsburg Manner."

Earthmovers on that hillside
Lie still now, and a jiggle
Of off-and-on orange flashes
Seemed, when I looked over there
Through reading glasses, a pulse
Of pain in the pink earth's wound.

My trustier bifocals
See lights atop the blazon,
Red on yellow, of
"Country Store" in this
Uncomplaining tract of
Tennessee disembowelled.

Among the supposedly fine
Arts, one at least has weaseled
Out of the tatterdemalion
Rear guard, and put its trust in
The double focus: "plan"
Enforced; then (optional) "manner."

Architects! co-workers
With Louis Sullivan once, you
Wink at as foolishly "dire."
My warning to your consumers:
The wider the range of manners,
The more inhumane the enforcement.

The American Scholar   DONALD DAVIE

WHITE PAGES

Today, all day, I gaze at a white wall.
The window panes are streaked or wreathed with webs.
The pages I have marked in my blue scrawl
lie all around me in a pile that ebbs
like water when I shut the windows and stall
the drafts. I watch the trapped bee burn. He stabs
the glass. He reminds me of my mind
that beats against its walls and is still blind.

Tonight I daydream at my desk, my head
in my hands hoping for a sudden line.
I drop it for a book and pick a thread
from the binding; let the leaves fall from the spine
and drift across my desk like a white spread
until the snowy pages settle; shine
in the lamplight, in the dark cloud of ink
that blues my arm and so I blink

and let my head slip down where, dreamless, full
of dark, it floats on my desk for an hour
until at last I grip this heavy skull
and force it still. I stare into the sour
eyepits, finding nothing but the same dull
light flowing and an image of the face
that wilts as it thins against the bone
into the mask I share with everyone.

The Southern Review   GLOVER DAVIS

THE APPLE TREE

(for my brothers)

There is not time to remember what is missing.
We have grown as old as the apple tree which leans
into evening. Save for one limb lost to lightning,

it is much as we left it. Each spring it is thick
with bloom and then the twisted apples of Ohio
weigh it down all summer. By fall, the armies of boys

are bored with it, the way we were. In winter,
there is nothing but the black bent trunk
and the tangled limbs against the stark white sky.

Each day it is saved by the dark, the way
this day, this February day, keeps me turning
the pages of the calendar back toward beginnings.

The North American Review   WILLIAM VIRGIL DAVIS

FAWN

Late summer dusk. Headlights along the road.
A sudden apparition by the hedge.
My car swerved aside of its own wish,
an instep arch crushed on the brake pedal,
and stopped in an instant. Jumped out
to learn whether we had killed anything
without a sound or click of contact.
Lying on asphalt, dazed but conscious,
half lay a spotted fawn, so scrawny that
I could not tell whether it had been struck
by hunger, illness, or accident. Over one eye
a slight cut, slightly bleeding. The fawn
blinked, lay still. Now other cars were halting.
Occupants were out, shouting advice.
The fawn reclined, dreamy and indifferent.
After a quarter hour of altercation
we heaved the passive, lally-legged baby
into a van, one of us holding a head
that did not need the holding, wary of
the hooves that did not move or strike,
and settled it inside a neighbor's barn
with a sheep-nipple, evaporated milk,
chlorate of lime, a bottle, barley-sugar.
Out of all these, warm deer-milk was concocted
and fed into the fawn with deep resistance
from one so weak, so wild, so uncomplaining.
Blowing into the corner of her mouth
triggered a reflex that would make her suckle
and take enough to help her stay alive:
most of the milk ran down along her neck
but some was kept. She lay with folded legs
unmoving, making no attempt to rise
when her feeders aproached, not attempting
to give more than a sniff of cooperation.
The second day we took her from the barn
and fed her on the lawn. Her keeper let her go,
and suddenly she found her feet, making for open
country, so weak she could not navigate,
staggering sideways, legs scissoring.
Now, when we tried to put her in the barn,
she flailed out at us with those edged hooves
and struggled till we feared not for ourselves
but her, that she might shatter against the wall.
The third and fourth days she was so much stronger
that her tail flicked up and down when she fed,
and she clattered back and forth in the dark stall.
We took her carefully into the sun,
fed her one last bottle, stood up and back,
and let her go. She walked, mincing forward,
then broke into a trot, and, as we watched,
she cantered down the lawn and onto the marsh,

tail held high, then out of view into the alders
that border on the marsh. There is no knowing
if she survived the winter, but it was a mild one.

The American Scholar   PETER DAVISON

THE DARK IS A DOOR

The dark is a door
you can open or a window
or a curtain that
will slide free, letting
you in. The dark is
a door that will open.
The dark is tonight,
with stars pendulous
as white buds,
bobbing and blinking on
a huge black bush,
always on the verge
of blooming open.
We go into. We go through
the dark door into
the hush and alien splendor
of grasses at night.
Of crickets whittling
away at something.
Of the cool, damp trunks
of trees. Of flowers closed
and still and dreaming
on their stalks. We do not
talk. We move carefully
into the dark. Deep to our
right and left, before and
behind, the night-things are
with us, awake and watching.
In this other world, something
in us aches of the familiar.
Dark, dark blood stirs.
We open the door of the dark
to enter a history, a memory.
Stones at our feet and gravel
reveal old faces. Noises
and whispers, wind in the leaves,
cries in the distance speak
with a voice that we've heard.
We enter these nights trying
to answer. Close to a secret,
we tremble with words.
But the dark is a door we can
only voicelessly enter;
a place before the word.

Touchstone   SUSAN STRAYER DEAL

LOOKING FOR POETRY

Don't write poems about what's happening.
Nothing is born or dies in poetry's presence.
Next to it, life is a static sun
without warmth or light.
Friendships, birthdays, personal matters don't count.
Don't write poems with the body,
that excellent, whole and comfortable body objects to lyrical
    outpouring.
Your anger, your grimace of pleasure or pain in the dark
mean nothing.
Don't show off your feelings
that are slow in coming around and take advantage of doubt.
What you think and feel are not poetry yet.

Don't sing about your city, leave it in peace.
Song is not the movement of machines or the secret of houses.
It is not music heard in passing, noise of the sea in streets that
    skirt the borders of foam.
Song is not nature
or men in society.
Rain and night, fatigue and hope, mean nothing to it.
Poetry (you don't get it from things)
leaves out subject and object.

Don't dramatize, don't invoke,
don't question, don't waste time lying.
Don't get upset.
Your ivory yacht, your diamond shoe,
your mazurkas and tirades, your family skeletons,
all of them worthless, disappear in the curve of time.

Don't bring up
your sad and buried childhood.
Don't waver between the mirror
and a fading memory.
What faded was not poetry.
What broke was not crystal.

Enter the kingdom of words as if you were deaf.
Poems are there that want to be written.
They are dormant, but don't be let down,
their virginal surfaces are fresh and serene.
They are alone and mute, in dictionary condition.
Live with your poems before you write them.
If they're vague, be patient. If they offend, be calm.
Wait until each one comes into its own and demolishes
with its command of words
and its command of silence.
Don't force poems to let go of limbo.
Don't pick up lost poems from the ground.
Don't fawn over poems. Accept them
as you would their final and definitive form,
distilled in space.

Come close and consider the words.
With a plain face hiding thousands of other faces
and with no interest in your response,
whether weak or strong,
each word asks:
Did you bring the key?

Take note:
words hide in the night
in caves of music and image.
Still humid and pregnant with sleep
they turn in a winding river and by neglect are transformed.

Antaeus   CARLOS DRUMMOND DE ANDRADE
—Translated from the Spanish by Mark Strand

TO A GIRL IN APRIL

It is April, mother of May,
Dress the dolls of life and play.
(Hide the origin of tears
For the later swamp of years.)
Loose your dreams and let them run
Like the horses of the sun.
Eat the manna of today,
April's short—and so is May.

The Arizona Quarterly   WILLIAM WALTER DE BOLT

OPOSSUM SPRING

This season of birth they seem to celebrate
self-slaughter. They squander on the berm,

in the ditches, splatter the concrete
like the gray shreds of a retreating army,

repeating the same slow-brained blunder
across the path where the man things hurtle.

I bend over one, brush the flies away, and touch
the whorls of grizzled fur, fur that kept it

warmer than dinosaur or mastodon.
Here the habitual curled lip, always

the toothy leer, as if at last it got the joke.
And yes, as always, the thickish, scaly tail,

curled in a perpetual question mark.
What vision echoed in your tiny skull?

What scrap worth clutching in those paws (so like
a child's spread fingers) made you start across

the asphalt in your shambling, nose-down way?
No time this time to feign death, but turn, face it

with your sort of addled courage. And then
the exploding glare, what must have seemed a sun

come down. And surviving all those eons,
here it comes again—one millisecond to gape,

grin your possum grin, and blink, and
wonder at this final rush of radiance.

The Yale Review   MARK DEFOE

SPEED LIMITS

*(Motorists caught speeding by radar-type devices . . .
in Dade County had their trials postponed Wednesday
after judges were shown a film in which a tree was
clocked at 86 mph.—ASSOCIATED PRESS)*

At high speed, bizarre things *are* possible,
Though statistics show that, of all of them,
Death's most likely: yardsticks shrink, clocks slow down,
Mass increases; familiar voices chit
In chipmunk's chatter. Suddenly, we lose

Our credibility. When the body
Sleeps, the mind speeds, and we dream. Like tortoise
And hare, body and mind can only race
Against reason. The stone-deaf man, the blind
Man—both exceed legal limitations

Of common sense: one has broken the sound
Barrier and gained a silent kingdom;
One has crossed the threshold of light into
A darkness that projects no depth. For them,
Experience has its hidden speed traps.

But for most of us, light and sound police
The world. When we wake from our harebrained dreams
In the morning, the trees are standing stock-
Still. And we slow ourselves down consciously,
Obeying the sirens and the stop signs,

Limiting life to what we can believe.

Southwest Review   JOHN DELANEY

THE BURIED ONE

The writer began his masterpiece.
A neighbor's child is dying of hunger.

The writer works ceaselessly at his work.
Now the starving child is worse.

The writer began to prune his great work.
The child is in a coma.

The writer abridges, synthesizes his work.
The child is in his death agony.

Now there's only one line left on the page.
The child is dead.

The writer has only the title left.
They've buried the child.

The writer
once again is facing his blank page.

Denver Quarterly   MANUEL DEL CABRAL
                                —Translated from the Spanish
                                    by DONALD D. WALSH

CATFISHING OFF THE WATEREE RESERVOIR BRIDGE

We bait our hooks, drop them into black water.
The bridge is a quarter mile long, one lane wide,
we share it with beer cans, bait cups, pine needles,
wooden boats that sail over the water in gusts.
A thunder storm is on the August horizon. Humidity is a suit
we wear, a tacky skin. Hot wind makes it worse. Mosquitos.
Men and boys in pick-ups pass, stop,
ask if we are lucky, how the family is; we nod,
give what we can, but we are unlucky, everyone is fine.

Lightning surrounds us with spikey ladders
leading up to a biblical Southern heaven none of us
will ever see. We are too full of beer, the devil.
Pines gather by the reservoir in a sappy, bitter
crowd, where red birds nest, mockingbirds, crows.
Towhee dive-bomb the updrafts inches from our faces,
teasing our lines that kick in the white-caps,
rifling across wide water, a sheet fluffed up,
settling down, kicked up again.

Night comes slow, no shooting stars, the crescent moon
is dipping into the pines, crickets rub their knees,
slow engines. The cloud-head breaks. We are side by side.
Our hearts grin on the end of fishing line,
bait dangling on the sandy bottom of our dreams;
"not giving a damn for hell or high water,
we have drowned our worms," have the widest part
of the bridge to ourselves. Reeling up, casting out again—
we hope something in us hooks a fish's memory,
whittles a notch into the railing we slowly drift away from.

Cedar Rock   KEN DENBERG

THE MAN ON MY PORCH MAKES ME AN OFFER

"Above all houses in our town
I've always loved this blue one you own
With its round turret and big bay window.
Do you dream about it the way I do?
Wouldn't you be just as happy
On a street with more trees
In a larger house, whose columned porch
Impresses every passer-by?
Does it seem fair that you've won the right
To gaze from these windows your whole life
Merely because you saw them first,
And consign me to a life of envy?
I'll gladly assume more than your mortgage,
More than the new brickwork and roof repair.
Often I've noticed your wife and daughter
Waiting on the porch, peering down the street
For your car, a handsome, modest pair,
And I'm sure I can make them happy,
Happier than you can,
You who have other projects to work on.
I would live for you the one life
You'd have wanted to live, had you stayed,
And you can walk free, away from town,
Out beyond the suburbs, to that quiet place
Where the small voice of your true self
May be heard, if anywhere, and each day
You can wake up feeling your powers
Still increasing, which is happiness,
While I lose myself in the life you made
And did not want enough,
Happy when the space you left is filled."

The Georgia Review   CARL DENNIS

ON COMMONWEALTH AVENUE AND BEACON HILL

(for William Saroyan)

Last year the magnolias flared
like candelabra bursting into flame,
quivering as if they had never bloomed
before, astonishing sight everywhere.

And if a soft rain fell it came
like angle breath, like gauze dispel-
ling the sweet excess of light.
This year the color is the same

and never was I more aware of fall-
ing petals. But only to compare
with those when we, a levitated pair,
walked above them all.

Yankee   DIANA DER HOVANESSIAN

NIGHTFALL

I was seven, the girl next door, thirteen,
with breasts and nipples new as grass,
and under her dress, warm, where
she hid me as a game
when my mother called me after dusk.
How could this girl know?—my face
on her thighs, my whole head
on her lap, the smell
of the secret under there. I want
to have my body there
yet, to be entirely small, and cling
with paws to one thigh. And I have
not left that girl, nor
my mother calling.

Images   PETER DESY

COMING HOME FROM THE DIVORCE

Things take their insignificance
from this. When I open the door
the house exhales its stale air at me.
The hall light burns
at low intensity. Under the table,
crumbs. And the oven, cold.
Each room silent as the pause
after a deep breath. All the plugs
pulled from their sockets. And dust
gathering dust.

Southern Poetry Review   PETER DESY

GOOD WOOD

It wasn't seasoned wood.
It stiffened where it stood.

Nor was it all that green.
It showed the paler sheen

Of olive, oozed the sweat
Of patience; and, once set,

Bore an ironic gloss.
This is what makes me cross:

It happily defies
Enthusiasm, lies,

Twenty centuries of Me.
Behold the man, the tree.

The Southern Review   THOMAS D'EVELYN

NEW DELHI, 1974

The city has spread quietly, suddenly. Everywhere
It springs up, this futile architecture, its garish forms

Shuffled and heaped, its grass sprouting sparse
And indifferent, its women brittle with paint,

Its wrists young and hairless, dipped into the pool
Where gold reflections rise, quiver at the rims of eyes.

The old scalps are dry, dead hair has lost its root,
And the mouth that once rehearsed its verses in these streets

Now is elsewhere. The monuments are black, rainblack
And shoulderless, and the plain that once stretched

Green towards the south is gray with dust and grime.
The old have nowhere to go now, in this new

City they have not built, and the impatient young
Are idle, and do not know where to turn.

Ariel   VINAY DHARWADKER

STRUGGLING AND SURVIVING

To struggle is only natural for us.
It is fighting the loneliness
When for-real brothers are few and far between.
It is explaining to the children why Malcolm is dead,
at least in the physical sense.
It is remembering the anguished cries of the ancestors
As they watched the ships slip beneath the horizon
And as we, chain-to-chain, stretched forth our hands
As if to touch once more the rich black earth of home.
To survive is only natural for us.
The drums yet beat in our hearts and the ceremonies yet
          remain in our memories.
Since the dawning upon the pyramids of time,

The African-American woman has nurtured the race
And kept its dreams ever stretching towards vivid reality.
We are queen, high priestess, warrior.
We are soft resilience, form and content,
Consciousness and development.
We do not struggle to survive;
We survive to struggle.

Black American Literature Forum   SCHAVI MALI DIARA

WINDOWS

are needed to put a frame around the landscape
which otherwise escapes into its own business.
Picture frames isolate what is the picture
from what is not the picture, and permit identification.
All these rectangular or square spaces
are similar; so is the printed page.

Open a book, the left page and the right page are equal.
The left brain and the right brain are equal.
This balance is significant, cities balance around squares
with a single warrior erect to the tip of his bronze sword.
He is historical because he is in his frame.
He is an agreement our brains have reached about him.

At its extreme, painting can dispense with objects
and see only the balance, the fact of containment
rather than things contained. That square information.
Now both the emperor and his clothes are needless.
Looking at an equation about emperors
their numbers vanish, and only an equal sign remains.

We can look in at the window, or out the window.
Windows are intended for safety between in and out.
In Amsterdam, the whores sit behind windows.
It is unnecessary to know what they are thinking.
They are there to be equal to what we are thinking.
If there were no glass, we would not know they are whores.

I have only met you, and already I find myself
thinking of taking photographs: your face,
your body to the waist, these civil squares
thinking to make you still, thinking to tame you,
thinking to look out or in at you through my square window,
through which I have watched so often these small elegies.

The Georgia Review   WILLIAM DICKEY

REUNION OF THE THIRD PLATOON

They drink while half the stars set,
laugh and talk lightly

of life and death with the Third Platoon,
their eyes bright with the ritual of telling—
heroic and proud
but still very much like aging clerks.

Telling of Dietrich and Chavez and Henderson
running through the flaming village,
drifting over the streets unaware of their legs.
How Maloney was pitchforked as soon as he landed—
staring up at the sky he had dropped from,
a small bubble of death on his lips.
Or Murphy, how he braced himself on a rock—
his machine gun barrel hot,
flies laying eggs in his wounded shoulder.

Now Anderson talking. Now Roberts,
his hands describing battles and barracks
but not the night he had DEATH BEFORE DISHONOR
tattooed on his arm—
half drunk on two beers
imagining medals on his first uniform
just fresh from the warehouse.

Never a word about Stein going mad
still keeping a pistol under his pillow,
dreaming pantomime battles
the same bullet burning his gut over and over,
or how Sergeant Bartoli grows sad and vague
if he sees a dead bird or a butterfly wing.
His wife says he sits too much alone.

No one mentions next year . . . or meeting again.
But they'll all be back
except maybe Peters, who seemed out of breath
several times tonight,
or Williams, who always acts restless
when they get together like this.

The American Scholar   JOHN DICKSON

CENTRAL SCHOOL

That's where I was once,
sitting at a desk that wouldn't fit me now.
And dreamy-eyed Miss Shaunessey scheherazading me
every afternoon with Introduction to Mythology—
Hercules cleaning out the stables,
Narcissus loving his reflection in the pool,
or Pygmalion's sculptured goddess
suddenly come to life.

And all the time me there singing back to her,
the sad silent cello sounds echoing inside me,
thinking that everywhere she walked

the schmaltzy violins would play bucolic melodies,
thinking I'd be holding her hair in my hands
if I were older.

O the sun takes forever to grow cold.
Where is she? Where is Miss Shaunessey now?
Decembering away on some hotel porch
rocking herself silly while time
slips through her hourglass figure,
or maybe puttering about in her landlady's garden,
or worse, being autopsied or something
where they find a schoolroom still behind her eyes
complete with blackboard, chalk, and thirty desks,
crayon drawings pasted on the windows—
and me the way I was
lost in her blur of faces.

The Spoon River Quarterly   JOHN DICKSON

IRISES

We have stood years
by the side of this house
unnoticed but by birds,
a black widow, ants, the cat.

Humans departing
by the back door
pore over the snow peas, cress, lettuce.
How the garden applauds
that repertory of panhandlers.
It wants no part of us.

When introduced,
they do not hear our names.
Hidden behind petalled hands
we daydream like spinsters
in the May afternoon
of love
and resurrection.
Our purple silences
light their faces.

*The Buddha was born
at the full moon in May,*
a broken voice says.
We irises, heads battered
by storms,
hang together shivering
in the middle of everything.

University of Portland Review   MARGARET TOARELLO DIORIO

JUST AROUND DARK

The hooded glow of households, just around dark,
of lampshades craned over empty sofas,
the ripe illumination of kitchens and off-white
silken fluency of hallways . . . Then a twitch, a blip,
the light fractured by a man or woman
drifting from entryway to parlor, corridor to bedroom.
It sends down no real shadow on the sidewalk,
on me, yet I feel its vagrant touch
justifying my form and place.
I fix that shadow, preserving its brief sanction,
and meet its inconsequential presence with no great
consequence in thought, only the mind slightly bent on change.

This imagining, to me, in this real surrounding
brings collaborative joy. To encounter one street's
undistinguished gift with a mild curve of spirit,
relaxed, but still prepared to pay a little attention.
And so I want to keep on talking about it,
to prove that there is never nothing left to say
when what's at issue is the fleet presence
of the world's smallest matter. I'd ask even more.
May the unseen unreal shadow of a householder
fall and fall again on me as I walk along.
Let a thousand instances of suchness break
from staid or rivering light of rooms in memory.

New England Review & Bread Loaf Quarterly   W.S. DI PIERO

TWO SEASONS

(for Seferis)

I never loved summer enough,
Racing from the platform to the sea,
The sea impossible to forget,
Always there, holding and withholding,
Tempestuous and merely quarrelsome.
I think of the infinity waiting
Beyond the dunes, calm days
When I dove into reflection and was released.

I made friends that time of year.
Work was over, we had little in common
But the train ride and the sea.
Their kindness was easy; they were not unkind,
Never did anything out of the ordinary.
Nothing to say, we shared
Like sailors who desired the same woman,
Each wondered quietly if she cared for him.

So here are my waterproof notebooks:
The promise of sets of waves, the tide

Moving in or out, and what's left on shore?
Seaweed for popping underfoot, fish heads
From Russian trawlers, oil and the iridescent
Film on the sand. Essentials:
Salt crusted on the lip of a shell.
No, I never loved summer enough.

And my friends? I remember them
When our coats make us strange as beasts,
When waves break out of earshot,
And the train ride goes underground.
People on platforms, people under signs,
Hands tucked in pockets, skin chapped and pale.
These days when my eyes, tired of reading,
Look aimlessly into the mirror that glares back.

Ploughshares   STUART DISCHELL

FARMHOUSE IN EARLY FALL

Today, our roof leaks.
Last night, a loose pane rattled
in a gust of wind, fell
into fragments two stories down.
Tomorrow, we'll find a new crack
in the ceiling, a new slit in the screen,
another mosquito, another ambush.
And now the anxious bees
are building a hive in our window frame,
depositing there a column of honey
and causing what sweetness, what terror.
It's the law of the season:
things want in: field mice, the stray dog
from the upper reach, an oak branch
scraping against our weathered shingles,
or even the invisible guardian of the place
whom we've half-created, half-heard,
who might have died laughing at December.
Such is the wisdom of old houses,
reminding us of what we sometimes keep
at bay, lose sight of: bad weather, fear,
decay, such things we've come to watch for
in each other. And here we are,
just a frail kitchen-wall away
from next winter's successes, failures,
scrambling with our pots and rags,
wedging in shims between the sash and casing,
spackling the cracks for yet another ruin.
Soon the stove will hiss like a snake:
a good sound to remember cold by,
and the heat which will reprieve us.
For better or worse, we'll guide ourselves

by what the house predicts, lets in.
If it snows in the bedroom,
I'll know to look for you elsewhere.
If the bough breaks,
there'll be a child at stake.
But now the moon's in the window.
Now your opened mouth is my own.
And now we lay us down, and fall
into each other and the arms
which will retrieve us.

The Georgia Review   GREGORY DJANIKIAN

CHINA NIGHTS

(The Journey In)

Nothing was ever so beautiful
As this. We stand
On the deck and watch
The mountains of China

Rise from the sea
Like dragons
As white gulls
Shower down the cliffs

Toward the wake of the ship.
Each sailor knows
That tonight Hong Kong
Will lift a million lights

Over this harbor
Called *fragrant* in Chinese.
Every eye searches
The face of the city

For the secret life
That waits
For the first visitor
Who will ride

Under a moon unveiled
Like a breast:
He will sail
Across rooftops

And over the harbor
Spread below
In a sheen of white-tipped
Darkness

To the mountains that sing
In the night for the sea.

Quarterly West   MICHAEL DOBBERSTEIN

THE GUN

Late afternoon light slices through the dormer window
to your place on the floor next to a stack of comics.
Across from you is a boy who at eleven is three years
older. He is telling you to pull down your pants.
You tell him you don't want to. His mother is out
and you are alone in the house. He has given you a Coke,
let you smoke two of his mother's non-filter Pall Malls,
and years later you can still picture the red packet
on the dark finish of the phonograph. You stand up
and say you have to go home. You live across the street
and only see him in summer when he returns from school.
As you step around the comics toward the stairs,
the boy gives you a shove, sends you stumbling back.
Wait, he says, I want to show you something.
He goes to a drawer and when he turns around
you see he is holding a small gun by the barrel.
You feel you are breathing glass. You ask if it is
loaded and he says, Sure it is, and you say: Show me.
He removes the clip, takes a bullet from his pocket.
See this, he says, then puts the bullet into the clip,
slides the clip into the butt of the gun with a snap.
The boy sits on the bed and pretends to study the gun.
He has a round fat face and black hair. Take off
your pants, he says. Again you say you have to go home.
He stands up and points the gun at your legs. Slowly,
you unhook your cowboy belt, undo the metal buttons
of your jeans. They slide down past your knees.
Pull down your underwear, he tells you. You tell him
you don't want to. He points the gun at your head.
You crouch on the floor, cover your head with your hands.
You don't want him to see you cry. You feel you are
pulling yourself into yourself and soon you will be
no bigger than a pebble. You think back to the time
you saw a friend's cocker spaniel hit by a car and you
remember how its stomach was split open and you imagine
your face split open and blood and gray stuff escaping.
You have hardly ever thought of dying, seriously dying,
and as you grow more scared you have to go to the bathroom
more and more badly. Before you can stop yourself,
you feel yourself pissing into your underwear.
The boy with the gun sees the spreading pool of urine.
You baby, he shouts, you baby, you're disgusting.
You want to apologize, but the words jumble and
choke in your throat. Get out, the boy shouts.
You drag your pants up over your wet underwear and
run down the stairs. As you slam out of his house,
you know you died up there among the comic books
and football pennants, died as sure as your friend's
cocker spaniel, as sure as if the boy had shot your
face off, shot the very piss out of you. Standing in
the street with urine soaking your pants, you watch

your neighbors pursuing the orderly occupations of
a summer afternoon: mowing a lawn, trimming a hedge.
Where is that sense of the world you woke with
this morning? Now it is smaller. Now it has gone away.

Antaeus   STEPHEN DOBYNS

BUT MOSTLY

I love the shapes your hands
make, mayapples shining
already with next year's green
and pendant fruit. In their
small turnings, a spring
so future its only sounds are seeds
waits in silence.
Each morning when I rise up
with you, the same
song meadowlarks once raised
to the sun in Oklahoma stubble
curves the light
your hands hold up
into the air.
In the days of my body I will
love you the way a small boy
loves the name the world takes
and gives back to him.
And when once again I am leaves
and wind and the sharp
astonishing taste of water
on your tongue,
I will love,
yea, and cherish you
in the perfect cup your hands
will make, lifting me up
to your eyes, your cheeks,
your warm thirsting lips.

The Chariton Review   WAYNE DODD

LINES FOR A YOUNG POET

1

You have looked
at death with awe,
at love gently,
at myths, cosmic space,
and too many told tales.
Living is an old story
done and done

and done before.
It will sound naive
if I tell you
sometimes there is joy in it.

2

Old people read obituaries,
perhaps to rejoice
they are not yet theirs,
to keep in touch,
or to practise mortality.
You study death
as if to find
whether you have
something it hasn't.
Let me comfort you:
Life,
its passion,
its pain,
will find you
in due course.

The Centennial Review   FLORENCE DOLGORUKOV

GRADUATION

This morning, Sunday,
the maples are at last in full leaf.
Late, I lie in bed.
Children play in the street below;
their voices rise to my window,
are lost in the green maple shade.

Yesterday, in the center of athletic fields,
we took the photographs that will
fill the albums of the children:
Parents and grandparents keep
still ritual in June sunlight.
The robed boy smiles into the camera.
His sister stands shyly behind
and the smallest brother watches, still.

My hand scrapes the headboard of this bed
given to me by my father, their first.
I think of them here,
in a different room,
a different town,
more than a lifetime away
and see us all
in dresses, flowered ties,
arrangements made to take the
time to mark its passing,

our cameras recording the generations
ranged on the yielding grass
that stretches out to maples
turned in the long wind
that lifts the ladies' hair,
that lifts the dust
and sweeps our sight up high
through the light-diffusing
deep and passive endless air.

Tendril   DAVID F. DONAVEL

EVELYN WAUGH ON THE YOUNG RUSSIANS

Of course they're charming. Everybody thinks they're charming.
They wear fur hats and make dramatic gestures like Marco Polo.
Gestures they hope can be seen 200 miles across the frozen snow.
Napoleon knew that snow. It stopped him cold before he got to
    Moscow.
The French were generous to them; they withdrew their troops
and left books; later Stendhal, Zola, Hugo, Baudelaire, Rimbaud.
They've never had a normal press; from Czar to Commisar.
They've never had the press you have in NY or Toronto or Paris.
They wear fur hats and make dramatic gestures like Marco Polo.
But what have they written since the fall of Dostoievski?
Their poets are all charming fakers in fur hats,
Mayakovsky, Essenin, Yevtushenko: droll ideologues at best,
no specificity, no true color, nothing exact;
they're afraid to describe a new idea or the society they live in;
they play around with the line of the poem and they boom—
and when someone says 'give' they talk about the Russian bear.

Poetry Canada Review   DAVID DONNELL

THE SMALL BROWN BAT

The bat's bad reputation's due, mostly, to rumor.
That he's hand-in-glove with night is no cause for alarm;
night is his hard-working day. Though in looks as grotesque
as a gargoyle, designwise he's handsome. From his toothpick toes
and the seashell whorls of his ears to the tiny thumbs

he can scratch the back of his head with, all's to the point.
The bat, a hunter like the lion which chases zebras,
pursues the mosquito. He tracks his game by echoes—
those ghosts of sound that are gone in a flash like faces
from mirrors—and he takes his prey not by clamping his jaws,

but like a butterfly-catcher, his wing his net.
He grazes air's pastures with speed—but so do others.
If a sharp-eared tiger moth crosses his path, he's in trouble.

That mimic by faking the bat's own signals and feeding him
false information can escape with his life. Not so

the less gifted mosquito. But bat or moth, the one
to hesitate is lost. Not needing to look before leaping,
the bat's in the air, doing his flying best
to be not only fast but first, and thus a success
at his business, existence, by talents made the most of.

America   DOROTHY DONNELLY

TWO EVENINGS AND A SNOWY MORNING

I've seen your wonder open
in the simple mouths of spoons,
or in the way a single fork
arranged on a white plate
constructs a bridge of shadows.
Tonight you've tied a scrap
of gray ribbon under your collar
as though you were a gift;
when I open the wrappings
I find a mirror, ornate
or severe. It's hard to see
into its silvered darkness,
or imagine what shines
in its smooth face when I'm absent.

The guests gone,
we step out into a September evening
where things seem to rush
away from us—houselights,
window candles, the crabapple's
thick-handed clatter—
allowing the dumb wind
behind them to tumble forward,
a dazzled acrobat shimmering
on cold grass.
It's snowing in all the mirrors
on this street. Startled, a little sleepy,
each of our neighbors eyes his face
above the bathroom sink through a delicate,
ghostly scrim like static on a tv screen.
No weather reports. Outside, the intersection's still
and everything's foreign: streetlamps,
trees, blue mailboxes so familiar
we thought they'd never startle us. Nothing moving.
Only ourselves, walking out of the house
into the stilled traffic,
the streets' quiet certainty.

Mississippi Review   MARK DOTY

TAKING IN WASH

Papa called her Pearl when he came home
late, swaying as if the wind touched
only him. Towards winter his skin paled,
buckeye to ginger root, cold drawing
the yellow out. The Cherokee in him,
Mama said. Mama never changed:
when the dog crawled under the stove
and the back gate slammed, Mama hid
the laundry. Sheba barked as she barked
in snow or clover, a spoiled and ornery bitch.

She was Papa's girl,
black though she was. Once,
in winter, she walked through a dream
all the way down the stairs
to stop at the mirror, a beast
with stricken eyes
screaming the house awake. Tonight

every light hums, the kitchen is arctic
with sheets, Papa is making the hankies
sail. Her foot upon
a silk-stitched rose, she waits
until he turns, his smile sliding all over.
Mama a tight dark fist.
Touch that child
and I'll cut you down
just like the cedar of Lebanon.

Ploughshares   RITA DOVE

DISILLUSIONED

I came expecting old-time magic
On a once-familiar street—
But modern pavements, hard and gray,
Were strange beneath my feet.

Time had built some barricades
And I had changed my ways.
This town was not as I remembered
From our enchanted days.

The music and the poetry
Were shiny scales that fell.
Time, that once worked miracles,
Could tear them down as well.

The Villager   IRMA DOVEY

OFF TO THE EAST

"Board, sleep, and wake to other shores and light.
Relax," well-seasoned travelers of the night
insist, "it is the only way to fly."
The moon's a broken wafer in the sky,
the consecrated host I'll never taste,
the fellowship with which I won't be graced.
And this is close to faith as I may come:
what it is I am hurled into or from
by some celestial, mechanistic will
is destiny. Indifferent, good, or ill,
it does not matter at thirty thousand feet
but to be done, if only with defeat.
Cold constellations bloom into pure space,
dying in flower, unchanged while changing place,
as meaning's adumbration drifts beyond
my dark face in this dark glass and is gone.
Off to the east the old sun's livid birth
lends definition to the blackened earth
toward which we sink, and I've not strength to keep
this vigil, nor despair enough to sleep.

The Southern Review   SUZANNE J. DOYLE

HOW MY FATHER TURNED THE NIGHT INTO STORIES

Nothing as common as sheep.
To fall asleep, my father told me
to count fish swimming inside the gray light bulb.
He said listen and I would hear their blind lips singing.
He said sleep was a mirror
they kept bumping into, trying to slide out.

After he left, I stood on my bed,
yanked the string as if it were a hand line
tossed into the sky.
I was sure I would see their bright scales
in this sudden flash of light.

Thinking he had lied
I snuck slowly down the stairs,
balanced the warm bulb in my palms like a miniature tank
of water.
            But in the basement,
although I saw nothing spill out
when I dropped it on the cold cement floor,
I felt my father surface upstairs,
gasping from a dream.

Now, middle aged, I dive each night
towards some murky bottom to find my own son
testing this same bedtime story

like an old lure he will never trust,
casting it far and deep into the dark.

Kayak   JACK DRISCOLL

CONSTRUCTION SITE

On girders where the 14th story
Would go, a riveter
Set down his tools and started
The lower half of a love
Duet in Italian. Torches
Stopped; pneumatic drills,
On the concrete below, stopped.
Only the wind made noise, a whistle,
And rumpled the canvas, and whipped
The men's shirts while he sang.
Then nothing but the wind.
Then all the hands above the city, clapping.

Poetry Now   JOHN DRURY

THE JOURNEY: FOR A MARRIAGE

We venture, bold,
Through inner seas,
And shatter old
Geographies,

Diffusing flesh
With flesh, till lands
Once bitter beneath
Our troubled hands

Transmute to silence.
There appears,
Unmapped, the axis
Of our twining spheres.

Studia Mystica   CLAUDIA JENSEN DUDLEY

DEAR GEORGE ELIOT

But for that wind banging
overhead in the dark—a sound
as of all the angry slogans in the world
at last gathered into the gale
that blows away walls and rains

rads into cellar holes—but for that
reminder, I could be reading
"Middlemarch" over again
by the warm stove, contented enough
(an eldering, well-wedded man)
to remember and be remembered. . .

Time was I could not have conceived—
any more than Dorothea and Will
could skip to a motel in Scituate
and unwrite a thousand pages
of honor and obligation—conceived
there could be such an elder, brain-
sick for a wayward thing
in her twenties—to parasitize
on that passionate oblivion!—as,
hearing the ominous wind pound
on the clapboards and knowing
no help for it—flinging the book down—
I remain.

The New Yorker   PETER KANE DUFAULT

IN MEMORY OF EIGHT FIREMEN

(Philadelphia, September 1974)

I saw a woman with binoculars
standing on a car hood,
a white cadillac with leopard spots
left by ashes blown across the water;
she'd found a furnace on the river,
the flames wrapped around refineries,
the dragon heat blown across the Schuylkill,

the whole conflagration,
oil, fire and brave men in fancy hats
falling to their deaths,
engulfed by fire and her prayers.
A terrible circus played on the edge of Philadelphia,
fires burned rings around tanks,
steel ladders rose in shining sections,

and through the ashes rising from infernal smoke
like flocks of black birds,
the firemen were sailors in a storm at sea,
going home for lunch in shifts,
coming back to rise and die,
tumbling through the air in awful somersaults,
becoming at last fire eaters.

America   LAWRENCE DUGAN

THE BATS IN SUMMER

Sunset . . . that is when they start to leave
The attic, at first the few we see, that hang
From rafters; toward night the unseen hundreds come alive,
Crawling at first, then taking off on wing
In search of food. We sleep as best we can,
Knowing they will not be evicted from the house,
Aware they will be winging back at dawn,
Trying to crawl back in through roof and windows.
We keep the windows shut—they bang against the walls,
Squeeze in through fissures in the roof, and gutters.
Every night I wrap my hair with towels.
I am going mad; all day the creatures
Occupy my mind. The doctor has no cure.
Get rid of them, he counsels, *or endure.*

Plains Poetry Journal   LORA DUNETZ

DIRECTIONS

How to imagine yourself a bird: first,
let every breath inflate balloons
inside your body. Let every breath
fill your bones with air.
Move most of your muscles to your chest.
Lean forward. Let your hips migrate
up backbone until your tilted body
balances. Move your big toe
to the back of your foot. Walk
on your toes. Replace your fingers
with strong primary feathers. Discard
the bones you do not need.
Cover your head and body and arms
with feathers, light and strong.
Shape the feathers on your arms to airfoils.
Hang your body in the air from outstretched
arms. Slide your shoulders
down your back until you balance.
Clap hands beneath your face. Feel
air twist the feathers at your wingtips.
Feel every feather at the tips of your wings
thrust you into air.
Feel air on your wings lift you up, hold you
firm. Construct a spacious curve
in the sustaining air.
Breathe. Fill your body with air. Fly.

How to imagine how I love you: first,
imagine yourself a bird. Imagine
that bird to be me. Imagine that you
are air.

Kansas Quarterly   MILLARD DUNN

THE UNIVERSE IS TOO BIG TO LOVE

Some nights it's better not to look up there.
  The stars appear broken from certain angles,
    certain imperatives of seeing.

Moods! Moods can alter mathematics.
  If only I believed I were unimportant,
    a speck, as a mystic does,

this heaviness in my chest
  wouldn't matter. I could make friends
    with a pebble.

But I'm both a speck *and* important.
  I'm the right size for love.
    Still, there's no reason

for you, out there turning these pages,
  to care about me.
    When a night falls apart

it reveals more night
  and this is true perhaps
    for only one person at a time.

Soon it will be your turn
  and I will be home reading a book,
    perfectly calm.

The Georgia Review   STEPHEN DUNN

IN THE SAN BERNARDINOS

It was boring going up the mountain,
my companions speaking of ponderosa
pines and the midsummer snow
on Mt. Baldy. My legs didn't hurt,
I just preferred that bar in Wrightwood,
halfway to the valley, where beer
helped the talk into surprise
and the pool balls clinked
and there was no obligation to beauty.
At 6000 feet, though, a wild red
flower grew solitary and I started
to anticipate others like it
growing amid rocks in small clearings,
no pattern to them, nameless
to me, and that's how I forgot
about the too-easily-loved view
and the top I didn't want to reach
and the insistent peacefulness.
Later, going down, I felt nothing
but the declension of my own movement,
saw only the blur of green

and Virginia's sweet human backside
in front of me. What could I say to her,
who loved it all, what could I say
to any of them who wanted calm,
who preferred this thin air
to sea level's hum and complication?
And what was I afraid of, up there,
and to what couldn't I yield?

We embraced at the bottom
as if all distances were bridgeable
by touch and recognition;
the beer in Wrightwood
solved the momentary general thirst
and on the drive back our shirts
stuck to our backs, we descended
into heat and more heat, everything
I remembered.

Antaeus   STEPHEN DUNN

TANGIER

There's no salvation in elsewhere;
forget the horizon, the seductive sky.
If nothing's here, nothing's there.

I know. Once I escaped to Tangier,
took the same face, the same lie.
There's no salvation in elsewhere

when elsewhere has empty rooms, mirrors.
Everywhere: the capital I.
If nothing's here, nothing's there

unless, of course, your motive's secure;
not therapy, but joy,
salvation an idea left behind, elsewhere,

like overweight baggage or yesteryear.
The fundamental things apply.
If nothing's here, nothing's there—

I brought with me my own imperfect air.
The streets were noise. The heart dry.
There was no salvation elsewhere.
I came with nothing, found nothing there.

The Yale Review   STEPHEN DUNN

HEAVEN

Today, in July, when there are supposed to be
waves of heat rising from the black highway,

it is raining and everything is wet and shining.
The clouds push down the horizon, the trees
that line the river darken, and the bridge is alive
as it drops back down behind a boat.
This must be heaven, smoke in the distance,
or is it fog running in with the tide.
All I see is green darkening and smooth gray.
And water, in the river, in the sky,
in the branches of these trees.
I talk as if you're here and can understand.
As if your eyes are green darkening, and your hair
is black and shines like the river, the highway,
the bridge beams, the car on the levee
moving away in its own smoke.
I wish I could tell you more things I know.
Your dark coats and dresses, damp eyes,
handkerchiefs willed with perfumed smoke.
I miss you always in rain, in this daytime
darkness, in the clam gray of this scene
you would love.

Quarterly West   QUINTON DUVAL

FALCON

It is a proud bird high and mean on a marble tower.
Black is its favorite color. If you must know. It is black.
Leave it alone, it does not think in colors. With crooked feet,
yellow and tight, it holds a kingly purchase on this height.
It is content; it has already fed. It will not stoop
to make you shiver, or to make you weep. It is a fierce
and quiet splash of black against this brittle morning.
It is smooth, sharp, and stark. Alert. Alone. And that small crack
of rage upon its face is just its smile. There is no bird
so glad in heaven on this bleak morning, no sad black bird
so fast upon a lonesome patch of sky as this mad thing,
keen plunger planted on the top of this tall cone of stone.
Imperiously ruling the horizon, all space and time,
it sees, with eyes that pierce, the blowing flowers, the rustle
of luscious, light-furred bodies far there in the grass, afraid,
below. It sees a star behind, a star ascending.
It sees the fountain, yes. It sees the trees. Yes, yes. It sees
everything you could show it, and it likes, if you must know,
not to be bothered with your bright attention. If you must know,
best it likes black; black; against its face.

The American Poetry Review   FRANK DWYER

WALKING OUT AFTER RAIN

How many times has it broken me,
this notion of perfect love?
The oaks in the park grow separately
though roots twine below, branches above.

Under the gleam of the trees
dark branches are still raining,
the sound of the water has become
a sudden rush of the tide.

I am lifted up onto a wide
ocean of love. I am some
boat with sails swelling and straining.
I am the breeze.

The Sun   RALPH EARLE

THE IMAGE EXIT

The tunnel through the mountain suggested terrifying power—
The dentist's drill, the auger; the little boring-in, the immense,
    contained, ruthless operation—
And right at the tunnel mouth the exquisite quaresma tree in
    purple flower.

The dentist may not let you go so easily again;
The engineer's crude ambition is absolutely endless:
The dentist smiles, quaresma offers you, for terror, this purple ruff
    around your pain.

So urban, tropic, images make their radical and rueful blend—
Aided by narcotics, I sat in the chair dreaming
Of how the mind kept thinking of the blossom, the tunnel that
    would never end.

It does, though, in an enormous sucked-through flower of sun—
Browbeaten by the light, you are as well bedizened:
Vision comes back, almost as heavy as flung jewels, to the propelled
    and punctured one.

Caves as compared with cavities, the elevator and the rising chair—
Were you told in a trance of the existence of a secret gold mine,
Vertical or horizontal—then shafted, shafted, without knowing
    where?

It has been years and years and years since I was there—the ultra
    South—
Many chairs, tunnels—*exeunt omnes*—the blinding nimbus just a bit
    too large to wear:
The doctor smiles, the open face of rock has a purple stain around
    the mouth.

The Midwest Quarterly   CHARLES EDWARD EATON

THE IDEAL AND THE REAL

The word that burned into a page
Destroyed time, but the page is still there,
    Blank.

It was so immediate it flew away,
But reality was reality when I was young,
    Singing.

When I was young I destroyed time
While lovingly I was discovering it.
    Flashing.

I knew the absolute of the immediate
When I looked at a lily in the thicket.
    Heaven.

I knew nothing of heaven but of earth,
Earth was heaven at eye and fingertips.
    Unforgettable.

How could I know that I was obliterating time,
Only that time should smudge the vision?
    Unsuspected.

The word I wrote on a page was absolute.
Everything was poetry, everything was real.
    Sensation!

The word burned into a page
That withstood the passion of my imagination,
    Another reality.

There was no death in the incredible garden,
Now age brings time on an open page,
    Inditing.

The timeless gives over to the labors of time,
Man's glimpse of perfection meets imperfection.
    Kingdom come.

The Literary Review   RICHARD EBERHART

NEW MARRIAGE

Marriage among the married
Is a new shoe on an old foot.
The foot-race is to the strong
Whether anybody is right or wrong.

Marriage among the married
Is a new progression and obsession.
Blood continues flowing
No matter which way the world is going.

If we cannot drink mead with the Persians,
Put it down to mischance and folly.
The worse the political weather
The closer we must bind ourselves together.

New marriage for old marrieds
Has to do with belief in living.
It is a matter of giving,
And it is a means of forgiving.

Let us rejoice at a new married pair
Whether or not married before.
It is good, it is something new
And all friends enjoy the view.

The single like to be double
For protection, to keep out of trouble.
Two against time are better than one.
If unloving, you may be undone.

Now let us be believing
In the charm of new perceiving;
These love-believers make us see
Freedom of a new reality.

The Literary Review   RICHARD EBERHART

CANOEING THE POTOMAC

As rivers go, this one isn't much.
It doesn't drain a continent; it doesn't
flow through wilderness; it isn't wild,
or wide, or deep. Between Antietam
and the Shenandoah, only scattered
mild rapids interrupt its calm.
What makes this river awesome
is its sadness: along these gentle
tree-lined banks, in 1861, a nation
shattered like a brittle stone.

Up ahead, at Harpers Ferry, abolitionist
John Brown captures the federal arsenal
for freedom, but he in turn is captured
by a West Point colonel, Robert E. Lee.
Behind us, three years later,
Lee's Confederate Grays are met
by George McClellan's Union Blues.
Cannon shot and bugles blare
the ranks of razored bayonets across
the fields littered with the cost
of John Brown's Glory.

The Union was preserved, of course,
but the sadness remains. Our sleek
canoes move in silence through the gap

between the violence of those years
and the violence we've inherited.
Moral people, principled and kind as Lee,
still apply their talents to the sword,
and people mad as John Brown still insist
their service to the noblest ends.
Saddest of all, Browns and Blacks, Blues, Grays,
Yellows, Reds, and Whites are still in chains
that bind us to the deadly past
out of which we seem this summer day
to glide with such apparent ease.

Samisdat   W.D. EHRHART

I, TOO, LOOK INTO THE FIRE

Forty years ago, in the forties, seventy he
was and I seven, we passed by
pelicans and storks; only years later (and Grandpa
already dead) I knew churches or napes of mosques
where coots and herons, all astir in morning mist
engulfed in half-light, stewed in the haze of swampy dusk.

Today, on this hairy hill, I tell the boy
riding on my back: everything has changed, the silence, the path,
    the shadow—
and he is quiet, looking down, then up, as if in search of a mountain,
sees a small donkey tickling his way up into the smoky yellow.

I, too, look into the fire rustling in the low brush
as in a faint golden picture I saw on some wall.
Where? When? There was a wall. I recall.

Suddenly someone beside me prays and weeps—
and that, God knows why, still pleases me

The Literary Review   ISRAEL ELIRAZ
                                          —Translated from the Hebrew
                                          by Beate Hein Bennett

ROOM 9639

Small rectangular plate
taped to your door:
raised metal letters—name;
date of birth, dash, & space
placed in parentheses below.
I see you're two years older
than I'd been told.

Inside, the window's bottom pane
props your x-rays:
clouds & wings—white, grey, black—

collage, symmetrically arranged.
That baseball—core of a bomb-blast—
may be what "indicates a mass."

Dismissing them with a gesture
your hand trembles, sweeping across
the narrow bed; a breathy voice,
"Part of my room's décor."

Eyes wander above the x-rays, bordered
by net curtains drawn to the side,
& stop, daydreaming, hypnotized
by the window's middle register,
film strip, the city there:

dark wide ribbon, the East River
dotted with boats by white banks
locked in ice. Only
thick charcoal from barge stacks
& clothing factories on shore
erupts, blows everywhere—
over the next-door helicopter pad
lightly powdered with snow.

Poetry   FLORENCE ELON

SATURDAY MORNING SERVICES

("I didn't like the ringing in my ears."
—Mary Baron)

From the women's section I
see my father and brother
and the older men
rocking under the hoods of their prayer shawls
in a *shul* that is nearly empty.
The gray chanting of the "Shmoneh Esray"
slurs inside my head
like a record played too slowly.

When some boys yelled out,
"Hey, ugly!" as I walked here,
their laughter rolled round and round
like the tires of their run-down car.

Standing alone, I look down at the black pumps
with felt bows my mother picked out.
She's at home now warming over lunch.

The parched voices of prayer
range through me insisting,
Modim anachnu lach,
we bow before you.

Mss   BARBARA ELOVIC

AND ECHOES FOR DIRECTION

*("Moreover, they [bats] have been heard to produce, while
hanging upside down in the depths of woods, strange,
solitary and lovely bell-like notes."—Lewis Thomas)*

Which they learned, no doubt, dangling
from stone arches in old belfreys.
Having been taught suspended animation
through hours of light, they found their night-wings
restless. So they took to the woods
all they knew of drift, air-currents,
foil and lift. And echoes
for direction. Moreover, memory
recalling not the wild fling of changes—
these they'd always fled in fright—
but the long pure tone sustained:
wind ringing the mouths of bells
head down in sleep, singing.

The Atlantic Monthly   Virginia Elson

"IF SATAN IN FALLING FROM HEAVEN . . .
HAD SWERVED SLIGHTLY AS HE FELL. . . ."

(from John Hollander's review of Harold Bloom's Anxiety of Influence*)*

Where were wings when his startled senses
first marked the rush of space, and he knew
he was hurled headlong? Was it pride's
conviction that this was choice: free-falling
toward a domination of his own design?

Suppose, instead, he had spread those vanes.
Planing a moment on the crest of a solar wave,
suppose he had trimmed sails for the broad reach,
a course not so straitly downwind of the starting line?

What a flying jibe against heaven that would have been—
veering off into original vastness
on an utterly new tack, no matter
from what quarter the gale blew!

Prairie Schooner   Virginia Elson

LAST NIGHT I DREAMED

I was a cat, my major qualification
being green-eyed (and left alone not growing
lonely nor bored). Immediate transformation

made me a pussyfooter in my glowing
sable so velvety the night winds were
as unaware of me as any mouse going

home before dawn. My enigmatic purr
was suddenly *there*, no winding up, no learning.
Wherever I went my feline savoir faire

made friends for me, though independence burning
was a fire I'd not imagined hitherto.
But the climax of my dream before returning

home was a biological breakthrough:
I knew I was witching, *and I knew I knew.*

Serpentine   ELAINE V. EMANS

OF YOUR FATHER'S INDISCRETIONS
AND THE TRAIN TO CALIFORNIA

One summer he stole the jade buttons
sewn like peas down grandma Ora's dress
and you, who loved that trail of noise and darkness
hauling itself across the horizon,
moths spiraling in the big lamps;
loved the oily couplings and the women's round hats
haunting all the windows
and the way he held you on his knee like a ventriloquist
discussing the lush push of grass against the tree's roots
or a certain crookedness in the trunk.
Now everything is clearer.
Now when the train pulls away from the station
and the landscape begins to come around, distant and yet familiar,
that odd crease of yellow light
or the woods' vague sweep framed in the window forever
remind you of the year you were locked up at the Hotel Fiesta
while father went out with fast black minks.
And how wonderful it was
when he was narrow as a hat pin in his tux
and to have come all that way on his good looks.
How wonderful to have discovered lust
and know that one day you would be on its agenda
like the woman who drank and walked naked through the house
in her black hat, the one you used to watch
through a stammer in the drapes.
In that small town of cold hotels, you were the girl in the dress
red as a house burning down.

The American Poetry Review   LYNN EMANUEL

THE COURTSHIP OF SUN AND MOON

(based on a Yaqui story)

Every morning the Sun knelt
in the courtyard of the Moon.
She would never let him see
quite all of her; cloud curtains
dropped at any sign of his advancement.
How he burned for her!
He compared her to seafoam, pearls,
hammered silver thin as rain.
He ached to marry her.

One day she agreed. "But you must bring me
a suitable gift which must fit
me precisely."

The next day he brought her a bracelet
made of red corral and dove feathers.
But it was too small! He gave her a cloak
to wear after her bath: it was too big.
He could never keep her constant.

They have never married. Moon saddened,
for he never spoke of the one gift
without measure and yet the measure of all things:
love.

The Malahat Review   ANITA ENDREZZE-DANIELSON

FLYING OVER ILLINOIS AT SUNSET

From this height I do not actually see the earth;
but I believe that it is there, turning beneath me,
white beneath the red clouds.

I believe there must be men walking in the white fields,
and that they wear the dark trace
into the snow of their fields.

I think how it must be to one standing on the earth,
looking out over what, at this moment, high
over Illinois, I can only imagine.

What I see, and what they perhaps imagine, is the swift
shadow of the wing upon the red clouds,
and how the clouds rise to the west

like mountains, and the sun falls behind the clouds as if
they were mountains. What I believe is that the sky
is snowing into the fields of the white earth,

and that in the fields, among the beautiful wheelings
of tracks, the turnings of roads, all
the spiralings-in

and roundnesses, serpentines of creekbeds, people
are walking, people are saying to themselves
that if in Illinois there were mountains,

they would seem on this day to be clouds.

The Georgia Review   JOHN ENGELS

FROM DUST TO DUST

I take my spade and turn over the ground
by the roses. It cuts clean, this spear
heart, in the dry soil, clean into the gray
flesh of the earth, gray like boiled meat,

gray like the clouds of incense ash,
or pickled bodies of the dead. So this is
the mixture roses use to make their blood.

I gave mother a rose that Sunday we drove
for steaks. We passed the cemetary where
father stays and I could not help notice
how her gaze lingered on the pastures

of stone, how she tried to say something
about a city of ash, and I, seeing her
go cold, knew her mind had hold of earth,

the gray dust of our end. I knew my gift
of a rose was a gift for the underworld,
the gift of fire against the claims of dust,
a touch-and-go attempt, like the very way

weeks later in a bar, that boy with skin
smooth as a rose played touch and go
with my desire, all night, till after many

vodkas I decided to ask him if he dances.
"Not very good, no!" he says.
I shut my eyes against the lights and din
and fall into his gray and separate dust.

Dalhousie Review   ROBERT KLEIN ENGLER

IN THIS HOUR

Even in the fog and dark wind
I can feel the tide coming in,
the steady wash and swell,
and sea salt along the shore,
and I try to make myself empty
to no avail.
      Somewhere ahead I imagine
an avenging angel, one of swift

shadow and sure ending, and I can
almost feel its beating wings,
a predator breaking from cover
in full autumn sail.
    But for now in this hour
the sea's lapping continues and
it's like an animal breathing
against the beach. I listen with each
light touch of the surf, and my hand
moves inside your silence, inside
your life and body's warmth.

Berkeley Poets Cooperative   CHARLES ENTREKIN

MANNEQUINS

This indecent procession of the undead
    invades the Avenue windows, dressed to kill,
sporting tomorrow's clothes and yesterday's faces.

One struts in a velvet shaft of midnight blue,
    slashed down the back in a diamond heat of lust,
gold crown at the wrist and throat, a garnet ring.
Here Lucie Anne side-slits a terry dress
    trimmed in Venetian lace
and petal edging on the camisole. There a lady,
    most unladylike, lounges
in silk of liquidly drapable muscadine,
    grinning the wine-red of wickedness. Another
borrows the schoolgirl's kiss, the cupie bow,
eyes round and empty as pots, and the apple cheek.
For we also yearn to join the innocent in their clothes:
    Jill in her jumper, Johnnie in his jeans,
sheep in their fleece, the pig in his narrow poke.

But I prefer them naked, the posturing frauds,
free from any trace of shame, and without nipples
    or the fur that friction-proofs our parts for love.
I like them headless, oh Marie Antoinette,
    what beauty knocked in the executioner's bucket!
I like them wigless, as a rack of bullets.
I like when a leg is kicked out of its socket
or an arm flings in some preposterous gesture
as if to say
"So happy to have missed the agony of meeting you,"
or
"We who are early salute you from the backs of our heads."
I love when the feet swivel for a fast retreat,
and the head jerks in wonder defying the neck.

But when they are assembled and decked out
they turn vicious, whispering through the glass:
"How have you achieved your shabbiness?
Where is your glamour, the youth you were born with?

Where, if you have one eye, is the other,
and if you have three limbs, where is the fourth?
Where is your hair, marcelled or carefully windblown,
your eyebrows, the artfully painted lips?
Put your face to the glass, you wretched snail,
kiss me, you desecration of a man."

The American Scholar   DANIEL MARK EPSTEIN

MIAMI

After years of stock-car racing, running
rifles to Cuba, money from Rio, high
diving from helicopters into the Gulf;
after a life at gunpoint, on a dare,
my father can't make the flight out of Miami.

Turbojets roar and sing, the ground crew
scatters out of the shadow of the plane.
My father undoes his seatbelt, makes his way
up the aisle, dead white and sweating,
ducks out the hatchway, mumbling
luggage was left at the dock, his watch
in the diner. Head down,
he lurches through the accordion boarding tube,
walks the shining wing of the airport, past
windows full of planes and sky, past bars,
candy machines and posters for Broadway shows.
Gasping in the stratosphere of terror, he
bursts through the glass doors and runs
to a little garden near the rental cars.
He sits among thc oleanders and palms.

It started with the Bay Bridge.
He couldn't take that steel vault into the blue
above the blue, so much horizon!
Then it was the road itself, the rise and fall,
the continual blind curve.
He hired a chauffeur, he took the train.
Then it was hotels, so many rooms
the same, he had to sleep with the light on.
His courage has shrunk to the size of a windowbox.

Father who scared the witches and vampires
from my childhood closets, father
who walked before me like a hero's shield
through neighborhoods where hoodlums honed their knives
on concrete, where nerve was law,
who will drive you home from Miami?
You're broke and I'm a thousand miles away
with frightened children of my own.
Who will rescue you from the garden
where jets flash like swords above your head?

The American Scholar   DANIEL MARK EPSTEIN

WHAT COMES BACK

Over the burnt hills a voice blows in.
A sound rises in my throat: yours.
My room grows cold and the night survives
itself, absorbing the country.

It wasn't like this in the old days.
Everyone sat by the fire and neglected tragedies
the wind swept in. The brittle debris of absence,
bathed in a river, became food for the garden.

There is a wish my affections make:
to see your name printed over the plains
as an arrangement of fine bones. I can hear them
click together, their sound carries westward.

When you plant rows of herbs and flowers
along the river this spring, a bit of us
will wound the soil. Our love is a strategy
of placement, a presence the clouds bring in.

The Georgia Review   ELAINE EPSTEIN

MOTHER AT THE KITCHEN WINDOW

Solitary dogwood, new with white flowers
Down by the pasture spring—
I watch for it always from my kitchen window.
Each Spring's return of petals
Makes obvious the Winter exodus,
Hinted at by earlier budding—
          now daily I witness their maturation.
Last spring the flowers failed in brilliance.
A deliquescent purity marked their whiteness.

Each year straining to see first flowers
   leaves sight diminished—
      Always, I saw the first flower.

Now the world moves around me unfocused, confused.
They tell me, old age,
        but I know the truth,
    I have found the truth,
   have seen it often
Dripping from the dogwood cross
To the green earth in waiting—
And back again.

Poem   PAUL C. ERWIN

TANTRIK X-RAY

One day he happened to notice it began to dance
while partially inside her, so he floated back,
detached, to see what meaning it could stimulate.
It took on a faint orange aura, becoming,
within the aura's haze, a kind of serpent man,
whose crocodile-like tail now seemed to writhe
in her brown triangle, no longer hair and flesh,
but cooking brown mud, or pollution, in which
this serpent king got hotter and hotter until his aura
turned into flames, and his arms became four,
to better gyrate or to handle more weapons,
lances on which little demons were perching
and unpulled though taut small golden bows.
The terror of the metamorphosis took time—
his smoking head grimaced and sprouted other
smoking heads until a temple of heads swayed
in the bonfire-like blaze around his body confined
to dance in this sandbox, archangelic play-space,
the size of a computerized explosion, male wrath,
hunger to destroy, hatred for generation within
the hose of himself. He saw the earth as a carpet of human
copulation heating up the atmosphere, and the stolen
serpent power, for she had been turned into an egg
and he the half born snake half out half in—

then I crawled away, full out of the shell—
no, into the hollow of a greater shell, the sky shell,
me, the tinker-toy me, the shard me.

Epoch   CLAYTON ESHLEMAN

FROM "THE PARIS HOTEL"

XV

Maybe someone died in this bed where I lie,
maybe these sheets momentarily
shrouded some corpse, some poor unknown stiff
the courts took into custody;
maybe someone died who'd come to settle
an affair, some business. Surely someone died
in this bed where I lie, any old night,
far from his home, his village, his family,
his barnyard and geraniums, his wife and parents.
Some teenager knelt on this bed,
dedicating his feverish hymn to Onan.
Someone couldn't sleep, pacing to and fro,
worried, smoking, up all night.
Maybe, one night, a woman gave birth,
a baby howled, a virgin cried out,

what they call adultery was committed.
Maybe, in this bed, a child died.

International Poetry Review   VICENT ANDRÉS ESTELLÉS
—Translated from the Catalan
by David H. Rosenthal

WISHES AND NEEDS

Sometimes, I am born in Boston.
I come of age in old mansions,
bricked and blue-veined. A Japanese

garden circles a sculptured pool.
Inspired by my mother, professor of
Eastern art, I attend Madame de Trop's

school for girls. At eighteen, trickles of
Latin and Greek and renaissance painting
flow from my brain, down the refined sinus

track into my classic nose and out of my
seasoned mouth. By twenty-one, I choose
for proper reasons either to research allergies

or to conduct the Paris Pops. Fatless,
each day I romp with African animals, swim with
Amazon fish from Brazil. Then, piranha-like

wishes are stilled. . . . Of real needs I write
good poems. Entertained, I propose with perfect
words the right toast.

Southern Humanities Review   SYBIL P. ESTESS

LEONARD MASSINGAIL: FATHERLY ADVICE

You don't know beans about girls
and you are going about half-cocked.
It will always be a wild-goose chase
until, by hook or crook,
you break the ice with her.
She'll let you cool your heels
as long as you beat about the bush.
It's no skin off my nose
if you can't cut the mustard
and act like a fish out of water.
I'm not talking through my hat
when I say you're asleep at the switch.
Getting a doll is no lead-pipe cinch,
and coming down with a case of cold feet
puts romance on the rocks.
She sure looks like the real McCoy,
so make hay while the sun shines.

Get yourself in the groove, son.
Go the whole hog, right now.
I'd sweat my good blood
to rule the roost with that chick.
Just be a chip off the old block
and you'll soon be on Easy Street.
If you're going to hem and haw,
I'm going to be madder than a wet hen.
Look, either fish or cut bait,
or you will always eat crow.
Damnit, take the bull by the horns!

New Letters   DAVE ETTER

A CHRISTIAN CHILDHOOD

My mother made me count
the cars of the freight train
clicking south toward Boston
that last year of the war.

They moved through the elms
with the slowness of newsreels,
in and out of sunlight,
guns and tanks secured,

box cars, flat cars—
one hundred and twenty-six
clicking south, the engine
already across the river.

Give, said my mother's voice
with a dusty resonance.
Give, Give, said the easing
of the ties as they rose and fell.

Give your blood and bones
if you have nothing else.
Give what the world is asking;
Give, said my mother's voice.

The Hudson Review   PRESCOTT EVARTS, JR.

AN OLD MAN PLAYING A PIPE

He is a sailor of uncommon
ships, and a mathematician
by degrees, calculating
the four careful winds with all
that remains of his senses
to find a proper corner
to set his stump and his hat.

Then, as if by virtue of the clay bird
a washwoman gave him once in Jaipur,
and the cold rain that fell for nine days
and caused its eyes to cloud,
as if by virtue of the goatherd
he met once in Samarinda
who wears discontinuance like a pearl hat
and washes it daily
in the clairvoyant mud of the Mahakam;
and as if by virtue of the daughter
of a brown princess he heard of in Kendari,
who was hidden at birth in a kettle drum
behind the fishmarket in Palangkaraja,
and who was stolen by the wolves who walk upright,
and who was raised up in their company
to do their bidding,
his pipe entreats you listen and contribute
to the timely coffer at the foot of the stump
and to pass judgment on no man
who carries his madness in a tune.

The Midwest Quarterly   DAVID EWICK

COMBAT

I keep dreaming that I'm back
in combat: the dead are like black rocks,
small boulders, they lie
strewn around me, all over
the countryside, in the fields, in the Normandy
orchards. I've been called back
to war, to the cold that walks through the bones,
to my consciousness narrowed to a pinpoint
in a universe that is nothing but death.
I've returned to the marches, to mess halls, to my
young life shrunken like a fallen crabapple,
and I see my friends receding,
crying out to me, their voices
thinning, growing transparent, crying
that they don't understand—their arms
outstretched, vanishing back in time,
calling out that our lives
exist like a war, like black rocks;
that our lives are stones, that there is no peace,
that we died with the dead whom we loved
a long time ago.

Plainsong   SAMUEL EXLER

OBSERVATIONS OF THE TOWER BLOCK

During the day, the building becomes a gigantic machine
collecting data from the whole district. At night,
a Cunard liner with every cabin occupied,
rigging decorated for the final gala.

Different patterns of lights. No matter how late I go
to bed or early I wake, there are always lights burning.
Nights of insomnia; when I look out the window,
someone else in the building is also not sleeping.

The lights glow pink and yellow, green and orange.
Is it from coloured bulbs, or filtered through curtains?
Who are the people who live in those apartments?

Illuminated lift-shafts, halls, and balconies.
The grid of the structure determines these lives,
     but my sightings
are too irregular to grasp their pattern or meaning.

The Hudson Review   RUTH FAINLIGHT

8TH STREET BAR

(from a photograph by Robert Frank)

The old couple in the booth
under the mirror, their lives
of work filling the glasses
between them. She speaks,
he in his suit and blue shirt
gazing up as if memory
with its gull wings hovered there.
I see them young, nude in bed
after making love, morning
sun turning the curtains
to a white glow like the jukebox
blazing now in the center
of the small dancefloor.
In the latticework of shadows
customers lift their drinks
delicately, admiring the gleam
along the rim, the uneven sheen
of the bar's veneer, the long, cool
remove from history. I can grow
old here. Someone will serve me,
will set the green bottle beside
the slender glass, and light will flow
endlessly from jukebox to mirror
to glass to floor. I can enter
the bed of the old couple,

lie between them as their child,
hands across my chest, and watch
the air bend and sag with sunlight.

North Dakota Quarterly   B. H. FAIRCHILD

JEWISH WIFE

When Risa crosses her long legs
the length of her
a lovely shyness on the couch
softens all the corners in the room

but when she lets down
her kerchiefed hair
all the wadis of Judea go streaming
in the rush of spring

Midstream   MARCIA FALK

UNTITLED

("Everything has a name")
—Solzhenitsyn

The place where shadows wait on moonless nights,
the passage of gestures with a stranger
who mistook you for his lover, a fragrance
hanging near the bush after roses are cut,
these are not *echo* or *wistful* or *galaxy.*
Some names will not stay where they're put;
the *ferry* slips its moorings and becomes
conifer and *phosphorus,* leaving *metaphor*
and *difference* in its wake. Some names
mingle like clouds, so flower and bone
are *rosehip,* branch and breeze, *woodwind.*

Remember the woman who raised a nameless animal?
She hid from it when it grew huge and black;
but it followed her everywhere
and when she died of fear, it sat on her grave
howling with grief. This is the consequence
of refusing to name what we feel,
that the names fall away from the sky
like shooting stars, and we are caught
in the dark where our hearts
hurtle together with a nameless speed.

The Georgia Review   LAURA FARGUS

THE HITCHHIKER'S ALTARPIECE

Beyond the dark mountains twilight expands. A
flock of birds speeds into the edge of the roof
and disappears. After the usual exchange of
pleasantries, he keeps silence, the way the
roller-coaster rider keeps that lump of faith,
his fist. The long smooth hood goes on swallow-
ing the road. We have our secrets. I begin to
think about the spoon on the dashboard, the cup,
our bearded faces set in the windshield, his
haloed with the brim of his hat. Smoke. The
cartoon mosaic of our possible sudden impact. Here
is an illustration for a faith in diminishing
distance. An imago mundi for disciples that is
modern, matter of fact from roof-post to roof-
post: valleys full of lights, siloes, stubbled
fields, brown rivers, neon, and the lane-stripes
flashing on the inward eye and vanishing behind.
The silence lasts. Up ahead, a brother and sister
scuffle in the rear of a station wagon. I follow
them for miles, hoping he'll see things my way.
Not a word. I look at his eyes set straight over
the top of the mountain. The telephone wires
keep cresting and falling through his dark head
like a pulse.

The Nantucket Review   ROBERT FARNSWORTH

SING JOY

Divinely dug from wilderness with grace,
The gardens in our town may well efface
From memory the uncouth, cluttered spots,
Obliterate completely all the blots
Hung in the mind's eye in another place.
Here, every spring, lost Eden blooms again;
Meridian, our home, is on the edge
Of bliss attained, trembling with flowers when
The mockingbirds awake upon their ledge
Of Mississippi glory, and sing joy.

Mississippi Poetry Journal   WINIFRED HAMRICK FARRAR

STRANGER

All my life, and today, too,
I have spoken this language
like a foreigner,
and they do not understand me.

Sometimes I have trouble buying things.
The grocer stocks white mice for me
and the barber offers me a bargain
in fishing poles and tennis shoes.
When I try to clarify my needs,
they laugh and assure me with a wink
that they do not understand me.

Once, at a dinner with the mayor,
when I promised him my vote,
he grabbed his lapels
and pulled them over his face.
The police escorted me to the door.

Last Friday, under a green sky,
when I told a woman I loved her,
she curled her lip and barked.

I know it is my fault.
With my limited vocabulary
I cannot round a meaning
with the word that fits
like a measured board.
If she is beautiful, I say so,
and never call her lovely,
exquisite or charming.
If I am wrong, I admit it
without resorting to disclaimers
like naive, ill-chosen or hasty.
If you are wrong,
I tell you, too.

You are wrong.

Four Quarters   BOB FAUTEUX

PARTIAL LIKENESS

My mother was a painter who
eluded words.
She glided through my childhood
mute as cloud shadows over the foothills.
When she stacked plates or dreamed
into the ivy, I followed her,
relentlessly confiding.

Sometimes, as if in answer, she'd say,
*I've caught the willows, that gold
is the first color of spring.*
Or, *My river is wrong.*
Her words: ochre, sienna, teal,
ultramarine. Through each still life
room she had arranged
I followed, hurling words.

Gently, from my door, she'd say goodnight,
then move down the gallery
past the languid glacial lake,
past the desert of pink rocks,
past the pine forest
with its caves of green-black silence
to my father. I used to imagine that
behind their door, color stopped
like a heart in the dark,
and she became real.

Primavera   SUSAN FAWCETT

A MUCH-MARRIED KING

(for EP)

You say the old
castle seems empty these days? I say
the damn place is well rid of the clutter &
claptrap. And, fancy, it's mine alone now,
the whole shebang. To sit in in the dark &
gobble candy bars, or soak my feet in the
throne room, 'neath moonlight caught
in tinseled wrappers.

So they're gone now. Good riddance.
Shed no tears for the high-stepping
queens who paraded thru these gates
to frolic a bit
then exit &, leaving, slam them
shut. What matter?

Not to me, of the hot palm
that handled more than four. That led them
in, bejeweled, big-eyed, yet knew they would
not stay. It's nothing to me now, no;
though time was I bowed & shook & pleaded.
Court jester, cadging love. Nights when
bedsheets crackled.

But in truth I cannot cry a loss.
No one rummaged my closets
nor ransacked my rooms—
bore off no jewels or myrrh
—ah, fools they were, too,
for it was all for them:

The gold doubloons, the furs, the pink-iced
coffee cake. All was theirs to take.
But not a smidge of this man's heart
was ever theirs.

The Hiram Poetry Review   THOMAS FEENY

NIGHTWALK

Late at night,
when the moon hangs red and guttering, cradled in the West,
when my wife and children are fast asleep
like the folded white buds of the drowsy flowering fig,
and the dew is sprinkling its dream glitter
over the misty countryside . . .
late each night
I walk alone down the sleeping sidestreets and lanes,
past the drowsy vegetation and the restless cats,
with the moon my last companion,
guttering like a smoky candlebutt,
sinking to the West.

Late at night,
on those lonely walks,
I become acquainted with myself:
I see a man is more than gathered dust,
more than the measure of grief.
Alone with the night,
with the silence overrun with stars,
I become immersed in who I am.
I sink like the moon
in the depths of myself,
in the very soul Heaven kindled in me.

I see there is no present,
only the future flowing from God;
like a long blue river it curls till it meets the past,
embracing it as its bride.

Let the dark lanes drowse,
steeped in lemon trees
and the dew that quivers and gleams;

Let the pines toss
like a wave from the heart
of a single dreaming seed;

Let the darkness rule the countryside,
let dawn be far away;

Let the soul of a man
flood the night
like a flowering lilac tree.

Midstream   CHAIM FEINBERG

FÜR ELISE

Lately I've been spending hours doing the piano practicing I
    didn't do
As a child. I'm up to *Für Elise.* A simplified arrangement
For a child's hands. I wish I knew more about music. Who

Was Elise? Some little girl whose rich parents sent
Her to Beethoven for lessons? Maybe the maestro felt bad
Yelling at her, and wrote this soulful Deedle Deedle Deedle
Deedle Dooo to soothe her. Or to mourn her, driven stark mad
By these chords cascading upwards ceaselessly to the needle
Notes near the top I can't seem to read. I should have started
As a child to compose myself. To gain some harmony.
Instead of laboring on like this in secret. Playing everything adagio
　　　and broken hearted
Because it's easier. The music's really my daughter's. What's hard
　　　for me
Is not to yell, "If you just practiced it ten minutes more . . ."
"You," she says, "are in a bad mood. And the tune's a bore."

Tendril　　　　　　　　　　　　　　　　　　　　　ALAN FELDMAN

ILLUMINATION

The miniature painters knew it was not simply
a question of castles, and lords and ladies
riding to the hunt, falcons on wrists. None of this

would have been possible without the peasants, ploughing
and sowing to put bread on the table, paring their corns
in the quiet season when they could do little

but feed and water the stock, sharpen the scythes
for next summer's harvest. Here are the farmer
and his wife, blowing on numbed hands in Winter, and,

innocent of underclothes, warming their private parts
at the fire while their small son makes water
through the open door, staining the snow; a hog roots

for stray morsels. These are the underpinnings
on which the turrets and spires rest,
and no less dear to the artist than the great lords

with their furs and damasks and tapestried walls,
keeping boredom at bay with minstrels,
jesters, pet dwarfs, and these breviaries.

The Malahat Review　　　　　　　　　　　　　　　RUTH FELDMAN

CLOCKS AND WATCHES

never let you forget, spy on you
everywhere, brazen on wrists, sly
in pockets! Quick as a tick

they conjugate time: it is always
past tense. Between one breath
and the next, the second hand,

invention of the devil, turns now
to then. Its moon face bland,
time hunts you down, smirking

from steeples, booming from noon guns.
Bulbs spell it out on the sides
of buildings. The tiniest timepiece

wields the same power as Big Ben,
gives you your marching orders.
No matter how you dig

your heels in, you advance,
with baby or giant steps.
Even if you stop the clocks.

Webster Review   RUTH FELDMAN

ACCORDING TO THE BAAL SHEM TOAD

According to the Baal Shem Toad
even frogs are croaking for us,
squeaking away, an improbable chorus,
floating like brown leaves, noses exposed.
"The point is singing and not hearing,"
"The point is hearing and not grasping,"
"The point is grasping and not holding"
—one frog's thoughts leap the thoughts
of the next, drawing out their commentaries.
They stare as frogs stare, past bare trees
into the folded and broken brown leaves.
In a few weeks, the same leaves, frogs believe,
will be turning green and starting over.
Frogs think of frogs as leaves, of course,
but more often think of leaves as frogs,
with a different speech, of another order,
probably related to toads. "Philosophically,"
one frog sings, "philosophically, I mean,
they must be frogs because of their beauty,
frogs by right of their intelligence and music,
frogs by virtue of their webbed feet,
their lithe bodies, their splashy techniques,
more dry and severe, less quick and sweet,
but all in all purely amphibian.
Each croak prolongs the breath in one key,
each croak arranges the air in short leaps,
each croak, so to speak, exhales a new leaf.
These frogs sing at a different frequency.
The point is singing and not hearing.
Nothing that croaks can be foreign to me."

New Letters   KEN FIFER

DOUBLES

I find and lose myself, assured, afraid;
I live and die, I see and do not see.
You make the darkness and the light agree
And bring my blackest storms ablaze with red.
My face which hides, and shows, with sorrow, joy,
My speaking silence and my muddy mind,
Reveal my errand to be gross and grand—
Such is the man despair and hope decoy.
Proud in my shame and full of shivery fire,
Blaming, praising, fleeing, seeking desire,
Half-brute, half-god, I look at you, once, twice,
And then, both kind and rigorous, you watch
Me light a match while putting out a match,
You blind clairvoyant, you, love, flame and ice.

The Malahat Review   ROBERT FINCH

YOU LISTEN FOR MY FOOTSTEPS—
I WALK ON AIR

Don't think because you sleep
I disappear.
Under your window, I am still
waiting.
When you enter I see through blades
of the fan.

I watch.
You have no secrets from me.
My patience takes root, probes deep,
deeper.

The way your hair breaks into waves
upon your pillow,
the white surf of your belly,
the white dunes of your thighs—
lie back!
show me where the well runs sweet
in that dark oasis.

Buckle   CHARLES FISHMAN

THE PORTRAIT

(*"I find that I have painted
my life . . . without knowing."
—Georgia O'Keefe*)

What I saw had so little to do with me,
or so I thought. I was the lens,

the clear glass through which all passed,
or was I a mirror, a still, sullen pool?
A delicate instrument? A recording device?
I could have accepted that.

Sometimes, to escape from the brightness,
I closed my eyes and felt my way through rocks,
shells, driftwood, seeking that sixth sense
of the blind. Or tasted fruit as if I were nothing
but lips, tongue, gullet. But the gold juice,
the air I sucked up pure, appeared on canvas
tinged with blood. No one had ever seen such
fleshy flowers, such landscapes of bones.

The Massachusetts Review   JANE FLANDERS

HEAVENLY BODIES

It is always night in the outhouse
and smells like a pig sty.
I unbutton my sunsuit, pull it down
and perch, feet dangling, on the rim of
the abyss beside a pre-war Sears catalogue.
The seat is silky from the buttocks of my
aunt and uncle and grown-up cousin.
I imagine them grunting away
year after year, in all weathers,
emptying themselves into this bowl
of sticky soup the flies love so well.
Sighing, I let my urine float
downward, outward through space,
marking this spot as mine, too,
knowing myself related to the universe
in yet another unspeakable way.

West Branch   JANE FLANDERS

SHORE STONES IN AUGUST
ON THE COAST OF MAINE

The water moves like fire ants across our feet.
The children have an hour before sun and moon
shift an ocean over their moats and keeps
and hide the stones we rifle for souvenirs.

Not one resembles the mathematician's
serene balloon, the perfect
blanched abstraction we skeletonized
on paper as students,

                nor even a planet
in miniature, gouged from its orbit

and left in this low-tide slosh and sand,
nor a gannet's egg, nor a speck
of dust grown monstrous.

       Not one conforms
in grayness: haphazard quartz streaks some;
scars mottle each in their way. Even now
the tide works time's abrasion on the one
we thought was Swedenborg's skull.

Among these thousand other vacationers, we watch
the distant shapes of children, the evaporative
dream we drift in, and hold each other's hand
so tight our knuckles whiten, then know
not all imagination could ever keep us whole.

Pendragon   RICHARD FOERSTER

SOMETHING CALLED A CITY

(New Orleans)

There are signals among a wreckage of flowers
struck clean in the earth's foaming hand,
something called a city
ruled by marching men, who sang and danced
and built their graves above the ground.
There are signals among a wreckage of humans
forced together, naked and unafraid,
lost surveyors of night's crescent fall
bound by rope and fire. The streets are rivers.
Who will unearth their gems and fat skulls?
There are signals without measure
like death uttered ten thousand years,
something called a city
ruled by marching men, who sang and danced
and built their graves above the ground.
There are brief signals
beginning and ending in the form of a child
with spiked fists and golden arms
who lifts a bird by its bright wing;
the ample, numbing proof of power,
something called a city
ruled by marching men, who sang and danced
and built their graves above the ground.

The Georgia Review   CHARLES FORT

LETTER NORTH

I am so far south that it's as if, to be
A birch, a tree must have touched a unicorn.

I need to live in a deciduous forest,
To have the seasons bang doors like children.
But I also want the sea, fraying its waves on the
Backs of the rocks, bringing together the threads
Once again and miraculously rebinding them. One day
I shall really talk of the sea, but tonight I cannot.
It is the wind tonight that reminds me of waves.
The wind running down the mountains
To the sea in pursuit of the moon. Tonight
All the unicorns are dead. The birches grow
Extinct by the hour. It is the hour when I wash
The white scarves in the basement tubs, the scarves
I will wrap the birches in, telling myself—see,
These are the birches, they were touched by unicorns.
Washing, I think of north, where the unicorns
Move—in Maine, in New Hampshire. Bending, I am
Thinking of the trunks of the old birches that are
Broken and are seen from the highway—moving on,
Ruthless. The high branches brought low and the white
Bark clinging like lichen. I am thinking that maybe
This summer I shall drive to Maine. But now I shall
Sleep, and when I awake the scarves will have
Grown cool and dry on the line.

Shenandoah   JAY BRADFORD FOWLER, JR.

THE BURNING FACTORY

As children, my sister and I watched our grandfather
grow senile. He would sniff the air
and ask *Is something burning?*
Our mother slapped us for laughing and said
he was remembering the factory fire
he witnessed at sixteen when he was
the youngest shoecutter in the city.
I can still smell that flesh, that cooked meat,
he'd say, as we grimaced and pedalled away on our bikes.
After a while, he began to wake up at night
thinking he heard those screaming factory workers again,
but it always turned out to be a late driver,
tires moaning as the car turned the corner,
or a howling dog left out for the night.

None of us imagined my sister, the family beauty,
the one with the bright red laugh,
would be pulled into breakdown after breakdown
as an adult. None of us knew
she, too, would sniff the air, conflagrations
more terrible than our grandfather's memories
searing the edges of her sleep.
Things seem okay for a year or two,
then she'll call, three thousand miles away,
and I'll hear the factory workers' terror

as it became clear they would not escape the fire
cutting through her voice.

Each time it happens, I weep and shake
as if it were the first, but I'm never sure
if I cry for her madness, or just for the
ordinary days of our childhood, the sweaty closeness
of living in one house, in one city, that our family
has lost. As my sister stutters into the phone, I cry
for the day my mother gave me a permanent
and I watched my sister's face like a mirror
as the curlers came out,
and for Sundays when all seven of us, grandfather and all,
climbed into the Chevy Impala
and went for a ride. If things had gone well
for my father at work that week,
he would turn up the radio on the way home
and we'd all sing as loud as we could,
while the orange sun spread out along the highway
like a distant and always benevolent fire.

The American Poetry Review   PAT THERESE FRANCIS

DOOR HANGING

Upstairs I have paced all day
hammering on intangibilities.
Downstairs in the kitchen
the old Finn kneels in shavings
finding a special grace
in the cough of plane on wood.
His tools circle him like toys.
Ancient hands dance
in the sweet music of grains.
This old man knows
the value of a snug fit.
The door and jamb will meet
as tightly as his beveled days.
When he leaves he says with a smile:
"Today I have made a door.
What have you made?"

Old man, perhaps for you
the setting sun latches into place,
but do not be fooled
by the confidence of tools.
Days, private worlds
cannot be engineered like cabinets.
Hard jobs cry for
(but cannot find)
the proper hinge.
We shim ourselves
not through well-made doors

but the empty spaces they fill.
The warps and cracks
that leave our frames out of square,
our lives mercifully ajar.

Passages North　　　　　　　　RANDALL R. FREISINGER

LIKE A MAN

To stop me sucking my thumb, my father
told me the story of Finn, who caught
a fish and, roasting it, was warned not
to touch. Touch it he did, burned his
thumb; he put it in his mouth to cool.

What my father didn't say was he liked
the taste so well, he chewed his thumb
to wisdom. Dad, I remind him now, Why
did you always half tell your stories?
He grins, Everything's allowable, kid,

everything labors for everything else.
Finn and fish and sin intersect at the
most crooked angles, we've got to fancy
ourselves in a blind alley with no dark
cuts for escape. Prepare the table right

there, cover it with our best cloth—you
to one side, your mom to the other—
and me coming down the drive with fish; now
eat him like a man so I can go to sleep.

The Centennial Review　　　　　　　　STUART FRIEBERT

WINDOW

Darkness outside,
then brightness.

A bumpy road
leading to a lake.

The water standing there
like a body.

Distance, that suddenly
clouds over with birds.

We look out
through sentences.

Tendril　　　　　WALTER HELMUT FRITZ
—Translated from the German
by Stuart Friebert

SHE

Entering the jewels of the northern tide,
sunlight hoisted in her hair
against the blue see-through day,
her body must melt like music
into bright threads.

She will weave, hip first, in a quiet
procession through the cool underwater,
resolving not to disintegrate like bread—
so, able to go on.

Whatever the water is—
a great upturned dish of tears
blistery with sunlight—
she desires it,
and fears.

Even when the damage of circles
of water in the sea
wears her out—her heart lies down;
her voice goes to pieces
like a rotted strand of pearls—

she will rest in the latitudes
of endless sand, composing
an answer to the thunderous question
in her veins,
Art thou in love?

Then, clothed in salt and anemones,
she will recognize herself again,
the threads of her song
designing their own supple fence
to tend the broken blue glass of her heart.

New Letters   CAROL FROST

SATURN IS MOSTLY WEATHER

Lying with her, watching the rain
pass through sunlight, I think about
the miles of love that lie
before me. Her eyes are closed
and she breathes in slow waves.
I can hear the rain washing off
the plumeria leaves, cleansing the tall
dirty palms.
          The distance ahead
must diminish, love by love,
and I delude myself in making a mask
of some god's face to see through.
We cannot share the mystery, she and I,
our dreams do not believe each other.

Her eyes circle around her self,
her sun, in the black starlit space
under her lids. Awake, I cannot help
her going, I can only listen to wet wheels
passing over wet light outside the window.

She will say my name and again
it will be someone else's. All those loves,
little suburban planets apart and bound
to my death, orbiting far ahead
in some still undeveloped photographs.
Meanwhile, if I am not in bed
beside this woman, I must be elsewhere
not hearing the suddenly awakened silence,
which I realize is the rain's deliberate
cessation.   More harshly the sun
streaks across the opposite wall,
and the shadows are harsher. Morning is late,
I am older, I don't want to shave
or even wash my face in the glass.
I will send her away; she shows up
only as a shade in my eyes' dim
and mustardy gaze.
                    Then her mouth opens
just a whisper when her face
rolls slightly away from me, so I hear
our separation as the last evidence
of a moth's wavering into the dark.
The cycles continue, nothing ever ends
completely until the gutters themselves
crumble into fiery mutilated air.
Her fingers twitch on my thigh
as if they had come from another land.

Poetry Northwest   GENE FRUMKIN

TO A DEAD RACCOON ON THE HIGHWAY

(between Chicago and Madison, U.S.A.)

Where are you going,
little ball of hair,
bit of gold—
raccoon of the woods?

Where are you going?
Why to the city?
Without putting on your shoes
or taking off your mask?

Were you going to hitch-hike?
Did you wish to commit suicide?

Didn't you know there were men,
that you are a Northamerican—
and that outside of your woods
the "turnpike" lies in ambush?

And all to eat corn . . .
You were not given time for anything,
no one knew how to tell you:
. . . that beyond the woods there are men
who eat up raccoons
with their elegant cars.

Oh little raccoon, why did you come
. . . to the city . . . ?

Poetry Now   GLORIA FUERTES
                                            —Translated from the Spanish
                                                by Dorothy Scott Loos

PLUMBLINE

(im memoriam: John Callahan)

The world could snore, wrangle or tear
itself to atoms while Papa sat
unnettled, bashful, his brain
a lathe smoothing thoughts civil
above fingers laced and pink

as baby booties; Papa, who said of any gambler,
roughneck, drunkard, just "I don't think much
of him," and in stiff denims
toted his lunchpail's spuds
down a plumbline of twelve-hour shifts:
farmed, lumbered and cow-kicked,
let the bones knit their own
rivet, oiled big wheels that bullied
water uphill, drank stout, touched animals only
unawkwardly, drove four-in-hand, and sired six.

My ideas are dumb: a fizz
mute and thick as the head on a beer
he once thought, who never thought
such clabber could whiz through
genes and seed and speak.

Poetry   ALICE FULTON

SOMETIMES I FEEL LIKE MY FATHER LOOKED

Sometimes I feel like my father looked.
Sometimes I feel his cold eyes

staring out of my skull, and feel my head
so full of all the things I'd always thought
his must be filled with to make him look so dark.
Sometimes, when he stayed away from me
with all but his eyes, I thought I saw
something like hell in those eyes.

                                        Now his grave

brings us closer; he can't stay
away much longer; soon we'll meet
on even terms, and stare
the hell out of each other.

The Midwest Quarterly   ROBERT FUNGE

PHOENIX

(for E.R.T.)

Lovely bird,
No need to fear your quivering wings.
        Though pinioned long
        They have not forgotten how to
                Move
        Through the air, to slice and caress
                the currents.

You, Beautiful bird,
        With purple fantasia-fluting song,
                Sing.
        You can sing those heart notes,
        Soul notes to those who will hear.

Golden winged bird,
        Consumed by the fire of your vision,
        You can rise again from your ashes to
                Live.

You, bird of matchless beauty
        Whom Egyptian mystics made immortal,
        You can soar.

        You can soar.

The Creative Woman   JOANNE V. GABBIN

MY FATHER SITS ON THE TOILET AGAIN

My father sits on the toilet again,
Midnight or *Star* spread out for his news.
The door is open. No one looks in.

He sits there nightly, regular as sin
and Walter Cronkite, whose views are his views.
My father sits on the toilet again

and blames our grief on unemployed Irishmen,
Blacks or Italians, vacationing Jews.
The door is open. No one looks in,

but he looks out, his hand on his chin.
A statue with pants piling over his shoes,
my father sits on the toilet again

believing in what? Being Polish? American?
Catholic? Becoming an old man whose
door is open but no one looks in?

If he had an insight we wouldn't listen.
We know he knows he'll die in his booze.
My father sits on the toilet again.
The door is open. No one looks in.

The Hollins Critic   FRANK GAIK

THE LAST MAN'S CLUB

My grandfather was always sad.
Sadly, as a boy, he paddled his canoe
along the beautiful Hudson River,
which was only then beginning to die.
During the first war
he was very sad in France because
he knew he was having the time of his life.
When it was over,
everyone in America felt like a hero—imagine.
Once a year on Armistice Day
he met with all his friends from the war.
They got drunk and recounted the stories
of the time when they had thought they were men
and the world had seemed entirely possible.
They placed empty chairs for certain of the dead,
and in the center of the table,
a bottle of cognac from France
for the last man of them to drink alone
in honor of the others.
Year after year they gathered to watch
each other and themselves disappear,
turn into empty chairs.
Sooner or later they all were sad.
Some of them must have realized
they didn't need to join a club for this.
Finally it was down to my grandfather
and a man named Oscar Cooper.
Neither one of them wanted to outlive anyone.
They couldn't remember what honor was.
When they drank the cognac,
it didn't taste like anything.
They threw the bottle in the river

as if they thought it meant
that neither of them had to live anymore.
When Cooper died the following year,
my grandfather took his rifle out into the yard
and fired three shots at the sky.
Then he went down to the river
and drank himself to sleep.
After that he was never sad,
not even when the river died.

Antaeus   JAMES GALVIN

RURAL FREE DELIVERY

What weighs heavy, like a letter, postage due,
is a certain silence, not of your own choosing, not
like a letter you've sent but one you haven't gotten.
All over Rural Free Delivery 1 and 2
people wait for answers mailed under cover
to questions asked so long ago they are forgotten
or didn't matter anyway. What has come
in time is the new *Saturday Evening Post,*
what has come is the new *Life,* promised once
a month, as glossy as the old one ever was,
and a gross of bills shouting for payment.
What has arrived, in briefs, is yesterday,
what we bought then, thought then, broke then:
slicing machines, old poems, State and Federal codes.
The man who was going to write, hasn't.
The woman who said she did, didn't.
What falls from envelopes unarrived in waiting rooms
is something as heavy and as soft as summer squash
thickening in the unpicked garden, yellow, silent.

The Hiram Poetry Review   MARTIN GALVIN

THE HOUSE

This is the house that all the questions
come home to. At night it fills up
with old light, makes broth and weak tea.

This is the time I like the best,
when daylight first invades the lightbulb.
Sudden is my favorite season.
I return to it like homesickness.

This is my garden, out of its mind
with flowers. The dogwoods bristle
on the lawn, one tree sends up magnolias
like a pale umbrella. Red is red here;
rose is something else.

This is memory; the past forgetting us.
At five in my red sweater, I was flight itself.
I can't remember everything I dream.

This is the house I built asleep.
The roof is a leaky slate-colored slate.
The dust runs through it like a flavor.
The things that I forget awake—
this house remembers. The ones that I re-call;

a pity. A red thread's unravelling.
It makes me sad, like supper getting cold.
Today drops stitches into night. This
weakness is my old nostalgia for myself.

Was it ever easier? Was the world
ever always vivid? What happened
after that, and that? Instead of sleep
I'm stretching around my body; building
a place to rest in from things
like flight that have forgotten me.

Cedar Rock   ROSANNA GAMSON

FLOWERS

Among dead leaves in the woods, my daughter
looks for wildflowers—trillium,
spring beauty, the petals
just opening, earth releasing
its blooms into her hands
for safekeeping. Bars
of shade fall across her cotton blouse.
Like any mother, I want to guard
innocence. *Not until she's ready,*
I say to stonecrop, those pure white
concentrations I would call stars
except that stars lose
their brilliance every morning. I watch her
as she moves deeper into winter damage,
off the trail. Already the delicate hunger,
vines, taking over.

The Hollins Critic   MARITA GARIN

SHORELINE

Here is a rock shaped
like a corrupted bowling trophy.
And here is one clenched in a root.
And here is a boulder, his offspring
around him, meek as potatoes.

Here is the end of winter.
The trees are less horrible now,
and the twilight behind them,
and the glazed shoreline.
You can believe only so long
in the malice of the crooked
and the cold. I think
I'll just sit here awhile
in this strange rock of my own body.
You other rocks, forgive me.
You waves, fall without me.

Plainsong   MAX GARLAND

BIRTHDAY

At my age, I should have known better
than to reenter this consciousness. Now
the worst has happened: left alone, my chronology
has unloosed itself, and the years that used to lie
folded and tied like a stack of old letters
are circling above my head as I lie on my father's
side of the bed at the close of a hazy afternoon,
slowly counting nine months backward
from this, the twentieth day of June.

I should be out somewhere walking a network
of fine lines, not retracing steps that preceded
mine or predicting weather for the last day
of a summer long since gone by.
In the garden behind my eyes, where the air is clear
as an unfulfilled wish, I realize my curious age
by searching among thick thorn-covered branches
for the stem that lost the white rose
to the dime-store glass it now is drinking from.
The sense of the rose reaches out to the corners
of the room, filling the void it travels through
with the surety of a voice that does not doubt itself—
I am worthy, I am worthy of you—or question
how thirst passes from milk to sweet dark rum
as the dappled shadows of trees blend back
into the gray-blue grass, and fireflies rise up
and are lit like candles, one by one by one.

The Georgia Review   CHRISTINE GEBHARD

FACE

Touch that deep-printed diaper,
pattern of garden, park, soft as a clump of leaves,
on this paperback's cover, and
you'll untangle a face, extradimensional.

Store fronts, sidewalks are swept and clean;
keep an eye on the ground; musing, I walk ten steps
   —gravel, insects—when suddenly I
spot an object. It lies upside down: oval brooch,

   gold frame holding a cameo;
turn it: monochrome, flesh; luminous, queenly face,
   serious, grown, and yet subtly young,
eyebrows, nose, finely cut; beauty, intelligence.

   Wonder now who the victim of
loss or theft could have been (mugging? a broken chain?);
   with that brooch in my palm, I stare
off toward far streets, I see. Solid pedestrians

   don't go staring at strangerfolk
(too preoccupied); most innocent citizens
   see no beauty, no softer face
(none by split-second glance) than my bijou showed me.

   In thick crowds, under traffic lights,
glance—don't stare. One may stand, study a work of art,
   browse—Rizzoli's. Revolving doors
leading out of a bank give her a handicap,

   run—she exits and disappears.
What's this? Eye-pick-and-chase? Am I a dangerous
   man, a mugger, whom women flee?
Slow down. Think of a far park where a strange young girl

   sits now, reading or knitting; low,
over benches, from boughs, blossom and leaf may touch
   hair and face, all you've come upon,
gently muted design, strong and articulate,

   intuition—she's being watched;
shudders, rises and leaves; and I am meant to know
   what poor finders of cameos
cannot find by design; feel that an accident

   may suffice to impress a shape
but for seconds; that I, I, in an earthly span,
   looking, studying, learn, and yet
will not fathom how eye, hand, and a tutored mind

   shape, assemble resemblances;
how one's glance, be it deep, clear, and discriminate,
   cannot find corresponding sight,
cannot, feature by line, measuring will by skill,

   match that art with reality.
Come tomorrow; let's say: what if you met the girl,
   saw her look for her lost-and-found
trinket? You could then say, "Here, Miss—I think that's yours."

   Never elevate certainty,
love and loss, to the doubt practical moments know;

take now, rather, another stroll,
evening, out to a park; thousands of shadows, leaves,

mime that soft-cover stock on your
book of spirit; then ask, has anyone lost a face,
hidden, foliage reversing out,
bright, or under a found brooch of a sister moon.

The Kenyon Review   EMERY GEORGE

AFTER THE GLEANING

(Nach der Lese)

We're striding up and down the lane of beeches,
Their leaves aglitter, almost to the portal,
And see across the field beyond the hedges
The almond tree a second time in petal.

We seek out benches where the sun still lingers,
Where no strange voices put our trance to flight;
In revery we're linked by twining fingers;
We savor long mild lethargies of light.

We're grateful for the hints of rays that glisten
From treetops down to us in weightless flood;
We look up only now and then to listen
When back to earth the ripened apples thud.

The Literary Review   STEFAN GEORGE
                                            —Translated from the German
                                                    by Peter Viereck

AFTER A LONG ILLNESS

It is a small damage
the wind has made in the maples,
and though now they bleed
and their frayed sleeves flap
slowly in the morning breeze
they are well and but worn in
more securely to this place,
warped more cunningly into
the branching bouquet in air
time leaves in its long wake.
Thus it must be. Flowering
in space, shifting the light,
and the light grazing your eye,
the small wheel spinning,
filling the spindle in your heart,
all this in a breath, all
this in the renewed waking.

We are here once more, though
it seemed but a moment ago
that the storm could not end
and that everything had gone
and was surely going into the
insatiate purse: darkness,
but the frail nitre, supplication
and the fiery, damp offering
of the body, titled and grave, won
through to this loose daylight,
a fluttering reprieve.

Yes, there's tea, if you wish,
and there's someone to see you.

Michigan Quarterly Review   LEE GERLACH

APOLOGIA: FOR THE SOCIETY
OF ORTHODOX JEWISH WOMEN

I sit in a room with my grandmother's
peers, Jewish women
who tell me I am not
Jewish because I do not speak
Hebrew, can't make *kugel.*

She didn't teach *kugel,*
wife, serve. In Yiddish
hot as horseradish, she taught me her religion
of college and virginity.
From the Pale to Ellis Island to tenure
in the sweatshops, she moved
to raising sons, then took me on,
girl grandchild, in her three-room flat
off a Brooklyn alley.

Too poor for private school,
I learned no Hebrew at P.S. 158
and never danced the *Hora.*
Yes, her cupboards banged
with dishes for meat and dairy,
separate as Jew and Goy,
but she showed me what was kosher
when she shooed me past
secretarial school to college.

And I first glimpsed holiness
when she said, *In America, Jews can be anything,*
the worklines in her face
melting in the Shabos candleglow.

Jewish Currents   PESHA GERTLER

THE UNSUCCESSFUL FARMER

works his fields
with stern deliberation
as though the earth
were his dirt enemy.

The vertical furrows
between his brows
stay plowed.

His hoe blade
stabs
with too much satisfaction.

He takes no time
to test an early cut,
to raise with naked hand
a fresh deep piece of dampest sod,
to put it to his nose, perhaps his lips,
to discover why the miracle will not work,
to know how close he must come to the earth
before it, in turn, will raise him.

Laurel Review   CHARLES GHIGNA

FLAME

That fish in the swim of haze over the city,
Sunsilvered fuselage slipping away to the east,
Sleek as a spike of ice in a stream speeding
Straight to the gleaming leap of a waterfall,
Flows to no finer goal than the gray ground,
To glide like a toy or fold its fins in flame.

Reading the future in no book of flame,
Seeing no gray but haze enfold our city,
Walking easy, though on ashen ground,
Breathing the bounty of the ambiguous East,
We count the nations slithering to their fall
On Fortune's hill or high on her wheel, speeding.

Leap of a shaft, twang of a string speeding
The shaft; then hands that tuned the twang; then flame
That fired the hand—then the black match, let fall.
Not out of the sky our furies sink to their city,
Nor swarm from our warded north, south, west, or east.
Nor rise up out of the sea or the underground.

Already with us, a long while, sure of their ground,
Breath of our breath, flesh of our flesh, speeding
On pleasure bent they please the gorgeous East
That holds the West in fee. On finless flame
They flaunt the mansions of a heavenly city,
They loft the flight of pride to no landfall.

Avid of fire they mount the last onfall,
Ready to rise and on predestined ground
Across the round of the world in a far city
Kindle a wick no treaties trim. Speeding
A long parade of flame to counter flame,
They preach a western peace to the arming east.

God shield us! whirled on a great globe into the east
Like travelers lulled in a plane's lift and fall
Till they awake reading a scroll of flame—
Rescheduled, look to each other and the ground
And rise to take the ramp together, speeding
Ticketed for impact, into Fortune's city.

Far on the east and voiceless now to the ground,
A plane is ranging away toward nightfall, speeding
To find a light, to circle a flame, a city.

Poetry   BREWSTER GHISELIN

THE DAYS

Up first, alone, only you
caught the earth dipping
just before dawn into silence.
The cars waiting outside
glistened in the dark with dew.
Then a mockingbird would go back
to the song it would break with a buzz,
and through the walls you'd hear
a few early workers, taking
the shortcut down our street,
gun it coming out of the S-
curve and leap into third for
the straight quartermile to the stoplight.

Pulling the door shut behind you
at six, by yourself on the porch,
you left us still asleep to fall
with the weight of the day
toward bottom, where we'd come
in late from an aimless, hours-long
cruise in the Fairlane and go softly by
your bed at midnight to the bathroom.
In a scratchy chatter two commentators
would be tallying late-season
farm-team hits and runs
from the floodlit stillness
of Busch Stadium. Then came
the studio insomniac's voice—
the all-night call-in debate on divorce,
gun-control, drinking . . .

till the produce and livestock prices
came on at five and you were up.

Occident   REGINALD GIBBONS

THE WALK

"Don't go so fast," I called,
but my father always forgot.
Helpless, I reached to clutch
his coattails until his hand
surrounded mine and towed me on.

What knowledge of me did
his hand record?
What angers were given
to my childish keeping—to await
this instant, years later,

when I'm reproached: "Go slow."
Memories swell. He stops to rest.
A small victory implodes. So brief
the time before my child
will triumph over me
for hurts I caused, unknowing,
back on our deep-rutted road.

Ploughshares   CELIA GILBERT

SIMPLICITY

(for E.)

Wishing to praise
the simple, the univocal, the one
word that falls like a ripe fruit
into an infinite well,
I watch

that easy old couple, limber
sixty-year-olds,
strolling, maybe just finished jogging,
under the plum trees.
Over their mild

gray heads the air
is pink with blossoms
accomplishing themselves;
under their tan, accomplished Keds
the sidewalk's pink with petals.

She turns to him and speaks, a word
that fills and falls like another petal,

easy, simple:
a word of thirst?—*milk? wine?*—
a word of love?—*good run?*—

whatever,
it befalls him
light as the stroke of a branch,
clear as color,
and he nods, smiles.

I want to learn that word, I want
to hold that word under my tongue
like a sip of milk,
I want to inhale that word
the way that gray-haired woman, now,

turns back to the tree
and inhales the lucid perfume
of a blossom that promises
ripeness, night, the sweetness
of the plum.

Poetry   SANDRA M. GILBERT

BURST OF COLOR

I gaze in disbelief
at trunk and gnarled dead branches,
skeleton pinned to the sky
by a sunlit web cradled in symbiosis,
then turn to the tree's other side:
a corsage of branches
weighted with flowering peach bloom.
What defiance of death to attract the insects,
to mantle the ground with sweet-scented progeny!

I used to think that fifty years
would see a faltering walk,
a gradual slipping on the path.
Now I know
we dance to the brink,
throwing our seed windward
until some sudden luckless day.

I lie in the sun and close my eyes
sealed tight from the blue.
A spider wheels red across the air,
his legs pumping him toward oblivion.

Green River Review   EVALYN P. GILL

THE SUNDAY NEWS

Looking for something in the Sunday paper,
I flipped by accident through *Local Weddings,*

Yet missed the photograph until I saw
Your name among the headings.

And there you were, looking almost unchanged,
Your hair still long, though now long out of style,
And you still wore that stiff and serious look
You called a smile.

I felt as though we sat there face to face.
My stomach tightened. I read the item through.
It said too much about both families,
Too little about you.

Finished at last, I threw the paper down,
Stung by jealousy, my mind aflame,
Hating this man, this stranger whom you loved,
This printed name.

And yet I clipped it out to put away
Inside a book like something I might use,
A scrap I knew I wouldn't read again
Yet couldn't bear to lose.

Poetry   DANA GIOIA

BIX BEIDERBECKE (1903-1931)

(January, 1926)

China Boy. Lazy Daddy. Cryin' All Day.
He dreamed he played the notes so slowly that
they hovered in the air above the crowd
and shimmered like a neon sign. But no,
the club stayed dark, trays clattered in the kitchen,
people drank and went on talking. He watched
the smoke drift from a woman's cigarette
and slowly circle up across the room
until the ceiling fan blades chopped it up.
A face, a young girl's face, looked up at him,
the stupid face of small-town innocence.
He smiled her way and wondered who she was.
He looked again and saw the face was his.

He woke up then. His head still hurt from drinking,
Jimmy was driving. Tram was still asleep.
Where were they anyway? Near Davenport?
There was no distance in these open fields—
only time, time marked by a farmhouse
or a barn, a tin-topped silo or a tree,
some momentary silhouette against
the endless, empty fields of snow.
He lit a cigarette and closed his eyes.
The best years of his life! The Boring 'Twenties.

He watched the morning break across the snow.
Would heaven be as white as Iowa?

The Ontario Review   DANA GIOIA

PHOTOGRAPH OF MY MOTHER AS A YOUNG GIRL

She wasn't looking
when they took this picture:
sitting on the grass
in her bare feet
wearing a cotton dress,
she stares off to the side
watching something on the lawn
the camera didn't catch.
What was it?
A ladybug? A flower?
Judging from her expression,
possibly nothing at all,
or else
the lawn was like a mirror,
and she sat watching herself,
wondering who she was
and how she came to be there
sitting in this backyard,
wearing a cheap, white dress
imagining that tomorrow
would be like all her yesterdays,
while her parents chatted
and watched, as I do
years later,
too distantly to interfere.

The Hudson Review   DANA GIOIA

GHETTO SONG

Within your bones my singing
melts like the snow's first flakes.
Within your starry eyes
an old joy reawakes.
Laugh, my darling child!
Sing, my grief, my prize!
Over an old wall
seven suns arise.

From the boughs and branches
a weary Sabbath weeps.
Beggarfolk sit dead
on all the gloomy streets.
Hush, my darling child!

Sleep, my tender flesh!
On your shiny platter
dances a golden fish.

Where your father passes,
the stars bestow their grace.
The moon's his dear possession
through the nightly chase.
Sleep, my darling child!
Kisses shut your eyes!
Over grieving ruins
a young dove flies.

The dove is you, of course;
your hands are its white wings.
Beside your hungry cradle
Mother sits and sings.
Shush, my darling child!
Just you hush and wait!
The good hands of your father
are opening the gate.

Midstream   JACOB GLATSTEIN
                              —Translated from the Yiddish
                                       by Aaron Kramer

GARGOYLES

Sunlight in the window,
a cup of lemon tea.
Nothing is about to happen.
This moment is mine—
I hold it in my hand and say
Yes, this is a new day,
I don't believe we've met before,
then lean on my porch,
pretending to be a man in shirtsleeves, smoking,
or a grandmother resting her years.

I can feel myself fitting into the long corridors
of balcony-loungers all over the city:
we are the gargoyles of the great cathedral.
It is our scrutiny which brings pink
to geraniums, red to the tiles of the roof,
a vivid blue to the ribbons
in a little girl's hair.

It is our vigilance that fills the air
with breakfast smells, and the memory
of last night's rain. We are
the attentive ones, the guardians,
drinkers of tea
in the cup of the day.

event   SUSAN GLICKMAN

THE GAS

That year, my mother was dying. And other things,
as well, stand out from what now seems that definable
block of time: a question of money; the way some poems
would only open at night, like certain
pale flowers; a woman whose smeary mascara would be
a flock of birds across my pillow weekend mornings,
often (even if accidentally) with the balance
of a Japanese woodblock print . . . It all comes back
when I fill up the car with gas. I know
how that sounds, but it's true. It's in the plume
of wavering gas-laden air that flows from the tank,
around the nozzle, just brushing the hand. The whole
year comes back then for me; I don't know why,
but it does. Perhaps the smell of the trays in the ward
when they cleaned up after her first
hit me as I stood in some station with snow
and neon falling across the Self-Serve bay; maybe
that, or a resolution having to do with debt
or language, or an understanding of how the lips
after love are sensitive instruments and pick up
signals from other inhabited planets . . . Maybe; and
maybe that's too easy, assuming a small event
in a larger one, if it recurs, reminds us
of the larger. I couldn't say. I'll only tell you
for sure that year comes back, it rides this
opulent feather of air for the moment it lasts,
that year and no other; and everything about it
moves into a clarity and back again, like figures
stepping out from behind a pane of pebbled glass,
then changing their minds. Of course the scent clings
to your hand for a while. You stop at a light
and a hint of it's still with you, and you think
what could be happening behind that door, that year
that won't come out but won't let you in; then the horns
behind you say it's time to step on it buddy and go.

Tar River Poetry   ALBERT GOLDBARTH

TEETH

We all live in dread of our teeth
falling out into our cupped palms.
We pray for our teeth, clattering
in the bone-chamber of the skull.
And when the little insanities
creep up from our throat, our teeth,
good soldiers holding their ground,
grind them down in our sleep. And praise
to the wolf with his sharp incisors,
the better to eat. And the ice-maiden's
teeth, sheathed in enamel, biting clean

through the bone. Oh we would never
depart from our eyeteeth, rooted dependably
above our unremarkable necks. And who
is not awed by the white buds of milkteeth
that sprout from red plushness and become
the cutting edge.

Poetry   BARBARA GOLDBERG

CELLO

Why does one say that the heart sings?
when it is not the heart, but the voice that does:
if the leg could sing, it might;
if the pump lodged in the chest
could sing, it would make such clear
deep sounds as only that cellist makes,
playing Bach, the man of the brook,
whose dark wood shivers with pleasure—

or it would make the hoarse, hurt sounds
of the deer bitten in the woods the morning
that our dog got to him;
over the frozen river,
dark wood, dark waters
under the leaping cross of the animal
as he seizes his pleasure with teeth,
with tongue, and the sail of his skin spread.

Should all abandon have such danger in it.
The air, given the faith of the cello,
sings with the innocence and stolidity of trees,
which bend, and also the human will
bends, the blades of its joy
folded like grass-tips, sunk
in the ice by the river, so many times;
they stiffen and thaw, the lip-like blades,
they open and sing.

Ploughshares   LORRIE GOLDENSOHN

FROM THE DIARY OF A ROYAL PSALMIST

Let me enjoy her and not sin.
Let me sin and repent.
Let me repent and be forgiven.
Forgive me in the future as in the past.

Let the Day of Atonement atone.
Let my sufferings be counted an atonement.
Let my death atone for all my sins.
Regard them as peccadillos, parden my dust.

I shall now write a psalm in praise of the Lord.

The American Scholar   JUDAH GOLDIN

POEM CONTAINING "SO, AND, SUCH"

And so they said the heavy usage of
such words as "so" and "and" and "such"
always gives away a woman writer,
also known as poetess. And we all know
what that means, do we not? A trifle
sentimental, and so personal, and so much love.
So that I studiously wanted to avoid
such easy give-aways so very much.

And then I had my first poems, so
belabored, relatively free of "so"
and "and" and "such." And I was married then,
and so I went to ask my husband once:
"Tell me, why is it that my women friends
always like my writing so much better
than do any of the men (whom
in parentheses, I'm begging to approve)?"
And he said, cautiously, he didn't know.

And so I had to ask myself
such questions over and over and over again,
until I had no choice but to grow up
with them into the shape of my own answer.

And frankly,
I would rather be a goddess than a god,
and so I must conclude
that I would rather be a poetess
than ever again a poet, straining hard
against my being, merely to avoid
such words as "so" and "and" and "such."

Anima   BEATE GOLDMAN

WHAT IT'S ALL ABOUT

Aha, I thought, this is what
it's all about. All of Life's
puzzles were miraculously
solved.

Then I was back in the room
with all the lights. My thighs
stretched wide; strangers peering
over masks.

"Isn't she pretty," said a nurse
in a green smock. "And just
as sweet," answered white-haired
Dr. Loomis, or was it God?

The vise started again, wrenching,
My spine was opening.
"Now, please!" I begged.

The sickening sweet cone suffocated
me once more. I floated through
the white clouds to the place
with the answers.

Now, where were we? Yes, yes.
I must remember this. All the ideas
kaleidoscoped into place. No more
mysteries.

Back again to Dr. God.

"A little patience, dear.
Press down, my sweet."

A cow-like moan. From me?
Through a flurry of busyness,
unbelievable pain, a little fellow
with the plumbing his father ordered
came.

Buffalo Spree   BOBBIE GOLDMAN

THE REFUGEE'S GARDEN

This is the nicest garden I have planted yet:
All flowers, early color for the Spring—
Narcissus, primrose and forget-me-not,
Fancy tulips even, begged from weary neighbors
Who wonder why I so persist.
We have such little hope of seeing it in bloom
That they advise me, "wait till later."
Perhaps *this* summer we shall all be home.

But I've forgotten how to wait.
Each year, as I was washed up on the shore
Of other people's wars—
Hopeless driftwood trailing seaweed
Like remembered roots—
I hid in foreign ground these coins of summer;
And though I have not ever been allowed
To claim or tend them,
I know my gardens grow like small fierce fires
To spite the holocaust.

Midstream   BARBARA GOLDOWSKY

LINES TO BAT-SHEVA

BAT-Sheva, daughter of seven,
daughter of the *Shabbas Malke,*
granddaughter of our gathering years,
tonight we heard you sing—

and it was different from all other nights,
for tonight you sang
in Yiddish!
The *mameloshen* was sweet as honey
rolling lyrically from your tongue.
You sang with the joy
of one who knows how to open
each day with song;
you sang with all the pride
of a nine-year-old
whose roots grow deep
in our people's history.
In your sweet, clear voice
pulsed the heart of your ancestors
who lived, loved, and even dreamed
in Yiddish.
The world they built
block by block
vanished in fire and smoke.
But tonight, you retrieved
that lost world for us,
and the frozen stars began to thaw.

This morning I awoke,
my face wet with hot tears.
I could hear your voice singing—
raising our half-forgotten hope
that the little ones who sang
in the darkness of the ghettos,
in the rubble of destruction,
will live again,
will sing again,
with your voice.

The Jewish Spectator   ROBERTA B. GOLDSTEIN

THE RAPTURE IS COMING

The frame church waits
By the tracks. I lean my shadow against the window,
Listening. My sister,
The believer, had told me, *the rapture
Is coming.* Voices swell out of air
Like a thin whistle rushing
To meet you and *light breaks,* she said,
Into a million pieces like stained glass.

She sits upright in the meeting room
And hears voices. They allow themselves
No instruments, only the beating
Of sinners' hands against breasts—and hearts,
Pounding, revealed to merciless daylight.

A train rumbles in the distance.
Over the hard, unforgiving country out here,
Sound travels for miles. The worshipers
Lift their heads. Judgment thunders
Less faintly and far away.

The train looms
Like a man over a bed, presses
Into me and is gone,
Into the blue. I've lived
A thousand deaths and resurrections. I straighten up.
The storm has passed and the rails die down.
Sister, I have sinned again and again
And found it good. Only lately
Has regret's saving grace come
To visit. Forgive me. We travel
Our different roads into eternity,
The fanned-out smoke against the sky.

The Georgia Review   ALISON GOLEMBIEWSKI

CIVILIZATION

It is not easy
to come to terms with eating meat.
There are those
who have become vegetarians,
        an impeccable choice.
But there are others
who have become hunters,
        stalking from their suburban homes
        and accepting, they say,
        the implications of their hunger,
        restoring the connection
        between necessity and action.
        (it is never, of course,
        because they like killing.)
I admit,
wary of the primal logic of their argument,
that on the farm we hunted and butchered,
        all the headless carcasses
        strung up outside the barn,
        draining into the red earth;
but it was a necessary chore,
no more than that,
abandoned with relief
for the cellophane-wrapped packages in stores—
        the consequence of income,
        of simple division of labour.
What purist could wish that away?

The Antigonish Review   LEONA GOM

VANITY

Gleaming with summer,
construction workers rivet
the vanity of steel beams and glass
into walls shimmering with traffic.

The buildings rise from blueprints,
gather like impudent heirs
around a clump of old buildings
ailing behind their brick facades.

The old buildings watch with dull eyes;
they hold fast to their legacy of permanence,
but it gets harder to remember
what was so important

about tiers of stone carvings,
gargoyles on the roof line, towering clocks,
and the tiled inscriptions of street names
that read like simple truths on the sidewalk.

Cedar Rock   REBECCA GONZALES

SIGNS

If the strawberry
Jam thickens at
The first boil, he
Will come for me.
If the wren builds
Again in the poplar,
I will bear him
A child.
If all the pole-
Beans come up
Strong, it will
Be a boy-child.
If the dough rises
In the bowl enough
For three loaves, I
Will die before him.
If the thread knots,
He will come late.
If the thread breaks,
He will not come.

Yankee   J. B. GOODENOUGH

A SWEET FEVER

I recently fell in love
with a Trobriand Islander.
We share a fondness for opposites
and sleep under the bald sun
of midday. When we wake,
the night is busy
shooting the small fish out of the sky
and they wash up on the shore,
more than we can eat.

Life is easy. We kiss
all night like the archipelago drifting
away from the equator,
and the mangoes fill our yard
with a sweet fever that all things alive
feel once or twice. There is nothing
we long for, children or music,
and the unendurable shyness
of our animal nature has ceased to exist.

Instead, we live in an oceanic
flight through silence, our bodies the tip
of one wave moving
through the longhouse
in a unison of touch—
no climax, no destination
but a prehistoric orchard
where fruit ripens and ripens
and will never fall.

Mississippi Review   MAREA GORDETT

THE BRIDGE REVERBERATES EACH STEP WE TAKE

(Bialystok Ghetto)

The bridge reverberates each step we take.
We stop a while and look below:
a train flies through, and here comes one in its wake,
and people nod at them hurtling through.
Just as they're standing now, I once stood there
spruced up in bright new sailor-shirt and shorts.
My father with his fingers combed my hair
and promised to send chocolates and torts.
The train's hoot mocked his hopes and plans.
You stand near me and fix your eyes
on me, and mine fix inward. I can feel your hands—
my throat senses your palm, my heart can recognize
your fingers. You're playing with me—and I'm
your child. Who told us love would be waving
more fiercely here on this bridge at this time
than the wind in the field—when the hoot of the train,

so fatefully harsh, wakes a tenfold craving
for joy? But here, where your hand slides over my skin,
tomorrow a bayonet will kiss me.
The hoot of the train, the roar of my fate,
caress, oh caress me . . .
It's dark, it's late.

New England Review & Bread Loaf Quarterly   JACK GORDON
—Translated from the Yiddish
by Aaron Kramer

YESTERDAY AND TOMORROW

MURDER is now
Suffering is now
And God is always yesterday

Pain is now
Injustice is now
And the Messiah is always tomorrow

The Jewish Spectator   NORMAN GORDON

BARGES

(to My Father)

They drift under bridges, huge as a city block,
restless as the migrating farmers who assemble
in the dark. While we sleep, their green lights

blink and expand. They are caught
by the river, willing to carry anything
in those sad, masculine forms.

Redwing, Lake City, Stillwater, Hastings—
the little towns wave like delighted women
from the parched shore. How could they love

these stubborn vessels, this iron
that hates its obsessiveness. The harbors
open their arms and the boats

roll drowsily away, dreaming of the ocean
waiting around the bend. Tonight
the barges are only barges and it is hunger,

a weakness that keeps them moving. So sad,
for the villages fear they will be forgotten.
But the barges store everything.

They remember a lover's sudden iciness,
the mother who whistles bravely,
and the houses starving

at their posts on the river.

Southern Poetry Review   SARAH GORHAM

PHOTOGRAPH

I have a photograph of a child
that is my mother, my grandmother,
and me. It has that light brown hair,
round face, the same smile.
I have odd objects that hold something of
my grandmother: silver candlesticks,
handkerchiefs, linen sheets, a silk teddy
—all worn with use and age.
When she was young she
had wanted to dance, but she
married young, was widowed young,
and lived alone. This I understand.
My mother was only eighteen
when her father died; I knew
the parallels in our lives,
and watched my father until
my nineteenth birthday (my grandmother
had been a posthumous child). My mother
married my father secretly
a year before the public ceremony.
I don't know what to do with myself,
wondering how much further
the parallels go: I'm the second daughter
of a second daughter of a
second daughter; neither dancer
nor wife—a child's face
in an aging walnut frame.

The Antigonish Review   NEILE GRAHAM

THE HOLY ONES

Invite them to your parties
Your meetings, your homes
Your *shuls,* your pools
Inquire after their numbered arms
Their darkened teeth
Their nightmares
Their sighs, their migraines
Do not hush
And never avoid their eyes

Celebrate their ambitious children
Their business success
Their decorator wallpaper
Their glittering memorial balls
Give them love
And belonging
And time
And listening

For they are the holy ones
Purified in hunger
Sanctified in whippings
Sacralized in the burning image
Of a bewildered mother
Pulled onto another line
Forever
They are our teachers
Our martyrs, our holy ones
They are our Death/ And our Resurrection

Midstream   BLU GREENBERG

WELDINGS

It was the tip of a match
that flew in this woman's eye.
And perhaps this woman
has always been blind.
I've gone slowly near-sighted.
The clinic is the top floor.
A tower is going up
across the street. Welders kneel
at the corners, blue torches
showering yellow ash.
When I looked up as a child,
they welded stars
to the corners of random constructions.
Now even white lettering blurs
when I'm on the streets.
The names in memory are perfectly clear.
The city and its piers
and all the blue of the bay
can be seen from here.
Even if only half-seen beauty like this
could send me to another
way of life far from this one
of simply recovering what is lost.
I think of my stepfather who died
this spring. How long it takes
to believe it, as truth comes slowly,
a kind of mercy.
Before we see it,
the world has already come apart.

Epoch   JEFFREY GREENE

HEART

He tells me I'm a risk:
he is small, blond, Mississippian. I trust him.

I am fighting my genes, he says; fighting
my father, at fifty-two pulling off the highway
that had become a gray blur
trying to call to anyone from a phonebooth
while it broke in his chest, calcified, knobby,
like an ankle bone;
and then again, over and over
in the hospital room while doctors
ran up and down the halls trying to stop
that sequence of explosions,
that string of firecrackers.

You see yourself as glass
for the first time, transparent,
shaken and fizzing, a bottle
of soda, and start watching
for potholes.
Or maybe you just learn to live with
a cart with square wheels
thudding in your breast,
trying to carry whatever it is
there
before it's too late.

This is how to become
old: worry only
about yourself.
So that if there come
bombs out of clouds,
or lovers into rooms, saying
goodbyes, learn
how to cup your hand around it, as if,
in a world of wind,
there is this one candle
that must be saved.

Poetry   WILLIAM GREENWAY

GOERING AT NUREMBERG

There are people in my country now
who wait for the rapture in living rooms,
by which they mean
to be gathered whole cloth to the arms

of God. As if to forecast
your later escape, you stood,
eighty pounds less of you stood in the dock
to be judged, your uniform draped like a flag.

What we failed not so much to imagine as
quite flatly to prevent was sponsored
bravado, the one small vial of cyanide burning
a hole through justice, by which

we sometimes mean revenge.
The hangman was left like a bride
forlorn. Malice absconded
and all its voluptuous ballast let slip

within our very walls. You'd colonized
the airier regions for years, had you not?
Wines the poets would envy, art,
as in "he's hung great art

on his walls," and one tubercular
Swedish wife, who suffered *grand mal*
as others among the chosen have suffered
great evil, to serve as a sign.

Like a bank account in some better
South America, this life of the spirit
accumulates. The dashing young flyer
is dashing again, though nearly out of time.

As good for the heart as conscious
election, as good for the profile
as a long silk scarf, the end of hope
is bracing as mountain air. Or so

you'd lead us to believe.
We can see how hope equivocates.
The lost don't send instructions.
Nobody trusts the saved.

Antaeus   LINDA GREGERSON

WITHOUT DESIGN ALL BEAUTY MELTS AWAY

It is cold this evening. One of the first
cold evenings of autumn.
I have your shirt over my own.
I am not hungry. I am starving.
And I look for the laws of all this.
I write down a new name, Cyrene,
beloved of Apollo. To look up.
To learn about it before spring.
To learn what the earth asks of us.
To know that would be happiness.
To go the right way. To carry what is not
known to those who will take it
and give me back something which is.

Ploughshares   LINDA GREGG

CHURCHILL DOWNS TOUTS

The railbirds
yell at the jockeys.

They yell at the horses.
They whoop and slap
their palms with flat programs
when the tote blinks photo.

These are guys who know about odds.

I like touts who get tense
in the grandstand,
bet heavy on fields of well-bred maidens,
figure the race with papers and bourbon,
yell at the horses,
yell back at the odds.

Give me a turn
away from the office.
Save me a place at the rail.

Mississippi Review   JOSEPH GRIECO

SPEED

Arrow hard my right leg slung
across the BMW, we bore
down on the straightaway, then
riding the pegs we took the curve
at 90. The boy on the Daytona-
500 did not know the forty-two year
old man, goggle-eyed and
helmeted; grinning in his spit.
He could have taken me, this
smooth-cheeked lad in denim; his
machine and nerves were newer than mine.
But at the last turn just before
the freeway he backed off, and I
shot by on my ancient metal steed,
laughing at my black gloved hands
that trembled too hard to wave.

Wind   WALTER GRIFFIN

STEVE / A LETTER

Steve, you have entered again
the world of whiteness and women,
the bombed look of patients, the fact
of reflection that once you explained in tears
could tell you nothing.
Yes. A father who beat you,
and those hard days of bucking hay
into the salt of Missouri.
For facts are liars, you said,

and art is how much money you make,
the way you live,
or the women you do not have.
You will be awakened daily to the chores of the insane:
basket weaving and food, the visits of doctors,
the hush of nurses' shoes.
In a blue sleep you tell yourself
plain facts do not change, do not
slide into one another like snakes.
Steve, it is not that way. Monsters are to be lived with.
And the glass of plain fact has never been hard.

Kansas Quarterly   JONATHAN GRIFFITH

CHILDREN, LIKE WHEAT

Children are raised, it seems, like wheat,
for a good yield average,
and best picked when sweet,
like corn before the starch sets in.

A good crop soothes the farmer's rage
against the sun, the rain, the wind,
the bank, the freeze, the constant weed,
the elements that make or break his children.

I'd rather be a cow grown for my meat
than raised a child between a farmer's rage, like wheat.
A harvest is its own reward from seed.
I raise my child because there's the need.

The Texas Review   PETER GRIVICH

SWING

Two grown men, men grown as I am,
play basketball one on one, giggling,
tripping and getting up fast
like children. The sun
glints in the sweat of their beards.
Eight times they miss before that orange ball
sinks with a cough through the chain net.
Strange, to call myself a man.
I sit on a swing, but when my hands reach
from my sports jacket pockets to grip the chain
I nearly fall,
then steady so I almost float, swing
like the windy maple shadow I played with once
that caught my feet in its raised roots.
I think this swing is what I mean:
the way I fall back and forth,

that I brighten and darken the grass,
how the sun falls in and out of my eyes,
the way it rubbed the skin of my leg in our maple
until I leap and land dizzy on the scraped earth
and the men on my right have gone, no longer play ball
like children, but children play ball on my left,
the limbs of their bicycles tangled in the grass.
The older brother, who's maybe eight, whose arm is
slung around his younger brother's shoulder,
tells how to throw a ball—
to bend your arm, then straighten out.
To swing from the ear.
The sun in our eyes says dinner, and across my legs
falls the shadow of the children linked, at play.

Mississippi Review   DAVID GROFF

IN THE LIGHT OF OCTOBER

(for V.G.M.)

The long red seam across her throat
shows where her thyroid, instrument
of checks and balances within
the body's greater, delicate machine
no longer lies. This afternoon,
the sleeve of light unravelling, she drank
a glass of radioactive iodine
to melt the last small edge
of poisoned tissue down.

Now for a day she radiates
in isolation like a minor sun,
closing the bedroom door to company;
and sits beside the window, looking down
on ranks of cattails autumn
thinned and scoured, the Sound's
blue mantle gently thrown
around the shoulders of the cove.

Her husband, for so many hours
unable to disturb her solitude,
sleeps and wakes in the cold livingroom
imagining the rose
she plucked a week ago
from one late-blooming bush:
how radiant around a central gold
the shadows held like petals, luminous.

The Hudson Review   EMILY GROSHOLZ

PORTRAIT OF A WOMAN

She rests restlessly
And is lovely. She is
Alive, full of vinegar

And the sweetest sugar
To be found. Her wrinkles
Are lovely; her sharp tongue

Is telling and mostly correct.
I would tell you about the crook
Of her arm or how her lovely

Breasts hang, or how she loves.
I could tell you how she lives
Her life—she is much her own

Person. I could tell you pages
In bad words, words that would not
Touch that original.

Rather say I have been
Spoiled for any other. There
Is no she but she.

The Spoon River Quarterly   HAROLD M. GRUTZMACHER

FOR MY WIFE, CUTTING MY HAIR

You move around me expertly like the good,
round Italian barber I went to
in Florence, years before we met,
his scissors a razor he sharpened on a belt.

But at first when you were learning, I feared
for my neck, saw my ears like sliced fruit
on the newspapered floor. Taking us back in time,
you cleverly clipped my head in a flat-top.

The years in between were styles no one had ever seen,
or will ever see again: when the wind rose
half my hair floated off in feathers;
the other half bristling, brief as a brush.

In the chair, almost asleep, I hear the bright
scissors dancing. Hear you hum, full-breasted as Aida,
carefully trimming the white from my temples,
so no one, not even I, will know.

Yankee   BRUCE GUERNSEY

CELESTIAL CONCERT

All the music we have heard
and all that we have dreamed
rises here in luminous figures.
They unfurl great wings, don rose-white
or flaming garments, cover themselves
with green feathers, like young buds,
wear halos of gold and emerald.
They have turned into angels
that touch lute and viola
with radiant fingers. They descend
toward us, a wavy stream, throwing off
sparks. Around them everything is music:
the pavilion with its light crenellations
poised overhead like trills, the decorations—
marble or leaves—interchanging, the sky
where all the colors wheel in a melodious rainbow,
mountain and shepherd's path,
blue castle and virginal lake;
and on its bank, closed in the secret
of its brown leaves, the rose burns.
Above all, she is music, the adored one,
lovingly gazed-at, in both the expectation and the fruit,
her transparent flesh veiling the spirit's fire
that kindles in the splendor of the Son.
At her feet even the simplest objects
are brightened by echoes and reflections: the cradle,
tub, the lowly pot
or a small jug . . . Will it be granted to us, too,
in an ineffable moment
to be nothing but light and music?

International Poetry Review

MARGHERITA GUIDACCI
—*Translated from the Italian
by Ruth Feldman*

THE QUESTION OF WINTER

The snow is heavy on the hedge,
Everywhere is white, burdened
With beauty brief as this cloudy day;
But here, now, the great mountains
Bending, the hills, the spruce by the house,
At night a gold window in it,
And the cedar and bare maple all over
With fallen glory far from April.

This asks answer, the grand gesture,
Of us, the earth rolling, blue,
Whirled cloudy blue from the viewpoint
Of the moon, this blue earth

With winter on it: What of that loss?
What has it, that other season of yours
When here now is naturalness, snow
Above the hills, along the road,
That cancellation is never made
In the insistent heart and its involvement
Held-to though the moment is now—
Of what is gone, of what will come?

The Malahat Review   RALPH GUSTAFSON

LILIES AT MOUNT ST. HELENS

Avalanche lilies break the earth,
Bugs appear at St. Helens.
Life returns.

I walk this path pumice-covered,
Fern and lupine cling
The banks; above the

Persisting world snow glistens.
I pick a blade to show
I control mortality.

There is nothing new to death
But the glory of renewal,
David's descent,

This Easter. I accept the ancestry; look down:
Above, the glory of uncertainty,
At my heel, while lilies.

The Malahat Review   RALPH GUSTAFSON

RETURN TO THE LOWER EAST SIDE

Four apartments in forty-four years—
the first two a forest of fears from each other,
both nesting tightly in rotted branches
overhanging perilous seas amid
stenches, cacophonies, sprightly visions,
I still call home—
the latter two, miles of decisions,
reams of revisions away,
within one chill compass of unruffled undefiled green,
a velvet field along serene seas
boasting odorfree, noiseless, permanent obsequies.

Can I also come home?
Can I breeze back from death to life?
Or is there no escape for me now
from the decayed root and branch that I am,
toiling its fruitless frayed unafraid pilgrimage?

My old father spoke frequently sagely of the *heim*
which was not my youthful home
but his own bold, broiling, grimy dell,
equally unreachable.

Midstream   LEO HABER

SPEAKING IN TONGUES

It is one and two and three
and close to four. No use
trying to sleep. I pad
down the hall. I heat
milk in a little brown enamelled pan
Made in Poland. Poland, sealed-off place.
Something is rotten in the state of Poland.
I stir in Nestle's Quik, my feet
frigid on the black, white
and grey linoleum floor,
which is blistered like skin from the time
some butter caught on fire
in this same saucepan. Memories—
pain, otherness, delight—
seep into me tonight
up through my two cold feet
as water through a pore.
I may not be able to sleep
but there are circumstances I can hold
against me through my nightgown in the cold.
My nightgown. I look down:
I thought it was sprigged with pink,
but even for four a.m.
it looks pretty pale and wan.
Oh. It's inside out.
I must have put it on
blindly in the dark.
I had been reading the old tongue again,
was back in the undertow, moving fast and frightened,
was trellised like a vine, branched and directed.
What was this edifice
whose humblest terrace I was trained to cover?
My family? my language? or not mine?
Through thick winter black
nostalgia winked a knowing wink
even when I had sprung from bed,
flung on my nightgown, hurried to the dead
kitchen, and was standing by the sink.
Figures sped by me, faceless.
They skimmed—or something skimmed—years off my life,
so much scum from the top of a cooling cup!
Now in the pan the cocoa raises up

its head like a cobra, hisses,
swells with self-importance.

The Threepenny Review　　RACHEL HADAS

LINES FOR MY MOTHER, AT 55

Women and men have gone mad
on land like this:
in winter, a white flint
of wind cuts the heart;
in spring, the windmill
never ceases its cry,
like a dying predator bird;
in summer, clouds of dust
stirred up from burning land
get into everything, leaving
grit between the teeth
and under the bedsheets;
and fall comes always
before the winter again.

They have gone crazy sometimes;
there are stories of Otoe women
found hanging in the oak-trees,
wanting so much to leave this earth,
of immigrant mothers wandering
over the skyline, calling
for dead children to come home,
of farmwives gone quiet, withdrawn
like doves protecting themselves.

Today as the blizzard moved in
I thought of you
out getting the cattle in,
lifting your face to see
how the weeping willow you planted
danced with the wind.

Southern Poetry Review　　　　STEVE HAHN

LOOKING OUT ON AFRICA

I slept inside a crib
in the corner of my parents' room
until I was six.
I lay between the safety
bars like a baby elephant
looking out on Africa, my parents
always hunting
each other underneath
their sheets.

They'd move into the unknown
territory and there
in that large space of bed
with no visible bars,
I'd hear the secret
noises of discovery
and see the shapes
of pleasure
and of discontent.

I don't remember thoughts
I had.
Memory merges with my own
geometry, becomes part of how
I dance
the foreign dance,
sing
the strange sounds.
All barriers invisible.

Poetry   SUSAN HAHN

MOTHBALL FLEET: BENICIA, CALIFORNIA

These massed grey shadows
of a distant war,
anchored among burnt hills.

The chained pitch and sweep of them
streaked with rust,
swinging in the sunlit silence,
hinges of a terrible labor.

Years before the last war
my father and I floated past them
on the Chesapeake;
our oarlocks and quiet voices
sounded in the hollow hulls.

And once again these shadows
crossed between me and the sunlight,
formations under flags of smoke.
They carried men, torpedoes,
sealed orders in weighted sacks,
to join tomorrow
some bleak engagement
I will not see.

They are the moving, the stationary
walls of my time.
They hold within them cries,
cold, echoing spaces.

New England Review & Bread Loaf Quarterly   JOHN HAINES

HOME

It is years since I've been here,
a small town, no bigger than when I left,
with diseased elms lining Broad Street,
and teenagers circling endlessly,
their cars humming in a pack
at the Dairy Queen, exhaust
settling like twilight. Not even
the movie theater has survived,
its doors boarded against vandals,
the lightbulbs which spelled its name
shot out one summer evening
of insufferable heat.

In the local newspaper there's a picture
of a newly-wed couple posing before
a field of tall corn: it envelops them
like a humorous statement on fertility,
when, in fact, it is no more than
the father's crop, the livelihood the son
will inherit. They will honeymoon
in Atlantic City and settle in a trailer
on the farm, and in four years she will
bear three children whose births
will be announced in this paper: Henry, Jr.,
Trisha, and Mark Anthony. Eventually
bovine, the bride will spend her days
vacuuming the wall-to-wall and leafing
through the TV guide.

When the corn is harvested in the fall
the land stretches for miles, its vastness
startling; so much land that it is unrecognizable,
yet familiar, like the faces I see when I walk
downtown. At the Acme there is a woman
who smiles and calls me by name, though
I have to read her name tag to return the
courtesy: "Julie." The lines that fan out
in faint symmetry from her eyes are disheartening,
as I recall how in fourth grade her twin sister
Judy drowned, and we walked as a class
from the elementary school to the church
in the rain, a parade of small umbrellas
and glistening yellow slickers. I look
at this woman and see both girls: one dead,
the other alive, bloated like a drowned person,
her eyes the color of the sea.

Poetry   VANESSA HALEY

BEREAVEMENT

In the rim of smoke
Above their poker
Table or beyond a fairway
Marker, when I miss them
So, for one moment,
Silently, I show myself.

Or in a classroom
Where the new woman
Hired to replace me
Lectures, when I miss them
So, for one moment,
Silently, I show myself;

But most often at home
When our five children
Talk or are all reading
Together, Oh, I miss them
So, and for one moment,
Silently, I show myself.

These and also others
I pass on my old feet
Or with my old hands touch
Their faces, for I miss them
So, and in that way,
Silently, I show myself.

Yet I know my skin
Of smoke, my transparent
Voice or children not enjoined
Signify that only I betray myself:
Neither my shadow nor my footprints
Are seen on the passing snow.

Tar River Poetry   JAMES B. HALL

WINTER IN TEXAS

A neighbor boy rings the doorbell
and asks if I have seen his black
Labrador. I have been reading Thirteenth
Century anonymous poetry and am thinking
of writing something about winter in Texas.
I stand in the doorway, holding my book
and a small notebook and a pen and I ask
the boy how long the dog has been gone,
what it looks like, its name. He tells me,
and there is anguish in his face and he is
anxious to get on to the next door.
Most of the poems I have been reading are
about loss. A young man has lost his loved

one, someone else has lost his illusions
of immortality. Another sees the swirling
leaves as a kind of loss. I see the boy
from the window by my chair, going from
house to house. I hear him singing out his
dog's name between the houses. These six-
hundred-year-old-poems still have their pangs.
Together they have made me recall my own
losses. I look out at the barren branches
of an anonymous tree across the street.
Beneath the earth I know its roots branch down
into a mirror replica of the tree; I know
that what we see above the earth is only half
the truth. I have a dog myself and I can imagine
its loss. I was a boy once, and once had a dog
which vanished into a neighborhood, and I sang
out its name over and over. I have knocked on
strangers' doors. Normally, I bury sadnesses
like this one. It is the Twentieth Century,
I have a name, it is winter in Texas. This
feeling won't survive. It will swirl away like
all the others. A boy's voice sings out all
through the neighborhood the name of his loss.

Quarterly West   JIM HALL

ROMANCE AND CAPITALISM AND THE MOVIES

To the child the movie is mysterious.
Like magic, her mother
always knows what will happen. "She slapped
his face," the mother says, "but in the end
they'll get married." Murders—
the child wonders how she knows who did it.
It seems fitting, the mother's like
that with the icebox too, no use
wiping up spilled milk. Does she
have eyes in back of her head? Can she see
into a child's heart?
One day at a school movie some kids whisper
in the row behind. "Just wait,"
a girl says, "that guy's gonna lose his money."
And the child realizes it's not magic,
not her mother, it's movies; if you see
enough of them you can gaze right into
the heroine's heart, her secret love for a brute.
You learn what the everyday fails to teach,
that love goes kiss-slap-kiss,
the filthy rich go broke, and honest
folk end up happy unless they're women
and radiant in sacrifice.

The Massachusetts Review   JOAN JOFFE HALL

REPAPERING THE KITCHEN

We probe and scrape and peel away the faded
Multicolored layers of a lifetime,
Like Schliemann
(Who? Grandmother asks)
Burrowing the many-layered Troy,
Yearning for a reenactment from another time
Such as comes to her like breathing.

There are fifty years and six or seven layers here:

Some full white flowers spangling a deep, yet muted pink
That even I recall;

An ivory vase of tiny purple blossoms
Clustered there since just before the war;

A simple cup and saucer and a china plate
Upon a background pastel blue.

As each new pattern breaks upon the light
The visions bud and bloom for her, and shimmer
Out, away
To bud and bloom and shimmer
Into bud and bloom

As she interprets to our blindness,
In anecdote and tale,
The echoed genealogies that linger here
Not far from flesh and blood.

Who can tell what time it is
In that one corner of the room
Where she sits in silence now,
And who or what she sees outside the window
Or in the pale reflection hovering in the glass?

Dialogue   RANDALL L. HALL

NIGHT SCENE

(for Bill)

The train passes through the night,
through tunnels like the night,
through open fields, at night.
The elemental racket of the rails
through the wine country of Umbria
keeps the two of us alert but saying nothing,
the wind whistling the second class

compartments, our train from Rome to Terontola.
We see from the corridor windows
two circles of fire in a wine field,
perfect red arcs circumscribed in the night,
burning lightly without sound.

This is a sight we both know
will mean nothing in retelling,

that the literal fire of the two
circles in the middle of the night
will be only another event, attached to nothing.
I am relating this event
far from the fact of the train ride.
The red of the flames might seem to us now
the color of local rubesco

or the deep red of Tuscan wines.
But this is something no longer important.
The train passed late in the night through
wine fields that held two perfect circles
of fire and we two, friends and silent,
watched it pass and at the time said nothing.
It was enough.

The Virginia Quarterly Review   DANIEL HALPERN

SUNDAY AVENUE

It's Sunday again, but there will be
no calls home, no walks east in Manhattan
to the docks, or to the bakeries south
of Houston Street. Only muted sun
off the Avenue and wilted endive
for a snack and Riesling
from Oregon. Geographical,
restrained, locked here
behind the finest cylinders abstract
fear can buy: Yale and Medeco. Sunday
afternoon behind a book with Sunday
photographs of New Orleans and Europe,
or old travel diaries: Morocco
and Cairo, a 1972
New York, New York. What is it
the black cat dreams of over on the sofa?
She is waiting for the spring and the spring
flies, waiting for the roof weeds
to rise up so she can again graze Sundays
when there is the terrace to sweep and pace.
In Pittsburgh my mother marinates fish
Sundays. In Los Angeles my sisters
cover their redwood fences with redwood
stain—old blood like the light of afternoon
air here, nothing to do but hold onto
what doesn't want to leave anyway. I
am thinking of you who left on Sunday,
another Sunday, dry like this one, and
although it's Sunday again, no calls home.

The Virginia Quarterly Review   DANIEL HALPERN

MY DAUGHTER AT HER GUITAR

(Christmas, 1981)

Sounds from Laurie's guitar
skip through the house like a child
in ponytail, bringing delight
into my basement study.

I cease my own laboring
on an unfinished poem to listen
to your latest composition,
a happy tune which breaks the ice
from winter's longing, evokes dreams
of warm skies, bouncing water,
the green laughter of grass.

For three days now we have sought,
you in your upstairs room, I here,
to find in thought, word, sound
the elements of harmony;
to fashion from false starts,
dead ends, rearrangements, discord
a music to live by.

Sitting at my desk, pencil stayed,
I trace in your voice a resilience
I had almost forgotten I, too, possess.
Can it be just a week ago
you leaned, sobbing, into my arms
and asked questions no mere father
could answer, except with love,
which must have seemed a frail prop
against youth's first betrayal.
Still, it's all we have,
and, as you now remind me,
it is enough: today you sing,
and grace my heart with your song.

Children, make music for your fathers.
Sing them from their graves.
Bathe them in melody, unstop their ears,
liven their bones to know every sunrise
proves the earth reborn, and agony
is only the sound the heart makes
being tuned for joy.

The Cape Rock   ROBERT W. HAMBLIN

SECOND GROWTH

(to Wendell Berry)

The woods beyond this house
were decimated long ago,

logged off and carried away
to San Francisco or on
down the coast. Now, at dusk,
I walk among second growth
down narrow muddy roads
leading out to the bluffs
above the straits the tides
pour through into Puget Sound.
Sometimes an eagle
slowly circles alder
and evergreens, sometimes
the ravens chase them hard
along the inland coast.

And I stand alone out there
waiting a long, long time
for what I cannot know.
The woods return, the
seasons come and go,
and at sunset a single star
winks and burns. Going home,
each step is slow: the ache
of back from splitting wood,
the ache of hands from
setting type. The work
warms the inner man, the fire
warms the outer. The woods
endure and return
and die and are born.

Take comfort in your chores:
to work and wait
and watch and learn.

The Malahat Review   SAM HAMILL

IN TIME

At the window above my desk, two flies
are beating out their lives against the glass.
Outside, the sun shines warm as memories
of ancient Mays: the hollyhocks all bloom
the week I celebrate my birth. Too late
for the ironies of April, too soon
to call the summer home, the time between
the brightest seasons settles in my bones.

What can a man come to in forty years?
The silence of open hands, empty hours
of meditation. I'm not old enough
to reminisce. The good and the bad, like leaves,
all fall away. Like flies, we understand
enlightenment comes slowly to the damned.

The Malahat Review   SAM HAMILL

CAMPING OUT LATE AUGUST

In the late summer haze we lie,
two spoons loose in the gathering
dark of night's drawer. And when
we shift in sleep, front to front,
how easily we match each other's
ragged breath. Our leggy dreams
of being chased run their restless
course. But as nightmare evens into
sleep, we're drawn from that cache
of visions. So we turn away, not as
duelists compelled to pacing distance,
but dancers drawn into the heart's
chamber of a slow minuet. Back to
back, we lodge under a sky of stars
with the cabinetmaker's eye for space
and woodsy closure, with the painter's
love of brushstroke, navy and white,
dazzling intensities of heat.

Separate Doors   KARLA M. HAMMOND

WEATHERING

(for May Sarton)

I have seen the day burn back on itself
where the cliffs meet the horizon in
one vast sweep of flame. Nothing is

what it seems. The male pheasant at your window,
for all his dazzle, is only a pheasant. And
your reflection from that view illuminates

the mere past. There is no present tense more
permanent than memory, no sky flushed by a sunset
that will not go down to an encore of darkness.

Pembroke Magazine   KARLA M. HAMMOND

LOVE'S FIRST LESSON IN SEMANTICS

Language being imprecise, precisely,
we gender it with pronouns: sex-it-up.
My breast, *your* loins, *his* lips,
her tongue. That failing to elicit
the expected response resort to
didactic unit archetypes, terse
& proven. *The* night in *the* country,
the bed together. Seducers are
lexicographers, sly drudgers of magic,

wise, lascivious & wizened. When
they say *the* ecstasy, *the* reference
of *the* article is shared with a style
appropriate to *the* other's lust.

Gryphon   KARLA M. HAMMOND

MOCKINGBIRD

I hear your knock in the chimney,
in the soot where you are locked
by glass. Your flutter trills,
its echo answers from the bush
full of thorns, dark wilted berries,
empty nests. Three frail
yellow beaks blather silent
for their feed. And their mother
is here, perched on the iron grate,
chirping so seldom she will stay
nearly all the daylight hours
before I find her. Escape, escape
will not come to her, closed eyes
against thirst. I shut off the house
and open the glass, the kitchen door.
Will she fly out, will she fly? No,
she's shut her black eyes and huddled
next to the blackened heat brick back
of the absent fire, too tired to budge.
I take a checked dish towel,
flag her across to open air.
I hold my breath, for she is flapping
her head into ceiling,
into molding, but then the open way
her wings are striped, white and black,
the way she doesn't turn back—I breathe
out, look up to dust away the down
spotting paint above my reach.
Straight to her nest, she beats the dusk.

Quarterly West   CATHRYN HANKLA

WINTER WINE

All winter we fought the cold.
Indoors, we baked bread and sorted
the golden lentils, drinking winter wine
that left a summer flavor in our throats.

In the unbearably white landscape
we watched the thin frost on the windowpane,
the candles dying in their roots,
our heads resting on hot pillows.

First we read Hamlet, then Macbeth,
and tasted three drops of blood within the wine.
We thought: what could betray us now, the snow
waist-deep, the cold earth unburdening the sky?

We drank iced wine beneath our frozen roof,
your eyes glinting like a mirror of ice.
We made love again as in love's first day,
reaching out to feel the scattering of snow.

Passages North   CHARLES HANSON

THE MYSTERY OF POTS

Here is our mystery: that the deep heart,
busy molding its own images to bless or blame,
still can bring itself to love some outer thing,
acknowledging a parallel to its own solitude.
Finished from the wheel, all pots
sing "I," but to their potter's tune.
And two pots, meeting on a stranger's shelf,
make subtle discord
if both were not turned by lovers.
As we do, who are most ourselves
only when we clearly hear
another potter's working song.

The Arizona Quarterly   HOWARD G. HANSON

DISTANCE MAKES THE DIFFERENCE

Distance makes the difference, as of memory, or dream.
Untroubled by the daily grind and grate, your image
rides the river of my love, as in a boat,
in serene and steady constancy.
Do not come in too close.
Do not put in to shore.
Do not pause here, testing my fragile bridge of will
above these waters.
I must rest nights
far from the destructive flood,
the discrediting of faith.
Distance makes a difference.

The Arizona Quarterly   HOWARD G. HANSON

FOR A FRIEND, AUTUMN 1978

A lust for love impales
us here, bringing us

together—one through
the other, companions in
some saintly crime. We are
friends here—somewhere
between heart
and mind.

When the time comes (as
the saying goes)—we'll part,
migrating south from here
for a winter's stay, clumsily
flapping age-old wings
along the way
to rest. Then (I trust) we'll
still be friends—one through
the other; perhaps heart
through soul, perhaps not. But
we'll be companions yet
in part—somewhere
in the mind
and heart.

Kansas Quarterly   PAUL HART

PARIS

Paris, the city of gesture.
There are a hundred ways
of saying, "why are you here?"
or "will you let me please you?"
And a thousand shaded ways
to say "No."
Paris, a city where the self
becomes an art,
explored, exploited,
extended to the last
fine gesture of loss.
Paris, the city of women
who are afraid of nothing,
not age or snobbery:
they will turn their collars
defiantly, lift a hem
to celebrate the end of illusion.
Paris, where men play checkered
games of possibility, surprised
by nothing except the beauty of speech,
the words an essence of gesture:
voiced, danced, shadowed into night.

The Massachusetts Review   RENÉE G. HARTMAN

QUATRAIN

Life is everywise a torment to me:
Women, in especial, are its grit and gall.
But I love life. Hence, inescapably,
I must love women: women above all.

Denver Quarterly   SATO HARUO
                                          —*Translated from the Japanese*
                                                    by Graeme Wilson

SIXTY-FIVE

not yet six   the wall begins its accusation   guilt
without crime   I force my eyes to close   an instant
trips them wide again to stare at flyspecks till the
waning night's small music is shattered   crescendo
of garbage trucks and grinding starters of curbside
cars   the hillside's dew-pearled   I find I have
been hearing mercifully without hearing the unending
anguished cooing of mating doves jays screaming the
chitter of insipid sparrows   the lark's on the wing
the newsboy's bike slips past my casement dropping the
inconsolable tears of yesterday's tragedies on the street's
doorsteps   7:49 exactly next-door junior executive
races his Fury off to the tool-and-die   a motorbike
splatters the air with compacted plosions   there are
horses neighing on far-off hills   8:15 and the sweet
young wondering voices drift by on perilous seas
      searching
hidden continents   my brain is tired   lying on my
suffocating pillow I follow the relentlessly diminishing
heelclicks of the block's pert secretary to the corner
bus stop   and all is momently still   the wall never
withdraws its accusation and I wonder whether God cares
that I turn over and try to close my eyes   there is
no need to rise

The Arizona Quarterly   LOUIS HASLEY

THE RUNNERS

The oldest dance on earth
begins and ends
with the heart.
No saying can enter
the sun wind, the hawk look,
the coyote foot, the ancestral
heart forever harking back.

I run on the coiled-clay shards
of those who were once

formed by sun, cloud, sand—
who came out of the earth
without logic.

I run on the
shapely bones
of those who
were once like us, the runners,
with feet of dust, who
begin and end
with the heart
and its singular saying
forever
harking back
without logic
to the oldest dance on earth.

The Arizona Quarterly   GERALD HAUSMAN

THINGS

Things are a problem.
I don't mean merely things
that clutter, should have been thrown out
as useless. Nor do I mean old people.
Or old friends or loves.
These are ephemeral.
But this carpet which has lain in many houses,
of which each knot was tied by human fingers
into a pattern left unfinished to praise Allah,
since worn by many feet,
chosen and cherished, lies where now it lies
in a cold room with a dead fire.
In its centre, a dry bone left by the dog.
It is the history of things
that troubles me.

The Malahat Review   RICHARD HAVEN

VARIATIONS ON THEMES

1. THE DEAL

Couldn't *someone* have managed to keep him quiet?
The deal was working out the way we'd planned.
The populace was eating out of our hand
Till little Big Mouth here started the riot.
Of course the Emperor knew. He's not a fool.
He knew that he was naked as a jay;
But who'd have thought a kid let out of school
To see the show would give the show away?

It could have worked out just as we'd arranged,
And kept top-secret. Why do you suppose
That we've been paid for non-existent clothes
If not for favors granted and exchanged?
But there's some rumbling in the neighborhood,
So let's get going while the going's good.

2. THE WIFE

I said, "I'm leaving you. And here's the reason.
I'm tired of furnished flats and rented rooms,
Of three-flight walk-ups, comfortless as tombs
Leased for a year at most, or for a season.
And never a bed or chair to call my own . . ."
I said to him, "I hate this rootless life.
I want a home. And if you want a wife,
You'll have to buy a house and settle down."

And so we did. We found this little place
In Pumpkin Hollow, really just a shell.
We'll finish the interior ourselves.
I'll sew, Peter can paint and put up shelves.
There's even a garden, and a lot of space.
And here at last he'll keep me very well!

The Lyric   SARA HENDERSON HAY

FROM A RICH FULL LIFE

(to Dinner)

We'll go with everyone: La Tour d'Argent.
O, ooo la, laa, the taxi driver cries,
Handing us over into white-gloved hands
That lead to other hands. Our names go on,
Whispering ahead. Past the great bowls in bloom,
We travel quietly, we waft above,
And there's the church below, the Seine below,
Contained and sculptured to the Paris view.
We do not order; rather, we discuss
How food and wine together pleases us.
Today's decisions—serious faces watch,
And serious faces somewhere, capped with toques,
Bend to the dedication of our meal.
The perfect food appears: as if we brought
No appetite, each presentation tempts
In color, texture, scent—it hasn't smells—
Yet every course is offered: something else
Will certainly, will instantly, be sent
Should any whim approach. But we're content:

As the wines marry, grow voluptuous,
We sip, we linger, nibble at something cold.
Money at last is mentioned. Silver, gold—
Swiss francs perhaps are best—the price is fair
For all the pleasures that are gathered there.

The Southern Review   ANN HAYES

WHISKEY IN WHITING, INDIANA

Watching them drink shots was best.
That fierce color as if it were burned
into the glass—the shot glass itself
so specialized, small and hefty the way
a bullet is. Shots made them talk tough
and say fighters' names: Mickey Walker,
Willie Pep, Beau Jack, Stanley Ketchel,
and Tony Zale. They talked cuts and
knockdowns and recalled whole fights by the
round. I got excited. I'd be Tony Zale, eye
brows obliterated, and told them so. "Jesus
Christ, no!" They'd cock their heads
at the glass, the bartender would pour
another shot. "Jesus, not you, Jimmie."
They did that. Get a dream up, then tell you
it was no good. Like how proud they talked
about the mill, how tough and dirty they got
and then made you promise to do homework
so as not to be stuck like them. They said
don't drink whiskey too. In the bathroom
when nobody was home I'd be famous
in front of the mirror with a shot glass
of Pepsi, watching myself throw one back.
This was after my title fight which I won
after taking awful punishment, just like
Tony Zale from Gary. I'd use my mother's
mascara and lipstick—to make
black eyes and blooded places on my face,
tuck cotton under to swell a lip. I'd study
their Jimmie in the mirror: everything
they loved and warned me not to be.
Sock down another shot, wince the way they did,
and watch myself defy them by loving
what they loved, by fighting my way into
their dreams of themselves and out of
their dream for me.

The North American Review   JAMES HAZARD

FOG AND GENDER

(for Lynn)

That winter night was cold, and I'd been
prescribing for myself a kind of woman.
Then, sometime in the dark, a warm fog
moved in and softened the crust of snow.
It stayed all day, easing about the precise woods.
In a hush, it filled the space between the trees,
wrapped around the arrogant spruce and dimmed them
into grace, gauzed the broken hands of elm and beech,
swaddled with shadow their ugly clutch at air—
did it all without a sound.

It could have been too much, all that
shadow and silence and comfort with itself.
But, exploring paths in woods,
I found clusters of red berries
and beads of drizzle,
a drop on each berry.
When one let go,
a brittle rag of leaf
flicked. Nearby,
something little
scuttled in the thorns.
Whatever moved,
pittered.

The warm shadow kept shifting into itself without moving,
and all the while that hush,
holding to its breast the twisted trees,
holding in its palm those flecks of sound.

Passages North   JOHN HAZARD

MOMENTS OF BEING AWAY

Today I walked through the house
to touch things I once knew.
It wasn't as a stranger I came
but more an uncertainty of where
I belonged. I mowed the backyard
as if hired to care for the property
and gave myself permission to pick
a panful of string beans. I found
a rabbit's nest with four little
white cottontails, a pair of brown
thrashers searched under an oak tree;
my neighbor's dog sniffed the hedge
all as much at home as if they owned
the place. A few clouds dipped
past a sun which has slowed down

two-thousandth of a second in
one hundred years, a southwest wind
brought up moisture from the Gulf—
nothing out of the ordinary
a usual summer day. Then two boys
asked to cross the backyard to fish
in Dry Run and a neighbor stopped
with a petition for me to sign and I
felt earth, mine, firm under my feet.

The Chariton Review   JAMES HEARST

GRAVEDIGGERS

They have done this so long
They could do it blind,
And some have—
This stocking every year
Of the dead's pond,
This going around at night
Closing all the flowers.
Yesterday I was sure
I could hear the screams
In the backs of their throats,
My neighbor's cats pacing
Down there in little
Cages of bone.
They are blameless
But that doesn't stop them
From digging, from winding
Their gold watches,
From staring out
Of their sheds when it's hot,
When all they can hear
Is the click-click
Of the sprinklers,
Like so many locks coming undone.

Sou'wester   ROBERT HEDIN

FOR AN EPIPHANY

Days like this in winter your mortality
weighs lighter, the thought of it doesn't pry
the backdoor of the soul so easily.

Go out in it, get loose in the great air.
Put off what makes you weary earlier
than usual and strive to say, I dare

you: I won't die today, I'm good for one
more, let it happen. Listen to the man:
he's giving sermons now. One afternoon

you'll find him on your doormat dressed to kill,
handing you a tincan in which a single
nickel clatters, and with a face so full

of radiance the tears start in your eyes,
so you go searching for the five twenties
you hid in any number of mattresses.

You'd give him anything for word like that.
This is the parlor of the Infinite.
Come in. It's good to see you. Have a seat.

New Letters   MICHAEL HEFFERNAN

LAST PERSON ON THE WALKWAY

(Kansas City, Missouri; 7/17/81)

Your life is a kind of architecture;
you have placed one stone on another,
and another, and a few logs, enough
for the brief passage or some process
you have discovered by necessity.
By now you have moved out of the cave,
your functional structures still intact.
Phantom of the atrium, no one
sees you come or leave. You have
not collapsed. You will believe—
or, unthinking, not disbelieve:
the parts of ample torque and tensile,
the pier shouldering its load. These
assumptions grow as you have grown.
They climb with you into the towers,
into glass-shafted elevators,
or this smart hotel gussied up
like a woman out on the town.
You can tread on solid rock, balancing
all those crystal buildings on your head.
You follow the flow of the music away
and crowd up high from the intimate bars.
You hum the tune, tap your foot,
bring down the sky and all those stars.

The Chariton Review   LLOYD HENLEY

THE DEALER

It's the night he likes, slick
as a fitted tux, the moon
a pearl button. Oh, ladies,
he loves
the clink of ice-filled glass,
the smokey passes he makes.

Yes, nights are fine and full
of money:
on the tips of his fingers,
out the side of his mouth.
At the edge of his eyes
the elegant claw of a footed tub,
a pink shimmer behind the curtain. Yes,

he's certain the money's there:
in the deal he's making, the spiel
he talks to himself
over and over
like a dollar bill from hand to hand—
the night bright
as coins in a fountain.

Yankee   MADELEINE HENNESSY

NATIONALITY?

Commando or SS,
Raff or Luftwaffe,
Dad's Army or the Volksturm,
English or German.

The fears are the same.
Living,
And dying.
Girlfriends and wives.

Children, evacuated perhaps,
Pretend to be their fathers
Killing Germans,
Or vice versa.

So many things
In common, and
Often, lastly,
Death.

New Letters   JAMIE HEPBURN

THE SKY IS OUT OF PRACTICE

Today the snow is falling neither
beautifully nor successfully.
Instead of gently floating down to
gradually make the earth virgin again,
it plods about, drunk,
forming a layer of grubby slush
that hisses its bad temper
at every step.
But it has been a long time

since it snowed last.
The sky is out of practice,
so it is no surprise that
these first efforts are stumbling
and tentative, like a guitarist
who has been too long away from
the instrument.
Soon enough, the stiff fingers
improve and become supple.
Soon enough, the sky
with a touch expert and deft
will turn the earth into a
blank sheet which we, in accordance
with the laws of nature,
will immediately and furiously fill up.

The Antigonish Review   PETER HERMAN

ORIGINAL

Those woods are a space now,
a fixed outline, a painting
you spoil every day,

trying to make the seasons fit
exactly as if the blackbirds
weren't racing in pairs

on either side of a line,
and the white moths of July
filling the small jar of the air

weren't the one thing you carried
alone into all that snow, saying:
Woods are for lovers,

the sun singling you out
among stems poised in their sap,
walking to a welcome

where no bird sings for an answer,
as if a song had to touch a song
in perfect time.

The Southern Review   NEVA JOHNSON HERRINGTON

BETWEEN FLIGHTS

In an airport television chair,
soap opera funeral to my left,
my own screen blank,
I lean back,
begin to doze as though in a hammock.
The afternoon drones, and darkens. . .

Those days when young when sick and home from school
but safe, in a flu haze,
household sounds around me,
comforting, I slept, dreamless,
or dreamed, or dreamed I woke,
or woke. . .

All around me this 20th century—
sunfish and roses in lucite paperweights,
jet engine whine heard through
plate glass panes and luggage ports,
strangers' commuting footsteps,
voices calling goodby—

so many, as I am, okay, or dreaming, or on the lam,
but safe here, for now, maybe, but far from home.

Poetry   WILLIAM HEYEN

THE DEMONS OF THE CITIES
[DIE DÄMONEN DER STÄDTE]

(December, 1911)

The midnight cities cower underfoot;
The demons trample through the urban graves;
Their skipper-beards, a sprout of smoke and soot,
Bristle like chins of Charons needing shaves.

Creeping on fog-shoes where the pavement drowses
And crawling forward slowly room by room,
Their shadows waver over waves of houses
And gobble street-lights in black gulps of gloom.

Their knees are kneeling on the city towers,
Their feet make footstools of the city squares,
And where the rain strews down its bleakest flowers
Their stormy pipe of Pan rears up and blares.

Around their feet each city's dark refrain
Is circling like a rondo of the waters.
An ode to death. Now faint, now shrill again,
The dirge ebbs into darkness till it falters.

The stream they stroll on is a snaky flow,
Its dim back speckled by the yellow glimmer
The lanterns—blanketed in black-out—throw.
The melancholy reptile wallows dimmer.

Their weight falls heavy on a bridge's railing
Each time their hands fall heavy into swarms
Of urban flesh, as if some faun were flailing
Across a slimy swamp his outstretched arms.

Now one stands up. He hangs a ghoul's black mask
On the white moon. The leaden heavens spill

Down darkly from a heaven darker still,
Crushing the houses in a jet-black cask.

A snapping sound. A city's backbone splits.
A roof cracks open, reddening its rent
With arson. Demons squat on it like cats
And ululate into the firmament.

A spawning mother bawls where midnight billows;
The steep crescendo of each labor pang
Arches her brawny pelvis from its pillows;
Around her the enormous devils throng.

She's tossed yet anchored. Overhead, her bed's
Whole ceiling shakes with howlings of the tortured.
Red furrow—redder, longer. Now the orchard
Brings forth the fruit. It rips her womb to shreds.

The devils' necks are growing like giraffes'.
The baby has no head. The mother lugs
It with her till she faints; a devil laughs;
Her spine is tickled by cold thumbs of frogs.

Tossing their horns, the demons grow so tall
They gore the very sky for blood to lap.
Their lightning shudders through each city's lap,
And earthquakes thunder where their hoofbeats fall.

The Literary Review   Georg Heym
                              —Translated from the German
                                      by Peter Viereck

WHY DO YOU COME SO OFTEN
TO VISIT ME?

Why do you come so often to visit me,
Dead souls, why do you flutter so frequently,
White butterflies, onto my hand,
Depositing a tiny mound of ash?

Dwellers near urns, haunting the home of dreams,
Crouched in eternal shade, the crepuscular room,
Like bats that congregate in catacombs
And start up noisily as night approaches.

Often in my sleep I hear the vampires bark
From the blotched moon's honeycomb. It sounds like laughter.
And then I watch deep down in hollow caves
The lights of wraiths without a habitat.

What is life? I ask. A brief torch
Surrounded by a flock of grimacing shapes
And some are pushing forward now and stretching
Emaciated hands towards the flame.

What is life? A small boat in the chasms
Of forgotten seas, grimness of torpid skies

Or the straying of moonlight which has lost its way
Across fallow fields before it vanishes.

Woe to the man who ever witnessed dying:
The moment when, unseen, in the cool autumn,
Death suddenly stopped beside the moist sick-bed
And bade one depart while the victim's throat

Expelled its final breath with a rattle
Like the frosty wheezing of a rusty organ.
Woe to him who witnessed dying: he'll forever
Wear the blanched flower of a leaden horror.

Who opens for us the countries-after-death
And who the gate of the gigantic rune?
What do the dying see that they turn up
So terribly the blind whites of their eyes?

Poetry Now
                                               GEORG HEYM
                                    —*Translated from the German
                                         by Francis Golffing*

THE DOG

A man sits in the night air drinking a last
cup of tea. He pushes aside the plates
and serving dishes and begins listing
the letters he must write, the bills he must pay.

Inside, his youngest daughter is practicing
the oboe. He never believed that anything
in his house could be that rich and lean, music
repeating the turns of its own thought, falling

and deepening to a twist of vines cut in the dark
wood of a door. The sound has nothing to do
with himself, and little to do with his daughter
who eats carnitas and dances at the disco.

The dog, sleeping on the tiles, turns
to listen. For a moment, there on his elbows
he is no longer dog but a bronze
figure cast by the moon, perfect shadow

and light. Then he scratches himself and wanders
into the kitchen: George, a dog of no breed.
Was the music illusion, too, the man wonders,
the gift of a good meal and solitude?

His daughter plays again. The intricate,
clear notes carve the air. He cannot doubt it.

The Virginia Quarterly Review   CONRAD HILBERRY

OPHELIA

Mr. G., my instructor, with wild eyes
And feet like a pigeon's, stands
In the shadows of the high school stage
Directing my speeches with his hand
In his hair. I'm his
Ophelia this year, naming the fistful
Of herbs that isn't there,
Trying to imagine my brief life closing
In this lunacy.
           Tomorrow, says Mr. G.,
You will fall in the river, free
Of Hamlet's intelligent disdain. Enunciate.
O how the wheel becomes it! You must see
The fennel and the columbines.

It's after school; the janitor's cart
Squeaks down the hall, then his soft wide
Broom sweeps the sawdust backstage.
Mr. G. comes closer, I am 16, he loves me a little.
He looks at me with infinite sorrow,
Then he straightens his glasses.

In a few years he's out of there, selling
Insurance. I can still do
That Ophelia he'd know anywhere,
stumbling, stuttering, never too clear.

The Threepenny Review　　　　　　　　　BRENDA HILLMAN

COLERIDGE, SLEEP YET GENTLY

This fine-edged morning should not
Lure you from your long hall or
Beckon out the ghosts of Keats or
Byron. It would be bad form for us,
Here now, to invite the spirits
Whose cranky, wrinkled thoughts on
Waking would reject the lumpish
Minds that lure an ugly century to
An ugly, fretful end.
           Do not rouse
Arnold, nor Shelly to test the
Locks that bind them to the dead.
They will not like it here. It
Will remind them of their misfortune
And bring another sleep of surly
Dreams.
           Content yourselves another
Thousand years in thoughts of quiet
Rivers running clear. If you must
Know what happens in this hour, send

Wordsworth, who was ever talking
Beyond the bounds of his own genius.
He will little note the emptiness;
Will gather enough to talk the
Millenium round and trance you into
Fitter sleep than we provide.
Lie still, and wait the coming of the day.

Ball State University Forum   WILLIAM C. HILTON

THE CRICKET

In vain we tried to banish him.
The roar of engines did not drive him away,
nor the asphalt with which we covered the fields.
We put up steel fences, walls of cement
                              and concrete,
Darkened the air with gas fumes
and shut ourselves in highrise buildings.

But he, like a password,
crossed every barrier unharmed.

And when we claimed victory
in the shade of a leaf, unseen,
his fine string music started again.

Its tone reeled off our forgotten friends,
                    our forgotten homes,
                    our souls.
It recalled to mind
the world's forgotten beauty.

Then we looked for him,
meaning to speak in friendship at last,
but in vain.

He was nowhere visible.
And only within us
still rang and rang his refrain.

The Hudson Review   KRASSIN HIMMIRSKY
                              —*Translated from the Bulgarian*
                              by Denise Levertov

NOVEMBER STREETS

I have been walking
a long time.
The same streets offer
homes sometimes
freshly painted

so I know the world
changes, or at least
the flat refusal of the world
to love us shifts.
And sometimes I feel
like running past the blue homes
reflecting white,
past mums and dahlias,
past roses rotting
on their urban stems.
Such sweetness in the pollens—
what gets passed.
I am walking with the odor
of a woman on my hands.
And see the line of trees engulf
as with a falling body, wind,
their great assembly of flat,
green leaves stirring
at the furthest tips
and down, as if some current
were being passed,
massive and with intent,
into the ground.
Is this the soul?
The drying out onto the air?

The Agni Review   DENNIS HINRICHSEN

IN SPITE OF EVERYTHING, THE STARS

Like a stunned piano, like a bucket
of fresh milk flung into the air
or a dozen fists of confetti
suddenly thrown hard at a bride
stepping down from the altar,
the stars surprise the sky.
Think of dazed stones
floating overhead, or an ocean
of starfish hung up to dry. Yes,
like a conductor's expectant arm
about to lift toward the chorus,
or a juggler's plates defying gravity,
or a hundred fastballs fired at once
and freezing in midair, the stars
startle the sky over the city.

And that's why drunks leaning up
against abandoned buildings, women
hurrying home on deserted sidestreets,
policemen turning blind corners, and
even thieves stepping from alleys
all stare up at once. Why else do

sleepwalkers move toward the window,
or old men drag flimsy lawn chairs
onto fire escapes, or hardened
criminals press sad foreheads
to steel bars? Because the night is alive with lamps! And
that's why in dark houses all over the city
dreams stir in the pillows, a million
plumes of breath rise into the sky.

National Forum   EDWARD HIRSCH

TWO IDEAS ABOUT THE WIND

For the coal black miner who rises from the mines
with a yellow lamp fastened to his head
and two black lungs smoking in his chest
the wind is still a hand touching his cheek,
a mother's warm palm, a daughter's cool
fingers pressing a damp rag to his face.

But for his wife, sleeping on a screenless porch
with a yellow lamp dimming in her mind
and a gaping hole opening up in her chest,
the wind is a restless stirring in the leaves,
a senseless weaving of shadows, the terrible
beating of wings moving beyond her reach.

National Forum   EDWARD HIRSCH

THE DEPARTURE

"What are you doing?"

He stood slouched in the doorway.
She finished folding her skirt,
put it in her suitcase, snicked
the latches shut—click—click.
It was an hour before dinner;
nothing roasted in the oven.
She checked her watch.
In five minutes, if it was on time,
the space ship would arrive.

She looked at him and smiled,
looked around the bedroom
as if it were an exhibit
in a museum she hadn't wanted to visit,
looked out the window
to the garden she wouldn't harvest,
looked back at him and smiled.

He followed her to the front door,
blinked stupidly when the cab horn beeped,

didn't even try to stop her as she brushed past.
His mouth was open like a fruit jar
as she pulled away not even waving.
She would call later, ask, "What are you doing?"
then hang up. She would do it every day
maybe for years. Until she was even.

event   ROBERT D. HOEFT

GAMBLING ON A DREAM

Driving down from Philly you
smell Atlantic City. The breeze,
scented saltily, wafts through
car windows lifting layers,
evoking memories.

Windblown waves topped with spray,
matched footsteps etched in sand,
sculptured castles, shell windows,
snail turrets, washaway stairs,
molasses, lemon, licorice saltwater
taffy pulled tautly into ropes,
pickle pins at the Heinz Pier and
samples of all 57 varieties;
the Human Cannonball at Steele Pier,
the Boardwalk carpeted with people,
a gleaming cornucopia of restaurants,
theatres, shops.

They say it's different now, Atlantic
City is held hostage; but after fifty
years of following a dream, I've paid
my ransom. I'm coming home.

Green River Review   MURIEL HOFF

SCRAPING THE HOUSE

Two rungs from the top, where you can see
what no one else could see, there are no more
handles on the world, I have to lean
against the warm cliff-face of my house,
cheek to cheek with wood, and, butting
the chisel's butt-end crosswise with one palm,
drive it, balking, under the lapped siding
to strip more cracked paint off, baring
more evidence.
            Below, I hear my children
laughing. A screen door slams. They don't suspect
I'm here. They don't care. The beautiful lie
of this October afternoon maintains

its poise, steadfast as those brilliant aisles
the sun is laying down over the grass
in layers. The end of weather. You almost
believe it. That somehow the damage is not
serious. And you will always wonder why
when no one says you must, you keep coming back
here anyway, obediently, all by yourself,
to this ladder on the northwest side
for your appointment, and go up quietly.

Poetry   JONATHAN HOLDEN

BEFORE THE MOVE, 1975

We are lucky here,
kidding ourselves again.
We have already told many stories
in front of the fireplace,
and we've sweated out paintings
and poems and songs and prints.
Studios for both of us
with wonderful French windows!
Yes. Well, it won't be long
before we will have to move again.

I wish I could see all of the furniture
lugged up these stairs over the years,
only to be taken down again;
and I wish I could see all of the people
who have loved these high walls
and went to these windows in the
          morning
dreaming like Matisse
holding hot coffee in hand.

I can see the building two blocks away
where my father came to live 45 years
          ago.
It was a nice place, he says,
but he shakes his head now.
He had just met my mother
and their life together
was a long time ago.

My dear Marianne, our life runs
right through these thick walls.
Our dreams bang right through
the ceiling like sparrows through the
          leaves.
Soon money will tell us politely to leave,
and money has no idea.

Washington Review   WILLIAM HOLLAND

VENETIAN BLINDS

On my window I have the new model,
The subtle modern kind: a little twist
Of the plastic rod, stiff with crystalline
Newness, will always show day to the night.

Surprise—morning already, and all the
Heavy light sifts into my room now, breathed
By the glistening landscape of water-
Towers and roofs. Summer, city, those two
Hot conditions that work the quick changes
On each other, melt and shimmer for hours.
It isn't Venice out there at all whose
Buildings wink and crumble like old jewels,
But another rich place framed in brackish
Sick sea, when the sun, still echoing stripes
Across my late bed, glares over Manhattan.

And it isn't a blond brocaded queen
Whose white body is bisected by the
Whiter blinds—look, here is a glimpse of breast,
There, the finer curves are compelled into
Anonymous shadows. It isn't Titian
Approaching the royal nymph to paint her

But a shabby man who sketches, a friend
Who looks up now from the burning grey street
As the New York girl, Renaissance-naked,
Stands half-hidden at the window and waits.

The Hudson Review   MARTHA HOLLANDER

THICK DAYS IN MIAMI

The sickening sweet smell of rotting mangos wakes me every
    morning.
I drink my coffee to the chattering green of parrots in the mango
    trees.
A fat green lizard as big as my arm sits on the roof of my car, its
yellow jaws slimy with the pulpy orange fruit, wagging its tail like
    a cat.

The angry vegetable traffic on US 1 creeps grimly on. I'm stuck
in my metal cell with the wildly posturing disc jockey. My head
    throbs
with the speaker, and I turn the volume a little higher. I want out.

I am surrounded by people caught in the same briar patch:
Men in sports cars with the top down tanning on their way to work,
women in pink Cadillacs with yapping toy poodles on the seat
    beside them,
people in Mercedes and BMWs with cocaine and expensive
    handguns in glove compartments,

Rusted-out pickup trucks with cement mixers in their beds.
People are adjusting their air conditioners, combing their hair in
rearview mirrors, tapping their fingers on steering wheels, rolling
down their windows and throwing out cigaret butts, shouting at
    their kid
in the back seat to shut up and settle down unless he wants a smack.
People remembering their dead mothers, and people forgetting
    them.

All of them have their eyes on the road and their hands on the
    wheel,
and they all wish they were somewhere else, but don't know exactly
    where.

I pay two dollars to park all day, and when I turn the key my car
    won't stop.
It chatters and coughs and shows no signs of stopping.
I sit covered in sweat and embarrassment until it finally dies, then I
wipe my face and leave the car.

But it takes a little longer every day.

Kayak   DAVID HOLLOWAY

HOME

South of here, it rains in autumn
When the leaves come up yellow
And the sun starts going down
Ridiculously soon.
Here, a part remains, dry,
Close-quartered and warm to the touch,
A kind of innocence,
A breath of something loving,
Internal,
Like violets blooming in bay-window boxes.
The cold air drives us home,
We're forced to huddle in—
Not safer, surely not—
But close enough to feel
The other bodies with us,
To touch the wreck and joy pressed up together,
Like peach-flesh gripping stones—
And all so hard,
Misunderstandable.
But here and inside, now and
All around through cold air
Gripping tightly down,
The fire burns in orange and licking
Makes an ash and tosses sparks
Against the coming of the cold and night.

Southern Humanities Review   JAMES W. HOOD

MY MOTHER, LONG-DISTANCE

On the telephone, something she told me . . .
Or was it that when I hung up
the receiver, a breeze at the screen
made me notice how warm the night was,
and the street, leafy with distance,
unsealed its rings
                    so that I hid outside
in our old neighborhood, playing
those games played before bed-time,
and saw, from the length of the yard,
the white light of the kitchen
and my mother passing the window,
separate, unable to hear
stars signalling leaves and branches
and my heart hammering *Find me . . .*
I notice how young she is, younger
that evening than I am now.

Tonight, alone in her kitchen,
she has finished the supper dishes,
peering outside at something
unseen that stirs in the dark.
Soon she will move to the porch,
hesitant now, and call.
Over the lawn, in the darkness,
a child is running.

The Centennial Review   PATRICIA HOOPER

IN A SUBURB OF THE SPIRIT

Everything has happened. Nothing is quite new.
Summer is so old it wrinkles at the edges.
Nothing is surprising. Nothing should alarm.
It's the same old rain over and over.
The sun is old, and the light is so decrepit
it lies flat on the ground and can't get up again.
Even your anger is old. It's large or small,
but all of your life it's been the same. Then

everything is new: nothing ever ages. There
was no wind until just now, no glacier until you
thought of it. Fish change every second; every glance
makes a new landscape, and the sea has a stiff new shine
as it moves around on crutches. Clouds are shaped
like typewriters. Things amaze. Nothing dies.

New Orleans Review   PAUL HOOVER

BUS TERMINAL

All seats are temporary.
The air's a market place
of smoke and odors too long
molded by the yeasty walls.

We sit in transit, sealed
as it were in a Mason jar
so the outside air, damp
and cool under dripping prairie clouds,

cannot fellowship.
A locker bangs. A girl
appears to pitch a frown
as she makes change for a Hershey bar.

The clock on the wall takes time
we're made of, ticks it past
each set of postures, each
ringed in by bridled muscle. Here

enclosed in waiting, staring
past a scallop of shoulder,
suitcase heavy at hand,
boredom disperses itself without

an echo, like idle talk
for which there is no listener.

Ariel   LEWIS HORNE

COAL MINERS AND OTHER PEOPLE

To someone who can see
through earth, we
are carving a deadly
shape, like a tree
with branches of air
thin enough to crawl through,
thick enough to keep us down.

After twenty or thirty years
the tree begins to feel like
home. We come
to love its form
so much we have
to breathe it in.

Soon, our lungs blossom,
go to dark seed, breed
black twigs and fruit
slippery with red drops.

Like the dream of all romantics,
we are becoming one

with nature, and there is nothing
we can do about it.

Denver Quarterly   ERIC HORSTING

DELAYED TRANSPORT

My Pegasus won't fly.
Some moulting barnyard hen
Displays more git and show
Than my sad, droop-winged steed.

He'll need a rasp-tongued voice
From Arkansas to make him go;
But Arkansas's as far as Helicon,
And even mule skinners know

That half a horse or half a bird
Can't practice airborne wizardry
When a dull rider, booted, spurred,
Drifts in the mists of lethargy.

The Hollins Critic   A. J. HOVDE

TIME

It is the crystal stuff that clocks
Spin out like spiders; that great web
That swings from star to star, in which
Hang all whom breath has visited.

How this fragile perilous net
Trembles with its living freight
Of wing-bound prisoners; how it sways
And sags beneath their struggling weight—

Time, the enemy of wings,
Time, who catches all that fly,
Time, who slowly sucks the blood
And leaves us dangling, drained and dry—

Time, whose minute filaments
Seem so light, so frail, to bind,
But tie and tie again, till steel
Would be more delicate and kind.

Out beyond the furthest star
There is a place where time's reversed—
Who so brave to venture there,
Daring Time to do its worst,

To wind Time back upon itself
Like a great skein of ravelled lace,

And toss it to oblivious air,
And leave Time lost in space!

National Forum　　FRANCES MINTURN HOWARD

THE FIELD

The breeze stops, the afternoon heat rises,
and she hears his back porch screen door slap shut.
She sits still, lets her mind follow him through
the swinging gate into the field, his shirt
and white flannel pants freshly pressed, his new
racquet held so loosely that it balances
exactly in his hand. Now my father
takes the stile in two steps. And now my mother
turns in the lawn chair, allows herself the sight
of him lifting the racquet as if to
keep it dry. This instant, before he comes
to where she sits under the trees, these two
can choose whatever lives they want, but from
the next it is fixed in shadow and light.

The Agni Review　　DAVID HUDDLE

THE YELLOW STEEPLE

On my way home from work, I jumped the fence
and cut across the Baptist cemetery.
As I walked over Sarah Pratt,
I saw a workman standing on a scaffold
and swatting a coat of yellow paint
over the peeling whitewash on the steeple.
He dropped a can of paint and, as it fell,
the paint dispersed into a mist
and spread a rain of yellow dots
across a corner of the cemetery—
the bushes, trees, headstones, and me.
It ruined my coat; I didn't care:
I felt like Danaë when she
was loved by Zeus in the golden rain.
Then, looking up, I saw a hawk.
It didn't move at all—not once—
but hung arrested in the air
till I released the breath I held
in awe of its pin-point, predatory grace.
Still watching it as I walked home,
I barked my shins on a marble angel,
slid down a bank of slick white mud,
fell in the creek and came up laughing.

It was one of those rare sustaining days
when you're absolutely sure you have a soul.

The Hudson Review   ANDREW HUDGINS

ON LOCATION

This superannuated Bavarian town
  of crumbling baroque and flaking facades
is the perfect backdrop for these shameful charades.
  It is a dull place which neither renown
nor notoriety has ever disgraced, so
  it is only fitting that this film crew
should choose to engender their legend of a Jew,
  his Aryan wife, and the Gestapo
here on this unhistoric square (for, after all,
  the innocent present is the fittest
set on which to play actions of the guilty past,
  since there we see the full ironical
force of historical fact). Thus, the director
  sits in his canvas chair smoking cigars,
snapping Hollywood commandments at timid stars,
  his belly in his lap, his green visor
pushed back into his straight black hair. Incessantly,
  the make-up girl paints, the clapperboard snaps,
and cameras capture the frail, final (perhaps)
  fitness of inevitability,
filming reality into fiction, fiction
  into reality: who can tell which?
With luck, this movie will make its producer rich,
  will even be seen on television
in Israel and the States, Japan and Germany.
  Tourists who visit this town in future
will tell each other that was Aaron's house, and there
  was where he said goodbye to Rosemary.

The Antigonish Review   MICHAEL HULSE

ACTAEONI (SOMEWHAT AFTER YEATS)

When I was fifteen, few escaped, few of the country club
ladies who came to swim, golf, tennis, or simply sun—
the summer we found the eyes in the knotholes of
the furnace room walls. Now had we been Rubens
or Renoir! Degas! To have "done" those ladies
in their baths! But *living* with that knowledge,
in all our stewing innocence: it wasn't easy at all.
The girls with whom we'd fallen out of trees, dissected toads,
and wrestled to falls: now "nubile," full of their springing
womanhood: Sylvie and Sallie, Di, Dee Dee, Kathy swaying
their turret breasts, towelling the moisture-beads from

their wonderful beards. The sullen older ones who
jiggled more. And the secretaries, clerks, teachers, tellers,
even sisters: all known, all discovered. We watched
from darkness, in darkness, and our sunny encounters
on the street and in the pleasant institutions of our lives
blinded us where we stored those awesome visions of planes
and mounds, clefts and tufts. For it was they
and not we who had put on power with our knowledge.
And who, pitiless, turned the not very delicate engines
of their unsuspecting wrath upon our deerlike hearts.

The Texas Review   JOHN HUMMA

TO A FORMER PROFESSOR

Looking back, I can see your need to be
The buffoon, keep us laughing—a sign that things
Weren't going well; and that story of the man
Who leapt from a window after reading
Sophocles—"Don't tell me Art isn't real."
But I always thought, somehow, that Lasarillo,
Moll Flanders and Emma Bovary
Would get you through your night.

But then that evening, the shotgun star
At your temple, and Art blown all to hell;
And those who had followed you
Were left bitter, and afraid.

Kansas Quarterly   MICHAEL ROBERT HURD

THE OUTCOME

North and South the clouds moved positive:
East, West, the sun.
Sky's spectaculars ready for battle,
Earth's histories won.

Soon said the leaves in a wild ultimatum;
Soon said the parched grain;
Soon said the clouds grown dreadnought to dreadnought—
Now said the warm rain.

The Southern Review   ROBERT HUTCHINSON

THE WEALTH OF METALS

Over half the sun eclipsed this morning and still the shadows
are crisp on the tin roof below my window,
brown and silver, deep Parisian colors
from the sun's daily, unownable wealth.

I remember huge abandoned farmhouses in the Middlewest
built when there was so much land the body's weariness
    was the edge of property,
and there was a room at the end of the upstairs hallway,
    never finished,
the grey plaster unpainted all the time the children grew up
    —"the empty room," "the extra room"—
still there when they moved into a trailer and gave up
    the unheatable house,
when they moved into town and the half-spirit of alcohol,
the Mesabi Range to the North and the red open-pit mine
    in Hibbing, deep as a city;
the tireless gasoline engines that drive all night in a gay,
    amphetamine joy;
farm boys out of college for the holidays, stopping for gas
    on Route 80 going west;
and it is night in Iowa or Kansas,
a telephone booth has tipped over in the snow,
the farms are quiet in the distance,
pulled back from the rest stop with its cheery dome of white light.

The Threepenny Review   LEWIS HYDE

AND REST WITH YOU

You who gave me birth between your sturdy legs
are dead. You who gave me food and drink
and washed my clothes, ironed my shirts,
took me shopping for a suit and coat are dead,
I alive, as if to bring you back to daily acts
of dusting with the mop and bending down
to scrub the wash and climb the two flights
down to feed the stove its coal and climb back
up again with labored breath, with long and silent
pauses on the landing step to gather strength
for one last flight of stairs. I watched
from up above, you waiting down below for strength,
and now that I am old I sing you back to stay
with me, companion that you were to me in youth,
to watch me from your resting place as now
I pause to gather strength to come
to where you are and rest with you.

Ploughshares   DAVID IGNATOW

IN THE GARDEN

And now I wish to pray and perform
a ritual of my devotion to the sun.
I will bow and sing beneath my breath,
then perform the dance of farewell

and my confidence in the sun's return,
a father I have always believed in.

All is dance: the sun glides along the horizon;
now the leaves sway;
now the earth spins.

The Georgia Review   DAVID IGNATOW

GOOD PACKING

When the Japanese came in
low that Sunday morning
attending to history, my
Mother read the *Tribune*
cover to cover and Dad
worked on those model planes
I marveled at years later
during the police action in

Korea. I inherited my keen interest
in voracious reading from Mom, I believe,
and from Dad I got that life's image
of his smoke-filled den choked
with model planes on white twine
crosshatching the afternoon.

By dark that Sunday night
everyone in the neighborhood was
aware of the bombing, and I've often wondered
just how many neighbors displayed increased devotion
toward each other the next few weeks.
For years now it's been my fond hope that
old, azure-veined Mr. Huddle made love
to his nagging wife before she died

Christmas Eve. I thought perhaps
one of the three uncles I was told
I had had died and gone to Purgatory,
the way my parents behaved December 7th.
Things were strange and still, and I'm positive
it snowed the morning of the 8th.

That evening we had the Motorola
tuned in as FDR made his reply
to the dastardly attack. Dad just
looked daggers and cleared his throat.
Mom didn't move a muscle for the longest time.
. . . Tuesday at school I got my first real
vaccination, and on the way home
throwing hard hurt my arm.

Four Quarters   RON IKAN

ANIMAL NATURE

When my mother mulls on the nature
of angels, ether, and clouds, I put
down my fork and study a fly,
its wingtips on my mutton chop,
before me a stack of plates to be
wiped clean like words on a slate.
Even in silence as I do the work,
I lose an argument to her, I, her
bastard daughter.

Slice off her head, tie up her tongue.
Tell her she's another captive to
the broodings of daughters eating
their mothers' grievances.

"We'll all arrive in a world of light
beyond desire"; she goes on to explain
how faith gives way to perfect love
in the afterlife.

Sometimes, when I see her
in the mirror, full-breasted and
intense, I start to believe
I was made from her animal nature.
My mother in the looking glass, behind
her the dark like an idle rumor
of nothingness devouring our lives.

The Virginia Quarterly Review   COLETTE INEZ

FIRST POEM

For me to write this song,
father,
in the Gaelic you were never
allowed to learn
is for us to forgive the world
for all that it has done
and not done with our lives.

And for my own son
to sit upon your lap
learning the language as you do now
in your old age
is to have tears dried,
wounds closed, and death forgotten.
It is to be asked:
"Who are you?"
It is to say and to believe:
"We are the Irish people."

International Poetry Review   DAN JACKSON
                        —Translated from the Gaelic
                        by Dan Jackson

TO MARK, MY RETARDED BROTHER, WHO LIVED
20 YEARS AND LEARNED TO SPEAK 300 WORDS

Nobody has any business but me, to tell how
you came home, a white ball up pitted concrete steps,
home to our grandmother's blue swirled carpet.
Knitted bundle, you wailed clues of that soft
rotten, that misconnection, that sever, that spasm
which broke your mother's heart into blank starts.
You drug your feet, child.
Across the wood floor the grind of your twirling
walker, the rattling dance lurched down
fourteen steps: you were never lucky.
Your spilled blood flowed like menses, expected
rupture, bombardment of corners, ridges, juts.
The red record player sat on the chest
by the window. I don't remember it new:
blood, spit and dirt where you plied
that delicate spinning with your scratched hands.
"Getting to know you," know you, you and Julie
Andrews on the vowels, one long happy drool.
Hollyhock ladies on the sill, I lined up for you.
With a towel, I held that white head
which smashed unknowing into the blank floor
and everything, I think, I could ever know.
You grew to be a white crane, your head
bobbling on the tops of your friends,
who took you to play with perfect aplomb.
Little citizens already, in the scruffy grass,
they calculated games you could not wreck.
I was the one who ran barefoot, terror light
to grab you loping onto Garland Street,
laughing. I could have bashed in your head,
unsubtle brother, smiling outline.
Angel face, pushing to break with rudiments,
the best word for you is unused.

So your ankles drew up solemnly,
wrists in. The spasm locked. When I came to you
in your sterile steel circus, the last clowns
had gone home. Malicious beard raked your face.
On your head, practical blonde hair razed at
short attention.
You seemed so heavy, you would never float away.
Then you sank into your coffin in flannel pajamas,
the warmest bed you ever felt.

Southern Humanities Review   FLEDA BROWN JACKSON

HOWEVER YOU SAY IT IS

I don't see how we can argue over
the name of that red, star-shaped

flower, nor do I understand
why it has chosen to bloom
here on this runway where Sam Houston
turned the Mexican Army away forever.

Lousewort, my friend calls it, a name
the cattle and sheep men gave it
because they dreamt their livestock
would be infested with lice if they grazed it.

It is nothing to the young couple
who have forgotten the names for everything,
even the love they make
on a blanket nearly out of sight;
and it is nothing to the young girl
raped last night in Fannin Park
who has learned how far it is
from one word to another.

It is hard to believe our words
that tell us only what took place in the past;
it is hard to believe how we can name the world.

And it isn't lousewort, either,
but Live-Forever, a single stalked flower
that blooms again from any piece of itself,
that covers the flatlands Sam Houston loved,
the name I bring back for you,
a simple flower we hope will tell us
what we will be saying years from now
since we let ourselves go a name at a time.

The Black Warrior Review   RICHARD JACKSON

ARA

Here I am.
You can see exactly how I am—
the contours of my body,
how it is opened to you.
Play me,
play me with passion and hunger.
Come to see how warm I can be.
Play me as you do to the most loved instrument you ever
        happened to play.
You don't need to be careful,
nor tender.
Just play me
with passion,
tonight.

Maize   TERESA JACOB

GEORGE LANG

Would close his eyes and sway,
his fingers drumming out a tune
on café tables after work.
He wasn't much for talk—
but when talk turned to music,
his voice and hands composed.
At midnight walking back, he'd stop
mid-block and conduct the air.
At his place he'd put on Chopin,
Mahler, Bruckner or Brahms,
and we'd stretch out on his window bed.
The music wove curtains and sheets
into the tone of that year.
It was music that kissed me
and ran its lips along my spine,
George lost in crescendos or diminuendos
of sound. He would hold off coming
until the climax of the piece
and always let me know just when that was
by the way he played the instrument
I had, by then, become.

Skyline   GRAY JACOBIK

HEARTS

"Look, I got my heart in my hand,"
        says my two year old son.

So a little boy
says what we all know:
our hearts always end up
in our hands, or thrown over our shoulders,
worn on sleeves, hats, lapels, pinned to our chests.

Some of us spend all our time
trying to give them away—
an open hand, a warm mouth, a lap—
and off the hearts go, sprung loose in the world.

Some place their hearts
up on closet shelves, in attics,
on ovens and refrigerators,
silent and sulking.

Still others share theirs,
exchanging hearts, holding onto someone else's,
which is too awkward and fragile,
which must always be returned.

In time,
our hearts appear again:

used, mauled, dried out or rotted,
on our shirts and coats,
in our arms and pockets.
They end up in our hands
and we carry them through our lives,
hearts held out in front of us, nearly raw,
bleeding each day
into the next.

The Centennial Review   DAVID JAMES

SOMETIMES, LATE IN THE NIGHT

I find to my surprise
that I'm not sleeping,
that my eyes are wide open,
and that I am following a sound
along the tracks of tube and bone,
a sound that grows richly brittle at crossroads,
and pulls its long load through slow arcs of darkness.

Now is the time the house cracks its knuckles,
and the refrigerator whispers out a song.
The noises of my pulsing body
echo and mix with the house,
the chattering trees,
and the rolling boxcars wailing south.

The whistle, the smoke, the square of moonlight,
the invisible ceiling of this hurtling room . . .
and then the distances of sleep.

And then the honest, morning sounds
of my feet on the floor,
the water splashing in the basin,
the urgent, waking life in which
the train runs silent and unseen.

Southern Poetry Review   PHILIP K. JASON

THE PRICE OF SURVIVAL

When we say we are all soldiers here,
it also means that this highway
is an aircraft runway,
this tourbus a troop-carrier
or an ambulance.

It means that this anchor
is a claw for scaling mountains.

It means that all these plowshares
can be turned to swords
and these pruning hooks to spears.

It means that this leather is armor,
these diamonds are bullets,
and these stacked crates full of oranges
are arsenals of bombs.

And do you know that
at the Technion in Haifa
we have engineered a giant Eucalyptus tree
a grove of which can drain the broadest waters
if by some chance they push us into the sea?

Webster Review   PHILIP K. JASON

LATE AFTERNOON IN CHINCOTEAGUE

I reel my line out of the channel,
cut off the chewed-up chicken neck,
tie on a fresh one,
and settle back to watch my father die.

The crustacean shape of a skull lurks
beneath the sparse white hair.
Yellow-stained teeth hint wryly
at their death grin.
Heaven only knows what
he looks like on the inside.
Booze and the years eroded
the less-than-granite flesh until
we figured each of the past four visits
would be our last.

I watch him change his line—
the crabs are smart this late in the season.
He tosses the scavenged shreds of bait
to a school of minnows waiting in the shoals,
pops the cap off a fresh beer
and resumes avoiding my eyes.

Fishing for small talk—
the price of clams,
the best mulch for his garden—
we skirt the edges of deeper waters.

He feels a tug.
The gaunt left hand scuttles
for the net by his side.
A real granddaddy—
eight inches across the shell.
He holds it up like a trophy,
washed-out blue eyes coming back
to life for an instant,
then lifts the lid off the plastic pail
and drops it in to struggle
with the other teeth and claws.

He winces himself down on the wharf,
pops another cap onto the pile.

The last bottle nestled in its cardboard crevice,
he is numb enough to face the night ahead.
I help him up.
We pack our mutilated catch and head home.
Lulled by soft liquid,
he dozes off in the front seat,
gone out with the tide.

Now not even small talk.

The Malahat Review   PAT JASPER

FALL

A dull distant booming in the mountains this
morning: constant, and there can't be all
that many rabbits and deer and boar and what
else? Quail? What's being hunted up there?

I picture quail and rabbits falling, bucks
staggering to their knees, does kneeling,
the thick sponge of brown leaves, mosses

and pine needles, mulch, the litter and
clatter of walnuts and chestnuts, and the
stalking and steady reloading: new shot.

The guns echo all morning in the valley:
fits, and starts. Down here the butchers'
windows are displaying trays of feathered
birds, their plumage more vivid and varied

than I'd imagined brown could be: a color
wheel of brown, a whole spectrum of brown.
Gamey forage to be filled with herbs and
mushrooms, maybe plunder from the rings

of wild mushrooms, innocent and sinister,
that poke their white caps up, bloodless
and surprised, in the high forest, just

begging to be plucked. The birds, herb
scented, mushroom stuffed, baked brown,
are probably delicious: but all this

morning, listening to that faint thunder,
I've been wondering what it's like there:
how wild is it up there? And just what do
they hunt, what are they hunting up there?

The Hudson Review   KATE JENNINGS

ALCOHOLIC

My father (didn't everybody's?) drank—
the Dread Disease, plague of his generation—
and we were patient, swallowed down his spite,
and understood him as he threshed and sank,
and all forgave (oh, life means brief duration!)
and all refrained from saying wrong or right.
We knew, in dry, bright Oklahoma City,
the only cure for drink was love and pity.
We knew the flesh was frail, with delicate breath,
and so indulged each other into death.

But when he dared me—cursing me, demanding—
and shuffling scrawnily down halls of my mind,
sagging his jaw, speaking with a tongue gone blind,
should I have answered him with understanding?
He cannot help the things he does, we said.
(He grinned and snitched a ten and drove off, weaving.)
His heart, we said, is spotless—but his head
disturbed. (Late I would hear him: racketing, heaving.)

Years after he was gone I think I saw
how we insulted him, drove him along:
His spirit we called nerves, said nerves were raw,
denied his holy sanction to be wrong.
The sonofabitch (God bless him) drank and died
because we understood away his pride.

Alcoholism   JUDSON JEROME

ENVOI: POEMS DURING COMMERCIALS

On the table beside your reclining chair,
beside your *Newsweek,* drink and ashtray, put
this book there,

and after dinner dishes and the laundry
is shaken, dried and sorted, put away
those bills piled on the desk. You couldn't
pay them anyway.

Give the evening up to self-indulgence.
You couldn't save the world now on a bet.
The kids are on the town, your mate is bowling.
Turn on the set.

Between your stockinged toes watch mortal danger
of spies or doctors or the famous dead
flicker and flash the room with sherbet colors.
Don't use your head.

But when the peacock spreads for a commercial,
squelch the sound.
If you don't need time for a pee or refill,
stick around

and pick a page at random. Drift my way.
A ninety-second spot is all I need.
Reclining, you are ripening like compost.
Here is the seed.

Cedar Rock   JUDSON JEROME

THE HONOR

At a party in a Spanish kind of tiled house
I met a woman who had won an award
for writing, whose second prize
had gone to me. For years
I'd felt a kinship with her in the sharing
of this honor,
and I told her how glad I was to talk with her,
my compatriot of letters,
mentioning of course this award.
But it was nothing
to her, and in fact she didn't remember it.
I didn't know what else to talk about.
I looked around us at a room full of hands
moving drinks in tiny, rapid circles—
you know how people do
with their drinks.

Soon after this I became
another person, somebody
I would have brushed off if I'd met him that night,
somebody I never imagined.

People will tell you that it's awful
to see facts eat our dreams, our presumptions,
but they're wrong. It is an honor
to learn to replace one hope with another.
It was the only thing that could possibly have persuaded me
that my life is not a lonely story played out
in barrooms before a vast audience of the dead.

The American Poetry Review   DENIS JOHNSON

REQUEST

Talk to me; talk to me
of anything at all,
that I might store the sound of your voice
in some small chamber of my mind
to bring out on a day, or night,
when loneliness storms
and threatens to break me all apart.
The memory could be board and batten
to save the inner core of me
against that plight.

And if not that,
(should, after all,
I prove more strong
than now it seems)
your voice remembered
can serve me well as warmth
when winter comes again
and you are far beyond my ear and reach.

It is not much to ask—
and time is running out.

Poem   HELEN JOHNSON

COYOTE SKULL: A LESSON FOR A CHILD

These two holes are where
his wet nostrils sniffed
the scent of his prey.

And these two are where
his keen eyes observed
the look of his prey.

And these two are where
his furry ears heard
the sound of his prey.

And this one is where
his sharp white teeth chewed
the flesh of his prey.

And this one is where
a hollow-point slug
smashed its thoughtless way.

The Texas Review   MICHAEL L. JOHNSON

INSIDE

Inside the sturdy
Maple I tell you
The sapling we planted
Remains

Exactly small, fragile, wearing
Like an oversize coat
The growth of two decades.

How right it feels to lie about this!
How right that nothing should change!

And we are the same ones
Who fight off the moment
Our parents

Call to us from the next room.
Call us by old nicknames out of childhood.
We are the ones
This embarrasses, the ones
Who hold for dear
Life to a vanished sapling.

The Hollins Critic   THOMAS JOHNSON

BOMB

Men came together,
making hate,
to swell this harmless metal egg.
Fetal now,
it awaits, impatient
at the altitude of labor,
the red morning of its birth.

Ball State University Forum   MARK JOHNSTON

TRIANGULATION

The Lubbock night is glittering, the shake roofs
glazed with starlight, and low in the west,
past the pale orange glow of the city,
a green pinpoint of light is blinking

on the wing outside the window from a stewardess
gathering trays. Her feet still sore from dancing
all night the night before, she now leans
back in the arms of nothing, making way
for the balding school-supply salesman from Dallas,
who, grasping each seatback, moves along the aisle
to the restroom in the stern. There he will sit
cramped and self-conscious on the vibrating stainless steel seat,
cursing his migraine, while the whole of space
drones in his ears and shrinks
to a small white pulsing point that

blips on the black grid of a radar screen
scanning the night sky over El Paso,
a city in a desert, a star on·the Texas map.

Black Warrior Review   DARYL JONES

LITANY

Here is the desk you undress by;
Here is the rug you lay your clothes on;
Here is the bed you sleep in, wrought-iron and dark;

Here is my shoulder you hold like a white bone;
Here are my breasts you pass your hands over;
Here are my hands;
Here is your voice, the body's husk exhausting November;
Here are your arms of suspicion and grace;
Here are the hours, I count them, I sleep at your side;
Here is the morning, rising like bread, rising as you rise in the white
    room;
Here is your body bending to dress, your scrotum folded like cloth;
Here is your mouth, your kiss, my ribs rising like birds as you leave
    me.

The Hiram Poetry Review   PAULA JONES

HAWKS

All the air shakes with a sound of hawks
Over the house. Brought back from memory
To stay again, their cries
Like tin parentheses scatter the light.

In shallow summer deepened by that sound,
Small creatures woven in the grass
Seem suddenly aware of a sky. Rabbits chew
Less lazily, their backs to the stone wall.

Now a garden snake, its emerald head raised,
Tongues an awareness of something above:
An old concern, forgotten for a time,
Reconjugates the primary tense

Attached to a terrible dream of flying
Like a pinned ribbon, away from earth: dizzy, helpless.
Surely too large for such a vehicle, even the cat
Stands mortised, looking up at the sound,

One paw raised as at the first spall of thunder.
Over us all, the fringed wings kite their shadows
To glide like innocent leaves; spin down,
Updraw then disappear, leaving holes in the light.

The Southern Review   LAURENCE JOSEPHS

SPRING CORN

Rubbing the damp morning
between our hands,
my father and I lift
the always heavy, rusty implements
to their appointed places on the tractor.
And with the cool light of
a March dawn
we hinge and bolt first the seed bucket

and then the pulley—and discs—
our fingers rusting with the effort.
Without wiping our hands,
we prime our contraption
with poison-pink corn seed,
making short trail furrows
before we get to the field.
There, we test again,
adjusting the seed timer,
finding the best depths
of seed and soil. . .
Then, when he's satisfied,
I see him glance up,
looking with assurance to the sun.

The Texas Review   S. M. JUDICE

THE SUNDIAL

Every path led me in a circle,
I serenely continued and, like a roundelay,
The luxuriant autumn drew its bows around me.
I saw waters there that are always silent. . .

Swans like an image of the beautiful, of the pure,
untouched in the autumnal decay,
And the asters that tremble like blue stars
In the morning-wind's breath.

But like a fragrance of the bitter, of the faded,
Which I had long, too long, forgotten,
It rose up about me and, as if through latticework,
I walked through the cypresses' green.

Between tendrils that strove toward the roof
In the vine's late-reddening foliage,
I read these words on the sundial:
Every hour hurts, the last one kills.

International Poetry Review   FRIEDRICH GEORG JÜNGER
                                       —*Translated from the German*
                                       by John C. May

ON THE FARM

The boy, missing the city intensely at this moment,
Mopes and sulks at the window. There's the first owl now,
    quite near,
But the boy hardly notices. And the kerosene lamp
Goes on sputtering, giving off vague medicinal fumes
That make him think of sick-rooms. He has been memorizing
"The Ballad of Reading Gaol," but the lamplight hurts his eyes.
And he is too bored to sleep, restless and bored. He thinks of
The city. . .

As, years later, he will recall, without blame,
The awful banalities of the long Julys — but, ah,
The bitterness of the lampsmoke now, the pure aloneness!
And the boy yawns, and the old dream of being a changeling
Returns. He hears the owl, and he thinks himself like this owl—
Proud, almost unnoticed—or like some hero in Homer
Protected by a cloud let down by the gods to save him.

Ploughshares   DONALD JUSTICE

FOR MY CHILDREN

After high school, I ran away to the coast,
slept in a pink Lincoln Continental, on blocks
in a deserted lot. By day, I body-surfed
the hollow waves. From orchards I stole fruit,
stuffed it in my tee-shirt like breasts
        I didn't have.

Boredom never troubled me.
At night, I travelled everywhere on LSD.
From the warm leather of the dead car,
I toured the rolling stars, or the great plains
spotted with buffalo on a beer can, the nearby
        sea rushing like a train,

earth turning beneath my seat like a carpet
yanked by some giant hand. Once I saw
my entire history in an avocado seed,
a quick replay of all my dawns,
until I stared, breathless, at the green pulp
        in my cupped palms.

Eyes like black noons from every bad trip
you ever heard. Next day I called my mom.
I spent my mayonaise jar of cash, saved
for a Mexican holiday on my ticket home,
then college, then this respectable job,
        with my name

embossed on creamy cards, my mail
arriving every day. I hardly budge.
This story isn't meant to warn: no shark
ever circled me, nor did local cops
plot my arrest for drugs or vagrancy.
        And don't fear

aging, stalling in your tracks,
a locked engine, churning in sand.
You're blessed, will remain,
for a time, unborn, without a past,
ignorant of change. This time is false
        and will not last.

Poetry   MARY KARR

TOO NEAR A CERTAIN DEATH

Moonlight mounts the windowsill,
a ghostly blade of light that cuts
across the carpet, sliding toward
the bed where you are curled
in sleep and I, awake, watch
as it moves unimpeded down the length
of bed, hallowing the space
between us; somewhere

I have read that lovers
sleep like seeds warm in the soil
of one another's embrace; we have always
turned our backs in search of solitude;
at first, I wondered if we feared we might
divulge some secret through
our skin, or touch
a wound that, hidden, had not healed; awake,

we bend often toward love; probing
the spot where pain and pleasure
merge, giving, taking back, forgiveness
like a benediction on our lips, and prayers;
and on those softer
nights explore, exposing gently what
in sleep we choose to hide; some call it

courting lies, this back-
to-back focusing on silent corners
of the room, as if believing that the body comes
to truth in sleep, and in a way it does;
always too near a certain death, one needs
to privately embrace the cold, one needs
to face the prospect of the grave; only
when we are still warm from where our hands
have left their mark, are we that brave.

The American Scholar   SUSAN KATZ

ROUND LAKE

I tell an easy story, all lies,
at parties. Ask me what I like,
I say digging pits, scrubbing sticks.
Ask me am I married. Easy.
I say no, divorced. You wonder
do I work. Sure, I drill two exact
pinholes in a block of steel.

You I'll tell two things: the summer
I was 12 I saw the rich men from Detroit
without their wives unravel sails
with the care I'd seen them count their cash.

Their hair was white and grey and brushed.
The big sails hooked a wind and then two boats
with even-handed men slipped by,
slipped straight in a hush into blue.
I knew that they were making deals out there.
I thought I'd swim sometime to check
but everybody else said, Oh yeah,
they'll hack some waves and yell,
back to your shack, girl. Git, git, git.
But I was sure the men would simply be precise:
Look, we'll tell you this, and this.

I learned to manage pretty well. And next:
when I was 17 and pregnant, I saw fire
spread across the lake in whorls,
the flames low, swirled, a richness
like embroidery, or golden robes.
I saw this for myself. And again
that winter, looking down through ice
in calms, in paths of blackened fish,
the sparks careened. A few like mica
flecked at the shores of eyes.
The lake steadied itself with lights
every season after.

                 Without leaving home
or reading anything I understood,
I knew what traveling could do.
Here I am with square knots tying lies
when all along it was the lake,
its blue and white and gold geometry,
the dressy fire, that took me in.

New Letters   JANET KAUFFMAN

THREE WAYS TO KILL A GOOSE

Here are three ways to kill a goose:

Praise her golden eggs, tell her that
No one lays them like she does, that
Nobody else can get that burnished glow, that
Effulgence, that lucidity.
Deluge the goose with praise,
Egg her on so that she confuses, silly goose,
Productivity with poetry.

Here's a second way:
Shame her into nesting,
Tell her that her eggs aren't bright enough,
Not quite up to contemporary Eggness,
That they, though gold, are only eggs, after all.
Deluge the goose with qualifiers until, humbled,
Silly goose, she confuses caution with craft.

And yet a third way, through love.
Say, "Gosling needs you, Goosie," and keep saying it
Until she hasn't time to lay a golden egg
And has not time to burnish it or nest.
Take a long view, tell her that
There will be time later
For all the laying, so that she confuses, silly goose,
What's good for the gander with gender, very tender.
Love's the best noose for the goose.

Descant   MARGARET KAUFMAN

FOR THE SIN . . .

Day of Atonement and the long walk
at sundown to the Wall. What the sun
does to itself, eating its lips
until they bleed, is already forgotten,
and the goat has gone out
of the Dung Gate with our sins.

The old man lifts his *shofar*
toward the gates of heaven,
blowing the notes to swing them wide
for the last time
before they are bolted for another year.

Now all our days
are measured in the book
against our repentance.

That's a small comfort.
A prayer is not a bird.

The Massachusetts Review   SHIRLEY KAUFMAN

RAIN

August watches from the porch, one hand
spread upon the screen like a star.
No stars. Lightning flares. He hears
large hounds prowling around the pond.
Thunder troubles the brim
where his wife's crysanthemums
color the water with their blooms.
Red rust, egg yolk, white plaster.

Every blossom like a bright crown
unwilling to bow
to the ground
in the gravity of rain.

The odor of a dark storm
swarms

in her hair, unribboned,
tumbling down her lilac gown.
In bed they listen to the rain
rattle the whole house now.
Roof, walls, porch, pasture.
All the earth saturated, shaken, still—

How long her hair is
rolling over his shoulder.
This is what he will remember after
forgetting her flowers. (There in the rain

they bow.)

New Letters   GEORGE KEITHLEY

THE FUNNEL CLOUD

It was something
foreign in these flat, watery parts
that rose, black and spinning over the woods
and carpeted the sky.
A machine
with debris and water aswirl in its center.
It came down in circles.
Downspouts and rain gutters shuddered,
a garage tipped its second floor.
Suspended and omnipotent, the giant toppled over,
smashed roofs, rained into chimneys,
sucked toys, bicycles, lawn furniture,
spat them out far as it could,
slammed doors on arms, tails, apron ties,
shook four creaking houses shutterless,
quivered over a flinching field,
shot up and hid in the smoky sky—
still blowing. We saw the rim inflame.
After, birds wired to slices of air
were not astonished at chairs nested there.
Flowers lay down, faced in one direction,
as if in prayer, some Mecca for storm clouds.

San Jose Studies   EMILY KELLER

THE SCHOLAR TURNS FORTY AGAIN

The years are revisions of other years,
So a scholar's birthday is no trivial matter,
Especially if he's forty and eager to forget
The crisis he's supposed to celebrate—
And the memories sneaking age brings to mind.
Again and again I turn forty. Forty-one

Is next: January twenty. Janus, one
Face looking back over the lost years,
The other gazing ahead wide-eyed, paying no mind
To the past. On the one hand (or face) it's matter
Over mind; on the other it's mind we celebrate,
Though both his faces we'd gladly forget,

Since they remind us how hard it is to forget.
Half way to eighty, thirty-nine past one—
Twice (January) twenty is forty. Celebrate!
Forty: a portentous age to be for one short year.
Enter my dear wife who begs me, "Age doesn't matter;
It's how you live and how you spend your mind."

I "appear to brood," and she warns me to get my mind
"Back on track." What track? Surely she forgets
I wrote a tract discussing that very matter
Several birthdays ago, and it didn't help me one
Bit. One little magazine kept it a whole year
Before returning it unpraised. Shall I celebrate

That? Still, I hope it's possible to celebrate
Some small victorious corner of the mind
That hasn't been stuffed with the junk of years,
When in she pops with more advice to help me forget.
"Why don't you write a sestina?" she asks one
Bright morning—as if this is an easy matter—

"It might help you figure out what's the matter
With you." Yes, I could review my ways and celebrate
My days and spit them into a sestina—one
Stanza tied to the next. I could remind my mind
Countless times, review, revise, erase—forget
My greying beard and bulging middle years.

Thirty-nine lines, forty years: for my mind's
Peace I try to fill them up. Remember or forget,
Celebrate or brood—days add up to years.

The Midwest Quarterly   MICHAEL J. KELLY

THE BOOK OF MOONLIGHT

("The book of moonlight is not written yet, nor half begun"
—Wallace Stevens, "The Comedian as the Letter C")

Writing the book of moonlight is a careful act:
The pages are November's air, crisp to the heart;
Ice snapping on a leaf in the dead of the night.

Imagine the sky as a lover, speaking to you
Of half-remembered hurts, of life as a question
Once asked. The dark promises only that suddenly

The book of moonlight can open, and you know,
The moment you forget the cold in your eyes,
Someone is home, warming your face to the light.

Yankee   GARY KERLEY

BALLAD

Driving south in sleet
I know you're coming north.
Take it easy, son,
whatever road you're on.

Hope the old car's safe.
Pray you stay awake.
Take it easy, son,
whatever road you're on.

Watch the ice at Great Bend.
Gear down in the dark.
Take it easy, son,
whatever road you're on.

Don't pass trucks downhill.
keep the music off.
Stay away from ghosts.
Stay away from thoughts.

Something sees us both
turning toward our town.
Take it easy, son,
whatever road you're on.

Mss.   MILTON KESSLER

ALCHEMY

Carpenters are in love with wood;
A hand on the bole of the living tree
tells them the number of running board feet.
Gnarl of hard winter, the limb lost to ice, might
save a tree, after all, for a season.
Carpenters are in love with the rasp, file,
the teeth of saws, the beat of hammers:
what transforms the exuberance of green
into something other (what's smooth under hand).

Bakers take fine flour (berries of wheat, rye,
threshed and ground by stone or steel rollers)
and yeast (that smells of loamy fields and grows,
there, in the kitchen, warmed with milk, water),
honey, knead alive the ball of dough; smell
the loaf baking in the killing oven;

break hot the new bread; dip it in butter,
salt it, and eat the whole—in the new house
that smells so sweetly of sawdust and loaves.

Time's fine chisel etches lines on faces,
molds the whole over into something else.
New shapes emerge from ball of baby, stretch,
smile, and stoop-shouldered, sink to sagging egg
of age perched uneasily on an earth
which waits for that further transformation.
Metamorphosis is what we know of time.
We are alchemists—loving change, not gold.

The Literary Review   MARJORIE DEITER KEYISHIAN

ON POETRY

Tonight sleep will not come,
I'm awake half the night.
I lie listening to sounds
I've never heard before.
Not new sounds, there are
no new sounds, only
ones the ear has been trained
not to hear, like those of
wood dying, cat sleep, a woman dreaming.
For an instant the ear rings true.
Each vowel, each word, each sound
becomes as fresh as milk poured
straight from the milker. On a cold morning
I carried pail after pail
from my father's barn, smelled
the mixed aromas of cattle and sweat.
I remember once five years ago
thinking farming a simple task,
my father a simple man. Tonight
I want to talk with my father
on farmland. We will bend,
put our ears to the ground,
and listen for hours.

The Ohio Review   ROBERT KINSLEY

MONDAY MORNING

I water the plants, watching
the water stand on dry dirt,
reluctant to settle, to soak
down to the roots. I am looking,
I know, into myself, the way
women do. Into folds of memory,

the soft surprise of revulsion.
Once I walked in on my mother's
bath, hated her breasts swimming
up at me. Now I see my body
is hers—there's no way
to deny it. Men are always
searching for fathers, or losing
their sons, seeing in them
the chance to let their lives
run clear. They want to carve
their names in stone. Women
don't care what they leave—
a wedding ring, the silver
tea set, the right way to iron
a shirt, a voice insistent
as guilt. We use our words
to ward off what we haven't said—
the dream of being barren
ground, hard and flat, rib and
pelvis indistinct, everything
picked clean.

The Georgia Review   JUDITH KITCHEN

WALKING GREAT ISLAND

Salt-licking its way around the barrier beach, scattering
the long-billed whimbrels, and backing fiddler-crabs
down their holes,
the tide advances, jamming its finger into the gut
—my complaint drowned in the roar.
When the sea is done, only the wrack endures.
I could tell you about desolation: seaweed ripped from its
          moorings;
ladder-shells—perfect spirals that led nowhere;
all the fallen angels that rode into shore on one wing;
the deposed horse-shoe crab; a stranded periwinkle
weakly clasping a piece of kelp.
And the gulls' shadows darkening the flats,
slivered white shrapnel,
a single glove stiffened with salt.
The couple at tide-line—how shall they stay?
—his driftwood scratchings,
her orange kerchief a brave scrap in the wind.
A battered dory's down to its chines,
each owner's color scraped back.
Where the tide fails, a spray sifts in:
the innocence of a weathered board, then splintered
chunks of someone's pier,
and so it goes until a whole house is cast adrift,
a logy mass of beams. Finally,
an island—its school and lighthouse—slides under the brine,

a corrugated shadow barely discernible on the neap tide.
And the ardent couple in the dunes, their plangent cries—
swallowed by the drone in a green bottle.

Boston Review   LINDSAY KNOWLTON

MORE GIRL THAN BOY

You'll always be my friend.
Is that clear, Robert Lee?
We go beyond the weighing
of each other's words,
hand on a shoulder,
go beyond the color of hair.
Playing Down the Man on the Field,
we embraced each other before
I discovered girls.
You taught me a heavy love
for jazz, how words can hurt
more than a quick jab.
Something there's no word for
saved us from the streets.

Night's pale horse
rode you past commonsense,
but you made it home from Chicago.
So many dreams dead.
All the man-sweet gigs
meant absolutely nothing.
Welcome back to earth, Robert.
You always could make that piano
talk like somebody's mama.

Ploughshares   YUSEF KOMUNYAKAA

AT THE OFFICE EARLY

Rain has beaded the panes
of my office windows,
and in each little lens
the bank at the corner
hangs upside down.
What wonderful music
this rain must have made
in the night, a thousand banks
turned over, the change
crashing out of the drawers
and bouncing upstairs
to the roof, the soft
percussion of ferns
dropping out of their pots,

the ballpoint pens
popping out of their sockets
in a fluffy snow
of deposit slips.
Now all day long,
as the sun dries the glass,
I'll hear the soft piano
of banks righting themselves,
the underpaid tellers
counting their nickels and dimes.

Southern Poetry Review   TED KOOSER

ARTLESS STORY

Chieko tells me that in Tokyo
There is no sky. Not real, real sky, she said.

Startled, I glanced aloft. High overhead
Between the cherry-branches' greenish glow,
Their budding leaves, the blue sky stretched away;
That sky I know so well and hold so dear.

On the horizon, pinkish and unclear,
Vague morning-shapes foretold another day
of humid summer haze.
                          My witless love,
Staring at distance from a vacant face,
Tells me that only in her native place
Are skies true sky, those skies that stretch above
The Atatara Mountains. There they lie,
Azure and open, skies that a soul can trust.
Or so Chieko tells me.
                          This is just
An artless-seeming story about sky.

Denver Quarterly   TAKAMURA KOTARO
                    —Translated from the Japanese
                    by Graeme Wilson

GYPSY

(for Janet)

Gypsy, honey,
you just love to love.
You know what goes on behind all those zippers
        as torso meets tambourine
        deliberately matching the rhythm of kept cobras
        in a room lit only by candles and cigarettes.
You tug at your own web:
        making wild promises with one set of lashes,
        seeking the outline of the door with the other.

Desperately now,
using your sea of red taffeta to part the crowd,
you try to suck in oxygen, push out opium
as your fingers slip from the doorknob.

The Bellingham Review   KAREN KOVACIK

THE CLICHÉ

I'd coursed through seven counties
of green and gold and blue,
eyes fixed on the macadam
whose every inch I knew,
while beaks around me flew.

We'd just swung off Route 80
onto the Garden State
when a breeze reached in through the window
invisibly as Fate
and made my brain vibrate.

I blush to confess the vibration:
it was just an anemic cliché.
By the skin of my teeth I triumphed
over my naïveté
and managed not to say
"How pleasant it is today!"

Perhaps it was that my nostrils
had cleared in honor of May;
perhaps it was for our daughter
and hers, twelve miles away;
I don't remember the visit
except there was food and play,
but I do remember the wonder,
and—even more—the dismay.

My wonder itself was the wonder:
whose edict do I obey
these thirty years, forbidding
the pulse to go astray?

There are some alive who remember
it was not always this way.
A thousand times at the Bay,
Fort Hamilton to Sea Gate,
in weathers glowing or gray
forehead fronting the spray—
a thousand times on the railroad,
clay against sweaty clay—
a thousand times on pavement
without one golden ray—
I have thought, yes, even whispered:
"How pleasant it is today!"

Wind Magazine   AARON KRAMER

THE YOUNG SKATER

I watch her ease about the rink. . .
Her slim young body fresh and supple,
young breasts formed and forming
in a tight tan cashmere sweater,
she glides along the ice like a
surfer on a wave, cresting one sure
leg and then another (oh the grace
in the flow of her white thighs passing).
Then her right leg reaches back
as she leans and hurls a twisted spiral
through the lifting air and lands,
her left leg twirling like a top
as her right leg follows in
the sway of the flying camel spin.

America   PETER KROK

A GOOD DEAL OF CHANCE

A good deal of chance
Is involved
Whenever a body
With breast, shoulder and knee
Begins to hover in the air,
And in this air
Meets another body
Like it
Along the way.

The atmosphere makes
Two inner torsos of them.
Unnoticed, their rapture describes
Tender lines in treetops.
Their whispering can be heard
For a long time,
And how they give
To each other
What is gentle.

Happiness always begins
A little above the earth.

But no one has been able to observe it.

International Poetry Review   KARL KROLOW
                              —Translated from the German
                              by John C. May

THE IMAGE-MAKER

A wind passed over my mind,
insidious and cold.
It is a thought, I thought,
but it was only its shadow.
Words came,
or the breath of my sisters,
with a black rustle of wings.
They came with a summons
that followed a blessing.
I could not believe
I too would be punished.
Let me watch,
at my casement window,
the acid wafer of the moon
slowly dissolving
in a scud of cloud.
Perhaps it is time to go,
to set this old body free
by pulling the night
like a sack over my head,
denying my affections.
But I am not in love,
nor ever shall be,
with the abolute dark.
I listen, but I avert my ears
from Meister Eckhart's warning:
"All things must be forsaken.
God scorns
to show Himself among images."

The Atlantic Monthly   STANLEY KUNITZ

THE GREAT POEMS

The great poems, surely they
are without people in them. For when people intrude
there are dishes, there is the smell of people,
of arms and eyes, of the brain having let the body slip.
But in the great poems there is only a flower or two,
and the wind playing leapfrog with itself. Perhaps
you do not understand or agree, but in the great poems
man arrives too late for the action, the accident
having occurred—he puts out his feeble hands, and
the blood is immense like the sea, or the bones
cannot be mended, or, dropped on its stem, the head
of the flower is down and its color gone. Lament
the loss. This is what the great poems do.
The bird which just now fled beyond your reach
or thought. The stone which the stream washes over and

over. Each day the sun creeps close over the earth
to free its colors.

The Georgia Review   GREG KUZMA

THE THIN EDGE

Enters, now,
the long cold in the bone:
the numb trees
turned in on themselves,
their branches empty;
badger and bear curled
in a hungerless sleep
and the seed sleeping.
Under the ice—slow silver,
the trout drift
into shadowy icons.
The sky swallows up light
like a stone mouth,
and birds, bronzed over
or pewter-coated,
keep to tbe stiff hedges.
The thin edge, we think,
watching the year slide
into its black crevasse.
Everything glints
with as bright malice
as the blade of a knife,
the sixth bullet.

Yankee   JOAN LaBOMBARD

STILL DANCING

You and I have not touched
for many nights.
In the same bed
we roll and turn
into ourselves, our lives
lashed together by one
peach-colored sheet.

It is your job to sleep
with your arms folded,
your body still stiff
with the day's fears.
While I fold myself
around two pillows,
hold all I can inside.

Sometimes it is weeks
before I look for your eyes.

Just inches away
we can not meet.
This is the dance
we were afraid of.
Feet together,
and no one leads.

Passages North   Margo LaGattuta

ALONG THE PACIFIC

A rock, white-stained by gull droppings,
cropped up in the blue furrows that the tide plowed
over and over at the moon's insistence. Waves
threw themselves like hysterical women at the cliffs, their white
        hair
blown forward over their faces; or like plumed
battalions, blue rank on rank, lay siege
to the land's end stone.
                        This was not
the immaculate blue expanse we would have made
an afternoon's diversion, wending slowly
over the Pacific highway's curves—something looked at drowsily
from the back seat after the first few hours, then awakened to
like sky after a picnic doze.
                        No, bigger than light and vision
this loomed up, and stayed there half the day—its blue calm
soothing at the proper height, murderous at a lesser distance:
those half-seen, jagged rocks, after a weightless pause
would crush a car's hull; those gulls, riding a cold down-draft,
would stab the eyes out of a corpse or tear flesh off
whatever, weakened by sea-rack, can't wave them away.

                        Better to return to the city
than watch this merciless inhuman beauty
fade to the bay window's blue
of these sleek cliff-houses, or learn to see it with a hawk's eye.
  Let it remain
the last unimaginable terror we imagine,
the last unfurled, furling mystery
to which we turn,
                from which we can return.

The Threepenny Review   Paul Lake

LONG ISLAND SPRING

(for Gerry)

It's sixty degrees and almost the end of April.
I wish so much you could be here

to see the beauty wrought before
it all happens. The weeping cherry
is full of flowers for the first time,
their color so delicate it burst upon me
before I knew it, amazing grace.

The wild crabapple is holding its buds for you;
too, the dogwood and dark leaved Hopa crab.
Flowers of myrtle, and violets, enjoy
visits from bees below my south window.
You'll miss the flowering almond unless you are quick.

Blue squills below the royal-purple magnolia
have mostly come and gone; frothy white clusters
of andromeda still ring their tiny wax bells.
The one at the north end of the garden died.
I kneel to receive the fragrance of poet's narcissi
as they march along the north.

I found two daffodils in the northeast woods
near the aging dogwood, thrusting up
through a pile of brushwood. I found a tiny new
Norwegian maple, two inches tall, growing
by the wild geraniums. I found a new sprout
of flowering cherry, the flowering cherry's child;
the diminutive fir in the iris bed survived.
The woods are laced with pale green gauze.

Woodpile is holding up, I've had few fires.
Cardinals await your more loyal hand, few lately;
mostly grackles, redwinged blackbirds
enlarging their red-and-yellow winged bars as they fly
or make love. So many doves, a couple of crows,
one robin bouncing along the lawn,
white-throated sparrows His eye is upon.

I called Fred this morning for help,
since Mark can come only once in a while.
I've finished cleaning icebox and stove
to make a fresh place for cooking you something.
Your bed is perfectly made with dark blue sheets
and the white and blue tufted spread with the fringe.

Come walk with me. Come home soon.

West Hills Review   RUTH LAKE

SEEING WILD HORSES

If only I could tell you how wildness shows
the space between us and the green world;
how an island is the same island with our
presence, but with that presence we lose
some hope of seeing, say, a horse, or the dead
gnarled limbs of an oak sunk in sand.
Edward Weston saw it in the folds of a pepper

and tried to hold not the succulent essence
of vegetable richness, but to take the divorce,
the gap between pepper and tripoded camera,
and catch purely the third thing,
the twisted surface perfect and singular.
Like now, soon after I wake I see

on the beach, unexpected, between sea
and shifting dunes, among the drifts
of kicking sand, horses running past, intent
on some distant grazable stand of island grass,
the word *stall* only a hiss in my mouth.
And to realize I've seen a wild horse the first

time, a swift knot of freedom, and I fight
some need to call it from that animal world,
then lose it in the shock of its leaving;
I call this the greed of human caring,
and count all my losses among its history.

Ploughshares   JOHN LANE

IN A MOMENT

How simple those words, how terrible.

In a moment I will have to imagine you:
your white blouse in the first of morning,
your hips as you walk, lifting and falling
as they cradle the seed of our night.

Your face has a deep sadness
as you sleep into dawn.
                    I cannot believe
how beautiful you are, the silver dust
dry upon your thighs, your back's curve
and your belly, its deep swell.

In a moment you will rise and shroud
your hips in cloth.
                    Like an animal,
naked and questing, my mouth searches
for you among these absences.

Descant (Canada)   PATRICK LANE

MUSIC FOR AN AUTUMN AFTERNOON

Under an ash tree, under October sky,
    Lies the quietness that only you and I
Compose and are composed of—ah, the wind
    Whispers, but all is quiet once again.

Beneath me lies the form, lies what is warm,
    Lies what, though silent, rivals any storm
In elemental sweep and unencumbered power,
    Though it is soundless in this blessed hour.

Above you lies suppressed thunder of
    The body and being made by love for love
That sometimes (as at the beginning) rages,
    But mellows, often, into mellow stages.

Beneath a sky that neither loves nor feels
    Lie we in shadows, two fire-flashing wheels
That spin at times (bright circles of desire)
    Then rest and burn here heatless when we tire.

Poem   STEPHEN LANG

TO-BE-AMERICA

America—
sea that rocks the great boat of the hemisphere.
Its woman-shaped shores that refuse to give birth,
sky that is never sufficient,
mountain that grows and grows in order to succeed in seeing what
    is there and what is not;
plains, this skin of earth and animal in a state of
    contemplation;
wind that blows in order to make everything clean,
desert that turns out to be impossible to desert,
islands that someday have to be united,
heat's milk that boils from the Tropic to Ecuador;
cold of the south, ice without north to save it,
river that arrives precisely from where one would want to go,
lakes in which the water is tired of waiting,
forests where the wolf always lives,
estuaries of clay with which someone molds the
    creature of this latitude;
man that can arrive at being Man is this vain
    enumeration that, almost forgotten,
inexplicably,
makes a bet on this man for All
or Nothing.

Denver Quarterly   CARLOS LATORRE
    —*Translated from the Spanish (Argentina)*
    by Mary Crow

THEY USED TO HAVE A HOMECOMING DAY

End of a hot day's drive on unimaginative
straight roads over the flat of the huge midland with its too much
corn; and the names come out of my past, Mahomet, the Sangamon,

Champaign-Urbana; threading the difficult point-to-point of U.S.
46. What a way to come back or not quite to
come back. Race and Green gloomed up, then the colossal

stadium. So to our motel. Phone book. No names, they must all
be dead. Unseen, Lincoln Hall, where I studied, where I taught
    Latin
and Philosophy, and sweated it out, and knew my future.

Shapes in the mist, shot by and lost. Flat streets, the rented
rooms, skinny breakfasts. Kicking leaves on the sidewalks.
The Press, alien now and I'm grumpy. Good bye, Urbana.

Known territory glimpsed, gone. No instant, no deferred replay.

The Hudson Review   RICHMOND LATTIMORE

SLAUGHTERING A BULL

*(Five years ago this June, in Dalton,
Pennsylvania, for my neighbor Jim)*

When you hit the right spot
midway between and slightly
above the eyes (and you can do it

with a hammer, too),
nothing
can have prepared you

for the surprise of it.
There's no momentum
to his magnificence, and whatever

wonder has been hidden there,
holding that great mass of cells
erect and dangerous, is now

instantly not there;
the mammoth shoulders, the fierce
white head and horns

don't even wait for the legs
to crumple: the earth attracts them
and all at once they drop. Quick—

gut the leavings before they stink.
And this night, Lawder,
may you sleep like a stone.

The American Scholar   DONALD LAWDER

WITH UNDIMINISHED FIRE

Louis, what the hell!
Let's bury the hatchet

(and this time not
in each other's neck or skull).
　　We're both grey around the edges
and facing ills that age brings:
arthritis, heaviness of gait,
loss of teeth and sight; the
weariness that sets in at the close
　　when life's seen as puppet show,
the colours fading from the stock figures;
and hate's fury or ambition's
sounding like tapes reeled backwards.

We've gone our separate ways
to Valhalla—so what?
　　We still keep our rage
for bourgeois and huckster,
still scorn the fashionable lies
of pulpit and marketplace;
still keep faith with Homer and Shakespeare,
John Donne and Yeats.
　　In that clamorous brotherhood
bound together by ties
mightier than nation or blood,
we invoke in the gathering dusk
the dear death-cheating names
of Glassco and Smith and Klein.

My left ear partly deaf,
I only half-heard your diatribes
　　and literary abuse,
the gossip seething in the streets
that malice grows from grin to crooked grin.
I hope, Louis, you were similarly afflicted
　　and only half-heard mine.
as for old fishwives' tales,
I know your famed humanity
stopped up your ears
till they fell to earth like tattered kites.
　　Dear friend, dear comrade-in-arms,
in the darker nights ahead
which the revolving sun
relentlessly spins for both of us,
　　let us forgive utterly
the long, divisive years, the pain,
and may each in his separate sky
with undiminished fire, shine.

Waves (Canada)   IRVING LAYTON

YEATS AT SIXTY-FIVE

Your warty lads are too shy to tell you
they burn to cover your body full length.

But I, a white-haired lecher and famous,
boldly apprise the world I do.

Dear maid, which will pleasure you most:
a young man's shyness or an old man's lust?

Poetry Canada Review   IRVING LAYTON

CLIMBING OUT

Five turtles on a fallen limb
that rises from the river; five turtles
motionless on the limb.
March sunlight skips from ripple to ripple
where water breaks over the rocks,
the fallen limb steady as a rock;
water breaks round it, whirls.
I stare into the sun, then drop my eyes to the trees;
how the branches whirl
(all the world spinning round the forming buds),
grow still again, the angular winter woods.
A truck rumbles over the old stone bridge
carrying what someone somewhere thinks he needs.
When did I climb out of the current?
Is it minute after minute or year after year
I've stood watching
five turtles on a fallen limb?

America   WARREN LEAMON

PAROWAN CANYON

When granite and sandstone begin to blur
and flow, the eye rests on cool white aspen.
Strange, their seeming transparency.
How as in a sudden flash one remembers
a forgotten name, so the recollection. *Aspen.*
With a breeze in them, their quiet rhythms,
shimmering, quaking. Powder on the palm.
Cool on the cheek. Such delicate
fragility the brittle wood, limbs snapping
at a grasp, whole trees tumbling in the winds.
Sweet scent on a swollen afternoon.
Autumn, leaves falling one on another, gold
rains upon a golden earth. How at evening
when the forest darkens, aspen do not.
And a white moon rises and silver stars
point toward the mountain, darkness
holds them so pale.
They stand still, very still.

The Midwest Quarterly   DAVID LEE

ONE-NIGHT STAND

She sleeps, half-draped,
half-innocent on the motel bed.
I stand at the window
watching sleet in the headlights
of passing trucks, feeling their rumble,
thinking of deer crossing the road.

Her young body twitches
like a moonlit rabbit
sensing the wingbeat of a gliding owl.

Nearly dawn, my body aches,
gripped in her sex,
an old orange squeezed dry.

There are muscles stiffening
where my heart used to be.
Yet I passed through her fire
with love, even god, on my lips.

She will escape with no wounds.
Tonight we broke her smooth
clear life like a champagne bottle
on this bed, and threatened
the world outside with jagged glass.

Now she sleeps like a flower
folded around my moisture.

This is passion: fooling
my loneliness in a strange girl's arms.
This is a haven, her breathing
unbearably soft beside the trucks' whine and roar.
Not till dawn will she need any armour.

Waves (Canada)   RICHARD LEMM

ODE'S BODKINS

If I were a god,
I'd sit in my professor's cloister
Like a bacchanalian Apollo,
Warping time and tight spaces
To allow a slow dance of revel
With all the maenads who prance
Among the elms and ivy,
Writhing their slight, curved
Bodies around my heroic proportions,
Sacrificing their sleek forms
To my eternal lines.
Alas, there are no gods but tenure,
And the birds sing of sexual
Harassment, not wine.

So I sit mutely upon their smiles,
As erectly flaccid
As a defaced herm.

The Classical Outlook   TONY M. LENTZ

TO HIMSELF

(A Se Stesso)

I've stopped it all, my exhausted heart,
Stopped it forever. That last, that fatal trick
Is all played out, though I thought it eternal. Played out. Yes,
Lying hearts like ours hold
Neither hope nor desire: it's dead.
So stop forever. You've throbbed
Too hard. There's nothing anywhere
Worth beating for, worth sighing for,
The whole world's not worth it. Life's
Gone bitter and boring, endlessly nothing over and over. This
     filthy
World! Never give it a thought. Give it all up
This one last time. Our kind is meant
Just to die. Wrinkle your lips and spit
At Nature, that ugly, mindless, invisible
Power in charge of everything, spit
At the infinite vanity of the universe.

The Literary Review   GIACOMO LEOPARDI
                                        —Translated from the Italian
                                        by Burton Raffel

ATLANTIS

Like buried layered
cities upon cities
centuries upon centuries
the metaphysics
metaphors of the mind
excavate explore
unfold before our eyes:
our minds the
scattered thoughts—
like vases, coins, busts
made by hands
envisioned by minds
like ours
as others will see
the artifacts
of our thoughts

buried layered
beneath our eyes.

The Arizona Quarterly   DOMINICK J. LEPORE

EARLY SEPTEMBER

(for My Father)

I look up from stirring the soup
to find you, four years deep in the ground,
smiling beside me, though it's not
my birthday or any anniversary
I'd note. This time I touch your face,
ruddy in the afternoon
sun this early September.

At last we're both warm. Last winter
when I couldn't eat I wore your thinness
against my skin, and understood how hard
I'd been to coax you with heaps of chicken
and bread, how when the body means
to give up food, it will not be tricked
like a mere hothouse flower.

See, I want to eat again. I remember
our lunch of pea soup and apple
dumplings that other autumn day before
either of us knew how to catch light
wherever it breaks. Now I ladle out
my soup and sip it slowly, slowly,
the way the moon grows, the way morning
ripens and feeds us, like love.

Carolina Quarterly   ELLEN LEVINE

THE CONDUCTOR OF NOTHING

If you were to stop and ask me
how long I have been as I am,
a man who hates nothing
and rides old trains for the sake
of riding, I could only answer
with that soft moan I've come
to love. It seems a lifetime I've
been silently crossing and recrossing
this huge land of broken rivers
and fouled lakes, and no one has cared
enough even to ask for a ticket
or question this dingy parody
of a uniform. In the stale,
echoing stations I hunch over a paper

or ply the air with my punch,
and soon we are away, pulling out
of that part of a city where the backs
of shops and houses spill out
into the sunlight and the kids
sulk on the stoops or run aimlessly
beneath the viaducts. Then we are
loose, running between grassy slopes
and leaving behind the wounded
wooden rolling stock of another era.
Ahead may be Baltimore, Washington,
darkness, the string of empty cars
rattling and jolting over bad track,
and still farther up ahead the dawn,
asleep now in some wet wood far
south of anywhere you've ever been,
where it will waken among the ghostly
shapes of oak and poplar, the ground fog
rising from the small abandoned farms
that once could feed a people. Thus
I come back to life each day
miraculously among the dead,
a sort of moving monument
to what a man can never be—
someone who can say "yes" or "no"
kindly and with a real meaning,
and bending to hear you out, place
a hand upon your shoulder, open
my eyes fully to your eyes, lift
your burden down, and point the way.

Antaeus   PHILIP LEVINE

LOON

Loon's a word I've always used:
calling her a loon for loving such a fly-by-night,
shouting "You're crazy as a loon!" at my husband
as he kicks off his shoes,
heads into snow, barefoot,
leaving a trail of black holes—

as if I knew just how crazy loons could be,
as if I'd seen loons all my life,
lived with them, catalogued their
most secret habits, knew they
couldn't walk on land
looking tipsy when they try.

Now, listening to the loons cry
night after night outside our lakefront window,
sensing it was loons I heard
our first night here,

their hollow song comforting me,
surrounding me like a necklace of o's,
a stippled lullaby from the dawn
of my childhood,

I can see they're not crazy at all
but subtle, graceful loners
who swim placidly along, then dive,
only to appear lengths of lake away
without a gasp, without a ripple,
their dark trickster bodies unafraid of day,
their crippled feet swift navigators of the lower depths,
the demented laughter an oracle
set to music.

The Malahat Review   HELANE LEVINE-KEATING

WINTER STARS

My father once broke a man's hand
Over the exhaust pipe of a John Deere tractor. The man,
Ruben Vasquez, wanted to kill his own father
With a sharpened fruit knife, & he held
The curved tip of it, lightly, between his first
Two fingers, so it could slash
Horizontally, & with surprising grace,
Across a throat. It was like a glinting beak in a hand
And, for a moment, the light held still
On the vines. When it was over,
My father simply went in & ate lunch, & then, as always,
Lay alone in the dark, listening to music.
He never mentioned it.

I never understood how anyone could risk his life,
Then listen to Vivaldi.

Sometimes, I go out into this yard at night,
And stare through the wet branches of an oak
In winter, & realize I am looking at the stars
Again. A thin haze of them, shining
And persisting.

It used to make me feel lighter, looking up at them.
In California, that light was closer.
In a California no one will ever see again,
My father is beginning to die. Something
Inside him is slowly taking back
Every word it ever gave him.
Now, if we try to talk, I watch my father
Search for a lost syllable as if it might
Solve everything, & though he can't remember, now,
The word for it, he is ashamed. . .
If you can think of the mind as a place continually
Visited, a whole city placed behind
The eyes, & shining, I can imagine, now, its end—

As when the lights go off, one by one,
In a hotel at night, until at last
All of the travelers will be asleep, or until
Even the thin glow from the lobby is a kind
Of sleep; & while the woman behind the desk
Is applying more lacquer to her nails,
You can almost believe that the elevator,
As it ascends, must open upon starlight.

I stand out on the street, & do not go in.
This was our agreement, at my birth.

And for years I believed
That what went unsaid between us became empty,
And pure, like starlight, & it persisted.
I got everything wrong.
I wound up believing in words the way a scientist
Believes in carbon, after death.

Tonight, I'm talking to you, father, although
It is quiet here in the midwest, where a small wind,
The size of a wrist, wakes the cold again—
Which may be all that's left of you & me.

When I left home at seventeen, I left for good.

That pale haze of stars goes on & on,
Like laughter that has found a final, silent shape
On a black sky. It means everything
It cannot say. Look, it's empty out there, & cold.
Cold enough to reconcile
Even a father, even a son.

The American Poetry Review   LARRY LEVIS

WINTER RAIN

My friend in Warsaw writes to me of rain, of the different types
of Polish rain—the filthy spray, the crystal mist, the warm, fat
droplets souring the earth—and of how this winter there will be
no winter by an order of the state. A continuance of autumn has
been declared. His letters mention endless names of towns—a
glottal litany, all consonants, that stumbles off the tongue—
and how unrest mounts incrementally, like water rising in a rain
gauge. He writes of how he spends whole days refusing visas to
potential emigrants who spend as many days inventing nonexistent
jobs and relatives awaiting them across the sea. And through all
of this—the knowing glances of the men who tail him everywhere
he goes, the card games in the dungeon of the embassy, the hushed
exchange of dying currency for lethal dollars—there is the rain
as agent of the state, which forbids the sweet release from autumn
into snow. Now I must write back to him. I feel I should say
something profound about survival in a foreign land, about the
intransigence of freedom when it's held in chains, about all rain

being relative and how he must, at last, remain aloof and cold.
I tear up a first draft, then a second, then a third as each
revision starts to seem redundant and obscene. And then, another
letter comes by mail. In it my friend reports the snows have
come at last, bringing with them much public celebration and
drinking of cold vodka. At last I come to know my jealousy, my
envy of a land so grim and strange. I look out my window at the
whiteness blanketing New York and begin a letter to my friend in
Warsaw, "Dear George, snow, in a free country, is only snow . . ."

Kayak   ROBERT J. LEVY

LUCILLE

We sit, jittery as birds before flight,
and deceive ourselves that there is something
more important than Lucille's return.

The long house surrounding us has kept
for twenty years. But it is as much Lucille's
now as the day she left this island.

Impatient for the sight of her, the ocean beats
at the shore the way it did when she and I,
at seventeen, explored the dark caves

Of our bodies. The sandpipers, frozen
in their frantic dances, stared at our sex.
We pitied their incapacities, forgave them

And marveled at waves glistering on our skin.
Something stronger pulled her away
these twenty years. A need, a promise, a man?

Now the wake of grief closes and the wind wheels
around my heart as she comes into the yard
like a procession of one, gay beyond description.

She comes to me, oblivious to all else.
She holds me like a baby.
She whispers, "Jeanette, Jeanette, oh girl. . ."

Passages North   J. PATRICK LEWIS

THE ACT OF LETTING GO

I know at last the hands, how they stay alive
in sudden weathers, only a twist of turquoise
to disguise their moaning. It is twilight
here where the hands wait,
though, out the window, the harbor water
is bright with ice. I remember
your face disappearing into my hands, asking
their protection when they
could barely keep themselves alive.

My hands have never been this cold,
as if my voice came from the hands alone
and not the throaty warmth of the page,
speaking to you, breaking
against you because
something must matter which already matters little,
is almost gone; I
do not know what it is, there isn't
a shadow of fist or caress left between us.

But I know the hands, even knuckle-hard, cannot
hold up anyone. It is hard enough the way
they drag their desires in front of them,
wishing to caress or rest
in a pocket, or simply be left alone.
And so I've let your face go.
Just like that I've thrown my hands
out and open. There is nothing
I can do for your hands, not even hold them.
They must be always going into the air.

My hands, held up now to the light,
have the bones of too delicate an animal.
I turn my hands over and see
they are like any hands—like yours, like those
unmet: they do their damage and repent.
To touch a curve of air, the angle of face, hands
may not even know each other: reckless
life like the reckless twist of water below ice,
all the small white boats remaining perfect, still.

Poetry   ELIZABETH LIBBEY

THE MENSCH

No dummkopf about God (prayer
    Worked in business; faith moved
    Money from red to black), Grampa
Had started out to become

    A rabbi. Unsentimental—sheepish
Or holy he couldn't feel—
He sided with God because God had
    A better head on His shoulders. God

Was the brains of the outfit, tough-
    Minded and ethical, nobody's fool *or*
    Saint. What God said just once
He *meant*, once-and-for-all,

    Took everyone at his word, could
See inside your head,
And never forgot your worst
    Thoughts. Grampa had known but one

Or two honest sellers
    Besides himself, but these had weaker

Moments when honor slept. True,
Only God kept a perfect

Vigil over base thoughts, quick
As weasels; but if Grampa felt
A weakening for *shiksas* or *schnapps*,
He swallowed temptation hard, and rarely

Hiccupped. The Old Testament,
In parts, tickled Grampa: whoever
Wrote the scriptures listened about half
The time, or less, to God's

Dictation. Grampa would fire absent-
Minded stenographers
On the spot, but he never blamed
God for leaning on a bad secretarial

Crutch. Only *poylishe goyim*
Would run the business and keep the books
And sweep the floors, too—not God . . .
God was a perfect *mensch.*

The South Carolina Review   LAURENCE LIEBERMAN

THE USED CAR LOT

In the used car lot
whore-cars wear too much body-paint.
Volkswagens go just so far for the money,
dress formal (if cheap)
and ask to be left at the garage at the proper hour.
Ferraris and Alpha-Romeos (that never grow old)
condone free love
but submit to no more than one owner per year,
while promiscuous Pontiacs, Buicks, Chevies
court a fast turnover of customers,
act solid for a week
to make a fast buck, and then collapse;
a little fresh paint, new plugs, a charge for the battery,
and back to the line-up.
Conscientious Fiats save up for abandoned sister-MGs
in forgotten parking-lots of cities,
and support grandmotherly
Bentleys in the ward of the city-dump.
Respectable jeeps
carry chrome-trimming bouquets to the auto graveyards
to honor the late ancestral Packard and Hudson,
the stillborn Edsel
and the never-to-be-forgotten Tucker
foetus, miscarried.

Kansas Quarterly   LAURENCE LIEBERMAN

IN COMPUTERS

In the magnets of computers will be stored
  Blend of sunset over wheat fields.
  Low thunder of gazelle.
  Light, sweet wind on high ground.
  Vacuum stillness spreading from a thick snowfall.

Men will sit in rooms
upon the smooth, scrubbed earth
or stand in tunnels on the moon
and instruct themselves in how it was.
Nothing will be lost.
Nothing will be lost.

Science   ALAN P. LIGHTMAN

NEVERTHELESS

(Horace Carmina 3.26)

Not long since quite attractive to the girls,
    I've fought with glory in love's battle-line;
But now upon this temple wall that guards
    The left-hand side of lovely Venus' shrine
Shall hang my arms, my lyre, her warfare done;
    Here lay aside the brands, the axes, too,
The crowbars threatening doors that would not yield.
    And one thing further I shall ask of you,
O Venus, who o'er happy Cyprus reign
    And Memphis, free from cold Sithonian snow,
Divinest Queen, with your uplifted rod
    Just give the haughty Chloe one sharp blow!

The Classical Outlook   ROBERT J. M. LINDSAY

ERASE TAPE

(Catullus 70)

There's none that she'd prefer to me
    (She says) to marry: so,
If Jupiter himself proposed,
    Her answer would be "No."

But, when a man's consumed with love,
    His girl's fond, foolish chatter
Should not be written on a page
    But on the wind and water.

The Classical Outlook   ROBERT J. M. LINDSAY

GOOD NIGHT

Light lies like snow along the branches,
the moon sits in a nest of shimmering haze;
it's a cold chaste world, still as a photograph.

I am standing in a darkened room—lights out—
while upstairs, mounded and oblong, John,
Michael, Una, Noreen, Patrick, and Therese sleep.

The clock ticks, and the cat's turned in
about herself. Nightly hibernation
in which, while mind rests, the inner

images play leapfrog, springs loosen,
and invisible tradesmen hurry
to the mending of the slack body.

Here the passions rest: fear,
ambition, hope and desire
and loutish hostility.

I pray that the horsemen of the night
draw towards the dawn
the fears and terrors of my children.

A father's job to close to the business down,
check defenses, and lull the house to sleep.
For a last look, I stand by the window and see

the light has frozen, the moon
is a cool drink, and I
am in the photograph.

The Antigonish Review   DON LINEHAN

IMAGES & LIES

Small things remembered.
Things words seem
foolish to describe.
The snow that falls in drifts on the cottage
Inside a frozen paperweight;
The musky smell of love on the sheets
That held us from the draft each morning,
Your screams of pain as you bore my spirit,
The tiny child who clings to her mother's skirt
Who sees me as a stranger now.
When I lift her up on the carousel
To watch her circle past, I imagine
Her waving as she passes. She manages
A smile, delicate and tenuous.
I notice the paint peeling
On the face of the wooden horse.
Make of it all you can.

Wascana Review   PETER HEARNS LIOTTA

SLOWLY THE EVENING: ATHENS

Earlier it had rained.
Now on the Sacred Way,
marble—the yellowish glow
of polished bone—
is stained with sunset,
holds little pools
pink as a child's hand
cupping water.

Below, the Agora
is gathering shadow.
It slips like a presence
into this ancient space
where Socrates and Plato
walked and spoke
among the heather
and the random stones.

The sun has dipped,
is setting over Corinth.
Opposite hangs Hymettus,
her flanks replete with honey
violet with evening.
Something is waiting
in this luminous air
that fades . . . that fades . . .

One tentative silver call
and the stillness trembles;
an answer, deep as doom.
Tone upon tone,
the city reels with ringing
as all the bells troll Angelus
and time itself soars up
to blend with night.

The Classical Outlook   SARAH LITSEY

FEAST DAY

God! The tears
of the poor in procession,
their vain hopes,
the eyes, identical and frightened,
of the children and the elderly;
the famished mouths of the beggars,
the flared nostrils
of the women who sell love,
the spinsters' pout—
this struck me
yesterday, on the feast day:

this is truth;
the rest, deceit.

Chelsea　　　Ordenio Loberto
—Translated from the Italian
by Lawrence Venuti

THE ASSESSMENT

(for Tom Lucas)

Beloved student, what makes you think I can still teach?
You came to me the first time five
years ago. Then I was younger.
Now I'm nearly sixty years old.
My memory grows shorter, though enthusiasm
is none the less. I could not teach number theory
anymore, nor Greek, biology, metaphysics,
as I did in my younger times—
and all of these are in my poetry, as you know.
You have been to Vietnam and you have studied Jung.
Sometimes I feel you are ahead
in what you write. You do not need
any academic weight to improve your smooth lines.
You have met Rilke, greatest one
of the twentieth century. I can't teach you him.
I can tell you to read Roethke—
that's one thing—and some Cavafy—
not for heft and greater literacy but for soul.
And I can repeat over the two cardinal rules:
First, that poetry comes from that
part of the personality that binds two in one,
the part that loves, no matter what
the militancy of the subject matter may be.
Poetry's form always brings a temporary peace,
brings a natural form of grace.
Second, that poetry is a ballet for the ear.
Without the dance of language,
the music and rhythm, nobody believes the vision.
I've said these things to you over and over again.
Maybe in these years you can train
in the regimen of these rules,
and I'll be glad, glad again that you've come back to school.

The Georgia Review　　　　　　　　　John B. Logan

WILD MUSTARD

(for Jeff)

I walked along the river today
with a boy of eight—not my

boy but a boy like the boy
in me: scattered
by excitements, like a flock
of crows startled from a tree.

I taught him the names
of wild edible herbs
and trees and flowers, said,
"Those yellow flowers
in the orchard are wild mustard flowers."
Later, I quizzed him and he called
bay dock, and dock bay
and the wild mustard in the orchard:
"Peanut butter flowers!"

How our hunger rules.

Through the trees, in the next field,
we saw a great cat
which had got stuck in the flood
last Spring, and it now looked less
like a ravenous machine
than a huge cricket dreaming,
peaceful, in the wild
mustard.

The Ridge Review   JONATHAN LONDON

CHELSEA

I'm comfortable here, on 50 mg. of Librium,
Two hundred bucks in my pocket
And a new job just a week away.
I can walk the streets in a calm haze,
My blood pressure down to where I'm almost human,
Make countless pay-phone calls from street corners—
Buzzing, they go by in near-neon trails,
People, people like me, headed for black-bean soup,
For screams in alleyways, for the homey click
Of the front door's closing, heading home
Past all those faces you know you've seen before,
Like a rear-screen projection in an old movie,
The actors pacing a treadmill or pretending to steer,
And the same '56 Dodge weaving in the background.

It's like walking into a room
And suddenly realizing you've had sex with everyone there
At least once, watching your friends' lives
Tangling as you all grow somewhat older,
Somehow more resolute. Bookshelves grow, too,
And you notice your handwriting becoming more matter-of-fact;
It's as if all that comic smartness we glided through in youth
Were somehow desperate. And now we come to terms

With the sidewalk's coruscating glamour,
The rows of dull but neat garbage cans,
Each with its own painted number,
The poodles and patrol cars, the moon rising high,
Like aspirin, over Eighth Avenue.

I get some cigarettes on a corner,
Catch my reflection in the glass. I'm neatly tranquillized,
And strangely happy just to walk out near the traffic,
Consider the asphalt intersections where kids lean on lampposts
    and fire alarms,
Where a man is shutting the iron gate on his ochre divans,
Where the beautiful taxis whiz and honk,
Clanking over sewer covers and smashing beer cans.
And windows light, one by one, like comic-strip inspirations,
And me, here, on your street corner,
In my second-favorite neighborhood in the world,
My index finger in the hole marked "9,"
Ready for anything, finally, and finally ready.

The New Yorker   ROBERT LONG

DUST

You can see it forming on a clear day,
a rose-sulphur haze, creeping up
the sky, swelling toward us, moving
fast out of the west.

The old ones finger their beards, nod
in resignation. They know these Texas
Plains. Already the light seems diffused,
as if filtered through yellow glass;

and the air imperceptibly dims, thickens.
Behind this quiet pervasion comes wind—
wind with its needles of sand, wind with
its layers of grit, that, uninvited,

now sits with us at table. We swallow
it with food, grind our teeth on it,
wear it in our clothes. We lie down
with it all night, while it seeks

our most intimate places. It bores
through the skin; we picture it attacking
the white bones, scraping away toward
the marrow. We wake, red-eyed,

the stubborn grains, big as pebbles,
grating beneath our lids. We rustle
as we walk from room to room, our feet
kicking up small clouds.

Cedar Rock   VIRGINIA LONG

HERE IS HOW THINGS ARE

My Mother dies slowly,
like kudzu, a rose giving itself
back to the winds, petal by tattered petal.
My Mother dies begrudgingly
while summer storms rampage, hurling hailstones down
upon the garden's young snowpeas, ragging the tender pods,
ripping, uprooting huge thick oaks.
My Mother dies like a carriage candle
in the midnight rain. The guttering flame dances,
spits, sputters, leaping higher, falling away.
She lays time by, misplaces calendars and clocks.
She withdraws, wraps silence about her crooking shoulders,
laughs at empty air, giggling like a mischievous child
at an errant memory. Her unfocused eyes scream
mute questions aloud, questions I cannot field.
Why must I keep fighting now?
If you think I'm enjoying this, you're crazier
than I ever knew. Which one are you?
Sometimes the sleeping Amazon queen of yesterday wakes.
Her head rears, a cobra's hood, aching to strike.
Words froth upon her straining lips.
She shakes her head, pees like a baby
everywhere, in her wheelchair, upon the living room carpet.
I strip the bed, roll her to and fro
like a lost top, smoothing the clean sheets
underneath her, then bathe her, rub baby oil
on her swollen legs. *I hate to see the sun*
come up again somedays, she says. *Don't worry;*
everything will be all right . . . while she ruffles my hair
with unsteady fingers. *You go to bed early*
and be ready come getting-up time.
My Mother dies like a light,
as she has ever lived, slow, full, to the hilt,
hard, hard, hard.

The Sun   VIRGINIA LOVE LONG

MY FATHER'S DYING

I thought you could not die until the sun stopped
and summer's shifting air parted into light's opening doors.
I never believed you would die until I stood clutching
the steel bed railings. Fragile flesh cracked
like a dropped egg. Your straining lungs heaved,
wheezing like a lumbering combiner lurching through ripened
    wheat.
Your sunken chest, my first safe pillow,
fluttered up and down like a frightened partridge.

Your hazel eyes clouded; speech trembled upon your lips.
Eternity slipped between us. You stared up at me
like a puzzled child and then turned back.
Your eyelids quivered shut. The hiss and spit
of oxygen stung my ears. It was the hardest work
I ever have known, covering your thin shoulders
with the sheet, squeezing your fingers, fumbling,
letting your hand drop and walking away.
It is harder now, letting go.
I greet callers at the front door in your place,
accept bags of ripe tomatoes and platters of grapes.
I pick out the softest bones from table scraps
for your bewildered dog. I nail the smiles on my face,
go hide, huddle on the running board of your pick-up in the dark.
I walk down to the pond, stand chainsmoking on the dam,
looking out over the water. Tomorrow at the family graveyard
we will plant your true seed, charred chips and broken shards
of shining bones, deep in earth's womb, with carnations and spider
    mums.
Daddy, you are the first man I learned to love,
the one man closest to a god I have ever known.
Foxes bark from the silent trees.
I flip my cigarette into the reeds, giggle, marveling again
how your Scots blood, your huge highlands heart
cheats the undertakers. Somehow I knew it,
all the time: how you have finished living,
how you will never die.

The Sun   VIRGINIA LOVE LONG

MEDITATION ON A DORSAL KNIFE-WOUND

If my field of vision were wider
and I were poised to dive down
a burrow at the passing of a shadow
or freeze at the scent of meat-breath;
if I knew the safe moment to drop

Out of a tree before the loggers
touch the bark with chain;
how to buy short and sell long,
when to mumble and when to shout
how much is plenty

And how much more is lethal—
and if I bore a calm and peaceful
bubble within my breast instead
or a carbonating jet within my brain—
we might have passed each other in peace.

Buffalo Spree   GRACE LONGENEKER

HIGH-SCHOOL PHOTO

smudged
where your hair
blurs into the crisp
edge of your grin
cool cocky
precise angle
of your cigarette
a moment removed
from your lips
there is confidence
in that lean stance
a world in the grainy
texture of denim
    now I see you in bars
holding onto a beer
wavering slightly as women
move around you shadows
to whom you offer
a grin your
cigarette flaring

The Malahat Review   LOUISE LONGO

VERMONT IN AUGUST

Already my breath is incarnated in mountain air,
and stars burn like asterisks of frost.
White bones underlie the flesh of summer
as granite underpins this soil.

Yesterday I walked among ferns and lichens,
hemlocks, peeling birches, and I noticed
some leaves had turned.

Today I swam in a pond fed by a mountain stream,
and dove into icy, black water,
as though rising into the night sky,
constellations printing themselves on my brain.
I remembered home, where Spanish moss drapes
oaks, and it's months yet until blackbirds
stream in vast banners overhead.

Tomorrow I'll follow the South Fork
down the mountain.
If I leave early, I'll see a wading fisherman
whipping line in whistling arcs
to drop, gently as a whisper,
a fly between boulders.

Wascana Review   RICK LOTT

THE SAME

(for W. E. Butts)

The night your father died,
you saw the stars screwed deeper
into the sky. Weeping,
you wished cheeks weren't waterproof,
and held your head in your hands
like an offering.
You hoped he'd learn to haunt.

It was the same for me
when my father died. He collapsed
in my arms, but I couldn't
lift him to heaven.

Because people die to have the dark done
to them, and graves guarantee,
the dead can talk to each other
only through their survivors. Listen to me.

The Hudson Review   ROBERT LOUTHAN

LULL

The pond is mute under shades of green
and choked with vegetation.
Between fringe-reeds several water beetles
swim its surface in tense pantomime.
A kingfisher breaks off a dive
to rise over it in a sudden arc.
As yet a movement of clouds
is still reflected in its face . . .

And still there is no sound
except the four flat stones
which turn in my hand.

Buffalo Spree   JONATHAN F. LOWE

SUNSET AT SOUNION

I shot this sunset with my Polaroid nine, ten years ago.
Not Ansel Adams, but I walked away with that sun
in my pocket. I'm like a kid over candy:
I can't wait, and I won't let go of what's
in my hand. When it comes to time, I am
a hedonist—I want the present now.
What other camera, the best of them, can give you that?
The moment you frame the object in your mind's
parameters, disintegration sets in. You send

the exposed film out to be developed, and by the time
you get it back you're lost in the forest
of memory. The journalistic who, what, when,
where, and even why are a blur of leaves
the light can't penetrate. It's ancient history
under a film of nostalgia that plays you tricks.
But this cute little box is a trap for time.
When I catch the birdie, it stays alive, palpitating
right here in my hand. And years later, at a glance,
I can still feel its warmth.
However Joshua managed
to stop the sun in its tracks, it wasn't long
before the sun dropped out of sight. Not mine.

The Hiram Poetry Review   ROBERT LOWENSTEIN

A CLOSED DOOR ALWAYS SAYS OPEN

More tempting than sin, for all the gifts
in a four-wall box are not noxious,
a closed door always invites transgression.
Find a door in the middle of the woods,
and you think open sesame. *There*
holds more treasure than *here*.
And what are doors but sentries to outwit
for access to the secrets they harbor?
One quick move and you catch them off guard.

The books leaning their heads together
on the shelf, were they talking about you
behind your back? That man in the painting
askew on the wall, was he about to sneak
out of the frame? And the squeak you heard
as you barged in—a body shifting in a chair?
two in bed? Even the dust betrays some presence.

You freeze, intent on picking up signs,
but already the room has clammed up
and feigns sleep as still as a hole.
Whatever invested the room closed, lurks
in it open, unconcerned. For you are
no longer there, but here.

Poem   ROBERT LOWENSTEIN

THE PEONY FIELDS

At harvest time which comes in Spring,
workers cut flowers and carry them to tents
where women bunch bouquets
to suspend on ice.
Inside the tent

laughter and mosquitoes
play with boredom and sweat
as each flower lines up
to be cut.

Later, their clear sap
dries to white flakes,
dissolves in water,
can be condensed and baked
into quivering Peony cakes.
So Happy Birthday, Happy Scent,
Happy Funeral, Lent, Christmas, Easter—
oh hell, Happy St. Valentine's Day Peony Massacre.

Eight crew members, we walked the fields,
picked the flowers, piled them on wagons,
thousands of colors, forever unmentionable.
Inside the tent, from Mission, Texas,
women,
tubs of ice,
the blooming Peonies
freshly cut.

The Georgia Review   TOM LUCAS

CLEARING MAYBE

A canary, first you've seen
out of a cage, leaves a branch
and dips over your head
before flying over a field
of corn, wondering why the ears
can't lift into the sky.
A book slides off your lap.
Wind turns pages the way
a calendar turns after 40.

Grass cut this morning makes
it easier to find something shiny
believed lost. Your hand climbs
a hill of trees along Route 5,
muffler of cars
going to Rochester and Buffalo.
Summer is gone quick as a minnow;
leaves start rounding up autumn.

Radio says clear tonight.
You think of stars, not sure if they
are periods of dark sentences
signalling a skyful of beginnings.

Four Quarters   SISTER MARY LUCINA

CONQUERING THE NIGHT JASMINE

Beneath the dining-room window
where everyone knows it should never
be grown, the night jasmine sends up
its devilish fragrance, sweet
as anything God imagined—
but with that tell-tale underscent
of abandon, of clove.

I must eat before eight each evening
before it begins to exhale through the screen,
making the dinner inedible;
peas, lamb and rice all honeyed alike.

Plain as a weedy potato vine,
it looks innocent all day,
its silence a dare
to accuse or uproot it.

I wouldn't. I know temptation
when I see it, and how to pass such tests.

Cestrum nocturnum, Cestrum nocturnum
I chant, and by nine it invades
the whole house, so all the air's sugary,
vulgar.

When I can bring
great panicles of the flowers in
as if they were fall hydrangeas, the tiny blooms
loose in Aunt Ellen's cranberry vase,
it will be victory.

I long for the hot summer night
I can keep my heart quiet
without the aid of marigolds.

The Georgia Review   SUSAN LUDVIGSON

SALAMANDER, SEVERED IN SPRING PLOWING

Salamander, speak!
The plow's blade has torn your hind legs
from your lungs (or are they gills?).
But the legend persists:
I cannot free you unless you speak.

So like a woman's body, your orange flesh
splayed out upon the half-turned loam.
Your mouth opens, closes, clutches
on the emptiness of air. Is it breath you seek,
or are you speaking now, so soft
I cannot hear!

The story states
that salamanders know the comings
and the goings in the earth. In that brain
resides the wisdom of white grubs
curled to sleep below the frostline.
Filed as in some great library,
you hold the organizational genius
of the ant, the impertinence of mushrooms.

Salamander, speak! I cannot let you go
until I know just what it is
you have to tell me. Is it true,
smooth perfect body, we have no choice
but death, imperfect lightless silence?
Is that the message coded
on your all-too-human lips?

The Massachusetts Review   DAVID LYON

I NEVER LOOKED FOR GLORY

I never looked for glory,
nor to leave my song
in the memory of mankind.
I love the subtle worlds,
almost weightless and genteel,
like soap bubbles.
I like to see them painted
in sunlight and scarlet, soar
under the blue sky, then
suddenly quiver and break.

Poetry Now   ANTONIO MACHADO
                    —*Translated from the Spanish*
                    by Willis Barnstone

TINTORETTO TO HIS APPRENTICE

Titian? that old hypocrite. You know
he was my teacher once, always lecturing me
on the virtues of earth colors—but I knew
what he meant. Finally he kicked me out
of the workshop; that dock is where
I went to ditch those touched-up sketches
he made me do. I stood there gloating
till they all sank. If those fat-head merchants
could see my smart ships, my Adriatic, they'd
forget his doges, his pious redeemers. Do you
see those masts as bare lines? and lower—
that yellow bird turning everything

below it blue. Good lad! Remember the light
in Milan: my Venice will emerge golder than that.
When my paintings are shown, Titian will see
that I can paint his landscape as pure color.
By now, he must be pondering purple; to him,
the mountains must seem like wreaths
and mourning robes. One of the framers
visited his studio yesterday, and there,
on his worktable, stood a giant candelabra.
And what was stuck in its stem-holders,
instead of candles, I mean?
nine brushes, stiff with black paint.

The Threepenny Review   GINNY MACKENZIE

JUST BORN

I think of myself just born
    blood and filth on my mouth
    air scorching my lungs
and my cry quivering in the air
    uttered not for nurses or doctors
    through the great spaces of the sky

and even up to God
    my fierce cry
    demanding an explanation
why this rape from the infinite
    into this question box of a world
why this imprisonment in time and space
    and in this animal body
    made for limitation and suffering

to be nothing and then suddenly something
to hardly feel and then to be in pain
to be in an envelope of flesh
    and then to be open to sound light and air
    to be pricked by numberless stimuli
to be all alone and then to be the center of touch
    circled by voices and eyes

much later in my crib
    I reached out to catch the birds
    that flew above the trees
when I opened my hands
    they were empty
I saw only my empty hands
    those symbols of captivity
as I grow shall I capture
    and retain

The Antigonish Review   R. J. MACSWEEN

THE HOUR BEFORE DAWN

It was the hour before dawn. I awoke.
The street lamp stared lamely at my window
and a world was quiet, bewildered
as though it were afraid it would be lost
among thoughts. I waited for a sound,
a rain to fall and tear this silence
between today and tomorrow.
On a distant tree a light breeze combed
the leaves of darkness without a whisper,
and through the window peered my love and fear
and dreams that were mere dummies to the hour.
Unknowing, I bring my palms together.
I remember the one I loved once,
but she seemed to have another face.
My father, sad-faced father! How very far you are
from this empty room filled only with myself!
Without a sound, the dark tree out there
struggles with its death in my life.
The silent world floats beside me;
tomorrow maybe I'll hear my father is dead,
but he might bear the face of my son.
This is the hour when there is
no distance between the two of them. The hour
of awakening, when my speechless voice
echoes only from my father to my son,
coming to rest on the lamp post like a weary nightbird.

The Hudson Review   JAYANTA MAHAPATRA

ISLANDS

If loves are islands
finger-tipping from below,
beckoning as if to say the palm trees
on this atoll are better,
the solitude deeper and richer with meaning
here with Circe;
if loves are strung out like beads
against a blue sky, each a different size,
marked sterling, will not tarnish;
if loves, like islands, can be washed by tides,
or occasionally, like Surtsey
erupt from the sea floor, or like Atlantis
disappear as if they'd never been;
if you can count islands you have known
throughout your life
like rosaries, saying a prayer for each one;
if loves are islands you swim toward
from the sinking ship upended in wet fog;
if these things hold, what then is the sea?

You may say hate, that separates you from your island
which you reach, gasping, to lie in hot sun,
but I say the sea is love.

Buffalo Spree   JEANNETTE MAINO

PLAYERS

The yellow ball just clears the net, skids low.
Your racket reaches, flicks, and floats it back.

We hit this poem together and watch it shuttle,
Weave against the green of someone else's youth,

The emerald pathos of a dozen different parks.
Back and forth, we build a rhythm, increase the pace,

Then break. With lobs, then steady strokes again
We stretch our rallies past the average-player five.

We make each other run, lunge to get what is past us,
Play off the impossible. We do anything to outwit

The average, this space that is nothing without us.
Sometimes I take advantage, hit out hard, but you

Still strain for the save, as if it were something rare,
Important as marriage. So the ball leaves yellow lines.

Once, near the ocean, time did a radiant slo-mo.
You raced with your racket extended and the ball towered

To a yellow spot in a sky suddenly storm-green;
It hung while you centered in your white dress: white,

Yellow, storm-green, white, the perfect centering.
Too excited, I watched my overhead splash the net.

Then as now, we come together at the net, our faces glad
With sweat, each telling what the other missed, or didn't.

Ploughshares   PETER MAKUCK

IN MY 57TH YEAR

This is the year my mother lay dying,
knocked down by tiny strokes she claimed
never once hit her, though when she lay
crib-like where they laid her there she wept
for shame to be confined so near her death.
This is the year the cancer inside my father's
groin began its growth to knock him down,
strong as he was beside his stricken wife.
This is the year I grew, ignorant of politics,
specious with law, careless of poetry,
English anti-semitic poets, Hebrew myth.

There were no graves. The prairie rolled on
as if it were the sea. Today my children make
their way alone across those waves.
Do lines between us end as sharply
as lines our artists draw upon the plains?
I cry out. They keep their eye upon
their politics, their myths,
careful of lives as I was careless.

What shall I say? It is too late to tell again
tales we never knew. The legends of ourselves
spill into silence. All we never said, father
to daughter, son to unmanned man, we cannot say
to count the years.
                    I no longer know time or age
thinking of parents, their time, their grave of names.
Telling the time, fiction consumes me.

Canadian Forum   ELI MANDEL

IN CLOSING

There being little to add about autumn,
I shall keep my remarks
brief. May we dispense immediately
with the easy assumptions,
those cozy cliches I know
you want to hear: that the season's
bare limbs are *reaching*,
that each fallen leaf
signals a promise
you'd like me to call *unspoken*?
Permit me to suggest instead
that those branches are wedged
in blankness, and every dead
leaf is fisted around
its own appalling emptiness.
And further (please bear with me),
you have no choice but to surrender
to that emptiness in yourself.
I see how quickly you have shifted
your gaze from your folded hands
to the window, your eyes
desperate for some sign
of rescue. A cardinal, darting
across the cobalt, would do. But
believe me, no such signs
exist: only the shocks of corn
waving their raw banners, the saw-
toothed maple leaves spiraling
through arrows of cold light.
In the interest of time, let's
be blunt: everything is falling.

I detect the twitch of a smile
on your face; you've glimpsed
a clot of rising smoke, or a pod
lifting on a gust, but I assure you,
what appears to be rising is simply
drifting, preparing for its final
descent. What you'd give to have me
admit that, even as you watch
the brittle refuse of this lost
season scrape across the pavement, we
are being rescued, and because the defeat
in the gesture of your upturned palms
touches me, I will confess:
if I close my eyes to the scattering
leaves, even I can imagine
it is the sound of everyone
I ever loved applauding.

The Seneca Review   KATHY MANGAN

LET US SING

Let us sing, simple and plain,
for everything homey, loved and held dear.
For old beggars who curse the cold
and for mothers who bless the heat of the fire.

For poor brides who light candles
in front of blind mirrors
and look for the faces
of men who have spurned their love.

For fortune tellers who speak in riddles
and charm the last coins
from widows who curse the world
and sneak out of back doors.

For servant girls who work bitterly hard
and hide the best bit of food
for the soldiers they sneak in at night
so that the gentle folk will not know.

Let us sing, simple and plain,
for everything homey, loved and dear.
For poor mothers who curse the cold
and for beggars who bless the heat of the fire.

For girls, who in the summer place
their bastard children at a stranger's door,
and shake in fear of the police
who can clap them into jail.

For organ grinders who scrape out music
on Fridays in the courtyards of the poor.
For thieves who have shown their hand
and scurry for freedom over roofs.

For rag pickers who scratch in the rubbish,
believing they'll find a treasure.
For the poets who have sought the stars
and have gone insane.

Let us sing, simple and plain,
for everything homey, loved and held dear.
For old folks who curse the cold
and for children who bless the heat of the fire.

Visions   ITZIK MANGER
*—Translated from the Yiddish
by Harold Black*

DAYS

Sensible days are rare. Prepared
all around a light blue as a see-through
palace. Wide open. Shoppers
arrive and depart. Cart
upon cart of crimson fruit. And pigeons
from hither to yon.
The landlord's elated. The height of the season
has come. Across the window trees in the breeze
a bold green. A powerful sun
stuns mountains and town. At its ease
the river flows to the sea. One
and all respond. Open
wide is the world. And pigeons
from hither to yon.

Even the evening is sensible. Sensible
the conciliatory steps.
A handful of gilded days. The stones in the wall
are prepared to accept
their human potential.
The skies redden and cypresses darken, vertical,
and the joy within sorrow parades
at the gates and halts for the quizzical.
And the mountains are no farther off, one reasons,
in the falling shadows. And pigeons
from hither to yon.

Poetry Now   YEKHI'EL MAR
*—Translated from the Hebrew
by Bernhard Frank*

A SUNDAY WALK

Where streets are like land spits
in a large faint meadow,
I walked through a new-built neighborhood

to see if it could take as sharp a measure
as those I cut through day by day.

Match-like trees bordering its distances,
the grass is still low—
no prairie for an old hero's dreams,
nor for a spinster poet's fainting bees.
Thin hedges restrain their tangled webs.
Dogs are few. Young passers-by
glance towards my shyness or away.

With each mail box a different sculpting
in iron, bronze, enameled paint—
angled and curved, varied and clean, modestly rich,
the houses root in the casual innocence
of profit and enterprise and ease.

Sou'wester   MORDECAI MARCUS

MEMORIES

All that year since November, it was
  blue with snow. We left by sleigh.
My grandfather didn't hunt. I wore
  a fur hat, fur-lined boots.
Did not dream. Did not write. I was happy.
The shadows flickered, the wind ran.
  The world was without limits.

That year I learned to know God,
  his beauty, his strength.
In the barns where the animals kept warm
  we talked for hours under gray tobacco smoke.

Very black coffee. Bacon sweetly burnt,
Sleep. The distant year, time fled.
I open the window. It snows. I embrace my wife.
  My child stirs.

Visions   YVES MARTIN
                                      —*Translated from the French*
                                                by Larry Couch

THE SUNDAY DRUNK

He sidewinds down the street,
calling his arms and legs back.
It's buck-and-wing into the parking meter,
then down to crack his old bone-head on the cement.
Crisp passersby try to mop him up—
but he'll have none of their gauzy good wishes. No,
he'll lie right there as long as they don't
want him to, pooling underfoot,

so that when he finally shakes them loose
their thin soles will go off printing red arrows
in his name. And with that many spare feet,
surely he can manage to rise and cakewalk home
in all directions at once: not exactly forward,
not exactly side or back, but something like
a broken box-step
where he wants to go.

Poetry   SUZANNE MATSON

INVERSE PROPORTIONS

Proverbs, aphorisms, epigrams
are designed to contain worlds
in solution: little goblets for
sampling whole seas and raging climates.

In this way would it not be good
to have one's life center upon something
private and small, such as
keys, names, sleeping tablets?

You could carry this secret
everywhere and fondle it like a lucky piece,
cool and heavy in the fingers . . .
perhaps like a coin minted in antiquity
by some old Emperor blurred by
the rub of dead thumbs for centuries,
engraved with words nobody alive
can read. Here would be salvation
and all the wisdom you'd ever need.

Poetry   JACK MATTHEWS

THE PSYCHOPATHOLOGY OF EVERYDAY LIFE

Just as we were amazed to learn
that the skin itself is an organ—
I'd thought it a flexible sack,
always exact—we're stunned
to think the skimpiest mental
event, even forgetting, has meaning.
If one thinks of the sky as scenery,
like photographs of food, one stills it
by that wish and appetite,
but the placid expanse that results
is an illusion. The air is restless
everywhere inside our atmosphere,
but the higher and thinner it gets
the less it has to push around
(how else can we see air?) but itself.

It seems that the mind, too,
is like that sky, not shiftless;
and come to think of it, the body
is no slouch at constant commerce,
bicker and haggle, provide and deny.
When we tire of work we should think
how the mind and body relentlessly
work for our living, though since
their labors end in death, we greet
their ceaseless fealty with mixed emotions.
Of course the mind must pay attention
to itself, vast sky in the small skull.
In this we like to think we are alone—
evolutionary pride: it's lonely
at the top, self-consciousness. We forget
that the trout isn't beautiful and stupid
but a system of urges that works
even when the trout's small brain is somewhere
else, watching its shadow on the streambed,
maybe, daydreaming of food.
Even when we think we're not,
we're paying attention to everything;
this may be the origin of prayer
(and if we listen to ourselves,
how much in our prayers is well-dressed
complaint, how we are loneliest Sundays
though whatever we do, say, or forget
is prayer and daily bread):
Doesn't everything mean something?
O God who composed this dense
text, our only beloved planet
(at this point the supplicants look upward),
why have You larded it against our hope
with allusions to itself and how
can it bear the weight of such
self-reference and such self-ignorance?

Antaeus   WILLIAM MATTHEWS

LEAVING OREGON

Trees by the Starlite Cafe
drip dew, a haze sticks
to the chortling Greyhound.
We stretch our legs and smoke.

In the rear, the dancer sleeps,
huddled under her sweater,
her mouth fallen open, as if
in speech, entering Idaho.

New Letters   KERRY PAUL MAY

ON BURNETT AVENUE

On Burnett Avenue in poor Kentucky where I lived
as a child, the declivity in our sidewalk never
got fixed. Nobody complained, not that anybody
forgot about it, but repairs or improvements seemed
without a function. Tall maple trees arose above
the pavements, and familiar bricks supporting gutters
invented moss gardens and little chirps of grass
that children could dip bare feet in on hot days.
There was a sweet deterioration that took over all
our land, against the suave contractors and their
villainous alterations. In snow, the pot-holes
held crystal; and in summer rains the water accumu-
lated, reflecting change, cloudy skies and branches
of sun, and gave differences to the otherwise not very
gorgeous terrain. Life was enjoyed, slightly crazy,
insolvent, and we didn't imagine it ever would be tamed.

The Hudson Review   JANE MAYHALL

IN THE GARMENT DISTRICT

Nothing like 10 in the morning
for making love—cats glaring
from the table opposite, the dog
watching gloomily from the rug;

and after, opening cans
of their food, you in the shower
singing while elevators ring up
through the sidewalk, carrying
their racks of dresses, the noises
of ordinary business:
unloading, loading.

Later, I stand at the window
watching a man in an office
through the arc of gold letters
that spells HESS REAL ESTATE.
He goes through his daily routine—
removes his brown jacket,
places it in a gray file drawer,
rolls up his sleeves.

And then, in the distinct light,
he stares down at the traffic.

He might, in his white shirt,
be wondering how to fill the day,
but he's perfectly still. He might,
framed in the arched window, be part
of the Hopper painting, precise,
painful, not quite come to life—

the empty office, file drawers,
a bald man with nothing to do
staring inward in the hard light . . .

And I know this memory of 20th Street
will come back often in the years
after we leave the city: bright sun
flooding the morning loft, you and I
loving, our animals arranged around us,
industry clanging on the sidewalk,
and across the street, a middle-aged man,
motionless, not quite anonymous.

Ploughshares   GAIL MAZUR

JEWELWEED

We were talking about sex, taking
the dirt road to town, walking
slowly in the hot afternoon.

I hardly saw the fields
shimmering in the heat, the goldenrod's
itchy impressionist glow,

the pale Touch-me-not,
or jewelweed, blooming in shade,
so skewed was my vision,

so interior. That day we agreed
never to touch each other,
passing the warm brown beds of pine

needles, the tiny graveyard. My face,
your face, reddened in August's ardent
flush; our hands clung to their pockets.

That conversation seemed harmless—
strange, that I still need
to put it this way . . .

Anyway, it must have been too far
to town. We turned back at a stone
marker to join our friends swimming

in a black pond deep in our past.
Now I am in the future where nothing
has happened, nothing happens.

What were we walking toward
that prickly summer day,
both of us suddenly guarded,

uneasy strangers, or greenhorns,
or children transported unprepared
to a heartless institution?

The Hudson Review   GAIL MAZUR

YESTERDAY'S CHILDREN

Dear, there are no rivers to divert
to clean the stables of our memory.
The horses have grown comfortable,
too old for stud, too tame to bolt.
Even mind's rush through winter to rebirth
is just as much a memory as a hope:
A yearning for those first green blades
of grass cutting through snow,
or the white blossoms of the apple orchard
wed to a first bouquet of pussywillow
I'll cut and bring to you—
not out of sentiment but to enchant
the eager children still within us.

We've mastered an endurance in their death,
as, in that winter, snow reached to
our second floor and, in the orchard,
drifts so buried trees
their tops seemed foreign bushes,
and we spent two long days digging out.
At first, we noted an occasional horse
chancing those drifts,
then a spinning glow of snowploughs,
and then perceived, like thaw,
a building flow of traffic.

Seeing these soft, dark, billowy clouds
of late summer now almost signal snow,
while fleeing flocks of geese,
like Stymphalian birds, head south,
let's cling to the survival,
throwing caution to our mood
or what those others might call love,
when you arrange the willows in a vase
and set the vase beside our window.
We know it as a labor sweet as sap
and as beyond us as
the skies or this onrushing winter.

The Literary Review   JEROME MAZZARO

STARSHIP

in this exploded diagram of my heart, the large
chambers, home of my love for you, are seen to enclose
constellations, memories of loves long gone, vague
designs hovering above the immense expanse of now.

watch as I try to bring one of these loosely-tied
bundles of light closer: a scene may form, hands & lips,
& stroke us both freshly as at first—but no, in coming
closer the stars move apart, identities dissolve. How

massive the past is, & the unknown! Everywhere faces gleam,
in every shadow, but recede or reveal other faces below,
beyond, beneath them.
     I am voyaging out, minute from many
perspectives, but where I am, a light, and drawn to light.

And here you are, vast as the sky, object of desire, source
of light, yet still surrounded & pierced through with night.

The Virginia Quarterly Review   DAVID MCALEAVEY

SECOND MARRIAGE

The sense of fifteen years of almost
anything shared is what she sometimes misses
with him, even the awful, silent suppers,
when, with everything already said,
she had longed for words, all over again.
In bed at night, his chest is not
the chest she wept on, learning,
where breast-hair inscribed her cheek,
of onset and ceremony, those whole and open places
that one may fully occupy, like the future.

How happy, even sadly, to have been
young together, to have held off loneliness
with the shiny locket of *we,* as if
whatever could not be found, must, nonetheless,
turn up inside that circle.
Now, neither memory nor need sustains.
She sees the land take shape beneath her,
as birds must, on the first migration,
trusting their bodies as they veer away.
This second love is possible, and chosen.

She wants him. Every broken edge of her
abuts the world, of which he is a portion.

New England Review & Bread Loaf Quarterly   LINDA MCCARRISTON

SONG: A CHANT FOR MICHAEL S. HARPER

What is most difficult
is to believe:

I say what is most difficult
is to believe:

When the sun
rises in the low, hard
grass

What is most difficult
is to believe:

When moon
comes night-certain
to the lake

What is most difficult
is to believe:

That Black children
gather a dream in their arms
and set that dream like a voice in their heads;
a vision so perfect, so inviolable,
a man might wade
through centuries with an undeniable reverence, a love:

What is most difficult
is to believe:

And son and daughter
once were son and daughter,
are son and daughter:

What is most difficult
is to believe:

And Black people
shall see sun
forever, the world inexhaustible,
the possibilities
infinite, like a Joshua tree or jazz:

What is most difficult
is to believe, I say:

What is most difficult
is to believe:

And believe we did,
as the world urged us onward
to shine, shout, our music the only truth
in this dead, forgotten city.

Black American Literature Forum   KENNETH A. McCLANE

FLOOD

The red line on the bridge-stilt goes,
and then it's true: flood, and the lights gone.
Is the rain crazy? Is your house a fish?
Please, you dream, leave the floor alone!
Have you a boat in your attic window?
When the last ditch fails, and the sand-walls,
there's always something to float on—roof,
table, the bottom drawer of the bureau.
All your flashlight will do is pick out the lumps
in the water, so leave it. It's everyone for himself,
but bring a rope and a pot to bang on or bell.
One daybreak the rain will stop; you'll see

rescue poking around in the distance.
The sky will smell like fresh paint in a church.
Then you'll hear the deep hum in the flood
as it moves in the old direction of the river,
and see all that isn't what it stood for.
Your sudden rage a softness huge as water
should have no mind will go numb
among the dead worms in the basement,
the mud fine as the membrane on an entrail.
Save what you can of the memory of fire.

The Nantucket Review   MARK MCCLOSKEY

OUR INHERITANCE

Saturdays we come to the old house
and walk the fields, or we sit
and swing under the oaks
and listen to the rush of leaves.
Later, we might row out on the pond
and listen to the slap of waves
against the hull of our boat.
When we lean over the side,
our reflections look pale
and unfamiliar, like ghosts
rising from the graveyard below us,
flooded for a hundred years.
Down there, sunlight goes through us
and slips into something else:
a fish or a white headstone,
a glass house with wide,
green verandas. A few paths
wind away toward forgotten crops
and forgotten people,
the wealth of sun-ripened days
grown mossy and rotten
under this parasol of green water.
Hour after hour we float
above it all like the fair sky
and reach down to match
our cool hands.

Southern Poetry Review   KEITH MCCLURE

WINTER AS REVELATION

I have always been angered
by winter's onset,
fall crippled,
giving up to lesser forces
a colorful

yet perennial defeat.
But today, at the winter solstice
fulcrum point in time
when light gains leverage
over darkness,
I see trees undressing
lean and vulnerable,
like lovers exposing themselves
to each other
for the first time.
I see branches assuming
an open upward pose,
like celebrants raising
arms in ritual awe.
I see forests
giving way to horizons,
lush overgrowth to
dark-boned silhouettes.
The essential unmasked
like some old blunt truth
rediscovered,
my vision widened
by the simple tilting of the earth.

Poem   MICHAEL MCCONNELL

VISITATION

(for Robert E. McCullough, 1908-1973)

On the beach, November, cold and alone, I lay there
looking up. I sensed you there and pulled to bring you
into focus. I started to cry and I could not cry. My
face was scrunched up like a baby's. It was trapped
inside me—a belt around my chest, a hand at my throat.
I called to you for help and you were there, above me
in the air, as you had looked at maybe 42, your eyes dark
and glistening. I told you that I had been the way I was
with you: recalcitrant, bristling, itching for a brawl
because I was afraid of you, afraid of becoming you—
a shy countryboy who crumbled cornbread in his buttermilk,
who knew nothing but work from Day One, whose only vices
were being too honest, too generous for your own good.
I could breathe now, sighing, and my eyes were open.
I said I understood, now, where it came from, the fear,
and that I accepted you, now, and wanted you to be with me.
That we never talked, is done with—no guilt on either side.
I have not been able to accept what *I* am, yet, and where
I came from. I want your help. I need you.
I held out my arms to you and you moved down
toward me steadily, and I could see your eyes as
you approached, fixed on mine—the reflections of me

lying there, confused, snotty-nosed, helpless, and you
merged with me in a nimbus of light, and I wrapped my
arms around you as you came to me and I sobbed, deep and
long, and thanked you for letting me let you in, at last.

Studia Mystica   KEN MCCULLOUGH

AGAINST THE ODDS

(After the TV series, "The Long Search.")

Wing above wing above wing,
Rainbow-tipped and burning,
The angels of Roumania
(As the Orthodox churches show)
Stoop to receive the souls
Of those released by death
From Industrial Communism.

In Bucharest, CITY OF JOY,
There is still baptism,
And out in the country among
Sheep and plough-horses
The people are faithful, the icons
Of Virgin and Saint saluted
Devoutly, and the bishop
Pacing through old villages,
Black-robed, black-mitred, black-bearded,
Is sure of their "Risen indeed!"
In response to his "Christ is risen!"
(In the Greek of St. Mark's Gospel,
Not Marx's.)

                        Bucharest's where
The wheat will be sifted. There
The tall dividing walls
Are going up, the tractors
Are fanning out from the City's
Modern assembly-lines
Into the traditional fields
Of Moldavia, blitzkrieging
The cows, the daisies, the serious
Human faces, capable
Of real sorrow, real joy; not chic
As in a TV commercial,
Or, alternatively, brutal,
Dedicated to celebrating
The Gross National Product
Or the success of a Five-Year Plan.

What can one on the sidelines do?
What can one do? I pray
That the Divine Mercy may forgive

The propagandists of Progress,
The technologists, the bureaucrats—
And I lay
My sagging American dollars
On the serious human faces.

Theology Today   HAROLD G. McCURDY

FLOOD FISHING

Upriver, the hens keep tumbling in
like lemmings. Fences flooded
by spring rains set them free to peck
worms washed up and sliding
to the river, luring the hens to banks
that crumble like frost.

All night down by the river you can see
white hens float by like chunks of ice.
All night you could cast and cast
and never get a bite. Crappie and bass
are feasting deep on the runoff of worms.
Like love, the only way is to feed them

what they want, dangling your line
along the bottom, the night fog coiling
over the river as if searching for survivors.
The woods are still on such a night.
But sometimes an alligator gar, thick as an arm,
reaches up and strikes, the white hen

melting from the river before your eyes,
the gar's broad tail splashing
as if the hen were still alive,
flapping to rise up on its wings
and fly, the dark trees on both banks
listening, the thin fog moving on.

Southern Poetry Review   WALTER McDONALD

POPPIES

(for Dana Gerhardt and Steve Hagel, and for Patti)

I can't find a book to help me out of where I am.
I remember the day we drove out to the fields,
Or rather the day I drove out with our friends.
You had to work, but you were with us just the same.
It was still an age of pet names and horizons.
I had been reading *The Mysterious Stranger* by Mark Twain,
And I climbed each hill hoping to meet him.

Nothing could have been more strange—
The California desert adazzle with poppies.

Drinking beer we thought of lions, tin, and straw.
We felt a little ashamed for thinking of them
For we were not in school any longer.
We were fond of reminding ourselves of what was real,
Then we'd run like hell for a movie or a book.
We didn't fight it when on a nearby hill we saw
A girl like you dancing in her ruby slippers.
Late in the day we split up and I climbed
Until voices called me back. Running,

I was Alice pursuing the white rabbit.
When I put my foot in a hole and tumbled down,
I was Jack with an empty pail of water.
Waiting for the pain to let up I imagined
"Around the World in 80 Days,"
My ankle soaring as crowds cheered.
Oh, yes, there were moments of delight,
Stories I felt a sure part of,
Days in which you and I were perfect.

The Hudson Review   ROBERT MCDOWELL

THE HERON

I've come to this place often enough
that I notice if a branch has fallen by the path
arching a sapling over.
I build my fire and walk a ways down the beach,
wander back to warm my hands
and cook supper over the coals. It's dusk.
A great blue heron lands offshore
on a patch of seaweed where it will fish.
Alert, poised, taut as a bow, leaning a little,
it strikes into the water with its sharp beak
then swallows, shaking its head, neck and wingfeathers
clear on down to its tail.
Life goes on. I think of you all the time.
It's not easy, living at a distance—
watching the days turn and turn, desire so close
to the surface you think you're going to break
open, you think you're going to burst.
When I bury the coals, the heron
is still there, fishing, barely a silhouette.
I pass the sapling in the dark (the grace
of it bending!) given over to a world
of things happening freely and without force.

Kayak   MARY ANN MCFADDEN

FACTS

(for my father)

In your orange flight suit, you approached the Renault
we knew might stall after a hard winter freeze.
With your pilot's hand, you turned the engine.
When it caught, I ran down the walkway you had shoveled.

Cinderella lunch-box under my arm, I climbed
in the frozen capsule, and waited for you
to clear morning like the path through snow:
hot water on the windshield. Ten below.

We skidded past our milkman, late with deliveries.
The paperboy's bright hand catapulted good-bye.
In your Scottish complexion, I recognized mine—
pink, freckled. Its color dissolved

in the heater's breath. That morning, the scarf
at your neck wound a jet stream like Lindbergh's in Paris,
but the brim of your cap was embroidered with oak leaves,
and stitched on the back, the words, *Tonkin Gulf.*

When we reached the schoolyard, I told you to take
care, my habit in leave-taking, as if care
were portable or compact like a parachute.
Your car veered toward the airfield and disappeared.

Those facts I have no use for; twenty years
I dream your death-plane back, down the foggy night
over the carrier, to the landing deck and hookmen's wire.
You kill the engine. Open the cockpit,

your hand raises a sign of hello. I keep this picture
for every mission you flew. You are always climbing out
of your plane, its wing flaps down, cool, hangar-bound,
to show me a way, if not around, then through.

Ploughshares   GARDNER MCFALL

PALOUSE HISTORY

The history of wheatfields
is not easily written.
Mostly it's wind
and the movements of dust,
shiftings of snow.
From below the surface
rocks and stones
keep edging up
as if they had
something to mutter to the sun.
Local history
comes and goes

in the stubble.
Like old men and women,
each crop thinks
it has something new to tell.
Here and there a shotgun shell,
a tuft of feathers,
a coyote's turd,
a beer can
offer their
temporary testimony.
One of the stones
may be an arrowhead.
On the rocky cilia
broken trucks and plows,
weathered combines
rust peacefully.
Board by board, roofs first,
old barns and houses collapse.
The wheatfields
write a quiet book,
only the cries of hawks and mice
for punctuation.
Yet at their vulnerable edges
thistle and ryegrass
wait.

Poetry Northwest   RON MCFARLAND

BUSTER KEATON

Into the frenzy of falling bodies
and chaos of pastry, apollonian
and sober even as an infant,
he came, just as decades later
he would calmly step into a frame
and never leave. In the curious
oracle of his face, distant and mute
and abstracted perfect as statuary,
the lesson of his life could be seen:
Patience. Be humble. Believe in grace
and miracles of our own foolish making.
Words are mostly waste. Laughter,
like love, is a rigorous discipline.
Think slow. Act fast. Persevere.
After the sacred grove of Hollywood
has babbled, flushed and scattered,
his image quietly endures, surviving
even when the small boat of his career
launches bottomward sudden as an anchor,
his body stubborn as a buoy or pile
fixed on the horizon, until he sinks
(soon to return, grave-faced) beneath

his flat hat floating on the water.
Or angled over some final tombstone:
the god of light, poetry and movies
still laughs at that one, Buster.

The Hollins Critic   MICHAEL McFEE

THE OKRA FLOWER

I stood in a ripe twilight
meaning to think about the mountains,
their brilliant hem all around,

but thought instead, I do not want
to die here, away from home, away
from her as she goes to the garden
to gather in this long light,
as she breathes the tang of tomatoes
and feels her forearms prickle
when she stretches to cut the okra.

I remembered how the okra flower
would be folded for the night,
how it held in itself the colors
of her face better than any picture,
the moon of her skin,
the rich purse of her lips.

I thought, when I get home again
I will stand at the kitchen window
and watch her stitch up the beans,
and a kind of healing will begin,
until the days ripen like a row
of vegetables on the bright sill,

until I can walk in the garden
on a late September afternoon
and look deep into the okra flower
without smell, without a freckle,
and not think of her, not her.

The Georgia Review   MICHAEL McFEE

TWO FIGURES, STILL LIFE

*(". . . there may be some secret communion, some whispering in the dark
between Daimon and Sweetheart."—Yeats)*

This is Longwood Road in Roland Park.
These houses turned the century and grew up together,
and went to sleep at last in the dark

neighborhood of oaks and elms and lindens. They never
make a scene, so why should I. But I miss
you, and you're not here, and the weather
is bad. Don't you have a poem for me? "This
poem," you whisper. But it's so sleepy and dull. Wake
us up and let me see your eye's blue iris.
Now will you give me your hand and let me take
you to this world we never made? When we lie
down in its dark light you and I will make
the green go very slowly today
to sleep once more. As I watch your hair,
you turn and seem to look so far away.
Already are you thinking of me tomorrow? Outside, somewhere
in Michigan where you are now, this poem is there.

Shenandoah   JEROME MCGANN

THERE IS AN ART

There is an art
to passive living:
the hours slip by
without a strain,

and in the mind
a silent voice
composes, softly,
drifting songs
of memory;

and every one
drifts by again,
revised, and made
a better thing,
until the last drifts by,
and then,
drifts by no more;

how often
in a single day
these drifters pass,
and with them pass
the hours,

until the ashtray
holds no more,
and you get up
to empty it.

The Antigonish Review   MELLO MCINTYRE

THE SACRING BELL

(for Michael P. Barrett)

The sound interrupts a thought
which goes slipping away: one
never knows whether to humbly bow
the head, or to lift it higher.
The ringing again! it conjures
a poem from the masks which hide
in the reds, greens and blues
of stained glass, masks lost
in the ritual of slender threads
of colored hope which spray grace
on the marble altar and raised
chalice of gold and blood.

Only you could bring me to
these doors now. Every May
you gather us together; here
is as good a place as any.
We kneel, cross ourselves

and remember more than dusty words.
We recall the voices and times,
your smells, your pall malls,
and the hacking cough which stole
our attention, bringing us, even
then, together, asking a blessing.

Harpoon   LOUIS MCKEE

BRAHMS ON THE WOODPILE

It is safer for me to listen
To Brahms while I am pulling
Weeds away from the pepper plants
Than to listen to him on a summer
Evening in a concert shed, my hands
Losing vigor with nothing to do.
Should I just sit there in row J
While the "Quartet in A Major"
Riots through me with no place to go?
There are laws against what I might do
When I sit with the music unadvanced
And screaming beneath my finger nails,
But there is a woodpile near my garden
From which a violin player sends Brahms
Through my hands against the dandelions,
The mosquitoes, and the eggplant
Whose purple is deep as my heart.

Cedar Rock   LUCIE MCKEE

WOODPECKER

No matter that your color, species, size
Remain a mystery to me, old friend.
The moment that I hear you tap and catch
Your shadow in the shadows of this pine,
Your presence heartens me and we begin
Again our little ceremonial,
Our quiet chat by August's fireside.
Right here, outside our cabin door, I share
With you the secrets of the year, and when
The other voices call, and I must leave
My boulder rocking chair, I hear you say,
In your non-singing way, endure, endure.

Studia Mysica   CARMELITA McKEEVER

QUILT

I'm on to you now, Grandma,
tough old lady,
despiser of religion and women
and, before you were through,
of Roosevelt, too, and all
that damned democratic daylight.

I know why you sat,
in uncharacteristic quiet,
those long kerosene-lit evenings
of flickering shadows,
bending over tiny stitches,
quilting . . .

And it wasn't economy, Grandma,
to save the scraps of old gowns.
Not sentiment, the memory
of their day of wearing.
Nor love . . . though you've provided
for us all.

It was for yourself,
to hold in your hand
bright colors compelled
to formal design.
Maps of your mind
when the land lay howling,
wild and desolate,
and cows quiet in the barn
and Grandad napping before bed-time.

Finally, it's doing that must be done
and it's wrapped in the work of your hands

that I sit . . . and I knit
carefully counting my stitches.

My afghans, too, glow in the dark.

Kansas Quarterly   JULIA McKEEVER

THE PEACE SIGN

From the back of a car,
two children
try the peace sign
on me. When I give
it back, they quickly
drop their hands
and look at one
another. I know
what they think: One
more for us,
perhaps.

The world
is at war, as ever.
The children, wise
in their cells, know
it is different this time.
They raise their fear,
sadness, hope
in a sign. Their fingers,
fragile, soft
as sprouting flowers,
ask to grow.

The Hollins Critic   RICHARD E. McMULLEN

OLD TREES

By the road
in the field
they stand, lifting branches

they cannot remember,
rocking shut
in the wind.

In some other world
they grew such trunks
and hurled their leaves

across the sky.
Now, emptyhanded,
they wait

for the end which has been
happening for years.
Nodding off

beside telephone wires,
tethered to farmhouses,
the old trees.

Ploughshares   WESLEY MCNAIR

LANDFALL

After the recessional,
when the last bell still
aches in mirage-rippled air,
and cobblestone clop
and harness creak and old mare snuffle
sign solemnity on the swearing place
at morning's end, and grandfathers
gather frayed old memories together
and pray over the capon that they'll last
as grandmothers know they won't
(Mere property, almost material, abandon such,
the women do not say, in wisdom),
and scolding daughters-in-law and dull-eyed sons
and bright-eyed babies and witty little girls
and cowering little boys and sullen adolescents all
are gathered at the table, then,
the scent of roses—man-bred flower,
vulnerable, demanding—comes
in through an open window,
and the sermon torpor dissipates,
and all the afternoon and summer Sunday evening
rise into the family's view,
like a new-found land,
to make of what they will.

The Georgia Review   THOMAS MCNAMEE

MARK'S USED PARTS

In come the wrecks to Mark's
and out the gear knobs, gas tanks,
visors, radiators, speakers, mufflers, ash
trays, hoses, handles. Bins of parts.

The crummiest clunker is worth
Mark's while. There's an avenue
of front ends—Plymouths, Buicks,
a '49 Nash,

an alley of chassis,
a park of gutted bodies piled on
one another like lovers. Everything has
a future.

All of which is very gratifying,
a sign
of what we'll amount to
in the after time.

The loosestrife will take this, the frog
that, creeks and clouds will value
our humus, the cardinal put us to use.
Dismantled, we'll go far.

The Atlantic Monthly   RENNIE McQUILKIN

IF I MAIL SEASHELLS

If I mail seashells,
Would you print them? instead of names?
Put them, voluted, pinkish, ridged, tar-stained, in rows
        instead of faces?
If I sent forgotten faces? on photographs in albums in these
        rusted cans the tide will upend soon? would you, then?
If I sent lists? frayed as mothwings, eggstained and brittle
        in fragile shades of gray—ah, wait.
If I just put in sand?
If I sent water only? this clear aquamarine—it's rare, for us—
        this pure and shining green, so clear the little fish glint
        through in every lifting wave? If I put those fish in?
Or yesterday's grey, steaming mist with high and numerous catcries
        that do not mean anything? I am more
Anonymous than these. I come
In forgotten envelopes, scentless and still
Unreflecting, small as three-cornered tracks done in by dawn
        and yet—ah, don't go, please, there's more—
I come to you a stutterer enormously convulsed,
Falling right down and twisting, casually repulsed, contorted
        with this effort
        —ah, somewhere here, there is,
It is here somewhere, I know
A certain bowl—
If I mail just the broken ones?
The whole?

Southwest Review   DODIE MEEKS

ROBERT FROST IN WARSAW

When I saw birches in Wasienki Park
leaning against the wind, I thought of you,

old ghost, so strongly have you claimed those trees
for us. Even here, four thousand miles away
from Derry or Franconia, your voice,
through foreign though familiar leaves, whispers
that the human heart can neither forfeit
nor accept responsibilities. Even
here, where storms far wilder, blacker, than those
which strike New Hampshire have torn up the stones
and thrown uncounted populations
into hells we only read about, your poems
proclaim ambiguous affirmation
in the dark. I sit here in a rented room
with you, heart pumping as I read your lines,
and think of parents, wife, and children
who travel with me complicated roads
beneath a winter sky that hides the stars.
They tell me you were selfish: it may be so.
I know you spoke to me through birches in
Wasienki Park, kindly, and brought me home.

National Forum   PETER MEINKE

TERRITORIES

As a child, when they swung
by me in petticoats, I tried to catch
what they were saying:
it was a throaty murmur of music,
a word here and there I'd know:
"ferry," "silver," "state."
They spoke about tin melting
deep in the woods,
night ferryrides through the ice-floes,
territories crossed by markers
almost buried in leaves.

At the bathing-houses,
as they unwound their long dark hair
and climbed the benches,
the other women silently gave way.
Once, they used our birch-twigs—
but their brown eyes never saw us,
and they didn't speak,
not even in the strange Gypsy dialect.
I longed to hear a word
like a silver fish in a stream of sound,
almost too quick to notice;
longed to be like them, draped
on the benches, cats without bones,
like the girl my age whose hair
ran in black rivulets
down the indentation of her spine,

the liquid curve of her hip. . .
the Gypsy sound hummed in her.
I could almost hear it about to spill:
a slowly gathering dance on the shore,
harbor, silver, tambourine.

Poetry   RIIKKA MELARTIN

THE HYPNOTIST

Hope is a woman with a gold watch chain,
swinging it right & left, left & right . . .
ordering everything to be under her control & to be dazzled by it.

So hope is a hypnotist
with the face of a woman who spent nights cramming for exams,
who was nearly ready to cheat on her medical exams
but said no to that sort of thing in the end;
& in the end did become a physician with a good practice in the
     suburbs
but gave it all up one day (as the story goes)
to become a hypnotist:
(best new trick in town).
Since then, she's been discriminated against by the rich and the
     poor.

But hope is a politician, a dictator, dictating hope
into people's lives on the weekend
(once organized a bingo game for the elderly & the sick).

Hope also drove across the country to see an eclipse of the sun
& took up mountain climbing in between.

Hope puts out her tongue to catch raindrops.
Hope confesses that she has a passion
for pistachio icecream on a TV talk show.

Hope likes jazz on a starry night.
Hope plays the trumpet to recharge her batteries.

Hope also wants to be a millionairess and a mother of twins
by this time next year, and at the same time maintain her reputation
& remain the one reason man cannot live by bread alone.

For the time being, hope is a bride, a midget,
who temporarily confronts rage with a smile.

Descant (Canada)   MARY MELFI

THE WAY OF THE WORLD

(December 1980)

Reading Duns Scotus, I find this passage,
a quotation from Avicenna:

Those who deny
a first principle
should be beaten
or exposed to fire until
they concede that to burn
and not to burn
or to be beaten
and not to be beaten
are not identical.

The Soviet Army masses
at the Polish border.
Larry Lee, a living soul,
is in Seattle.
He is singing.
Later tonight I'll read poems
by Rudenko, who is in prison
for speaking out for the beaten.
And you, my unscathed wonder, tell me:
The curtains. The colors are wrong.
Oh my dear.

Poetry   ASKOLD MELNYCZUK

NORTH BOULDER PARK

There is no one at the park.
For dusk gathers itself early
here by the foothills,
and the blue evening is waning.
We have come for a last
game of catch, our bodies
after all this time
sure and practiced in their motions.
Step and snap the ball away;
duck and stretch and vie with the
gloved hand, a trap sprung upon the ball
like the nighthawk's beaks above us
on their bugs. Over and over
across the ripe green grass
we make our play. The white ball
passes back and forth between us,
the afterimages of its flight through
the dusk like streamers of our
concordance. Until the dark
marks our finale. Then I throw
the ball as far as I can,
looping it into the night, and follow,
easily running, to fetch it.
When I reach it, it has
gone gray. When I take it in, and turn,

you will be gone. The summer
will be over.

The Fiddlehead   LYNN L. MERRILL

RETURNING ALONE

I move by memory in the dark rooms.
The rain-dampened air speaks
of dust, unemptied ashtrays, and plums
ripening on the kitchen table.
A farrago of perfumes from your shower
lingers in the upstairs hallway, Ivory
soap, bath oil, wet towels. Careful
not to touch you, I ease into bed,
alive to the cool freshness of the sheets.

Your breath sighs against my cheek
its song of a dark moon inside you.
Drifting off, I am falling, letting myself
fall; I am breathing deep the scent
of my own neglected flesh. I see a wheatfield
catch the house in its golden arms.

Passages North   RICHARD E. MESSER

UNDER THE RESTLESS CLOUDS

Under the restless clouds
the wind stepped by
like a homeless animal.

You hid your face in my neck
as if it were hopeless
to find a hiding place for our happiness
as restless as the clouds
and homeless as the wind.

International Poetry Review   HANNY MICHAELIS
                    —*Translated from the Dutch*
                    by Rob Hollis Miller

WHERE I SAT

I sat between Grandmother
and Aunt Etta.
I never had a chance.

Grandmother would point to
her forearm, the numbers
tattooed there, and that's

how I learned to count.
Aunt Etta told lies about
men who had loved her
when she was a young
coquette. I sat

like the silence
between train whistles
and dreamt

of the first woman
that took me to bed.
She was so beautiful
I never had a chance,
her skin
as smooth
as her silence. I heard
bells and sat

like a boy mid-bath,
between curiosity
and my own nakedness.

I sat between Grandmother
and Aunt Etta.
Between spoonfuls
of regret
they fed me—
from this you shouldn't know,
and may you never forget.

Midstream   RICHARD MICHELSON

IN JUNE

Today we stick to the front porch
and don't talk much.
New leaves stuff each bush.
Attic-hot, the day leans in on us,
cluttered with doubts we'd forgotten.
And cramped: whichever way we turn,
we have each other, each other.
The perfect weather is over.

And today the fire officials
test June's sorry sirens.
All's well. Our backyard apples swell
like fevered glands or hearts.
Last night a storm toppled the peonies
and after, that false cool
endured for maybe an hour.
Then it was back to the attic and you
so "bored" you missed your mother's.

Oh the lilies-of-the-valley go limp.
How is it that we can still trust the whole

dull heaven to give back
the spindly flowers and all that matters?
We do, we do.

Carolina Quarterly   LORETTA MICKLEY

NARCISSUS IN DEATH

Persuaded by illusion to the true, I breathe
The water's face, crowned with the wreathing sprays of
    curls
Pulled down by the sinking brain. Locks of clouted gold,
Unwinding, serpentine, spoil of the ruffling waves
Collapsing over me in death: the shallow wraith
Who peers reflects what you emblaze, the heartsick mind
Defaced, compelled to meet the phantom it disdains.
Beyond the famous pain, bewildered by a kiss,
I drift in the soundless swells of sleep, through panic
Into bliss, silent and darkening to a dream of thought,
Dimmed image of my own apostasy. Whose mind
Contains the beauty that I saw, so singular
And still, enlightened wake of perfect countenance
I gazed upon and fell? Betrayed by breath I find
These rippling visages, elusive and divine,
Glimmering, in the distant presence of the sun,
Lost aureoles, ever-widening, out of reach.

The Classical Outlook   DAVID E. MIDDLETON

DOMESTIC VISION

There is something to be said
for solitude. When everyone
is working the night shift
or shape shifting in their sleep,
sirens are a kind of company,
sounding the empty avenues
and dead ends, the shallow grave
of morning.
                    Everyone wakes
to a whiter noise, wind
whisking the leaves into light
reflections, windows within
green windows, the cacophony
of pots and pans inescapable
as the smell of cinnamon rising
from the apartment downstairs.
Acute, unamazed, you find
small things become large,
every table and chair hints
at the virtue of being
useful, and you wonder if
it is you who are superfluous.

How rare to be a chair
and know it!
                  But burdened
with memory, you know
it would not be enough,
you would want to be
human again, to stand
before a picture window
spangled with blue glories
comtemplating the sun and all
the tables and chairs.

Mississippi Review   ROBERT MIKLITSCH

THE INITIAL-TREE

I found the old initial-tree,
our names diseasing an entire branch,
and took my knife to carve some bitter words,
and stopped—death will spread
without my help, and the limb,
ten years feeble now, speaks effectively
for two who could not speak themselves.

Poetry   MICHAEL MILBURN

THE PORE PERSUET

Years of marking essays
may have done it,
or some genetic weakness
prodded by the flexibilities

of married life and fathering.
Or too much drink.
My words won't work.
My thinking's fine,

I think, but half my words
when spoken couple with the wrong
halves of the other half
as though my brain had lost

the war in Europe, or my train
turned over in a tunnel.
I have forgotten how to write
and when I mean men,

I type mean,
mean fact type ract
squirrel squarrel—
sometimes the lightest touch

can alter centuries.
Even my children are infected:
a son like Humpty Dumpty
and a daughter puzzled

that man's laughter
is a criminal offense.
The young around me occupied
with idol gossip, the old

with nothing, my own
generation unregenerate—
I here commit myself (1883)
to the pore persuet of poetsy.

Canadian Literary Review   RON MILES

THE SORCERESS

(for Teri)

This room holds no magic,
even in darkness. No stars
gather here, no wild birds,
no sorcery of wind and sea
timbres the night with song,
        until you cross its threshold—

And a savage sweetness fills the air,
orchids burst into bloom at your feet,
moonflowers sprout from your fingertips,
papagallos flash through the forest of your hair
and waterfalls tumble deep in your throat, tumble
and surge between your breasts to the sea
while jaguars prowl the thickets in your thighs,
brinking the night with a gorgeous roaring—

Bonfires blaze in your eyes.
I am drawn to their heat,
their light, the promise
of conflagration, my flesh
in yours, perfect destruction
and resurrection in love,
the two become one: being,
burning, blossoming: one.

Studia Mystica   AARON MILLER

PATIENCE IN THE CENTRAL VALLEY

On this dark day in San Francisco, the wan
light presumably struggles against
rainclouds. I think how the bare, ruined choirs

of grape vines in my native San Joaquin Valley subsist
until Spring, finally burst in a panoply of
lush grapeleaves (man having laced the valley
with now-dry ditches, soon to be brimming full,
replacing the raging watercourses formerly favored—
just as the stately, grand Valley oaks, resorted
to by indigenous Miwok or Yokus or Patwin, for
sustenance have been replaced—the former violently—
by cultivated, irrigated peaches & plums). O what damned
fools we've been & are! Patience, a virtue long since
pogromed, cries out from miles on miles of
empty ditches & yawning oak stumps, while, outside
my Twin Peaks-ward window, the potted geraniums
patiently await Springtime resurrection.

The Antigonish Review   HUGH MILLER

FERESHTEH

Students still play tennis on the courts
below the dormitories.
This summer I saw an agile dark-haired girl
serving on those courts

and recollected how we played there Sunday mornings
in the Fifties—the dark-haired Celt
from the Appalachian woods,
the sweet Iranian girl who vowed she'd never
go home, and never did.

And she was dead, even as I remembered.
Later I read it with the helpless horror
I felt the first time her serving arm
came out of socket and hung,
so odd—irreparable, I thought,
like a broken wing.

What I didn't dare do that awful first time
I learned to do routinely—give
her arm a yank and pop it back in place!

Now everything has changed
and nothing's changed.

Iranian students still mistake me
for a countryman.
They cross on campus, speak to me in Farsi.
Sounding like Andy Griffith, I reply
in Northcarolinian

and think of her.
The notice in the alumni magazine
didn't say whether she won
the fight to save the dunes in her town—
only that she led it.

Nothing has changed,
everything has changed.

Kentucky Poetry Review   Jim Wayne Miller

JEALOUSY

All evening I have noticed
that desire is not complete
in his eyes, and I don't want
to share that confusion of wishes.

I have a right to what
I have touched. If that is denied,
my hands will not behave in my lap
and I will talk, talk
to be heard, or stand up
to be looked at.

See how all my choices
have paled, and circumstance
chooses something worse than loss:
the possibility of it,
white asterisks of need surfacing
on my skin, telling
that man I am ill with it.

Every gesture begs and taunts.
He knows, he doesn't know—
there is no flower to be
torn apart for an answer,
no spell to be cast
by a wizard with distorted tricks.

And he wants me to watch
the one stunt I can't bear,
to recognize how small
I need a room to be,
so I can fill it.

The Georgia Review   Leslie Adrienne Miller

UNTITLED

Even among this maze of lighted houses
Arises the disorderly smell of raccoon:
   the bandit,
   the fierce organizer,
   one-who-walks-in-a-huddle.
They come down from the dry hills
by who knows what paths—
   surely not along the road—
Come to overturn garbage

and seethe at the dull and domestic:
   dogs, cats,
      people's toys.
They freeze in the sudden light
and growl with a body improbably deep.

Late in the night
They and their energetic children
   root and roust beneath your house
As if building a place of their own
Down there. Their tricky hands
   turn out halfhuman noises
   which time and time again
Poke cleanly through your dreams.

The Sun   PATRICK MILLER

BLOOD BROTHERS

I am slicing raw meat, pink rounds
of fragrant, fresh veal; it brings
the cat to the kitchen, his claws
scratching the air, his groans
deep, his mews, shrill, clean to
the bone, as he circles the table,
leaping, before I can blink, then
seizing a fat slice to chew up in
a corner with firm, careful bites,
growling with pleasure, giving me
the bad eye as he swallows it down,
the cold stare, not of victor,
but of one blood brother to another.

Poem   PHILIP MILLER

SUMMER—1981

It is summer and Norway
   in my heart.
Commerce spent, day's tasks unraveled,
I travel the country of mountain kings who live
High in the halls that smoke and flame
When the sun sets fire to the sky.
I am where oceans have thrust their fingers
Into rock, carved fiords into eternity. The
Centuries are calm here,
Subdued and humble. If I were
A boy still, I could be one forever,
For daylight is motionless with awe,
And time is reduced to a whisper . . .
Slow, silent, sliding,

Stronger than granite,
                More gentle than water—
                Deeper even
        Than history.

The Spoon River Quarterly   ROBERT MILLS

VENI CREATOR

Come, Holy Spirit,
bending or not bending the grasses,
appearing or not above our heads in a tongue of flame,
at hay harvest or when they plough in the orchards or
        when snow
covers crippled firs in the Sierra Nevada.
I am only a man: I need visible signs.
I tire easily, building the stairway of abstraction.
Many a time I asked, you know it well, that the statue
        in church
lift its hand, only once, just once, for me.
But I understand that signs must be human,
Therefore call one man, anywhere on earth,
Not me—after all I have some decency—
And allow me, when I look at him, to marvel at you.

The Paris Review   CZESLAW MILOSZ

YAHRZEIT

Some things we cannot translate.
We must travel far and suffer
our travels as long winters
to learn the value of imprecision,
which is a pitiful satisfaction.
Jahreszeit, for example, in German
means *season*, and is feminine.
In Yiddish, however, anniversary—
in this case, of the dead. A candle
is lit in the home, an unceremonious
occasion that seems to honor the ordinary,
as death must be. In our house
I remember how the ring of light
accented the old, a bruised apple
collecting dust at the soft hollow
of the stem, bananas going black,
and the napkin holder turned out
in plastic to be a log cabin
with no roof. The small erratic flame
was a young girl, alone on a pond,
learning to skate, and the gray wind
wrenched like a train through the valley

where the river ached beneath its floes.
At night I listened to the traffic,
the thrum and whir through the hobo
dusk that wintered in tobacco fields.
What would I have you believe
that another would make different
and simpler? I have not shouldered
such meaning this distance simply
to convince you. The candle burned
one night and one day on top of the refrigerator.
The smaller the wick, the greater
the scope of its light until
soon the whole kitchen was one season,
precise and incomplete.

Tendril   LARRY MOFFI

TWO IN TWILIGHT

Between you and me on the overlook
an underwater brightness flows, distorting
the outline of the hills, and your face too.
Against that wavering depth, every gesture you make
is cut away from you, appearing without trace,
then disappearing, in that medium which fills
every wake, closing over your passing:
you beside me here, within this air that settles down
and seals
the gravity of stones.

                    And I, overwhelmed
by the power weighing around us, yield
to the sorcery of no longer recognizing anything
outside myself: if I lift my arm
just a little, the act becomes a different
thing, shatters on crystal, its memory
unknown and leached away, and now
the gesture is no longer mine;
if I speak, I hear an astonished voice
descending to its lowest range
or dying in the unsustaining air.

Such is my bewilderment: lasting
to the point where it resists the wasting
consumption of the day; then a gust
lifts the valley in convulsive movement
upwards, wakes from the leaves a tinkling
sound that dissipates
in rapid puffs of smoke, and the first lights
sketch in the piers.

                    . . . the words fall lightly
between us. I look at you in a soft
quivering. I don't know

whether I know you; I know that never have I
been so divided from you as in this late
returning. A few instants have scorched
all of us: all but two faces, two
masks which, with a struggle, carve themselves
into a smile.

Antaeus
EUGENIO MONTALE
*—Translated from the Italian
by William Arrowsmith*

PARABLE OF THE CICADA

It's unwise to let me into your garden;
One locust can undo the work of centuries.
I am legion, faceless in my blunt
Helmet, my descent sudden
And clumsy, a rape of wires.

You have ordered your life; its
Fevers lap backward, the
Deliberate rose sucks
Velvet.
Listen,
Around the edge of the grass,
My hoarse breathing—
I have nothing to lose.

It's another summer, all
That's lovable, cruel,
Drained off.
Your soil is not friable:
I dig holes in it,
Tick like a bomb
In the alley under the rose.

The plant is dying.
You heap new chemicals
Around its legs;
They neutralize.
You try dung from the greenhouse;
Its worms, its borrowed oils
Drip backward into the rock.

At the end of summer
I plunge out of control
In my metal car,
A last wild trip through the branches—

You hear nothing,
Nor do you see
The shell I leave behind me,
Nailed like an abrasive map to the bark.

Denver Quarterly
BARBARA MOORE

THE LETTER

You want it back, mailed in an unbalanced moment.
The box on the corner gulped it
like a slick pill. And now you want it back.

You live on the rim of a careening hope
that the mail truck will wreck,
contents burn beyond recognition.

But even fire is not fatal.
Once you received a dress in autumn colors
always smelling of smoke
and a letter from home
singed around the edges.

To stop your words would take
an act of nature, a possum in the drop box
chewing words into riddles.

It happened in Front Royal, Virginia,
but no one believed. It will not happen again.
Not to you.

Travelling through heat, rain, snow and sleet,
your words are still whole and readable.

The Chattahoochee Review   JANICE TOWNLEY MOORE

BLUE EYES

With you on my bike
I crashed into a car
but we both escaped
what should have been
a total smash-up
or shambled remains.
An hour later,
as we sat in deck chairs
drinking tea,
you mentioned casually
it was your birthday.
Slowly a thin tear
played on my eye
and I saw how,
climbing once
on hands and feet
the unknown side
of the mountain,
I had come upon
the mouth of a gorge
where under tangles of vines
a rill pushed through rocks,
poured over a sandy floor

making an oasis.
The spell had got me,
and I slid into the pool
scooping out as I lay
precious handfuls
of the first grains of the earth.
But what took my breath away
was a soundless explosion
of a thousand butterflies
sifting the sieved light
of the noon sun,
and in that beatitude
I had remembered
what I now see
in depths before me:
your blue eyes.

New Letters   P. RAMA MOORTHY

THE BRANCH BANK

When the bank fathers were feeling expansive,
they put up a branch office.
It looks like an ice cream parlor:
steep gables, spires, trellised windows.
They thought the town would grow toward the East,
with a shopping center and a new car agency.
Dead wrong, the fathers made the best of it.

So they tried marketing: pens, alarm clocks,
and, finally, the ultimate china. Failure.
Now and then a child, drifting uncertainly,
asks for pistachio nut in a sugar cone.
Once a man filled out loan papers
for a nine-year-old Chevrolet. Off the books,
that car stunned the branch to life.

Planted in geranium, aster, chrysanthemum,
the drive-in window becomes the seasons;
and the two women, the manager and teller,
leave the vault teasingly open.
"Where is Sundance? Where is Butch?
O for the life of possibility!"

The Southern Review   RONALD MORAN

PORCH SITTING

In the summertime,
after dinner, after dishes,
after the street lights went on,
we would sit on the porch,

Mom in a housedress on the glider
breathing in time to glider squeaks,
fingering the close night air
like dark rosary beads,
a beatific smile behind the darkness;
and Dad on the green metal chair,
cigarette for a mosquito-chaser,
one leg propped on the
rustoleum over rust railing;
he and a glass of ice tea
would sweat, listening to Ernie Harwell,
Tiger Baseball on the air;
and I would fidget on the steps,
thigh sticky against a vinyl cushion
(so I wouldn't get piles),
arms and legs folded, unfolding,
tense and teetering like
some young night bird,
wondering how these two could
sit so quiet so long.

Tar River Poetry   JANICE E. MORDENSKI

IRVINGTON

In the dawn freshness, when the mists are slowly rising
       from the great lawns and only a few early delivery
       trucks move silently down the lanes,
when the house is quiet but for sounds of deep breathing
       behind closed doors and the subdued creak of your
       footsteps on the stairs,
to walk out barefoot on the dew-damp grass spotted with
       dandelions, where dragonflies are already hovering
       and veering, settling now and again on the glinting
       croquet wickets,
across to the garden of peonies and snapdragons, of
       marigolds, nasturtiums and pansies
pale-hued in muted early light and revealing in the
       pensive gazing-globe their subtle, enigmatic
       presences—

to walk down the gravel drive, stones sharp underfoot, and
       out through the great hedge onto the open road,
to run, feet slapping the tar, for pure joy of feeling the
       wind rushing past your heedless frail body,
to feel cotton shirt and shorts light as leaves on the airy
       child body,
to hear in the distance a screen door slam, a dog bark
       sharply, a woman call out (as you catch fresh whiffs of
       frying bacon from the kitchen of the house across the
       road),
to look down on the great river far below as it moves slow

and strong in the early sunlight, hearing the whistle
and rattle of the 6:00 A.M. train that is just now
pulling out of the vine-covered station—
to stop stock-still and close your eyes, remembering the
night, its mists and derangements,
recalling its shaded ambiguous faces, its paths of guilt
outside your window,
then to breathe cool air in freely, deeply, feeling with each
breath the self intensify in keenness
as you shout out to the kindling dawn, as you catch up
from the road's green verge a huge rough rock and
hurl it!—

to feel with your forehead the sun's strong touch that
greets you at the peak of being,
recognizing there a self in opposition to your own—
to be alone, to be glad in aloneness, to be at one with all
that surrounds you in strength of your aloneness:

to be aware—translucent—as it were for ever—in
brightness of that opening world.

Ploughshares   FREDERICK MORGAN

THE PARTING

I stood in the pine wood waiting for my friend
by the path along the water—
night falling, the last lobster boat
throbbing in from the bay.
I wished to say farewell, *bonne chance!*
I would not be seeing this man again.

"It's the end, I guess," he said, "but first
I'm glad we can share such a moment.
You've loved this place for years, quite as much as I,
and must surely know what I'm feeling
now that my time has come to leave it behind.
What a heart-breaking sunset! Yes, I'm glad you're with me . . .

"Still, you'll agree, I haven't been lucky here,
and maybe this moving on will help me find
whatever it is I've always wanted.
I feel like being alone somewhere high in the mountains—
the Rockies, or Switzerland:
I might find what I need there—and if I die, all right."

We watched the red sun as it sank behind granite islands,
and stood for a time not speaking—then shook hands.
"Goodbye," I said, "Prevail.
May life be kind while it lasts!
But I'm sure you and I will be called as one, in the end."
He smiled . . . I pulled from my hip the flask of brandy,
and we each took a sip before he turned and went.

The Southern Review   FREDERICK MORGAN

ANAKTORIA

Now that you have made your great renunciation
do you think of us, in our cold city,
those many of us who loved you,
those who have held you close—
do you remember our faces, the touch of our hands and lips?

Something about you had been secured from death,
or so we felt
(fresh, perhaps, from your strong embrace)—
and to watch you when all thoughtlessly you danced
was to share a fierce joy we couldn't quite comprehend.

Now, you move beneath a desert sky
among foreigners, are touched by other hands—
but at night, when the moon rises coldly above our avenues,
we recall old days of triumph
and see you again in our midst:
lean body, candid profile, glittering hair.

The Southern Review   FREDERICK MORGAN

DUST

in my scraggly beard and the first
sweat of the day glistening on my arms,
I lay on a canvas cot, thinking of you
and of another woman too raw for that land.

Burnt flakes of shale, jeweled peppergrains
of moletooth, limbbones packed in stone,
a fence, a track through sagebrush, colors
mute, regions of advanced decay: these
inarticulate inhuman cries are somehow mine.

That August, back in the Village,
an intimate catastrophe:
your pale, cream-colored buttocks, lady.
All the years haven't taken away
what that day turned up missing.

Given a life to spend, a bank of bones,
two bodies tough as any blossoms, we
took each other in hand. So this
is what it means to live on earth:

pressing warm skin within your skin, not
tentative, not innocent, not knowing

that would come later.

Permafrost   JOHN MORGAN

THERMOMETER WINE

Always hung on its plaque
on the porch like a mounted
icicle, but was so old
already the painted numbers
were peeling and hard to read.
Only Daddy could tell
the measurements—he'd known
the instrument since a boy.
At ten below it really
meant twenty, being slow
with age, he said. At
ten above it was roughly
accurate, but on a hot day
he added twenty to its reading.
I watched the red needle
rise in the dog days and
marveled how the tiny
hair was both sensitive
and significant.
The blood rose in that stem
just a capillary of
bright, as though the day
were sipping through its ice
straw that special wine,
and about to taste the
color from the drop at
the bottom that never clotted
or dulled no matter how
far up or down it wrote,
always chilled as snake or worm.

The American Scholar   ROBERT MORGAN

LABOR DAY AT WALDEN POND

(". . . they know whether they are well-employed . . .")
            —H. D. Thoreau

Both narrow shoulders of Rte. #126
(marked "No Standing" for 3/4 of a mile
past the Pond to the Concord town limit)
are jammed with cars single-file, parking free.
The $2-buck lot in front stands almost empty.

Citizens with the law in their own hands
mill through big pines on Walden Reservation.
The master's words fly on the cool west wind:
Where there is a lull of truth, up springs the
state's Department of Natural Resources.

Bathhouse, johns, lifeguard, lots of sunbathers
crowd the east end. The far shore still looks fresh.
Waves peak and sparkle in late afternoon.
One frog is croaking to a different drummer:
you have to call this much water a lake.

A path along the northern shore—the deep side—
leads past a cove to a bare clearing where
Thoreau lived a year in a shack that cost
$62.00, including food and clothes.
No clouds today. No boards left on the site.

A small crowd watches where the great man worked
more trades than he had toes or fingers. Profit,
like the railroad, still rides us. Men with jobs
run out of work. We disband toward wherever
we must—a shrinking week. Summer is over.

The Nantucket Review   EDWARD MORIN

IN THE ALBUM

In moments we appeared,
In sixty seconds blossoming on the paper.
Brilliantly we are there, this whole bookful of us
With not a thought in our paper heads.
And everywhere we are smiling. Always
The idea seems to be to turn our backs on
Something tremendous—the South Rim, say,
Or Niagara ruining behind us.

Now we all stare with my stare.
For I am here chiefly as the point of view—
Invisible but the without-which-nothing.
My business is composition, keeping
Us close together inside the hard edges
Where we pause for these moments of reflection.

Though the dyes are unstable and the manufacturer
Does not guarantee the chemistry that arrests us,
And the light disappearing into the spaces
Between the pictures gives back a flat blackness,
Tonight, rightly, by lamplight we just look
At the pictures. We stare us in our faces,
Ignoring everything that lies about us.

The Yale Review   JOHN N. MORRIS

SEA BED

I could live gently here,
rise from a bed with the tide,

pull the long horizon in,
weave smoke and clouds
into a child's quilt.

Last night i dreamt
black porpoises
dancing in a line of waves,
slick mermaids, elaborate gowns;
houseguests waiting.

I could build a house
from salt and drifted wood,
my window the door
to the Pacific,
my roof the ray of sun,
sleet of October morning.

I could live empty here.

The Malahat Review   NADENE MORTON

TURTLE-BACK

My father loathed snapping turtles; and why not?
They ate his goslings, or bit them one-legged.
They were tough, very hard to kill.
(No use firing from shore with a .22).
And I was almost a baby, but I too
Must have picked up some rancor/fear.

It was a twisting, ominous thing
That my fishline raised through water dimness, up near
The surface. It shattered *now*
Into grisly *then*. My nerves spasmed
As though to trigger a death shriek
From a food-thing grabbed by the lizard-fanged antique.

But then—in a sudden settling
Of nerves that cleared the day, and more than the day,
I saw the turtle clear and diminish, and plunge
To the innocent bottom in algaed innocence.

Turtle and I have journeyed. It's tempting
To fancy further journey. Recalling
He's tough, very hard to kill,
Can make land passages, long ones, over rock and hill
From water to better water—how would it be
If (forgiving his feeding habits, his stink, and his temper)
I should mount pickaback some traveling shell?
Would he portage me back to the pond of innocence and goslings?
Forward to the place the dolphins ferried souls?

Yet turtle and I are tangible flesh; the future
Lacks tangibility. He wrenched free of hate;
I'd better wrench free of—something. He got off

My hook; I'd better get off his malodorous back.
And wait.

Kansas Quarterly   W. R. MOSES

MADONNA WITH CHILD: VIETNAM 1975

The village was not unlike others couched
In rain forest, pummeled by sun. Until ranks
Of bandoliered soldiers began charging the barbed buttresses
To wet hot dusty streets with their blood.
I lay low by a well where the marketplace stood

And shot my fill of reel war.
Retreating soldiers, until the tanks came,
Hustled old rice-hatted women
Piggyback, and carried by twos, blood steeped
Blankets tied round poles, looped

Under like killed game. Gathered in tall
Grass, we watched nine civilians
Break from a hit café like tree-startled
Crows, almost make cover, then swoon
In billowed heaps beside the Buddhist shrine.

Later, after the tanks came returning thunder
For thunder, we lumbered to the still, huddled,
Black clad shapes to find something weirdly
Sacred amidst all this slaughter:
A live girl bearing forth a daughter

Between bloodied thighs: solemn, scared
Like a lame horse, tearless as the tank's
Thunder flourished and crackling volleys rained
Against a roiling sky to a Buddha's serene smile
And eight dead crows and Madonna with Child.

The American Scholar   GREG MOSS

BLOOD ORANGES

In 1936, a child
in Hitler's Germany,
what did I know about the war in Spain?
Andalusia was a tango
on a wind-up gramophone,
Franco a hero's face in the paper.
No one told me about a poet,
for whose sake I might have learned Spanish,
bleeding to death on a barren hill.
All I knew of Spain
were those precious imported treats
we splurged on for Christmas.

I remember pulling the sections apart,
lining them up, sucking each one
slowly, so the red sweetness
would last and last—
while I was reading a poem
by a long-dead German poet
in which the woods stood safe
under the moon's milky eye
and the white fog in the meadows
aspired to become lighter than air.

Ploughshares   LISEL MUELLER

LIVES OF THEIR OWN

The day gray, the sky falling, laden with light
that can't burst through. The noisy jays:
I covet their blue wings, remembering his body, loose
beside me. Making love in the morning seemed right,
before separating into the dailiness of self.
He asked if I could see his fear. He forgot
how I held him as his dreams struggled like small fish
to leap away from sleep and assume lives of their own.

I wonder at this other body, how like quicksilver
we take each other in; this other mind,
a twin filament, conducting a singular circle
of light. Outside, the traffic never stops; brakes screech
through open windows, reverberate the length of the house.

Loving him feels so right,
like loving Daddy,
who after work at night
told me story after story,
and sang. I flushed
as he swept me up. His heart beat
through his T-shirt. His whiskers stung my cheek.
"Whose girl are you?" he'd ask.
I teased back, "I'm Mommy's girl."

Lately, when I'm alone, I imagine a man
standing just outside. Sometimes the kitchen door,
sometimes the bedroom. I feel his shadow.
He is my old boyfriend, my new lover, the guy across the street.
When his eyes begin to draw their blue from my breath,
when his fingers form and reach,
I lock the door.

Tendril   MARY JANE MULHOLLAND

ALABAMA MEMORIES

Houses with peeling skins of gray paint,
with swaybacked wooden porches furnished with dingy sofas

and wringer washing machines perched on old-fashioned legs.
Houses with muddy yards and dirty chickens,
with no indoor plumbing,
with outhouses leaning at tipsy angles.
(I remember being embarrassed to pee
in a red-rimmed white-enameled chamberpot
on a rainy night at somebody's house.)

Sounds of buzzing flies
and screen doors banging in the summertime.
Dirt roads where the dust flies up in your face
and a grassy field where a mule chews slow and thoughtful-like.
(Some men have caught a huge turtle
and are dragging it down the road at the end of a rope.
An old woman wearing a faded print dress held with a safety pin
says, "That'll make right good soup.")

I ride all over our polished hardwood floors
on a fuzzy red piggy bank,
I play in the thick green branches of a tree
knocked down in a storm;
I eat all the orange candy in the aspirin bottle
and sleep for two days,
wake up wearing a wrinkled dress;
I steal a doll and my mother makes me give it back.
Agnes lets me help her in the kitchen,
weaving a lattice of white strips of dough for apple pie.

All these things return in one moment,
bubbling up with the aroma of nutmeg and cinnamon:
Alabama memories returning
like an old familiar dream.

Southern Exposure   HARRYETTE MULLEN

LOGIC

The fog slides inland and the day goes
Grey. There's someone cutting a tree
Somewhere nearby
And the sound of the power saw
Fills the air. Autumn is strict here, precise.
Never over the even
Lines.
I hate that sound.
That whine and naaaaaah—it sounds like
What it is, the world
Coming apart, being dismantled, disjointed, the saw
Coming down where the tree swerves,
Where you make up your mind
Again. And the shape, the discovered shape,
Does it hang in the air, the good idea
You can't let go of, chapel of space

To no religion, above the clean edges
And dust? This is history;
The clothes you grew out of
But kept, the small
Answer and the question riding outward on the water,
Ring after ring. And the dead
Leaves
Had already fallen,
Weights on the tug of their shadows.
Now they have none.

Poetry Northwest   LAURA MULLEN

GRANDFATHER

Sleep, Old Friend. Your pain is gone now. All
Of us have said goodbye to you, each
After his own fashion. In the hall
The family gather, careful that their speech

Is not so loud as usual, circumspect
As the occasion warrants. All of those
Who came tonight, to show their deep respect
For you, are quiet. Now and then one goes

Outside and wipes the hot rebellious tears
Away. But now a funny anecdote
Remembered rushes round the gathered ears
And smiles break out. The Sunday tie and coat

Come off, and loving laughter starts to break
As we remember. Somehow there's a rhyme
Between the laughter and the sobs. Our ache
Will come at us again, from time to time,

But now the sadness and the love require
Laughter so that we may *truly* say
Goodbye to you. We know you must retire
In the twilight of this autumn day.

Ball State University Forum   CECIL J. MULLINS

THE SCREEN

We watch films of actors suffering
From love or axe wounds:
Pain's causes fail to matter
Since we marvel only at the swoons,
Mad scenes,
                    the bitter partings
Into which we substitute ourselves.
Our lips move in the dark.

We choose the sides of those most wronged
And least able to get even.
Crushing the soft drinks in our hands,
We yearn to get even.
Even.
        Such misery is bearable
If everybody bears it as the actors do,
Beautifully, fine taste in clothes intact.

When they can hold it in no longer
They maim themselves,
                        or relatives or strangers.
We understand why. Our palms crease
In the same places.
They make love the way we'd like to,
In furious waves,
                        breath steaming off
The places kissed.
The body redefined in fire.

Whether these films end well or grimly,
Concrete life waits for us outside
Like a patient spouse.
We are late getting back to it.
                        The slow walk
Up the aisle carpet creates static in our souls.
We come out charged.
                        We have escaped.
But those we love insist we never change.

The Chariton Review   FRED MURATORI

TURNING THIRTY

While tonight, upstairs, my children
remember how to sleep,
I light thirty candles and stay awake,
trying to remember everything.
Slowly, the corners soften, walls
fall forward to meet the glow
of these thirty small flames
unable to heat a single room.
In this flickering of years, I
stand in my skin, my shadow drawn
behind me like the entrance to a cave.

What pours in is the great silence of time,
flecked with stars, like black rainwater
brimming in a barrel.
There's a kind of knowing that leans close
and is gone; tonight, above the house,
a stray comet, gathering and leaving its breath,
chases its tail across the wide night.

Out there, a child—
you know his face—is lost.
It is his breath under the door
that licks at the flames.
With a finger, in the grey frost
my breath makes on the windows,
I write his name, calling him home,
and turn away before morning comes again
and burns it clean.

Calliope   GEORGE E. MURPHY, JR.

WINTER SERMON: NORTHSIDE CHICAGO

On Hubbard Street, among factory signs
And the gay bars further west, this winter
In the ditch does not mean enough.
With innocence, a melodrama of duty
Is played by the big Pole city workers
—flinging rock salt, unplugging sewers
In defense of a surprise freeze.
Their smiles, like habits, break hard.
Their black stocking caps appear
Stark and vulnerable to the young men cruising
Past hand-in-hand, swimming at noon
Toward darkened theaters and bargain hotels,
Requiring sweet ambush, a ration
Of luxury. These filthy buildings don't care,
Can't whistle insults. Soon the Poles,
Immutable as mud, will have picked
These streets clean of ice
And loitering glances, will filter
Home to dinners of wurst and bock beer,
Laying odds against more snow.
And slowly, in its timeliness, a clothesline
Of color will string through the city,
Flapping proudly, ready for collision
With high blue skies, like old lovers
Tossing again in a warehouse loft, straining free.

Southern Humanities Review   G. E. MURRAY

FAIRY TALES

It seems to me, no matter where I go, that
People come into and go out of my life
And touch me where I feel it.
Then they leave me only with the memories . . .
Like fairy tales of children,
Easily forgotten
Since one never really knows them wholly.

How can I know
Who I am seeing for the last time?
I don't know how I can make a halt
With those I once have known,
Nor how I can protect these fairy tales
Without their losing all their magic.

And now with you . . .
Okay, come on . . .
Get entangled with my life's fences.
And stay just long enough
For us to get to know each other.
For if you dare stay longer,
I will want you with me
After it becomes impossible.

But come, anyway.
Our fairy tales
Are the most delightful ones we know,
And then, big books are made
From smaller chapters.

Denver Quarterly   MARJORIE A. MYERS

MAGIC

When you come,
the closed room opens
and lets in the seas.
You touch the walls and magically
transform them
to luminous vaults.
When you stay,
the stars get wings of fire
that quietly sink
in timeless sun-night
and take root
on the ocean floor.
When you leave,
unseen wind
flutters through the room.
The walls crumble
and moist stars
rise and unfold
fugitive wings.

Poetry Now   KATE NAESS
                          —Translated from the Norwegian
                          by Nadia Christensen

THE LAW

All around us things hold together
by a tense balance of forces, the lonely
negative side of one joined
to the lonely negative side of another, and all
without the slighest hope, as water
has no hope or stone, but is faithful
out of necessity.

So when I read your letter a third time
and it still said no, I finally saw
that some marriages are made
in refusal devoutly forever and ever,
and the freedom given therein
is to love elsewhere and even often—
but without necessity.

Northwest Review   LEONARD NATHAN

OLD CHARLIE

he always made me wonder

eyes crowfooted from sun
on snow
body slumped
from slack times

he lived
out there on
the Pine Ridge Reservation

in a gutted '49 Ford

army blankets on the floorboard
made his bed

Sunkist orange crate
along the door
held flour and sugar and
Annie Green Springs

Coleman stove
in the hump
of the trunk
warmed his food
and body

and up front
floor to windshield
a raw pineboard
bookcase
bulged

with Miller and Michener
and Freud

Buffalo Spree　　　SHERYL L. NELMS

A LIFE

(for Robert Francis)

A man lived a simple life.
No, it isn't true—
no one lives a simple life,
certainly not him.
But if we describe a Chinese painting
which shows, say, a scholar standing near
a single twisted tree,
with a waterfall in the distance,
and a third of the silk is blank,
as having a beautiful simplicity,
then, in that sense,
we might use the word for him.
He lived alone.
Forty years ago,
when not many people wanted to live there,
he had a small house built
at the edge of town
on a pasture knoll gone back to woods.
A fireplace of native stone,
the walls unpainted pine,
the kitchen stove cast iron,
the refrigerator (in winter)
a box outside the window.
The bedroom only twice as wide
as its single narrow bed.
He lived as inexpensively as possible,
and didn't need to earn much money—
taught off and on.
He ate no meat.
He planted a garden,
but the garden got smaller
as the trees (and he) got older.
He wrote poems.
He lived alone.
If you visited him
you had good (and careful) talk.
If he asked you to stay for "a light supper,"
he was true to his words—
a dish of potato salad maybe, saltines,
a little piece of cake
soaked with dandelion wine.

Writing poems
and the quiet satisfactions of the senses

and the mind finding its outlines—
it isn't much to sustain a person.
But if he is married
to his denials
as to the things he loves,
he will be all right.
But it isn't simple—
not in the ways
we usually use the word.
Nearly eighty,
he says in a letter:
"The winter wind is roaring
as I write these words,
and on my hearth
a bright fire is blazing."

Poetry East   HOWARD NELSON

ON GROWTH AND FORM

Young ones, when your distant grownup kin
At gatherings admire your new height
And say such standard silly things as that
They knew you when you were just so high, or, worse,
When you were just a glint in your father's eye,
Command your high displeasure that it turn
To wonder like the wonder they must feel
And you may feel one day under the roll-
ing wheels of heaven that make up age and time,
At the procrustean miracle of growth
That tripled your length and turned it into height;
And, if you don't take care, may cube your weight,
And being struck with *sagesse* and regret
At having not a verse to bless yourself,
Must mark the moment with a silly say.

The Massachusetts Review   HOWARD NEMEROV

A BIRD BELOVED AND STRANGE

He who, with his magic, spellbinds a thousand eyes, can't spellbind
his own. He who conjures up a skyful of birds from
his hat may fail to conjure up the bird of his soul.
The silvery, distant birchwoods, the snow on the tall
slow-rising mountain, the intensely grey sky,
the white hand and smiling face as recorded
in memory.   It all comes back, comes back but does not come.
        The last watch already. Already steps in the garden
or rain or dreams. Your hand dropped, your fingers on the pillow
fumble like roots for richer soil. It isn't sleep

escaped me. Nor dreams. I'm better off now than dreaming.
The white and the frigid turns river, the bold green
rises in the cheeks of fields and years and the magician is spell-
    bound
by that magic. From his hat sprouts a bird beloved and strange.

Poetry Now   ELI NETSER
                                    —Translated from the Hebrew
                                        by Bernhard Frank

HUNGER

Our thoughts ascend this holy day,
and self-examination consumes us.
We abstain from food. We escape for a day
from the mouth's demands. We taste hunger,
as with parched lips we utter supplications.
We taste hunger, just taste, for we know
the fast will end and we shall feast.

There's another hunger, hunger to be free,
and yet another, the hunger of the freed,
the hunger that day's end does not end,
that renews itself with each new day;
the hunger of the ingathered
still eating the bread of affliction—
in Israel! Three hundred thousand poor.
They eat. Of course, they eat.
They eat their frustrations.
They feed on grievances.
They chew on resentments.
They gag on idleness.
They swell with bitterness.
They retch forth their hopes
in the land of milk and honey,
the promised land.

Who shall extend a helping hand?

Midstream   ERNEST NEUFELD

BOUNDARIES

It is not enough to step through the night
enclosed in our separate bodies;
your arm floating across my back,
your fingers lost in my hair.
The darkness parts before us
and slams shut as we pass
with absolute finality.
I cannot see the orbit of your eyes,
the dark side of your face,

the wisp of cloud behind your ear.
You press me to your side, close as a wing
and I seep through my skin
to lodge between your flesh and the air,
surrounding you like water
around a drowning child.
I grasp your hand, reminding myself
I am real. As real as the night. As real as you.
And we are both alone, and we are both alive
stranded like sand under this moonless starless sky.

The Sun   LESLÉA NEWMAN

ODE TO MY HIPS

Move over boy
these hips are coming through!
These hips'll knock you off the street
if you don't make room for them to move!
These hips sway
these hips sashay
these ain't no Brooke Shields teenage
boy size 3½ slim hypocritical hips—
these hips are woman hips!
These hips are wide
these hips hypnotize
these hips fill a skirt
the way the wind fills a sail.
These hips have chutzpah—
they think they can change the whole world!
When I take these hips out for a walk on the street
and the sun is shining
and my bones are gleaming
I place my hand on these two hips
and know they speak the truth.

The Sun   LESLÉA NEWMAN

THE SWEETWATER

At dawn, crossing the Sweetwater River
in Wyoming, I dream of old songs,
girlfriends. My brother-in-law
lights up, opens a window. His
wife tries to quiet their child.
The wind is cold, the ground
bare. My wife and boys are asleep
in the back of the van. Twenty-four
hours out of Wisconsin, everyone's
waiting for Utah, Nevada,
to unravel beneath our spinning

wheels. Waiting for California,
family Christmas. Sweetwater,
Sweetwater. At forty-three, I'm
sentimental and weary. Why
am I thinking of past loves?
The van is full of cameras, film
rolling endless as the West,
to frame our togetherness. Somewhere
out here—I've crossed it—
there's a poison river. In Iowa
my father is dying. Have I told you
lately, Sweetwater, that I love you.

Passages North   HERMAN NIBBELINK

ELEGY

(for Marion, for Jane)

I

Death and the maiden

Were you, as old prints have shown,
armor over props of bone,
scythe on shoulder blade asway,
here's a word or two I'd say:

When you met that lady now
—she of the amused cool brow—
which of you with more an air
carried off the occurrence there?
Held—the buoyant head so high—
every fascinated eye?
Stole, as half in mischief too,
scenes *you* strutted front to do?

Which at last, when curtains met,
had us leaning forward yet
in the dark?—to breathe and rise,
odd elation in our eyes.

II

"one day anyone died I guess"

Here she lies, poor dancing head,
in the world we know of, dead.
Every sense avers: The End.
Yet we're hedging (who'd pretend
our five portholes on the night
gauge the seven oceans right?)
hedging: past a world in stream,
past the learned journal's dream

(quark or quasar, beta ray),
what's that glimmer? limbs at play?
Something there? a curtain stirred?
Laughter, far and teasing, heard?

Where such awesome laws are set,
honey, misbehaving yet?

The American Scholar   JOHN FREDERICK NIMS

TREE TOAD

My field has dried up
Near my neighbor's field,
Though people say:
The sad ones cry on the nearby shore
Among sad ones.
When, O messenger of cloudy days,
O tree toad,
Will it rain?

On the worthless carpet
Inside my dark hovel
Where not an atom of happiness exists
And the screen of reed-ribs
By the wall of the room
Cracks with dryness,
Like the hearts of friends
Separated from friends,
When, O messenger of cloudy days,
O tree toad,
Will it rain?

International Poetry Review   NIMA-YUSHIJ
—*Translated from the Persian
by Munibur Rahman*

TURQUOISE, I LOVE YOU

Turquoise, I love you
as if you were my girlfriend,
as if you were mine;
you are everywhere:
you are just washed,
just recently sky blue,
just fallen from above—
you are the sky's eyes:
you slice through the surface
of the shop, of the air—
blue almond,

sky talon,
bride.

Poetry Now   PABLO NERUDA
—*Translated from the Spanish (Chili)*
by James Nolan

THE VAGARIES OF TWELVE YEAR OLD LUST

Once a week I'd roar up her driveway
on my lawnmower,
stones pinging off her garage door,
and, opening her backyard gate,
I knew she'd be there—
her face lost in the window's glare—
watching me cut the side
of that green hill,
the lawnmower almost on two wheels,
my muscles extra-tensed.

And I'd recall times
I had watched her from next door,
her stomach swelled with child,
shirt billowing,
as she'd so carefully bend over
to trim about the fence.

Yes, I could mow down her grass
and trim most all her edges
except the one
where she'd come out on the back porch
and, in calling my name,
raise herself up on her toes a bit,
asking could I come in
for a glass of ice tea.

Berkeley Poets Cooperative   BRUCE NOLAN

THE WRITER-IN-RESIDENCE'S POEM

He was one of those kids who say they want to be poets.
"This one is pompous and not overly bright," I thought
as I thumbed through the typewritten lists he had handed me
of words like "lonely" and "love" and "Apocalypse,"
and listened to him say he knew he had talent and only
          wanted to be told
whether he was heading in the right direction.

The worst of it was he didn't know when to go—and knowing
when to go is far more important
than being talented or wearing clean underwear.
He sat in my living-room for one hour, two hours, three—
with me aching to say, "Go away, please, you're making me
          so lonely
that if you don't leave soon I may burst into tears."

Still he stayed.
        He had an irritating manner
of putting his hand in front of his mouth and half-turning
        away when he spoke
as if afraid of what might come out,
and when I spoke to him, which was less and less often
as the evening wore on, he scowled as if concentrating
so hard it was painful.

"Thank God, that's over," I thought when he left.
It wouldn't have been so bad if it hadn't been
for those disgusting mannerisms. Then I realized why
his gestures had seemed so familiar—that hand
in front of the mouth, those shifty eyes, that scowl;
and I almost ran after and embraced the poor bugger.
For he had been labouring to be me—
me in the flesh, I meant, out of his longing
for what he innocently imagined me to possess
and believed that he wanted to be.

The Fiddlehead   ALDEN NOWLAN

MY WIFE SWIMMING

A little madness, a little grief,
a few years' accumulation
of intimacy and reproof
(knives in the dark,
rare flowers, and trivia)
to demonstrate our ignorance
and the audacity
of such an enterprise.

My wife squats on the sand,
I astride a rock,
smoking my pipe,
wrap thoughts around the day
cautious as footnotes —
sunlight, the shadow
of a passing thundershower, shrieks
from the children in the shallows.
Today
I am sober, she a little drunk.

Suddenly
she is swimming, flung
full length into the plash,
her arms thrashing, face
contorted with laughter,
all clothed in
the hilarious small waves, beating
towards me, or away from me
(I cannot tell),

her dress
billowing around her
like the wings
of some strange bird.

Waves (Canada)   LESLIE NUTTING

THE USE OF FICTION

A boy claims he saw you on a bicycle last week,
touring his neighborhood. "West Cypress Street!" he shouts,
as if your being there and his seeing you
were some sort of benediction.
To be alive, to be standing outside
on a tender February evening . . .
"It was a blue bicycle, ma'am, your braid was flying,
I said hello and you laughed, remember?"

You almost tell him your bicycle seat is thick with dust,
the tires have been flat for months.
But his face, that radiant flower, says you are his friend,
he has told his mother your name!
Maybe this is a clear marble
he will hide in his sock drawer for months.
So who now, in a world of figures,
would deny West Cypress Street,
throwing up clouds into this literal sky?
"Yes, amigo"—hand on shoulder—
"It was I."

Antaeus   NAOMI SHIHAB NYE

MY FATHER'S SHADOW

Holding the ladder for
my father, I followed
the sun around the house:
"sun side in the morning,
shadow side in the afternoon."
I felt the ladder bounce
with each ascending step,
felt it sway as he swiped
with the five-inch brush,
looked up to see the rails
converging on him: my father
against the sun-blanched siding,
his lengthening shadow like a
long-legged fly upon the stream.

Now I am on the ladder, still
following the sun, my son
below me: son following the sun,

holding the same spackled ladder,
encrusted paint like pigeon droppings,
and the same mute tools: blunt scraper,
wilted brushes, their handles bleached
with the acid of my father's sweat.

I scrape the siding, fleck off
paint like brittle parchment.
I wipe the weathered shingles,
as beautiful as driftwood.
And then I see my shadow.
Or is it my father's?
I am *my father's shadow!*

I grab the five-inch brush,
slap on sun-dazzle white,
smooth it out, and watch the
luster harden. The brush strokes
come out, the shadow sets in.

Kansas Quarterly   WILLIAM P. O'BRIEN

THIS POEM IS FOR MARGARET

who picks apples
who climbs the long ladders
toward handfuls of fruit
who nests apples in canvas
rapidly without bruising them.
This poem is for Margaret
who comes from Minnesota
who says "the hardest work I ever done"
who at the end of the day is perfumed with apples,
Black Gilliflower, Macoun, Winesap,
who disappears north with the harvest.

That is the direction of sorrow
and her laughter
slow and deliberate
as farm children.
Margaret, this poem is for going north
and for all those traveling
and for your eyes liquid
with the hard, red fruit.

The Georgia Review   ED OCHESTER

SOURCE OF LAKE OCHRID

(Yugoslavia)

Bees in the fennel and blue everlastings.
Here, in September with the tourists gone,

moulting peacocks graze like geese
in the suits of exiled kings, stabbing short
quick mouthfuls from the pepper stalks.
Disturbed, the grasstips shower balls of dew
that fall like oil on struggling ants.

Past grape and asphodel and medlar
the path leads, past three wasps in ecstasy
at rotting windfall plums, then over
dunged earth to this shrine or urinal—
patched decayed plaster, empty haloed eyes.
A trickle comes up between the Saint's feet
like a hose beneath damp leaves, turns
to a runnel, a stream, a pond, then cascades
into Lake Ochrid, the South Slavonic sea:
steep-banked, so clear and limestone-hard
that milfoil rises rope-like from the floor
through fourteen metres of reflected sky
to thrust its florets in the wind. And deeper still,
green willow tresses swing, reversed in water.

Poetry   MARK O'CONNOR

IRON

Some pains are like an iron suit
That's soldered up the front with iron rivets
And ends at a metal ridge around the neck.
My head sticks up, polite as a department store dummy's.
Everyone tells me how straight I walk.
Inside my molded glove my fingers are slow;
Out of my careful eyes I watch and watch,

Because iron understands only itself
And its face like a pitted pot.
But somewhere under my shoulder there's that other kind of
    hurting.

I wake at night, you're by my window.
But my iron sleeve is so heavy
I can't reach out to touch you.

Yankee   DIANA Ó HEHIR

SHE PLEADS GUILTY

A woman of seveny-one years
stands before strangers
and whispers her plea
She does not ask for mercy
She knows she is a criminal
and the bar of justice is austere
Her daughter stands up with her
and strokes her hair

Not the harridan drape of her dress
not her bag, or its emptiness
not the young grocer who pressed the charge
not the poverty
not the judge, nor the law
for none bears animosity
But the embarrassment
She cries openly

Brecht might have
brought a crowd into the street
Neruda might have
woven a garland for her of wheat
Lorca might have
torn out his heart to offer its wingbeat
She needed less
Thirteen dollars worth of vegetables and meat

New Letters   ADRIAN OKTENBERG

LOOKING AT MY FATHER

I do not think I am deceived about him;
I know about the drinking, I know he's a tease,
obsessive, rigid, selfish, sentimental,
but I could look at my father all day
and not get enough: the large creased
ball of his forehead, slightly aglitter like the
sheen on a well-oiled baseball glove;
his eyebrows, the hairs two inches long,
black and silver, reaching out in
continual hope and curtailment; and most of
all I could look forever at his eyes,
the way they bulge out as if eager to see and
yet are glazed as if blind, the whites
hard and stained as boiled eggs
boiled in sulphur water, the irises
muddy as the crust on a live volcano, the
pupils glittering pure black,
magician black. Then there is his nose,
rounded and pocked and comfy as the bulb of a
horn a clown would toot, and his lips
solid and springy. I even like to
look in his mouth, stained brown with
cigars and bourbon, my eyes sliding down the
long amber roots of his teeth,
right in there where Mother hated, and
up the scorched satin of the sides and
vault, even the darkness on the back of his
tongue. I know he is not perfect but my
body thinks his body is perfect, the
fine stretched coarse pink

skin, the big size of him, the
sour-ball mass, darkness, hair,
sex, legs even longer than mine,
lovely feet. What I know I know, what my
body knows, it knows; it likes to
slip the leash of my mind and go and
look at him, like an animal
looking at water, then going to it and
drinking until it has had its fill and can
lie down and sleep.

The Agni Review   SHARON OLDS

A RECITAL BY RUDOLF SERKIN

Music, oldest of arts,
Unlike all others
Moves immediately upon the mind,
Presents no Lear for pity,
No awakening Adam for wonder;
We exult or grieve, unable to say why;

Nor can we say how it was
That suffering, thought, toil
Became the fleeting touch of a fingertip,
How the insensate instrument
Shook the insensate air
To make passion into sound, sound into passion,

How a man became music;
We became that music,
All the many listeners became one,
Differences like discords
Resolved in concord;

Nor how, through such tremblings of common air,
The splendid Presences were summoned then
To speak in tongues unknown yet understood
Of what Man might have been
And still might be.

The American Scholar   ELDER OLSON

THE TARN

The horn of the hunter singing
in the clear air drew me
through the latticework of trees
to a tarn where the mountains
began. I had not known
my garden
went back so far.

And now all has become
quiet. I sit beside
these waters and watch
the reflection of leaves and
sky and beyond them many
far off things rising
towards me. Anything
I wish for
I can call.

And then comes what I had not known
to call. Unfolding, moving
upwards through leaves to this
still surface; though I lean
towards it, it
is too far away as yet
for me

      to touch. Why, then,
as I lean to the pool do I feel
myself so surrounded,
caressed
by something unseen in this
most secret place?

If I turn around quickly, will I see it?
I think if I did, my calling might not be enough.
The sound of the horn is gone. What is it I want?
I rise and go farther, climbing
the stiff side of the
mountain beyond the tarn.

Studia Mystica　　　　　　　　　　　　　　　MARIJANE OSBORN

TAKING THE SHUTTLE WITH FRANZ

A search for metaphors to describe the thick
Pig faces and large torsos of businessmen.
I am encountering a fiendish wall
Of these on the Newark-Boston 9:35 shuttle flight.
My friend Franz Kafka has his nose in a book,
As ever, preparing his lecture notes, while I
Weave among the strangers, spindling and unspindling
My boarding pass, and am aghast with admiration for the cut
Of their suits, the fineness of their shirt
Fabrics, and the deep gloss of their shoeleather.

But what amazes me most is the vast expanse
Of clothing required fully to cover them,
So that one fancies a little mustached tailor
Unrolling hopefully bolt after bolt of excellent
Woolen stuff. How lucky they are, after all,
That stores sell jackets, trousers, etcetera,
In these palatial sizes.

What if they had to clothe their nakedness
With garments made for lesser men?
In patches it would have to be, perhaps

Even with stretches of raw flesh showing.
As it is, they look good
Enough to ski on. And they talk
In firm but thoughtful voices, about money.
Only about money. It is not my aural delusion.
It is commodities, it is securities.
"Franz," I whisper, "take a look. What do you think?"
Of course I cannot consider them human, any
More than I would consider the marble columns
Of an Attic temple human. Franz agrees,

But sees them more as resembling something Chinese,
Perhaps the Great Wall. Similarly, they,
Although they speak of money,
Glance from their eye-pouches at us, low
Of stature, ineffably shabby (we
Have dressed our best), with "Intellectual"
Scripted messily in Parker ink across our foreheads.
Now as they do so, the athletic heart
Throbs within them, under cashmere and cambric:
"Vermin," they think, imagining stamping us out.

Poetry   ALICIA OSTRIKER

STOP SENDING NOW

Stop sending now the signal of danger,
stop the laments of hysterical sirens
and let the helm go in the hands of the storm:
the most frightful shipwreck would be that we are saved!

What then? Shall we return again to boring Ithaca,
to our stingy concerns and our cheap joys,
and to the faithful spouse who weaves as a spider's web
her love around our life?

Again shall we know before tomorrow what will be,
and shall we not feel any desires to complete,
again to liken our dreams to those sunless fruits
which wither and fall rotten to the earth?

Since daring failed us (and will always fail us!),
let us go alone from our narrow smooth bed
and free, like men at the dawn of the world,
let us take the unknown and great roads

with a light step like a bird on the earth;
and as our soul shivers like leaves in the breeze
let us not miss this opportunity to become
the plaything of the wild waves,

whatever that may bring! As tentacles, the waves
of the sea are able to pull us down the shadowy depths,
but also they are able, with their rush, to raise us up
on high—where with our forehead we touch the stars!

The Classical Outlook   K. OURANIS
—Translated from the Greek
by Karelisa Hartigan

LEADING THE BLIND

I will lead you
with my dark eyes.
My eyes of ash, shadow, earth.
My eyes that are secrets

the darkness keeps
and never gives back.
This is the season of night.
It is the landscape

of sleep, dreams, and death.
We will not talk to
the features of the moon.
There is no way to complete

the light that starts stars.
Even the heart can show
its hidden form.
And the random world

will receive us as it falls
into the nearest shapes.
You will follow me
as an alphabet follows sound,

blind to what light imagines.
These words, these syllables
of the dark will
be your reliable guide.

Ploughshares   SUE OWEN

AN UNPETRARCHAN SONNET

I wake at midnight, facing surgery
Tomorrow. Since my sweet, officious nurse
Decrees one sleeping pill's enough, I curse,
Then stare at shadows as sick summary
Of us kills night. You spat out savagely,
In bitter rage, I was spoiled, perverse
Big baby. How you said it next was worse,
Since it was phrased and toned so clinically.

But, as a patient, once again I'm "hon"
And "darling"; you're the sweet, supportive wife:
This marriage could revert to early fun
And games, if daily I'd endure the knife!
Enough. Let's get our operation done,
Put up with pain, recuperate to life.

Poem   JOHN OWER

IBIS

The drought persisted. Mornings he would stand
Among the hogs on one leg, balancing
Half sunk in that rich filth he had to probe,
To peck at curd, extending his thin neck

As if for slaughter: Bird, who having not
Invented justice, charged no violation,
Claimed no dignity his need could shame—
Just bird alone, who came at dawn, cried out

And went on feeding. By late afternoon
The offal in his feathers dried. He preened,
Puffed his warm breast out wide, then circled off
Across the cow kraal, raising a harsh cry

From dung to heaven. Sought no witness, made
A job of drift between baked laterite
And fertile sty: flew fast, as if his wings
Could scrape the bright rust from an arid sky.

The Atlantic Monthly   HARVEY OXENHORN

FIRE-FOE

You don't forgive
what can't occur.
You tell me: "Live!"
as if there were
no virtue in the negative,
all valor in the stir.
Fire's flailing through a sieve,
for you to catch,
for me to watch.
You snatch, I flee;
you thrive, I fail;
yet ice will trail
through you and me
equally.
The lustful and the tame
come to just the same.
This so, why blow

higher higher
the scaffold of desire?
Gallows and bellows,
graveside fellows:
easier by far to go
under the exacting snow
when the blaze is ashes-low
in the barren bush of No.

The Literary Review   CYNTHIA OZICK

SINCE THEN

There was a time (centuries ago, nobody remembers)
when we were together, months on end,
from dawn till long past midnight.
We talked all there was to talk.
We did everything there was to do.
    We battened
on fullness and failure.
    And in a short while
we burned up the measured days.
    It became impossible
to survive what we had been together.
And since then eternity
has furnished me with a brief and worn vocabulary:
"absence," "forgetfulness," "lack-of-love," "far-away."
And nevermore, nevermore,
    never, never.

Denver Quarterly   JOSÉ EMILIO PACHECO
—Translated from the Spanish
by Anthony Kerrigan

CLEANING THE FISH

Mom says she won't; we'll have to clean them, though
she used to do it when I fished with dad.
Dad's illness wore her down; I think she felt
relief after he died, and didn't mourn
him long enough before she married Sam.
I know there is an art to cleaning fish.
In ancient times, prophets could look into
the future by examining the entrails
of an animal; they'd burn it then
to satisfy their chosen deity.
Hold down the tail, and use a scraping knife,
stroking the scales to get right to the skin.
Slice through the vent and open up the fish,
just like a box. Then pluck the organs out:
liver, bladder, stomach, and gills; cut off

the head and tail, and wash away the blood.
This tissue here—this irridescent film
that runs along the whole back-bone—must be
removed with care. How smooth the small heart is!
It will continue beating for a while.
Fish don't feel pain as people do; they go
right into shock without the fear of death,
like other animals, because they have
no thought of time extending after them.
They don't know what loss is; you musn't feel
sorry for them. Don't be upset with mom.
It was because of us that she remarried
so soon following dad's death. She knew
we needed money and a healthy father
in the house after those draining years.
When Sam bought you that dress with yellow birds
you've wanted for a year, you hardly said
a word of thanks. But I predict that he'll
be kind to you and mom. I've told him how
dad sang to you before you went to bed,
even when he had lost the melody,
until the very end. Sam understands
the way the dead still live within our minds.
The clearest memory I have of dad—
he's pasting in his stamps, studying them
with his magnifying glass, looking for
the special marks that make them valuable.
The ones he loved the most were animals,
bright red and blue, I think from Africa.
He told me that he never traded those.
I saved his whole collection for a while,
but then I had to sell it to a friend.
Enough of that! Today we concentrate
on fish! First, rinse it in cold water, dry,
then lightly rub with salt, inside and out.
A shallow dish is what we use, and top
with sherry, soy and peanut oil. Later,
I'll give you all the measurements. Sprinkle
with parsley, garnish with some shredded scallions,
and, behold, a two pound fish should steam
for twenty minutes and be done! Take out
mom's crystal glasses, grandma's silverware,
the yellow tablecloth, and light the candles
when the sun goes down; they shine with orange
merging into purple blue, almost like
the inside of the fish. When you grow up
and marry someone whom you really love,
you'll teach your daughter how to clean a fish.
If dad were still with us, he'd show approval
with his eyes: "Life must serve life," they'd say,
"here's to good food!" And Sam, well, we'll find out
whether he has an appetite for fish!

Ploughshares   ROBERT PACK

HARD TIMES

They asked the man for his time
so his time might be added to History.
They asked him for his hands
because in hard times there's nothing
like a pair of hands.
They asked him for his eyes
(which had shed a few tears),
so that he might see the good side
of things—especially the good side of life.
(To look on misery, a stunned glance will do.)
They asked him for his mouth's lips,
parched as they were and cracked, so that he might affirm,
and with each affirmation build a dream
(the tallest Tall-Dream).
They asked him for his legs, tough and gnarled
(his restless roving legs),
because, in hard times,
is there anything like a pair of legs
with which to work on a construction site.
or dig a trench?
They asked him for his woods, where
his yielding tree had brought him up.
They asked him for his chest, his heart, his shoulders.
They told him
that all those things were absolutely necessary.
Then they explained
that all these donations were useless
if he didn't hand over his tongue,
because, in hard times,
there is nothing like a glottal stop
to block opprobrium or memory.
Finally they asked him to
"Please go along."
Because, in hard times,
that would be, no doubt, the decisive proof.

The Malahat Review   HEBERTO PADILLA
                                                 —*Translated from the Spanish*
                                                    by Anthony Kerrigan

THE BATON TWIRLERS

Soon we will sit in little rooms
and watch ourselves on a screen.
Strange anyone should think our job
is simple, is easy.
The sequence unfolds as we
watch our arms and legs
make movements impossible
to any but the faithful

who rise each morning
before the dawn and put down
the silver wand only with the last
swirl of sun. The white polish
of our boots shines like our
even teeth and is every bit
as important in the quick
routine as making our grace
appear natural and easy,
like the shimmering shadows
of leaves. But skill is not the reason
we would win the viewers' love,
nor beauty luxurious with the smell
of sex. There's more to admire
in any art than tossing sticks.
Somewhere inside these nimble
pirouettes and high-kneed steps
there's untold significance
that like all religious gestures
must finally be taken on faith
even if it shows nothing of itself.

Mississippi Review   WILLIAM PAGE

THE SWING

The yellow metal seat flashes
in the casual summer sun.
His four daughters, all under twelve
and desperate to be pushed,
circle around him
as he waters the garden.

Swing *me,* Daddy!   Swing *me!*

You'd shoot the hose at us.
The water was hard and cold—right in August—
but there was a sudden tilt to your laughter.
The neighbor paused to watch your girls
running, bare feet springing the dandelions,
skin sparkling and dripping.

When I pass the park at night now,
I imagine a father swinging his daughter,
pushing her higher, and higher.
The park echoes with long trailing screams of pleasure
as the thick familiar hands propel her small body,
her skirt opening to gather the dark.

April
and there are no
pieces left
to assemble.
But there is myself,
older than you ever were,

who hasn't yet come
to the full dark bloom.

Tar River Poetry   GAILMARIE PAHMEIER

EACH OF US HAS AN ODYSSEY

Each of us has an Odyssey,
a morning setting-out with a boat of wood or of iron,
a journey
with frigate, schooner, or caique
on broad fog-covered seas;
            around
all of us the arms of war wander,
the hum of the wind, the rose-colored evenings of
bloody battle.
We will all hear enraptured some lustful sirens,
we will do battle with sword or word against the cyclopes
or the barbarians,
we will fall—sometime—with a banner of sentiment into
the arms of a Circe.
All my brothers, we have one fatherland,
for all of us there awaits somewhere that day of return,
since
each of us has an Odyssey.

The Classical Outlook   P. PANAGIOTOUNIS
                                        —*Translated from the Greek
                                        by Karelisa Hartigan*

THE NIGHT: ENSENADA

Somewhere a tiny Sanctus bell
is ringing in a mud church.
To the woman falling asleep
under her black shawl
it is the glitter of a lost instant
in some other life.

Alone in Ensenada,
a boy stands up drunk
in the dark of a small room
wanting a woman,
staring at the lights
on the water of Bahia Todos Santos.

All the saints of the water
rise with him in the dark
to the street music of mariachis,
to the moaning of cattle on the docks,
and soft rumbling of ships
ready to sail before dawn

where men smoke
and women burn in the rising
and falling of the coals,
or bathe in small phosphorescent waves
that follow each other to shore;
and the woman who steps from the waves
with the glitter of the sea
in her hair turns

and leaves him standing there,
fourteen, drunk, and alone,
staring out the window
at a path of emerald light
laid across the bay
that a boy might row or swim
all the way
to Punta Banda, or further,
to some other life.

The Georgia Review   GREG PAPE

SWIMMING IN LATE SEPTEMBER

We listen:
the hush of apples falling through a dark,
the crackling of pines.
A slow wind circles the pond
like an ancient bird with leathery wings.

I float, my belly to the moon,
lifting my toes through cold, black water.
You brush against me, fanning your hair,
so close we are touching head to foot.

Frog-eyes sparkle in the ferns
as if they wonder
who would be swimming in late September.
Already the crickets have lost their wings;
the woods are brittle yellow.

But we go on swimming, swimming.
It is part of our love.
We give off rings of chilly waves
from one still center. Tonight
there is nothing but skin between us:
the rest is water.

The Southern Review   JAY PARINI

GRANDAD

The curtains are pulled,
thinning the light.

He sits
in his favourite chair
the way sediment
settles in liquid,
newspaper furled
beside him.
He's grown too old
to unfold the world.
Pottering thoughts
cross his face
as he plays
with jigsaw pieces
of his life
he can no longer
fit together—
all the colours
have converged to fade.

Now and then
the wind lifts
the curtains
letting in measured light,
light where dim memory
and another age live.

The Atlantic Advocate   NANCY PASSY

THE PRINTER

(for Roland Hoover)

Baskerville, Perpetua, Garamond:
I thought you were naming a dance,
but the only minuet is typeface moving
across the page, and you in your apron, bowing—
journeyman to the letter, apprentice to the word.
The smell of ink, like the smell of bread,
signifies morning, a bleeding of color
at the horizon, the horizon itself
a line of boldface too distant to read.

In this world there are as many letters
as leaves, as birds, as flecks of ash;
whole armies of alphabets march across
margins of pavement, margins of snow.
Now there's a smudge on your forehead
where your hand strayed
making those architectural gestures,
the Pleasure of our Company is requested,
the ceremonial announcement of birth or death.

Your press is as fruitful as a wine press,
the sound of its motion like surf, hour after hour

reams of paper spreading their deckle-edged foam.
At night you distribute the type as carefully
as if you were placing your daughters in their beds.
Dark enters, a time before language,
but the sky is printed in white indelible stars,
with God's own signature—that thumbprint of moon,
like the printer's colophon
on heaviest Mohawk Superfine.

The Georgia Review   LINDA PASTAN

WE COME TO SILENCE

We come to silence slowly.
Washed into the world
on a wave of sound
we leave it later with closed mouths,
our tongues grown heavy
as stones to anchor us
in earth. Now we hear
wind in the noisy leaves,
a hubbub of water
over the rocks,
the musical warfare
of the birds.
Consider the ear
shaped like the bass clef,
but empty.
Consider the spaces between stars,
soliloquies of light.
It is almost time
to hush the children,
to quiet the dogs.
Even your words grow muffled
in my hair, soon
it will be only touch
I know you by.
These are the corridors
of silence; enter
on tiptoe.
Here Orpheus sleeps,
his harp unstrung.
Here the sound
a leaf makes
falling to ground
may deafen us.

The Georgia Review   LINDA PASTAN

WINTER APPROACHES

Winter approaches. And once again
The secret retreat of some bear
Will vanish under impassable mud,
To a tearful child's despair.

Little huts will awaken in lakes
Reflecting their smoke like a path.
Encircled by autumn's cold slush,
Life-lovers will meet by the hearth.

Inhabitants of the stern North,
Whose roof is the open air,
'In this sign conquer' is written
On each inaccessible lair.

I love you, provincial retreats,
Off the map, off the road, past the farm.
The more thumbed and grubby the book,
The greater for me its charm.

Slow lines of lumbering carts,
You spell out an alphabet leading
From meadow to meadow. Your pages
Were always my favourite reading.

And suddenly here it is written
Again, in the first snow—the spidery
Cursive italic of sleigh runners—
A page like a piece of embroidery.

A silvery-hazel October.
Pewter shine since the frosts began.
Autumnal twilight of Chekhov,
Tchaikovsky and Levitan.

The Hudson Review   BORIS PASTERNAK
                    *—Translated from the Russian
                    by Jon Stallworthy and Peter France*

ONOMATOPOEIA

Metaphor is the delegate of the text,
a mind within an act of the mind,
writing's icon of fusion within the text.

Metaphor is to the text as text
is to the world. In its fusion we find
metaphor is the delegate of the text

within itself. In metaphor, one object
links with another to form a kind
of writing's icon of fusion within the text.

One link creates all links to reject
no possibilities. Due to its velocity we find
in metaphor, as delegate of the text,

the delicate co-life of simultaneous facts
concerning both objects; metaphor binds
writing's icons of fusion within the text

by keeping them apart. Equal and perfect
dwell objects' facts in us. As it upholds the mind,
metaphor is the delegate of the text,
writing's icon of fusion, within the text.

The Arizona Quarterly   RICARDO PAU-LLOSA

A GARDEN

Whoever loves a garden fears seasons.
It is the highest of civilizations,
a bed in the earth. Great fears are the reasons
for each garden. Simple devastations—
fake death, false dreams, hungers only imagined
—are just the magic of habits compared
to fear of dirt nature, its crouch, the lesioned
back of earth. The swamp's spilled stomach is stared
down by eyes in a garden. Seasons terrify,
they terrify with their strict endurance
and strict abandonment, like parents. Why?
To garden is to love the instance, the dance
of one's reason and the season, a time
seized to be eased: a garden is a rhyme.

The Georgia Review   MOLLY PEACOCK

AND YOU WERE A BABY GIRL

I loved your smell when you were a baby
high above me lying in your bassinet
amid cotton, flannel and rubbery
talc. I stood in the mock diaper I'd wet
(a dishtowel pinned around my rear end) and sniffed
upwards past the trousered and wool-skirted knees
toward you, taking in a uriney whiff
of the light but deep sweet smell of fleece
that was your infant skin thirty years ago.
When we lie close together now on the beach
on our towels in the wind near the undertow
in a flower of years whorled against the crease
of sand by the tin waves, I catch the tender
spark of the faint comet of your infant
smell, still, and am shocked and won't surrender—
and then do—it is all the years have meant,

the damp baby smoke of rivalry unfurled
beyond the salt and oil of the practicing world.

Mississippi Review   MOLLY PEACOCK

ONCE WHEN I RETURNED TO THE SEASIDE

Once, when I returned to the seaside,
I went searching at night
through the warm streets
for my onetime companions . . .

Like a crazed wolf I smelled
the hot shadow among the houses.
The old and empty odor drove me
to the vast beach by the open sea.
It was there I found
the clearest bitterness
and my lunar shadow clinging
to the ancient odor.

Poetry Now   SANDRO PENNA
                              —Translated from the Italian
                                  by W. S. Di Piero

SEQUELS

Each time we decide to
   shake out the blanket
      downwind and go home,

turning our backs on the ocean,
   something happens, and you
      stay a little longer.

A seagull begins a crazy cadenza
   as if a bone is stuck in his throat
      and suddenly cuts and runs, or

a single scallop shell seizes
   one ray of the lowering sun
      in a color without a name, or

some mysterious beach-being
   has scrawled its *mene-mene-tekel*
      on the sand wall of the sea

which you need to understand, the why
   and where under the beach it sank,
      leaving its last meaning.

I call: *Time to go!* But you are upwind
    listening to sequels of thunder, the long
      moody equivocations

of the beast that is both life and death
    which you aren't able to believe
      for all my blows, my kisses, my frothing
        logic, old man's love.

Passages North   EDMUND PENNANT

EGYPT AFTER THE HAIRDO

You have just sprung coiffed
from beauty's den & now
we have come to Egypt
through the portals
of an exhibition.

Three thousand years of culture
float before us under glass
& there you stand—
culture facing coiffure,
each fixed upon the other.

Circling,
spiralling inward on the figurines
& etchings, hieroglyphs & mummery gifts,
you remark with wonder,
butterflying brilliantly through time.

From Memphis to Thebes
& finally to Alexandria—
which sifts across my tongue like lust—
you grow more marvellously ringed
& ringleted

Until, arriving at the Nefertiti profiles
hewn in stone,
your glance cuts through the glass
& streams across all time
like hair,

Bright as the black Nile,
braceleting my wrists & neck & ankles,
promising me everything
so fundamental
in your newest way.

National Forum   ALAN PERLIS

STUDY

For three weeks rain pocked January drifts
with a sound like footsteps
of many tired people,

then soaked a dirty pile
of leaves and earth scoured
in the fury of clearing snow . . .

Ambition leaked from me. I was willing
to donate my life
to plumped pillows, the comfortable armchair . . .

But instead I drove past a little farmhouse
with a big cordwood stack
like its blind solid shadow,

past the shuttered farmstand
where soon the paddock gate
would be thrown back, and pots of marigolds—

those easy flowers—set out on sawhorses
for customers who couldn't wait for bushel baskets
to overflow with peas, and crates with green lettuce-roses,

and I thought, soon the shadow beside the house
will shrink in noon heat, and the sign on the door
flip from CLOSED to OPEN—HAVE A NICE DAY . . .

Once in my study,
I felt every minute, *You can't
work any longer.* But I worked.

And when I couldn't write,
read, without anxiety,
thumbed-over paperback books . . .

The New Republic   JOYCE PESEROFF

A TOUCH OF IMPATIENCE

I was patient at the start,
full of diplomatic art;
you were young: I played my part
    with delicate good taste;
asking nothing but your heart
    I kept our courtship chaste.

Now you've reached a riper stage;
now the fire begins to rage;
now my virgin's come of age,

with breasts new-grown and waiting—
wasted if we don't engage
in something less frustrating.

Since we've coupled mind with mind,
let's be physically entwined:
wrestling's a delight, you'll find,
　　if you'll relax your guard.
Sweetest flower of all, be kind:
　　let's play with no holds barred!

Grapes are luscious things to squeeze;
sucking honey's nice for bees.
What's my meaning? Darling, please
　　accept a full translation:
not in language; what you'll see's
　　a graphic demonstration.

The Malahat Review　　　　　　　　PETER OF BLOIS
　　　　　　—Translated from the twelfth century Latin
　　　　　　　　　　　　by Fleur Adcock

UPSTATE LILACS

Up the spring hillside where the dug road went
Before the county realigned it, past
Broken stone walls and grown-up fields, we find
The old foundations folding. Round about them
The lilacs stand, stiffly, with none to please
Or take account of. By the ruined sills
They wave their heart-shaped leaves and shake their blooms,
Flouting the fact that those who planted them
Gave up the homestead. If the shallow wells
Went foul, if rains and snows of yesteryear
Escaped the catchments, if the summer sun
Turned on the crops, leaving the fields burnt straw,
If three hard winters cracked the will to plough,
Or if, simply, there was no special reason
To stay on high ground when the Indians
That held the river valley had moved on,
We cannot know, although these old maids might,
These gnarled old maids, the hardiest of whom
Stand round about in green and lavender,
Heedless of man, preferring their perfume.

The American Scholar　　　　　　　　DONALD PETERSEN

THE OLD POET LOOKS AT THE NIGHT SKY

When I was young, watching this same moon, huge,
rise through the gap-toothed houses in the east,
and hearing the March wind wrestling the black-topped elms
till their branches scraped the eaves, I dreamed the power
that lived in that moving darkness lived in me.

Now, having done all that I could, and failed,
I am content tonight to feel it still,
out there, moving through the barren, moon-tossed branches,
and know when I am dead it shall live on,
though not in me—having served it with my life.

The Arizona Quarterly   PAUL PETRIE

A RAINY DAY

(after a photograph by Jeanloup Sieff)

What luck to come across
gartered buttocks
hanging out a window!
I'm sure she feels the light
(and perhaps my eyes)
on the sharp grain of her skin.
I wonder if she is coming out
or going in, or if
it is possible to fall in love
with only a part of someone?

I think I have been in love
with a woman's calves
when she is wearing heels;
with a thirty-year-old dancer's
prematurely gray curls
drenched in sweat;
with the eyes (I am without shame)
of a five-year-old girl.

I consider turning the page
but hang around instead
like a notion,
or a kid at seventeen
when the air was always erotic
with cigarettes and Juicy Fruit.

The Malahat Review   ROGER PFINGSTON

AT THE CONCERT

Teeth are everywhere,
wall-to-wall teeth:

American-beauty teeth like toothpaste ads,
unwholesome teeth, wolf teeth,
but all smiling,
trying to be friendly.
Trying to show who they are,
big square blocks of white
or thin-skinned yellow,
lipstick flecked, tobacco flecked;
still, all pretending to be full sets,
even those that are false.

Everyplace I turn
I am walking on teeth:
they are in my hair, nipping
at my ear, my rear,
my private parts.
The skin of my hand catches
on a fang,
my clothes are in shreds,
saliva drips from the air.
Everything is wet from smiles
when clatter ceases
and music begins.

Kayak   RICHARD PFLUM

THE LAND: A LOVE LETTER

This hill and the old house on it
are all we have. Two acres,
more or less—half crabby lawn,
half field we mow but twice a year.

Some trees we planted, most gifts
of the land. The pine by the kitchen?
Grown twice as fast as our son. The bald
elm lost the race with my own hairline.

The mulberry—so lively with squirrels,
chipmunk chases and birds—
fell like a tower in the hurricane.
My chainsaw ate fruitwood for weeks.

And the juniper, the one that all but
obliterated the view? Men cut it down
to make way for the new well and water
pump. That pump should pump pure

gold: we lay awake, engineering
ways to get it paid for. But we'll never
leave this mortgaged hill: this land
is changing as we change—its face

erodes like ours—weather marks,
stretch marks, traumas of all sorts.

Last night another limb broke in the storm.
We still see it sketch the sky.

We've become where we have been.
This land is all we have, and this love
letter is addressed to anyone
who ever loved and married the land.

The Paris Review   ROBERT PHILLIPS

I DO NOT KNOW

(Thereiyavillai)

I see the mountain
as rock and stone!
to carve a statue,
to build a temple,
     a compound wall round a bungalow.
To metal the road,
a peak to conquer. . .
All this I see,
but not the mountain as mountain.

I see the flower:
bait for tender love,
to distil a perfume,
arrange in a vase. . .
All this I see,
but not the flower as flower.

I see myself:
as a stone pillar
supporting an unseen society,
as the icy pinnacle
of all evolution,
as the last link
in the chain of generations. . .
All this I see,
but not myself as myself.

New Letters   NA PICHAMURTI
                                    —*Translated from the Tamil*
                                    by P. G. Sunderarajan

VALENTINE CONFESSION

All right. After all these years, yes:
I do not love you more than your fragile replicas.
I love you in another curve or design.
I admit, I cannot cleave only to you.

I get homesick for my mother's lips on my forehead
and the reflection I see in my father's eyes.

It's true: while you pounded between my thighs
I have let others tap on your shoulder.
How many? I never knew or counted.
And now that I've started and your tears pelt
my shoulders like stones, I'm glad
I opened this pressed heart.

There were times I blessed the blood curse.
Sometimes your demands stain
me dark-faced. And even this, I confess.
I have placed you in a casket and hid my smile
behind the black veil and it was not enough.

On occasion, I wiped you from my days
as easily as the kitchen sponge cleans spills.
Are you satisfied, now that you've seen the uneven cut
of my heart? Can you grasp my lip-warm touch on the tip
of these words and believe I love you, as any woman loves
her man after twenty years?
And now that the air is strained by truth,
does my love sting your eyes?

Passages North   DEANNA LOUISE PICKARD

SHORT PORTRAIT FROM EXETER

All my family is like that: petty, concerned
With moments, the short view. Which is why
I'm rarely home. Usually, it's the park,
The library, the supermarket. Rows of canned

Peas and corn, tomato juice, bottles and jars;
All reasonable and exactly the things that
Shadow an afternoon. When the sun is high,
And the trees lonely, I prefer to walk

Toward the river, where ducks, a few swans,
Paddle in silence. My feet immersed in
Slow water, grubs and butterfish, a perch in
The shade. All life is like this in the summer.

But winter is more of the same: rows of books
Panthered on shelves, ready to spring
At a moment. Which only brings me back to
My parents. There's no hope; there never was any.

Only two people, the same age, one taller
Than the other; both seated at a kitchen table.
Between them they've buttered so much bread
The slices stack out the door, lead out of town.

Tendril   JOHN PIJEWSKI

JOGGING ON THE BEACH

I jog past a grin
in the claw a crab
left behind and homes
that stilt along the shore
in case the tide gets high
enough to want more beach.

I follow cloud and gull
like a ship on a sweat voyage
with a wake of foot prints
in sand surf pounds flat
as the stomach I will kiss tonight.
But the ocean is calmer
this evening than the bay
I saw last week where
my heart still floats.

A few dunes more
and what I thought
was a buoy becomes ship.
I keep jogging until we
are nose to bow and I stop to
watch it catch whatever
the sea has to offer.

What was cruel in my life
is lost now and this beach
is what church once meant.
I realize, too, that surf is white
because wherever prayer begins,
it ends in foam.

The sun sets the sky pink
enough to know why tourists
come, and to blush the cheeks
of a young girl asked
to waltz at her
first dance in the music
this wind brings.

I then turn to walk back.
The squawk in the
throat of a gull could be
what it takes to make me
love again.

Poetry   KEVIN PILKINGTON

THE OLD MAN

When flesh and expectations shrink, the old
man is like a tree-root sunk deep on a lonely

homestead. He drinks dark waters and gains
strength from rock-strewn field and thorny hedge.

Waiting for the dark days to come, he shies
away from the abundance of the world. He embraces
the loneliness of lanes and the muted oboes of
autumn. Sadness is his shield against despair.

The Arizona Quarterly   WILLIAM PILLIN

AUTUMN DROUGHT

(Stanford University 1976:
to the memory of A. Y. W.)

November brings no rain. Brown stubble blackens.
Torn paper litter, wind-blown with the leaves,
Piles up against dead stems. As traffic slackens,
Nightfall brings fear, and always now one grieves.

Where I once listened, lonely as these young,
But with some hope beyond what I could see
That meaning might be mastered by my tongue,
Anonymous process now claims them and me.

Perhaps the enterprise of mind is vain:
Where hucksters sell opinions, knowledge fails,
Wit pandering to the market for gross gain
Corrupted words, false morals, falser tales.

Though one I loved taught here, provoking strife
By speaking truth about the human word,
And died—as few men do—ready for life,
I teaching in his absence seem absurd,

Seem almost unremembering, unawake.
And should his poems live—some consolation
To those who knew him and to those who take
His measure by their worth—their celebration

Will not be here, not where the idle gaze,
Touristic, slides past phoenix palms to stare
Where Mount Diablo dominates through haze
The ever-diminishing waters and the glare.

The Southern Review   HELEN PINKERTON

RECALLING ROETHKE, I REMEMBER JOY

("I trust all joy."
—from Theodore Roethke's notebook)

You triumphed over everything:
The dames who bugged you half the night;

Papa's flowers and unfriendly ghost;
Your own madness and boozy breath—
Even the grudging honors heaped by those
Who did not bother to read your books.
Words remained your only joy.
But re-reading them today,
I can feel their energies taking root,
The leaves of the collected work
Sprouting their heads off,
Waving like something very close to joy.
I trust it more than I do myself.

Green River Review   SANFORD PINSKER

VISITING HOURS

The stern-faced lady at the hospital desk
Hands me a pass. The elevator ascends
And I am in post-intensive care—
A visitor to the chronically ill.
My mother watches the "Happy Anny Show,"
Her face blanker than *tabula rasa.*
She does not recognize her tanning son
Who has given up this hour on the beach.
But I nod. Make more small talk than I believe.
We no longer quarrel about Art
Or the physician I might have become.
The afternoon drags on like endless dactyls.
The nurse assures me she is confused;
Her unused bedpan confirms the fact.
I plant a kiss on her chalky forehead
And depart. Tomorrow will be the same.
Look out for me, Ma. I'll be back at 2.

Midstream   SANFORD PINSKER

DEATH & DYING: LESSON #1

Nobody dies enough for someone else:
We only imagine what it might be like
As the face contorts, the breath zooms out.
Death comes hard as a grunting lover
Until, in a wink, a life is over.
Whatever the lesson in all that,
You shrink back, fail to learn.
But wait: No doubt you will get a turn—
And somebody else leaning over with a mirror,
Hot for a glimpse of your afterlife.

San Jose Studies   SANFORD PINSKER

AFTER WHISTLER

In his portrait of Carlyle, Whistler builds
from the color out: he calls it an arrangement
in gray and black and gives it a number in order
to commit us to the composition—to the foreground
first, in profile, before we go on to a wall
that seems to be neutral but is really the weather.
Carlyle is tired, beyond anger, and beautiful,
his white head tilted slightly toward the painter.
He is wearing a long coat and has his hat in his hands.

When I was born, I came out holding my breath, blue.
The cord had somehow rotted at the navel—
I must have lain alone for hours before they would let
my father's mother, the other woman there, give blood.
She still had red hair and four years to live.
The place on my arm where they put the needles in
I call my mortality scar. When I think of my grand-
mother lifting me all the way to the kitchen counter,
I think of the weight by which we are doubled or more

through the lives of others. I followed her
everywhere, or tried to. I was her witness.
When I look at Whistler's portrait of Carlyle
I think of how the old survive: we make them up.
In the vegetable garden, therefore, the sun is gold
as qualified in pictures. She is kneeling in front
of the light in such a way I can separate skin from bone.
She is an outline, planting or preparing the ground.
For all I know she will never rise from this green place.

Even the painter's mother is staring into the future,
as if her son could paint her back into her body.
I was lucky. In nineteen thirty-nine they still
believed blood was family. In a room real
with walls the color of buckwheat she would sit out
the afternoon dressed up, rocking me to sleep.
It would be Sunday, slow, no one else at home.
And I would wake that way, small in her small arms,
hers, in the calendar dark, my head against her heart.

Antaeus   STANLEY PLUMLY

WEEKEND AT THE BILTMORE

("I'll meet you under the clock.")

When, set loose like children
Kept in through the long winter,
Spring finally came,
And the old hotel seemed theirs, all New York,
Each moment announcing its presents,

Fresh, self-invigorating pleasures
To be sought out again and again,
As if eyes and brains and nerves
Can only absorb so much
Before they're overwhelmed, and must start over,
Slower, more patiently, this time,
Or, like children,
Are blessed with wondrously short
Wandering spells of attention
That dart like eager headlights
Viewed from the top of a tall building.

In their brown room, in taxis, in bars,
Through sex and shopping,
And long dinners in restaurants,
They chase the floats and banners, horns and
High-steppers of a parade that keeps going on,
And sweeps them up, and does not stop for anything,
Just as they cannot stop—
Not even to say their unhappiness:
She in flight from her parents, and a small town,
Their teeth already sunk too deep . . .
He gunning engines, pressing the landscape
For a road that does not double back to himself—
And hold still long enough to hear,
This is not it, you haven't been saved,
And, wrapped in each other's arms,
That nothing will come of these days
But themselves wrapped in one another's arms—
A clock going round and round to please itself.

Ploughshares   ROBERT POLITO

JERUSALEM

(This year here,
but next year in Jerusalem.
—The Hagadah)

And what will the pious Jews
in Jerusalem
pray for, this year?
As always,
they will pray and sway,
"This year here,
but next year in Jerusalem."
For Jerusalem, even to them,
is visible only
on top of the edge of
the horizon, a chimera,
shimmering in the sun. . . .

New Letters   FELIX POLLAK

OUR ELDEST SON CALLS HOME

(for David)

To-night you break a week's still absence
to assure us you are safe and well.
Still the father I was years ago,
I am unable to neglect the shadow of
the child I fear, at times, may haunt you.
But though I strain for nuances of loneliness,
regret, your voice demands our confidence.
So, for the moment, I am relieved—
unlike that monstrous day I recollect:

Crimson in infantile rage,
our eyes briefly negligent, you stiffened,
turned and fell from the open crib.
Then, like a lifeless doll, mother crying,
"My God, he's dead!," we swept you up
into our arms and ran, abandoning the house.
Half-naked and insane with grief and guilt,
we screamed our way through plodding traffic.
Only the next day when they pronounced you
wondrously whole could we deride our frenzy.

Now, beyond the wooded lakes and
distant prairies, you're telling us
of climbing high onto those cool alluring slopes
where you've observed small nestling eagles.
Prayerfully I listen, simply ask you
write us soon and just be careful
—sense the aging of my arms.

The Antigonish Review   DON POLSON

A MIDDLE-AGED DREAM

Dead December has blown itself
Up my shirt sleeve,
And I stand under half-
Forgotten snow and rumored winds,
Frozen in this summer park,

Years away from fields gone wide
In winter-remembered light
Where a boy walked with a man called father
Through day's last shadows,
Through youth's last years.

America   LARRY COE PRATER

RELATIVITY

(for Lotte Jacobi)

As we go down in the dark the slight
Icy slope to the car, the grip of your hands
On my shoulders tells me you're right

Behind me and upright. I don't understand
Relativity, but forty-some years ago
You photographed Albert Einstein, and

Today I saw his soft eyes, below
The fine accumulation of his hair,
Random, gentle, abstract hair, as though

His thought like pipesmoke issued on the air;
I saw his sailboat drifting, his violin
Waiting his hands. And always I felt you there,

About the age I am you must have been,
Holding your camera as if you took a friend
By the shoulders to show him something you'd seen.

If the universe is a slope all things descend,
If the speed of light is the only absolute,
What every atom dreams of as its end,

On this icy path, if I should slip, would we shoot
Like lasers into the dark, a double star?
Old hands on my shoulders, be my parachute,

Help me go slow. And so we reach the car,
Waiting to take us wherever we're headed tonight,
And laughing, say to each other, "Here we are!"

The Atlantic Monthly   C. W. PRATT

BLOOD ORANGE

The zipper has glided over your back
and every delicious turn of your amorous flesh
right in the middle of darkness
has shone suddenly
And your dress falling on the waxed floor
has made no more noise than
that of an orange peel falling on a carpet
But under our feet
its small pearly buttons crackle like seeds
Blood orange
pretty fruit
the point of your breast
has etched a new line of fortune
in the hollow of my hand
Blood orange

pretty fruit
Sun of night.

Prism International   JACQUES PRÉVERT
                                  —Translated from the French
                                       by Harriet Zinnes

LOSS

A thousand years from now this hill will be
a little smaller, smoother, rounder,
and as empty of my standing here as it will be
the moment that I leave
. . . that I should have happened at all!
those connections that produce us,
the blunders, chance encounters,
the ironies and histories other than my own,
the delicate unlikelihoods
of randomness and fate
. . . a commonplace of miracles.

A thousand years ago
this hill was bigger, rougher, sharper, and
as empty of my standing here as it will be
the moment that I leave.
. . . but one can't expect to be relieved
of one's miraculous inconsequence;
meaning forms its place.
Holes in the rocks through which time sounds,
we are shapes of being having been. Invisible,
as we must be to rocks and trees before we leave,
our absences remain: the common place,
direction, of our lives, the view
from which to have without possession.

Occident   V. B. PRICE

YOU DO NOT COME

Spring is waking and stretching its arms,
Flowers weave their silk threads
For the festival of colors.
You do not come.

Afternoons grow long,
Red has touched the grapes,
Sickles are kissing the wheat.
You do not come.

Clouds are gathering.
Earth opens its hands to drink
The bounty of the sky.
You do not come.

Trees murmur enchantment,
Airs from the woodland wander
With lips full of honey.
You do not come.

Seasons wear their beauty,
Night sets on its brow
A diadem of moon.
You do not come.

Again the stars tell me
That in my body's house
A candle of beauty still burns.
You do not come.

All the sun's rays vow
That light still wakes
From the death sleep of night.
You do not come.

New Letters   AMRITA PRITAM
                            —Translated from the Punjabi
                                    by Charles Brasch

ONCE I MOVED LIKE THE WIND

(from the surrender speech of Geronimo)

Nobody tells the wind
where to hunt or when to sing
or when to dance—
the wind whirls and shouts if it pleases;
it is the freest thing we know—
our men were like that,
unhurried, bold.

And the wind goes down to the river
and watches the moon walking there.
It moves as quietly as a butterfly
where the maize is planted.
It brushes past
the sweet-smelling tassels,
it touches the bean vines
and the blackberries—
our women were like that.

Sometimes the wind tosses the birds
and worries the trees,
sometimes it goes off by itself
and, other times, it calls to the sun
to look at what it is doing—
our children were like that,
like the wind in the spring.

Anima   KATHARINE PRIVETT

OXFORD, ON AN ANCIENT CROSSROADS
BESIDE THE THAMES

We meet in the park because it is ancient
and well-planned.
It feels particular,
our walk becoming part of a miniature order.
The crocuses look stemless,
set down like teacups by a careful hand,
and the footbridge is formed
in a curve of suspension.

You tell me that once black swans
imported from Australia floated on the Thames.
Because it is final,
our conversation is distilled,
comes down to objects.
Goldfish circle the ornamental pond.

I never told you that sometimes I went alone
to the Botanical Gardens,
slipping into the greenhouse
to smell the lemon scent of the foppish magnolias.
There were nights in Mississippi
so dark you could see the green hay
begin to smolder in the barn,
and the cows moved without substance
through the barbed wire fences.
I had a treehouse,
its cypress planks scaled down, child-size,
to hold one body.
It would drift like a raft on the branches.
Though my brothers worked ropes through the trees
for sending messages,
there was sadness in their intricate system.

We have lost disorder.
I talk of the monkey-puzzle trees
that we are passing
and wallabies with insatiable appetites for roses.
You recognize it is only information,
as we become by talking.

Though we could rig up pulleys
to carry things between us,
the operation would be make-shift and small.
It is good that you are leaving.
The figure we made together has symmetry here
and will stay, provided for, on simple ground.

SUSAN PROSPERE

IF WE HAD NEVER MARRIED

What if we had never married, what if
just before the wedding, foreseeing
the pain we would cause each other,
we broke it off, goodbye.
I see us meeting again after 10 years,
each of us married to people we like
but don't love;
     there is a deep, sober longing
in your eyes, an airy wish too late made conscious
turned into the steady flame of regret.
We recognize in each other's gaze
what was missing, what has been not quite right
about these years. I wonder if it's not too late
to change it all; you pull your skirt up
and straddle me, nostalgically.
The pain we forsook each other to avoid
we know now could be nothing compared to this,
seeing each other in the fragments
of the mirror we shattered so long ago,
for peace of mind, if we
had never married.

Ploughshares   BILL PRUITT

LETTER HOME

This afternoon I saw a deer inside that narrow
strip of woods between the rose gardens
and the Northway. She bolted, paused, turned,
twice. I wasn't going to move much closer,
and I was willing to feel like the intruder.
But the noise she made dismissed me—
two chuffs of annoyance or disgust.
And then on the road back three groundhogs
in the long grass heard me coming and rushed
beneath the cottage. Jennifer, I think
you would have laughed out loud to see
their lopsided, ungainly waddle—
foolish creatures, and not designed
to hurry gracefully. But I imagine
fear was what they really felt.
Someone who knows more about these things
might tell us even that's too human
a word to work exactly. One sound
that doesn't fit—my heavy step
on the path—triggers the instinct to escape,
and afterwards what passes
for the usual allows their tentative return.
Also, I know the birds don't sing for gladness,
although it's hard not to want to think so

when we're happy. Which is also to suggest
that the big smile you inscribe upon the sun,
saying, each time you explain a picture,
"Look, it has a face," makes that face your own
laughing kindly back at you, and sometimes
I choose to believe it's mine as well.

The American Scholar   LAWRENCE RAAB

GREECE

Past and present mingle in timeless spirit.
Listen! St. Paul speaks to the men of Athens,
cypress groves echo the lute as Orpheus
mourns his beloved.

Under gnarled olive trees flocks are grazing
where once on moonlit nights Grecian maidens
flung their garlands in the maddening dances
of Bacchic ritual.

Bees still hum in the thyme of Hymettus,
sunset gilds the Parthenon's creamy columns
as when the Argonauts, sailing homeward,
saw it from starboard.

The Classical Outlook   CHRISTINA RAINSFORD

GIFTS FROM GAMBERAIA

To the old man walking by
I am just pawing dirt again, cropping
bricks, piling wood, mixing fresh cement.
He waves as usual. Inside,
the vacuum grates at carpet's edge,
wet clothes spin in cycle.
I hear my name called,
but I am off

to Gamberaia
through Tuscan breeze
into lemon trees
and garden pools bright as topaz,
turf viale long and green as youth.
Fiesta I say, and freedom,
my breath
troweling sand, stakes, string
into simple lines.
Rows of cypress frame the Val d'Arno.

Still, my son says
I am here
and hands me nails to brace

a bungled row of wooden slats
and salt for strength
and hard rock sounds to shake
the roots I tear from brittle soil.

But I am gone
into balustrades,
into gray eyes of stone dogs,
into words one might say to gods.

Tomorrow, repentant as usual,
I will bring a nightingale
back home, and ilex trees
and indigo blue water from a fountain.

The Literary Review   PHILIP RAISOR

SYLLOGISM

If every good boy deserves favor, and all cows eat grass,
then music, like milk, is made of sly croppings
of green blades glistening some mornings in dew
and desire, of the wish to be better and do more.

Nothing returns whole unless transformed.
The insinuant twitter of birds in the barn when the boy
does chores before school—these sounds will return
when his drink is stronger, his love of life weaker
perhaps, but better for being not duty but desire.

Sing something, solemn boy, and press your head deeply
into the flank of the cow while the music of milk
deepens in the bucket. All flesh is grass.

The Georgia Review   BIN RAMKE

FINDING WILD STRAWBERRIES

(for my mother)

I.

In your terrible austerity of grief
after his funeral, you said a thing
so shocking I held my hands out, warding the blow—
    "I know I'll never be happy again,
    not in the old way, never."
The man's death upon them both,
what son's a consolation to the widow?
Fathoming your loss as though I'd never
been born, I stood corrected there,
a map of scars in either hand.

II.

Five years—Mother, who am I
to testify that you are happy now, or never?
Yet, hiking with us over Bunchgrass Ridge,
rangy as your grandkids, you are first
to smell the wild strawberries underfoot
and bring us to our knees around you
in the morning grass, and find each one
his perfect berry, dropping them like rubies
in our eager hands.
Am I the only one to notice who is missing?
I search your smiling face for evidence
of loss repealed by joy.
The brief sweetness of a berry
burns my tongue.

The American Scholar   JAROLD RAMSEY

MIDDLE AGE

The groundhog we dumped in the woods
is back in the yard
where he lies with his head in a cloud
of lice, an aura of flies,
a pale apple-green shimmering.

You say the dogs bring him back,
wanting praise, claiming credit.
At first I thought him but one more proof
of Spring, like wasps in vents,
ticks in children. All I know is he's there
when I walk to the mailbox,
when I lie in the sun,
when I look up at the stars
to say we're all nearer
to each other than we are.

He's a message from my father,
refusing to settle with the dead,
warning me I lack the skills
to keep them buried. Something's trying
to keep me from grief, but I'm not fooled:
love doesn't come back
like this, nor second chance.

Children gather to poke the remains,
then go fishing. I'm left
where the dead and the young
would keep me, cleaning up the mess.
What a mess they leave.

The American Poetry Review   PAULA RANKIN

SEEING DAUGHTER OFF

"Blind are still the eluded eyes."
That's Swinburne, who would not interest,
hardly an author for this trip
taken away from me, this time
by your own choice, not your mother's.
I smile, you flash inflamed brown eyes,
letting me see that no good will
and certainly no money paid
to the lady clerk who helped you
choose your fashions could change a fact
of life so basic. This anger
degrades your youthful beauty. Yet,
hat atilt, now you're like some darling
movie star or cowgirl. New boots
from Argentina filled the bill,
and you've got the family dimples,
dark hair framing the oval face.
You choose the smoking section now,
half-turn to mock at my concern.
A week now I've heard you cough, rough
as a Skid Row bum or tragic
artist in the movies, dying
of consumption in Mallorca
between bouts of rain and preludes.
And yet you preach right on about
ecology and the fine health foods
you got to be an expert on
in that hippy school where teachers
gave no grades, just scrawled "I love you!"
and summed it up, "You've grown a lot!"
All this in bright blue crayola.
I haven't said a word all week
about your habits but you know
I care, and caring is a vice
you'll not forgive. None of your friends
care, after all, and we know they're
wonderful. That mad man Swinburne
said in an old verse, "Thou art far
too far for wings of words to find."
As you retreat into your plane,
the muzak on and hostess bland
with sisterly concern, I fall
back to his poem. He says our dreams
"pursue our dead and do not find."
And it's enough for me that same
good poet understood, still helps
me grieve as I too watch the light
fail us in these elusive skies.
He names a thin flame that I see
now where your plane slips through the clouds.

Ploughshares   DAVID RAY

THAW

(for my mother)

It is spring, although the trees
are crazed with ice,
dogwoods clouded by snow
mounded in each cupped cluster
of twigs. Rhododendrons
emerge out of drifts,
holding up their waxy buds
like tapers ready to be lit.
All winter we haven't spoken,
but I know how you approach spring.
You will be at a kitchen window
watching the lithograph of birds
over the alley. Redpoll.
Evening grosbeak. Always looking
for one you haven't seen.
Staring past snow in the yard.
At the door a child stands, wanting
to complete the scene;
she is glass
through which you see the sun.

Pendragon   SUSAN REA

TIME

Budgets
Battles
Phone calls
Hassles.
Letters
Meetings
Luncheons
Speeches.
Politics and
Press Releases.
News conferences
Delegations
Plaques and
Presentations.
Travels
Briefings
Confrontations
Crises
Routines
Mediation.
Eight years pass swiftly.
But I look out the window.
The elm in the park looks
        just the same.

Tendril   RONALD REAGAN

ONCE MORE O YE ETC.

In what heaven or hell
do you, Bob, booze?
If heaven, there's gin
sempiternal; you wake on a cloud,
press a button
and an angel comes in
with an enchanting tinkle;

or, if you're allowed
in the Elysian Fields
(why not? you
boozed an epic amount),
you'll wander till
you find that stream
of gin, of gin, more gin,

and life eternal
will be one colossal
binge; you'll tell
your odd little stories
in that phony accent
and the angels will clap
and everyone will dance . . .

or if hell (semblable, frère),
you'll roll forever—
liver caved in,
crying for the pain,
crying because you're afraid,
crying for the one
thing that consoles you, gin.

Ploughshares   MICHAEL RECK

AT THE RESORT POOL

The lifeguard sat above us,
Hair baking in a bun.
Now, long wet and lively,
Its blades flash in the sun.

The lifeguard guards a motley,
All shapes and sizes here,
Most of them bagged and beaming
With hashish and with beer.

A child is crying, "Marco,"
"Polo" shouts another.
The first one, lunging blindly,
Bumps into his mother.

An old guy's here with "daughter,"
Another's with his "niece,"

Laid out mid the lithe and lovely
And the shamelessly obese.

Into the pool dives daughter
About to swim her laps.
In his mind the old guy's with her,
But soon the old guy naps.

Niece makes like a mermaid,
Legs hidden in the pool.
Above bikini hip bones
Don't help her old guy's cool.

Old gentlemen are patient,
They lie here hot and still.
They could prove entrapment,
But I don't think they will.

A child is crying, "Marco,"
"Polo" shouts his brother.
The first one, lunging blindly,
Bumps into their mother.

The lifeguard mounts her ladder,
Her hair back in a bun.
Adored, she sits above us
All burning in the sun.

The lifeguard guards a motley,
All shapes and sizes here,
Getting it on together
With hashish and with beer.

The Southern Review   ENNIS REES

MORNING WATCH

Slung in your hammock of comfortable dreams,
woven of the thickest strands
of night—but broad-stitched at this hour,
like a fishnet, letting light
pour through the web like water—
before you raise an eyelid from the pillow,
do not think that there is a world out there.
The sound of distant traffic in your ear is really
the rush of blood humming from its hive,
eager for nectar from the opening flower of morning.
Sight? A fire plays on your eyelids
and, like a child, insists you play with it.
Do, and by playing, shape it
as a baby's head is shaped by its journey to the light,
or a child takes on the shape of its pursuits—
the architect rising from stacks of wooden blocks,
the mother stitching her image together from rags
her love has warmed to life.

Now, with this in mind, open your eyes and
warm your world to life.
Go to the window and lift the blind: see,
it is not glass, it is the eye of your house
(which is itself the body of your most homebound soul),
and those headlights are the eyes of roving souls
up and out before you,
scissoring the mist, carving and stacking the blocks.
Only where their light knits with the light of your eye
can morning
rise from a restless dream
and wear the warm, close weave of day.

Descant (Canada)   JOHN REIBETANZ

A FAREWELL TO CONRAD SADORSKI

There is just one tree*
on Groesbeck Highway that I recall.
But you found it one drunken
night a month ago and wrapped
your soul around it. All of us
must one night face alone our own
fatal crashing that might've been
avoided if we'd only called a cab.

Back in 1981, at our class reunion,
we had a few drinks together.
It was pleasant enough. And I was glad
you never asked me what I remember
most about you. For that was
in eleventh grade, when we were
playing ping pong in your basement.
Your mother was unloading clothes
from the Maytag dryer. She was not
an attractive woman, but
she was wearing that day
a loose-fitting robe and whenever
she leaned over to fold some sheets,
her breasts swayed like a lullabye
and I thought that lady lovely.

When Greg Zane fell from a helicopter
to his military death, I remembered the smile
of his girlfriend. When Chris Fetzer
died of cancer, I thought about the leather
jacket he so uncomfortably wore.

Conrad, forgive me if you can,
but I can't forget your mother's breasts
on what was probably the last day I ever
really looked you in the eye.

Passages North   JOHN REINHARD

SCHILFGRABEN

is German for "reedy ditch." I read it yesterday
on a plaque under a painting of marshland.
When I reached the top of the spiral-tiered gallery,
I stared six stories down at a fountain jetting
and thought of particulars, the proper
names for ferns and vine-hungry moths.

I make a wish for Clara, whose hair was straw yellow.
In my journal one summer I called her "my willowy reed."
I wrote: "Clara's waist-long hair made me feel
like Rilke beside her today as we hiked down a slope
toward the Danube over swampy areas
locally known as The Sedge."

Not one straw-yellow strand lasts, saved
between the pages of my journal, to tell me
she is more than the hollow stalk of a phrase.
Yet I wrote: "She wore a barrette
and braided the dough she baked
in ovens that made me think of Treblinka."

I think of half-tracks, tanks,
the dominance of one idea
without regard for particulars.
Then I imagine Clara hatless in 1980,
leaning over a rolling pin or pounding
dough with her fists.

Shy as a marsh bird, mired behind a counter,
she bags pumpernickel, rye,
says Auf Wiedersehen to a customer,
and scribbles on a pad: "These tablespoons,
these numbered measuring cups,
dole out the bread of life."

The Hudson Review   JAMES REISS

AUTOGRAPHS

The dusty back room bookcase holds my past.
I once retrieved it briefly: fumbling for
An old forgotten piece on some curmudgeon
Poet, thumbing through the random stacks
Of lives and works, I came across the lines
Still clear, the tattered marginalia
That fuse me to so many others living,
Dead, forgotten, lauded, present, past.
I read one donor's hasty scribble on
A page of Orwell's *Catalonia*
(A ribald physicist who brought me fifths
Of Johnnie Walker, I recall). Below
That shelf I found my roommate's pencilled quips,

Her prim irreverence in the *Rubaiyat*.
And on another flyleaf yellowed with
The passage of so many years, I read
The small inscription, delicately penned,
Extolling all my tireless efforts with
The index of a book I'll never read.
Its author was a Spaniard. Courtly, kind,
He bowed to all the women, wore starched shirts
And Continental suits, leaving his door
Ajar, the office somehow redolent
Of olive trees and ripened oranges,
True to all the honored stereotypes.
They seem almost reproachful now, the mute
Lines *con profunda gractitud*. He left
Soon after, lives I think in Salamanca.
I saw a onetime lover's *Leaves of Grass*,
The dog-eared pages echoing the hours
Of eager talk and hungry touch, the time
When no one thought of time. At last
I found my uncle's battered Webster, old,
Discolored, bearing still the street address
Of some unpainted rooming house a few
Blocks from the university. The year
Was 1939. He's dying now.

Outside, the fog rolls in so quietly,
Enfolds the naked branches of the trees.
A single rose explodes upon the bush.

Inlet   CAROL C. REPOSA

LOVE POEM

*("He makes the smallest talk I've ever heard."
—John Woods)*

The smaller the talk, the better.
I want midgets in my mouth.
I want to sit with you and have us
Solemnly delight in dust; and one violet;
And our fourth night out;
And buttonholes. I want us
To spend hours counting dog hairs,
And looking up who hit .240
In each of the last ten years.
I want to talk about the weather;
And detergents; and carburetors;
And debate which pie our mothers made
The best. I want us to shrivel
Into nuthatches, realize the metaphysics
Of crossword puzzles, wait for the next
Sports season, and turn into sleep

Holding each other's favorite flower,
Day, color, record, playing card.
When we wake, I want us to begin again,
Never saying anything more lovely than garage door.

The Georgia Review   JACK RIDL

POET AND NOVELIST

(to Barry Spacks)

The poet is reading a novel.
One line, then another line,
they are all linked!
It's all in there—"The German columns
advancing like banks of clouds!"
They make a sense which
escapes him.
That brother
who was left behind with an uncle
in the third chapter
turns up now, trying to recapture
his heritage.
The poet,
intent on the vanishing
charms of a heritage,
its music,
its verbal cadence,
had forgot all about him.

The novelist has read three novels this evening already.
He picks up a volume of poems. He begins at the beginning!
He is astonished by all that is left out.
There are no moon, no shoulders, no conversations.
Ideas? Yes, but he was taught what Mallarmé
Taught Dégas: "It is not with ideas that one
Makes sonnets, but with words." He has always wanted
To *depict* that scene: M's apartment up one flight
Of tall stairs. The furniture, the windows—the paintings!
My God, the Impressionist paintings all over his walls!
D's physique, mesomorphic, paint-flecked.
And the outlines of figures Dégas sets against his walls!
The novelist is nothing if not an enthusiast.

Around the poet the ghost of his novelist
Hovers upside-down like an image in a shiny doorknob.
Wherever he goes, it moves with him,
Glossing his wide blank margins with invisible notes.

Ploughshares   JOHN RIDLAND

A TIME OF PEACE

Noontime on the quiet esplanade . . .
The silken waters show
A lethargy of their own.
The June sun everywhere is perfect.
I am lounging on one of the deck chairs
Freshly painted for the season.

It is Odessa maybe . . . near the Black Sea,
Or Brighton, circa an earlier time.
A gull swoops down and something
Tugs at my memory like a day of
Revolution or of war. The world
Seems to be waiting for news of the world.
An entire sea is burning before me, and
There was never so much light
Or so much terror . . .

Ascent   RUBY RIEMER

BEN'SMOTHER

As custom in a certain African tribe,
A mother is renamed after her eldest child;
Thus I would be: Ben'smother. The name,
They say, adds beauty.

And as I look at you, Ben, sleeping, I
Don't doubt it, and re-name myself . . .

A child's skin is the perfect blend: earth-
Air-fire-water, irridescent as sunset
Over a rolling mile of land,
Unplanted. Shadows
Of a few dark birds
Mark it with a dream . . .

I see, for the first time, hundreds
Of tiny, pale-gold hairs
Soft upon your temple
That grow into the rusty field:
Your thick auburn hair . . .

Each day I know you a little better
As I know any Future—
And when I am aged to a balance of dust
I will give you back
Your name . . .

Having traveled awhile in a foreign
Land, I am content to sleep at last
In my own mother's
Word.

Studia Mystica   JOANNE M. RILEY

CHILDHOOD

The long anxiety of school and waiting out
the time flows past slowly, in pure dullness.
Oh loneliness, oh heavy passing of time.
And then outside: the streets sparkle and ring
and the fountains flow in the squares
and the world grows so distant in the gardens.
And going through all that in a little suit
so differently from the way the others did.
Oh strange time, oh passing of time,
oh loneliness.

And, in all that, to look out far off:
men and women; men, men, women
and children who are different and colorful;
and sometimes a house and sometimes a dog
and terror silently alternating with trust.
Oh sorrow without cause, oh dream, oh dread,
oh groundless depression.

And so to play ball and ring and hoops
in a garden which faintly fades,
and sometimes brushing against adults,
dazzled and disorderly in hopes of tagging,
but in the evening, quiet, going home
with stiff little steps, held onto tightly.
Oh ever escaping understanding,
oh anxiety, oh burden.

And kneeling for hours at a time
at the big gray pond with a little sailboat;
forgetting it because other similar,
more beautiful sails sail around in a circle,
and having to think about the pale little
face which seemed to be sinking in the pond.
Oh childhood, oh vanishing comparisons.
Where to? Where to?

The Greenfield Review   RAINER MARIA RILKE
                                        —*Translated from the German*
                                        by Norbert Krapf

DEAR NEIGHBOR GOD

Dear neighbor God, if sometimes I disturb
you in the middle of the night with my knocking,
it's because so often I can't hear you breathing
and know: you're alone over there.
And if you need something, and no one's there
to fill the cup and put it in your fingers,
I'm always listening. Only say the word.
I'm right here.

Only a little wall stands between us,
built by chance: for this is all it might take—
one cry from your mouth or mine,
and it would break down
and not make a scene, or sound.

    It is made up of all your images.

And your images stand around you like names.
And if just once the light in me burns high
that shows the way to you from deep inside,
it goes to waste as glare spilling on their frames.

And my mind, so soon to stumble and go lame,
wanders away from you, homeless, exiled.

The Literary Review   RAINER MARIA RILKE
—Translated from the German
by Steven Lautermilch

LIKE WATER

Put out my eyes, and I will see your face.
Shut my ears, and I will hear your voice.
Take my feet, and I will not forget the way.
Take my mouth, and your name will remain on my lips.
Break these arms, and you will find me holding
you with this heart as though it were a hand.
Make my heart stop, and my brain will start to pound.
And if you set fire to my brain,
I will carry you like water in my blood.

The Arizona Quarterly   RAINER MARIA RILKE
—Translated from the German
by Steven Lautermilch

PHARMACOPOEIA

Marigolds an aphrodisiac, periwinkle
a cure for poison. Field daisies
to curb lechery. Cuckoopint to ward off snakes
and melancholy. Columbine for impotence.
Strawberry for cholera
and spleen. The garden grows, mystical and vain,
gathering arcane powers from the earth,
up through tender roots, a bright eruption
of petals, green tangle of leaves and stems,
mingling magic and hope, knowledge
and wishful thinking. They will plant the seeds
and harvest the flowers, catching the potency of the earth
in cordials and compounds, a bitter taste
to kill off memory and bad dreams,

bad things the body shrinks from, dies from.
The garden is theirs, in bloom, spread out,
mute dialogue with the summer sky. Distilled primrose water
to calm mad dogs.

Southwest Review   NICHOLAS RINALDI

SKIN-GAME

I move blue sheets under the flutter of green-and-white moths,
and see my thighs veined as the wings of moths
or leaves half-drained of their chlorophyll,

And I know your skin touching mine till I moved
is freckled and blotched forever by a malevolent sun
and you also now are shaped like a dolphin, but

I quickly flick the sheet back over my thighs
or hide within my orange sarong like a chrysallis,
for although I can love you for playing

An agonized violin or washing my floor
after we've written and loved and danced and drunk wine all night,
and you so important to half the world,

So I accept your piebald skin and intransigent wrinkles
and put up with your churlish temper, yet
I suspect you'd prefer

Some skinny blonde from Ohio, thighs tanned and smooth as a
        peach,
cool as a julep, making no claims on your nebulous future,
ready to spit you out like a pit when you want to be free,

Not caught in a net of veins where blood runs green and blue as
        the sea,
or trapped as I am in a patch of heat
and blinded by sun and the splashing of dolphins.

Poet Lore   ELISAVIETTA RITCHIE

AT LEAST

The statues, he said, they too die if you don't look after them.
I've often seen them fallen down, with eyes half-closed. They're
        waiting
to see if anybody notices them; then they get up again. Maybe that's
        why
the stores on the main streets, both inside and out,
or the small-change shops in the suburbs, are full of mirrors,
small, large: all kinds. Hung on the walls,
they shine dully—as though indifferent—in secret expectation;
        they mirror
one another among themselves or sometimes a bit of the street:

the bakery smokestack, a medlar-tree, two women,
the wheelbarrow from the small flower shop with its empty clay
   pots.

Late in the evening, around eight, when the stores close, the
   mirrors
empty all at once. Everyone—clerk or owner or customer—
takes a mirror and shuts himself up in his room,
while in the streets outside the stillness of insomnia already begins
   to jell.

Antaeus   YANNIS RITSOS
                            —Translated from the Greek by Edmund Keeley

WORDS ARE WORDS, ETC.

It must be true
that pieces of oneself stick around
any old place;
don't be surprised to find
some stupid thought or other
tricked out
around here,
shamelessly remembering that it was yours
though now you disavow it.

Also there in ambush lies the troubling certainty
of the leftovers—
the fact that we abandoned
our best laughter in a hotel room,
or on a walk by the riverbank.
Those expressions that didn't come out
in the photographs
are not recovered either:
a lock of hair lodged on your forehead,
bits of madness like a glass
half-full on the nightstand
(someone assured me he had seen,
eight months after it happened,
his own reflection
in the window of a shop downtown).
So I don't doubt
you can find
among the pleats of the simplest dress
a memory
completely on its own.

Nor would I be amazed
should you encounter
—in the city far away—
a page, or maybe a shoe,
that speaks of me
to you.

Denver Quarterly   ELIANA RIVERO
                                        —Translated from the Spanish
                          by Leland H. Chambers and Eliana Rivero

FIRST DAY OVER 60°, APRIL 1980

No love on a day like this is to scorn
the green just beginning to rumor
through the lawn, the awkward aim for sky
our apple graft is making. Juncoes
come and go thanklessly, which is good. Their
complacence is a kind of love that won't choose
us over the scattering of wild seed,
the crumbs of park bench or trash bin.
On a day like this, no love means to love
unevenly, to not embrace it all.

So you are the bridge by which I come to love
the death of friends, leaf-rot, armies, marigolds,
myself. These lawns hopscotch down our street
and whisper to their homes the new law.
I begin with loving you: not less
but by opening my arms around you,
turning the palms out toward whatever else.
Days like this I could hold you all, forgive
the hell in me, welcoming any light
my own darkness had refused. I could believe
I'd improve on grace, and continue. Well
into days below zero, I'd go on.

Quarterly West   RICHARD ROBBINS

FIRST KISS

When that blue-black cloud
came over the sand lot with drops
of rain big as marbles, we ran
down the dark alley into Big John's
orchard where we leaned, then
clutched the other's shivering body
and I had my first kiss.
But what I remember most is the running,
how our wet clothes hung to our skin
and the clouds actually billowed up
as lightning struck the hill.
And the smell of cut grass getting wet,
the sense of chill coming,
the wanting to go home and the wanting never to leave,
just the two of us, who didn't love,
barely liked each other,
breathing, holding hands
the way we'd hold an apple slick with rain,
or a slingshot stone, lightly,
ever so lightly.

Quarterly West   LEN ROBERTS

TRANSPLANT

I'm not a native of the Little Balkans—
Here sixteen years and still I don't belong.
The natives look back many generations
And hunt for ethnic spellings of my name.
Perhaps, if I assemble special evidence,
My children will not be transplants like me.

My grandfathers both labored hard in Kansas.
My daddy's daddy came to dig the coal
When things got tough in poor Sebastian County,
Arkansas; he left and headed north.

My other granddad started as a teamster;
Not a union man, he drove a team of mules.
He made the drive from Fort Smith to Fort Scott,
About six weeks' round trip, when roads were good.

I have some odd relations in the Ozarks
(Not strange relations, that's a local phrase).
Raised poor like most of Southeast Kansas people,
I've pulled myself up by my own bootstraps.

I'm not a native of the Little Balkans—
But I'm home.

The Little Balkans Review   ROBERT J. ROBERTS

EURIPIDES:
IPHIGENIA AMONG THE TAURIANS
(1138-51)

If only I could follow
the sun's shining horses
home to Argos
I would fold restless wings
in my room upstairs.
I would stand among the girls
at the wedding dance
and I would whirl and dip
at my mother's side
daring all the swaying girls
to a contest of loveliness—
a melee of luxuriant hair
and embroidered veils—
and my long dim hair
would shade my cheek.

The Classical Outlook   DIANA ROBIN

WHITESBURG BRIDGE

There was something about Whitesburg Bridge
that made people want to jump off.
It arched high over the Tennessee River
to stay clear of tug boats that pushed
barges full of coal underneath.
With its silver-painted braces and beams
it looked like a big erector set.
We liked to jump off the barge docks and swim
just a hundred yards down river from the bridge.
The docks made for a pretty high dive themselves.
The water was dark and you couldn't see
more than a foot below its surface.
Once Larry Stone jumped in and stayed down
a long time—over a minute and a half.
He scared the hell out of us all.
He came up with his face all white saying he'd
touched something at the bottom with his foot.
Said it felt like a human head,
with hair, eyes, and a torn-up face.
But Larry was a dare-devil and a bluff,
liked to make something out of nothing
just for the thrill of it.
Like when he said he could do a swan dive
off the Whitesburg Bridge
and never let his feet spread apart.
Frank Little and Johnny Cole egged him on
until he went up and stood about half-way
across the river for twenty minutes or so.
Traffic slowed to see what was going on.
Then damned if he didn't do it;
but he didn't keep his feet straight.
They were flopping all over the place.
When he kept on staying down
we just shrugged and thought
he must have found another human head.

Poem   JAMES MILLER ROBINSON

SPARROW

It doesn't forget. It doesn't go away,
this wily urchin
of our life. Always
borrowing, aimless,
anonymous, walking here,
washing there, stubborn,
underfoot.
What does it look for in our dark
life? What love does it find
in our hard bread?

It already gave the dead to the air,
this sparrow that could
fly away but stays
down here, secure,
putting in its breast
all the dust of the world.

Denver Quarterly   CLAUDIO RODRIGUEZ
—*Translated from the Spanish
by David Garrison*

7:00 A. M. LAKEFRONT

When the wind roars in from the east like this,
the lake is all spray shot up
like island palms splayed against the sky.
At each rock the surface bursts
then heals itself against the shore.

Back in the grass,
wrens sputter themselves clean in a pool of sand;
on the beach a passionate couple grapples
on a paisley blanket, and waddling gulls
suddenly fling themselves up in a single motion
netting the sky with their wings.

Out there no land is in sight, no safe harbor
in the heave and spasm vacant as sea.
From where I stand, the sun-glazed waves
look solid enough to walk on. So it may
have seemed to you in April, 1932,
when you stepped from the deck of the *Orizaba,*
giving up your body to the sea.

Poetry   PAULETTE ROESKE

MIRAGE

This sheer white page of empty writing paper
staring at me, as barren as the moon,
reveals no trace of heat or light or vapor,
but suddenly becomes a distant dune.
There's no oasis, not a single palm,
no coal black sky alight with piercing stars.
No straggling caravans destroy the calm
nor spitting camels bearing golden bars.
My fancy will transform this wilderness
by penciling cool caves along its edge
so tribes in white burnooses may process
past holy men and pools of ruffled sedge.
Then let the moon with houris in her train
entice young desert warriors in vain.

The Arizona Quarterly   BERNARD ROGERS

THE MOUNTAINS DRAW A GREAT CIRCLE AROUND US

Morris says the reason the Los Alamos scientists
crack, become alcoholics,
is that the desert and pure blue mountains,
secure at the edge of sight,
remind them they can't control the universe—
no matter how many pieces they compress, explode,
they can't move the heart of things one inch.
Looking at tall pines
makes me unable
to believe in a world
we can manage: stone kneels before cloud,
the world changes, unflowers: it only happens
if we watch. Slow circles move out,
healing falls on our arms like hot light through pine-needles,
traces its way through grass to our feet,
a ray of light like the woman singing
at the hoedown at Westminster—"Me and Jesus."
We stood in calm dust, or sat on baled hay,
finding our way back through years
to the time we were innocent
as rainwater in a trough.

We need the trees, light through linked branches,
to wait until the mountains make us whole.

Cedar Rock   DEL MARIE ROGERS

THE ART OF BECOMING

The morning, passing through narrowing and widening
Parabolas of orange and spotted sunlight on the lawn,
Moving in shifting gold-gray shawls of silk lying low,
Thinning and rising through stalks of steeplebush
And bedstraw, through the first start of the first finch
Streaking past the vacancy in the sky where the last
White stone of star was last seen, can only be defined
In the constant change of itself.

The particular leaf, pushing its several green molecules
Outward to a hard edge of photosynthesis, microscopic
In its building and bumping continuously
From one moment to the next, only becomes magnolia
In this prolonged act of its dying.

Realization itself is the changing destruction
And process of cells failing and rising constantly
In their creation of thought. If every white glint
On the surface of the holly, every clenching hair
In the amber center of spirea, every sleight of insect
Wing and cactus spire, the creviced tricks
Of fern segment and sunfish blade were halted right now,

In this moment, one instant caught perfectly and lasting forever,
Then "now" would be the only and final statement of this work.

Immortality must only exist in the sound
Of these words recognizing, through the circling and faltering
Of oak peaks, through the knot of midnight tightening
And loosening, through star-streams inventing destination
By the fact of their direction, in the sound of these words
Recognizing their need to pray over and over and over
For the continuing procedure of their own decay.

The Georgia Review   PATTIANN ROGERS

IN YALTA

New York, back in 1943,
and Itzik Feffer was bidding me good-bye,
and smilingly he slapped me on the back,
—*Nu,* you'll come see us once again in Kiev,
and we'll ride down to Yalta
and bathe in the fondling Black Sea waters.

Now I sit here in Yalta
and, from my balcony on the sixth floor
of the deluxe Yalta Hotel,
I hear the swishing of the waves
of the dark blue-green Black Sea.
They chant a hymn to the encircling hills,
to the beauty of Massandra Park,
and a choir of birds erupts in serenade.
And people point out that over there,
in that white house Chekhov once lived,
for the last time gazed upon his seagulls.
And Lev Tolstoy came here to take a cure
(not far from here a street is named for him),
and Pushkin, Gorky, Nekrassov and Mayakovsky
sang out here, together with the birds,
the song of freedom and peace.

And I wander about alone, alone,
longing for Itzik Feffer,
and the aroma of lilac, jasmine
cannot pacify me;
and I know I have come to pay homage to the dead,
to Feffer, Markish, Bergelson and Shlomo Mikhoels,
in beautiful Massandra Park, by the Black Sea.

Jewish Currents   I. E. RONCH
—Translated from the Yiddish by Harold Aspiz

THE OLD HORSESHOER

In late spring the horseshoer navigates
Our soggy road, his Studebaker truck
Clanging an anvil, tools of the trade,
Iron shoes in a barrel. Stooped, Days Work
Mixed with mustache, he sets up under
Cottonwoods, keeping one eye on the corral
Where Sugar, PeeWee, wary Shorty are waiting.
Their coats are patchy, winter hair
Shedding unevenly, "bellies a little gant."

He hasn't come for small talk. Remembering
The last time, he picks out Shorty first,
Ties him high by a heavy halter-rope.
Wearing leather apron with pouches for nails,
The old man lifts a foot, swears, wields
His curved hoof-knife—spits—neatly clips
The edge with rusty pinchers, rasps it level.
He bends the calked shoe by a squint,
Pounds, fits, refits, gauging the ellipses
Against soft blue and Shorty's cautious eye.

His mouth bristling with nails, he works
Under the raised front leg, a circus
Act, gray cap on backwards, hammers near
The quick, twisting and clinching nails down,
Mutters to himself, the horses, the light
Green morning opening to sun. Shod in muddy
Boots, he limps around Shorty, picks up
One hind foot easily as a tired lover,
Asks if we've heard the first meadowlark.

Descant   ROBERT RORIPAUGH

MANTA RAY

Quite by chance I caught something
from the looking glass bay that leaped up
with devil's wings, its whip-tail
smashing the water into shards.

I was after cud-chewing fish
lounging in the warm sea, and this beast
as it rose through a trapdoor
tugged at my trembling line like dread.

Capsized on the mussel-crusted rocks,
he was my fellow-creature, mortal,
a shrunken star. In this dark world
of penance the day was bright.

I let him go, chastised by love,
and he was dragged back

by the tide to vast-flowing night.
He was the thought, and I the thing.

Ball State University Forum   D. M. ROSENBERG

CARVING PUMPKINS

(for My Father)

Being small, I chose
the largest I could find,
thumped the yellow rind
like a melon, then watched him carry it home.
On the concrete patio out back
he placed it gravely on the Arts and Leisure,
and with a mild look of censure
drew from his pocket a red jackknife.
He worked with an engineer's precision:
First the top—lifted off with a smell
of ripe decay. We scooped out strings of seeds, made ears,
small hoops of light; the slanting eyes.
Sometimes I took the nose—a jagged
"o." But with great care we carved the ragged
grimace tooth by tooth,
two dark bent heads grinning,
pumpkin-like ourselves,
taking turns till the last
tooth was chiselled clean.
Running, I'd go for candles, though the awful
boys would later seize it in their hands
and hurl it to the street for trash.

But at the moment of first lighting,
when the crooked mouth glowed,
and his dark curly hair bent in delight
over the jack o'lantern, and stayed bowed
in some adult musing that aimed
for that other woman, fussing
among the pots and pans—then the world
held off an instant,
till a smoky wind could twist and rise,
and evening's purple shadow,
like a shadow of the dream that held him,
would first darken, and then fill, his eyes.

Michigan Quarterly Review   L. M. ROSENBERG

THE STATE OF THE ART

In my youth, that far-off time,
Strict was meter, sure was rhyme.

In this, a more permissive day,
Every doggerel has its say.

The Arizona Quarterly   F. C. ROSENBERGER

KADDISH DE RABBANAN

Grandfather Graybeard
ate a three-minute egg each morning.
Looking like a guest just come in
with his hat on,
he blessed breakfast;
he blessed the bread,
he blessed the egg,
and the giver of eggs—God.
Something always eluded him.
On its way in
the egg dripped and caught,
shone viscous and yellow in the bristles of his beard,
a bauble for children;
while framed,
the rabbis of every principal city in Russia—
the Rabbi of Minsk and the Rabbi of Pinsk, for instance—
sat on the wall like handwriting.

Grandfather walked down the hall
in his white underwear (with his head well covered)
or wore black broadcloth.
Sometimes he performed the penny-bestowing ceremony.
This was private and confidential.
Produced mysteriously from his pocket,
the gift of dull, thumbed copper
gleamed, winked at us from between fat fingers,
left off being common coin,
became a thing of value.

Southwest Review   MARJORIE STAMM ROSENFELD

PUNISHMENT

I wonder how he felt
when the switch hit the wall
and the juice cooked his brain like a golden sponge
Blindfolded between the spaces
did he himself become the current
that sizzled through and through
and scarred the fragile wax inside his ears
Or did it only seem
his icy heart had never felt so warm
his ophidian mind so like a man's
and the instant of death the very first

> he could want to last
>   and last

The Ohio Journal   JOHN B. ROSENMAN

A STRANGER IN THE WEST IN AUTUMN

Over the wide-open hymnal
of the plains
the grasses bow down
broken-willed
and muttering,

the sumac in terrified covens
chatter out
prayers of wood,

the dark pines are damned
while the aspens ascend
on the gold
of their angel leaves.

And though it once brandished
a rainbow I might have believed in,
this brimstone sky appalls me,
confesses me empty with wind,
forgives me nothing.

I'm not among the chosen
of this country,
not one with its martyred antelope,
not minded to suffer
like grass.
I'm only a stranger here,
and I was never schooled

in fierce religions.

Sou'wester   ABBY ROSENTHAL

THE MEETING

(for Aaron Kramer)

Our hair thinner, otherwise fit,
We meet at the artificial waterfall
Splashing down the concrete wall,
A pocket park in the city's stone—
Two poets, ammunition spent
On the right things in the wrong time,
Nevertheless cheerful: we're still alive.

I say, "Even an artificial waterfall
Has something for the soul and ear."

He replies, "Another generation—
And who'll remember the real thing?"
We exchange memos, small ambitions.
There is between us an unacknowledged
Feeling of keeping the past alive.
We keep our battle scars hidden,
Our eyes have a secret praise.

A girl moves by, shimmering; her step
At once dissolves the web. We lean
Toward music now, we've got the essential
Sun on our faces. Even the fake
Waterfall seems in place.
"Lovely perfume, farewell," I say.
"Poetry ever onward!" he grins,
And departs into the common world.

I walk down the street again,
Into the dense forest, birds
Swarming everywhere in the foliage,
And deeper on, the real water.

Michigan Quarterly Review   NORMAN ROSTEN

COUÉ REVISITED

Silly platitude . . . . I cannot repeat it any more:
"Day by day in every way . . ."
Because it's not getting any better—it's getting worse.
Science and technology are better—
We have better bombs—better buttons to push to unload them.
Greed and strife run riot while ambassadors of many nations
parley and bargain for peace—hoping to make it.
But in spite of technological progress it still eludes them.

Me—I'm trying to make it—trying to eat, pay rent, insurance,
and the monthly light bill on the dollars I earn.
But in spite of all the scientific know-how of man,
Most of the products I buy are inferior in quality
and a waste of money I cannot afford to waste.
(Chiefly because someone rich wants to be richer
is why my little household items are made skimpier now.)
Frustration surrounds me—there is nothing I can do to
change things . . .
But I'm trying to make it.

Statesmen scramble for countries and pieces of countries
and rights to the waterways—hate seeps in
nationally and individually—leaders are trying to ease
the tension, trying to make treaties work.
Young couples in the supermarket hold hands
making small talk over the vegetables,
choosing words—each adjusting to the other's opinion
and temperament—

wanting no arguments—nothing to ruffle the sea
of elusive happiness, yearning to hold the moments,
fearing they are temporary, trying to make it with love.

It all frightens me—the greed, confusion, hate, and envy,
and all of us trying to make it . . .
Oh God! Please—let somebody make it!

The Little Balkans Review   DOROTHY RANDOLPH RANGEL

THE OTHER

In the night window your body becomes visible
like a memory or an old lover returned.
The dim lamplight and willing glass
conspire to flatter you, to deny
the pull of long hours on your face.
The woman reflected watches you,
writes something on moon-white paper,
watches you again, looks through you,
sees what you did yesterday, the stain of regret
on your back. Vulnerable, love addicted,
your thoughts fog the glass.
She makes note of that, scratching hurriedly
on the paper, mice racing between walls.
She knows your weaknesses, your lies,
how you drive yourself at night
beyond dull endurance, though the unmade bed
beckons like repressed desire.
You will do anything to feed your needs,
glutton of never enough.
As you write the fiction of your life
she makes a second copy,
gives it to the darkness as a joke.

Poetry   BECKE ROUGHTON

WORDS TO ACCOMPANY A LEAF
FROM THE GREAT COPPER BEECH AT COOLE

Deep shade and the shades
Of the great surround me.
In the distance, the house
Is a ghost over grass.
You can see clear through it.

This tree is standing still,
Great names gnarling the bark
Like the names of lovers.
What were they but lovers
Of this shadowing tree?

Last evening at Kilkee
The whole sky was westward
Over the Atlantic,
No nightfall but nightfall,
Dark with the local drink.

Then, early this morning,
A small mist followed me
Halfway to this garden
Along the Galway road
And then gave way to light.

What are we but lovers,
The one web of our lives
Veined nearly visible
Over the Atlantic
As this leaf shot with light

Though its veins are darkness?
Your face is before me,
Your green eyes shot with light.
What are we as lovers
But the one leaf only?

This tree will bear others.

Ploughshares   GIBBONS RUARK

LINES AT MY FATHER'S GRAVE

If I had written you in Lexington
And said what sons should say to fathers
Freezing in the white withdrawal rooms,
Would you be in the body now, free
Of all the needles, the doses you devised,
A druggist locked into his cabinet,
Hooked on sleep, squeezing the ampules of hope,
Of every poppy dreamed on Turkish graves?
My silence was the knell, the needle deeper
Than the lies I carved into your stone.

The Southern Review   LARRY RUBIN

AW SON, AW HELL

When things got tough, I'd turn to him,
catch him on the porch staring at the fields,
useless now out there, but wise and willing
to offer what he could. He'd know by my
face whether I needed humor or comfort,
motion me over to the steps to sit and talk.
His face hung loose, gravity pulling
him toward the grave, he said,

but his eyes were as bright as sin
and his words worth sinning for:
deep and heavy with the past,
delivered to the fields as much
as to me, head turning like an owl's.
"Son," he'd say, "the present don't matter
one whit: what is ain't going to be long.
Things change with the sun and wind,
and that's the way it's always been.
What's left is best. Aw son, aw hell,
it ain't who you are or what
but who you been and where
and what you've lived to tell."

Wisconsin Review   PAUL RUFFIN

RED BIRD IN A WHITE TREE

(for Philip Booth)

Today, his chosen dogwood
bursts into lace. Whistling
possession, the cardinal flashes in,
brighter than blood, to pose
among patterns of light.
For this, he braved midnights
deep in pines, risked
empty feeders, held off
ice. For this, he trusted
weather.
            The bird is what
he feels himself to be.
He knows his scarlet impact
among the blossoms' foam.
The life he lives is precisely
what he means, not a blurred
photo of strange plumage,
super-imposed.
            He sees
as though he learned
the fallacy of dark before
the fact. He glides
among dependable branches.
And when he starts to sing,
he is not choked
by all the slow unyielding
half-truths of the heart.

Black Warrior Review   MARIÈVE RUGO

DOGS AT THE VETERANS' HOSPITAL

Walking in the slate cold afternoon,
I hear their barking carrying in clear air,
Compounded in its echoing off walls,
The antiseptic enclosure,
Metal cages stacked like books.

Their tired voices
Fading, I wonder idly
What provokes such hysteria—
The daily hosing?
The slow movements of some aging veteran
Whose task it is to feed them?
Perhaps only that he talks to them
As he monitors their hunger, the weights
Of their small defecations.
When I get home,
None of this matters . . .

Later, the house quiet,
I read, sinking into the sofa
Until I doze. And wake
Hours later cold and absent
And having dreamt of dogs
Asleep on the warm chrome of their cages,
Their legs twitching, soundlessly
Running in their dreams of running.

Quarterly West   LEX RUNCIMAN

NEW YORK THRUWAY, THREE A.M.

Remembering her words, like angry wasps
brushed from their spoiling fruit,
and the hanger I twisted while she talked,
I blink my sore eyes in silence, fixed
on the road. I shake my drowsy head.
The car beams flicker, strafing roadside bushes,
the pavement curves and climbs and curves.
The miles, the pointless wishes unwind.
And out of the moonlit night ahead,
vague shapes loom gradually clear—
steep, rock-walled mountains rise up through mist:
the solid things, the masters.

Skyline   LAWRENCE RUSS

CHILDHOOD, OR THE HOBGOBLINS' HOLIDAY

In those days, the overhead pipes
throbbed with heat and wishes in the night.

And each time you twisted the faucets,
emotion splashed into your hands, affection or hate,
bewildering angers, or dumbfounded grief . . .

Mother gave you indelible gifts:
a promise made of lead, like a painted soldier,
stolid, forever on guard,
and a nest of electric train-wrecks,
a candy made from the dust of moths' wings.

With her litany mournfully intoned—
"Your father's not . . . Your father will never . . .
I worry, you can't do anything right . . ."—
she made you a choirboy bearing candles to her altar;
she left you open to the devils she feared.

And Father? Father was a wrong-way sign
on a one-way street, a cab without running lights,
a washed-out bridge.
Father of "You don't know how hard life is,"
and "Why don't you try to do something worthwhile?"

He wobbled on the high-wire, distressed.
Father was a fun-house mirror that forces
the child to see himself ridiculous, squashed.
Father, the crippled elephant king
in a country overrun by rancorous mice.

All the years of four-lane dreams
and wild bumper-cars of desire!
All the glass hearts dropping their delicate rain,
and the child a clown without an umbrella
to save him from getting drenched . . .

O, let's have done with it, once and for all,
those memories like a cartoon vampire gnawing
your scrawny, but rubbery neck—
that childhood, like a carnival
that terrifies the child.

Mss   LAWRENCE RUSS

A LONGING

(for Peter)

Against distant hills, a bruised slant
of storm clouds lowers over the hay fields.
They've been mowing, the fields cropped,
studded with rolled hay,
luminous creatures in this charged,
hurried dusk.
A man in a blue shirt, pants
the color of clay, hand on a rake,
wipes his mouth on his shoulder.

Here in the car my knee rests
against a bag of groceries: asparagus,
wine; the promise
of a dinner I will have alone
because you are away;
a plate of vegetables, wine,
rain on the back porch roof,
clinking of fork on plate,
glass opening upward.

I need to know the old man
who paused in the open field.
It's the same with these houses I pass,
which become houses I loved once
and will never again enter.
Where are you?
In the lighted room of a house I pass,
a window is lowered by a graceful arm
against the rain.

So it was when we first met.
I felt, stopping by the barn
to lean on the fence,
that I had already been sleeping next to you
years and years.
It's as when we first wake
from a place to which we, neither one,
can pursue the other.

Skyline   LISA RUSS

HELPLESS DAY

What can we say
on a March evening
with the sun half down
neither winter nor spring?
Inside, it's like that, too,
deep inside where all
the loam and memories are.
Lamplight shades off, ignoring
the corners, the hours vague,
bleeding away. An evening of magazines,
the manic crossword,
the cruel discourtesies
of solitaire—the last king buried
forever. But what do we want?
Statues on roller skates?
Fish with mustaches? Tattoos
on our hearts? No tattoos;
we have those already, exact
duplicates of sidewalk cracks—
so intricate, yet

we remember how each arrived.
But even the sum total of old
grief turns trivial
in this dim light, the night like
some dream we cried in
but can't remember why.
Something we lost is near us
but won't appear
until we call its name, and we can't
remember if it's seven down—
six letters—or lies buried
with that last lost king.

Quarterly West   VERN RUTSALA

THE PARTING

Without good-byes you left, and without tears;
    for this now must I weep?
You did not grieve because you'd lavished years
    of kisses in my keep.

Some loves perdure, and hold unto their ways,
    beyond a lifetime too.
I know a love that lasted thirty days,
    and it was true.

Occident   UMBERTO SABA
                                    —*Translated from the Italian*
                                    by Felix Stefanile

AFTER A DISAPPOINTING VISIT WITH OLD FRIENDS, I TRY IN VAIN TO RECOVER THE JOYS OF CHILDHOOD

Exhausted by excess, obsessions of our age
—the passage of time and eternal decay—
I take a walk through the crust of fallen snow:
just a dusting, so the grassless ground shows
through like a scalp on a balding head. It's ugly,
but not shamelessly so, and I by-pass the safety
of our small house for the smaller patch of timber
behind it. Here, after crossing the fallen wire
and four-post fence, I find, next to a tangle of
vines and thorns, old milkweed pods, snapped-off
and stepped on, hollow and stiff. I rub the shells
in my palms and a few feathers drift down and fall.
I wish I could say they had a certain dignity.
My wife thinks I sulk too much. Truth is, I'm happy,
solitary, and if I close my eyes as I sit on the downed
oak log, I can almost hear the shouting children
who, summers before, scanned this ground for arrowheads,
for fossil prints on stone, for the formica shine

in beds of quartz. It didn't take much to please us.
Any oddity of surface became Geronimo's last arrow,
and we could make the dullest stone shine
with spit or with squinting against the sun.
So when I think the banal thought that time is loss,
that my modest home lacks the grace of past imaginings,
I can't forget the false but valued treasures
I once found breaking ground: the triangular rock
a friend unleashed which missed my eye by inches.
We must be given happiness revising pleasure,
the patch of frosty pine we turn into a forest,
the simple fiction of the dig. I see it now, I feel it
on my forehead, door to memory: an indentation, tiny scar,
archeology of loss, the once saved stone released.

The Yale Review   IRA SADOFF

NO OTHER GODS

(for C.)

"Thou shalt have no other gods
before me," the first commandment
warns, and so I warn myself,
first thing in the morning,
my face breaking into song
at the sight of you: the
hymn of your hair, its dark
chords, your lips half open,
themselves on the verge of song.

Sleep rises from you,
your breath is wet,
my first kiss winds around
your last dream. I whisper,
"I love you." My words drop
into the well of the world.
I hear the splash, make my
wish. You open your eyes,
it's granted.

My joy is a high note.
Too high? I wonder.
A long walk I took,
with my sainthood
for a crutch, and my eye
on love's horizon. Up the
mountain I went, and kept
going. There you were,
eyes closed, dancing.

The Sun   SY SAFRANSKY

FOR ART

The news of your dying
reaches me faster than
the news of your living.
But why complain? So
we didn't have more time
together, and I hardly
wrote. I reached where
I reached, like you,
only sometimes knowing why.
Is death more mysterious?
Aren't these days like ashes,
scattered here and there?
Job, family, standing on line—
where it goes is no clearer
to me than where you go now,
free of your body—
as the wind,
dying,
is free of a kite.

The Sun   SY SAFRANSKY

MARY TO SHELLEY

The book in your back pocket
Is soaked, swollen,
But still I can read the line:
"Bright star! Would I were steadfast . . ."
Identifiable words that identify your body.
It appears I am a girl in some story:
Wrapped in a shawl, watching
A bonfire on the beach;
I could mention the waves, the requisite gulls,
Or describe the sky as overcast,
But I won't. I want you
To apologize for dying, for refusing
To learn to swim, for dying young.
And I want to thank you
For those nights when we sat stoned
In a circle, terrifying each other
With horror stories, trying to lose
Ourselves in other bodies.
Words are lies.
It's history I believe in now,
Not love, as my redemption.
I want to engrave myself in time,
A brown, line-drawn figure,
Recognizable to herself.
The girl I was is gone:

Wild, reckless, fierce,
Stolen out of her father's house.

The Hollins Critic   MIRIAM SAGAN

FROM THE SIDELINES

Great decisions are being made:
wars declared,
new weapons discovered and discarded,
with every tear in the night
admitting sun.

Great decisions are being made,
and I am casting words on needles,
knitting socks and sweaters for the men
who wrap their tears in handkerchiefs
and smile while they march
and wave goodbye.

Great decisions are being made.
I'm melting down my words,
shaping them into bombs,
pouring them into bottles stuffed with rags
ignited by the sun.

Great decisions are being made:
you think we women are patient still,
but I tell you, we're hardening our fists,
we're painting off our smiles.
We're preparing more than pies
in the steaming kitchen of our eyes.

event   LAKE SAGARIS

AWAY

(for Charles Hyatt)

I hold a banyan of memories of home
in my head; I have a Rio Bueno of slides:
an unbroken flow of air mail envelopes,
their zig-zag borders carrying on and on,
until the unseen sender returned and died;
someone else, just as faithful, a Harriet
who stayed beside me but who also died;
a large dining-room blackboard on which
singular verb matched singular subject;
that end-and-beginning-of-year Swift ham,
brown with sugar and jabbed black with cloves;
the slow, slow understanding of '38;
those very painful examination years;

the inconsolable lack of a community bell;
abeng, broken again and again, and discarded;
the lizard on its back; the waste of men;
the long line of women at the bottom of the hill;
the warmth that goes for nothing; the lies;
the story no leader will tell; the drift;
the blaze of poinsettias; the sunset at sunrise;
the burning image of West Kingston as hell.

The voices in my room say something, perhaps
nothing, at all, that really means anything.
And yet, they persist. They claim they have a way
with history, with all the people who make it.
Meanwhile, the everlasting banyan spiders the earth
and slowly penetrating Rio Bueno flows and flows.

The Massachusetts Review   ANDREW SALKEY

PORTRAITURE

To sit through a painting is to be taken away.
Raped.
You are left with no illusion of self,
no corner for hiding.

You are the victim
of another's need. The mask that sees
everything and nothing at once
bears down from above, merciless.
You squirm
beneath the painter's stare.

Like love
that has turned hard and won't go away
ever, it is bad business
but perfect art:

this penetrating down,
down to a core.

When it is over,
it is not over. The image remains
floating,
like the sense of having lost
something unknown
but known by its absence to be lost.

The painter has taken it away.

Southwest Review   ALBERT SALSICH

AT CENTER COURT

Backcourt to backcourt,
the ball whips flat
across the net by an inch
or ovals over in a top-spin.

Now the players converge
at the net, their racquets
turn animal, the ball leaps off,
instincts bared to the quick.

For three hours we've watched
them sweat their bodies to invade,
to defend, one arm lengthened
to sting or caress the air.

At last they are being applauded
into sweaters along the sidelines.
What remains is the stubborn
geometry etched on the same ground

we all walk on. It is still divided
by a wall we can see through
and stretched tighter than nerves,
strung on muscle-frames, can bear

for more than a few hours in the sun.
These rectangles laid down rigid and white
as bones along the packed earth are not now,
are not even a game, are always

a later day, another year, younger bodies.

Michigan Quarterly Review   ERNEST SANDEEN

TELESCOPE

It lies interlocked in your hands
compact with things it has held, extended,
holds nothing, then fills back inside
from where you direct it to see—
horses and ships, hills, trees, stars,
two does and two fawns stepping
a freshly ploughed field from furrow
to furrow.

        Outside, coherence
is shaping to enter the lenses
which must by reversal turn small;
and you, if you're quick, will spy
glints from silica spectra

detached at the eyepiece, where
what was left watching still serves.

Queen's Quarterly   PETER M. SANGER

THE BEGINNING OF AUTUMN

The day has barely lifted before
the rain begins, and I sit down
at the desk littered with unanswered
letters and look out into the garden
abandoned now to ragweed and sour-
grass. The gentians we planted
have been dead for weeks, but still
their stalks turn strangely green,
and the spent leaves, too, scattered
on the ground around them: it is
the illusion of water and light,
of light playing on water, playing
in the mind, until the mind becomes
part of the illusion. A few hours
ago, waking in the dark, I could see
beyond the window those same clouds,
heavy and back-lit by the moon,
coming up from the south, and all
I could think was I could not hold
them back, could not keep them out
of our lives . . . But look, instead,
what a quiet now is settling
on the world: at the other end
of the house, Lynne is still sleeping,
the fir trees are murmuring above
their pitted roots, the dry earth
softening to shadow. And it seems
that hours from now, though everything
else might have changed again, this
same slow rain will still be filling
the air with that warm and ineffable,
that uselessly inturning light.

Ploughshares   SHEROD SANTOS

A FAREWELL

For a while I shall still be leaving,
Looking back at you as you slip away
Into the magic islands of the mind.
But for a while now all alive, believing

That in a single poignant hour
We did say all that we could ever say
In a great flowing out of radiant power.
It was like seeing and then going blind.

After a while we shall be cut in two
Between real islands where you live
And a far shore where I'll no longer keep
The haunting image of your eyes, and you,
As pupils widen, widen to deep black
And I able neither to love or grieve
Between fulfillment and heartbreak.
The time will come when I can go to sleep.

But for a while still, centered at last,
Contemplate a brief amazing union,
Then watch you leave and then let you go.
I must not go back to the murderous past
Nor force a passage through to some safe landing,
But float upon this moment of communion
Entranced, astonished by pure understanding—
Passionate love dissolved like summer snow.

The Paris Review   MAY SARTON

WOMAN SMOKING

A woman is in the next room, smoking and reading.
It's late winter and she likes to think about
the rainy, pared down trees she saw once
in the Dutch *wouds,* though sometimes the rain
is too beautiful. The sparrows, a concert
of them, are suspended above the shaking hedgerows.
One afternoon she watched the sun
as it touched water at the far end of a canal,
the sun coming apart in the depths like an aspirin.
Spinoza noted the tendency of light to organize
around the descriptive parts of a text,
but the significance here is the woman's arm
slipping from the arm of her chair
and the fact that nothing else in the room moves.
In the dark, though, it all begins to loosen.
A breeze catches somebody's wash
on the line, every shirt bellying
out, the line itself
loping gracelessly between the poles.

The Ohio Review   ROGER SAULS

STORY

No one ever knew this story:
She came that night to my place
And sat down silently,
Hung her head,
Never said a word,
Her eyes avoiding mine.
For a long time
She was no more in love with me.
This pain wore me out:
Does she love someone else?
I began to weep in her lap,
Cries whose memory makes my body tremble.

She caressed my head,
Sat near me;
She gave me a kiss,
But I knew
Her heart had become cold toward me.

International Poetry Review   HUSHANG IBTIHAJ SAYA
                                    —*Translated from the Persian*
                                        by Munibur Rahman

THE GADGETS

My coat is full of gadgets, the magic
that stunned aboriginal man, consigned him
to the cross and the singing computer.

My wristwatch-calendar-radio alarms me
in languages from continents adrift
or burning.

My knife can slice, snip and saw,
open bottles and cans, loosen or
tighten three types of fasteners.

I compute at a touch vast sums
and differences, irrational roots
and functions, unnatural powers.

Conversation spools into my pocket.

The snapshot smaller than a stamp.

I look at and listen to
what I've made of you,
transparent, off color blur
and something rising, refractory.
The scratched voices,
pale ghosts of content,
like the marks on the mountain,
show which way the ice ran

when the spring of the world
shone down.

I can almost resolve what it is.

I can almost repair what is wrong.

The Antigonish Review   AARON SCHNEIDER

STARS, FISH

It was your silence that hooked me,
so like my father's. We were fishing
the Blackfoot thirty miles from Ovando.
I always think of us by that river.
Fisk sulked in their green house—
the intelligent browns, the beautiful
cutthroat. So deep in the stream
you were of the stream, the small bats
brushing your shoulder.

Or was it your past that got to me—
when you worked double shifts
in the zinc mines of Pennsylvania
stoned on opium, weaving one dream
into another, in the humid blur
of the steam pump? We fished
till stars came out, till night
filled the woods with smoke.

Now it's as though on the other side
of this life, figures move against a screen
in silhouette. You are among them: there,
where there is no language.
You brought that silence back
and burdened me with it. Is it in denial,
then, we find our true voice?

                    Tonight
I'll name stars: Deneb, Aldebaren, as though
the great North listened, rising up like spruce,
like smoke through the trees and stars,
and the great spaces among them
of which we never spoke.

The American Poetry Review   NANCY SCHOENBERGER

EVERYTHING IS ONLY AN IMAGE . . .

Everything is only an image in a mirror
that reflects another mirror—
Reflection behind reflection,
ad infinitum.

Everything is only a dream
in a dream
in which you dream
that you dream.

Until death shatters the mirror
and awakens the dreamer.

The Literary Review   ERNST SCHÖNWIESE
—Translated from the German
by Beth Bjorklund

SATURDAY MORNING

So much is unexplained. There was
The death you knew about, could smell
Months in advance, the sun riding
On water the day he died—his mouth
Not firm, one eye sagging, hidden
Almost in the imperfect shadow.
Was it for you with your composure
Unfaltering in the June heat? Forgive him?
You had hardly spoken for years.
Now you've awakened at dawn to shudder,
Remembering. He was your father.
That somehow complicates the present.

A week ago you walked in the morning
Down to the newsstand on the corner.
She was riding a bicycle, lean
And sober, eye on the wandering cars,
Threading traffic in light rain.
And seeing her face you half remembered
The time when all you were concerned with
Was just as simple as a ride
Through heavy traffic in light rain,
Saturday morning on a bicycle
In a town that looked something like this.

The Southern Review   JAN SCHREIBER

GRANDMOTHER BRYAN

I watched a scorpion shiver through the door
And bend its knees beside the kitchen stove.
When it was crushed, its hate-filled curve of tail
Still arched at them, in jerks,
The way a woman arched, long lives ago,
Convulsing to give birth,
Writhing out in fierceness far past strength
The inborn, God-willed poison of her wrath.

And years ago a snake my husband killed
Lay twisting hopeless halves before my feet.
Its mouth lashed death into the tranquil air,
Its quick tongue knowing, full of desperate will.

Where I sit, there are ninety years before,
And all their vehemence lies curdling here.
My hands twitch and my mouth, but most my brain.
I sit and reach for some last course of power,
For some Lear act of hatred or of love:
For any act—connection—some last sting!

The Threepenny Review   GLENDA SCHROCK

"LET THERE BE TRANSLATORS!"

("And the Lord said, 'Behold, the people is one and they
have all one language . . . Go to, let us go down, and
there confuse their language, that they may not understand
one another's speech.' "
—Genesis xi: 6, 7.)

When God confused our languages, he uttered,
in sapphire tones: "Let there be translators!"
And there were conjurors and necromancers
and alchemists, but they did not suffice:
they turned trees into emeralds, pools to seas.

God spoke again: "Let there be carpenters
who fasten edges, caulk the seams, splice timbers."
They were good.
                    God said: "Blessed the builder
who leaves his tower, turns from bricks and mortar
to marvel at the flames; the smith who fumbles
for prongs, wields andirons and prods live coals,
who stokes the hearths and welds two irons as one."

Praised was the man who wrote his name in other
handwriting, who spoke in other tones,
who, knowing elms, imagined ceiba trees
and cypresses as though they were his own,
finding new music in each limitation.

Holy the one who lost his speech to others,
subdued his pen, resigned his failing sight
to change through fire's change, until he saw
earth's own fire, the radiant rock of words.

Shenandoah   GRACE SCHULMAN

LOSSES

Life's gains are losses: water leeches rock,
rivers erode and deltas restore the land;

the sun melts ice, turns rain to clouds of mist.
Wind that spins palms in circles like propellers
squanders its force; the fire that feeds destroys.

Each morning burns what night had bound together,
waking us, amazed, staring in wonder
that bodies rivetted could break apart
to forfeit wholeness and regain the light.
So for all things neglected, nights refused,
I turn, as ships spill wind to change their course:
Just as the sea recedes, I grow large with loss.

The Georgia Review   GRACE SCHULMAN

PUMPERNICKEL

Monday mornings Grandma rose an hour early to make rye,
onion & *challah,* but it was pumpernickel she broke her hands for,
pumpernickel that stank up the neighborhood & for which she
    cursed
in five languages if it didn't pop out fat as an apple-cheeked peasant
    bride.
But bread, after all, is only bread & who has time to fuss all day
& end up with a dead heart if it flops? Why bother? I'll tell you why:
For the moment when the steam curls off the black crust like a strip
of pure sunlight & the hard oily flesh breaks open like a poem pulling
out of its own stubborn complexity a single glistening truth; & who
can help but wonder at the mystery of the human heart when you
    hold
a slice up to the light in all its absurd splendor; & I tell you
we must risk everything for the raw recipe of our passion
every moment of our lives.

The Kenyon Review   PHILIP SCHULTZ

FUNNY BONES

Looking past the shunt of your breasts
toward the round lift of our age, its stillness,
its fat blunt hands, the dark crust
of burnt coffee, I pull up against the headboard
stiff as a bog king, a peat king, bloodless.
You too sleep like one of the last:
full, deep, fossil. This heavy bed, this hoard
of too much believing, sinks into the dust
as you turn from the sun. The suddenness
hurts—not so much your motion as your war
against waking—as if I did not want your rest
as well. I stretch my hands along your collar
bone only as a sign of love, but lust
is quicker than nostalgia; you shake and toss

and twist up to me, ardent. Can we afford
passion at this end, when any moment just
a certain single indiscretion could mean loss
and the tumbling in of earth against the shored-
up ridges of this featherhearted place? Yes,
you say, there is nothing else now for it
but coupling; all the rest is sediment, husks
of light; and you settle over me, lord
and lady, stone and staff, leering sorceress.
It is sex, then, the antic deposit, the fuck
and funk and tackle of sex, that keeps us
specific to this lime bed, this deep gorge.
They find us in their time entirely by luck
groin to groin, jaw to jaw, and as they brush
away the dirt and fiber from the trapdoor floor
that is our joke, we collapse: heaven or bust.
You would have it that way, a kind of humor,
a last screw to the artifacts, a bird in the bush.
As you lie back, old as I am and exhausted by our trust,
pleased that we have come, as we have, this far.

Hampden-Sydney Poetry Review   HILLEL SCHWARTZ

PARIS

    those who come later
    are forced to learn
    to love what's left

    I never had the chance
    to fight on the barricades
    of '71 or '68
    I never sat in the cafés
    of Glassco's Montparnasse
    or paid my respects
    on Saturday nights at the rue de Fleurus

    first time I came was 1970
    the Métro was en grève
    an old whore was patrolling
    the alley outside our hotel

    the skyline is broken: neon
    flowers above the Luxembourg trees

    and like a patient lover
    who will not admit he's abandoned
    I sit at the café Bonaparte
    watching the crowds of St. Germain
    fire-eaters and magicians
    the tourists rush past ignoring
    la rue Guillaume Apollinaire

    it is enough: those of us
    who come later must learn

        to love
        whatever is left

Poetry Canada Review   STEPHEN SCOBIE

IN THE RAINS OF LATE OCTOBER

These are the Iron Days
when the heart
knows something is coming,
and animals
bellow and spook in their pens.
The birds of summer are gone.
Windows are closed,
and the spirit wants to curl up
in a warm room by a wooden table
with the smell of coffee
and leave nothing,
nothing exposed.

So I sit here alone,
watch water drop
from leaves of the maple,
turn from all
appliances,
and listen to the rain
stream from eave to granite
in an almost dream.

Western Humanities Review   MOLLY SEE

BRIEF FLIGHT

The heel of her hand pressed hard against his back.
Her face turned toward the window, greeting
the breeze. Faint as wands of feathers, it dried
the sweat that formed in the bends of her knees.

Tomorrow would be cooler. Rain would cleanse
the air to respite the legustrum's cloying scent.
Against his shoulder she rubbed her lips, traced
with the tip of her tongue a figure eight.

Flashes of light outlined the tree around whose trunk
wound trumpet vine. His face bending gently over
hers so that the flesh hung loose from the bone, and
the lines around his eyes crinkled like heavy paper.

Unless the rain reneged. Then she'd rise
before the heat accumulated, and the air would touch
her cheek like wet breath. The sun no stronger
than a candle cupped in morning haze,

yet all around plants whose roots demanded
saturation. A bounty there. A plushness born
of variegation. Its ripeness satisfied, lifted her
the way the wind transports the autumn seeds.

New England Review & Bread Loaf Quarterly   LYNDA H. SELF

ON NUDITY

(Quoi! Tout nu! dira-t-on,
n'avait-il pas de honte?
Tout est nu sur la terre,
hormis l'hypocrisie.
—Musset, Namouna)

Naked we are born, naked
inspected by doctor,
army, phys. ed. prof.

Naked, on operating table,
in hospital bed,
in winding sheet.

Naked in love to see one another,
to feel the skin of other bodies and,
the more we penetrate,

to have the jolt and the rub
that tell us how far we have penetrated.
Naked always, even in what doesn't matter.

Why, then, are there those who fear so
the nakedness of others? Could it be
they fear, less than the ugliness

of many, the beauty of
a few, or the fascination of
the splendid parts

of some special ones? And that, paralyzed
(with envy), we let the world and life
scud rudderless

toward naked liberty?

Denver Quarterly   JORGE DE SENA
—Translated from the Spanish
by Alexis Levitin

FROM HOLLAND

(Amsterdam)

It was chance that took me one Sunday morning
between nine and ten

turning at a bridge, one of the many, to the right
along the half-frozen canal. And not
this is the house, but only
—already seen a thousand times—
on the unpretentious plaque: "House of Anne Frank."

My companion said later: it should not be
that of Anne Frank, memory
shouldn't play favorites. There were so many
who collapsed from hunger alone
without time to write about it.
She wrote about it, it's true.
But at every turn at every bridge beside every canal
I kept searching without finding it again,
finding it over and over.
This is why Amsterdam is one
in its three-four variable elements
that it fuses into so many recurrent unities,
in the three-four putrid or harsh colors
its space perpetuates throughout;
spirit that, steady and limpid, illumines
thousands of other faces, everywhere—
seed and shoot of Anne Frank.
This is why Amsterdam is vertiginous on its canals.

Poetry Now   VITTORIO SERENI
—Translated from the Italian
by Ruth Feldman and Brian Swann

TRAPEZE ARTIST

After the clowns have shambled from
the ring, the circus lights are lowered
and the background music assumes
a quieter, yet more threatening, note.
An expectant silence holds the crowd
until the trumpets and a roll of drums
direct attention to the Acrobat.
Something from his childhood makes him proud.

He flings aside the ceremonial cape
with practised nonchalance. All eyes
are focused as he squirrels up the rope
deftly synchronizing hands and knees,
his rhinestone epaulettes and belt
changing colour in the spot's kaleidoscope.
But at the scaffold he appears to falter.
Something from his childhood makes him ill-at-ease.

Tonight he stands alone. Partnered in turn
by blonde, redhead and spry brunette
who risked more than their bodies to his grip,
he stalled, misjudged the timing, or thrust

each into the hated archetypal shape.
Lucky those few who reached the safety net.
So far as co-performers are concerned,
something from his childhood breeds distrust.

Now the apparatus is set in motion
and trapezes pendulate at different heights.
Falconlike, he swoops across the gulf,
barely touching the crossbars on his mission
through space, swings steeplejack high, drops low
in somersault, then, hanging by his teeth, rotates,
airing a compulsion to prove himself.
Something from his childhood makes it so.

Something from his childhood pre-empts the show.

The Antigonish Review   HOWARD SERGEANT

THE NATIONAL ANTHEM

I could hit the high notes, I said,
the ones at the top of the Star-
Spangled Banner and the teacher said yes, yes,
you may lead today and I jumped for the first bar
and it was fine, a little high maybe, but wasn't it
fine when I sang *OH-o say* and they were all
behind me, Mrs. Kipp's sixth graders: Richard, who just
that day said I was flat, and Donelyn, with breasts the object
of all our desires. I could see they were all
for me: Junelle, Annetta, and Betty
who'd never seen snow; Warren, and Kim the musical
genius, soft Shawn, and Karen the new girl, and Debbie
who told Karen to avoid me—all in it together
at the twilight's last—buck-toothed Frank and Bernard, the reverse
swallower always gargling 'round the rugged rocks; fragile
Patty whose grandpa was buried with all our get well
cards—all that brave class, still with me at *the ramparts*
and after *so gallantly streaming* it was no good
going back, too late to stop, nowhere to go
but up, up to the inevitable *rockets'*
red glare and up once more with *the bombs*
bursting and down, Oh god, back down *through the night,*
    grateful
that our flag was still there, bracing myself for the final
ascent toward *the land of the free*—a height
my thin soprano barely reached and where I knew no one
would follow.

I still sing it softly at ball games,
changing keys with the crowd or taking cover
under some great Voice. But they come back:
thirty faces straining for the one *glare*, even Mrs. Kipp's
chevron smile flagging as she heard where I intended

to take them. Thirty red faces for my solo breaking
free, for the shame of starting too high
and finishing alone.

Poetry   ROBIN SEYFRIED

POVERTY

I am weary of a toil
Not mine;
I am sitting on a ground
Not mine.

I have lived with a name
Not mine;
I have cried with a pain
Not mine.

I have found life in a pleasure
Not mine;
I surrender my life to a death
Not mine.

International Poetry Review   AHMAD SHAMLU
                            —Translated from the Persian
                                by Munibur Rahman

LONG DAYS

These are the long days when
the sunlight breathes
out of the shadows on the ground
and into leaves;

days when the air is nervous
with the sound of birds;
when through the trees from other gardens
the faintest words—

fragrant with all distance—
come to your ear:
each one, a wish that vanishes
before you hear;

each one reminding you
you must beware:
when all you've ever wished for comes
to all you are.

The Southern Review   ALAN SHAPIRO

BROOKLYN HEIGHTS

1.
I'm on Water Street in Brooklyn,
Between the Brooklyn Bridge
And the Manhattan Bridge,
The high charge of their traffic
Filling the empty street.
Abandoned warehouses
On either side.
In the shadowed doorways, shades
Of Melville and Murder Incorporated.
Five o'clock October light.
Jets and gulls in the fleecy sky.
Climbing the hill to Columbia Heights,
I turn to see the cordage
Of the Brooklyn Bridge, and, behind it
The battle-gray Manhattan.

2.
This room shelved high with books
Echoes with my midnights. Pages
Of useless lines swim in it. Only
Now and then a voice cuts through
Saying something right: No sound
Is dissonant which tells of Life.
The gaudy ensigns of this life
Flash in the streets; a December light,
Whipped by wind, is at the windows.
Even now the English poets are in the street,
Keats and Coleridge on Hicks Street,
Heading for the Bridge. Swayed aloft there,
The lower bay before them, they can
Bring me back my city line by line.

Epoch   HARVEY SHAPIRO

ON A SUNDAY

When you write something,
you want it to live—
you have that obligation, to give it
a start in life.
Virginia Woolf, pockets full of stones,
sinks into the sad river
that surrounds us daily. Everything
about London amazed her, the shapes
and sight, the conversations on a bus.
At the end of her life, she said
London is my patriotism.
I feel that about New York.
Would Frank O'Hara say, Virginia Woolf,

get up? No, but images from her novels
stay in my head—the old poet
(Swinburne, I suppose) sits on the lawn
of the countryhouse, mumbling
into the sun. Pleased with the images,
I won't let the chaos of my life
overwhelm me. There is the City,
and the sun blazes on Central Park
in September. These people on a Sunday
are beautiful, various. And the poor
among them make me think
the experience I knew will be relived again,
so that my sentences will keep hold
of reality, for a while at least.

The Paris Review   HARVEY SHAPIRO

BLUES REMEMBERED

Plastic chairs anchored
in boundless cement:
the War Memorial Auditorium,

Boston, back
in the middle 'sixties—
is time, is place a part of performance?

Old Son House
could hardly carry
himself, let alone his guitar onstage.

Lighting was no more
subtle than the décor.
In a white shirt he was high-grade coal.

He sat a minute
limbering till
his fingers loosened. Then played like hell.

Once, between numbers,
he looked down at us
and said in a voice like a spade raking gravel:

"I love Gawd.
I love everybody.
If you got religion you know what I mean."

No one said a word.
Then a girl giggled.
We clapped, embarrassed, and waited, blank.

for him to lift up
slag-heavy hands,
to span and grapple with steel once more,

to play a song
whose words, half mumbled,
would cover up silence. At last he did.

The Yale Review   ROBERT B. SHAW

SCAR

The ferry moves from shore
towards the islands, quiet as sleepers.
My last time here
I didn't have a scar. Now, from the maze
of tall buildings, old men rummaging
through garbage, slow throb
of lights, I've entered again
this calm.

Each night as I fall off to sleep
I still think of the knife
the rapist held beneath my eye.
Part of my mind ticked abstractly on:
the knife, it is beautiful, a hardened flame,
a flame that will not die.

The ferry moves forward through the night,
the pale moon slowly eclipsed
by the clouds.

I had a friend who lost most of his face
before he died, the cancer like ants
eating him alive.
He wore gauze to cover up the scars
so strangers wouldn't flinch.
Sundays we went fishing.
I looked into his eyes and was afraid.
Together we rocked in our little boat.

Sometimes I touch the scar beneath my eye
as if I could reach down inside it
and find the rapist's face
still sneering, talking to itself,
wet and soft as a fetus.

Sometimes I stare into a fireplace
and see in the ashen, crumbling wood
my friend's ruined face.

The ferry bears its few lights
towards the islands, through what appears
to be emptiness, without end.

The Virginia Quarterly Review   LAURIE SHECK

LEARNING TO RIDE THE TRAIN

Grandmother, I am here again,
rocking on the half-knitted shawl in your lap.
We could see for miles
along the coast, to the penny arcade
where the neon clown juggled
red balls of light above the roof.

You would kibitz about my future,
then lick the salt on your lips
and take me with you—the light in your eyes
sweeping back to some unfinished history
of a European terminal, the last whistle still blowing.

I know the tracks: how you clawed like dogs
under barbed wire, your father's flayed skin
already lighting the way. I see every station
sweatered in Yiddish—ancient Aunt Fanny,
young then, married to a *mensch,* and Uncle Ben,
so anxious to depart, he had *spilkies.*
All of you, thank G-d, caught trains winding West.

The steamer into Manhattan and the stogie-hollowed
gray man, young then, who helped you with luggage,
later pumped and showered into you the strain that
could reach me.
All this, in summer salt, on the Maine coast,
bouncing on your lapboard, I listened.

And I learned to ride the train.

Now, as I stand this time alone at the platform,
I feel the rails going on both before me
and behind: I see you in the slow formal train of Jewish ceremony,
the old men *dahvaning* you into the cemetery,
calling that I should follow.

And I have remembered this air—
every part of us touched by the great waves.
You said the lighthouse beacon sweeping over us
on shore was a message of the hidden
shoals just off the coast. These memories
sweep the span from your shore to mine—
the lights juggled above the roof
in the arc of remembering.

The Southern Review   NEIL SHEPARD

MY HEIRESS

No use telling them again who she was,
this portrait of the lady on my bedside table,
ancestress of theirs and mine who died

before they were born.
                    I who knew her then
am the last from whom she can inherit.

My bequest has nothing to do with wreaths
or the perpetual care of her grave.
She inherits only while I live. When I die,
no one will remain to offer her so much as
the substance of a wraith.

The Southern Review   PEARL ANDELSON SHERRY

MY FATHER'S GARAGE ON CHRISTMAS NIGHT

Back after all these years, and older,
The silence better, more like
Friendship, two neighbors
Rooting for the same team.
Rafters filled with the detritus
Of mutual lives:
                    a tent we used
For camping at the lake,
A punching bag nobody hits now,
My sister's furniture.
And your workbench piled higher
Than ever with a hundred
Accomplished or forgotten
Repairs and adjustments—
Power sander and soldering iron askew,
A wood box filled with broken things
Waiting to be renewed.

This is what you end up with:
A garage domain, a world of certainty,
Perfect fits.
                    I don't question it anymore.
Perhaps half lost
                    in realms of idea
                    and perplexions of beauty,
I even envied this yoga
Of wood and metal
Tightly joined,
Of things held down by nails and bolts.

Admiring this platter you once fashioned—
Quail in flight on smoky plastic—
I praise it perhaps too much,
Or awkwardly,
                    meaning a hundred appreciations
Left unspoken, meaning
You weren't what I thought—
That you never understood
The anger of your sons,

The drugs, the grasping for roads—

(America has nothing to do with
this)—

There's just the two of us, looking
More alike than we realize, feeling
What we don't know how to say.

The Sun   MICHAEL SHORB

THE GOING-PART

Time was a more private matter when it was hidden
in the fob of a man's trousers. In double-darkness
there it ticked and moved its hands,
in darkness again its springs and wheels,
winding down against the hours of the day
until waking; man intervened upon the stem
to set it right again. There was a ritual
to keeping it: a man had to be faithful.
Time was something mothers taught their children—
about the big hand and the little hand;
it was basic childhood stuff,
like tying shoes and reading Seuss.

In time, old faces will be something
we show children from scrapbooks. Hickory-dickory
tales will bore them, they will not understand
O. Henry, Big Ben, or Sherlock's seventh clue;
syncopation will be obsolete,
and among the attic-relics of great-grandfathers
and station-masters, a chain, if it is not broken,
will lead us to the scratched case
of a retired friend, a familiar face that spoke
reliably as long as we did our part,
and to a working order that stayed the life span
of a man who lived when fobs were still in style.

Poetry   SUSIE SHULMAN

CANOE AT EVENING

On the mirror-still water, its widening vee
covering the lake's enormous vowel,
our canoe glides out from shore.

Each eddy slows and flattens. Only a tremor
reveals where we have been. In our wake
a loon trolls for walleyes, moths flirt and dip,

waterbugs scribble and vanish.
A slow flush spreads in the west, the firetower's
stick-figure against it and the first small

flakes of stars. We pull over narrow shoals
past a white float into the long shadow
of the Jameses' shore where abandoned birches

double themselves on the water.
We talk of many things, hanging there
in a green twilight between two heavens.

A loon's laugh shakes from the darkness,
gathering behind Vicker's Point. We turn
and once again crease the salmon-edged bay—

paddles rising and flashing—
toward the waiting cabin whose red lamps blink
through leaves still green in the afterglow.

Easing the canoe on shore we walk uphill,
partridge-berries nodding against our ankles,
leaving the lake to itself,

the loon's indecipherable laughter,
and stars that rise to its surface
like fry to shimmer and feed.

America   ROBERT SIEGEL

CHUMLEY/TACONIC STATE PARK/1950

I can hear her call him, "Ray, don't
take the boy. It's not morning yet,
and rainy. He'll catch his death
or you'll have a wreck."

But my father, mild as a rule,
drives us across the Manhattan Bridge,
the lights blurring in the rain,
through the still dark city,
upriver, to Route 22.
Just the two of us. So excited,
I can't speak, and he doesn't either.
Each time the lightning cracks
I can see his face,
his large hands on the wheel.

At Bish Bash Falls, Father baits my hook.
He shows me how to cast.
We keep quiet so the fish will bite.

Later, we strip and swim.
Then he takes me back to the narrow
beach and tells me to wait there.
As in a silent movie, my father
swims, breast stroke,
his head above water, sleek as an otter,
toward the center of the lake.
I am three years old and wait for him,

awed how soundlessly he glides
beyond reach
of my voice,
my longing for him a straight line
between the fixed point of my heart
and the back of his head.
He dives, and for a moment
I'm an orphan
breathless and dumb
until he comes up, a black rock out there.
He pulls toward me.
The silvery distance narrows.
So I wait,
learning to love what moves away
and may return.

New Boston Review   MAXINE SILVERMAN

YOUR SPACE

(from the Cycle, "The Altar of Isenheim")

The empty jacket on the hanger,
the jacket that still bears your imprint,
the folds used to your way
of moving in the world—
the jacket so big
I can't even give it away
because there's no one on earth
of your same stature.
This jacket—
with its pen, glasses, the handkerchief
sticking out of the pocket—
this
is what death is:
in the shapeless magma of existing,
the unfillable space of being.

International Poetry Review   PIERA SIMEONI
                              —*Translated from the Italian*
                                 by Ruth Feldman

BLACK ANGEL

There is a cemetery I walk to
in the stiff breath of autumn,
in the lengthening sequence
of dwindling days, where
the bald knolls and hollows
fold in on one another, hide
one thing from the next:

the yew tree from the crepe myrtle,
the garland from the path,
the hole in the land from
the hole in the heart—
I walk there to hide myself
from myself.

                    And still
I come stark halt upon
the monument people call
Black Angel—black as a shadow
in deep water, big as a man;
and I wonder, as some must,
drawn again
into its sunken glare,
who would raise such a memory
to himself, to another,
to break from the grave's
belly of snow and stare
the living down, to say
the dead are dead
and don't come back.

                    Each
night I wrestle my own
black angel, who comes upon me
like a sudden mirror,
so that I can feel the black
wings wrenching my shoulders,
see the black lips broken
by desire, by grief; so that
I must wrestle each night
until I am exhausted enough
to wake, to walk back
into the world of things
as they are, one step
and its consequence
after the next.

Quarterly West   JIM SIMMERMAN

FIRST SUNDAY OF ADVENT, 1967

Today it's nearly dusk
when the snow gathers, finally,
on the lawn, the tired side

of the wind turned white
and settling down.
I watch the steady storm

from my mother's rocking chair
upstairs, all roomlights off.
The house below is quiet.

My father, too, may be staring
out the window, straining to see
the fender of the Chevrolet

he banged up on a tree this afternoon;
he will not speak for hours, or days.
My mother, having trouble reading

in the intricate silence,
lays down her book and glides into the kitchen:
she adds potatoes to the sizzling roast.

Up here it hardly matters what they do.
Through the lulling constancy of snow,
I hear the muffled grunts and spatters

of their need, and still I sit,
a dream apart from love. For who am I
to cry, entranced with the night,

and lost to them as if,
unseeing, I looked down
from the darkness of heaven?

The New Republic   THOMAS SIMMONS

LIVES IN ONE LIFETIME

Sometimes you get what you ask for—
to be left alone. All day
not once the sound of a motor,
one sailboat only with a yellow flag waving.

From this shore I see where sky begins,
a shaft of blue touching ground
between oaks on top of the ridge.
Across Chatuge, lake made by man,
a whole mountain rises out of the water.

I have no boat and no way to cross over
this flooded valley except to walk.
Where the road was, my feet can touch asphalt
if I let myself sink.

                    Here the house stood.
There is the roof of the barn, buried forty years.

Yes, I am sinking in doubt.
Rubble from lives in one lifetime passes before me.
This is the end, the new start,
rock I remember, and clay soft beneath my feet.

An old logging road leads me to the top of the mountain,
where trees stand apart,
where sky begins.

The Georgia Review   NANCY SIMPSON

SHE AND I

The sky was shining
When we both met.
The moon was up
When we both met.
The world was jealous
When we both met.
But we smiled
When we met.

The love days
Were liked only by us.
The world felt jealous
Even of hearing about us.
The dim bathroom light
Shone brightly when we met.
But both of us were unaware
Of the cruel wide world.

Our last meeting was seen
Only by the bathroom light.
We went our different ways then.
She was taken by the cruel world
And I by loneliness.
Oh, the cruel world.

New Letters   SAMIR PUNIT SINGH

POSSESSIONS

The small bird that walks in its sleep
belongs to me. And the old man
who trips on a dirt road at dusk,
one strand of white hair blown straight
above his head like a thin flame,
he also belongs to me.
The ragged essence of green
like a heavy curtain at the forest's
edge, and the sky that disappears
as I shut my eyes: mine.
But not the clouds. The cables
I throw to them pass through
and fall to my feet;
no one owns the clouds.
The news, the bad news that arrives
in threes, and leaves in one
body is mine. And the tiny belief
I swallowed like a seed
years back: dry leaves rattle
in my lungs, branches open into hands,
roots that once ripped through
thick leather, fray: still mine.

Friends, all the lies you've inhaled,
all the snuffed prayers
for happiness whispered in my
presence belong to you—
I could do nothing with my own.
Only the dappled wren
that smashes itself against
the kitchen window, the crumpled dress,
the drop of blood on the white sill,
and the sullen one, sitting alone
in the alcove, dark master of my childhood
who will no longer look me in the eye,
is mine, is mine, is mine.

Kayak   JEFFREY SKINNER

SEEING WIND

That morning, in December light,
rain was so heavy my child claimed
to see wind in its sideways flight.

She stared. The visible wind shamed
me for seeing a sixth straight day
of rain, for the failure she named

blindness. Child, though not blind I may
no longer see as you do now,
or hear what you do when you say

zebras live in fir trees whose boughs
kick outside your window at night.
Mine is the age at which one vows

to find vision and song, delight
simply in the seen and heard. But
seeing wind in rain's sideways flight

is seeing only rain and not
a thing more. I have understood
where I spend my life and on what

grounds such rain beats as if for good
all day as the old year ends, and
I dread the next more than I should.

Southwest Review   FLOYD SKLOOT

BLOOD IS SAP IS DESIRE

Blood is sap.
The only kind I know on sight
is mine. I always thought
the Queen would bleed in blue.

My arms look like royal forests,
fine blue trees
that can't hold off the future
from my wrists
anymore than a maple
can hold its sap all year long,
way up in the branches,
spiney fingers
sucking out the sunlight.

Sap is desire.
My body feels empty of you
because I love the curve of your wrist.
I know the pause
longer than a breath, and then some;
and then like a diver come deep into me
knocking out sounds I don't know
from my searching throat.
I want to come inside you
with more than emotion,
to have your body surround mine,
to have you depend on my deep movements
for your language, your need.
I want to fill you up
from root to blossom,
fill your head with warmth and confusion.
Watch me now,
as I begin to part the leaves
from about your body.

The Malahat Review   CAROLYN SMART

BATS

Still in sleeping bags, the promised delivery
only words as usual, our lives upside down,
we are transients lost in thirteen rooms
built by a judge who died. The landlord says
they mean no harm, the bats, and still I wake
at the shrill whistling, the flutter overhead.

I fumble to a tall window open among maples.
A car crawling a hill splashes my face with light
spread fine by mist that had been summer rain,
a sweetness that drips from black-palmed leaves.
The breeze I feel is damp, edged with mown hay,

enough to make me think the thumps and titters
I hear might be the loving pleasure of parents
unguessed, a long quarrel ended, a thrilling
touch that trails to muffled play. Slight shadows,
these are bats, residents of the house elders
built to last, the vaulted attic tall as a man

holding them hung in rows daylong like words
unuttered above the yard where children romp.
Flashlight in hand, I pass through the parlor
papered in silk for marriages the judge made,
and stand beneath the hidden door. The truth is,
nothing can drive them out or contravene those
fretful, homespinning voices we cannot help
fearing, as if they were the all-knowing dead.
Yet if I had one chair to stand tall enough on,
I would climb with my light and shaking voice
to see whatever has lodged in their wizened eyes.

Under a room I have never seen but know, I stand
like one of the unblessed at the edge of dawn.
Smelling mold, I hear a dog's hopeless howl
and think of the stillness in the deep heads
of creatures who hang in sleep that is like love

in the children we cannot keep forever, absolute.
Each one near me unfurls a homekeeping song no
darkness or deed can kill. With them, all green
from the field clings beyond each flood of light.
As if I had never been out of this room, I listen.
The sound is like rain, leaves, or sheets settling.

Ploughshares   DAVE SMITH

AND HAPPY PEOPLE

the only pain i remember about being poor
is how often our houses were sold from us
how often we couldnt pay rent there anymore
and would have to find another place
and the pain wasnt clear to me
i enjoyed the commotion of moving

the galloping exploration of the new
empty house on a sunday afternoon
and then seeing the old furniture
shape itself in the new rooms
the pain is in the remembering
all the grownups smiling

as if they were excited too
and had chosen a smaller house
for some adult purpose they couldnt
explain to us—oh, if i could hold
those faces in my hands now
and press the tears out of them

New Letters   PATRICK SMITH

PERFORMING MY MORNING ABLUTIONS

The pump's out again,
but water's everywhere from last night's storm.
I bring the well bucket in and fill
the basin you gave me,
the white one with a thin red rim.
In the translucent lens
I try to see my face as you saw it shine:
a flower one might use for making wine.

A crisp sun makes this day resemble
the one of our last "nature walk"
where you smiled at wrens
and the hummingbird like a petal
and named each wild bloom
like Eve adrift in Eden and ordaining
names she found in a dream:
bittersweet, bindweed, loosestrife, rue,
dewdrop, heartweed, true wood sorrel,
sad false asphodel.
Illogically, you proclaimed,
"Some day these will all be ice."
You filled your arms with colors and their smells.

I should go to the woods to cut some fresh ones.
The room is dull, although
the sun's new angle has danced
the window glass to
a dandelion blur of light I can feel,
and one vase you shaped from clay
holds its pale bouquet of boneset,
whose leaves, the Cherokee believed,
had properties that could heal.

Buffalo Spree   R. T. SMITH

NOTHING

We are driving east on Glebe Road
when a rabbit is caught
in the sudden snare of headlights.
My father eases off the gas,
downshifts, and the rabbit escapes
into marsh grass.
I'm twelve and can think of nothing
but Nancy Simmons naked,
how at Clausen's pond
I'd heard her laughter
and seen her pale body hidden
among the bleached reeds.
My father asks what I am thinking
and I cannot tell him

of breasts ripening
somewhere in this soft darkness.

Twenty-five years
and I'm driving with my son
on a summer night.
In the radio's blue glow
I see on his face
that look I could not see on my own:
the eyes of a startled animal,
life bearing down
with the instancy of light.
"What are you thinking?" I ask,
and he answers,
as we all must,
"Nothing."

Green River Review   STEPHEN E. SMITH

COMMEMORATIVE

(Edna St. Vincent Millay, American Poet)

Within an oval frame, inside a square,
Her profile and her red-gold hair outshine
The postage stamp, too delicate, too fine
To risk to commerce, to her name unfair.
Yet poets must go public now to share
Her lyric voice along its classic line.
She leads us upward to a towering pine
Revealing transient youth, its fresh despair.
With her I weave a tune to succor tears,
I clutch remembered pages, saffron, worn.
The harp, the figs, the thistles where I stood,
An everywoman's maiden fraught with fears
Of tangled spirit, love's Renascence sworn,
Recalling three long mountains and a wood.

Lincoln Log   VIRGINIA E. SMITH

LIFE

I, my own prisoner, say this:
life is not spring dressed in light-green velvet,
or a caress that one seldom gets;
life is not a decision to go
or two white arms to keep one from going.
Life is the narrow circle that holds us prisoner,
the invisible ring we never break through;
life is the imminent happiness which passes us by,
and the thousand steps we are not capable of taking.

Life is to despise oneself
and lie motionless at the bottom of a well
and know that, high above, the sun shines
and golden birds fly
and arrow-swift days shoot by.
Life is to wave a short farewell and go home and sleep . . .
Life is to be a stranger to oneself
and a new mask for each person one meets.
Life is to deal carelessly with one's own happiness
and to push away that solitary moment;
life is to believe one is weak and does not dare.

Calyx
EDITH SÖDERGRAN
—Translated from the Swedish
by Christer L. Mossberg

CALLIE LIDA'S PAIN

*("Today Tom told me that he is Billow Man, as I had suspected. But even so
I find it hard to believe, and keep thinking he was only kidding, and pray-
ing he's only kidding. . . ."—from Callie Lida's diary)*

I get up, and shut the door, locking out my fear.
But you're everywhere, Tom, a shadow crossing the refrigerator,
green light through the grill striping the balcony,
a reflection in the window when I look up.
There's a stillness of shattered light inside me
that could congeal at any time into pain.

Last night I walked 34th Street past men
crouched over sack paper in phone booths.
I hardly even cared about getting mugged.
I wanted to soar up above the buildings—
wanted a super-power of my own, to don a lavender costume
with wings, go up and find you where nothing would matter,
where the world's troubles would be as distant
as the voices and honking drifting up to us from Broadway.
The air, it's so peaceful; why can't it. . . .

Tom, if you're Billow Man—could I love you nonetheless?
And would you be happy with me, me locked onto earth,
stuck to a mere body, not bending crowbars or rippling sidewalks,
only a narrow face looking up each time
you push aside curtains in favor of the night?
Could I live always waiting for you,
praying each time the curtains swing back
that it will be you?
Could I live in a sadness hardened to indifference,
and blot out the thought of you maybe killed by criminals,
the bored police shifting from foot to foot
as they hand me the papers to sign at our front door?

Mississippi Review
JAMES SOLHEIM

ACCUSATIONS 4

I am going to bury you in a telephone booth
   when you die. I will hook you up
    to lots of WATS lines
so you can still be in on all the conference calls.

   Centuries hence,
    they will puzzle over your artifacts:
   intricate intercom devices,
    flashing hold buttons,
a great tangle of tightly coiled long lines,
    even a closed circuit set
hooked up to a poolside cabana
    in Beverly Hills.

        They will think it's medical.
    They will figure out
that all that incredible tangle of stuff
   is a complex dialysis machine
   or a mammoth pacemaker
    that kept your pulse going.
   They won't understand.

I am going to erect
   an enormous antenna for a tombstone.
   You will become one
with almighty American Tel and Tel;
   you will be connected up
    to everything.
I'm going to do that for you—
   if I don't die first.

Sojourner   JANE SOMERVILLE

PROXIMITY

How do we hold the world,
if not too close,
this bouquet of earth and animal,
its fragrance half heavy with decay?
Times I back away from the riddle's edge
and would crush it underfoot:

Distance,
I call for distance.
Clear the land,
I'll assume affections from afar,
building a high world on stilts,
letting the river down to marsh.
Here there are no soft paws
or even a semblance of small hands.
Everything is the cold child
of another marriage.

Swallowing hard, I watch the world
scuttling on, always ahead,
like a raccoon filled with dawn.
I do not even hear the leaves turn.

I've come to the underside of riddle,
cleared to stone and forgetfulness.
The only clue makes for the trees.
I can't recall its name.

College English   KATHERINE SONIAT

FOURTEEN

Whatever became of blue-eyed Jeannie
whose breasts were magnetic fields
that seized our boyish eyes like iron fillings?

In our coltist play of bump and push,
we teased and ran from discovery's edge,
ran like scolded pups from her mock chiding.

That summer's sudden rounding of her body
caught us unaware at September's return;
the thrust of her womanliness was thunder
rolling into the past, our boyhood summers
provoking a new surge like volcanic anger
that drove our nights into new wonder.

The Malahat Review   GLEN SORESTAD

SASKATOONS

You must understand the ritual,
know when the fruit has reached
its moment of beauty, for the saskatoon
is a fragile berry, and its sweetness,
its delicate moment of perfection,
captured on time only.

This you told me when we were young
as we walked, fingers intertwined,
through aspens laced with saskatoons.
And I surrendered to this rite,
your dark eyes daring mine.

Waves   GLEN SORESTAD

GETTING SERIOUS

I shave my face, comb my hair
Back on the sides, and I'm different

From the posture I assumed in a grunting sleep.
It's time to get serious,
To cough delicately into a hanky,
To weigh each meal on a fork, not my unbalanced tongue.
I've turned thirty, brighter
By an espresso and paper back translations,
And my task is to be polite:
I hold open a door, and people rush in.
I help my wife with her coat,
And she smiles like a red coal blooming under wind.
So it is. I'm crisp
In slacks, a stiff collar,
And I'm off to witness a french romance.
This will take years. I turn 35,
Still crisp, and the theater is weeping,
Its lap full of popcorn and hands
Petting one another's love so it won't be sad.

Poetry   GARY SOTO

BOARDED WINDOWS

Will I die while thinking of
dull gray houses in the rain,
attics where moths eat our clothes,
closets where mice sleep,
drawers that won't open,
doors that have lost their knobs,
newspapers piled in the cellar,
or faded yellow wallpaper?
Will I die while thinking of
apples rotting on the kitchen table,
white sheets on the line,
dull knives, rattling pans,
rugs asleep in the hall,
shoes thrown in the corner,
or red curtains pulled shut?
I don't want to die in the silence of
a black telephone waiting to ring,
floorboards waiting for footsteps,
old coats waiting to be worn,
mirrors waiting for eyes to look at them,
windows waiting for hands to close them,
or flowers on a table waiting for water.
I don't want to die
because death reminds me of an abandoned secret
wanting to be told.
The secret is
nothing can alter the sequence of events
that have led me to make certain wrong decisions.
The secret is
my wrong decisions will crowd around me in the end

like apologetic children
trying to convince me of their good points.
The secret is
my past will seem suddenly less habitable,
like a quiet house with boarded windows.
And so, I will refuse to think.
I will simply be aware of the rain
falling into the empty street
when I feel my body being pulled,
as if by gravity,
toward the end of things.

The American Poetry Review   MARCIA SOUTHWICK

IN THE GARDEN AT MIDNIGHT

Do trees ever sleep? The flowers close,
and the lawn lies down with the moon to dream,
and you and the other animals
drift through the dark with your totems . . . but leaves,

in the stillness, the leaves of the trees seem to wait,
absolute in the garden at midnight,

as if in the dark still they breathe the light.

The Hudson Review   BARRY SPACKS

PRAYER TO THE LORD OF SPEED

O grant me the reins of a chrome horsebeast.
And sweet cubes of fuel for its hungry mouth.
Roll the road out smooth and endless, my carpet
Of blacktop. At my right hand, place the shaft
That changes gears and lives. Let me hear the tires
Keening high as dynamos. With the heat
Of my passage, make the world melt into shapes
Of blurred rushing, its colors merging. Let
The air scour me with cries of being hurtled through.
I beseech you to grant me your ever-swelling
Essence—*acceleration*. As I pass the speed
Of light, make my skin wear away, flaking off:
A husk I need no longer. And let
My buried light explode upward, rocketing
On and on and on into the heavens,
Returning like a comet to its birthplace
Among the stars! Speed without end, amen!

Portland Review   MICHAEL SPENCE

AUDEN'S FUNERAL

(to Christopher Isherwood)

I

One among friends who stood above your grave,
I cast a clod of earth from those heaped there
Down on the great brass-handled coffin lid.
It rattled on the oak like a door knocker.
And at that sound I saw your face beneath
Wedged in an oblong shadow under ground:
Flesh creased, eyes shut, jaw jutting,
And on the mouth a smile: triumph of one
Who has escaped from life-long colleagues roaring
For him to join their throng. He's still half with us,
Conniving slyly, yet he knows he's gone
Into that cellar where they'll never find him,
Happy to be alone, his last work done,
Word freed from world, into a different wood.

II

But we, with feet on grass, feeling the wind
Whip blood up in our cheeks, walk back along
The hillside road we earlier climbed today,
Following the hearse and tinkling village band.
The white October sun circles Kirchstetten
With colours of chrysanthemums in gardens,
The bronze and golden under wiry boughs
From which a few last apples gleam like agate.
Back in the village inn we sit on benches
For the last toast to you, the honoured ghost
Whose absence now becomes incarnate in us.
Tasting the meats and wine, we hear your voice
Speaking in flat benign objective tones
The night before you died. In the packed hall
You are your words. Your audience read
Written on your face the lines they hear
Ploughed back and forth criss-cross across it,
The sight and sound of solitudes endured.
And, looking down at them, you see
Your image echoed in their eyes,
Enchanted by your language to their love.
And then, your last word spent, bravo-ing hands
Hold up above their heads your farewell bow.
Then many stomp the platform, entreating
Each, for his hoard, your still warm autograph.
But you have slipped away to your hotel
And lock the door, and lie down on the bed,
And fell out of men's praise, dead on the floor.

III

Ghost of a ghost, of you when young, you waken
In me my ghost when young, us both at Oxford.
You, the tow-haired undergraduate
With jaunty liftings of the hectoring head,
Angular forward stride, cross-questioning glance,
A putty-faced comedian's gravitas,
Saying aloud your poems whose letters bite
Ink-deep into my fingers lines I set
In 10 pt. Caslon on my printing press:
AN EVENING LIKE A COLOURED PHOTOGRAPH
A MUSIC STULTIFIED ACROSS THE WATERS
THE HEEL UPON THE FINISHING BLADE OF GRASS.

IV

Returned now to your house—from which we first
Set forth this morning—the coffin on a table—
Back to your room blood-drowned in memories—
The poems deserted, empty chair and desk,
Books, papers, typewriter, bottles, and us—
Chester, blessed on your lips named there 'dear C',
Now hunched as Rigoletto, spluttering
Ecstatic sobs, already beginning
Slantwards his earth-bent journey to you:—summons
Opera, your camped-on heaven—music—bodiless
Resurrection of your bodies,
Passionate duets whose chords conclude
Quarrels in harmonies. Remembering
Some tragi-jesting wish of yours, he puts
Siegfried's Funeral March on the machine.
This drives out every word except our tears.
Summary drums, cataclysmic cymbals,
World-shattering brass uplift on drunken waves
The hero's corpse upon a raft that's borne
Beyond the foundering sunsets of the West
To that Valhalla where the imaginings
Of the dead poets flame with their lives.
The dreamer sleeps forever with the dreamed.

V

Then night. Outside your porch, we linger,
Murmuring farewells, thinking tomorrows
Separate as those stars in space above.
Gone from our feast, your ghost enters your poems
Like music heard transformed to the notes seen.
This morning dwindles to a photograph,
Black and white, of friends around a grave
That dark obliterates now. Buried,
The marvellous instrument of consciousness
With intellect like rays revealing

Us driven out on the circumference
Of this exploding time: but making
Paradigms of love, your poems
That draw us back towards the centre,
The separateness of each within the circle
Of your enfolding isolation.

Antaeus   STEPHEN SPENDER

CRAZY QUILT

Each night, eyes closed, I walk the crazy rows:
no up or down, no north or south
to guide me, I zigzag, dizzy and drunk,
my heart, like the quilt's, off-center.

The sun and moon, at odds with one another,
shine darkly from different corners.
Random stars point this way and that.
A dog barks. A calico cat meows.
An owl hoots, not unkindly, "Who? Who?
Who are you looking for?"
Before I can answer, it disappears.

A house, a heart, a tree.
This must be childhood, a road
leading through unreasoning, moonlit fields
I almost remember. The only rule is simple:
for each step forward, take one step back.

I find a piece of silk from my mother's
wedding dress, still gleaming whitely,
a tie my father used to wear.
Each thing I touch initialled and pieced-in
carefully, my birth, a wedding anniversary.
But something's always missing.
"Not for a child's ears," they said
when I asked, "Who's dead? Who disappeared?"

Each night I walk the quilt in circles,
retracing the past, waiting for morning
to call me back. "Mother, where are you?"
I call and call, my voice travelling
beyond me, echoing back. I hear her answer,
so near, so far within the quilt's
dark borders, "I'm here. I'm here."

The Yale Review   ELIZABETH SPIRES

PHOTOGRAPHY AS THE EFFECT OF LIGHT

Your body, a stooped critical question mark:
what is the meaning? You are looking

through thick plate glass
at me, at the children,
hoping the lens
will make us larger than we are,

so faraway and bright.
More focused than we should be, we recede.
The children wave.
You see their moonlit faces;
blinking, you make them disappear
onto the screen:
you are trying so hard to love!

Now you're the projectionist as well.
I'm standing in a field of daisies,
skirt blowing, shading my eyes
from your penetrating glare.
I hold our children's hands:
the movie slows
and in a burst of flower-like flecks
the film goes dark. Your view of us,
your brain, the flashbulb, blows.

The American Poetry Review   KATHLEEN SPIVACK

TROUBLED HOUR

Towards evening, as fishermen in the harbors ready their boats
At ebb tide, the brown masts trembling before the wind,
You throw yourself into the sails, starved for those distant coasts
Which have risen, night after night, in your unslumbering mind.

Or are you perhaps fiercely compelled by planet-rule
To seek out whatever is shoreless and far away,
To roam across the wide waters while hurricanes pound the ship's
      hull
And sky and ocean are fused in the same dull grey?

Do you rage in the dark against what you hold dearest, then
      anguished, awake at last,
Eyes dim and blood burnt beyond remedy,
To watch with vacant stare, tight-lashed to kismet's mast,
The day sullenly break above a shuddering sea?

Poetry Now   ERNST STADLER
                  —*Translated from the German by Francis Golffing*

BEYOND APPEARANCES

1.

Wherever the next place is, here comes
a shaft of sun. It has found Earth,

become local gold—you can catch it
in your hand. (Like anything precious, it weighs
nothing.) For a minute as a reflection
your face knows whatever light
there is. The world in its onward course
for a minute has a halo of brightness around it.

2.

Sometimes the end of a sound comes
where you are—someone is singing far
off and a footprint of the song fades
away in your cupped hand by your ear,
or a bird has left its passage hanging
in the air: wherever you go, not spilling
the past, you hold the end of the sound
in the tilt of your head ever after.

3.

A little excitement among the minutes
may mean a story is gathering: you lean
forward a certain way and let
what is coming have all your life—a ripple
begins, a beaver head has appeared,
a still pool comes alive; and all
the world that looked at you from the surface
lets down, down, into the dark.

Southwest Review   WILLIAM STAFFORD

LITTLE ROOMS

I rock high in the oak—secure, big branches—
at home while darkness comes. It gets lonely up here
as lights needle forth below, through airy space.
Tinkling dish-washing noises drift up, and a faint
smooth gush of air through leaves, cool evening
moving out over the earth. Our town leans farther
away, and I ride through the arch toward midnight,
holding on, listening, hearing deep roots grow.

There are rooms in a life, apart from others, rich
with whatever happens—a glimpse of moon, a breeze.
You who come years from now to this brief spell
of nothing that was mine: the open, slow passing
of time was a gift going by. I have put my hand out
on the mane of the wind, like this, to give it to you.

The Hudson Review   WILLIAM STAFFORD

YOU DON'T KNOW THE END

Even as you are dying, a part of the world
can be your own—a badger taught me that,
with its foot in a trap on the bank of the Cimarron.

I offered the end of a stick near the lowered head:
space turned into a dream that other things had,
and four long grooves appeared in that hard wood.

My part that day was to learn. It wasn't folklore
I saw, or what anyone said, when I looked
far, past miles of the world around me:

Wherever I went, a new life had begun,
hidden in grass, or waiting beyond the trees.
There is a spirit abiding in everything.

The Chariton Review   WILLIAM STAFFORD

VOCABULARY

("Consciousness is a singular
of which the plural is unknown."
—Erwin Schrodinger)

Turning from you to pick up a starfish,
I wonder if anyone has the right
to know me this well,

the way we know the particular
habits of the day—how the rabbit
will cross the lawn after supper,

which birds fly to which trees—
and the way we fit into the double
hollows of the summerhouse beds.

Though I know the names of little enough,
when I say "that's eel grass"
or "that's a periwinkle," it pleases you.

In your lab, when you gave voice
to the microscopic while we looked
through twin eyepieces at cancerous cells,

you labeled the parts, then asked,
"Are you thinking of your mother?"
I was so startled I could hardly reply.

A year ago on the tide flats
I walked alone and could not speak
the name of anything.

And now you turn me to you,
touch my face and say:
lips, philtrum, iris, *you.*

Poet Lore   SUE STANDING

THE WOMAN ON THE ISLAND

I have tried to tell you how it was on the island,
left alone, the village deserted, the path
growing high with grasses,
the days passed in watching.

Always the same, the same gulls
haunting the rock face, their white wings
hovering over the shallows,
their cries constant as the sea's mutterings.

Once in a while I climbed the cliff by the shore
and watched for the ship that was sure to come.
But the years passed like leaves, where I recorded the seasons.
Notch after notch, first the moons, then the changes
from green spring to summer
to the fogs of autumn and the cold
wind bringing rain.

Still, sometimes I looked out over the sea
past the coastal shallows, where the swells
rose like the gray humps of whales
going southward in springtime.

I forgot the moons, then the seasons.
Only the years returned. I forgot the look
of the sea where it lay in its own
blue vast widening circle round the island.

Yankee   Ann Stanford

KATI AT FIFTEEN MONTHS

Seven blocks high there is this unsaid
glee spilling in the alphabeted room
where every speck's a great surprise
and every sound a mystery moving air
where your small hands are birds in spring
and all your movements sing discovery.

Age waits patiently in other rooms
while into your eyes the whole world
tumbles—
like morning into apple groves,
like lovers into bed.

Dalhousie Review   Ken Stange

MUSEUM PIECE

Young lady, your face is a sight for sore eyes
that have looked on beauty: you are real,

I admire the swing of your skirt,
    not the pertness of your demeanor
among the catalogues, the lacquered vases
that, breaking, would break the patron's heart.

So the first fruit of beauty is this,
the last. Lights burn in your mind
        as you contemplate the marble floor
        where Pan might cavort in state,
but only after you have written him down—
Miss Museum, you are indeed a Muse.

It is a delicate hammer you ply, dear girl,
that flashing, felt-tip pen. It puts me down
        along with the broad-beamed Venus from Sardinia,
        the pug-nose Priapus from Rome.
We are all on that thick list you carry,
daughter of Plato, from the Greek Room to the tea-room.

Plato, it is written, felt a fear
of the divine madness we might comprehend
        only at great peril. Heavenly tantrums,
        leave them to heaven, he said.
Now we have left them to you. They are put away
in the warehouse you represent, whose lofty ceilings

remind me both of Plato and the state,
and the state is no poet. Neither are you.
        Though your conversation is sprinkled
        with the pious jargon of art,
your words will summon no flutes. Pan is as frozen
on his pedestal as is your stare

who watch me making faces at Pan and Priapus
as I saunter past you, conscious of the effect.
        Such misbehavior before the work
        of masters! Surely danger lurks
in the museum, as well as downright bad manners,
such disrespect before the caged, bright madness.

Occident   FELIX STEFANILE

THE REASON OF NATURE

I came deep into the woods.
And, by the drooping of the branches,

by the growing quiet of the creek,

by the attention that welcomed me,
I thought—

this veneration before my presence . . .
Understandable . . .
A recognition that this creature is I.

Nature is rudimentary . . .
A few instincts for life,
some reflexes for survival . . .
Only people can bring it out,
transform it, make it more.

Suddenly a jay called,
Be careful, someone is here!
Instantly the woods closed in,
bright, imperceptible, quick.
Something sank into the shadows.

International Poetry Review　　　NEVENA STEFANOVA
—Translated from the Bulgarian
by Juri Vidov Karageorge

RHYTHM OF DISHES

Water steaming in the teakettle,
she tied an apron on me,
took down the silver dishpan,
big and shiny as a shield.
I took the towel; she handed me
the willoware, each dish
with its little scene in blue—
cabin and trees, chimney
with spiral of smoke.
　　　　　　　　Hand
to my hand, and hand to mine again.

And when the plates were put away,
she stood at the screen door,
light behind her, pinning
and repinning her thin hair.
I hung the dishpan on its peg, then saw
the kitchen there, the same but small—

table, chair, teakettle,
grandmother, child.

Ball State University Forum　　　KAREN STEINER

THE RED COAL

Sometimes I sit in my blue chair trying to remember
what it was like in the spring of 1950,
before the burning coal entered my life.

I study my red hand under the faucet, the left one
below the grease line consisting of four feminine angels
and one crooked broken masculine one,

and the right one lying on top of the white porcelain
with skin wrinkled up like a chicken's
beside the razor and the silver tap.

I didn't live in Paris for nothing and walk
with Jack Gilbert down the wide sidewalks
thinking of Hart Crane and Apollinaire,

and I didn't save the picture of the two of us
moving through a crowd of stiff Frenchmen,
and put it beside the one of Pound and Williams,

unless I wanted to see what coals had done
to their lives, too. I say it with vast affection,
wanting desperately to know what the two of them

talked about when they lived in Pennsylvania
and what they talked about at St. Elizabeth's
fifty years later, looking into the sun,

40,000 wrinkles between them,
the suffering finally taking over their lives.
I think of Gilbert all the time now, what

we said on our long walks in Pittsburgh, how
lucky we were to live in New York, how strange
his great fame was and my obscurity,

how we now carry the future with us, knowing
every small vein and every elaboration.
The coal has taken over, the red coal

is burning between us and we are at its mercy—
as if a power is finally dominating
the two of us; as if we're huddled up

watching the black smoke and the ashes;
as if knowledge is what we needed and now
we have that knowledge. Now we have that knowledge.

The tears are different—though I hate to speak
for him—the tears are what we bring back to the
darkness, what we are left with after our

own escape, what, all along, the red coal had
in store for us as we moved softly,
either whistling or singing, either listening or reasoning,

on the grey sidewalks and the green ocean;
in the cars and the kitchens and the bookstores;
in the crowded restaurants, in the empty woods and libraries.

The Paris Review   GERALD STERN

FOR THE FARM GHOST

Your barn needs work.
The warped boards are diaries of rain,
quietly incoherent
and, more than ever, neglect speaks
for distance, letting termites comb

years out of wood.
All day long, in a living gesture,
it seems to lean slowly toward evening.

Our eyes become lost on the inroads
of the place
as luminous dust veers into breath
and walls read like love
for loss, for the green
of essentials mulched by age.

Around here, as the saying goes, a soul
will follow the grain
and, though a century's gone,
a caul of silence clings
when I allude to you
in the shattered panes and split beams,
in the foothold of sky
on a dangerous roof.

Poetry Northwest   BARRY STERNLIEB

TRANSPARENCIES

The almond tree next door
leans on a splintered limb,
its leaves—crisp but still gray-green
as though nurtured by some force
pushed through the still morning air—
whispering
that fall will reward those who wait
on its harvest.

               A raven
struts through the thistles,
its dark bill snapping. Behind me,
on the bed,
my wife arranges the white linen sheet
around her shoulders,
smiles and slides back into a dream

as far from my fingers
as the raven

or the whispers
that bind me
to these transient things.

America   ROBERT JOE STOUT

INTERLUDE

I have this whole long day
before me; the cats sleep

in puddles of sun on the floor,
the plants press their green hands
against my window: shadows
on the page, the pen upright
and moving.
                    Until you call.
The phone bursts into the house
like a challenge, like an intruder,
like a gossip gone half-mad
to see the sky falling. You say,
it's been three weeks now. You say,
how long the waiting. I lie on the bed
alone and listening, my hand pressed to my eyes,
staring through red fingers at the sun
inside to answer or cry, pinned
by my own heat to the undone sheets—
and his shirt left empty and hung
to the hook on the closet door.

event   BETSY STRUTHERS

IN A DIFFERENT HOUSE

In a different house
even stairs take footsteps
cautiously: the silence rearranged.
I turn left, past rooms
with strange curtains, books and beds.
In a different house
working mornings is discovery:
the sky moves north; at the back door
a mountain range of conifers,
ferns in a shelf over the sea.

From small panes of glass in your study
all I see is a barricade of trees,
white spokes of porch guard-rail
like unfinished picture frames,
and a photograph of your woman
pinned onto the wall.
In a borrowed study, the words I find
also belong to you.

Maine in drifts of fog . . .
I begin to listen for something
else: harmonies in rain,
how to read this wild, unfamiliar light.
I look beyond to your bare birch
and fix on the one branch
aloof as antlers,
deer ghost. The bone of life
        caught in frost between earth and sky.

The Georgia Review   HARRIET SUSSKIND

THE STALLION

Walking the dry winter woods,
I reached the hidden pasture
And paused to admire the mare and stud
Till he came after me, the bastard.

He ran right at me, reared,
And whipped around to kick.
I hollered, "Hyah!" but he didn't hear,
So I retreated, throwing sticks.

He'd always been shy and mild,
But the mare was so fat with his foal
He'd suddenly grown wild,
Proud as a prince, powerful.

He chased me half a mile,
Till I rolled beneath a fence.
He stood there sweating, male,
Magnificent. I dusted off my pants.

"So long," I said, "you son of a bitch."
And headed home. The sky was red and violet.
Reeds and cattails rattled in the ditch.
I felt a wonderful violence.

The Lake Street Review   BARTON SUTTER

DANCE FOR THE SUN

Hopi: *We sacrifice to the rain god. Sometimes*
it rains, sometimes it doesn't.
Zuni: *We cry to a shaman to cure our sick. Sometimes*
we get well, sometimes we don't.
Navajo: *We dance all night for the sun to rise.*

Our bodies pool and break
like a moon over water.
I know then no candle
need be lit: when the sun
comes, I will be awake
and watching you. And so

a skin forms over each caress,
turning it into something
to take home: a bottle
of ship, its billowing sails—
an impossibility like that.
Silly as any virgin, I plan

a honeymoon: two palms shaking
from a moving hammock. Why?
No cruelties are set out yet:
Curled, skewered and repeating

as in a tray of hors d'oeuvres
from a party that's gone on

too long. I don't worry that
you won't be my lover. It's an odd
knowledge, a kind of control—
like in the Indian tale, the sun's
tinder's set, its match is already

crossing the cover.

The Georgia Review　　　　　TERESE SVOBODA

LOOKING AT A PAINTING OF CONSTANTINOPLE
BY PAUL SIGNAC

The minarets spire vaguely through a mosaic
of small shells of paint: like oyster-shells,
mussels, abalone. But these odd, green waters

have no odor, no dark movement under the surface.
When we step back from the canvas, the shells
blur, fade, become a sea-mist, through which we

see the unreal city. Boats without oarsmen,
yachts without tillers, mosques without muezzins.
Any sound we could hear over these waters would

seem like a sigh. This sea is not a sea, with
foam and wave, but a gauzy veil taking on the
light of green yachts, the reflection of white

minarets, grey domes, beige walls. And the city
is not a haven we reach after a pleasant voyage;
but a mirage we gaze at, starving, thirsting.

If I step back far enough, it's green haze, white
smoke. I'm lost. I'm lying down. Sea-sick.
On the ferry-boat from Yalova to Istanbul. The

walls of the cabin tilt down, then rise up, tilt
down, then rise up. The faces of my friends,
oblique, are strangers; are doctors surrounding

a puffed-up bed. "Would you like some water?"
"Some orangeade?" "Some lime juice?" The walls
tilt down, rise up. The portrait of the captain
on the wall looks like Conrad, though a Turk.
"It's very bad to throw up on a Turkish ship.
They make you clean it up." I hear a laugh

chasing those words across the dry floorboards.
I look for a face. It's Lester. He's brought
me a Pepsi. "Where'd you find that?" "A little

'abi' had it. Only a quarter." I sit up. Motion
Lester to sit down. The wood of this bench is worn,
old, warm. The ship creaks as it moves in its slow

trough of water. I feel OK. The captain looks like
Signac. He's able. He knows his business. Bright
bells. A slowing. We're coming in to Istanbul.

The Hudson Review   ROBERT SWANSON

FOREST LAWN

Like an amusement park, the cemetery grounds
are divided into themes.
Gardens of Memory, Babyland, Slumberland
look out over the valley where palms
punctuate the smog, standing on one leg
like molting, Disney waterbirds.

Turned to stone, Norman Rockwell kids
snuggle each other in the Great Mausoleum
on an overstuffed marble armchair while
the curtain in the main hall pulls electronically
to display da Vinci's *Last Supper* in stained glass.
A recorded voice speaks to rows of folding chairs
to silence as the sun moves in the stillness
along marble thighs of *Playboy* nymphs in the nude,
who cavort and weep along the hallways where
the dead lie tidily labeled in their marble drawers.

Under the vaulting mimicry of this Gothic attic
or outside among immigrations of Italian cypress,
the American dead reside in subdivisions,
their gentility guarded by cloned angels—
Michelangelo's David and the Little Mermaid—
in this park whose theme is death and reproduction.

Salmagundi   KAREN SWENSON

WAKING AT NIGHT

It would be easy to dismiss them—
"They're bored," I'd say,
Meaning those people across the alley
Who gather past midnight, alone or in pairs,
At the all-night convenience store.
And some of them probably are.
Under hell's own rinsed-out lighting,
They bump down the submarine aisles
Looking for something to eat or drink,
Something to put on a scratch or, worse,
Take home to a pet nearly starving.
Searching gives them something to do,
But not much and not for long:
The clerk keeps asking, "Hi, can I help you?"—
Knowing damn well no one can.

Not tonight, anyway, in this condition
And sleepless as well, which makes it hurt.

Who am I to judge them? My own window opens
To the street and the teenagers
Racing their cars by the pumps.
There's a tree gone numb with the resting weight
Of birds that come nightly to nest.
I don't know what I expected to see,
But those shapes like high-flung bowling pins
Are disturbing, crowded in sagging rows.
Earlier, in bed, I dozed briefly
But rose before some dream could take me;
A churning in my stomach signaled
Some fear, but nothing I could locate or name.
That's how the unconscious speaks to us—
Cast adrift, a message bobs in our sluggish blood
With a warning to keep awake, keep watchful.
The worst can happen, don't we all know it,
And probably already has—
If not to me, then to one
Of these neighbors I keep my sleepy eye on.

Chelsea   THOMAS SWISS

RESIGNATION

Here is the key to the writing desk
and here the one to the cabinet with the files.
In the folders, there
lie the copies;
in the other one
the originals and the forms.
This for the information of my successors:
The reports are complete,
the statistics up-to-date.
If one should perchance
somewhere between the pages
find my used-up
shrunken life,
throw it
in the wastepaper basket.

The Literary Review   WILHELM SZABO
                                  —*Translated from the German*
                                        by Beth Bjorklund

THE POINT OF ORIGIN

Open a window and touch the sun,
or feel the wet maple leaves flicker in the rain.

Watch a blue crab scuttle in clear water,
or find a starfish in the dirt.
Describe the color green to the color blind,
or build a house out of anguish and pain.

The world is more than you surmise.
Take the pines, green-black, slashed by light,
etched by wind, on the island
across the riptide body of water.
Describe the thousand iridescent needles
to a blind albino Tarahumara.

In a bubble chamber, in a magnetic field,
an electron spirals and spirals in to the center,
but the world is more than such a dance:
a spiraling in to the point of origin,
a spiraling out in the form of a
wet leaf, a blue crab, or a green house.

River Styx   ARTHUR SZE

EVERYDAY ENCOUNTERS

Whenever we meet,
You talk to me about your stone houses,
Your metal horses,
Your machines which wash, iron
And sew for you.

You never tell me
How many drops of joy
Are still left in your heart,
How the pupils of children's eyes light up,
Or how a cobweb of spring wind
Shines between your fingers.

Poetry Now   DEJAN TADIC
                          —Translated from the Serbo-Croatian
                                  by Stephen Stepanchev

FROM A FRENCH TRAVEL JOURNAL

1. A PARISIAN GIRL (1874) BY RENOIR

Look how she wears the whole sky,
look at how all the paintings that she looked at,
    and that Renoir and Monet looked at,
wore the colors and songs of the rainbow and the skies
    very lightly;
she as a matter of pedestrian fact being her self,
    and seeing in the joyous and
    heavenly way that

was most essential to us, would stroll on the boulevards,
    could walk in all gardens, could
    enjoy the many best
Impressionist paintings and consequently create all
    heavenly forms of change;
she also has a blue bonnet.

2. RENOIR AND OTHERS AT VERSAILLES

Can you find yourself invisible between
    Renoir and Monet looking at
    each other?
Can you find yourself growing more visible
    and invisible between Renoir or
    Monet looking at
    a landscape?
Can you between two inescapable songs, God's,
    the world's, can you make
    your growing self
    somewhat like them?

New Letters   JOHN TAGLIABUE

SONS

My hair's gone white, my skin both dry and wrinkled
And, of five sons, not one is my own kind.

A-shu, sixteen, is the laziest lad in the world;
A-hsuan, late fourteen, appears to find
Refinement loathly to the point of hate.
The next two, both thirteen, have minds so crude
They still can't tell their sixes from their sevens.
The youngest, nine, thinks only about food.

Thus, sourly served by an ungrateful heaven,
Who would not drink to drown ingratitude?

Western Humanities Review   TAO CHIEN
        —Translated from the Chinese
        by Graeme Wilson

LAUDE

He was a face
photographs improved:
gaunt, Phidian, scrupulously shaved.
Old pictures gave him a foreign body,
grinning in the mineral light
of Athens, or the islands, his arm linked
loose around some friend his age.

Teaching at home, he loved
the particular histories of things:
etymologies that reached toward verbs,
a recipe for avglolemono soup,
the mahogany clock that made the hour
sound large in his white apartment.
He sat with his back to the window.

Autumn and spring he led me
through the *Iliad,* clause by clause
to the death of Hector, spent a week
on the last great feast, began the *Philoctetes*
and never finished. Just once, before commencement,
we digressed, laying aside the copy
of Sophocles we shared—and worked instead

on the Sappho papyrus discovered by accident
in strip-papers winding a Coptic mummy.
Eighteen years old, half in love
with love-and-death, I churned
through the harsh dactyls and the unfamiliar verbs
of longing, till he lifted the book from my lap
as if to forgive me and read the poem

through in the low voice.
What did I know? It was late
in the afternoon. Over his shoulder
the rain had ended, Commonwealth Avenue
gave up a grey light and men wrapped
in bright metallic cars, shining toward destinations,
flew to the right and the left of him terribly fast.

Epoch   STEPHEN TAPSCOTT

POEM TO SOME OF MY RECENT POEMS

My beloved little billiard-balls,
my polite mongrels, edible patriotic plums,
you owe your beauty to your mother, who
resembled a cyclindrical corned beef
with all the trimmings, may God rest
her forsaken soul, for it is all of us
she forsook; and I shall never forget
her sputtering embers, and then the little mound.
Yes, my little rum runners, she had defective
tear-ducts and could weep only iced tea.
She had petticoats beneath her eyelids.
And in her last years she found ball-bearings
in her beehive puddings, she swore allegiance
to Abyssinia. What should I have done?
I played the piano and scrambled eggs.
I had to navigate carefully around her brain's
avalanche, lest even a decent finale be forfeited.

And her beauty still evermore. You see,
as she was dying, I led each of you to her side;
one by one she scorched you with her radiance.
And she is ever with us in our acetylene leisure.
But you are beautiful, and I, a slave to a heap of cinders.

Tendril   JAMES TATE

OVER THE RAINBOW

Over the rainbow, under the rainbow, does it
Matter where?
Just so you know you're there

Digging your fingers in diamonds, grabbing the gold.
Getting yours
As in the literature

Describing some green garden or Emerald City.
Let it be
Some submarine glory,

Just so it's got the glamour you want, what you
Don't know,
The shards of the rainbow

Rationed in story, packaged in pleasing fiction.
Call it Oz,
Call it heaven because

Somewhere over the rainbow Judy Garland sinks
Down deep, deep
In red poppies to sleep.

New Letters   JOHN TAYLOR

VISITATION RIGHTS, SUMMER, 1968

I have a snapshot in my head,
"summer, 1960," scribbled below:
you in a battered hat and an army shirt,
sun on your teeth and narrowing your eyes,
behind you the outboard motor, then,
stretching to the far dark pines,
a blue lake deepening the sky,
swirled by the blades skimming the boat along.

I cannot see you as you are.
Between us a child runs on sturdy legs
to gather leaves to give to you:
"Daddy," she says, and grins,
thinking maybe this time you will come home,
read *Goodnight Moon,* beer in your hand
and supper to come, the long evening's
presence as she drifts in her bed.

Still as I look, your pale skin has the tan
you acquired so deliberately, your hair
is confined by an old Stetson bound
with a beaded belt, the white shirt
lurches to olive drab. Who have you become?
I can't guess, don't even want to try. Solemnly
you take the leaves, stare away, mentioning
time, friends, meetings—never the blue sky.

The Cape Rock   LAURIE TAYLOR

LIFE AMONG THE WHITES

in brussels i saw jews and arabs fighting
in the doorways
and the old gargoyled square a memorial
to human bondage
in kopenhagen as the last fruit fell from
the trees doors closed on house and heart
for the winter
       long winter months in which to
carve live images of dead eskimos
in london i learned what pancake makeup meant
and that you need false teeth to keep a
stiff upper lip
in nyc i saw fear a constant in any
man's jungle
in sf i saw the hand outs of rotten bread
and the same old stale circus show
as the forked tongue lapped the boot
of power
i've lived in houses of last ditch dreams
filled with closets ready to scream
as the obvious becomes clearer
and the fall much nearer
i've seen the confusion of what to do now
as the truth of the dupe includes all
i've seen women and children huddle in
the basements of their hearts and minds
feeding on american realism and bubble gum
living without music and lost without love
i've seen the men move without feature who have
forgotten about pride, nothing is worth
fighting about, it's just a matter of waiting
to die
       and now and again i wish that i could
gather them all together in my arms
gently sway them sing a song
and when they have rested and fallen into
peaceful sleep dump the whole load of
them into the hungry waiting briny deep

Washington Review   GREGORY TEBRICH

THE YELLOW CHAIR

Sitting in the yellow chair with its orange cushion,
I am looking at a photograph of you
sitting in the same yellow chair
looking out the door on a sunny morning.
I hold you, surrounded by sunlight
looking out over a sunlit world, in my hand.
Even the tides in the picture are running full.

Here it is an autumn evening.
Far away a dog is barking. A man is yelling
beyond the haze that is hanging over the water.

The tide is running out, leaving the piers
stained and covered with snails.
The first rain is beginning to fall.
You would not recognize the place.

I have tried to describe it to you many times,
but you insist on getting out your photograph—
the way it is in the picture.
So when I hold you in the palm of my hand
as you sit in the sunlight, I must look up.
I must look out. I must look away.

New Letters   VIRGINIA R. TERRIS

PICTURES FROM AMERICA

Because a soldier had almost
taken me, just born in the last weeks
of the World War, with him
over to America, I often dreamed
about waking up in America
with jeans and tennis shoes,
the baseball bat under my arm.
I dreamed of a green terrace
before the high school, of pink toothpaste,
and pineapples out of the can. Certainly
I'd have spoken American with a broad accent,
and later I would be driven, so I dreamed,
in a Cadillac to my high-rise office.
But later I was still
here in Mannheim and rode every morning
on a bicycle without gear shifts
into the docks to the export division.
And still later I saw young
Americans, as old as I,
being led away because they
had burned their draft cards.
I saw the smokey houses
in the ghettoes of black people, and I saw

the National Guard in uniform
against barefooted students, saw the
riot sticks of the policemen that were
as long as baseball bats.
Now I hardly still dream
of America, not even anything bad.
But I ask myself, often, what kind of
country it may be, the pictures of which
have changed so, so quickly
and so fundamentally.

International Poetry Review   JÜRGEN THEOBALDY
                          —Translated from the German
                          by Wayne Kvam

THE MYTH

My dead father was coming! Thrilled, I said, *Lord!*
I hope I don't run out of things to say,
like when my sister came home, after twenty years,
and I ran out of words on the drive from the airport.

All the same, my sleep bloomed autumn in winter,
I was dreaming in bronze, while rain was beating my house.
He would love these English colors; and yet, I knew,
New England in the fall was also vivid.

When we met, I told him the good news:
the Reds had beaten Camborne, the old enemy.
Catching a high kick, the blind fullback
burst through to score the winning try.

I was pleased, but not thrilled as I would have been
in the days when we watched together.
Though in some ways I'm still the boy my father
thrilled with the myth of the great prewar team.

The news was more a way of breaking the ice.
His harrowed face cracked into a smile,
as if he was pleased, but not thrilled;
as if the years made it remote from him also . . .

When I awoke, I thought much about life
and eternal life, and the blind fullback
racing up by instinct to field the high
garryowen and bursting through to win the match.

The American Scholar   D. M. THOMAS

THREE TINY POEMS

1.

When I see you, I remember
birds
in the pepper tree at daybreak.

2.

In your absence the years
seem never to go anywhere,
as a hawk hangs still over its prey.

3.

Tonight will be silence and snow.
Tomorrow at your window, looking out
at white, all white, will be
like lying down to sleep at nightfall,
the light in your eyes still linger,
your eyelids the last leaves sinking.

The Southern Review   HARRY THOMAS

THE WOMAN WITH THE SHOPPING BAG
KNOWS THE CORRECT TIME

In the night, in a subway station
coated with dirt, the woman with
the shopping bag sleeps with one
eye opened, pinned to the exit sign,

where she knows shopping bag snatchers
not above wrestling her grimy
to the ground, swarm in the shadows,
waiting for her to close down for the night.

But the years of sleeping sitting up,
of walking on the sharp edge of things,
have not gone unrewarded; the woman
with the shopping bag does not blink.

And she knows the correct time,
what year it is, what her children
are doing, what her husband has said
about her: her wisdom is in that one

eye on the exit sign, not in the black
matted hair, not in the rusted iron skin,
not in the layers of found clothing, not
even in the shopping bag, but in that

one unblinking eye. Before daybreak,
she rises and walks through a world

of silent strangers, where other shopping
bag people avoid her; and on Sundays,

if she's not too tired,
she stands on a park bench, screaming
hoarse statements at the clouds floating white
above her, and jabbing her finger into the blue sky.

Dark Horse   TED THOMAS, JR.

RETURNING

In my old neighborhood again it's cold; November
and the reds and golds of maple, gingko I collect

are far too vivid for memory. I walk, holding a handful
of leaves speckled with rot. I turn the familiar

corner past the Lacy's house, and I'm twelve years old.
The sound of wind through white pine and sweet gum

soothes, as necessary as a lullaby. When a cat at ten yards
emits a sound like speech, I stop to answer her.

The wind nudges, mouthing a script in the leaves
scattering like children across the high green lawns.

Now at the school yard, drawn by the screech and cheers
of recess, the teacher stands, poker stiff in the wind,

watching a game of kickball. Her blue skirt and brown sweater,
her dark glasses firm against the winter sun.

The tall pines brush each other like shy girls.
The woman stands, still watching me

racing against the ball, my foot cocked—
I turn the corner, allowing memory and childhood

their moment near one another, so quiet,
these patient neighbors.

The North American Review   JEANIE THOMPSON

HYPOTHESIS

Slowly the world moves into nursing homes,
yet we keep the gnomon, the figure left
after one parallelogram, smaller, is removed
from the larger that touched it at one corner.

If I plant a tree beside the sundial,
the style will change its shadow indicator,
not interpreting the day correctly;
yet my tree is hidden in their forests.

Today is cloudy and the gnomon stops.

Having found its certain path, the ancients
never questioned what the young would question.
What dark days produced their elaborated theorems
and their clocks whose styles move
no matter what?

I see a strange gnome, hunched indicator
of my parents' passing sun, tangental
to the moon, which, in the narrow eyes
of minutes, calculates certain dark.
I am one parallelogram removed
from their graves.

San Jose Studies   JOANNE THOMPSON

I RECALL THE WAY

I recall the way the curtains of our room
Hung across the window—
The color of the carpet on the floor—
And the sound of children in the street below.
We touched, made love to children's voices
As a chorus, a capella.

Early autumn with the leaves dulled green
And the sleepy-stillness when the birds have gone
And only the crickets would sing us to our bed.

I remember, and crickets sing our love
Daily, daily. It was love
And light and new-green
And shone like new leaves in the rain,
And the crickets in my house all winter
Tell me so, singing. I sing them back.

Poem   JUDITH THOMPSON

A BRIDGE TOO NARROW

We meet on a bridge too narrow to pass,
Over waters too dark to fathom.
I dare not look down.
We meet on a bridge too narrow,
Over water too deep, too swift for comfort.
I cannot swim.
You cannot fly.
We must remain forever face to face,
Not touching,
On this narrow plank of wood—
Or one of us must turn and lead,
And one of us must follow.

Poem   JUDITH THOMPSON

CRUST OF LIFE

The things we love, the scientists have said,
the mountains, trees, the seasons, and the seas
and all the pulsing life beneath the sun,
are no more than a crust upon a ball
of heavy breathless molten metal ores.
Like arctic ice, the continents themselves
float and shift and break apart and melt,
and only the brief span of human life
impedes the knowledge that we dwell with hell
beneath our feet, that we are accidents
of evolution, born from death to die.

There may be other planets in the sky
beyond the range of our small voice, where life
like ours, or quite unlike, perceives our sun
as only a small, dim and yellow star
and does not guess one of its worlds is blessed
by a thin crust where life has come to be.
They, like we, perhaps have sent a voice
to voyage, and ask if anybody's there.
The preachers say all this will pass away,
the mountains, trees, the seasons and the seas,
and all the pulsing life beneath the sun,
and only the illusion of our breath,
transfigures death and subjugates the soul.

This crust of life above this molten soul
cries plaintively to the eternal sky
for confirmation of its ecstasies
and pains, for proof it lives, and proof it is
not merely ruled by heavy breathless hell.
I yearn upon the beauty of the doe
and the fragility of dogwood trees
that raise pale buds against a dark March sky,
and search the shining eyes of friend and child
for images of God. The hand I hold
is all I know of immortality.

Webster Review   MARILYN THRONE

POEM FOR MY MOTHER ON HER 50TH BIRTHDAY

As another year of silence
falls from the calendar,
I imagine her exploring malls,
reading cheap romances, staring
for hours at air, photo albums,
the drafting degree
beside the welfare cheque;
imagine her taut gaiety
braced for breaking,

her body fat with boredom
massed in front of me,
obstacle, reminder.

Ten years since he left,
yet love for my father
still ticks in her heart
like a perfect clock,
timeless.

I imagine peeling
the decade from her face,
finding her as she was
and, somehow, understanding.

event   EVA TIHANYI

LUCANIAN CEMETERIES

Little Lucanian cemeteries,
hidden among the mountains
and in the green of the valleys,
you are more beautiful
without shining marble,
funeral eulogies,
hothouse blossoms.
In your paths, redolent
with wild roses and rural flowers,
one smells the breath of the past
and between the rusted iron crosses
the echo of invisible tears resounds.
How many times in the train's flight
have I seen you appear on the horizon
and at once vanish in the distance?
Everything's the same:
with the tall, severe cypresses,
the red roofs, the white roads,
and the endless sleep of the dead.
Little Lucanian cemeteries,
hidden among the mountains
and in the green of the valleys,
I see you again one by one
and in this dim sunset
that mounts the horizon
with a long sob,
I offer you the flickering light of a candle,
and my quiet tears.

Chelsea   FRANCO TILENA
                          —Translated from the Italian
                              by Lawrence Venuti

LOVE AND RESISTANCE

In early evening
you sit again at the head
of the field, before weed and clover,
a majesty of patience, a .22
across your thin legs.

You watch for rabbits and argue
with yourself because I
will not take part
in your death.

It is not a question of love
or resistance. Behind you, the garden leans
into something we no longer recognize
or care for. Summer is late. Its hours tease
and curl around our necks.

I think now of your legs
with mine, the pull of muscle—
and we are young, younger
than the long line of cancer in you.
I think of that dark blood
as a mistake we will erase. I think of
the weddings of children,
the delicate shadings of loss.

You tremble now, the light tremor
of pain. The sun flattens and washes
the sky. The first rabbit nears, rounds the pine.
The horizon opens, ready. I close my eyes
to focus on nothing.

College English   MICHAEL S. TKACH

STEPPING INTO SPRING

(after Tu Fu)

Awakened by a square of sunlight
on my bedroom wall
translating the bending trees to
sinuous shadow strokes,
up I get.

Outside the house, I look
into blue air, depth beyond depth:
even as I pause, spring arrives.

Already the air is mild.
My thoughts are warmed: words
come and I mustn't waste time.

Rubbing my hair back, I face into
the descending road and walk: everything
my eye picks out delights me.

Bending over a fence post,
leaning my weight, my head feels like
thick cords had snapped.
In the air, the dull hum of awakening bees;
soon farmers will be pacing out their fields.

Nearby, the homes of two old friends;
bread and wine are waiting:
what a rarity nowadays
their wise tranquillity!

I still avoid rich and ambitious men:
their voices' hard ring hurts my ear.

Queen's Quarterly   R. D. WAYNE TOMPKINS

PESADAMENTE

Like the shadow of a bird on bright water, the word
crosses my dream, rests on the tongue when I wake
soft as one body over another, foreign body.
There are languages we can never hope to master.

But this one word, pesadamente, as it leans,
heavily, into the quick light, I comprehend.
Love, in its presence, becomes loss.
How can you deny it?

Like gray cloth fallen to the floor, like gray cloth
gathered and, long before dawn, put on . . .
pesadamente . . . the heavy eyelid, the sad
baffled face . . . pesadamente . . . the weight
of the mouth . . . pesadamente . . . the slow
low voice saying, "I am almost always lonely,"
. . . pesadamente . . . the echo . . .
"by choice."

Northwest Review   HEATHER TOSTESON

LANDSCAPE

September evening. The dark shouts of shepherds sound sadly
Through the dusky village. Fire spurts at the blacksmith's.
A black horse rears powerfully; the girl's chestnut hair
Strains for the warmth of his red nostrils.
The cry of the doe freezes at the edge of the forest
And the yellow autumn flowers bend speechless
Over the blue face of the pond.
A tree burns in red flame; the dark faces of bats fly up.

Poetry Now   GEORG TRAKL
                    —Translated from the German by Paul Morris

NECESSITY

As a physician, I can understand
the passion for money.
I myself, after four
or five hours in the operating room,
prefer an object that won't bleed,
that is durable.

The human heart
is more than a muscle.
Having cupped it in my palm
I find that warmth fugitive.
I have held and felt it
tender, anxious as a polyp,
slippery as a squeezed grape.

If my hands were not chill
they would be sticky.
The cool symmetry of figures,
the daily placebo of dimes,
is not enough.
I keep my wallet in my breast pocket.
Sometimes I hear it beating.

Canadian Forum   RHEA TREGEBOV

RE-ENTRY

Over the Sahara to Paris in December,
connections loose as hanging threads.
I come into civilization all thumbs,
everything startles me.

Absence of sound, absence of smell,
crusts of white hanging on each body.

I'm a tourist again, passing through
museums, fade in a crowd of Metro passengers.

Clocks again, water from faucets,
water spouting out
mouths of fine gray monuments.

All signs lead this way/that. Glass doors
swing closed. I cover myself
in pieces of wool, fall into days of
eating and drinking, eating and drinking.

Months later, back in America, I enter
a small grocery store that smells of white bread,
stand there with strange coins in my hand,
waiting to buy candy.

The Hollins Critic   MARGOT TREITEL

HOW MANY TIMES

How many times in the long dream of years
will I wake in the night, sick with longing
for nothing I can name?
                            Midnight, full moon,
a fast freight moaning on the grade. Heard once,
it is always there, part of the memory
we live by.
                And the other sounds too, cats
on the ridge, the partridges drumming.
There was a ramshackle cabin in the woods,
trails fanning out to every lake, river
in twenty miles.
                    At night I have stood here
and let every question have its way
with me, and still there is nothing more
than this landscape in shadow, this I,
this high, wheeling canopy of stars.

New Orleans Review   ERIC TRETHEWEY

IN THE CLINIC WAITING ROOM

This is no Lourdes, though we come in faith.
We wait our turn at Bethsaida's pool.
Yet which of us will be healed is still
as arbitrary and unfathomable
as sudden sun, or hope, or a rush of wings.

Poem   MEMYE CURTIS TUCKER

HOMAGE

The baseball is
also known as the fruit whereby man lost his innocence.
No one shouts, "Throw the old peach." It is
the Old Apple,
and when the air here greens and violets dab purple,
while the leaves still keep their pure forms before
ravenous generations of insect commence to ravage,
the Apple is thrown.

It is new, fresh with purchase, of
amazing whiteness.
It is like no other white hereabouts in a June field, too
early for the daisy.
It is a whiteness that begins and stuns
and lasts one day.
If you hold the ball in your hand, you cannot stretch your arm
far enough so that it may appear

less than the sun.
If you let your eye follow its wandering seam, it
recedes as mysteriously as horizon and refuses to end, sly
in hand, in mind.

It is sometimes given to outfielders grazing
in the depths of a well-pitched game, far
from the violence of batter and pitcher, as far
as the dreamer from his pillow, at the edge
of the game, at the August-edge of summer,
to understand.

Ploughshares   TOMMY NEIL TUCKER

POWER OUT

A boom like a house exploding
lowers the sky: thunder.
Gray sponges of cloud, heavy
with rain, wring in the atmosphere.
The day turns dark as winter.
The kitchen flickers once, and again.
Then out—dead coal.

When a house loses its power
nothing can hold back the dark.
It knocks on your roof.
It walks in without opening a door.
Suddenly it's everywhere, like a landlord,
claiming your rooms,
dismissing your furniture,
cutting your appliances off.
The look on its face stops clocks.

You know what it is.
Still, you don't believe it's here.
When you enter a room
you reach, like a habit, for light.
But the switch mocks you,
clicking a hollow castanet,
rattling a dry tongue.

Your hand drops.
You stand alone in the dark.
Your house is a plain pine box
and silence shuts the lid on you.

Slowly, as though off in the distance,
then nearer, a sound comes:
the current of your blood is humming.
Your heart, a power cell, flashes its beam.
Behind the clear white of your eyes
the sun dazzles you.

Kayak   CYNTHIA TUELL

PAPER WHITE NARCISSUS

Awake or asleep,
the brain dreams at midnight,
roused by the furnace tenderly clanking,
or the errant perfume of the narcissus
forced from midwinter, hard as a kiss.

It dreams its good-bye
to the swindler at the door,
who turns into the granular snow light,
away. And good-bye, tense new hearts
into which the rough hand and its pallor
already have reached.
Grief makes its bouquet the hour
the fire colored pollen starts to fall.

The wicked flowers of memory
are also white, and bloom anywhere.
Far away, in summer,
the pit loosens in the peach,
and the ring slips off
into tall grass, and is lost.
Love comes to nothing.

Nectar dampens the starry clots
that the bees do not visit.
No loveliness, no fragrance or longing
brings on the black honey of forgetfulness,
though grief is perennial.

The Massachusetts Review   CHASE TWICHELL

BEFORE THE HARVEST

I leaned at the window in your blue room
under gables. Through the glass,
rooftops and treetops blurred in the dark,
stars over them, the small galaxies like powder,

dust on an apple. You sat behind me
on the edge of the bed, your brush
crackling faintly as it swept your hair.
You switched on a lamp, spoke my name.

Your shelves were arranged with antique dolls.
Moving toward you, I imagined eyes rolling
open, the dolls stepping from satin
and spinning through the room—

porcelain, porcelain and auburn hair.
Once, I watched you undress and knew the body
is fruit—who are you waking with now?
I wish the apple could rise again to its branch

and blossoms drift up to constellate.
Holding you, I watched your back in the mirror,
how you slowly relaxed. You were still brown
from the sun, russet flecked with light.

Poetry   JAMES ULMER

EASTHAMPTON-BOSTON BY AIR

Oh no!
the plane is so small the baggage
is stuffed into its nose

and under its wings,
like the sacs of a honeybee!
There are six of us, mostly women.

We crowd in, crouching
in our summer denims and shades,
settle, buckle, inhale. Oh

no, we are aloft! like that,
with just a buzz, and Shelter Island
flattens under us, between

the forks of Long Island—the twisty
legs of a dancing man, foreshortened,
his head lost in tan mist.

The plane is too little!
It rides the waves of air
like a rowboat, of aluminum,

slewing, dropping into the troughs,
giving out with a shuddering frug motion
of its shoulders—one, two!

I sit facing
the ladies I am flying to Boston with,
only one of them my wife

but all of them grimacing,
shutting their eyes with a sigh, resting
forehead on fingertips as in sick prayer.

Eyeballs roll, breasts bounce,
nostril-wings turn pale, and hair
comes sweaty undone, untended.

We tip! tip as a body,
skid above some transmitting antennae
in Rhode Island it must be,

stuck in the Earth like knitting needles
into a ball of yarn; webbed
by wire stays, their eerie points rise.

We are high, but not so high
as not to feel high;
the Earth is too clear beneath us,

under glass that must not be touched,
each highway and house and the sites
of our graves but not yet,

not yet, No! Bright wind
toys with us,
tosses us,

our eyes all meet together
in one gel gaze of fear;
we are closer than in coitus;

the girl beside me,
young and Jewish, murmurs
she was only trying to get to Maine.

And now Boston
is its own blue streetmap beneath us;
we can feel in the lurch the pilot

trying to pull in Logan
like a great fish
by the throat of the runway.

What invisible castles
of turbulence rise
from the complacent, safe towers!

What ripples of ecstacy
leap
from the wind-whitened water!

The seawall, the side-streaming asphalt;
we are down, shouting out
defiance to our own momentum,

and trundle unbroken
back through the static gates
of life, and halt.

Had that been us, aloft?
Unbuckling, we trade
simpers and caresses of wry glance

in farewell, our terror
still moist on our clothes.
One by one

we crouch toward the open and drop,
dishevelled seatbelts left behind
us like an afterbirth.

The American Poetry Review   JOHN UPDIKE

"I IMAGINE SAYING . . ."

I imagine saying the right thing to amaze
you forever, though it occurs beyond
where we stand, the stage-scenery over-tall,
horses not tame enough, music too electronic.

Or I shut us up in a dream's aquarium
where slow legs of light walk patrol, the year ambles,
and water herds our humanity. There I can
hardly look at you or think what to say.

Does some eye oversee my craze and will not help?
Come, clever words, give harness to this wheezing.
Mark the bareness of winter with an engrossing
phrase. Explain me to her in love's ways.

The Southern Review   STEPHEN UTZ

READING IS SUCH AN INTIMATE ACT

Reading is such an intimate act: see how my finger traces
your spine, delicately runs along the edge, touches
the hollow space between the binding and your back,
and lingers, hovering breathless and poised above the cover,
deferring the moment, the dazzling second of opening
your secrets, devouring your pleasures, my lover, my text;
give me your words, your images, your cleverness,
while I, eagerly turning the stiffened tips of your pages,
delight, exult in this shy creature of sudden, burning
whiteness whose eloquence I bespeak and share,
as diving between the covers, savoring the best parts,
I surrender to your manly grace, my text, my lover,
        my lover, my text.

RE: Artes Liberales   NOEL M. VALIS

SPRING AT ARM'S LENGTH

Leaning out of my Boston window
hearing the winos arguing,
I realize this is spring.

Nothing convinces me like these voices,
not the trees in small green flames
nor the pink unretouched arms

of women who've grown younger
in long sleeves and vinyl boots
all winter, but now in spring

leap, leap toward age.
The winos stay sleeved and stained
and gray all seasons.

In winter they find furnace rooms,
spring-cleaning niches in buildings
held up by walls of other buildings,

and, like rivers under ice, do not exist.
But brushes prickle walks; it's spring.
It's spring when the winos

come flapping against the curbs
and take hold of benches,
and curse each other and inflation.

Curse is the life force;
so is the bagged bottle going around,
life by ritual, life . . .

As for me, I'm through
with my discovery and coffee break,
through shortly with temptation.

This is a disease ceremony,
like factory labor, wrong to celebrate,
but a gift. A gift to look in the mouth.

The Georgia Review   CHARLES VANDERSEE

THE TWO WALDENS

(for Mary Sherwood)

The book is actual as its namesake pond,
Its lapping words are real as lapping water.
It exists as much as a tree, or flower.
Ah, the movement of matter, the event
Of human thought, secreted by the brain,
Working quietly as the earthworms tunneling
The greatest luxury of all, the earth.
Weaving Walden-words like any bird
At work upon its nest, here was Thoreau,
A monument of sensitivity,
A texture, stratum, an embodiment
Of all the faith that man has placed in nature;
And so we have this charm, this living book,
This Concord quality, a bread that's good
To cast on water. Then, then as a sign,
Let one with much adventure in her go
And immerse *Walden* in Walden Pond so that
Each page may merge, may blend with it and be
As married to nature as was its author—
The man who wrote, "All nature is my bride."

Thoreau Journal Quarterly   WADE VAN DORE

HIGH WATER: PETERBOROUGH BRIDGE

Pood Weetz spits on his bait for luck:
Did so, they will tell, on the May day
He put his doughball at the eddy
Off the center piling of the Peterborough Bridge.
The sixty pound flathead lying there
Inhaled that bait (asleep some say)
Or, figuring Pood Weetz wasn't much,
Took it in to measure old Pood's rod.

The first thing Pood knew, the pole arched
As the line sang taut upstream,
And on the riffles Pood saw a shadow
Larger than the rocks the fish's belly touched.
The fin broke the water like a snag.

And Pood admired what he'd take to town
Dead over his handlebars, small eyes downward
Over the spokes; stiffening tail locked
Between Pood's pumping legs. Pood rode
That flathead three times to town, they say:
At five o'clock when the mill let out,
At three o'clock when the fish turned back,
And, at five till three, just before
The doughball hit the water.

Ball State University Forum   PATRICIA VAN DYKE

"THERE IS A SKY ABOVE THE ROOF . . ."

There is a sky above the roof,
   how blue! how placid!
There is a tree above the roof,
   its foliage rustles.

There is a bell in sight,
   softly tolling.
There is a bird in sight,
   sadly calling.

Oh, Lord, my Lord, all life is there,
   innocent and slow.
That gentle murmur rises there
   from the town below.

"What have you done, O you there,
   crying without surcease,
say, what have you done, you there,
   with the days of your youth?"

Descant (Canada)   PAUL VERLAINE
                                    —Translated from the French
                                       by Bernhard Frank

ASHES

Ashes fan across the snow.
I leave the ash pail on a rock.
Wind knocks it into the creek.
All day over the ice
the pail rocks side to side
whispering ash.
No one sees the snow cover it.
Find an old paint can to empty ashes.

In March, the wind blows straight down the chimney,
smoke sinks in the drapes.
The mushrooms unbuttoning the wood I burn
cause it to smolder
half in, half out of the flame.
The floors are cold, smoke stuffs the stove

and one day, hauling out ashes,
the paint can lists to the side
jumping its handle, and ashes
fill the kitchen air.
An avalanche of moths slides
from the window I open.
I spot the pail down by the culvert,
pooling the creek around it.

Suddenly it's spring.

The Virginia Quarterly Review   JOHN VERNON

A FALKLAND 'NO' TO
FASCISTS RIGHT AND LEFT

("Britain's Fleet Sails to Falkland Islands"
—News item, April 5, 1982)

We pre-Viet vets of the last just war,
Once knowing what Britain was bleeding for,
Now hoped for one clear NO or YES:
Are her daughter islands motherless?

She who gave us Shakespeare's theater,
She who gave us Milton's meter,
She who gave us James's Book,
What will she do for the Land of Falk?

She did it when Philip came warring,
She did it to Sun King and Boney;
Her RAF did it to Goering
When the mother of islands stood lonely.

Who'll serve our slandered Churchillian cause
Against Right and Left twins?—we who've witnessed
A bear with Polish blood on his paws
And a gaucho with Jews on his hit-list.

Let Empire end, but why betray its islets
To cop-docs who lock up the sane,
Or a wheat-vending junta whose "Christian" pilots
Daily dump Christ from a plane?

Dead Churchill, dead Orwell, come ghost-write the Falkland story:
When Auschwitz and Katyn were tearing Poland to shreds,
You gave us a Brown-baiting Tory
And a socialist baiter of Reds.

Has Britain's brow lost its laurel?
Is the Munich umbrella aspirant?
. . . Came a NO to a fascist tyrant.
Came a YES to you, Churchill, you, Orwell.

The New Leader   PETER VIERECK

A POSTER

It's harmless enough,
merely a government poster,
like a painting that's holy
to be worshipped by masses.
Read it, the voice of the gods,
conveying the message,
statistics, thousands
of promises. Read it,
help spread the word,
how our prestige has gone up,
how prices have fallen,
how the World Bank has sanctioned
an enormous loan, then another,
all for our industry,
linked to fabulous employment.
And all this generates millions,
rupees recycled
into ever new glories.
Think of the profits,
ripe as a harvest.
Then we'll build houses.
The poor shall have shelter.
No more sleeping in gutters,
no more love on the sidewalks.
Let the wretched shout out
Jai Hind! Hallelujah!
But, between you and me,
the poor man's afraid, afraid
to stand there and read,
afraid to read. And, my friend,
if the poor can't read
and can't write, why bother
to print all these posters?

Why bother to promise him?
Why bother to notice him?

New Letters   KUMAR VIKAL
                        —Translated and adapted from the Hindi
                        by Mrinal Parde and David Ray

REPETITION

Memories are everything, and endless
repetition:
            to return to a place
time after time and listen
to the years' echo, perhaps
rediscover a stone we'd always thought
was there, and now there's neither voice
nor stone.
            To do it, nonetheless,
is a way of life.
            The mermaids call
in the harbor. No, now I remember them.
No, I've made them up.
Nothing calls.
And except for those who must now
be suffering,
everything's fine.
            Soon another day
will dawn.
            I turn on
the light because the night is ending—
but the other night has just begun.

International Poetry Review   JOAN VINYOLI
                        —Translated from the Catalan
                        by David H. Rosenthal

FATHER TO FATHER

Children, Father—
how strange each day
to see more of you in me,
more of me in them.
This is one game for which
you never taught me rules;
and now, as I begin to feel my age
move in me like lodestone,
perhaps we have something
to talk out after all—
two old men unsure
of where it really starts or ends.

I sit up late
scratching something out
while all my darlings sleep,
and curse the noisy neighbor
or the barking dogs—
that never wake them anyway.
This seems to be my job,
to play their night
like some shadowy Orpheus—
I, who can remember only the dark,
a father 30 years ago at a kitchen table
moving toward first light
with bread, milk, and *Reader's Digest.*
What was it *you* heard—
you, who understand
neither sons nor poems?

Perhaps this same thing I pass on,
so one day all that's given
is returned.
Love? Duty? Fear? Hard words
for men who speak so sparingly.
Tonight it's time to say it, Father,
what's taken all these years:
I have daughters, you have a son.
Only the name ends here.

The North American Review   MARK VINZ

I'VE LOST THE MORNING

I've lost the morning.
It was here, a minute ago.
I'm certain; I caught all its clues:

the birds waking up at 5, the cats
out prowling at 6:30; and the garbage
man at 9. and then, of course,

there was the light. it just
kept rising, filling the sky.
I'm sure I had it in my hand.

I held it like a shovel or an ax.
It was as solid as a kiss, as clear
as day, and then I lost it; it slipped by.

Now, not a thing remains to dredge
it out of memory but memory itself.

Already I miss the afternoon, the
splendor of the sunset. Already
the stars begin to fade.

The Sun   LES VON LOSBERG

SEEING SILVER

Sure that the cold would find us, or maybe a snake,
I worried over every little choice:
where to put the sleeping bags, the tarps,
the food, the dog and her lead, her water, and most
of all, the light. You worried with me, explaining
every move you made, patient, controlled,
knowing my love of the desert, my fear of cold.

And just when the three of us began to settle in,
seven or eight coyotes began to howl,
so close, so plaintive, so delicate in the moon,
that it felt as if they were a part of us.
Lupi, colored and shaped like a coyote herself,
began to shake. Spasms of eagerness rippled
along her spine; holding her ground, she trembled
with the hope of meeting an unknown one of her kind.
But the howling died down, and none of them ever came out,
though each of them had been close enough to touch,
immobile in the sweet-smelling, darkened brush.

Too alert, I rearranged myself,
restless, sleepless in the narrow bag,
until you unzipped yours and drew me in.
You wrapped me in laughter, wrapped me up in heat,
amused, supportive, comfortable with the rules.
For a night, it was the old system again:
I was feeling afraid, and more than a little dependent,
but trying not to show either; you saw them both,
and my pride as well. Calm, you accepted it all.
You held me in, and I felt the cold withdraw.
Overhead, the moon was all I saw.

For no reason, Lupi suddenly whined.
From nowhere came a presence we could sense
but not identify: crossing the barriers
we had set up (campstove, tool box, and tire),
it came in like a cat; quick with the light,
you took it by surprise, as it did us:
the silver head of a fox was fixed for an instant,
there, among us, before it spun and ran
and all we saw was the wild flash of the tail
across the darkness, faster than we could act.
For a while, all three of us shared a sleeping bag.

You, who sleep lightly at home, slept soundly that night.
When I knew I could move without your feeling it,
I sat up and looked around. Only the low,
rough shapes of sage were visible in the moon.
The desert was calm. At our backs the dunes rose up,
imperceptibly growing in the night.
The night before, they rose three feet, in a storm.
But tonight the desert was warm; there was almost no wind.
Lupi watched with me awhile, then curled herself

in a circle and slept, sure the surprises were done.
But I, not quite as certain, stayed awake,
her body warm on my left, yours on my right,
and watched stars come out in the coal-black sky,
one by one, each bright as a fox's eye.

The Southern Review   CORY WADE

RETURNING TO THE CITY BY BOAT

A young girl stiffens her arm
in the shrill of a whistle.
Her cheeks harden and she points ashore
to a square light in a far building
echoing 'home home'
as if she'd come home
from school this way for years,
shuffling these lights
like stones along the street.

And facing these lights,
trembling as the boat draws
near, I watch this girl beside me
fingering the hem of her lace
dress, holding it to her knees,
keeping warm. And hear mother
in the next room stitching
clothes at night, waves
of cloth piling onto the floor,
darker as the hems grow deep.

And I remember, as the bay
drifts into harbor and twelve
herons watch the city dredge
stars from the night,
that we have no home, but space
between two hems:

The girl lowers her thin arm,
wind falls into a pleat
of waves. My dress curls around my white
knees and the young girl clutches
the iron railing and leans
over, far down, home into the streets.

The Midwest Quarterly   KATHY WAGNER

SOME OTHER BODY

All the boys I danced with were deserters.
Feet nervous as rodents,
they'd leave for something better.

Under lights in the school gym I sweated
and swallowed lemonade and knew
that we deserved each other.
One asked me kindly what my father did.
Along the wall, girls strained to hear my answer,
their ball-gowns stiff as a hedge of conifers.
"My father plays the harp," I said,
hoping no one remembered the week
in seventh grade I left to bury him.
The music either could not hear
or did not wish to know me.
With shame that bodies die,
my thighs turned into stone.

But death is a dance we all finally learn
practicing small desertions the dead teach us.
I write this down to keep it straight.
My father turned to face the wall the way
a harpist bends fretfully to touch the strings.
His arpeggio still shivers on my backbone
while I pick lemons in the supermarket,
while I patch my bedspread
in the arc of light I now call home.
He was the first deserter
who hurled the score away in contempt
and played by ear all those notes
which call me like gravity
to some other body than earth.

The Georgia Review   JEANNE MURRAY WALKER

GRANDMOTHER GRACE

I didn't give her a goodbye kiss
as I went off in the bus for the last time,
away from her house in Williamsburg, Iowa,
away from her empty house with Jesus
on all of the walls, with clawfoot tub and sink,
with the angular rooms that trapped my summers.

I remember going there every summer—
every day beginning with that lavender kiss,
that face sprayed and powdered at the upstairs sink,
then mornings of fragile teacups and old times,
afternoons of spit-moistened hankies and Jesus,
keeping me clean in Williamsburg, Iowa.

For three months, lonely, in Williamsburg, Iowa,
I sat in that angular house with summer
dragging me onward, hearing how Jesus
loved Judas despite his last kiss,
how he turned his other cheek time after time,
how God wouldn't let the good person sink.

Months later, at Christmas, my heart would sink
when that flowery letter from Williamsburg, Iowa,
arrived, insistent, always on time,
stiff and perfumed as summer.
She always sealed it with a kiss,
a taped-over dime, and the words of Jesus.

I could have done without the words of Jesus;
the dime was there to make the message sink
in, I thought; and the violet kiss,
quavering and frail, all the way from Williamsburg, Iowa,
sealed some agreement we had for the next summer
as certain and relentless as time.

I didn't know this would be the last time.
If I had, I might even have prayed to Jesus
to let me see her once again next summer.
But how could I know she would sink,
her feet fat boats of cancer, in Williamsburg, Iowa,
alone, forsaken, without my last kiss?

I was ten, Jesus, and the idea of a kiss
at that time made my young stomach sink.
Let it be summer. Let it be Williamsburg, Iowa.

New Letters   RONALD WALLACE

WORDS, WORDS

Why is it I always love best
what I cannot see—
the children with their affectionate
nattering, the old house
with its cracked siding and broken door,
you with all your various perfections?
Why is it this loveliness I dream of
vanishes in the thunder of familiarity and use?
So that even now, at this very moment,
faced with all this good life holds for me,
I'm thinking of some love I once threw over—
the sherry of her hair, the glint of
sunlight in her eye,
the sweet words enrapturing my tongue.

Poetry Northwest   RONALD WALLACE

FOR EVA ON HER SEVENTIETH BIRTHDAY

I promised myself and you a villanelle
Or, failing that, a sonnet or an ode,
To celebrate the ten times magic seven
Of the decades you condescend to number.

But now it comes in blank verse, though nothing of you
is blank to me.

        Well, here am I, forever
Three years behind, and now a foursquare four.
Shall I complain about your precedence?
No, be my voyageur, track the lakes and rivers.
My own canoe will follow after yours.

I know, Dear Heart, you have some modest wrinkles,
And I brown spots. Our hair races to gray.
We fall asleep reading a gripping book.

Some things have changed, but not in one direction.
I loved you then, I love you more this day.
If I could wipe my slate clean I would marry
The magic girl of forty years ago,
Beget four daughters, and for bonus have
A double four of children of my children.
And I would spend a life—and spend it well—
Learning to love and know you.

The Literary Review   Chad Walsh

MY FATHER

He is a wolf
that lit out
for the high timber
at first sight of me
rounding out his wife's belly.
But it didn't take too many
tough winters
to drive his range
downward
to the sheep.
My mother's breath
on my neck
is the name
I know him best by
on mornings
when I could freeze
dark the windows
with a whisper,
watching
for just a sight
of him passing.

The American Scholar   Harry Walsh

WILD JACK

Sounds so Irish when you say it,
you said, grinning in Leprechaun.
I am Irish, I say, nibbling a shamrock.

Sweet young, young man: charmed,
your innocence a catholic irony
spilled on my sheets and kneecaps.

Guilt takes a walk: you wear
no underwear, eat no red meat,
Piscean, swimming into me

again. You are a cradle
where my cravings have been napping.
They wake stiff-jointed, hungry.

What a robbery. I am armed, dangerous;
you hand over the goods, twinkling,
humming an Irish lullaby.

South Carolina Review   ANGELA WALTON

PELICAN

Over the inland wave of commerce that curls
on the Tampa side and froths over the sound
like traffic to Longboat Key and the mangroves
awash with curios and bait and seafood
shacks and trailer parks beached on stilts, and over
the fishing piers and marinas and gulf sands
and the chumming tour boats and rusting shrimpers
and the snub-nosed mullet fleet butting the tide
offshore,
          this unlikely, omnivorous bird
plunges through time like hunger incarnate,
gross, prehistoric, right at home anywhere.

Pendragon   MICHAEL WALTON

THE LAST GREAT PARADISE

You talked of Montana like the last
great paradise, meaning wilderness:
the streams followed their own clear courses,
elk ghosted through the forests unseen,
and the deer still paused in flight to stare
quizzically at the rare tourist.
You said the mountains were still unskied,
and the plains stretched from sight unfenced.
And most of all, you said, land was cheap.

Pendragon   MICHAEL WALTON

IN THE GREEN STREAM

Entering the Yellow Flower River,
Each ripple flows in a green stream
From the mountain brooked by countless turns,
An elegant journey of a hundred miles.

Its sound rushes wildly from the stones,
But it is a quiet color, like that deep within the pines.
Water chestnuts float in waves upon waves
That are so clear they reflect reeds and rushes.

My heart is pure and quiet here,
Like this fresh, clear river.
If only I could stay upon this rock forever,
Dangling a hook, my self giving what it finds!

The Literary Review   WANG WEI
                                           —Translated from the Chinese
                                                by Joseph Lisowski

THE TWO OF US

I said to you: O, dog of conscience and desire tugging
at the leash that keeps us together and apart,
I know you care nothing for what I have to say.
Nose to the pavement, leg cocked, hips hugging

the hydrant, you are almost in your heaven. You pull
me headlong, satisfying nearly all your needs,
nearly but for me, yanking you back, my voice
griping that it is I who wants relief, who is overfull

of your bullying, doggy needs, simple as they are:
to be fed, to be walked, and even so to be cleaned up after;
in short, to be attended to whenever you demand,
regularly and insistently. How I wish a car

would put an end to our misery together! But, pity
striking, yes, and remorse at the thought of losing
the company of your winning ways lead to petty
stroking, and we turn the corner into the wind as ever,

the two of us, perceived by the neighbors as one.
Tonight you will appear suddenly on the floor of my dreams,
tomorrow you will address me with your impassive eyes,
asking only more of the same. You speak and it is done.

Shenandoah   MATTHEW WARD

CONNECTING

I think of all these telephones, linking us
like veins in the larger body: memory, dreams,

and seasons changing, like voices.
I bless Mr. Graham Bell, who invented the body/
voice split, and I bless Mrs., who probably
made tea, or drew shutters
against the cold that might have stopped him
had she not been there. Our voices go flying
through crowded and invisible air, through
rain and wires thinner than our nerve ends.
How is this done? I marvel each time.

How is this done? Against small irritations
(the intercept, the disconnect, the staccato
busy/busy/busy) that accumulate like penance,
I pay my way
into the eventual, astounding presence
of your voice. My love, this is a small price
to hear what we want
to hear. Hello—are you there? I am here.

Yankee   LARKIN WARREN

BREAKING THE CODE

The world around us speaks in code,
Or maybe something like the old Indian sign
Language of the Great Plains—all with a load
Of joy and/or despair. And in all of which you must resign
Yourself to ambiguity, or error. The road
Markers are often missing, or defaced. Is
The message the veery tries at dusk to communicate benign?
Does the first flake of snow from a sky yet blue
Mean *that* or *this*?
Is the owl's old question—"*Who?—who?*"—
Addressed to your conscience, and you?

In dawn light does the scroll-mark of wind-swirl in night snow,
Or later the bleeding icicle tip from the eaves,
Tell you a truth you yearn to know—
Or is it merely an index of the planet's tilt?
And what of the beech's last high leaves
Of hammered gold, or glint of sunlit gilt?

What do the eyes of a mother, dying, say or perceive
As your heart compresses in the torturing twist
Of a fist,
And do you know
Whether you feel a ghastly relief—or grieve—
As with glazed eyes you go
Forth, alone, under winter stars, and try to weep,
And try again, and yet again,
For only undefinable tears will serve such a paradox of pain?
Later, of course, you sleep.
Oh, for the longest sleep!

But, no, for later you may see a beloved face
Wreathed in raw rage,
And see a timeless beauty clawed, in a flickering moment, by age.

It is hard to break the code in our little time and space.

The Southern Review　　　　　　　　　　　ROBERT PENN WARREN

ILLUMINATION

We heard it first, a high-pitched
incandescent whine,
and then the bone of the moon
rattled loose from the hill
and lodged in the thick of the night.

It had to be the moon, or
the stiff black legs of the moon
moving to the murmur of our consent.
Could the moon's heart break?
Could the moon strike a bargain?
Could the moon ever mean what it said?

We were so white, there by the pond
in the fragile light, in the
sibilant weeds,
and so black, our future
as meaningless as stars
whose names have yet to reach the earth.

Poetry Northwest　　　　　　　　MARY ANN WATERS

THE FAITHFUL

Sometimes, when the world
no longer seems capable of surprise,
when your wife rehearses
the usual gestures of affection

and birches offer their annual
assortment of autumn leaves,
you forget how small the heart
might be, how fragile.

One morning, rushing to work,
you brush past a stranger
more beautiful than the dark
bruise of adolescence—

your fingers tracing a breast
at fourteen, your tongue
blooming with the moisture
on your sweetheart's throat—

and the world fashions a frail
shell, a pale rind,
the air within billowing
with the scent of buds unfolding,

so that in the story
you'll tell tonight to your children,
the cobbler in a barren country
lets fall his apron

to find, not nails, but
the breathing, miraculous roses.

The Georgia Review   MICHAEL WATERS

CHANDLER COUNTRY, 1954

Dancing in a white jacket at the Beach Club,
who knew Raymond Chandler lived down the road
of that "reluctant suburb," La Jolla,
with its Pink Poodle ice-cream parlor,
swank shops and quaint little Library?
It may have been the same prim librarian
who was tempted to throw his latest book across the room,
"except there was something about the writing."

And, close by, the city—San Diego—deceptively sunny,
where the damp brought bronchitis out at night,
its streets waterfront-seedy or window-box residential
with an occasional profusion of gladioli—
and, of course, the perpetual palm trees
watching over every drive. The seals performed daily
and humans flapped their hands in hot applause
at the fabulous zoo.

Who knows what private eye watched and noted
mysterious characters entering and leaving,
refugees from god-knows-what California crime,
holing up probably in Coronado, where the old hotel
poked its dowager hulk into the Bay?

Pikestaff Review   EDWARD WATKINS

CAMPUS MEMORIAL, OCTOBER, 1982

Young faces blow by me like leaves,
As if I could forget how flesh
Will fix itself in memory,
Seeing how Plato's archetypes are boys
Rosy in athletic sweaters,
Blond and doomed as elms
Bending in October's holocaust.

So this one reminds me of that one,
Michael looks like Kip who looks like David
Who went to school with me at sixteen,
Or was it college, or someone I taught
In the palmy days of graduate school?
No, it is David drifting like a shade
Where the mind's murky undergrowth untangles,
David, the nimble one,
Adonis and warrior of the soccer field.

Of Danang, that travesty of autumn trees
Lurking like skeletons in outer darkness
And orange agents defoliating night,
The less we speak the better.
David would be thirty now,
Stalking his youth on lost campuses.
His face, anomalous and pale,
Became a searing sacrament of leaf.
It kindled bloody, then flamed out to gold,
Burning and burning in the emerald air.

Studia Mystica   WILLIAM COLLINS WATTERSON

PLAYING FROM MEMORY

Mother had never played for us—
not once. I was practicing
when she sat next to me on the bench.
Without a word
she began that burst of music,
her vein-backed hands
making the keys ripple, waking
her childhood in our living-room.

She seldom played after that—
even if we coaxed—
and then only that one piece. Always
the beginning would come back to her
and always at the same arpeggio, that stumbling,
starting again, stumbling—those few notes
like the name of the piece
always escaping her. She would stand

to lower the fall-board, hinge by hinge.
Everytime it happened—
not just the music breaking in half
or that chord like framed glass
shattering in place,
or even the wood clanking against wood
but the silence afterwards—
the keyboard closed on all our pasts.

The Massachusetts Review   JANE O. WAYNE

THE FUTILITY OF BREEDING

When the great red, bloated sockeye,
Plump with the spawn of future generations,
Swim to their ruin on ripe gravel beds,
The whole river reeks
With the futility of breeding.

Cruel water, cruel stone,
The air the gills barely breathe:
All elements become their enemies,
All creatures predators.
Bear, coyote, osprey, gull—
And the frivolous otter,
Content with a single bite—
Converge and gorge.

Yet no enmity is greater
Than their own:
Even as the olive heads bow down,
Trophied with the leprous blight
Which blossoms before death,
They slash and bite.
The gills flutter for the final breath
And the crimson bellies
Turn inexorably towards
The darkening sky.

The faint inhalations of evening,
The aroma of bramble,
The pine resin's sharpness:
These fail to sweeten the fetid air.

Queen's Quarterly   JOHN WEBB

LOOKING OVER THE EDGE

It doesn't bother me
to walk on the dam.
Even though a flash flood
may crash down the canyon
and wipe us away,
or a tiny leak may crack bigger,
and the dam collapse
like a tiger in a pit.

When I was little,
my family came here.
What does it look like
over the edge?
Dad grabbed me under the arms,
leaned me over the edge.
Driftwood tapped against the side,
duck feathers clung to a dead carp.

The overflow shot out
in a rainbow arc,
belly-flopped the river.
Dad pushed, re-grabbed,
laughed at his joke.

I know what's over the edge.

Nexus   DIANE WEBSTER

FOR THE WIFE BEATER'S WIFE

With blue irises her face is blossomed; blue
Circling to yellow, circling to brown on her cheeks.
The long bone of her jaw untracked,
She tries to save herself in our kitchen;
He sleeps it off next door.

Her skinny chicken legs tucked under her,
She is frantic with lies, animated
Before the swirling smoke.
On her cigarette she leaves red prints, red
Like a cut on the white cup.
She pulls her sweater around her like a skin.
She's cold;
She brings the cold in with her.

She hides in our kitchen,
He sleeps it off next door, his great
Stomach heaving with booze.
She tells the story again and again
As if the details ever changed,
As if blows to the face were somehow different
Beating to beating.

We reach for her but can't help.
She retreats into her cold love for him
And she looks across the table at us
As if across a sea.
He claws out of sleep.
She says she thinks she'll do something
With her hair tonight, after all.

New England Review & Bread Loaf Quarterly   BRUCE WEIGL

LIVE LIFE NOW

(Horace Carmina 1.11)

Seek not what end the gods decree
For mortals—it is wrong to guess.
Tempt not the Babylonian seers
Their calculations to profess.

Endure with equanimity
Relentless Jove's unyielding fate:
Are countless winters yours or is
This storm-bound season ultimate?
Now wisely strain the seedy wine,
Long hope ignores life's brevity;
Throughout our talk time's ticking fast.
Live now! Trust not posterity.

The Classical Outlook   SUSAN K. WEILER

MEDITATION

The self-consuming mind
            Attempts to find
Respite from turbulence
By taking leave of sense.

In order to assuage
            Its constant rage
For rest, it would dismiss
Particular, past bliss;

And turning from the haze
            Of future days,
It fixes the mind's eye
On what it must descry:

Will and desire cease.
            Unstructured peace
Abides, as evidence
That passing time presents

No reason to exist,
            But to subsist
On current being's ground,
Inhumanly profound.

Nothing at all there will
            Relieve the still
Moment. The only stress
Is to be motiveless.

The Southern Review   DAVID WEISSMANN

CARVED BY OBADIAH VERITY

Once when I was looking at some decoys
carved a hundred years ago,
curlews and plovers, ruddy turnstones,
I thought of how they began,
as stutters in wood, gouges and flutes,
skewers and judgments of beauty.

They were simple things,
in their heartwoods the grains ran on,
the primitive music of fibers.
And as I stood there I began to imagine
Verity working, the acts of his hands,
the pauses, in which he kept

mounting something finer than skin
on those things. And what came over
the years was more than a touchable
silence. There was something
in those shore birds I was supposed
to pass on, from Verity,

like the deep intelligence of love;
and I left that place full of
breed, and brood, and cross-hatching.

Blue Unicorn   DON WELCH

ON FLYING

Birds dawdle in the grass;
they peck and mumble
like old ladies at bingo in the church basement.

Each bird is the size of a pair of hands
clasped in prayer;
each black back is freckled
with gold spots, gold coins of grace.

A note strikes, and the congregation all rises
in a pounding of wings
and silence.

The flock lifts overhead,
arcs over the display of houses.
Then it twists back, dives,
and collects in an empty tree,
filling it in the sunlight;

each pair of hands flutters
at the offering, the winnings,
the loneliness of flight.

The Hiram Poetry Review   WARREN WERNER

REMEMBERING ROSALIND

Ah these misty September mornings—
as though you could take the trees by their shoulders
and slide them lightly here and there
over the bumpy ground.

Like dancing with the drunken girl, Rosalind,
shuffling and laughing across the wooden floor,
ripe as a melon going on nineteen,
her shoulders firm beneath her sweaters . . .

Morning: a marble rolling in your pocket,
a cricket in the coal cellar,
the earth tilting under your feet.

The earth has been going on four billion years.
But when were there ever days like these?

The Ohio Review   BRUCE WETTEROTH

PENELOPE AND ME

The same people pattern our lives
in and out of time, always.
They are the threads we weave
into our lives' fabric, like Penelope;
and, like Penelope, we unravel
at night what we weave during the day
while we move, like shuttles,
in and out of our crowded tapestries.
From the moment they stitch their names
on our mind's embroidery, they declare
themselves our friends, and we compete
against them with handshakes and smiles.
We lie through our smiles, confident
that our mythical Odysseus
will return to us and make himself
real to us again; and so we sustain
our suitors and patiently wait
for a moment of insanity to deliver us,
when in that moment's tense clarity,
unlike Penelope, we take up
our scissors and cut through the threadbare
metaphors woven in our shrouds.

The Arizona Quarterly   ROBERT F. WHISLER

THE HOBO BLUES

Always thought I'd like to be a hobo:
ride the empty cars
on the Orange Blossom Special
and backpack up the levee
from New Orleans to Memphis,
sleeping on the ground,
walking into cities to take a bath
and mail my postcards home.

But in the back of my mind
stands my late grandmother,
67 years a Southern Lady,
saying, Don't Talk to Strangers;
and deep in my mind
that light flashes on
a thousand times a minute:
Stay Home After Dark Because
Women Get Raped.

So I'm singing those
Female Closed-Door Blues,
making do with what I can get,
telling myself I'm successful,
and a beachcomber's life
is a cop-out after all.
And I try to believe
Mother Nature's not a bitch
for making me rapable . . .
and men are really okay . . .

Oh brothers,
it's not the corporate boardrooms
I envy you:
it's those empty cars
on the Orange Blossom Special.

event   GAIL WHITE

A NATURAL THEOLOGY

Once again a spring has come around,
And many of the best I think I know
Are going crazy.
                    Light on the warm ground
Is almost God requiring them to grow—
Or, at least, to change—the usual song
And arrogant demand that nature makes
Of moral, thoughtful people all gone wrong,
So far as they can see.
                    Their hands hold rakes.
They comb what later are attractive lawns.
They harrow in their ways, then drive the stakes
Up which flowers and food will climb their dream
Of this one season right.
                    They pick up sticks
To make the whole thing work, then plant a tree.
Spring. Spring. They take it personally.

The Southern Review   JAMES WHITEHEAD

DEPARTURE OF A FRIEND

The going is slow, last-minute
borrowings, a shared meal, angry
words smoothed over,
nothing to indicate it isn't an ordinary day
but the sweep of the second hand
and sudden nightfall.

         A silence
will descend in the loft for three weeks;
you will mutter through your days,
glad for the silence but looking
at the calendar, sorting through
the mail, waiting for the sound of a door
opening, a violin scratching,
a voice through the wall.

Waves (Canada)　　　　　　　　　　CLIFTON WHITEN

SHIBBOLETH

Let's say the overcast that has made gray
  Our air for years suddenly clears. The sun
Comes out in a flash, triumphing. Let's say
  For centuries no gentleness has won
    More than a passing compliment, but now
      All mankind opens yarely to the heart.
    Say, though till now we've all been quick to allow
      Divorce, how in one glance none feels apart.

Let's say that's how it is. The sun shines and
  Our quarrels are the pastimes of our feeling
Of solidarity. We understand
  Everyone with the need to be concealing
    His need, though we can't force him to display it
    In the one way we know, which is; "Let's say it."

Shenandoah　　　　　　　　　　MAX WICKERT

COUPLES

       I see them
everywhere
          sitting at stop lights.
      Sometimes one will be smoking,
talking,
      the other listening, nodding,
tapping fingers on the steering wheel.
      Sometimes they are laughing;
other times shaking their heads,
        arguing.

At other times they are looking at each other,
    smiling
        at some shared secret.
And there are those frozen in time,
      staring straight ahead,
      seeing nothing.

    The most intriguing are the ones
who smoke.
      I remember
      being young
      in Ridgefarm, IL,
seeing Charlie and Edna
parked downtown at night, watching people who
    passed by. I couldn't really
      see them. I just knew
        who they were.
    All I could see was
        the glow
of their cigarettes
weaving like fireflies as they chatted. That is
what has seemed to me so intimate
about cigarette smoking all these
years, that masculine
flip, that
feminine inhalation.
    And in the dark
    the playing with fire.

The Ohio Journal   JEAN WIGGINS

THE RIDE

The horse beneath me seemed
To know what course to steer
Through the horror of snow I dreamed,
And so I had no fear,

Nor was I chilled to death
By the wind's white shudders, thanks
To the veils of his patient breath
And the mist of sweat from his flanks.

It seemed that all night through,
Within my hand no rein
And nothing in my view
But the pillar of his mane,

I rode with magic ease
At a quick, unstumbling trot
Through shattering vacancies,
On into what was not,

Till the weave of the storm grew thin,
With a threading of cedar-smoke,
And the ice-blind pane of an inn
Shimmered, and I awoke.

How shall I now get back
To the inn-yard where he stands,
Burdened with every lack,
And waken the stable-hands

To give him, before I think
That there was no horse at all,
Some hay, some water to drink,
A blanket and a stall?

Ploughshares   RICHARD WILBUR

ORCHARD TREES, JANUARY

It's not the case, though some might wish it so,
Who from a window watch the blizzard blow

White riot through their branches vague and stark,
That they keep snug beneath their pelted bark.

They take affliction in until it jells
To crystal ice between their frozen cells,

And each of them is inwardly a vault
Of jewels rigorous and free of fault,

Unglimpsed by us until in May it bears
A sudden crop of green-pronged solitaires.

Kansas Quarterly   RICHARD WILBUR

WASHING WINDOWS

All day we make our clockwise circle around the house,
you on the inside, me on the out,
going through the motions, the awkward ballet
            of some purgatorial experiment,

our polishings the matched waves,
            one pressed against the other,
nodding, tapping, rubbing out this streak and that.
What is that you're saying? mine or yours?

I shout trying to remember what I did at the party last night.
Did you really do your kickup dance from the *West Side Story*
and did I, late, whirl around with a lamp shade on my head,
arms out in hilarious mockery of the cliché and myself?

Nevertheless finally it's done, and having spent
just a few hours from our lives we're back
to where we started, grinning at one another, at our prospect:

to sit inside for one moment of the year purged at last,
completely sober, watching the wind outside,
that vagrant never so transparent staggering around the
    neighborhood.

Michigan Quarterly Review   PETER WILD

RESPONSIBILITIES

I

"Come on. Get up! It's time. Let's go!"
Nightgown, soakers, new shawl, slippers, brassiere:
with her overnight case overflowing, we depart.

The morning traffic: veer through there, yield here,
touch-and-go. . . . Suddenly, Beth's water breaks.
"Easy now," she winks, "we'll get there."

II

They take our names and numbers, they impart
responsibility
on us to hold the hospital to no
responsibilities. I sign below.

Smoothed brow, set jaw, Beth pants
as she was taught instinctively she knew.
I slowly do the rhythmic breathing too,
intensely minding what I know nothing of.

"You coach: say now, 'relax' . . . and now, 'shove'."
So, her moon tutors my tides: wind, unwind.

Enters the doctor, charming, with his glove.
"Ouch!" "Good, four fingers wide,
one more to go . . . Now push." Again the womb
tips up, again firm in the clench of love.

Beth's arms restrained, her legs
in stirrups raised, the hard lights sharply blaze.
Masked, capped and green, scrub suits whisk back and forth . . .

We both are pushing now. *You* have begun
to swell out, blonde and wet,
more and more your long fall into our daze.

The Hampden-Sydney Poetry Review   ROBERT WILJER

FRIDAY EVENING PRAYERS: CRESTON, IOWA

This is less a rural evening than a blessing
delivered in mist, wind, and warm rain
moving the darkness in the heart
of the ain't-what-it-used-to-be USA.

I am happy to be in this far town,
away from the blather of suburbs
where Friday evenings are gloomy with neglected prayers,
and no blessing flickers over the continuous car noise,
the slick seam of sound that binds
all the Bushy Tail Roads and Pumpkin Hollows of the land.

The varied sounds of spiritual life may be heard here.
Tonight, for example, the mist is torn beauteously apart
by the crying white flying squadrons of geese
settling near the lakes north of town,
crying as they circle their refuge,
descending in snowy whirls on the stock fields
to rest this Sabbath,
crying out and trembling in the dark
like a crowd of *daven*ing Jews,
who also pause, even in flight, chanting and swaying, to pray.

Midstream   MELVIN WILK

OUTLAW

The dog slept as usual
in his worn place in the dirt under the kitchen window.
The cattle stood as usual
in the spattered afternoon shade of mesquite
as the hills around heated.
In her bedroom, with wallpaper
yellow-twilit by drawn shades
and the throb of the air conditioner, he
took her gently,
she half his age of thirty-four,
had never parted herself to any man
before him, her father's cousin.
The radio was turned off.
She guided her mind only on love,
divorcing the image of his divorced wife,
taking to herself his smooth back,
lightly freckled shoulder.
She clenched her eyes, clenched
love up against her,
clenched her mind away from the scripture
that no fornicator shall inherit
the kingdom. He had been often
to church with her. They would
go again, permitted somehow,
marry somehow permitted,
God would still love them.
She listens
in fear of a car door slamming,
her tall mother, two younger sisters,
father sun-burnt and crew-cut,
who leads in prayer

but who, moved to black anger,
can go a little crazy.

Descant   CHRIS WILLERTON

NORMANDY BEACH

The waves on the Normandy coast jump heavily toward us.
Somewhere above the roiling, ocean-thick air
soldiers are lining up in a rising light.
The name we have come to find is whitely there.

We stand awhile above the ragged beach
where the German gunnery crews held hard
and spread the beach with bodies that still sprawl,
appearing and disappearing. A silent charge

comes out of the lifting fog, vague visions of men,
some of them drowning, some digging holes in the sand,
some lying on the sand with waves washing their boots.
We watch as the bodies fade away in the sun.

We find his name, Lieutenant, Arkansas.
To leave you there alone I turn around
to a curving monument, The Spirit of Youth
Rising Out of the Sea, what might be found

as frontispiece in a book of Romantic verse.
It must have suggested solace to someone:
arms that might be wings, and flowering waves,
what Shelley as a sculptor might have done.

I watch the statue standing over the stones
and think of what the living do to the dead.
Then suddenly what you came to do is done.
We stop in a dark store for cheese and bread

and a bottle of wine. We find that famous room
where tapestry runs like a frozen picture show
the slow invasion that went the other way
over eleven hundred years ago,

princes and knights and horses in feathers and metal
changing the names of things. An iron cross
leans from an iron gate at the foot of a hill
where careful Germans step out of a touring bus.

I don't want to make a bad metaphor here—
and everything is suddenly metaphor.
We head the Fiat south in a sundown light
and follow the back roads. Beside a river

we make the wine outlast the food and sit still
and watch the water run. Thought after thought
comes into my head and goes. Lonely companion,
there's something I have to tell you but I don't know what.

The Southern Review   MILLER WILLIAMS

ALL SONGS

There's belligerence rumored in the wind.
All men's songs, hap-hazard,
Catch the wind with the grace of trees.
Consider prayer a song.
What odd music intolerance brings,
Sifting out harmonies,
Silencing strings.
God alone is one voice.
Who are we to silence one another?

Midstream   MORISSA LOU WILLIAMS

A CURIOUS FANCY

I think I cried for Italy
The morning I was born;
I think my crumpled body lay
In the ruins of Pompeii,
And my fleeing soul found refuge
In the new American morn.

Then when my eyes first focused
On Texas' amber hues,
This sharp desire within I found
For Roman sights and Roman sounds
And cruel Vesuvius smiling down
On the sea's electric blue;

For though I am a Westerner
And walk the Western way,
My feet ache to be sandal-shod,
To feel smooth stone on Roman road,
And my eyes long to see the crowd
Along the Sacred Way.

The Classical Outlook   ROSE WILLIAMS

SPANNING THE GAP

Oh, give us words that fly from earth to sky,
Synaptic bridges linking mind to mind.
Spell out in seismic tongue each rock's own cry,
The alphabet of custom redefined.
Entice our eyes from stare to quantum leap,
From powered lens to panes of unframed space,
From Attic heights to lowlands wide and deep,
Engaging their full focus in the chase.
And should the furrowed specialists complain
Of feasts too varied for their single need,
Plead for the picky, anorexic brain

That fancies bits of sugar in its feed.
Let's share the light that ranks all knowledge one,
Its least small ray synecdoche for sun.

Geophysics: The Leading Edge   GRACE WILSON

THE PROMISE KEEPERS

We come like memory,
that shaft on which we turn, wheeled by the past,
geared thickets of motive, guilt, and blame.
We come, obedient as water
to those we love and no longer love,
those who can call us to living account
and the dead.
Across the watershed of moral age
we belong less to ourselves
than to an intricate field of promises;
like gravity, like natural law,
we slope to them.

Promises that support us, even against ourselves, light
doubled by the river.
Promises that use us up, like a long illness,
with no expectation of mercy.
Promises we inherit like a genetic oath.
Promises that enfold us, cradling against the urgency
of chance and change, or fix us, still twisting, to the felt,
the glass already sliding into place.
While time, our devout custodian, bears us up and along,
the itch of circumstance cruising in murky jags.

And the world whispers "sucker"
and parades the merits of adjustment, the plausible harvest
of opportunity, singing the provisional
anthem of itself.
What can we know?
Only what the world exacts
and our countersong,
the keeping.

The Georgia Review   MILES WILSON

COURTSHIP

"Can marriage survive passion?"
My friend's question again in my ears
this morning as I lie alone
looking out at thin fingers
of trees.

Here, on my back, I remember
a lover's "Yes!"
I had put my wedding ring in a drawer.

Now I marry myself:
I am learning my skin,
the sound of my voice,
the stretch of my legs.

Tonight, my husband and I
will drink tea, break bread,
see the dark coming on.

College English   BARBARA WINDER

YOUR WHITE BREASTS

Your white breasts—
how yellow
by the light of the moon.
Your breasts, small as fists,
sprouted in the palms of my hand—
two large flowers,
and you said not a word.
The silence left the house
for the grey of morning:
Soon now—we shall be statues,
far from each other, with
wings transparent in the wind.
And the heart mottled with the lights' shadows
shall learn the vast wanderings
of renunciation.
Your small breasts have sprouted since
in the palms of my hand
like two invisible flowers.

Poetry Now   MANFRED WINKLER
—Translated from the Hebrew
by Bernhard Frank

HUNGER

The fox watches.
Cat dog, he sees
the rabbit move
from dandelion flower
to flower,
consuming
these ragged yellow disks.
Rabbit ears twist
toward fox breathing,
but more blossoms

beckon to soft eyes.
Mobile mouth nibbles
petal after petal.
Dandelion suns warm.
Fox ears twitch forward
as only animal movement
behind muzzle-high grass
stirring in green spring breeze.
No cry flies upward
out of flurry of fur
and sudden blood.
It is done at tooth point.
Quick and lethal,
appetite overpowers
appetite.

Ball State University Forum   HOWARD WINN

SEMI-OLDIE

The new 30-watt Sony with metal capability
woofs a semi-oldie
as Saturday Nite Fever [with its grooves still intact]
roars into the kitchen.
Flinging the dish rag aside,
I strike an attitude: let's dance!
The kneecaps ache, a floater in one eye swims;
an upper tooth shrieks with intermittent pain
loud enough to look for sacks, to drown cats in—
a toe throbs; digits lock . . .
Screwing a lid, the protein particle momentarily sinks
into the lower quadrant;
I swallow two Motrin to stabilize the joints—
grind the incisor,
ignore the nerve dying inside the enamel.
The plaintive bridge of the Bee Gee's gurgling overwhelms:

> *"I'm going nowhere,*
> *somebody help me!"*

I twist. Pivot. Clap. Stumble. Sway. Shimmy. Grimace. Mumble.
Smile. Turn. And, turn again . . .
When the last sweet note has encircled the spindle,
the system shuts itself off.
My system, too, is beginning to shut down.
I look down at my hands that have just typed prophesy—
(do they possess foresight beneath the matrix?)
Like ten endowed unicorns,
fingers hover the keyboard and print:

You'll dance in your poems
and the paper will twist. Pivot. Clap. Stumble. Sway. Shimmy.
Grimace. Mumble. Smile. Turn. And, turn again . . .

Broomstick Magazine   BAYLA WINTERS

HIGH SCHOOL GRADUATION BANQUET

(for Daff)

They mass around the punch, pushing,
the made-up mothers with new perms,
loud polyester-suited fathers with cigars
and hip-flasks. The air hangs heavy
with perfume, drink and flowers.
Accustomed to jeans and sweaters,
the students move awkwardly
in their long dresses and rented tuxedos,
greeting each other with giggles,
introducing parents to embarrassed friends.
We sit at long tables and try to eat
a dismal catered dinner. The men get high.
Nervous students, over-rehearsed,
stumbling and expressionless,
reel off speeches. Everyone laughs
too hard and too long at the jokes.
Voices drone. Someone sings.
I reach for another cigarette.

What is this for? It's a ritual
of affirmation, I suppose, but parents
chatter and shout and tell old stories,
the waitresses are bored and harassed,
and above fixed smiles sharp inquisitive
eyes move round in judgment.
And yet it's working for you,
flushed and lovely in your yellow dress,
attentive to every word, every movement.

I'm glad for you. I understand.
You feel that life stretches open miles
just ahead, bright and beckoning.
But it hurts to watch you like this
in the candlelight, knowing that before
too long the world will glaze and darken
that shining in your eyes.

event   CHRISTOPHER WISEMAN

THE OLD SAILOR

He feels the seas pull, in his finger-tips,
Its swell, around his now unsteady feet,
And when he walks the quiet elm-treed street,
He thinks of wind-blown billows, and the ships
He sailed on voyages where a strange sun slips
Into the depths as sky and ocean meet,
Of busy ports, where alien tongues would greet
The freighters from their long, land-hidden trips.

He looks above him now at inland skies,
Thankful for pleasant days of well-earned ease,
And friendly talks beneath green leafy trees;
Yet often, waking in the night, he sighs
For the immensity of endless seas
That startled, long ago, his youthful eyes.

The Lookout   KAY WISSINGER

WINESBURG

Twisted were they, lonely and grotesque—
those people in a small American town?
I read about them at my boyish desk,
lit a Lucky up, my parents gone
to supper at the Presbyterian Church.
I turned the light out so the moon streamed in
and in the darkness felt my young heart lurch—
the smell of summer and the cricket din!
It wasn't Winesburg, not midwest or then,
but I was sighing for the way things were—
the book of strangenesses lay glimmering open,
a far off whistling train rushed others elsewhere—
toward brilliant cities—love and hope and learning—
while I sat groping there and yearning, yearning.

The Hiram Poetry Review   HAROLD WITT

SWITCHYARD

I've woken up again with the sweet singing
in my ears. Another world
must begin at the end of our road,
the empty boxcars coupling and uncoupling,
their steel wheels ringing where they squeeze the track.

I can hear my sister.
From the woods behind our house
where I am sharing with the turtle,
the brown bird and the worm my loneliness,
I think she is raising the flute to her lips,
she's trying for the high clear notes

And I can hear in the harbor
the boats coming home filled with mackerel,
with panic. The fisherman is tired of his life,
his whole day reaching into the water, working so hard
in his imagination. I can hear the winches
squeal lifting the big bucket up out of the hold.

You can see I keep coming back.
I'm lying perfectly still in the dark,
still awake, still in love with you. Soon enough

I'll dress, and leave in the direction of these sounds.
I'll come to the tracks, a locomotive moving this way
and that, selecting cars like words in a sentence.
I'll find the hobos stumbling
through the cinders like stunned angels.
When they ask for a little change I'll be ready.
I'll have my whole life there with me.
I'll give it to them.

The American Poetry Review   JOHN WITTE

BIRTHDAY

On your birthday the pictures of your father
tactfully vanishes and the gray room
grows elegantly silver. I bring flowers:
symbols. You think my fine regalia,
dusty silk and cedar-smelling vest,
indicative of wishes
unfulfilled. Cloaked in black,
you remember your death souring outside the window.
On this, the anniversary of your separation,
you admit the umbilical pull of the time
before time. Your feet skim the blood-red floor
unsupported, as I, bound to you head
to head, eye to eye, float over you
like the bride's veil just lifted.
Year after year I fly above you
in a wild parody of the love
I remember. Finally,
I slip the rose sachet
into your hand as I do every year. Again
you make me promise: no more
will day follow day follow day.

The Antioch Review   ELLEN WITTLINGER

FISHING FOR BLUES

The sleeping muscle awakens. In the leaves of the sea
Schools of fish stir and gather, a blue wind with teeth
Bared toward winter. Little by little the body
Rediscovers its habits only to be lost in a daytime
Sleep no dreamer can dream. I woke up this morning

And it was winter, out of nowhere. I wondered
About the cold, the cloud patterns. I could go on
For years waiting for the southwesters. Nobody
Seems to mind. Down on the beach the tide is out, leaving

The sand shell-shocked and marbled with names sinking
Back into the earth. A man calls his dog and the dog

Comes. A woman is turning her face to the sun.
The bare hook is tuned to the sound of thunder,

And under the sound the water shakes. Schools of fish
Explode and flash, first secret like wind, then in view,
Flames I have fed, food I steal from gale to gale.

Carolina Quarterly   CARY WOLFE

LOST CHILD

This is the new world. I keep forgetting that.
Not long ago, there was nothing here.
So, it doesn't make much sense to ask what's
wrong or what's missing or what's disappeared.
There hasn't been time, you see, for sadness.
We've been busy with . . . whatever. With business.
Only now. there's this feeling of losing ground,
as if we once had more love than we have now—
as if, walking to the bus one day,
it had just vanished—without a trace.
Enough to notice. Enough to see the space
left in the crowd and be able to say
the height, the weight—even to recognize, at last,
the face that proves that time goes past.
We post that face in every storefront glass.
We stamp it: *Still Missing—No Questions Asked.*
And then we forget. You see? We have to forget the facts.
This is the new world.

The Threepenny Review   DANIEL WOLFF

WALK

(for Janet)

Fond of vague, local expeditions, we
   Decide to go for a walk.
The elms are lifeless. The clouds are magenta.
      We talk
   About the prospects for disarmament,
My back pains, how in Maine each spring is "late."
         None of this
      Precipitates any debate
On the part of the woodpeckers or frost-spilled walls
   Or the hillside's seasonal waterfalls.
After awhile our voices have had enough of themselves,
         We listen
   And in our aimless footsteps detect something else,
      Something lulling and May-sweet.
      We try to repeat ourselves but fail.

The gloss of description or the extraction of a moral
　　Won't do.
　Notions of grandeur and humility pale.
　　We sense the vacant truth:
　　　Peace is a motion.
　　We head back home
Through the beech grove and unfurling ferns.
　　　On the path
　Between silence and talk
　We are learning to walk.

The American Scholar　　　　　　　　　　Baron Wormser

THE MYTHOLOGY OF GUNS

The rifle's beside you
like a lover
when I crawl into bed.
The barrel gleams in the dark,
an acceptable emotion.
Boxes of ammo shells
by the nightstand are unconditional
terms for love.

Your aim's not calculated,
not a bargain struck with a father
training his misaligned sights
on you, cocking the hammer
of his numbered days,

but your personal myth—
the basement stocked with survival
rations for a world you swear
you're not a child of.
Every catalogue you open
lists early death for price.

I flip the light switch on.
Your eyes blink dreams back
for the showdown: a Socrates
hated unto hemlock, a Peter
crucified head-down for love. Already
I am one of the survivors.

The Georgia Review　　　　　　　　Carolyne Wright

LAGUNA BLUES

It's Saturday afternoon at the edge of the world.
White pages lift in the wind and fall.
Dust threads, cut loose from the heart, float up and fall.
Something's off-key in my mind.
Whatever it is, it bothers me all the time.

It's hot, and the wind blows on what I have had to say.
I'm dancing a little dance.
The crows pick up a thermal that angles away from the sea.
I'm singing a little song.
Whatever it is, it bothers me all the time.

It's Saturday afternoon and the crows glide down,
Black pages that lift and fall.
The castor beans and the pepper plant trundle their weary heads.
Something's off-key and unkind.
Whatever it is, it bothers me all the time.

The Paris Review   CHARLES WRIGHT

MY DEAD PELICAN

Lumped onto the sand, she rested dead
to the passing eyes of friends and strangers.
We know not how she died or what she fled.

Such evidence needs the surgeon's answers.
We can only stare on, our feet awash
in twisting surf. Our ears want to transfer

the day's silence into the cries of harsh
departure from this earth. This pelican
melts so slowly into the sand and marsh

of my seashore. I do not want this land
to grow from carcasses left as debris
by death's random visit and casual hand.

My beach is my sanctuary. My sea
does not belong to death, my enemy.

Fiddler Gram   FRED. W. WRIGHT, JR.

HEART ATTACK

Throwing his small, blonde son
into the air, he begins to feel it,
a slow motion quivering, some part
broken loose and throbbing with its own pulse,
like the cock's involuntary leaping
toward whatever shadow looms in front.

It is below his right shoulder blade,
a blip regular as radar, and he thinks of wings
and flight, his son's straight soar and fall
out of and into his high-held hands.
He is amused by the quick change
on the boy's little face: from the joy

of release and catch, to the near terror
at apex. It is the same every throw.
And every throw comes without

his knowing. Nor his son's. Again
and again, the rise and fall,
again the joy and fear, squeal and laughter,

until the world becomes a swarm of shapes
around him, and his arms
go leaden and prickled, and he knows
the sound now is no longer laughter
but wheezing, knows he holds his son
in his arms and has not let him fly

upward for many long moments.
He is on his knees, as his son stands,
supporting his father, the look on the child's face
something the man has seen before:
not fear, not joy, not even misunderstanding,
but the quick knowledge all sons

must come to, at some age
when everything else has been put aside,
the knowledge of death, the stench
of mortality, the fraction of an instant
even a child can know, when
his father does not mean to leave, but goes.

Quarterly West   ROBERT WRIGLEY

THAW

Plump from her winter over-feeding,
my cat Coco sits glued to the window,
gossip-minded as any pensioner.
Outside, a sudden thaw.
Snow floods our road
and wood thrushes, round as my cat,
assemble, strangely placid, on the oak
branch not five feet from our window.
In the moment's harmless winter
Coco's tail thwacks and her teeth
chatter as if, in wished-for Spring,
she were plummeting upward . . .
Today the thrushes,
quiet as park squirrels,
would eat out of your hand.
They have come out of shelter
as if a war were abruptly over.
They are happy to have us near them.
No foot-sound startles them;
they have forgot we are dangerous.
Up and down the street tame shovels
scrape the black wet road, car wheels,
half a foot in snow and water, night frost
promised on the news. The mailman,
in knee-high boots, waves to my cat,
oblivious on her window sill, dreaming

how the air tastes of feathers.
Under the grey sky, on the sodden branches,
the birds appear in color.
I rummage in the pantry for stale bread,
bolt downstairs, and don't notice
until water soaks my toes
that I've run into the puddled road
in socks, wool socks.

The Southern Review   JIRI WYATT

STARS

The astronomer-sage
who first imagined constellations—
how frightened he must have felt
of stars scattered all over the universe;
I know.

Stars are really frightful.
            Or lovely.
Stars never set.
Eyes dimmed by the lustre of the sun
Can't see them, that's all.

Early morning,
when stars start disappearing one after the other,
only the broken shape of leaves
of the opposite *neem* tree-top
comes to the rescue of eyes.
Beauty, when not frightful, can be so fragile.
That's the reason why at times
I wish to take my eyes out of their hollows
and place them on a mountain top
to see the beauty of stars from near them
—without a thought for my safety.
In these ugly lanes of the sun
I'll manage with a stout stick.
But
then
I remember my beloved's momentary face.
—I need my eyes.

New Letters   SITANSHU YASHASCHANDRA
                              —Translated from the Gujarati
                                        by Varsha Das

IN THE CLOCK SHOP

All day there is no silence
between ticks

listen, you can hear
the new clocks tightly coiled

outrunning the old
preparing to strike the hour
before its time

but the clockmaker refuses
to interfere

he has heard it all before
and knows it is the way
with new clocks
and only time
can change it

listen, it is dusk
and in the back of the shop
you can barely hear
the first clocks winding down,
the slow click of bones
the tap of a blind man's cane
the sound of night
holding its breath

Writers Forum   Michael Yots

ELEGY IN THE FORM OF AN INVITATION

(James Wright, b. 1927, Martin's Ferry, Ohio;
d. 1980, New York City)

Early spring in Ohio. Lines
of thunderstorms, quiet flares,
on the southern horizon.
A doctor stares at his hands.
His friend the schoolmaster
plays helplessly with a thread.

I know you have put aside your voice
and entered something else.

I like to think you could come back here now,
like a man returning to his body
after a long dream of pain and terror.

It wouldn't all be easy:
sometimes the wind blows birds
right off their wires and branches,
chemical wastes smolder on weedy sidings,
codgers and crones still starve in shacks
in the hills above Portsmouth and Welfare . . .
hobo, cathouse, slagheap, old mines
that never exhaust their veins—
it is all the way you said.
But there is this fierce green
and bean shoots poking through potting soil,
and in a month or so the bees
will move like sparks among the roses.

And I like to think
the things that hurt won't hurt you anymore
and that you will come back
in the spring, for the quiet,
the dark shine of grackles,
raccoon tracks by the river,
the moon's ghost in the afternoon,
and the black earth behind the plowing.

Ploughshares   DAVID YOUNG

JOZEPHA—1900

October's sky fills with sun and swift, white
clouds. So unlike Poland's pale autumn dawns.
Coffee scent spills out to the porch where I
stand to watch Walter hitch the mare. He takes
the sweet corn five miles to market. Last
night, I whispered, "At summer's height, a baby's
due. Perhaps a boy." He roared, swung me
around. His joy shook our sturdy home.

I trembled, throat tight, when I first saw
Walter. Tall, dark auburn hair glowing with
sun-sparks as he strode to Papa's door, claimed
me as his bride. Then he warmed my shaking
hands, called me sweet Jozepha. Gentle, like
the flow of Uncle Casimir's flute on summer
nights. The Russians caught Uncle Casimir
when he swam the ice-thick Prosna to celebrate
secret Mass. Two days later, they took Papa.

Poland lies only in my heart now. The land,
schools, all Russian. And Walter says,
"We are American! Our children will live
with freedom, pride!" He even changed our
last name to sound American, Walter waves
from high atop the wagon seat, I wrap
my arms around the life inside. When warm
winds curve through trees with the sigh
of flutes, I will sing Polish lullabies.

Southern Humanities Review   REE YOUNG

PAPER CUT

Opening her letter, I got a paper cut
On the whorl of my thumb.
Thumb-sucker, then a hitch-hiker,
I had a vision.

Of Carol Thompson as she was
Twenty years ago, twelve years old

In the beauty of her tomboyhood,
Half sleeves in the Indian summer.

She uncradled the .22 from her blond arm,
Slung the sack with the dead squirrel in it
Onto the bank, and sat me down at the apex
Of sunlight, triangled by glints from the brook.

I squinted at her
As she kissed me on the lips, then slapped
My cheek, put my hand on her breast,
Then twisted my wrist.

Soon I was sobbing and whimpering,
Eight years old, too stupid to blow my own nose.
She wasn't laughing, she was studying:
Trying her charms on a boy.

The dazzling pain of small outrage—
Now it comes back because of a letter,
A marriage dissolving
Out west, where the aspens are turning

Around a clear well I used to draw from.
Beside it, a bucket brims shining.
I shade my eyes with my palm.

Pendragon   WILLIAM ZARANKA

SUBURBAN SUMMER

Compressed, compact, the little houses stare
on airless quiet, choked and thick and still.
Sit on the doorstep, child, and comb your hair
heavy as city sunlight, and as warm,
as stifling and as dense as the few torpid trees—
release its reluctant beauty to your knees.

Or let your window songs—muted as air,
as faint and fine—rise in thin elegy,
resenting the long seasons rooted where
the frail tenacious flowers of tender hue,
cold time has scattered on such troubled winds.
Or rest strained eyes on heavens grown dim and small,
and listen to the railroad's whistling call:

The universe runs by through shuttered blinds.

New Letters   MARYA ZATURENSKA

THE NEGLECTED GARDEN

One rose that straggles shyly, another bush reveals
few peonies that flaunt an uneasy glamor.
My soil is poor this year. It gives with niggard hand
where once profusion reigned and showered the land
with multicolored flames, compelling fragrances.

My purple and white phlox cannot compare
with the displays the skillful gardeners raise,
yet what I have can glorify my days.
They too must fade as others do, and raise
new fires at last to face the winter's gloom.

But now in living air, in powerful light,
in nervous beauty, their soft signature
blazes through uncut grass, untended trees.
My day will come, and theirs, my forsaken flowers,
when we will bud and blossom, through some care.

New Letters   MARYA ZATURENSKA

IF I FORGET THEE

If I forget thee, O Jerusalem,
standing here on the ledge of Abu Tour
among the chartered buses and souvenir peddlers
looking west to the Wall, the Mosque, the Basilica,

while grinning Arabs place kaffiyehs on squealing tourists,
and hoist them onto camels for two dollars a head—
if I remember thee not,
let my Nikon forget its cunning.

Here, to the City of David
I have returned from my diaspora
bundled and greased against the sun,
my tongue cleaving to the roof of my mouth

even as I recall yesterday's climb
into the Judean hills,
oleander and hibiscus blossoms
among the trucks left by the roadside.

On this, the day of my chiefest joy,
a *Satmar Chasid* in caftan, beard and earlocks,
told me the State of Israel does not exist
as the Messiah has not yet come.

The Literary Review   DAVID ZEIGER

OLD WESTBURY GARDENS

Here is this other flower,
exquisite even under glass—
the young model they are
so busy photographing
in the famous garden room.
She bends beside a chintz sofa
pouting into a mirror.

I press against the French door
inches away from her,

shamelessly staring, enjoying her,
the curve of her orange mouth,
the little flat nipples,
the swivel of the hip
in orange satin.

I am her duenna
with dark hair above my lip
and maybe a wen on my cheek.
My rough hands bathe her,
perfume her, dress her in
gauzy underthings.
I am in love with her—

And I know about loving.
I am the root that knits the earth.
I am the worm that makes things happen.
And, more than anything else,
I want to be the flower.

West Hills Review   LILA ZEIGER

YIZKOR

Am I a man?
Yes, you say.
But you are wrong:
I have only
The appearance
Of a man.
Actually,
I am made of corpse-fat
Scraped from the undying
       death-camps
Of Christian Europe.

Was I hard to make?
No, you say.
But you are wrong:
For six long days
God sweated over my carcass
And, then, just before
He rested on the seventh,
He lit the wick
Of my
Jewish mind.

Does it pain me?
Yes, you say.
And you are right:
The flame sears through me all
The years since,
Every waking moment of my life.

And when, at last, I sleep,
It burns my
Jewish dreams
To ash.

Midstream   CHAYYM ZELDIS

SNOW

Love is all we could manage, its particles
Floating from the hard rim of the air.
Our tracks were clear as a book
In the fresh chance heaven threw behind us.
And the pain went on searching
Behind your face, the snow went on falling.

Once I felt your tongue
Work so gently into my brain,
It took root in the mind-dark
And branched forth again as song.

Character is a failure of love,
And I want to love you this morning.
I want to love the birch trunks
Invisible against the snow,
And your hand fishing warmly in my pocket.
I want to love the darkening blue at the sky's edge,
Our thoughts like mittens fumbling to hold on,
Our breath-smoke warming the air
Before it dissolves into a hard February day.

The Paris Review   PAUL ZWEIG

SCARECROW

I'm sure I've seen him
roll his eyes
each time I come
to pick the corn.

I think of him
knee-deep
in crickets
reciting
their wisdom.

Twice he's been
an umbrella
for finches,
shouldered
two species
of garden snake,

and provided shade
on numerous occasions
for field mice
and garden hens.

But when the sun
was finally down,
I saw how hanging
from a simple pole
was his only trick.

event   FREDRICK ZYDEK

BREAKFAST

(for Margaret Atwood)

The sound the eggs make
sucking against the pan
like a baby's mouth
sucking a full breast:
moist music.

You trust me, so you sit
at my table, while I
play at playing a role:
solicitous bride.
This is not a game;
this is serious
business, feeding
and eating.

These odors, this clatter
of fork against plate,
these brilliant yellow eyes
will never converge again
like this. The scene
is not set for promises,
only for breakfast.

Kansas Quarterly   MARIANNE ADAMS

BLOOD GRAVY

During the war Aunt June
was left standing at her kitchen sink
holding a piece of honey bread on her tongue,
peeling onions and staring out the window
while a pot of blood gravy simmered on a back burner.

That first spring
she turned her mirror against the wall
and worked the farm like a man,
until one day on her way toward the house
she saw Christ's face in her kitchen window screen;
when she looked closer it was
an old woman's face.
The next day she invited three young men
for supper and to see her screen.

After they soaked up the last gravy with bread
and wiped their mouths on their sleeves,
one said he saw his dead mother in the window,
one said he saw Christ,
one said he saw nothing but a window screen
that hadn't been stretched tight on its frame,
and he'd be around about four o'clock
the next afternoon to fix it.

Tendril   JANE BIRDSALL

FUGUE

The body replicates itself not quite perfectly
every seven years, the doctors say. When I
was twenty-eight,
four times my skin had shed,
four times the meat replaced itself inside; nothing
but a few nonreplicating cells remain—
the brain. The liver, maybe. I forget.
The hand that offended me at fourteen is gone.
Long gone the eye that screwed me up at twenty-one.
Where are they now? Have they
found coordination to peer, to clutch
from among the bricks in some garden corner?
And what of the rest?
The legs, now a half dozen, that wanted
only to run and never harmed a soul.
The hearts, the toes.
The intestines, veins and nerve bundles
unreeling by the mile through my past.
This bitter death—it neither comes nor goes.
It lingers, taking only little bites in passing,
as if I were a buffet.

Passages North   ROBERT BIXBY

IT IS

It is true, that at midnight
it gets cold in the forests of summer,
but the moon is getting round again.

It is true, that at midnight
stars jump from twig to twig
very curious
and still searching for Heine.

It is true, that at midnight
heaven overlaps
with nothing but love and transcience.

It is true, that I go and everything goes along,
the young trees, and also the old,
and the benches underneath
that stand so still through the day.

I go and go
and change the geography.

The Chariton Review   ELIZABETH BORCHERS
                                              —Translated from the German
                                              by Gudrun Mouw

TELEPHONE CONVERSATIONS

(After Discussing William Faulkner with George Kent)

Telephone conversations
are little lives.
Their tempers and temperatures
fall and get up and fall.

Each one is New.
There is the birth—
easy or difficult.
The little baby prospers or declines.
Sings. Sobs.
Limps. Lulls.

But suddenly
(sometimes)
an Imminence of Light.
Ribbons of fire and music.
A democratic transportation.

Black American Literature Forum   GWENDOLYN BROOKS

FASTING

My father could eat eggs Sunday morning
because he didn't believe.
He dipped warm bread in the yolk,
and we scraped his plate with our stares,
but still had to wait three hours
before Communion. We held our veils
down with bobby pins and followed
my mother up the winding stairs
to the choir loft. Long pipes
on a wall warmed with music as she sang
by an organ with pedals as big
as the man who played them.
I loved the sun pouring in through
the saints' bright robes, and my mother's
red hair, her long red hair. I saw him touch it—
the organist, where the stairs curve
into the church basement,
but I didn't care. Mass was over.
We were going down there
for sweet rolls, sweet rolls with butter.

Mississippi Rivew   DEBRA BRUCE

EPIGRAM

I still remember that street with its yellow lights.
The full moon among the electric wires,
that star on the corner, a distant radio,
the belfry of La Merced when it would strike eleven—
and the golden light of your open door in the street.

Poetry Now   ERNESTO CARDENAL
                                    —Translated from the Spanish
                                    by Steve Kowit

WITHOUT FLOWERS

He calls from the house, "In this light, your dress
is the color of the cornflowers under the stairs."
She remembers when they planted their garden
and thinks this suggestion of the light
on her dress is unfair. She leans over the porch
and searches the flowers that border the footpath.

She wonders why he reminds her the path
wears flowers as she wears a dress—
to hold her, like this, to the porch,
to keep her from taking the stairs

for the last time? But when he calls from the light
of the house, when he calls on the garden,

does he believe in that memory, in the garden,
or only his power to direct her path
with his words? In the half-light
she stands in, she sees her arms and dress
are the color of nickels. The stairs,
the mailbox, the cracked urn on the porch

are all silver. Alone on the porch,
she thinks that except for the garden
they planted together under the stairs
they've never understood things the same. Now the path
he asks her to take leads back to where her dress
will be blue again, in the light

of the house, as if that particular light
could redeem them from this scene on the porch;
as if, to have her clothed in a dress
the color of their garden
will make their separate paths
come together again. He approaches the stairs.

And entering the half-light of the stairs,
he leads her even further from the light
of the house, taking the path
that leads from the porch
to the black night and the garden,
extinguishing the color of her dress.

The Threepenny Review   MARI REITSMA CHEVAKO

LOST CHILD

Far from town and road,
a narrow trail leads straight through woods
where a mockingbird vaunts its high
freedom, smooth limbs of an ash
wind like stalled snakes across the path
tempting him to leap, with delight,
for this limited human flight.

Looking back to mark how far he's come
since leaving home, ages ago,
he sees, like pictures shaping the past,
diminishing tracks in melting snow.

In search of new sights to redeem
what's lost, he crosses an old bridge,
climbs fast, trying to flee the self left
behind, a curved way to a tangled ridge;

hearing the snow, his boots kick back
dropping softly down, as in a dream,

like someone following; he turns to seek
what's lost on the far side of the stream.

He's soon off every trail in dark woods,
turned around, bewildered, wandering
into the new unknown, as in childhood
when all felt strange, surprise or wonder,
hoping he'll make the right turns, come
on human tracks, another's or his own,
and in good time find a way back home.

Poem   ARTHUR CLEMENTS

WHEN THE ROCKS ARE CINNAMON

In my vineyard
the sumach's grape clusters
are limp with desire,
and there is a shudder
in the maple's pomegranate.
Autumn's blaze
is heavy with passion and sadness
and my love is here,
and away.

On a sultry afternoon
when the rocks are cinnamon
and cicadas cannot wait till dusk,
my thoughts quench their thirst
in saffron lakes,
and the wind's winepress spices with honey
my longings,
wooing the sun to be my lover
and I his Shulamite.
And though we drop our veils,
and I let him kiss
my uncovered dreams,
we sleep together
unrequited.

Midstream   DONIA CLENMAN

REFLECTIONS AT DELPHI

1.

HEADLESS SIBYL

There, in a ceaseless movement of stone drapery,
she sits beside the sacred way,
a nun unique, cloistered in ruins.
Vainly to her the taste of the salt spray comes;
out in the bay in vain the dolphins flash.

She cannot smell the cypress-laden breeze,
nor hear Castalia falling, cold, to the rocks below.
Bride of the god, she waits.

But if at last some true believer comes,
he may rouse her to duty, and the Lord Outcast
startle her to awareness with accustomed touch.
Then, beauty like frenzy rising in her breast,
she will rage far out on the mountain,
and cry out, as once, the wisdom of the god.

2.

THE LYRE-kNARLED FINGER

The lyre-knarled finger moves across the strings;
the cypress bends
to hear the strange somnambulent music that befriends
a god's rememberings.

3.

VENUS ARISING

Venus arising blue above the fane
steps from the delicate shell of twilight.
On the night's dark plain
attendant stars are blossoming
like asphodel.
Venus genetrix, mother of all things,
knew not this cool Apollo, bore no sons
to this great lord.
Mated with blood and lust, mated with fire,
sated with love's quicksilver, in this one desire
her failure lay. This temenos alone
offered the mistress of the doves no throne.

Was it that in her were no little leaves,
no green shoots budding?
That her roses sprang
forth from that fertile womb full-blown?
His need was of the future, of its promises.
She was the past and present, held no secrets
from her lovers. Venus was the known.

Though she send down each night her star-love's beam,
it cannot pierce the shadow where he lies
wrapped round forever in a laurel dream,
and Daphne, who denied him, is his queen.

The Classical Outlook   MARTHA DREADIN DAVIS

ONE ROOM

The one-room school
sitting for its photograph
could have been my students,
and the faces
are not happy June ones—
one girl worried
about her dark dress
amidst the light frilly ones,
two boys uncomfortable in jackets,
the rest scolded solemn
as if the teacher were taking
mug shots.
I know that the lad on the left
who climbed the schoolyard pine
and threw down the hawk's eggs,
bombing the future,
died later by drowning,
dumped from his canoe.
I wonder if the girl in the middle,
blessed with alcoholic parents,
now buys overshoes compulsively
so her child will never wear
plastic sandals in January.
And I still see the ones
who brought garter snakes,
carried water for the drinking urn
and pounded blackboard erasers
bending over me
after the baseball knocked me down
at recess and asking if I'm okay.
I am, and long
to ask them the same.

Saturday Night   DIANE DAWBER

DIGGING LILACS

She wants to plant vegetables this year.
I offer to take out her old lilacs—
her husband, a revered electrician, wired
my house, and I, naturally reverent and
fascinated by electricity, am in his debt.
She offers to pay. I gracefully decline.
Working conditions are ideal: flowers blooming
in the garden, lawn curving down to the bay.
At least the tide is out and rain threatens.

Raising my mattock, I poise it artfully,
then bring it smoothly down. The head
jars against the stump, the handle

rings with current. Transfigured,
I hack and rip the crazy provocation.
My hair blossoms with chips, my eyes
shed humus, my lips sputter with sap.

In time the old couple stop by—he's
jovial, offers locker-room encouragement,
she's concerned, uses "splendid" several times—
then drift down the garden path. I dig again,
this time with cunning, encircle the root,
cut it off from its romance with earth.
Piecemeal, it yields. It goes better.
There is time to save a tulip, probe
carefully, feel for the bulb,
lay it gently on the side.

And so, systematically, I reach the final root,
mind blank, body enervated. It comes,
bears no surprises. Only then
I look and see my path: bits
and heaps of earth, lilacs
strewn upon the ground.

Passages North   DINO FABRIS

SLEEPLESS NIGHT

Night, when can I hope from you beyond
The sombre vaudeville of memory
and the lean dreams confessed to light applause?
But never night, remorseless night, do you give to me
Soft glide and softer skid of sleep,
Nor sleep into my nostril breathing
Sleep, oh, not all night.
Until there finally stirs a creeping color
In the east, and suddenly
The huge and shivering eye of light
Flies open in the sun
And morning sits astride the mountaintop.
Sleep, not till then, thou black and lovely one,
Do you enter my house at every door
And stroke the four corners of my bed.

Yankee   HILDEGARDE FLANNER

1928

i imagine heisenberg sitting down at his desk
to write us a long letter telling us
that physics is not the world
physics is so very simple
and the world is not
and between his index finger and the typewriter keyboard

so much happened
which only proved his point
if he waited five minutes longer to write
he'd have five minutes' more evidence
for what he wanted to say to us
and if he waited till tomorrow
or the next day
surely the proof would be insurmountable
so i imagine him sitting back at his desk
which looks a lot like the desk i am writing at now
and letting the world flow by
these waves
washing away the letter he is trying to write
these particles
scattering their own message where he'd meant to write his
the world in all its vast complexity piling up
faster than he can get down
in black print
on a simple piece of white paper
the news that the world in all its vast complexity is
piling up faster than
i can get down
on this simple piece of white paper
the news of the world in all its vast complexity
and the long letter heisenberg will never write

The Georgia Review   ALVIN GREENBERG

THE PROFESSOR'S MUSE

Divinest Plato was in essence right
when he condemned all art as specious lies.
Petrarchan sonnets will not shed such light
as falls from half-articulated cries.
Indeed, what truth submitted to the test
of stern unyielding form and rhythm and rhymes
can withstand such devils as give no rest
as poets poised on the edge of time?

But what is that to me? When bid, I must arise
and show the truth embedded in the page
that all can read, but few can understand—
the grit enshrouded in the pearl of lies
must lead in fact the choosing few from age
to age and on to Form's eternal land.

The Classical Outlook   E. R. GREGORY

I GOT

When I see myself and touch myself,
me, Juan without Nothing only yesterday,

and today Juan with everything,
and today with everything,
I turn my eyes, I look around,
I see myself and touch myself,
and I ask myself how it all got to be.

I got, lemme see,
I got the pleasure of walking round my country,
boss of everything in it,
looking real close up at what I didn't use
to have and couldn't have.
Sugar harvest I can say,
countryside I can say,
city I can say,
army I can say,
mine for always now, and yours, ours,
and a broad glow
of sunbeam, star, flower.

I got, lemme see,
I got the pleasure of going,
me, a compesino, a working man, a simple guy,
I got the pleasure of going
(just for instance)
to a bank and talking with the manager,
not in English,
not in Yessir,
but calling him compañero like we say in Spanish.

I got, lemme see,
that just because I'm black,
nobody can stop me
at the door of a dance hall or a bar.
I got . . .
Or maybe at a hotel desk
shouting at me that there ain't no rooms,
just a tiny little room, not a great big room,
a little room where I can get some rest.

I got, lemme see,
that there ain't no troopers
to grab me and lock me up in a barracks
or drag me out and shove me off my land
out into the middle of the highway.

I got that because I got the land I got the sea,
not country club,
not high life,
not tennis and not yacht,
but from beach to beach and from wave to wave,
gigantic, blue, open, democratic:
that's it, the sea.

I got, lemme see,
that I've learned how to read and how to count,
I got that I've learned how to write

and how to think
and how to laugh.

I got that now I've got
a place to work
and earn
what I got to have to eat,
I got, lemme see,
I got what I have to have.

The American Poetry Review   NICOLÁS GUILLÉNS
—*Translated from the Spanish
by Donald D. Walsh*

DEATH AND THE DISSERTATION

I scarcely noticed
when my mother died.
I was busy
shuffling papers, moving cards
from one pile to another.

I went of course
and said all the proper things.
She was old,
had lived a long and useful life.
Wasn't it wonderful
she didn't have to suffer?
I want to go like that.

I felt, I'm sure,
although I never said it,
it was commendable of her
to be so little bother.

We buried her.
I hurried home
to finish up,
to get it typed
to study for the orals.

My diploma came today
and for the first time since,
I cried.

Because the only one
who would have cared
to see my name in fancy script
was dead,
and I had scarcely noticed
when she died.

Ball State University Forum   LAVERNE HANNERS

BEETHOVEN

("O Freunde, nicht diese Töne!")

Not these tones, my friends!

Not this dense pity,
whispered eye to eye
behind the deaf man's back . . .

Stop scribbling those
demeaning lies
to soothe the still
unbelieving terror
of my ear's
strident night.

Terror indeed!

Hammering at the temples:
my sealed Caucasus
where bitterness flashes
unsurrendered phrases,
spiting the fetters
with brazen themes.

The eagle always swoops down;
I defy his beak, his talons
with my every mutinous sensation,
bled out in clefs
my once soundest hearing
could not invent.

Somewhere within the core
I laugh—
and score my chains
with titanic fury
or orphic touch
upon these amoral boulders.

If there is little justice
among the living,
friends,
I shall compose my own

to raise its purple thistles
across the yellow grave.

National Forum   HANS JUERGENSEN

FATHER POOLE

Lord, it is time.
Let my ghost tumble down
and my priest's hat go riding in the wind.
At nightfall, women by the fountains

go over and over their beads, their hair loose,
and the youngest knows I yearn.
The sparrows fly like stones.
Yours, Lord, is a fabulous claim.
Whole nights I wait beside a candle
or I feel the four black limits of the wall,
my cowardice more fixed. You do what you must.
I can't divide another moment on this tower into two,
three; now, now, if ever, Lord, direct me
to the guarded world of those whom you distrust.

Skyline   KATHERINE KANE

MY FATHER AND THE MISSISSIPPI

He had a special fondness for the river:
The Mississippi cleansed an increment
Of sins, he said, as on a holy day
He tossed out crumbs of bread. His litany—
"Don't die, don't die, don't die, don't die, don't die."
I have been talking with my father lately:
Standing at his grave. I could remember shame
For anguished silence in a troubled time
(Every man's father will return to him).

He laughed on waking from a dream that he
Had come to own a thousand moving steers:
Dying poor in the city, owning pain,
He left the memories of his charities.

Now that the years of protocol are past,
We speak with ease concerning hunger, pride.
Late in the day, yet still time to discover
How the mute teach the alphabet of love.
Remembering is free of pain, for I
Can sense the world's end in my private glaciers,
And feel death's elephant approach to drag
Bones and shadowings of fertile brains to where
In time my interlocutor will come
(Every man's father will return to him)
Requesting just a modicum of time
To soften forgotten little interludes.

Southern Humanities Review   ALLEN KANFER

OUR ISLAND

Our father's ship
has entered the mist.
His charmed cargo
will grow precious in the hold
but will never spoil,

salted, as it is, by tears.
He's charted a course
for the birthmark
you have on your back,
I in miniature on my forearm.
Once, dripping from the shower,
laughing, drunk and steaming
in the cold motel room,
he stretched the blue-veined skin
of his scrotum into a map
and showed us the same marking.
I wish him safe passage.
I hope you do, too, Theresa Rene.
I wish him safe passage
from this world of banks and prisons
so he may haul his cargo of outrageous needs
into his own blood and search always
for our island. May he be a hero
unto himself and may you
never forget
that though I do not know
the woman you've become,
you were my first lover
lying upside down next to me
so we could tickle each other's feet.
Come here, turn over, I'd whisper,
and in the dirty light from street lamps
illuminating our room,
I traced with my best finger
over and over
the coastline of your island
till you slept.

The Antioch Review   RICHARD KATROVAS

CALLING

Falling asleep in the afternoon
I forget that my father has died.
I anticipate him calling me up,
asking me how my writing is going,
and am I thinking about having children.
Making a joke or two. "Don't worry,
Mom and I will never be lonely."
Then I fall into deeper sleep, he
loses me, traveling in his car, the green
chevrolet, to old baseball fields
which are sweet with rye grass
and lush stadiums, his pals throwing
him the ball—"Give me some pepper, Al."

The Sun   JUDY KATZ-LEVINE

LABOUR DAY

A last fling out to the cottage, ritual swims
in the mild rain: we sit on the deck, observing
a few leaves already golden. Fall
is hard upon us as our children grow,
aching as they endure
schoolyard initiations,
not knowing why; for them,
the future seems straight lines.
We who have grown devious, turned aside,
must learn to hold our peace. It is a time
for recognitions, disconnecting power:
in air-tight jars we preserve last fruit, seal off
our sadness, facing winter.
After the long drive back
to the city's sodden dusk, I feel
the year evaporate.

Queen's Quarterly   CHRISTOPHER LEVENSON

NEW MATH

(for Judy & Gerson)

we were three, we children,
now we are six/
we were five, in the family,
now we are eight—
with the children eleven.

we were six for a while,
the family,
then seven,
then six again,
then, with the children,
seven and eight—
then we were nine
and another child, ten.

now we are eight,
with the children eleven.

the sum of the parts
is greater, at last,
than the whole
and the limits on addition
are subtracted by physical law.

we were three,
now we are six—
the fraction of love
is the difference.

Ariel   DAVE MARGOSHES

EMILY DICKINSON'S WELCOME HOUSE

On this small house's stone steps,
hearing you walk about
I want to perch on the porch
in this dawn's fragrance
reaping the earth with harvest
and willows in the stillness.
Concealing my quickened sighs,
now shuffle the whispers
of the poet long gone, yet close,
sensing the secret terrain
of her end of shade garden,
the white curtain fears
which lift and the lever listening
even to my voice, whenever a poet
with morning between us in safety
opens a welcome on my child-like palms.

The Hollins Critic   B. Z. NIDITCH

BREATH OF GOD

Come, my heart, come,
Come, my wing, come;
And harp, come
Run with mirth,
Like flying fingers strum
O'er the island Earth.

Beat, my heart, beat,
Beat O wing, O pulsing sweeping chord
And silver ivory word, breathe
From lip to line
The love our word defines.

Breathe, O sweet breezes,
Breath of God,
Breathe anew the symmetry of seasons
Till wakening gods come forth to stand
O'er the island Earth.

Holy, holy, holy land,
Garden thrice anointed.
At thy Beloved's hand
Comes thunderous wave upon wave upon
Symphony of voices.

O still, my heart, still;
Rest, my wing, rest,
Silent harp, peaceful flesh
Embraced within an emerald breast,
The Emerald island Earth.

The Emissary   STEPHANIE CELENE SARBECK

MORNING MEDITATION

Morning: my eyes robins and sparrows singing,
yet sleep still mulches. The first body chores:
kissing the devil: yet fibers of morning meditation.
I like the solitude of the house now,
I like those I love a voice away,
protected by the sleep I forget.
The walk to the bus, the simple waiting,
the boring man I sit next to each ride,
who talks as if he had been dead ten years:
a part of the fabric of my plenitude.
I arrive at the library an hour early;
I bring in the papers, I make coffee,
the news I read, crusts of bread
on the winter snow of world history.
These little acts are a waiting, a preparation,
for those who will walk into my life.
For people are my real solitude,
their lives arms about my loneliness,
their concern an antidote for the cacophony—
without them my life has an incurable flaw.

San Jose Studies   ALAN SEABURG

MESSAGES

I.

I am almost there, driving the interstate
Only slightly over the speed limit, Mother,
And I see the rich late afternoon sun
Burnishing the spring-soft hills,
Turning the dogwood blossoms gold.
And there is a roadside cemetery,
The kind you used to take me to
Full of Illinois ancestors years ago.
This one belongs to strangers
And a van, its doors open,
While a golden girl pushes an eager mower.
Oh, my dead mother, I think of you
In this glimpse of a grasscutter's simple soul
And I send you across all time these words,
This message that, of all places in the world,
That is where I'd most like this moment to be—
Trimming the grass and pulling the weeds
From the edge of your far-distant grave.

II.

Now it is another day,
Another winter turning past,
And I travel the same roads again.

The cars and the causes are not the same,
And the colors and calendars have changed,
But the long-haired girl is there once more,
Her brown van parked on the hillside road,
Clearing away the remnants of snow,
Thinking of someone who lies buried there,
Remembered, loved, worth caring for,
As I still care for you
And wish that I could rake away
Not only sticks and stones from winter storms
But distances as well, and time,
Somehow to tell you once again,
As I said too seldom long ago,
How good you were, my parent, my friend,
And that I love you. Now.

Laurel Review   BARBARA SMITH

THE GIRL ON THE EDGE

Rising too soon from sleep, my head singing
with absent love, I see the neighbour's child
walking her collie, wind and a bright sun
teasing the fur into a white spray on the neck
of the muscled beast. The girl stands on the edge
of the slipping cliff, fist full of cold chain, shaking
gold hair at the empty lake letting her harmless hips
sway in sweet ignorance of choice and consequence.

Clouds between light and land accumulate
banality, love baits its double trap
of brief denials and long acceptances, and the dog
drags its chain homeward. I turn from my window
to the wide bed, rumpled on one side.
If sleep is denied now I will make coffee
to start up the day, while my wife of many years
stays tending her garden in the north.

Poetry Canada Review   FRANCIS SPARSHOTT

LOVE IN THE VACATION

You were my freckled summer girl,
palm slender, soft and tart
as ripe persimmon. The sun
was a day-glo tennis ball
bouncing languidly from bay to ocean.

Your mother made mint-chocolate cake.
We shared chocolate lips and tan
on your bay-view porch, ate hot dogs

with sand and salt, got boardwalk
splinters and soft ice cream.

the evening your mother brought us
to her club, potted palms and pop-calypso,
we slipped away, kissing and clinging
in her white Ford, me fumbling
with your tight party clothes.

I was so "good," wanting your sweet
white pulp, wanting to tear the nylon
skin, Maybelline smile to sobbing rags;
confused as radio static,
sentimental as old rock and roll.

Visions   BRADLEY R. STRAHAN

THE EPILOGUE

It was a dream delivered the epilogue—
    I saw the world end; I saw
Myself and you, tenacious and exposed,
    Smallest insects on the largest leaf.
A high trail coasted a ravine
    Eves could not penetrate because a wood
Hung down its slope; a fugue of water
    Startled the ear and air with distances
Around and under us, as if a flood
    Came pouring in from every quarter.
Our trail and height failed suddenly,
    Fell sheer away into a visibility
More terrible than what the trees might hide:
    Fed by a fall, wide, rising—
Was it a sea claimed all the plain
    And climbed towards us, smooth
And ungainsayable? We turned and knew now
    That no law steadied a sliding world,
For what we saw was an advancing wave
    Cresting along the height. An elate
Despair held us together silent there
    Waiting for that wall to fall and bury
Us and the love that taught us to gorget
    To fear it. I woke then to this room
Where first I heard the sounds that dogged that dream,
    Caught back from epilogue to epilogue.

The Hudson Review   CHARLES TOMLINSON

Index of Titles

Index of First Lines

Books of Poetry by Contributors

*This bibliography is included as an aid for those who wish to
locate additional poetry by authors whose work appears in the
Anthology.*

A

Aberg, William: *The Promise Of Morning.* Blue Moon Press, 1983.

Ai: *Cruelty.* Houghton Mifflin, 1973.
—*Killing Floor.* Houghton Mifflin, 1979.

Aleixandre, Vicente: *World Alone* (translated by Lewis Hyde and David Unger). Penmaen Press, 1983.

Aleshire, Joan: *Cloud Train.* Texas Tech University Press, 1982.

Alina, Marta: *Seeing Stone* (under the name of Marta Zaborska). Black Moss Press, 1978.

Allardt, Linda: *The Names Of The Survivors.* Ithaca House, 1979.
—*Seeing For You.* State Street Press, 1981.

Allen, Dick: *Anon And Various Time Machine Poems.* Delacorte Books/Delta Books, 1971.
—*Regions With No Proper Names.* St. Martin's Press, 1975.
—*Overnight In The Guesthouse Of The Mystic.* Louisiana State University Press, 1984.

Allen, James B.: *See The Lighthouse Burning.* Peter Quince, 1977.
—*Beggars Could Ride.* Seaview Publishers, 1981.
—*If Wishes Were Horses.* Seaview Publishers, 1983.

Almon, Bert: *The Return.* San Marcos Press, 1968.
—*Taking Possession.* Solo Press, 1976.
—*Poems For The Nuclear Family.* San Marcos Press, 1979.
—*Blue Sunrise.* Thistledown Press, 1980.

Amabile, George: *Blood Ties.* Sono Nis Press, 1972.
—*Open Country.* Turnstone Press, 1976.
—*Flower And Song.* Borealis Press, 1977.
—*Ideas Of Shelter.* Turnstone Press, 1981.
—*The Presence Of Fire.* McClelland & Stewart, 1982.

Anderson, Jon: *The Milky Way: Poems 1967-82.* Ecco Press, 1983.

Anderson, Maggie: *The Great Horned Owl.* Icarus Press, 1979.
—*Years That Answer.* Harper & Row, 1980.

Andrea, Marianne: *The Fifth Corner.* Mohansic Press, 1976.

Anson, John S.: *A Family Album.* Robert L. Barth, 1983.

Armand, Octavio: *Poems With Dusk* (translated by Carol Maier). Logbridge-Rhodes, 1983.

Armour, Richard: *Light Armour.* McGraw-Hill, 1954.
—*Nights With Armour.* McGraw-Hill, 1958.
—*Our Presidents.* Woodbridge Press, 1983.
—*Have You Ever Wished You Were Something Else?* Childrens Press

Astor, Susan: *Dame.* University of Georgia Press, 1980.

Atwood, Margaret: *Procedures For Underground.* Little, Brown, 1970.
—*Power Politics.* Harper & Row, 1972.
—*You Are Happy.* Harper & Row, 1973.
—*Selected Poems.* Simon and Schuster, 1977.
—*Two-Headed Poems.* Simon and Schuster, 1979.
—*True Stories.* Simon and Schuster, 1982.

B

Balazs, Mary: *The Voice Of Thy Brother's Blood.* Dawn Valley Press, 1976.
—*The Stones Refuse Their Peace.* Seven Woods Press, 1979.

Barber, Dave: *Overwater.* Cornell Press, 1983.

Barnes, Mary Jane: *The Opposite Shore.* National Poetry Association, 1961.
—*Delta Portraits.* Swordsman Publishing Co., 1962.
—*A Puff Of Smoke.* Candor Press, 1969.
—*Vignettes: American.* Henricks Association, 1976.
—*Look East Of The Mountain.* National Poetry Press, 1976.
—*Rising Tides Of Splendor.* Tri-State Bible College Press, 1976.
—*Shadows On April's Hills.* World Poetry Society Press, 1981.
—*Songs From An Islander.* Scotts Valley Printing, 1982.

Barth, R. L.: *To Be Brief: X Poems From The Latin.* Privately printed, 1982.
—*Forced-Marching To The Styx: Vietnam War Poems.* Perivale Press, 1983.
—*Anniversaries, Hours, And Other Occasions.* Privately printed, 1984.

Bartlett, Elizabeth: *Poems Of Yes And No.* Editorial Jus (Mexico), 1952.
—*Behold This Dreamer.* Editorial Jus (Mexico), 1959.
—*Poetry Concerto.* Sparrow Poetry Series, 1962.
—*It Takes Practice Not To Die.* Van Riper & Thompson, 1964.
—*Threads.* Unicorn Press, 1968.
—*Twelve-Tone Poems.* Sun Press, 1968.
—*Selected Poems.* Carrefour Books, 1970.
—*The House Of Sleep.* Autograph Editions, 1975.
—*Dialogue Of Dust.* Autograph Editions, 1977.
—*In Search Of Identity.* Autograph Editions, 1977.
—*A Zodiac Of Poems.* Autograph Editions, 1979.
—*Address In Time.* Dufour Editions, 1979.
—*Memory Is No Stranger.* Ohio University Press, 1981.
Behm, Richard: *Letters From A Cage & Other Poems.* Raspberry Press, 1976.
—*This Winter Afternoon Of Angels.* sun rise falldown artpress, 1978.
—*The Book Of Moonlight.* Moonlight Publications, 1978.
—*Simple Explanations.* Juniper Press, 1982.
—*When The Wood Begins To Move.* Jump River Press, 1982.
Bell, Marvin: *Things We Dreamt We Died For.* Stone Wall Press, 1966.
—*A Probable Volume Of Dreams.* Atheneum, 1969.
—*The Escape Into You.* Atheneum, 1971.
—*Residue Of Song.* Atheneum, 1974.
—*Stars Which See, Stars Which Do Not See.* Atheneum, 1977.
—*These Green-Going-To-Yellow.* Atheneum, 1981.
—*Segues: A Correspondence In Poetry* (with William Stafford). David R. Godine, 1983.
—*Drawn By Stones, By Earth, By Things That Have Been In The Fire.* Atheneum, 1984.
Bensko, John: *Green Soldiers.* Yale University Press, 1981.
Bergman, Roger: *Under One Roof.* High Window Press, 1979.
Berry, Ila: *Come Walk With Me.* Wuerth Press, 1979.
Bishop, W.: *Second Nature.* Tideline Press, 1980.
Blumenthal, Michael: *Sympathetic Magic.* Watermark Press, 1980.
—*Twice-Born Matches.* Viking, 1984.
Bly, Robert: *Silence In The Snowy Fields.* Wesleyan University Press, 1962.
—*The Light Around The Body.* Harper & Row, 1967.
—*Sleepers Joining Hands.* Harper & Row, 1973.
—*The Morning Glory.* Harper & Row, 1975.
—*This Body Is Made Of Camphor And Gopher Wood.* Harper & Row, 1977.
—*The Man In The Black Coat Turns.* Dial Press, 1981.
Booth, Philip: *Letter From A Distant Land.* Viking, 1956.
—*The Islanders.* Viking, 1961.
—*Weathers And Edges.* Viking, 1966.
—*Margins.* Viking, 1971.

—*Available Light.* Viking, 1976.
—*Before Sleep.* Viking/Penguin, 1980.
Bosworth, Martha: *Bright Sand.* Lemon Tree Press, 1979.
—*All The Lost Children.* Lemon Tree Press, 1981.
Bouvard, Marguerite G.: *Journeys Over Water.* Quarterly Review of Literature, 1982.
Bowers, Neal: *The Golf Ball Diver.* New Rivers Press, 1983.
Bozanic, Nick: *Wood Birds Water Stones.* Barnwood Press Cooperative, 1983.
Brosman, Catharine Savage: *Watering.* University of Georgia Press, 1972.
—*Abiding Winter.* R. L. Barth Press, 1983.
Broughton, T. Alan: *Adam's Dream.* Northeast/Juniper Press, 1975.
—*In The Face Of Descent.* Carnegie-Mellon University Press, 1975.
—*The Others We Are.* Northeast/Juniper Press, 1979.
—*Far From Home.* Carnegie-Mellon University Press, 1979.
—*Dreams Before Sleep.* Carnegie-Mellon University Press, 1982.
Bruce, Debra: *Pure Daughter.* University of Arkansas Press, 1983.
Bruchac, Joseph: *Indian Mountain.* Ithaca House, 1971.
—*Entering Onondaga.* Cold Mountain Press, 1978.
—*There Are No Trees Inside The Prison.* Blackberry Press, 1978.
—*The Good Message Of Handsome Lake.* Unicorn Press, 1979.
—*Translator's Son.* Cross-Cultural Communications Press, 1982.
—*Remembering The Dawn.* Blue Cloud Press, 1983.
Brummels, J. V.: *614 Pearl.* Abattoir Editions, 1982.
Brush, Thomas: *Opening Night.* Owl Creek Press, 1981.
Bryan, Sharon: *Salt Air.* Wesleyan University Press, 1983.
Buckley, Christopher: *Pentimento.* Bieler Press, 1980.
—*Last Rites.* Ithaca House, 1980.
—*Cider-Light.* Moving Parts Press, 1983.
—*Blue Hooks In Weather.* Moving Parts Press, 1984.
—*Five Small Meditations On Summer And Birds.* Bieler Press, 1984.
—*Blossoms & Bones: Monologues On The Life And Paintings Of Georgia O'Keeffe.* Pentagram Press, 1984.
—*Other Lives.* Ithaca House, 1984.
Buell, Frederick: *Theseus And Other Poems.* Ithaca House, 1971.
—*Full Summer.* Wesleyan University Poetry Series, 1979.
Bullis, Jerald: *Pastoral Meditation: An Eclogue.* Anglefish Press, 1970.
—*Taking Up The Serpent.* Ithaca House, 1973.
—*Orion: A Poem.* Jackpine Press, 1976.

—*Adorning The Buckhorn Helmet.* Ithaca House, 1976.
—*Inland.* Collectif Generation (Paris), 1978.
Burden, Jean: *Naked As The Glass.* October House, 1963.
—*Journey Toward Poetry.* October House, 1966.
Burns, Michael: *When All Else Failed.* Timberline Press, 1983.
Burns, Ralph: *Us.* Cleveland State University Poetry Center, 1983.
—*Windy Tuesday Nights.* Milkweed Chronicle, 1984.
Burrows, E. G.: *The Arctic Tern And Other Poems.* Grove Press, 1957.
—*Man Fishing.* Sumac Press, 1969.
—*The Crossings.* New Moon/Humble Hills Press, 1976.
—*Kiva.* Ithaca House, 1976.
—*Properties: A Play For Voices.* Quarterly Review of Literature, Poetry Series, XXI/1-2.
—*On The Road To Bailey's.* Fallen Angel Press, 1979.

C

Cairns, Scott C.: *Finding The Broken Man.* Window Press, 1982.
Carter, Jared: *Early Warning.* Barnwood Press, 1979.
—*Work, For The Night Is Coming.* Macmillan, 1981.
Cassian, Nina: *Blue Apple* (translated from the Romanian by Eva Feiler). Cross-Cultural Communications, 1981.
Cherry, Kelly: *Lovers And Agnostics.* Red Clay Books, 1975.
—*Relativity: A Point Of View.* Louisiana State University Press, 1977.
—*Songs For A Soviet Composer.* Singing Wind Press, 1980.
Childress, William: *Burning The Years.* The Smith/Horizon Press, 1971.
—*Lobo.* Barlenmir Press, 1972.
Citino, David: *Last Rites And Other Poems.* Ohio State University Press, 1980.
—*The Appassionata Poems.* Cleveland State University Poetry Center, 1983.
Clampitt, Amy: *Multitudes, Multitudes.* Washington Street Press, 1974.
—*The Kingfisher.* Alfred A. Knopf, 1983.
Clarke, George Elliott: *Saltwater Spirituals And Deeper Blues.* Pottersfield Press, 1983.
Coffin, Lyn: *Human Trappings.* Abattoir Editions, 1980.
—*The Poetry Of Wickedness.* Ithaca House, 1981.
Cohen, Marion: *The Weirdest Is The Sphere.* Seven Woods Press, 1979.
—*The Temper Tantrum Book.* WordWorker, 1983.
—*A Child's Grave.* Centering, 1983.
—*These Covers To Crawl Under.* WordWorker, 1983.
—*Seeking The Fourth Perpendicular.* Warthog Press, 1984.

Conn, Jan E.: *Road Of Smoke.* Colophon Books, 1983.
—*Red Shoes In The Rain.* Fiddlehead Poetry Books, 1984.
Cook, Paul: *Casa De Luz.* Porch Press, 1979.
Cooley, Peter: *The Company Of Strangers.* University of Missouri Press, 1975.
—*The Room Where Summer Ends.* Carnegie-Mellon University Press, 1979.
—*Nightseasons.* Carnegie-Mellon University Press, 1983.
Corey, Stephen: *The Last Magician.* Water Mark Press, 1981.
—*Fighting Death.* State Street Press, 1983.
Cosier, Tony: *With The Sun And Moon.* Privately printed, 1979.
—*The Verse Master.* Privately printed, 1983.
Crooker, Barbara: *Writing Home.* Gehry Press, 1983.
Curtis, Tony: *Preparations.* 1980.
—*Letting Go.* Poetry Wales Press, 1983.

D

Dana, Robert: *My Glass Brother & Other Poems.* Constance Press, 1957.
—*The Dark Flags Of Waking.* Qara Press, 1964.
—*Journeys From The Skin.* Hundred Pound Press, 1966.
—*Some Versions Of Silence.* W. W. Norton, 1967.
—*The Power Of The Visible.* Swallow Press, 1971.
—*In A Fugitive Season.* Swallow Press, 1980.
—*What The Stones Know.* Seamark Press, 1982.
Daniels, Jim: *On The Line.* Signpost Press, 1981.
Davis, William Virgil: *One Way To Reconstruct The Scene.* Yale University Press, 1980.
—*The Dark Hours.* Calliope Press, 1983.
Davison, Peter: *The Breaking Of The Day And Other Poems.* Yale University Press, 1964.
—*The City And The Island.* Atheneum, 1966.
—*Pretending To Be Asleep.* Atheneum, 1970.
—*Walking The Boundaries.* Atheneum, 1974.
—*A Voice In The Mountain.* Atheneum, 1977.
—*Barn Fever And Other Poems.* Atheneum, 1981.
Dawber, Diane: *Cankerville.* Borealis Press, 1984.
Deal, Susan Strayer: *No Moving Parts.* Ahsahta Press, 1980.
De Bolt, William Walter: *Second Spring.* Candor Press, 1976.
—*Mist From The Earth.* Candor Press, 1980.
—*Bricks Without Straw.* Candor Press, 1981.
DeFoe, Mark: *Bringing Home Breakfast.* Black Willow Press, 1982.
Dennis, Carl: *A House Of My Own.* George Braziller, 1974.
—*Climbing Down.* George Braziller, 1976.
—*Signs And Wonders.* Princeton University Press, 1979.
Der Hovanessian, Diana: *How To Choose Your Past.* Ararat Press, 1979.
Diara, Schavi Mali: *Growing Together.* Agascha Productions, 1973.
Dickson, John: *Victoria Hotel.* Chicago Review Press, 1979.

Diorio, Margaret Toarello: *Listening.* Falcon Books, 1970.
—*Bringing In The Plants.* Icarus Press, 1980.
Di Piero, W. S.: *Country Of Survivors.* Rasmussen Publishing Co., 1975.
—*The First Hour.* Abattoir Editions, 1982.
—*The Only Dangerous Thing.* Elpenor Books, 1983.
Dodd, Wayne: *We Will Wear White Roses.* Best Cellar Press, 1974.
—*Made In America.* Croissant & Co., 1975.
—*The Names You Gave It.* Louisiana State University Press, 1981.
—*The General Mule Poems.* Juniper Press, 1982.
Donnelly, Dorothy: *Trio In A Mirror.* University of Arizona Press, 1960.
—*Houses.* Burning Deck Press, 1970.
—*Kudzu And Other Poems New And Selected.* Pourboire Press, 1978.
Dove, Rita: *The Yellow House On The Corner.* Carnegie-Mellon University Press, 1980.
—*Museum.* Carnegie-Mellon University Press, 1983.
Doyle, Suzanne J.: *Sweeter For The Bark.* Robert Barth, Publisher, 1982.
Driscoll, Jack: *The Language Of Bone.* Spring Valley Press, 1980.
—*Twin Sons Of Different Mirrors* (with Bill Meissner). Spring Valley Press, 1984.
Dunn, Millard: *Engraved On Air.* Kentucky Arts Council, 1983.
Duval, Quinton—*Guerilla Letters.* Quarterly West Press, 1978.
—*Dinner Music.* Lost Roads Press, 1984.

E

Eaton, Charles Edward: *The Bright Plain.* University of North Carolina Press, 1942.
—*The Shadow Of The Swimmer.* Fine Editions Press, 1951.
—*The Greenhouse In The Garden.* Twayne Publishers, 1955.
—*Countermoves.* Abelard-Schuman, 1962.
—*On The Edge Of The Knife.* Abelard-Schuman, 1970.
—*The Man In The Green Chair.* A. S. Barnes & Co., 1977.
—*Colophon Of The Rover.* A. S. Barnes & Co., 1980.
—*The Thing King.* Cornwall Books, 1983.
Eberhart, Richard: *Selected Poems.* Oxford University Press, 1951.
—*Collected Poems, 1930-1960.* Oxford University Press, 1960.
—*Quarry: New Poems.* Oxford University Press, 1964.
—*Selected Poems, 1930-1965.* New Directions, 1966.
—*Shifts Of Being: Poems.* Oxford University Press, 1968.
—*Fields Of Grace.* Oxford University Press, 1972.
—*Poem To Poets.* Penmaen Press, 1975.
—*Collected Poems, 1930-1976.* Oxford University Press, 1976.
—*Ways Of Light.* Oxford University Press, 1980.
—*Four Poems.* Palaemon Press, 1980.
—*Survivors.* Boa Editions, 1980.
—*New Hampshire/Nine Poems.* Pym-Randall Press, 1980.
—*Chocorua.* Nadja Press, 1981.
—*Florida Poems.* Konglomerati Press, 1981.
—*The Long Reach.* New Directions, 1984.
Ehrhart, W. D.: *The Samisdat Poems.* Samisdat Press, 1980.
—*The Awkward Silence.* Northwoods Press, 1980.
—*Matters Of The Heart.* Adastra Press, 1981.
—*Channel Fever.* Backstreet Editions, 1982.
Eliraz, Israel: *Via Bethlehem.* Sifriat Poalim (Tel Aviv), 1980.
—*Five Chapters.* Dvir Co., 1981.
—*Things Within Things.* Sifriat Poalim (Tel Aviv), 1982.
Elson, Virginia: *Where In The Sun To Stand.* State Street Press, 1982.
Emanuel, Lynn: *Oblique Light.* Slow Loris Press, 1978.
Endrezze-Danielson, Anita: *Burning The Fields.* Confluence Press, 1983.
—*The North People.* Blue Cloud Quarterly Press, 1983.
Engels, John: *The Homer Mitchell Place.* University of Pittsburgh Press, 1968.
—*Signals From The Safety Coffin.* University of Pittsburgh Press, 1975.
—*Blood Mountain.* University of Pittsburgh Press, 1977.
—*Vivaldi In Early Fall.* University of Georgia Press, 1981.
—*Weather-Fear: New & Selected Poems, 1958-1982.* University of Georgia Press, 1983.
Epstein, Daniel Mark: *No Vacancies In Hell.* Liveright/Norton, 1973.
—*Young Men's Gold.* Overlook/Viking, 1978.
—*The Book Of Fortune.* Overlook/Viking, 1982.
Eshleman, Clayton: *Fracture.* Black Sparrow Press, 1983.
Etter, Dave: *Go Read The River.* University of Nebraska Press, 1966.
—*The Last Train To Prophetstown.* University of Nebraska Press, 1968.
—*Strawberries.* Juniper Books, 1970.
—*Voyages To The Inland Sea* (with Lisel Mueller and John Knoepfle). University of Wisconsin-La Crosse, 1971.
—*Crabtree's Woman.* BkMk Press, 1972.
—*Well You Needn't.* Raindust Press, 1975.
—*Bright Mississippi.* Juniper Press, 1975.
—*Central Standard Time: New And Selected Poems.* BkMk Press, 1978.
—*Alliance, Illinois.* Kylix Press, 1978.
—*Open To The Wind.* Uzzano Press, 1978.
—*Riding The Rock Island Through Kansas.* Wolfsong Press, 1979.
—*Cornfields.* Spoon River Poetry Press, 1980.
—*West Of Chicago.* Spoon River Poetry Press, 1981.

—*Boondocks.* Uzzano Press, 1982.
—*Alliance, Illinois* (complete edition). Spoon River Poetry Press, 1983.
Exler, Samuel: *Ambition, Fertility, Loneliness.* Lintel, 1982.

F

Fairchild, B. H.: *C&W Machine Works.* Trilobite Press, 1983.
Farnsworth, Robert: *Three Or Four Hills And A Cloud.* Wesleyan University Press, 1982.
Farrar, Winifred Hamrick: *Another Fountain.* Privately printed, 1940.
—*Thru Our Guns.* Privately printed, 1945.
—*Rumshinsky's Hat.* Thomas Yoseloff, 1964.
—*Cry Life.* South & West, Inc., 1968.
—*The Seeking Spirit.* South & West, Inc., 1974.
Feinberg, (Harvey) Chaim: *Cock Of The Morning.* Crossing Press, 1972.
Feldman, Alan: *The Happy Genius.* Sun, 1978.
Feldman, Ruth: *The Ambition Of Ghosts.* Green River Press, 1979.
—*Poesie Di Ruth Feldman* (bilingual). Editrice La Giuntina (Florence), 1981.
Fifer, Ken: *Falling Man.* Ithaca House, 1979.
Finch, Robert: *Poems.* Oxford University Press, 1946.
—*The Strength Of The Hills.* McClelland and Stewart, 1948.
—*Acis In Oxford.* University of Toronto Press, 1961.
—*Dover Beach Revisited.* Macmillan, 1961.
—*Silverthorn Bush.* Macmillan, 1966.
—*Variations And Theme.* Porcupine's Quill, 1980.
—*Has And Is.* Porcupine's Quill, 1981.
—*Twelve For Christmas.* Porcupine's Quill, 1982.
—*The Grand Duke Of Moscow's Favourite Solo.* Porcupine's Quill, 1983.
Fishman, Charles: *Aurora.* Tree Books, 1974.
—*Mortal Companions.* Pleasure Dome Press, 1977.
—*Warm-Blooded Animals.* Juniper Books, 1977.
Flanders, Jane: *Leaving And Coming Home.* Quarterly Review of Literature, 1980.
—*The Students Of Snow.* University of Massachusetts Press, 1982.
Flanner, Hildegarde: *Young Girl.* Nash, 1920.
—*A Tree In Bloom.* Grabhorn, 1924.
—*Time's Profile.* Macmillan, 1929.
—*If There Is Time.* New Directions, 1942.
—*In Native Light.* Privately printed, 1970.
—*The Hearkening Eye.* Ahsahta Press, 1979.
Frost, Carol: *The Salt Lesson.* Graywolf Press, 1976.
—*Liar's Dice.* Ithaca House, 1978.
—*Cold Frame.* Owl Creek Press, 1982.
—*The Fearful Child.* Ithaca House, 1983.
Frumkin, Gene: *The Hawk And The Lizard.* Swallow Press, 1963.
—*The Orange Tree.* Cyfoeth Press, 1965.
—*The Rainbow-Walker.* Grasshopper Press, 1969.

—*Dostoevsky & Other Nature Poems.* Solo Press, 1972.
—*Locust Cry: Poems 1958-65.* San Marcos Press, 1973.
—*The Mystic Writing-Pad.* Red Hill Press, 1977.
—*Loops.* San Marcos Press, 1979.
—*Clouds And Red Earth.* Swallow Press, 1982.
Fulton, Alice: *Dance Script With Electric Ballerina.* University of Pennsylvania Press, 1983.
Funge, Robert: *The Lie The Lamb Knows.* Spoon River Poetry Press, 1979.

G

Ghigna, Charles: *Plastic Tears.* Dorrance & Co., 1973.
—*Stables.* Creekwood Press, 1974.
—*Cockroach.* Contemporary Drama Service, 1977.
—*Divers And Other Poems.* Creekwood Press, 1978.
—*Circus.* Creekwood Press, 1979.
Ghiselin, Brewster: *Against the Circle.* Dutton, 1946.
—*The Nets.* Dutton, 1955.
—*Country of The Minotaur.* University of Utah Press, 1970.
—*Light.* Abattoir Editions, 1978.
—*Windrose: Poems 1929-1979.* University of Utah Press, 1980.
Gibbons, Reginald: *Roofs Voices Roads.* Quarterly Review of Literature, 1979.
—*The Ruined Motel.* Houghton Mifflin Co., 1981.
Gilbert, Celia: *Queen Of Darkness.* Viking Press, 1977.
—*Bonfire.* Alice James Books, 1983.
Gill, Evalyn P.: *Dialogue.* Green River Press, 1980.
Glickman, Susan: *Complicity.* Signal Editions/Vehicule Press, 1983.
Goldensohn, Lorrie: *Dreamwork.* Porch Publications, 1980.
—*The Tether.* L'Epervier Press, 1982.
Goldman, Beate: *A Well-Behaved Skeptic.* Celadon Press, 1978.
—*Letters To A Stranger.* Washington Writers' Publishing House, 1981.
Goldowsky, Barbara: *Ferry To Nirvana.* National Writers Press, 1983.
Golembiewski, Alison: *The Bone Orchard.* Porch Publications, 1980.
Gom, Leona: *Kindling.* Fiddlehead Poetry Books, 1972
—*The Singletree.* Sono Nis Press, 1975.
—*North.* League of Canadian Poets, 1980.
—*Land Of The Peace.* Thistledown Press, 1980.
Goodenough, J. B.: *Hill Country.* Cleveland State University Press, 1984.
Gordett, Marea: *Freeze Tag.* Wesleyan University Press, 1984.
Graham, Neile: *Travelling In Place* (with Harold Rhenisch). Saults and Pollard, 1980.
—*Seven Robins.* Penumbra Press, 1983.

Greenway, William: *Pressure Under Grace.* Breitenbush Books, 1982.

Gregerson, Linda: *Fire In The Conservatory.* Dragon Gate, 1982.

Gregg, Linda: *Too Bright To See.* Graywolf Press, 1981.
—*Eight Poems.* Graywolf Press, 1982.

Griffin, Walter: *Bloodlines.* Windless Orchard Press, 1972.
—*Nightmusic.* Pale Horse Press, 1974.
—*Machineworks.* Sweetwater Press, 1976.
—*Port Authority.* Brevity Press, 1976.
—*Skulldreamer.* Border Mountain Press, 1977.
—*The Dark Eaters.* Long Run Press, 1982.

Grivich, Peter: *Four Poets.* Medicine Wheel Press, 1983.

Grutzmacher, Harold M.: *A Giant Of My World.* Golden Quill Press, 1960.
—*Generations* (with Stephen Grutzmacher). Spoon River Poetry Press, 1983.

Guernsey, Bruce: *January Thaw.* University of Pittsburgh Press, 1982.

Gustafson, Ralph: *The Golden Chalice,* 1935.
—*Alfred The Great,* 1937.
—*Epithalamium In Time Of War,* 1941.
—*Lyrics Unromantic,* 1942.
—*Flight Into Darkness,* 1944.
—*Rivers Among Rocks,* 1960.
—*Rocky Mountain Poems,* 1960.
—*Sift In An Hourglass,* 1966.
—*Ixion's Wheel,* 1969.
—*Selected Poems,* 1972.
—*Theme & Variations For Sounding Brass,* 1972.
—*Fire On Stone,* 1974.
—*Corners In The Glass,* 1977.
—*Soviet Poems,* 1978.
—*Sequences,* 1979.
—*Gradations Of Grandeur,* 1979.
—*Landscape With Rain,* 1980.
—*Conflicts Of Spring,* 1981.
—*At The Ocean's Verge,* 1982.

H

Hadas, Rachel: *Starting From Troy.* David R. Godine, 1975.
—*Slow Transparency.* Wesleyan University Press, 1983.

Haines, John: *Winter News.* Wesleyan University Press, 1966.
—*The Stone Harp.* Wesleyan University Press, 1971.
—*Twenty Poems.* Unicorn Press, 1971.
—*Leaves And Ashes.* Kayak Press, 1974.
—*In Five Years' Time.* Smokeroot Press, 1976.
—*Cicada.* Wesleyan University Press, 1977.
—*In A Dusty Light.* Graywolf Press, 1977.
—*News From The Glacier.* Wesleyan University Press, 1982.

Hall, James B.: *The Hunt Within.* Louisiana State University Press, 1973.

Hall, Jim: *The Lady From The Dark Green Hills.* Carnegie-Mellon University Press, 1976.

—*The Mating Reflex.* Carnegie-Mellon University Press, 1980.

Hall, Joan Joffe: *The Rift Zone.* Curbstone Press, 1978.
—*The Aerialist's Fall.* Ziesing Brothers, 1981.

Hall, Randall L.: *Mosaic.* Utah State Poetry Society, 1979.

Halpern, Daniel: *Traveling On Credit.* Viking/Compass, 1972.
—*Street Fire.* Viking Press, 1975.
—*Life Among Others.* Viking/Penguin, 1978.
—*Seasonal Rights.* Viking/Penguin, 1983.

Hamill, Sam: *Petroglyphs.* Three Rivers Press, 1975.
—*The Calling Across Forever.* Copper Canyon Press, 1976.
—*The Book Of Elegiac Geography.* Bookstore Press, 1978.
—*Trianda.* Copper Canyon Press, 1978.
—*animae.* Copper Canyon Press, 1980.
—*Fatal Pleasure.* Breitenbush Books, 1983.

Hankla, Cathryn: *Phenomena.* University of Missouri Press, 1983.

Hanson, Howard G.: *Ageless Maze.* Robert Allen, 1963.
—*Future Coin Or Climber.* John F. Blair, 1967.

Hart, Paul: *A Crossing.* University Microfilms, 1983.

Hausman, Gerald: *New Marlboro Stage.* Bookstore Press, 1971.
—*Circle Meadow.* Bookstore Press, 1972.
—*Sitting On The Blue-Eyed Bear: Navajo Myths And Legends.* Lawrence Hill & Co., 1975.
—*Night Herding Song.* Copper Canyon Press, 1979.
—*Runners.* Sunstone Press, 1984.

Hay, Sara Henderson: *Field Of Honor.* Kaleidograph Press, 1933.
—*This, My Letter.* Alfred A. Knopf, 1939.
—*The Delicate Balance.* Charles Scribner's Sons, 1951.
—*The Stone And The Shell.* University of Pittsburgh Press, 1959.
—*Story Hour.* Doubleday, 1963/1982.
—*A Footing On This Earth.* Doubleday, 1966.

Hayes, Ann: *For Sally Barnes.* Privately printed, 1963.
—*Amo Ergo Sum, Amo Ergo Est.* 1969.
—*The Dancer's Step.* Three Rivers Press, 1973.
—*The Living And The Dead.* Carnegie-Mellon University Press, 1975.
—*Witness: How All Occasions . . .* Rook Press, 1977.

Hazard, James: *Fire In Whiting, Indiana.* Juniper Press, 1983.

Hearst, James: *Country Men.* Prairie Press, 1937.
—*The Sun At Noon.* Prairie Press, 1943.
—*Man And His Field.* Alan Swallow, 1951.
—*Limited View.* Prairie Press, 1962.
—*A Single Focus.* Prairie Press, 1967.
—*Heartland: Poets Of The Midwest.* Northern Illinois University Press, 1967.
—*Voyages To The Inland Sea, II: Essays And Poems By Felix Pollak, James Hearst, John Woods.* University of Wisconsin-La Crosse, 1972.

—*Dry Leaves.* Ragnarok Press, 1975.
—*Shaken By Leaf-Fall.* Kylix Press, 1976.
—*Proved By Trial.* Juniper Press, 1977.
—*Late Harvest: Plains And Prairie Poets.* BkMk Press, 1977.
—*Snake In The Strawberries.* Iowa State University Press, 1979.
—*Landmark And Other Poems.* JiFi Print, 1979.
Hedin, Robert: *Snow Country.* Copper Canyon Press, 1975.
—*At The Home-Altar.* Copper Canyon Press, 1978.
—*On The Day Of Bulls.* Jawbone Press, 1979.
—*County O.* Copper Canyon Press, 1984.
Heffernan, Michael: *Booking Passage.* BkMk Press, 1973.
—*In Front Of All These People.* Blue Period Books, 1977.
—*A Figure Of Plain Force.* Chowder Chapbooks, 1978.
—*The Cry Of Oliver Hardy.* University of Georgia Press, 1979.
—*To The Wreakers Of Havoc.* University of Georgia Press, 1984.
Hennessy, Madeleine: *Pavor Nocturnus And Other Poems.* Washout Publishing Co., 1979.
Heyen, William: *Depth Of Field.* Louisiana State University Press, 1970.
—*Noise In The Trees.* Vanguard Press, 1974.
—*The Swastika Poems.* Vanguard Press, 1977.
—*Long Island Light.* Vanguard Press, 1979.
—*My Holocaust Songs.* William B. Ewert, 1980.
—*The City Parables.* Croissant & Co., 1980.
—*Lord Dragonfly: Five Sequences.* Vanguard Press, 1981.
—*The Trains.* Metacom Press, 1981.
—*Along This Water.* Tamarack Editions, 1983.
—*Erika: Poems Of The Holocaust.* Vanguard Press, 1984.
Hilberry, Conrad: *Encounter On Burrows Hill.* Ohio University Press, 1968.
—*Rust.* Ohio University Press, 1974.
—*Man In The Attic.* Bits Press, 1980.
—*Housemarks.* Perishable Press, 1980.
—*The Moon Seen As A Slice Of Pineapple.* University of Georgia Press, 1984.
Hillman, Brenda: *The Train To Paris.* Penumbra Press, 1980.
—*Coffee, 3 A.M.* Penumbra Press, 1982.
—*Ellipsis.* Wesleyan University Press, 1984.
Hinrichsen, Dennis: *The Attraction Of Heavenly Bodies.* Wesleyan University Press, 1983.
Hirsch, Edward: *For The Sleepwalkers.* Alfred A. Knopf, 1981.
Hoeft, Robert D.: *Exhibits At A Retirement Home.* Wings Press, 1982.
—*Tools.* Mosaic Press, 1983.
Hoff, Muriel: *Animal Alphabet Rhymes For Children Up To Ninety.* Inter-Collegiate Press.
Holden, Jonathan: *Falling From Stardom.* Carnegie-Mellon University Press, 1983.
—*Leverage.* University Press of Virginia, 1984.
Holland, William: *How Us White Folks Discovered Rock And Roll.* Some of Us Press, 1973.
—*Snapshot.* Dryad Press, 1984.

Hoover, Paul: *Letter To Einstein Beginning Dear Albert.* Yellow Press, 1979.
—*Somebody Talks A Lot.* Yellow Press, 1982.
—*Nervous Songs.* L'Epervier Press (forthcoming)
Horne, Lewis: *The Seventh Day.* Thistledown Press, 1982.
Hovde, A. J.: *Selected Poems.* Fairhaven College Press, 1981.
Huddle, David: *Paper Boy.* University of Pittsburgh Press, 1979.
Hutchinson, Robert: *The Kitchen Dance.* Alan Swallow, 1950.
—*Standing Still While Traffic Moved About Me.* Eakins Press, 1971.

I

Inez, Colette: *The Woman Who Loved Worms.* Doubleday, 1972.
—*Alive And Taking Names.* Ohio University Press, 1977.
—*Eight Minutes From The Sun.* Saturday Press, 1983.

J

Jackson, Richard: *Part Of The Story.* Grove Press, 1983.
James, David: *A Heart Out Of This World.* Carnegie-Mellon University Press, 1984.
Jason, Philip K.: *Thawing Out.* Dryad Press, 1979.
—*Near The Fire.* Dryad Press, 1983.
Jennings, Kate: *Second Sight.* Iron Mountain Press, 1976.
—*Thirtieth Year To Heaven.* Jackpine Press, 1980.
Johnson, Denis: *The Man Among The Seals.* Stone Wall Press, 1969.
—*Inner Weather.* Graywolf Press, 1976.
—*The Incognito Lounge.* Random House, 1982.
—*Angels.* Alfred A. Knopf, 1983.
Johnson, Thomas: *Swerving Straight: Poems Selected & New.* Alembic Press, 1981.
Josephs, Laurence: *Cold Water Morning.* Skidmore College, 1964.
—*Six Elegies.* Greenfield Review Press, 1973.
—*The Skidmore Poems.* Skidmore College, 1975.
Juergensen, Hans: *I Feed You From My Cup.* Quinnipiac College, 1958.
—*In Need For Names.* Linden Press, 1961.
—*Existential Canon.* South and West, 1965.
—*Florida Montage.* South and West, 1967.
—*Sermons From The Ammunition Hatch Of The Ship Of Fools.* Vagabond Press, 1968.
—*From The Divide.* Olivant Press, 1970.
—*Hebraic Moods.* Olivant Press, 1972.
—*Journey Toward The Roots.* Valkyrie Press, 1976.
—*California Frescoes.* American Studies Press, 1980.
—*The Record Of A Green Planet.* Linden Press, 1982.

—*Fire-Tested.* Lieb-Schott Publications, 1983.
—*Roma.* Serious Press/Konglomerati, 1984.
Justice, Donald: *The Summer Anniversaries.* Wesleyan University Press, 1960.
—*Night Light.* Wesleyan University Press, 1967.
—*Departures.* Atheneum, 1973.
—*Selected Poems.* Atheneum, 1979.

K

Kane, Katherine: *Ferry All The Way Up.* Porch Publications, 1979.
Katrovas, Richard: *Green Dragons.* Wesleyan University Press, 1983.
Katz, Susan: *The Separate Sides Of Need.* Song Press, 1983.
—*Two Halves Of The Same Silence.* Confluence Press, 1984.
Katz-Levine, Judy: *The Umpire, And Other Masks.* 5 Trees Press, 1976.
—*Carpenter.* Firefly Press, 1979.
—*Speaking With Deaf-Blind Children.* Free Beginning Press, 1983.
Kauffman, Janet: *The Weather Book.* Texas Tech University Press, 1981.
Keithley, George: *The Donner Party.* George Braziller, 1972.
—*Song In A Strange Land.* George Braziller, 1974.
Kitchen, Judith: *Upstairs Window.* Tamarack Press, 1983.
Komunyakaa, Yusef: *Lost In The Bonewheel Factory.* Lynx House Press, 1979.
—*Copacetic.* Wesleyan University Press, 1984.
Kramer, Aaron: *Another Fountain.* Edward Rosner Press, 1940.
—*Till The Grass Is Ripe For Dancing.* Harbinger House, 1943.
—*Thru Our Guns.* Privately printed, 1945.
—*The Glass Mountain.* Beechhurst Press, 1946.
—*The Thunder Of The Grass.* International Publishers, 1948.
—*The Golden Trumpet.* International Publishers, 1949.
—*Thru Every Window.* William-Frederick Press, 1950.
—*Denmark Vesey.* Privately printed, 1952.
—*Roll The Forbidden Drums!* Cameron & Kahn, 1954.
—*The Tune Of The Calliope.* Thomas Yoseloff, 1958.
—*Moses.* O'Hare Books, 1962.
—*Rumshinsky's Hat.* Thomas Yoseloff, 1964.
—*Henry At The Grating.* Folklore Center, 1968.
—*On The Way To Palermo.* A. S. Barnes & Co., 1973.
—*O Golden Land!* Dowling College Press, 1976.
—*Carousel Parkway.* A. S. Barnes & Co., 1980.
—*In Wicked Times.* Black Buzzard Press, 1983.
—*The Burning Bush: Poems And Other Writings, 1940-1980.* Cornwall Books, 1983.
Kuzma, Greg: *Adirondacks.* Bear Claw Press, 1978.
—*Village Journal.* Best Cellar Press, 1978.

—*For My Brother.* Abattoir Editions, 1981.
—*Of China And Of Greece.* Sun, 1983.
—*A Horse Of A Different Color.* Illuminati, 1983.
—*Everyday Life.* Spoon River Poetry Press, 1983.

L

LaGattuta, Margo: *Diversion Road.* State Street Press, 1983.
Lake, Paul: *Bull Dancing.* New Poets Series, 1977.
Lane, John: *Quarries.* Briarpatch Press, 1984.
—*The Small Losses.* Charles Street Press, 1984.
Lane, Patrick: *Poems, New & Selected.* Oxford University Press, 1978.
—*The Measure.* Black Moss Press, 1981.
—*The Mother.* Oxford University Press, 1982.
—*Women In The Dust.* Mosaic Press, 1983.
Layton, Irving: *The Improved Binoculars.* Jargon Press, 1956.
—*The Collected Poems.* McClelland & Stewart, 1971.
—*For My Neighbours In Hell.* Mosaic Press, 1979.
—*A Wild Peculiar Joy: Selected Poems.* McClelland & Stewart, 1982.
—*The Gucci Bag.* McClelland & Stewart, 1983.
Lee, David: *The Porcine Legacy.* Copper Canyon Press, 1978.
—*Driving And Drinking.* Copper Canyon Press, 1979.
—*Shadow Weaver.* Jawbone Press, 1983.
—*The Porcine Canticles.* Copper Canyon Press, 1984.
Lemm, Richard: *Dancing In Asylum.* Pottersfield Press, 1982.
Lepore, Dominick J.: *The Praise And The Praised.* Bruce Humphries, 1955.
—*Within His Walls.* Branden Press, 1968.
Levenson, Christopher: *Cairns.* Chatto & Windus (England), 1969.
—*Stills.* Chatto & Windus (England), 1972.
—*Into The Open.* Golden Dog Press, 1977.
—*The Journey Back.* Sesame Press, 1978.
Levine, Ellen: *Notes On The Pumpkin.* Lynx House Press, 1979.
Levine, Philip: *On The Edge.* Stone Wall Press, 1963.
—*Not This Pig.* Wesleyan University Press, 1968.
—*Red Dust.* Kayak Press, 1971.
—*Pili's Wall.* Unicorn Press, 1971.
—*They Feed The Lion.* Atheneum, 1972.
—*1933.* Atheneum, 1974.
—*The Names Of The Lost.* Atheneum, 1976.
—*Ashes.* Atheneum, 1979.
—*7 Years From Somewhere.* Atheneum, 1979.
—*One For The Rose.* Atheneum, 1981.
Libbey, Elizabeth: *The Crowd Inside.* Carnegie-Mellon University Press, 1978.
—*Songs Of A Returning Soul.* Carnegie-Mellon University Press, 1981.
Lieberman, Laurence: *The Unblinding.* Macmillan, 1968.

—*The Osprey Suicides.* Macmillan, 1973.
—*God's Measurements.* Macmillan, 1980.
—*Eros At The World Kite Pageant: Poems 1979-1982.* Macmillan, 1983.
Litsey, Sarah: *Legend.* Privately printed, 1936.
—*For The Lonely.* Favil Press (England), 1937.
—*The Oldest April.* Golden Quill Press, 1957.
—*Toward Mystery.* Golden Quill Press, 1974.
London, Jonathan: *In A Season Of Birds: Poems For Maureen.* Mudborn Press, 1979.
—*Between The Sun And The Moon.* Lawton Press, 1979.
—*All My Roads.* Beehive Press, 1982.
Long, Virginia: *Song Of America.* Aquarian Truth Press, 1976.
—*The Armadillo From Amarillo.* Image Press, 1980.
Long, Virginia Love: *After The Ifaluk And Other Poems.* Thorp Springs Press, 1975.
—*The Gallows Lord.* John F. Blair, 1978.
Lott, Rick: *Digging For Shark Teeth.* Anhinga Press, 1984.
Louthan, Robert: *Shrunken Planets.* Alice James Books, 1980.
—*Living In Code.* University of Pittsburgh Press, 1983.
Lowe, Jonathan F.: *Practical Insanity.* S.W. Press, 1982.
Lowenstein, Robert: *Twice A Boy.* Privately printed, 1982.
Ludvigson, Susan: *Step Carefully In Night Grass* (under the name of Susan Bartels). John F. Blair, 1974.
—*The Wisconsin Woman.* Porch Publications, 1980.
—*Northern Lights.* Louisiana State University Press, 1981.
—*The Swimmer.* Louisiana State University Press, 1984.

M

MacSween, R. J.: *The Forgotten World.* Antigonish Press, 1971.
—*Double Shadows.* Antigonish Press, 1973.
—*The Secret City.* Antigonish Press, 1977.
Maino, Jeannette: *Speeding Through Lost Landscapes.* Compass Maps, 1977.
—*Islands.* Compass Maps, 1981.
Mangan, Kathy: *Ragged Alphabet.* Rook Press, 1978.
Matthews, William: *Ruining The New Road.* Random House, 1970.
—*Sleek For The Long Flight.* Random House, 1972.
—*Sticks & Stones.* Pentagram Press, 1975.
—*Rising And Falling.* Atlantic/Little, Brown, 1979.
—*Flood.* Atlantic/Little, Brown, 1982.
Mayhall, Jane: *Givers & Takers, 1.* Eakins Press, 1968.
—*Givers & Takers, 2.* Eakins Press, 1973.
Mazur, Gail: *Nightfire.* David R. Godine, 1978.
Mazzaro, Jerome: *Changing The Windows.* Ohio

University Press, 1966.
McAleavey, David: *Sterling 403.* Ithaca House, 1971.
—*The Forty Days.* Ithaca House, 1975.
—*Shrine, Shelter, Cave.* Ithaca House, 1980.
McCarriston, Linda: *Talking Soft Dutch.* Texas Tech University Press, 1984.
McClane, Kenneth A.: *Out Beyond The Bay.* Ithaca House, 1975.
—*Moons And Low Times.* Ithaca House, 1978.
—*To Hear The River.* West End Press, 1981.
—*At Winter's End.* Emerson Hall, 1982.
—*These Halves Are Whole.* Black Willow Chapbook Series, 1983.
McCloskey, Mark: *Goodbye, But Listen.* Vanderbilt University Press, 1968.
—*All That Mattered.* Greenfield Review Press, 1977.
—*The Secret Documents Of America.* Red Hill Press, 1977.
McCullough, Ken: *The Easy Wreckage.* Seamark Press, 1971.
—*Migrations.* Stone-Marrow Press, 1973.
—*Creosote.* Seamark Press, 1976.
—*Elegy For Old Anna.* Seamark Press, 1984.
McCurdy, Harold G.: *A Straw Flute.* Meredith College, 1946.
—*The Chastening Of Narcissus.* John F. Blair, 1970.
—*Novus Ordo Seclorum.* Privately printed, 1981.
—*And Then The Sky Turned Blue.* Briarpatch Press, 1982.
McFarland, Ron: *Certain Women.* Confluence Press, 1977.
McFee, Michael: *Plain Air.* University Presses of Florida, 1983.
McGann, Jerome: *Air Heart Sermons.* Pasdeloup Press, 1975.
—*Writing Home* (with Janet Kauffman). Coldwater Press, 1978.
—*Nerves In Patterns* (with James Kahn). X Press, 1978.
McKee, Louis: *Schuylkill County.* Wampeter Press.
McMullen, Richard E.: *Chicken Beacon.* Street Fiction Press, 1975.
—*Trying To Get Out.* Crowfoot Press, 1981.
McNair, Wesley: *The Faces Of Americans In 1853.* University of Missouri Press, 1983.
McQuilkin, Rennie: *An Astonishment And An Hissing.* Texas Review, 1982.
Meinke, Peter: *The Night Train And The Golden Bird.* University of Pittsburgh Press, 1977.
—*Trying To Surprise God.* University of Pittsburgh Press, 1981.
Melfi, Mary: *The Dance, The Cage And The Horse.* D Press, 1976.
—*A Queen Is Holding A Mummified Cat.* Guernica Editions, 1982.
—*A Bride In Three Acts.* Guernica Editions, 1983.
Middleton, David E.: *Reliquiae.* R. L. Barth Press, 1983.
Miller, Aaron: *In The Eye.* Writers' Workshop (India), 1961.
Miller, Leslie Adrienne: *Fortissimo.* Narcissus Chapbook Series, 1978.

—*Hanging On The Sunburned Arm Of Some Home Boy* (with Matthew Graham). Domino Press, 1982.

Miller, Patrick: *Line For Line: Poems, A Story & Type.* Privately printed, 1979.

Mills, Robert: *Brown Bag.* Spoon River Poetry Press, 1979.
—*Toward Sunset At A Great Height.* Spoon River Poetry Press, 1983.

Moffi, Larry: *10 Poems 10.* Stanboy Press, 1976.
—*Homing In.* Ridge Road Press, 1977.
—*A Simple Progression.* Ampersand Press, 1982.

Moore, Barbara: *The Passionate City.* W. D. Hoffstadt and Sons, 1979.

Moran, Ronald: *So Simply Means The Rain.* Claitor's, 1965.

Morgan, Frederick: *A Book Of Change.* Scribners, 1972.
—*Poems Of The Two Worlds.* University of Illinois Press, 1977.
—*The Tarot Of Cornelius Agrippa.* Sagarin Press, 1978.
—*Death Mother And Other Poems.* University of Illinois Press, 1979.
—*The River.* NADJA, 1980.
—*Refractions.* Abattoir Editions, 1981.
—*Northbook.* University of Illinois Press, 1982.
—*Eleven Poems.* NADJA, 1983.

Morgan, John: *The Border Wars.* Musk Ox Press, 1978.
—*The Bone-Duster.* Quarterly Review of Literature, 1980.
—*The Arctic Herd.* University of Alabama Press, 1984.

Morgan, Robert: *Zirconia Poems.* Lillabulero Press, 1969.
—*Red Owl.* W. W. Norton, 1972.
—*Land Diving.* Louisiana State University Press, 1976.
—*Trunk & Thicket.* L'Epervier Press, 1978.
—*Groundwork.* Gnomon Press, 1979.
—*Bronze Age.* Iron Mountain Press, 1981.

Morin, Edward: *In The Late Gnat Light And Other Poems* (anthology edited by Dallas Wiebe). Cincinnati Art Association, 1965.
—*The Dust Of Our City.* Clover Press, 1978.

Morris, John N.: *The Life Beside This One.* Atheneum, 1970.
—*Green Business.* Atheneum, 1970.
—*The Glass Houses.* Atheneum, 1980.

Moses, W. R.: *Identities.* Wesleyan University Press, 1965.
—*Passage.* Wesleyan University Press, 1976.
—*Not Native.* Juniper Press, 1979.

Mueller, Lisel: *The Private Life.* Louisiana State University Press, 1976.
—*Voices From The Forest.* Juniper Press, 1977.
—*The Need To Hold Still.* Louisiana State University Press, 1980.

Mullen, Harryette: *Tree Tall Woman.* Energy Earth Communications, 1981.

Murray, G. E.: *A Mile Called Timothy.* Ironwood Press, 1972.
—*Holding Fast.* Bonewhistle Press, 1974.
—*Gasoline Dreams.* Red Hill Press, 1978.

—*Repairs.* University of Missouri Press, 1980.

N

Nathan, Leonard: *Western Reaches.* Talisman Press, 1958.
—*Glad And Sorry Seasons.* Random House, 1963.
—*The Matchmaker's Lament And Other Astonishments.* Gehenna Press, 1967.
—*The Day The Perfect Speakers Left.* Wesleyan University Press, 1969.
—*Flight Plan.* Cedar Hill Press, 1971.
—*Without Wishing.* Thorp Springs Press, 1973.
—*Returning Your Call.* Princeton University Press, 1975.
—*Coup And Other Poems.* Windflower Press, 1975.
—*The Likeness: Poems Out Of India.* Thorp Springs Press, 1975.
—*The Teachings Of Grandfather Fox.* Ithaca House, 1976.
—*The Lost Distance.* Chowder Chapbooks, 1978.
—*Dear Blood.* University of Pittsburgh Press, 1980.
—*Holding Patterns.* University of Pittsburgh Press, 1982.

Nemerov, Howard: *The Collected Poems Of Howard Nemerov.* University of Chicago Press, 1977.
—*Sentences.* University of Chicago Press, 1980.

Newman, Lesléa: *Just Looking For My Shoes.* Back Door Press, 1980.

Niditch, B. Z.: *Elements.* MO.O.P. Press, 1980.
—*Freedom Trail.* Wings Press, 1980.
—*A Boston Winter.* Realities Library, 1981.
—*Unholy Empire.* Browns Mills Review, 1982.

Nims, John Frederick: *Selected Poems.* University of Chicago Press, 1982.
—*The Kiss: A Jambalaya.* Houghton Mifflin, 1982.

Nutting, Leslie: *Personal Effects.* Manoeuvres Press, 1982.
—*Not Honesty.* Manoeuvres Press, 1983.
—*Theseus.* Manoeuvres Press, 1983.

Nye, Naomi Shihab: *Tattooed Feet* (under name of Shihab). Texas Portfolio Press, 1977.
—*Eye-To-Eye* (under name of Shihab). Texas Portfolio Press, 1978.
—*Different Ways To Pray.* Breitenbush Books, 1980.
—*Hugging The Jukebox.* E. P. Dutton, 1982.
—*On The Edge Of The Sky.* Iguana Press, 1982.

O

Ochester, Ed: *Dancing On The Edges Of Knives.* University of Missouri Press, 1973.
—*The End Of The Ice Age.* Slow Loris Press, 1977.
—*A Drift Of Swine.* Thunder City Press, 1981.
—*Miracle Mile.* Carnegie-Mellon University Press, 1983.

O'Brien, William P.: *Starting From Paumanok.* Despa Press, 1971.

Olds, Sharon: *Satan Says.* University of Pittsburgh Press, 1980.

—*The Dead And The Living.* Alfred A. Knopf, 1984.

Ostriker, Alicia: *Songs: A Book Of Poems.* Holt, Rinehart and Winston, 1969.
—*Once More Out Of Darkness, And Other Poems.* Berkeley Poets Co-op Press, 1974.
—*A Dream Of Springtime: Poems 1970-78.* Smith/Horizon Press, 1979.
—*The Mother/Child Papers.* Momentum Press, 1980.
—*A Woman Under The Surface.* Princeton University Press, 1982.

Owen, Sue: *Nursery Rhymes For The Dead.* Ithaca House, 1980.

P

Page, William: *Clutch Plates.* Branden Press, 1976.
—*The Gatekeeper.* St. Luke's Press, 1982.

Parini, Jay: *Anthracite Country.* Random House, 1982.

Pau-Llosa, Ricardo: *Sorting Metaphors.* Anhinga Press, 1983.

Peacock, Molly: *And Live Apart.* University of Missouri Press, 1980.

Pennant, Edmund: *I, Too, Jehovah.* Scribners, 1952.
—*Dream's Navel.* Lintel, 1979.
—*Misapprehensions & Other Poems.* Lintel, 1984.

Perlis, Alan: *Skin Songs.* Thunder City Press, 1977.

Peseroff, Joyce: *The Hardness Scale.* Alice James Books, 1977.

Petrie, Paul: *Confessions Of A Non-Conformist.* Hillside Press, 1963.
—*The Race With Time And The Devil.* Golden Quill Press, 1965.
—*From Under The Hill Of Night.* Vanderbilt University Press, 1969.
—*The Academy Of Goodbye.* University Press of New England, 1974.
—*Light From The Furnace Rising.* Copper Beech Press, 1978.
—*Time Songs.* Biscuit City Press, 1979.
—*Not Seeing Is Believing.* Juniper Press, 1983.
—*Strange Gravity.* Tidal Press, 1983.

Pfingston, Roger: *Stoutes Creek Road.* Raintree Press, 1976.
—*Nesting.* Sparrow Press, 1978.
—*The Presence Of Trees.* Raintree Press, 1979.
—*Hazards Of Photography.* Writer's Center Press, 1980.
—*The Circus Of Unreasonable Acts.* Years Press, 1982.

Pflum, Richard: *Moving Into The Light.* Raintree Press, 1975.
—*A Dream Of Salt.* Raintree Press, 1980.

Phillips, Robert: *Inner Weather.* Golden Quill Press, 1966.
—*The Pregnant Man.* Doubleday, 1978.
—*Running On Empty.* Doubleday, 1981.

Pijewski, John: *Dinner With Uncle Jozef.* Wesleyan University Press, 1982.

Pillin, William: *Dance Without Shoes.* Golden Quill Press, 1956.

—*Pavanne For A Fading Memory.* Alan Swallow, 1963.
—*Everything Falling.* Kayak Books, 1971.
—*The Abandoned Music Room.* Kayak Books, 1975.
—*To The End Of Time: Poems New And Selected.* Papa Bach Editions, 1980.

Pinkerton, Helen: *Error Pursued.* Stone Wall and Cummington Press, 1959.

Plumly, Stanley: *In The Outer Dark.* Louisiana State University Press, 1970.
—*Giraffe.* Louisiana State University Press, 1973.
—*How The Plains Indians Got Horses.* Best Cellar Press, 1973.
—*Out-Of-The-Body Travel.* Ecco Press, 1977.
—*Summer Celestial.* Ecco Press, 1983.

Pollak, Felix: *The Castle And The Flaw.* Elizabeth Press, 1963.
—*Say When.* Juniper Press, 1969.
—*Ginkgo.* Elizabeth Press, 1973.
—*Subject To Change.* Juniper Press, 1978.

Polson, Don: *Wakening.* Fiddlehead Poetry Books, 1971.
—*Brief Evening In A Catholic Hospital.* Fiddlehead Poetry Books, 1972.
—*In Praise Of Young Thieves.* Alive Press, 1975.
—*Lone Travellers.* Fiddlehead Poetry Books, 1979.
—*Moving Through Deep Snow.* Thistledown Press, 1984.

Price, V. B.: *The Cyclops' Garden.* San Marcos Press, 1969.
—*Semblances.* Sunstone Press, 1976.

Privett, Katharine: *The Poet-People.* San Marcos Press, 1976.
—*The Dreams Of Exiles.* Holmgangers Press, 1982.

Pruitt, Bill: *Ravine Street.* White Pine Press, 1977.

R

Rainsford, Christine: *Timeless Moment.* Golden Quill Press, 1962.
—*Upland Pasture.* Golden Quill Press, 1969.
—*Spring Laughter.* Golden Quill Press, 1980.

Ramke, Bin: *The Difference Between Night And Day.* Yale University Press, 1978.
—*White Monkeys.* University of Georgia Press, 1981.

Ramsey, Jarold: *Dermographia.* Cornstalk Press, 1982.

Rankin, Paula: *By The Wreckmaster's Cottage.* Carnegie-Mellon University Press, 1977.
—*Augers.* Carnegie-Mellon University Press, 1981.

Ray, David: *X-Rays: A Book Of Poems.* Cornell University Press, 1965.
—*Dragging The Main And Other Poems.* Cornell University Press, 1968.
—*A Hill In Oklahoma.* BkMk Press, 1972.
—*Gathering Firewood: New Poems And Selected.* Wesleyan University Press, 1974.
—*Enough Of Flying: Poems Inspired By The Ghazals*

Of Ghalib. Writers Workshop (India)
—*The Tramp's Cup.* Chariton Review Press, 1978.
—*The Touched Life.* Scarecrow Press, 1982.
—*Not Far From The River: Transcreations From The Gatha-Saptasati.* Prakrit Society (India)
—*On Wednesday I Cleaned Out My Wallet.* Pancake Press, 1984.
—*Not Far From The River.* Prakrit Society (India), 1984.

Rees, Ennis: *Selected Poems.* University of South Carolina Press, 1973.

Ridland, John: *Fires Of Home.* Scribner's, 1961.
—*Ode One Violence.* Tennessee Poetry Press, 1969.
—*The Lazy Man.* Christopher's Books, 1975.
—*In The Shadowless Light.* Abattoir Editions, 1978.
—*Elegy For My Aunt.* Abattoir Editions, 1981.

Riley, Joanne M.: *Earth Tones.* Seattle University Press, 1979.

Rinaldi, Nicholas: *The Resurrection Of The Snails.* John F. Blair, 1977.
—*We Have Lost Our Fathers.* University Presses of Florida, 1982.

Ritchie, Elisavietta: *Timbot.* Lit Press, 1970.
—*Tightening The Circle Over Eel Country.* Acropolis Books, 1974.
—*A Sheath Of Dreams And Other Games.* Proteus Press, 1976.
—*Moving To Larger Quarters.* Artists and Writers Collaborative, 1977.
—*Raking The Snow.* Washington Writers Publishing House, 1982.

Robbins, Richard: *The Invisible Wedding.* University of Missouri Press, 1984.

Rogers, Del Marie: *Breaking Free.* Ironwood Press, 1977.
—*To The Earth.* Trilobite Press, 1982.

Rogers, Pattiann: *The Expectations Of Light.* Princeton University Press, 1981.

Roripaugh, Robert: *Learn To Love The Haze.* Spirit Mound Press, 1976.

Rosenberg, L. M.: *The Angel Poems.* State Street Press, 1984.

Rosenberger, F. C.: *One Season Here.* University Press of Virginia, 1976.
—*An Alphabet.* University Press of Virginia, 1978.

Rosten, Norman: *Return Again, Traveler.* Yale University Press, 1940.
—*The Fourth Decade.* Farrar & Rinehart, 1943.
—*The Big Road.* Rinehart & Co., 1946.
—*Songs For Patricia.* Simon & Schuster, 1951.
—*The Plane And The Shadow.* Bookman, 1953.
—*Thrive Upon The Rock.* Trident Press, 1965.
—*Selected Poems.* George Braziller, 1979.

Ruark, Gibbons: *A Program For Survival.* University Press of Virginia, 1971.
—*Reeds.* Texas Tech University Press, 1978.
—*Keeping Company.* Johns Hopkins University Press, 1983.

Rubin, Larry: *The World's Old Way.* University of Nebraska Press, 1963.
—*Lanced In Light.* Harcourt, Brace & World, 1967.

—*All My Mirrors Lie.* David R. Godine, 1975.

Ruffin, Paul: *Lighting The Furnace Pilot.* Spoon River Poetry Press, 1980.
—*Our Women.* Abbott House Press, 1982.

Rugo, Mariève: *Fields Of Vision.* University of Alabama Press, 1983.

Runciman, Lex: *Luck.* Owl Creek Press, 1981.

Russ, Lawrence: *The Burning-Ground.* Owl Creek Press, 1981.

Rutsala, Vern: *The Window.* Wesleyan University Press, 1964.
—*Laments.* New Rivers Press, 1975.
—*The Journey Begins.* University of Georgia Press, 1976.
—*Paragraphs.* Wesleyan University Press, 1978.
—*Walking Home From The Icehouse.* Carnegie-Mellon University Press, 1981.

S

Sadoff, Ira: *Settling Down.* Houghton Mifflin, 1975.
—*Palm Reading In Winter.* Houghton Mifflin, 1978.
—*A Northern Calendar.* David R. Godine, 1982.

Sagan, Miriam: *Dangerous Body.* Samisdat Press, 1976.
—*Vision's Edge.* Samisdat Press, 1978.
—*Aegean Doorway.* Zephyr Press, 1983.

Salkey, Andrew: *Jamaica.* Hutchinson & Co. (England), 1973.
—*Away.* Allison & Busby (London)/Schocken Books (U.S.), 1980.
—*In The Hills Where Her Dreams Live.* Black Scholar Press, 1981.

Sandeen, Ernest: *Antennas Of Silence.* Contemporary Poetry, 1953.
—*Children And Older Strangers.* University of Notre Dame Press, 1961.
—*Like Any Road Anywhere.* University of Notre Dame Press, 1976.
—*Collected Poems, 1953-1977.* University of Notre Dame Press, 1979.

Sanger, Peter M.: *The America Reel.* Pottersfield Press, 1983.

Santos, Sherod: *Elkin Pond.* Porch Publications, 1979.
—*Accidental Weather.* Doubleday, 1982.

Sarton, May: *Encounter In April.* Houghton Mifflin, 1937.
—*Inner Landscape.* Houghton Mifflin Co., 1939.
—*The Lion And The Rose.* Rinehart & Co., 1948.
—*The Leaves Of The Tree.* Cornell, Iowa, Chapbook, 1950.
—*The Land Of Silence.* Rinehart & Co., 1953.
—*In Time Like Air.* Rinehart & Co., 1957.
—*Cloud, Stone, Sun, Vine.* W. W. Norton, 1961.
—*A Private Mythology.* W. W. Norton, 1966.
—*As Does New Hampshire.* Richard R. Smith, 1967.
—*Plant Dreaming Deep.* W. W. Norton, 1968.
—*Kinds Of Love.* W. W. Norton, 1970.
—*Bridge Of Years.* W. W. Norton, 1971.
—*A Grain Of Mustard Seed.* W. W. Norton, 1971.

—*Faithful Are The Wounds.* W. W. Norton, 1972.
—*A Durable Fire.* W. W. Norton, 1972.
—*As We Are Now.* W. W. Norton, 1973.
—*Collected Poems, 1930-1973.* W. W. Norton, 1974.
—*Crucial Conversations.* W. W. Norton, 1975.
—*The Small Room.* W. W. Norton, 1976.
—*A Walk Through The Woods.* Harper & Row, 1976.
—*A World Of Light.* W. W. Norton, 1976.
—*Selected Poems Of May Sarton* (edited by Serena Sue Hilsinger and Lois Brynes). W. W. Norton, 1978.
—*A Reckoning.* W. W. Norton, 1978.
—*The Fur Person.* W. W. Norton, 1979.
—*A Shower Of Summer Days.* W. W. Norton, 1979.
—*Halfway To Silence.* W. W. Norton, 1980.
—*A Winter Garland.* William B. Ewert, 1982.
Schoenberger, Nancy: *The Taxidermist's Daughter.* Calliope Press, 1979.
Schreiber, Jan: *Digressions.* Aliquando Press, 1970.
Schulman, Grace: *Burn Down The Icons.* Princeton University Press, 1976.
Schultz, Philip: *Like Wings.* Viking/Penguin, 1978.
—*Deep Within The Ravine.* Viking Press, 1984.
Schwartz, Hillel: *Phantom Children.* State Street Press, 1982.
Scobie, Stephen: *Babylondromat.* 1966.
—*In The Silence Of The Year.* 1971.
—*The Birken Tree.* 1973.
—*Stone Poems.* 1974.
—*The Rooms We Are.* 1975.
—*Airloom.* 1975.
—*les toiles n'ont peur de rien.* 1979.
—*McAlmon's Chinese Opera.* 1980.
—*A Grand Memory For Forgetting.* 1981.
Seaburg, Alan: *Thoreau Collage.* Brodeur, 1978.
See, Molly: *Sleeping Over.* Lynx House Press, 1979.
Shapiro, Alan: *After The Digging.* Elpenor Books, 1981.
—*The Courtesy.* University of Chicago Press, 1983.
Shapiro, Harvey: *Battle Report.* Wesleyan University Press, 1966.
—*This World.* Wesleyan University Press, 1971.
—*Lauds & Nightsounds.* Sun, 1978.
—*The Light Holds.* Wesleyan University Press, 1984.
Sheck, Laurie: *Amaranth.* University of Georgia Press, 1981.
Sherry, Pearl Andelson: *Fringe* (under the name of Pearl Anderson). Will Ransom, 1923.
—*Arch Of A Circle* (with Doris Vidaver). Swallow Press, 1980.
Siegel, Robert: *The Beasts & The Elders.* University Press of New England, 1973.
—*In A Pig's Eye.* University Press of Florida, 1980.
Silverman, Maxine: *Survival Song.* Sunbury Press, 1976.
Simmerman, Jim: *Home.* Dragon Gate, 1983.
Simpson, Nancy: *Across Water.* State Street Press, 1983.

Skloot, Floyd: *Rough Edges.* Chowder Chapbooks, 1979.
Smart, Carolyn: *Swimmers In Oblivion.* York Publishing, 1981.
—*Power Sources.* Fiddlehead Poetry Books, 1982.
Smith, Dave: *Mean Rufus Throw Down.* Basilisk Press, 1973.
—*The Fisherman's Whore.* Ohio University Press, 1974.
—*Cumberland Station.* University of Illinois Press, 1977.
—*Goshawk, Antelope.* University of Illinois Press, 1979.
—*Blue Spruce.* Tamarack Press, 1981.
—*Homage To Edgar Allan Poe.* Louisiana State University Press, 1981.
—*Dream Flights.* University of Illinois Press, 1981.
—*In The House Of The Judge.* Harper & Row, 1983.
—*Gray Soldiers.* Palaemon Press, 1983.
Smith, Patrick: *Xmas Sutra.* Pancake Press, 1976.
—*Photo Fiends.* Pancake Press, 1977.
—*Zen Mover.* Pancake Press, 1977.
Smith, R. T.: *Waking Under Snow.* Cold Mountain Press, 1975.
—*Good Water.* Tamarack Editions, 1979.
—*Rural Route.* Tamarack Editions, 1981.
—*Beasts Did Leap.* Tamarack Editions, 1982.
—*From The High Dive.* Water Mark Press, 1983.
—*Finding The Path.* Black Willow Press, 1983.
—*Roosevelt Unbound.* Tamarack Editions, 1984.
Smith, Stephen E.: *The Bushnell Hamp Poems.* Green River Press, 1980.
Smith, Virginia E.: *Lion Rugs From Fars.* Dan River Press, 1982.
Sorestad, Glen: *Wind Songs.* Thistledown Press, 1975.
—*Prairie Pub Poems.* Thistledown Press, 1976.
—*Pear Seeds In My Mouth.* Sesame Press, 1977.
—*Ancestral Dances.* Thistledown Press, 1979.
Soto, Gary: *The Elements Of San Joaquin.* University of Pittsburgh Press, 1977.
—*The Tale Of Sunlight.* University of Pittsburgh Press, 1978.
—*Father Is A Pillow Tied To A Broom.* Slow Loris Press, 1980.
—*Where Sparrows Work Hard.* University of Pittsburgh Press, 1981.
Southwick, Marcia: *What The Trees Go Into.* Burning Deck Press, 1977.
—*Thaisa.* Singing Wind Publications, 1979.
—*The Leopard's Mouth Is Dry And Cold Inside* (with Larry Levis). Singing Wind Publications, 1979.
—*The Night Won't Save Anyone.* University of Georgia Press, 1980.
—*Connecticut: Eight Poems.* Pym-Randall Press, 1981.
Sparshott, Francis: *A Divided Voice.* Oxford University Press (Toronto), 1965.
—*A Cardboard Garage.* Clarke, Irwin, 1969.
—*The Rainy Hills.* Privately printed, 1979.
—*The Naming Of The Beasts.* Black Moss Press, 1979.

—*The Cave Of Trophonius.* Brick Books, 1983.
—*The Hanging Gardens Of Etobicoke.* Childe Thursday, 1983.
Spires, Elizabeth: *Globe.* Wesleyan University Press, 1981.
Spivack, Kathleen: *Swimmer In The Spreading Dawn.* Applewood Books, 1981.
Stafford, William: *Braided Apart.* Confluence Press, 1976.
—*Smoke's Way.* Graywolf Press, 1978.
—*Stories That Could Be True: New And Collected Poems.* Harper & Row, 1978.
—*Things That Happen Where There Aren't Any People.* BOA Editions, 1978.
—*Sometimes Like A Legend.* Copper Canyon Press, 1981.
—*A Glass Face In The Rain.* Harper & Row, 1982.
Standing, Sue: *Amphibious Weather.* Zephyr Press, 1981.
Stanford, Ann: *In Narrow Bound.* Alan Swallow, 1943.
—*The White Bird.* Alan Swallow, 1949.
—*Magellan: A Poem To Be Read By Several Voices.* Talisman Press, 1958.
—*The Weathercock.* Viking Press, 1966.
—*The Descent.* Viking Press, 1970.
—*Climbing Up To Light: Eleven Poems.* Magpie Press, 1973.
—*In Mediterranean Air.* Viking Press, 1977.
Stern, Gerald: *Rejoicings.* Fiddlehead Poetry Books, 1973.
—*Lucky Life.* Houghton Mifflin, 1977.
—*The Red Coal.* Houghton Mifflin, 1981.
Stout, Robert Joe: *Moving Out.* Road Runner Press, 1973.
—*Trained Bears On Hoops.* Thorp Springs Press, 1974.
—*Camping Out.* Samisdat Press, 1976.
—*The Trick.* Juniper Press, 1976.
—*Swallowing Dust.* Red Hill Press, 1976.
Strahan, Bradley R.: *Love Songs For An Age Of Anxiety.* Black Buzzard Press, 1981.
—*Poems.* Black Buzzard Press, 1982.
Struthers, Betsy: *Censored Letters.* Mosaic Press, 1984.
Sutter, Barton: *Cedarhome.* BOA Editions, 1977.
—*Sequoyah.* Ox Head Press, 1983.
Swiss, Thomas: *Rounds.* Blue Buildings Press, 1982.
Sze, Arthur: *Two Ravens.* Tooth of Time Books, 1976.
—*The Willow Wind* (2nd edition, revised). Tooth of Time Books, 1981.
—*Dazzled.* Floating Island Publications, 1982.

T

Tagliabue, John: *Poems.* Harpers, 1959.
—*A Japanese Journal.* Kayak Press, 1966.
—*The Buddha Uproar.* Kayak Press, 1970.
—*The Doorless Door.* Mushinsha-Grossman, 1970.
Tapscott, Stephen: *Mesopotamia.* Wesleyan University Press, 1977.

—*Penobscot.* Pym-Randall Press, 1983.
Tate, James: *The Lost Pilot.* Yale University Press, 1967.
—*The Oblivion Ha-Ha.* Atlantic-Little, Brown, 1970.
—*Hints To Pilgrims.* Halty Ferguson Press, 1971.
—*Absences.* Atlantic-Little, Brown, 1972.
—*Hottentot Ossuary.* Temple Bar Bookshop, 1974.
—*Viper Jazz.* Wesleyan University Press, 1976.
—*Riven Doggeries.* Ecco Press, 1979.
—*Constant Defender.* Ecco Press, 1983.
Taylor, Laurie: *Changing The Past.* New Rivers Press, 1981.
Tebrich, Gregory: *Untitled Collected.* Privately printed, 1970.
—*Life Among The Whites.* Privately printed, 1974.
Terris, Virginia R.: *Tracking.* University of Illinois Press, 1976.
—*Canal.* Channel Press, 1981.
Thomas, D. M.: *Two Voices.* Viking Press, 1968.
—*Logan Stone.* Viking Press, 1971.
—*Love And Other Deaths.* Elek (England), 1975.
—*The Honeymoon Voyage.* Secker (England), 1978.
—*Selected Poems.* Viking/Penguin, 1983.
Thompson, Jeanie: *Lotus And Psalm.* Baltic Avenue Press, 1981.
—*Tinder Dreaming Of Smoke.* Holy Cow! Press, 1984.
Tihanyi, Eva: *Gutter Star Regenesis.* St. Clair College, 1972.
—*My Own Mind's Land.* St. Clair College, 1973.
—*Excelsior.* St. Clair College, 1975.
—*A Sequence Of The Blood.* Aya Press, 1983.
—*Prophecies Near The Speed Of Light.* Thistledown Press, 1984.
Tregebov, Rhea: *Remembering History.* Guernica Editions, 1982.
Trethewey, Eric: *In The Traces.* Inland Boat/Porch Publications, 1980.
—*Dreaming Of Rivers.* Cleveland State Poetry Center, 1984.
Twichell, Chase: *Northern Spy.* University of Pittsburgh Press, 1981.

U

Updike, John: *Telephone Poles And Other Poems.* Alfred A. Knopf, 1963.
—*Midpoint And Other Poems.* Alfred A. Knopf, 1969.
—*Tossing And Turning: Poems.* Alfred A. Knopf, 1977.
—*The Carpentered Hen.* Alfred A. Knopf, 1982.

V

Vernon, John: *Ann.* Iris Press, 1976.
Vinz, Robert: *Winter Promises.* BkMk Press, 1975.
—*Letters To The Poetry Editor.* Capra Press, 1975.

—*Songs For A Hometown Boy.* Solo Press, 1977.
—*Red River Blues.* Poetry Texas, 1977.
—*Contingency Plans.* Ohio Review, 1978.
—*Deep Water, Dakota.* Juniper Press, 1980.
—*Climbing The Stairs.* Spoon River Poetry Press, 1983.
—*The Weird Kid.* New Rivers Press, 1983-84.
Von Losberg, Les: *Granulated Sugar/Raw Cocaine.* Poets Union Press, 1974.
—*A Dangerous Life.* Poets Union Press, 1978.
—*Making Sense Of Foreign Currency.* Poets Union Press, 1982.

W

Walker, Jeanne Murray: *Nailing Up The Home Sweet Home. Cleveland State University Press, 1980.*
—*Necessary Angels.* Dragon Gate Press, 1984.
Wallace, Ronald: *Installing The Bees.* Chowder Chapbooks, 1977.
—*Plums, Stones, Kisses & Hooks.* University of Missouri Press, 1981.
—*Tunes For Bears To Dance To.* University of Pittsburgh Press, 1983.
Walsh, Chad: *The Factual Dark.* Harper, 1949.
—*Eden Two-Way.* Harper, 1954.
—*The Psalm Of Christ.* Westminster, 1963.
—*The Unknowing Dance.* Abelard, 1964.
—*The End Of Nature.* Swallow, 1969.
—*Hang Me Up My Begging Bowl.* Swallow, 1981.
Warren, Larkin: *Old Sheets.* Alice James Books, 1979.
Waters, Michael: *Fish Light.* Ithaca House, 1975.
—*Not Just Any Death.* BOA Editions, 1979.
Wayne, Jane O.: *Looking Both Ways.* University of Missouri Press, 1985.
Weigl, Bruce: *Executioner.* Ironwood Press, 1976.
—*A Sack Full Of Old Quarrels.* Cleveland State University Poetry Center, 1977.
—*A Romance.* University of Pittsburgh Press, 1979.
Welch, Don: *Dead Horse Table.* Windflower Press, 1975.
—*Handwork.* Kearney State College Press, 1978.
—*The Rarer Game.* Kearney State College Press, 1980.
Werner, Warren: *The Structure Of Desire.* Riverstone Press, 1983.
Wetteroth, Bruce: *Life In Progress.* Ohio Review, 1982.
White, Gail: *Pandora's Box.* Samisdat Press, 1977.
—*Irreverent Parables.* Border-Mountain Press, 1978.
—*Fishing For Leviathan.* Wings Press, 1982.
Whitehead, James: *Domains.* Louisiana State University Press, 1966.
—*Local Men.* University of Illinois Press, 1979.
Whiten, Clifton: *Putting The Birthdate Into Publication.* Clarke-Irwin & Co., 1969.
—*Various Titles.* Sandpiper Press, 1979.
—*One Poem: Poems New & Selected.* Mosaic Press, 1984.
Wickert, Max: *All The Weight Of The Still Midnight.* Outriders Poetry Monographs, 1972.

Wilbur, Richard: *The Beautiful Changes.* Reynal & Hitchcock, 1947.
—*Ceremony.* Harcourt Brace Jovanovich, 1950.
—*Things Of This World.* Harcourt Brace Jovanovich,
—*Poems 1943-1956.* Faber & Faber (London), 1957.
—*Advice To A Prophet.* Harcourt Brace Jovanovich, 1961.
—*Poems Of Richard Wilbur.* Harcourt Brace Jovanovich, 1963.
—*Walking To Sleep.* Harcourt Brace Jovanovich, 1969.
—*The Mind-Reader.* Harcourt Brace Jovanovich, 1976.
—*Seven Poems.* Abattoir Editions, 1981.
Wild, Peter: *The Afternoon In Dismay.* Art Assn. of Cincinnati, 1968.
—*Terms And Renewals.* Two Windows Press, 1970.
—*Peligros.* Ithaca House, 1971.
—*Wild's Magical Book Of Cranial Effusions.* New Rivers Press, 1971.
—*New And Selected Poems.* New Rivers Press, 1973.
—*Cochise.* Doubleday, 1973.
—*Tumacacori.* Two Windows Press, 1974.
—*The Cloning.* Doubleday, 1974.
—*Health.* Two Windows Press, 1976.
—*Chihuahua.* Doubleday, 1976.
—*House Fires.* Greenhouse Review Press, 1977.
—*Barn Fires.* Floating Islands Publications, 1978.
—*Rainbow.* Blue Buildings Press, 1980.
—*Jeanne D'Arc.* St. Luke's Press, 1980.
—*Wilderness.* New Rivers Press, 1980.
—*The Peaceable Kingdom.* Adler Press, 1983.
Williams, Miller: *Recital.* Oceano (Santiago, Chile), 1963.
—*A Circle Of Stone.* Louisiana State University Press, 1964.
—*So Long At The Fair.* E. P. Dutton, 1968.
—*The Only World There Is.* E. P. Dutton, 1971.
—*Halfway From Hoxie.* Louisiana State University Press, 1973.
—*Why God Permits Evil.* Louisiana State University Press, 1977.
—*Distractions.* Louisiana State University Press, 1981.
—*The Boys On Their Bony Mules.* Louisiana State University Press, 1983.
Winn, Howard: *Four Picture Sequences Of Desire And Love.* Front Street Publishers, 1978.
Winters, Bayla: *Tropic Of Mother.* Olivant Press, 1969.
—*bitchpoems.* Olivant Press, 1971.
—*Mothers And Daughters, Daughters And Mothers.* Women Writers West, 1983.
Wiseman, Christopher: *Waiting For The Barbarians.* Fiddlehead Poetry Books, 1971.
—*The Barbarian File.* Sesame Press, 1974.
—*The Upper Hand.* Enitharmon Press (England), 1981.
—*An Ocean Of Whispers.* Sono Nis Press, 1982.
Witt, Harold: *Family In The Forest.* Porpoise Book Shop, 1956.

—*Superman Unbound.* New Orleans Poetry Journal, 1956.
—*The Death of Venus.* Golden Quill Press, 1958.
—*Beasts In Clothes.* Macmillan, 1961.
—*Winesburg By The Sea: A Preview.* Hearse Press, 1970.
—*Pop. By 1940: 40,000.* Best Cellar Press, 1971.
—*Now, Swim.* Ashland Poetry Press, 1974.
—*Surprised By Others At Fort Cronkhite.* Sparrow, 1975.
—*Winesburg By The Sea.* Thorp Springs Press, 1979.
—*The Snow Prince.* Blue Unicorn, 1982.
Wittlinger, Ellen: *Breakers.* Sheep Meadow Press, 1979.
Wormser, Baron: *The White Words.* Houghton Mifflin, 1983.
Wright, Carolyne: *Stealing The Children.* Ahsahta Press, 1978.
—*Returning What We Owed.* Owl Creek Press, 1980.
—*Premonitions Of An Uneasy Guest.* Hardin-Simmons University Press, 1983.
Wright, Charles: *The Southern Cross.* Random House, 1981.
—*Country Music/Selected Early Poems.* Wesleyan University Press, 1982.

Wrigley, Robert: *The Sinking Of Clay City.* Copper Canyon Press, 1979.
—*The Glow.* Owl Greek Press, 1982.

XYZ

Young, David: *Sweating Out The Winter.* University of Pittsburgh Press, 1969.
—*Boxcars.* Ecco Press, 1973.
—*Work Lights: Thirty-Two Prose Poems.* Cleveland State University, 1977.
—*The Names Of A Hare In English.* University of Pittsburgh Press, 1979.
Zaranka, William: *A Mirror Driven Through Nature.* Sparrow Press, 1981.
Zeiger, L. L. (Lila): *The Way To Castle Garden.* State Street Press, 1982.
Zeldis, Chayym: *Seek Haven.* Reconstructionist Press, 1968.
Zweig, Paul: *Against Emptiness.* Harper & Row, 1971.
—*The Dark Side Of The Earth.* Harper & Row, 1974.
Zydek, Frederick: *Lights Along The Missouri.* University of Nebraska-Omaha, 1979.
—*Storm Warning.* Inchbird Press, 1983.

PART TWO

Yearbook
of American Poetry

The Yearly Record

The following bibliography lists books of and about poetry that were published, copyrighted, officially announced, distributed or otherwise appeared in the United States and Canada in 1983.

(1) COLLECTIONS OF POETRY BY INDIVIDUAL AUTHORS

A

A-Se-Gi (Julia Gibson)—*Words From The Earth.* Privately printed

Aal, Katharyn Machan; Crooker, Barbara—*Writ-Writing Home: Poems.* Gehry Press

Aberg, W. M.—*The Promise of Morning.* Blue Moon Press

Abse, Dannie—*One-Legged On Ice: Poems.* University of Georgia Press

Achtenberg, Anya—*I Know What The Small Girl Knew.* Holy Cow! Press

Ackerman, Diane—*Lady Faustus.* Morrow

Adkins, Geoffrey—*A Difficult Peace.* Ceolfrith Press

Adonis—*Transformations Of The Lover* (translated by Samuel Hazo). Ohio University Press

Ahern, Tom—*Superbounce.* Burning Deck

Ai Qing—*Selected Poems Of Ai Qing* (edited by Eugene Chen Eoyang). Indiana University Press

Aichinger, Ilse—*Selected Poetry & Prose* (translated by Allen H. Chappel). Logbridge-Rhodes

Akhmadulina, Bella—*Three Russian Women Poets: Anna Akhmatova, Marina Tsvetayeva And Bella Akhmadulina* (edited and translated by Mary Maddock). Crossing Press

Akhmatova, Anna—*Poems* (selected and translated from the Russian by Lyn Coffin). W. W. Norton
—*Three Russian Women Poets: Anna Akhmatova, Marina Tsvetayeva And Bella Akhmadulina* (edited and translated by Mary Maddock). Crossing Press

Akillian, Michael—*The Eating Of Names.* Ashod Press

Alban, Laureano—*Autumn's Legacy* (translated from the Spanish by Frederick H. Fornoff). Ohio University Press

Albert, Liz—*Nothing You Can See.* Glavin Press

Albert, Sam—*As Is.* Wampeter Press

Alcuin—*The Bishops, Kings And Saints Of York* (edited by Peter Godman). Oxford University Press

Alegria, Claribel—*Flowers From The Volcano* (translated by Carolyn Forche). University of Pittsburgh Press
—*Changing Centuries: Selected Poems Of Fernando Alegria* (translated by Stephen Kessler). Latin American Library Review Press

Aleixandre, Vicente—*World Alone* (translated by Lewis Hyde and David Unger). Penmaen Press

Allen, James B.—*If Wishes Were Horses.* Seaview Publishers

Alpert, Michael—*Darkwood.* Puckerbrush Press

Amichai, Yehuda—*Great Tranquility: Questions And Answers* (translated by Glenda Abramson and Tudor Parfitt). Harper & Row

Ammons, A, R.—*Lake Effect Country.* W. W. Norton

Anbian, Robert—*Bohemian Airs & Other Kefs.* Night Horn Books

Anderson, Jack—*The Clouds Of That Country.* Hanging Loose Press

Anderson, Jon—*The Milky Way: Poems 1967-1982.* Ecco Press

Andrews, Jenne—*Reunion: Poems.* Lynx House Press

Anglesley, Zoe—*Something More Than Force: Poems For Guatemala, 1971-1982.* Adastra Press

Anglund, Joan Walsh—*The Circle Of The Spirit.* Random House

Anson, John S.—*A Family Album.* Robert L. Barth

Aplon, Roger—*By Dawn's Early Light At 120 Miles Per Hour.* Dryad Press

Applewhite, James—*Foreseeing The Journey.* Louisiana State University Press

Ariosto, Lodovico—*Orlando Furioso* (translated by Guido Waldman). Oxford University Press

Aristophanes—*Knights* (edited and translated by Alan H. Sommerstein). Aris & Phillips/Humanities Press

Armand, Octavio—*Poems With Dusk* (translated by Carol Maier). Logbridge-Rhodes

Armour, Richard—*Our Presidents.* Woodbridge Press
—*Have You Ever Wished You Were Something Else?* Childrens Press

Arnstein, Flora J.—*Light Widening.* Privately printed

Ash, John—*The Goodbyes.* Carcanet New Press/ Humanities Press

Ashman, Russell Smith—*A Sword From Words.* Privately printed

Axinn, Donald Everett—*The Hawk's Dream And Other Poems.* Grove Press

B

Baca, Jimmy Santiago—*What's Happening.* Curbstone Press

Bailie, Anne—*In The Soul's Riptide.* Chantry Press

Baker, Donald W.—*Formal Application: Selected Poems, 1960-1980.* Barnwood Press

Balakian, Peter—*Sad Days Of Light: Poems.* Sheep Meadow Press

Balaz, Joseph P.—*After The Drought.* Topgallant Pub. Co.

Baldwin, Deirdra—*Totemic.* Burning Deck

Baldwin, Deirdra; Davis, Gene—*Inside Outside.* Brooklyn Museum

Baldwin, Michael—*King Horn: Poems Written At Montolieu In Old Languedoc, 1969-1981.* Routledge & Kegan Paul

Bamberger, Paul—*Crossing.* Unhinged Voice Press

Bangs, Carol Jane—*The Bones Of The Earth.* New Directions Pub. Co.

Baranski, Johnny—*Pencil Flowers: Prison Haikus.* Holmgangers Press

Barber, Dave—*Overwater.* Cornell Press

Barfield, Owen—*Orpheus: A Poetic Drama* (edited by John C. Ulreich, Jr.). Lindisfarne Press

Barker, Cicely Mary—*Blossom Flower Faeries: Poems And Pictures.* Philomel Books

Barker, George—*Anno Domini.* Faber and Faber

Barlin, Paul—*Lovers Lately: Poems Of Relationship.* Privately printed

Barnes, Dick—*A Lake On The Earth.* Momentum Press

Barnes, Djuna—*Creatures In An Alphabet.* Dial Press

Barnett, Anthony—*A Forest Utilization Family.* Burning Deck

Barth, R. L.—*Forced-Marching To The Styx: Vietnam War Poems.* Perivale Press

Becker, Robin—*Backtalk: Poems.* Alicejames Books

Bell, Marvin—*Segues: A Correspondence In Poetry* (with William Stafford). David R. Godine

Benenson, Michael—*Alcman Ape.* Los Poetry Press (England)

Bergin, Thomas G.—*Under Scorpio.* Solaris Press

Berrigan, Ted—*The Sonnets.* United Artists Books

Berry, Wendell—*The Wheel.* North Point Press

Berssenbrugge, Mei-mei—*The Heat Bird.* Burning Deck

Bishop, Elizabeth—*The Complete Poems 1927-1979.* Farrar, Straus & Giroux

Bizzaro, Patrick—*The Man Who Eats Death For Breakfast.* Backstreet Editions

Black, Charles—*The Waking Passenger.* New Orleans Poetry Journal Press

Black, Patsie—*Tapestry, A Finespun Grace & Mercy.* Multnomah Press

Blackburn, Kate—*Four North Carolina Poets.* St. Andrews Press

Blake, William—*William Blake's Works In Conventional Typography* (edited by G. E. Bentley, Jr.). Scholars' Facsimiles & Reprints

Blasing, Randy—*To Continue.* Persea Books
—*The Particles: Poems.* Copper Beech Press

Blazer, Stuart—*Ricochet.* Copper Beech Press

Blessing, Richard—*Poems And Stories.* Dragon Gate

Blotnick, Elihu—*Storm Year.* California Street Editions

Blunden, Edmund—*Selected Poems* (edited by Robyn Marsack). Carcanet New Press/ Humanities Press

Bly, Robert—*The Man In The Black Coat Turns: Poems.* Penguin

Bodecker, N. M.—*Snowman Sniffles And Other Verse.* Atheneum

Bolls, Imogene L.—*Glass Walker.* Cleveland State University Poetry Center

Booker, Stephen Todd—*Waves & License: Poetry.* Greenfield Review Press

Bottoms, David—*In A U-Haul North Of Damascus.* William Morrow

Bowering, George—*West Window: The Selected Poetry Of George Bowering.* General Publishing Co.

Bowers, Neal—*The Golf Ball Diver.* New Rivers Press

Boyle, Charles—*House Of Cards.* Carcanet New Press/Humanities Press

Boyle, John E. Whiteford—*Graffiti On The Wall Of Time.* Wheat Forders

Bozanic, Nick—*Wood Birds Water Stones.* Barnwood Press Cooperative

Bradbury, Elspeth—*Is That You This Is Me.* Fiddlehead Poetry Books

Braham, Jeanne—*One Means Of Telling Time.* Geryon Press

Brander, Harry—*What Rhymes With Cancer?* (translated by Judy Schavrien). New Rivers Press

Brandi, John—*Rite For The Beautification Of All Beings: A Poem.* Toothpaste Press

Brandt, Jorgen Gustava—*Selected Longer Poems* (translated by Alexander Taylor). Curbstone Press

Brathwaite, Edward Kamau—*Sun Poem.* Oxford University Press

Breytenbach, Breyten—*In Africa Even The Flies Are Happy: Selected Poems And Prose 1964-1977* (translated by Denis Hirson and John Calder). Flatiron Book Distributors

Bridges, William—*Common Places.* Privately printed

Britton, Corburn—*Second Seasons.* Horizon Press

Britton, Dave—*New Mystery Poems.* Villa Publications

Britts, Maurice W.—*I Will Survive: Survival Poems.* Guild Press

Brodsky, Louis Daniel—*Mississippi Vistas.* University Press of Mississippi

Brome, Alexander—*Poems* (edited by Roman R. Dubinski). University of Toronto Press

Brosman, Catharine Savage—*Abiding Winter.* R. L. Barth Press

Broughton, T. Alan—*Dreams Before Sleep.* Carnegie-Mellon University Press

Brown, Sterling A.—*The Collected Poems Of Sterling A. Brown* (selected by Michael S. Harper). Harper & Row

Brown, Steven Ford—*Erotic Mask: 18 Prose Poems.* Lunchroom Press

Brown, William Hill—*Selected Poems And Verse Fables 1784-1793* (edited by Richard Walser). University of Delaware Press

Bruce, Debra—*Pure Daughter.* University of Arkansas Press

Bruchac, Joseph—*Remembering The Dawn.* Blue Cloud Press

Brunish, Corey (see listing for Paxston, Laura)

Bryan, Sharon—*Salt Air.* Wesleyan University Press

Buckley, Christopher—*Cider-Light.* Moving Parts Press

Buning, Sietze—*Style And Class.* Middleburg Press

Burns, Michael D.—*When All Else Failed.* Timberline Press

Burns, Ralph—*Us.* Cleveland State University Poetry Center

Burns, Richard—*Black Light: Poems In Memory Of George Seferis.* Los Poetry Press (England)
—*Roots/Routes.* Cleveland State University Poetry Center

Burrow, J. A. (editor)—*Sir Gawain And The Green Knight.* Yale University Press

Bursk, Christopher—*Place Of Residence.* Sparrow Press

Byron, Lord—*Don Juan* (edited by T. G. Steffan, E. Steffan and W. W. Pratt). Yale University Press

C

Calais, Jean—*Villon.* Pick Pocket Series

Campbell, Roy—*The Selected Poems Of Roy Campbell* (edited by Peter Alexander). Oxford University Press

Caratheodory, A. M.—*Amphibian Dreams.* M. and R. Wolfe

Carey, John—*Hand To Hand.* Curbstone Press

Carmi, T.—*At The Stone Of Losses* (translated by Grace Schulman). University of California Press

Carpelan, Bo—*Garden/The Courtyard* (translated by Samuel Charters). Swedish Books (Sweden)

Carver, Raymond—*Fires: Essays, Poems, Stories, 1966-1982.* Capra Press

Cassell, Douglas—*White Magician.* Privately printed

Catullus—*The Poems Of Catullus: A Bilingual Edition* (translated by Peter Whigham). University of California Press (reprint)

Cavafy, Constantine—*Poems Of Constantine Cavafy* (translated by George Khirallah). Privately printed

Caws, Ian—*Boy With A Kite: Poems.* Sidgwick & Jackson/Merrimack Book Service

Cercamon—*Cercamon And Jaufre Rudel: Poetry* (edited and translated by George Wolf and Roy Rosenstein). Garland

Cervenka, Exene (see listing for Lunch, Lydia)

Cesaire, Aime—*Aime Cesaire: The Collected Poetry, 1939-1976* (translated by Clayton Eshleman and Annette Smith). University of California Press

Chandler, Keith—*Katt's Rebellion And Other Poems.* Carcanet New Press/Humanities Press

Chandra, G. S. Sharat—*Heirloom.* Oxford University Press

Chang, Diana; Greco, Leonard; Willitts, Martin, Jr.
—*The Horizon Is Definitely Speaking; Union Regulations; Exit Laughing.* Backstreet Editions

Chatterjee, Kishore—*Broken Fingers.* Writers Workshop

Chaucer, Geoffrey—*The Miller's Tale* (edited by Thomas W. Ross). University of Oklahoma Press
—*The Nun's Priest's Tale* (edited by Derek Pearsall). University of Oklahoma Press
—*A Variorum Edition Of The Works Of Geoffrey Chaucer, Volume II, The Canterbury Tales* (edited by Paul G. Ruggiers and Donald C. Baker). University of Oklahoma Press
—*Chaucer's Poetry: An Anthology For The Modern Reader* (selected and edited by E. T. Donaldson). Scott, Foresman (reprint)

Cheatwood, Kiarri T-H—*Psalms Of Redemption.* Lotus Press

Chisholm, Scott—*Desperate Affections.* State Street Press

Chmielarz, Sharon—*Different Arrangements.* New Rivers Press

Chretien de Troyes—*Percival, Or, The Story Of The Grail* (translated by Ruth Harwood Cline). Pergamon Press

Citino, David—*The Appassionata Poems.* Cleveland State University Poetry Center

Clampitt, Amy—*The Kingfisher.* Alfred A. Knopf

Clare, John—*Clare's Countryside* (selected by Brian Patten; edited by Eric Robinson). Heinemann/Quixote Press/David & Charles, Inc.
—*The Rural Muse.* Carcanet New Press/Humanities Press

Clarke, George Elliott—*Saltwater Spirituals And Deeper Blues.* Pottersfield Press

Clarke, Gillian—*Letter From A Far Country.* Carcanet New Press/Humanities Press

Cloutier, David—*Soft Lightnings.* Copper Beech Press

Clucas, Lowell—*The Death Of Alexander.* Poetry X Press

Codrescu, Andrei—*Selected Poems, 1970-1980.* Sun

Cohen, Marion D.—*The Temper Tantrum Book.* WordWorker
—*A Child's Grave.* Centering
—*These Covers To Crawl Under.* WordWorker

Colby, Joan—*How The Sky Begins To Fall.* Spoon River Poetry Press

Coleman, Wanda—*Imagoes.* Black Sparrow Press

Colum, Padraic—*The Poets Circuits: Collected Poems Of Ireland.* Dolmen Press/Humanities Press

Condee, Nancy—*Explosion In The Puzzle Factory.* Burning Deck

Conn, Jan E.—*Road Of Smoke.* Colophon Books

Conrad, Earl—*The Tumblin World Of Tom Mac-Whorty.* Privately printed

Cook, Gregory M.—*Love En Route,* Fiddlehead Poetry Books

Cooley, Peter—*Nightseasons.* Carnegie-Mellon University Press

Cooney, Rian—*Icarus.* Kastrel 3

Cope, David—*Quiet Lives: Poems.* Humana Press

Corey, Stephen—*Fighting Death.* State Street Press

Covino, Michael—*Unfree Associations.* Berkeley Poets Workshop & Press

Coward, Noel—*Spangled Unicorn.* H. Frisch

Cox, Carol—*The Water In The Pearl.* Hanging Loose Press

Crane, Stephen—*Prose And Poetry* (selected by J. C. Levenson). Literary Classics of the U.S./Viking Press

Crashaw, Richard—*The Complete Works Of Richard Crashaw* (edited by A. B. Grosart). AMS Press (reprint)

Creeley, Robert—*The Collected Poems Of Robert Creeley: 1945-1975.* University of California Press

Crews, Judson—*The Clock of Moss.* Ahsahta Press

Cronin, Anthony—*New & Selected Poems.* Carcanet New Press/Humanities Press

Crooker, Barbara (see listing for Aal, Katharyn Machan)

Crosson, Robert—*Abandoned Latitudes: New Writing By 3 Los Angeles Poets.* Red Hill Press

Cruz, Victor Hernandez—*By Lingual Wholes.* Momo's Press

cummings, e. e.—*Etcetera: The Unpublished Poems Of e. e.* cummings (edited by George James Firmage and Richard S. Kennedy). Liveright

D

Dacey, Philip—*Gerard Manley Hopkins Meets Walt Whitman In Heaven And Other Poems.* Penmaen Press

Dahl, Roald—*Roald Dahl's Revolting Rhymes.* Alfred A. Knopf

Dante Alighieri—*Purgatorio.* University of California Press

Dasgupta, Pranadendu—*This Life.* Writers Workshop

Davie, Donald—*Three For Water-Music.* Carcanet New Press/Humanities Press

Davis, Gene (see listing for Baldwin, Deirdra)

Davis, Jon—*West Of New England.* Merriam Frontier Award

Davis, William Virgil—*The Dark Hours.* Calliope Press

Day, Jean—*Linear C.* Tuumba Press

Daya, Gulu—*Awakening: Paths & Pursuits Of Pure Knowledge.* Daya

Deahl, James—*In The Last Horn's Call.* Aureole Point Press

DeFoe, Mark—*Bringing Home Breakfast And Other Poems.* Black Willow

DeFrees, Madeline—*Magpie On The Gallows.* Copper Canyon Press

De Luca, Angelo—*Chimera And Cosmos.* Great Society Press

Derricotte, Toi—*Natural Birth: Poetry.* Crossing Press

Dick, J. P.—*Homing.* Los Poetry Press (England)

Dickey, James—*Night Hurdling: Poems, Essays, Conversations, Commencements And Afterwords.* Bruccoli Clark Publishers
—*Puella.* Doubleday
—*The Central Motion: Poems 1968-1979.* Wesleyan University Press

Di Piero, W. S.—*The Only Dangerous Thing.* Elpenor Books

Dixon, Melvin—*Change Of Territory: Poems.* University of Kentucky

Dobrin, Arthur—*Out Of Place.* Backstreet Editions

Doolittle, Hilda (see listing for H. D.)

Doria, Charles—*The Game Of Europe: A Comedy Of High Gothic Romance Frankly Rendered Out Of The Senseless.* Swallow Press

Dougherty, William F.—*Owl Light.* Wings Press

Douskey, Frank—*Rowing Across The Dark.* University of Georgia Press

Dove, Rita—*Museum.* Carnegie-Mellon University Press

Dovichi, A.—*The Morning After Midnight.* Iron Press

Dubois, Rochelle H.—*Timelapse: A Book Of New Poems.* Lunchroom Press

Duff, Gerald—*Calling Collect.* University Presses of Florida

Dugan, Alan—*Collected Poems.* Ecco Press

Dugan, Thomas—*A Modern Bestiary.* Cordella Books

Dunn, Millard—*Engraved On Air.* Kentucky Arts Council

E

Eaton, Charles Edward—*The Thing King.* Cornwall Books

Edda, Saemundar—*Norse Poems* (translated by W. H. Auden and Paul B. Taylor). Athlone Press/Humanities Press

Efird, Susan—*The Eye Of Heaven.* Abattoir Editions

Eigner, Larry—*Waters, Places, A Time.* Black Sparrow Press

Ekelof, Gunnar—*Songs Of Something Else: Selected Poems Of Gunnar Ekelof* (translated by Leonard Nathan and James Larson). Princeton University Press

Elder, Karl—*The Celibate.* Seems

Eller, Vernard (translator)—*Pearl* (Middle English poem, author unspecified). University Press of America

Elsberg, John—*Home-Style Cooking On Third Avenue.*

White Ewe Press

Endrezze-Danielson, Anita—*Burning The Fields.* Confluence Press
—*The North People.* Blue Cloud Quarterly Press

Engels, John—*Weather-Fear: New & Selected Poems, 1958-1982.* University of Georgia Press

Enright, D. J.—*Collected Poems.* Oxford University Press

Eshleman, Clayton—*Fracture.* Black Sparrow Press

Esteban, Claude—*Transparent God* (translated by David Cloutier). Kosmos

Etter, Dave—*Cornfields.* Spoon River Poetry Press
—*West Of Chicago.* Spoon River Poetry Press
—*Alliance, Illinois* (complete edition). Spoon River Poetry Press

F

Fabian, R. Gerry—*Elemental Women;* Faslund, Elysabeth Nancy—*The City Of The Dead.* Raw Dog Press

Fairchild, B. H.—*C&W Machine Works.* Trilobite Press

Farnsworth, Robert—*Three Or Four Hills And A Cloud.* Wesleyan University Press

Farruggio, Philip A.—*Please Read Me.* Privately printed

Farrukhzad, Furugh—*Bride Of Acacias: Selected Poems Of Furugh Furrukhzad* (translated by Jascha Kessler and Amin Banani). Caravan Books

Feirstein, Frederick—*Fathering: A Sequence Of Poems.* Apple-wood Books

Feldman, Irving—*Teach Me, Dear Sister.* Penguin Books

Feliciano, Margarita—*Window On The Sea.* Latin American Literary Review Press

Ferry, David—*Strangers: A Book Of Poems.* University of Chicago Press

Finch, Robert—*The Grand Duke of Moscow's Favourite Solo.* Porcupine's Quill

Fisher, Aileen—*Rabbits, Rabbits.* Harper & Row

Fishman, Sam—*The Restless Mind.* L. Stuart

Flook, Maria—*Reckless Wedding.* Houghton Mifflin

Fortner, Ethel N.—*Nervous On The Curves.* St. Andrews Press

Fowlie, Wallace—*Characters From Proust: Poems.* Louisiana State University Press

Foye, June E.—*Many Rooms, Many Faces: New And Selected Poems.* Privately printed

Fraire, Isabel—*Poems In The Lap Of Death* (translated by Thomas Hoeksema). Latin American Literary Review Press

Frank, Jacqueline—*No One Took A Country From Me: Poems.* Alicejames Books

Freedman, Neil—*Green: In Loves Season.* Pryor-Pettengill

Friedlander, Ginny—*The Last 1000 Years.* Charles Street Press

Frost, Carol—*The Fearful Child: Poems.* Ithaca House

Frost, Robert—*North Of Boston: Poems* (edited by Edward Connery Lathem). Dodd, Mead

Fuller, Roy—*The Individual In His Times: A Selection Of The Poetry Of Roy Fuller* (edited by V. J. Lee). Athlone Press/Humanities Press

Fulton, Alice—*Dance Script With Electric Ballerina.* University of Pennsylvania Press

Funkhouser, Erica—*Natural Affinities.* Alice James Books

G

Galarza, Ernesto—*Kodachromes In Rhyme: Poems.* University of Notre Dame Press

Gallo, Philip—*Some Roses.* Abattoir Editions

Galvin, Brendan—*Winter Oysters: Poems.* University of Georgia Press

Gama, Jose Basilio da—*The Uruguay (A Historical Romance of South America* (translated by Richard F. Burton; edited by Frederick C. H. Garcia and Edward F. Stanton). University of California Press

Gardner, Silvana—*When Sunday Comes.* University of Queensland Press

Gascoyne, David—*Collected Poems.* Oxford University Press

Geller, Leslie M.—*North Cape And Other Poems.* Publication Arts

Gibson, Grace—*Drakes Branch.* St. Andrews Press

Gibson, Julia (see A-Se-Gi)

Gibson, Margaret—*Long Walks In The Afternoon.* Louisiana State University Press

Gidlow, Elsa—*Saaphic Songs: Eighteen To Eighty.* Druid Heights Books

Gifford, Larry—*Beautiful Phantoms: Selected Poems 1968-1980.* Tombouctou Books

Gilbert, Celia—*Bonfire.* Alicejames Books

Giles, Lllewellyn Ivory—*Songs From My Father's Pockets: Poems.* Shadow Press

Gilliland, Mary—*Gathering Fire.* Ithaca House

Gillis, Everett A.—*Far Beyond Distance.* Pisces Press

Gillon, Adam—*The Withered Leaf: A Medley Of Haiku And Senryu.* Astra Books

Gilson, William—*Old Poems.* Wickwire Press

Giovanni, Nikki—*Those Who Ride The Night Winds.* William Morrow

Gizzi, Michael—*Species Of Intoxication: Extracts From The Leaves Of The Doctor Ordinaire: Poems.* Burning Deck

Gleason, Marian—*Bystanding.* Golden Quill Press

Glickman, Susan—*Complicity.* Signal Editions/Vehicule Press

Gluck, Louise—*Firstborn: Poems.* Ecco Press

Goacher, Denis—*If Hell, Hellas.* National Poetry Foundation

Godfrey, John—*Dabble: Poems 1966-1980.* Full Court Press

Gogou, Katerina—*Three Clicks Left* (translated by Jack Hirschman). Night Horn Books

Goldbarth, Albert—*Original Light: New And Selected*

Poems, 1973-1983. Ontario Review Press/Persea Books

Goldberger, Iefke—*The Catch.* Sol Press

Goldowsky, Barbara—*Ferry To Nirvana.* National Writers Press

Goldsmith, Otto—*Some Thoughts That Seem Important.* Myriad Moods

Goldstein, Sanford—*Gaijin Aesthetics.* Juniper Press

Goodman, Miriam—*Signal-Noise: Poems.* Alicejames Books

Gosney, Michael—*We Are It.* Avant Books

Gosvami, Satsvarupa Dasa—*Remembering Srila Prabhupada: A Free-Verse Rendition Of The Life And Teachings Of His Devine Grace, A. C. Bhaktivedanta Swami Prabhupada.* Gita-Nagari Press

Graham, Jorie—*Erosion.* Princeton University Press

Graham, Neile—*Seven Robins.* Penumbra Press

Grahn, Judy—*The Queen Of Wands.* The Crossing Press

Gray, Thomas—*Selected Poems* (edited by John Heath-Stubbs). Fyfield Books/Humanities Press

Greco, Leonard (see listing for Chang, Diana)

Green, Rose Basile—*Songs Of Ourselves.* Cornwall Books

Greenway, William—*Pressure Under Grace.* Breitenbush Books

Gregerson, Linda—*Fire In The Conservatory.* Dragon Gate

Gregor, Arthur—*A Longing In The Land: Memoir Of A Quest.* Schocken Books
—*Embodiment And Other Poems.* Sheep Meadow Press

Grenfell, Cynthia—*Stone Run: Tidings.* Sunstone Press

Gresser, Sy—*Fragments & Others.* American Studies Press

Griffin, Larry D.—*New Fires.* Full Count Press

Grosholz, Emily—*The River Painter: Poems.* University of Illinois Press

Grossman, Richard—*The Animals.* Zygote Press

Grutzmacher, Harold and Steven—*Generations.* Spoon River Poetry Press

Guillaume de Lorris; Jean de Meun—*The Romance Of The Rose* (translated by Charles Dahlberg). University Press of New England

Gullans, Charles—*The Bright Universe And Other Poems.* Abattoir Editions
—*A Diatribe To Dr. Steele.* Symposium Press

Gurney, Ivor—*Collected Poems Of Ivor Gurney* (edited by P. J. Kavanagh). Oxford University Press
—*War Letters: A Selection* (edited by R. K. R. Thornton). Carcanet New Press/Humanities Press

Guro, Elena—*The Little Camels Of The Sky* (translated by Kevin O'Brien). Ardis Publishers

Guthrie, Ramon—*Maximum Security Ward And Selected Poems* (edited by Sally M. Gall). Persea Books

H

H. D. (Hilda Doolittle)—*Collected Poems, 1912-1944* (edited by Louis L. Martz). New Directions Pub. Co.

Hadas, Rachel—*Slow Transparency.* Wesleyan University Press

Hague, Richard—*Ripening: Poems.* Ohio State University Press

Halperin, Mark—*A Place Made Fast.* Copper Canyon Press

Halpern, Daniel—*Seasonal Rights.* Viking/Penguin

Halpern, Moyshe-Leyb—*In New York: A Selection* (translated by Kathryn Hellerstein). Jewish Publication Society of America

Hamburger, Michael—*Variations.* Carcanet New Press/Humanities Press

Hamill, Sam—*Fatal Pleasure.* Breitenbush Books

Hankla, Cathryn—*Phenomena.* University of Missouri Press

Hansen, Dorothy Lee—*Africa To Me.* Adinkra Press

Hanson, Kenneth O.—*Lighting The Night Sky: Poems.* Breitenbush Books

Harder, Uffe—*Paper Houses.* Curbstone Press

Hardy, Thomas—*The Complete Poetical Works of Thomas Hardy: Volume I—Wessex Poems; Poems Of Past And Present; Times Laughingstocks* (edited by Samuel Hynes). Oxford University Press

Harjo, Joy—*She Had Some Horses.* Thunder's Mouth Press

Harmon, William—*One Long Poem.* Louisiana State University Press

Harrington, Anthony—*Tersery Versery.* Hendricks Publishing

Harshman, Marc—*Turning Out The Stones.* State Street Press

Hart, Paul—*A Crossing.* University Microfilms

Haskins, Lola—*Planting The Children.* University Presses of Florida

Hauser, Gwen—*Gophers And Swans.* Fiddlehead Poetry Books

Hayes, Dorsha—*New Poems From The Bell Branch.* Dragon's Teeth Press

Hazard, James—*Fire In Whiting, Indiana.* Juniper Press

Hazen, Rachel A.—*Words Ready For Music: Poems Of A Young Teenager.* Branden Press

Hazo, Samuel—*Thank A Bored Angel.* New Directions Pub. Corp.

Heath-Stubbs, John—*Naming The Beasts.* Carcanet New Press/Humanities Press

Henri, Raymond—*Dispatches From The Fields.* Dragon's Teeth Press

Hepburn, Brent—*Wrought Iron Blossoms.* Privately printed

Hemingway, Ernest—*Complete Poems* (edited by Nicholas Gerogiannis). University of Nebraska Press (reprint)

Henrichsen, Dennis—*The Attraction of Heavenly Bodies.* Wesleyan University Press

Henryson, Robert—*Selected Poems* (edited by W. R. J. Barron). Fyfield Books/Humanities Press

Herbert, George—*The Bodleian Manuscript Of George Herbert's Poems: A Facsimile Of Tanner 307.* Scholars' Facsimiles & Reprints
—*The Complete Works In Verse And Prose Of George Herbert* (edited by Alexander B. Grosart). AMS Press (reprint)

Hesiod—*The Poems Of Hesiod* (translated by R. M. Frazer). University of Oklahoma Press

Hess, Linda; Singh, Shukdev (translators)—*The Bijak Of Kabir.* North Point Press

Hikmet, Nazim—*Human Landscapes* (translated by Randy Blessing and Mutlu Konuk). Persea Books

Hinrichsen, Dennis—*The Attraction Of Heavenly Bodies.* Wesleyan University Press

Hoccleve, Thomas—*Selected Poems* (edited by Berard O'Donoghue). Fyfield Books/Humanities Press

Hoeft, Robert D.—*Tools.* Mosaic Press

Hoey, Allen—*Hymns To A Tree.* Tamarack Editions

Holden, Jonathan—*Falling From Stardom.* Carnegie-Mellon University Press

Hollander, John—*Powers Of Thirteen.* Atheneum

Hollis, Jocelyn—*Twentieth Century Sonnets* (edited by J. Topham). American Poetry Press

Holub, Miroslav—*Interferon, Or On Theatre* (translated by David Young and Dana Habova). Field

Honig, Edwin—*Interrupted Praise: New and Selected Poems.* Scarecrow Press

Hood-Adams, Rebecca—*Biscuit Soppin' Blues.* Proscenium Press

Hooker, Jeremy—*A View From The Source: Selected Poems.* Carcanet New Press/Humanities Press

Hoover, Paul—*Somebody Talks A Lot.* Yellow Press

Horace—*The Complete Works Of Horace* (translated by Charles E. Passage). F. Ungar

Howard, Mitchell—*Always Seeking The Edge: Poems.* Amphibian Publications

Hudson, Marc—*Afterlight.* University of Massachusetts Press

Humes, Harry—*Winter Weeds: Poems.* University of Missouri Press

Hunt, Connie—*Reaching.* Pulsar Publications

I

Ignatow, Yaedi—*The Flaw: Poems.* Sheep Meadow Press

Inez, Colette—*Eight Minutes From The Sun.* Saturday Press

Isherwood, Christopher; Mangeot, Sylvain—*People One Ought To Know.* Doubleday

Islam, Kabirul—*The Home-Coming.* Writers Workshop

J

Jabes, Edmond—*The Book Of Questions: Yael, Elya, Aely* (translated by Rosemarie Waldrop). Wesleyan University Press

Jackowska, Nicki—*Earthwalks.* Ceolfrith Press

Jackson, Richard—*Part Of The Story: Poems.* Grove Press

James, David—*Surface Streets.* Applezaba Press

Janowitz, Phyllis—*Visiting Rites.* Princeton University Press

Janssen, Martha—*Silent Scream.* Fortress Press

Jason, Philip K.—*Near The Fire: Poems.* Dryad Press

Jean de Meun (see listing for Guillaume de Lorris).

Jenner, Thomas—*The Emblem Books Of Thomas Jenner: Photoreproductions* (introduction by Sidney Gottlieb). Scholars' Facsimiles & Reprints

Jennings, Elizabeth—*Celebrations & Elegies.* Carcanet New Press/Humanities Press

John, Da Free—*Crazy Da Must Sing, Inclined To His Weaker Side: Confessional Poems Of Liberation And Love.* Dawn Horse Press

John Paul II, Pope (Karol Wojtyla)—*Collected Poems* (translated by Jerzy Peterkiewicz). Random House

Johnson, D. C.—*Much Toil, Much Blame.* Read Weather Press

Johnson, Denis—*Angels.* Alfred A. Knopf

Jones, David—*The Roman Quarry, And Other Sequences* (edited by Harman Grisewood and Rene Hague). Sheep Meadow Press

Jones, Gayl—*The Hermit Poems.* Lotus Press

Jones, Seaborn—*Drowning From The Inside Out.* Cherry Valley Editions

Jones, Susan—*The Unmarked Landscape.* Glavin Press

Jong, Erica—*Ordinary Miracles: New Poems.* New American Library

Joselow, Beth—*The April Wars: Poems.* Sultan of Swat Books

Joseph, Lawrence—*Shouting At No One.* University of Pittsburgh Press

Judson, John—*North of Athens.* Spoon River Poetry Press

Juergensen, Hans—*Fire-Tested.* Lieb-Schott Publications

K

Kakavelakis, Demetris—*Massa Confusa: A Vision For America* (translated by Athan Anagnostopoulos). Hellenic College Press

Kallet, Marilyn—*In The Great Night: Poems.* Ithaca House

Kaminsky, Marc—*A Table With People: Poems.* Sun
—*Daily Bread.* University of Illinois Press

Katrovas, Richard—*Green Dragons.* Wesleyan University Press

Katz, Susan A.—*The Separate Sides Of Need.* Song Press

Katz-Levine, Judy—*Speaking With Deaf-Blind Children.* Free Beginning Press

Kavanaugh, James—*Who Will Love Me In My Madness?* Dutton

Kazantzis, Judith; Roberts, Michele; Wandor, Michelene—*Touch Papers.* Allison & Busby

Keats, John—*Complete Poems* (edited by Jack Stillinger). Belknap Press/Harvard University Press

Kelly, Robert—*Under Words*. Black Sparrow Press

Kennedy, X. J.—*Did Adam Name The Vinegarroon?* David R. Godine

Keyen, William—*Along This Water*. Tamarack Editions

Khairallah, George—*Academe*. Privately printed
—*The Making Of Americans*. Privately printed

Khatchadurian, Haig—*Shadows Of Time: Poems*. Ashod Press

Kherdian, David—*Place Of Birth*. Breitenbush Books

Kilmer, Joyce—*Trees & Other Poems*. Larlin Corp.

Kinnell, Galway—*Selected Poems*. Houghton Mifflin

Kirk, Norman Andrew—*Panda Zoo*. Bitterroot-West of Boston Press

Kirkpatrick, Margaret—*Slow Rush Of Time*. Sycamore Press

Kitchen, Judith—*Upstairs Window*. Tamarack Editions

Kitrilakis, Thalia—*Biting Sun*. Kelsey Street Press

Klepfisz, Irena—*Keeper Of Accounts*. Persephone Press

Kline, Shaya—*After The Chebron Pogrom*. Sand Ridge Books

Kloss, Phillips—*Selected Poems Of Phillips Kloss*. Sunstone Press

Knight, Hilary—*Hilary Knight's The Owl And The Pussy-Cat* (based on the poem by Edward Lear). Macmillan

Knobel, Paul—*Events*. Orianna Press (Australia)

Knott, Bill—*Becos: Poems*. Random House

Knox, Caroline—*The House Party: Poems*. University of Georgia Press

Koch, Kenneth—*Days & Nights*. Random House

Koehn, Lala—*Forest Full Of Rain*. Sono Nis Press

Kostelanetz, Richard—*Fields/Turfs/Pitches/Arenas*. BkMk Press

Kostiner, Eileen—*Love's Other Face*. Curbstone Press

Kotzwinkle, William—*Great World Circus*. Putnam

Kowit, Steve—*Lurid Confessions*. Carpenter Press

Kramer, Aaron—*In Wicked Times*. Black Buzzard Press
—*The Burning Bush: Poems And Other Writings, 1940-1980*. Cornwall Books

Krause, Tina—*I Am As Dark As Your Smile November*. Black Willow

Krenshaw, J. C.—*Ugly Sneakers Are Cool!* Whirling Dervish Press

Krishna, Valerie (translator)—*The Alliterative Morte Arthure: A New Verse Translation*. University Press of America

Krishnan, Gopi—*Milestones To The Sun*. Writers Workshop

Krishnasami, Christine—*Iris In Dark Water*. Writers Workshop

Kumin, Maxine—*Our Ground Time Here Will Be Brief*. Penguin Books

Kuzma, Greg—*Of China And Of Greece*. Sun
—*Everyday Life*. Spoon River Poetry Press
—*A Horse Of A Different Color*. Illuminati

Kyger, Joanne—*Going On: Selected Poems, 1958-1980* (selected by Robert Creeley). Dutton

L

LaGattuta, Margo—*Diversion Road*. State Street Press

Lall, Emmanuel Narendra—*Blue Venda*. Writers Workshop

Lally, Michael—*Attitude: Uncollected Poems Of The Seventies*. Hanging Loose Press

Lamont, Corliss—*Lover's Credo*. W. L. Bauhan

Lamport, Felicia—*Light Metres*. Perigee Books

Landor, Walter Savage—*Landor's Imaginary Conversations; Landor's Poems, Dialogues In Verse And Epigrams; Landor's Longer Prose Works* (edited by Charles G. Crump). AMS Press (reprint)

Lane, Patrick—*Women In The Dust*. Mosaic Press

Larsen, Marianne—*Selected Poems* (translated by Nadia Christensen). Augustinus/Curbstone

Lasker-Schuler, Elsa—*Your Diamond Dreams Cut Open My Arteries: Poems* (translated by Robert P. Newton). University of North Carolina Press

Lattimore, Richmond—*Continuing Conclusions: Poems*. Louisiana State University Press

Lawson, Helen—*Live Me A River*. Blue Spruce Press

Layton, Irving—*The Gucci Bag*. McClelland & Stewart

Lear, Edward—*The Owl And The Pussy Cat*. Holiday House
—*An Edward Lear Alphabet*. Lothrop, Lee & Shepard

Lee, David—*Shadow Weaver*. Jawbone Press

Lengyel, Cornell—*Late News From Adam's Acres*. Dragon's Teeth Press

Lenhart, Gary—*One At A Time*. United Artists Books

Lenier, Sue—*Swansongs*. Oleander Press

Leopardi, Giacomo—*The Moral Essays*. Columbia University Press

Lermontov, Mikhail—*Narrative Poems By Alexander Pushkin And By Mikhail Lermontov* (translated by Charles Johnston). Random House
—*Major Poetical Works* (translated by Anatoly Liberman). University of Minnesota Press

Lesser, Rika—*Etruscan Things: Poems*. George Braziller

Levertov, Denise—*Poems, 1960-1967*. New Directions Pub. Co.

Lewis, Roger—*The Carbon Gang*. Cherry Valley Editions

Lieberman, Laurence—*Eros At The World Kite Pageant: Poems 1979-1982*. Macmillan

Lifshin, Lyn—*Madonna Who Shifts For Herself*. Applezaba Press

Lily, Peter—*The Great Riding: The Story Of De Soto In America*. University of Arkansas Press

Lindskoog, Kathryn Ann—*A Child's Garden Of Christian Verses* (adapted from Robert Louis Stevenson). Regal Books

Lipsitz, David—*Illusions On The Road*. Bragdon Books

Little, Geraldine C.—*Hakugai: Poem From A Concentration Camp.* Curbstone Publishing

Lobel, Arnold—*The Book Of Pigricks.* Harper & Row

Lohmann, Jeanne—*Steadying The Landscape.* Privately printed

Loring, David M.—*Coastal Conversations.* Panorama West

Louthan, Robert—*Living In Code.* University of Pittsburgh Press

Lowell, Robert—*Lord Weary's Castle; And The Mills Of The Kavanaughs.* Harcourt Brace Jovanovich

Luhrmann, Thomas—*The Objects In The Garden.* Wesleyan University Press

Lum, Echo R.—*Poetic Reflections.* Privately printed

Lumpkin, Kirk—*Co-hearing.* Zyga Multimedia Research

Lunch, Lydia; Cervenka, Exene—*Adulterers Anonymous.* Grove Press

Luria-Sukenick, Lynn—*Houdini Houdini.* Cleveland State University Poetry Center

Luton, Mildred—*Little Chicks' Mothers And All The Others.* Viking Press

Lynch, Laura Bethany—*Poetry To Read Alone At Night.* Artefact Co.

M

MacAdams, Phoebe—*Sunday.* Tombouctou Books

MacBeth, George—*Poems From Oby.* Atheneum

MacInnis, Jamie—*Practicing.* Tombouctou Books

MacLow, Jackson—*From Pearl Harbor Day To FDR's Birthday.* Sun & Moon Press

MacPhee, Rosalind—*What Place Is This?* Coach House Press

Maddox, Everette—*The Everette Maddox Song Book.* New Orleans Poetry Journal Press

Mahon, Derek—*The Hunt By Night.* Wake Forest University Press

Mahra, Rooma—*Sunshadow.* Writers Workshop

Mailman, Leo—*The Handyman Poems.* Applezaba Press

Makuck, Peter—*Where We Live.* BOA Editions

Malanga, Gerard—*This Will Kill That.* Black Sparrow Press

Malloy, Merrit—*We Hardly See Each Other Any More.* Doubleday

Mandelstam, Osip—*Selected Poems* (translated by Clarence Brown and W. S. Merwin). Atheneum

Mangeot, Sylvain (see listing for Isherwood, Christopher)

Margolis, Gary—*The Day We Still Stand Here.* University of Georgia Press

Mariani, Paul—*Crossing Cocytus.* Grove Press

Martinez, Maria—*Sterling Silver Roses.* La Morenita Publishers

Martone, John—*Ocean Vows.* Copper Beech Press

Marz, Roy—*The Island-Maker.* Ithaca House

Matlin, David—*Fontana's Mirror.* Boss Books

Matson, Clive—*On The Inside.* Cherry Valley Editions

Mayer, Bernadette—*Midwinter Day.* Turtle Island Foundation

McAuley, James J.—*The Exile's Book Of Hours: A Sequence.* Confluence Press

McBride, Mekeel—*The Going Under Of Evening Land.* Carnegie-Mellon University Press

McClane, Kenneth A.—*These Halves Are Whole.* Black Willow Chapbook Series

McClure, Michael—*Fragments Of Perseus.* New Directions Pub. Co.

McDaniel, Wilma Elizabeth—*Sister Vayda's Song.* Hanging Loose Press

McDonald, Agnes—*Four North Carolina Poets.* St. Andrews Press

McDougall, Jo—*Women Who Marry Houses.* Coyote Love Press

McEwen, Phyllis—*Hystery And Other Tools For Women.* American Studies Press

McFee, Michael—*Plain Air.* University Presses of Florida

McFerren, Martha—*Delusions Of A Popular Mind.* New Orleans Poetry Journal Press

McGrath, Thomas—*Echoes Inside The Labyrinth.* Thunder's Mouth Press

McKain, David—*The Common Life.* Alicejames Books

McKee, Louis—*Schuylkill Country.* Wampeter Press

McKee, Martha—*Single Circles.* Landfall Press

McKuen, Rod—*The Sound Of Solitude.* Harper & Row

McLaren, Ken—*Yes With Variations* (edited by William Packard). The Smith

McLaughlin, William—*At Rest In The Midwest.* Cleveland State University Poetry Center

McNair, Wesley—*The Faces Of Americans In 1853.* University of Missouri Press

McPherson, Michael—*Singing With The Owls.* Petronium Press

McPherson, Sandra—*Elegies For The Hot Season.* Ecco Press
—*Patron Happiness: Poems.* Ecco Press

Meehan, Brian—*Plain Song.* Symposium Press

Melfi, Mary—*A Bride In Three Acts.* Guernica Editions

Merriam, Eve—*Love Poems.* Alfred A. Knopf

Merrill, James—*From The First Nine: Poems 1946-1976.* Atheneum
—*The Changing Light At Sandover.* Atheneum

Merwin, W. S.—*Opening The Hand.* Atheneum
—*Finding The Islands.* North Point Press

Messerli, Douglas—*Dinner On The Lawn.* Sun & Moon Press

Michelson, Peter—*When The Revolution Really.* Thunder's Mouth Press

Middleton, Christopher—*Woden Dog.* Burning Deck

Middleton, David—*Reliquiae.* R. L. Barth

Midler, Bette—*The Saga Of Baby Divine.* Crown

Miles, Josephine—*Collected Poems, 1930-83.* University of Illinois Press

Miller, Jane—*The Greater Leisures.* Doubleday

Mills, Robert—*Toward Sunset At A Great Height.* Spoon River Poetry Press

Milton, John—*Paradise Lost: A Prose Rendition* (edited by Robert A. Shepherd, Jr.). Seabury Press

Miranda, Gary—*Grace Period.* Princeton University Press

Mitchell, Susan—*The Water Inside The Water.* Wesleyan University Press

Mizejewski, Linda—*The Other Woman.* Signpost Press

Moffi, Larry—*A Simple Progression.* Ampersand Press

Monteiro, George—*The Coffee Exchange.* Gavea-Brown

Montes de Oca, Marco Antonio—*Twenty-One Poems* (translated by Laura Villasenor). Latin American Literary Review Press

Moody, Shirley—*Four North Carolina Poets.* St. Andrews Press

Moore, Clement C.—*The Night Before Christmas.* Golden Press

Moore, Marianne—*The Complete Poems Of Marianne Moore.* Penguin

Moore, Richard—*The Education Of A Mouse.* Countryman Press

Moretti, Josephine B.—*Love Is Where.* Golden Quill Press

Morgan, Edwin—*Poems Of Thirty Years.* Carcanet New Press/Humanities Press

Morgan, Frederick—*Eleven Poems.* NADJA

Morgan, Robin—*Depth Perception: New Poems And A Masque.* Anchor Press/Doubleday

Morice, Dave—*Poetry Comics! A Cartooniverse Of Poems.* Simon and Schuster

Morris, Herbert—*Peru.* Harper & Row

Morrison, Madison—*O.* Working Week Press

Morrow, Bradford—*Posthumes.* Cadmus Editions

Mosby, George—*Population.* Hanging Loose Press

Mudd, Harvey—*The Plain Of Smokes.* Black Sparrow Press

Mulvihill, Michael—*Bodies For A Small Museum.* Cambium Press

Munro, J. A.—*Lines From Lincoln Land.* Adams Press

Murdoch, Royal—*The Disrobing: Sex And Satire* (edited by Winston Leyland). Gay Sunshine Press

Murray, Les A.—*The Vernacular Republic: Selected Poems.* Persea Books

N

Nelson, Yvette—*We'll Come When It Rains.* New Rivers Press

Newth, Rebecca—*Finding The Lamb.* Open Book

Newton, Alice Spohn—*Have A Cup Of Bygones.* Golden

Nelson, Paul—*Days Off.* University Press of Virginia Quill Press

Nicholson, Norman—*Selected Poems, 1940-1982.* Faber and Faber

Nordbrandt, Henrik—*Selected Poems.* Augustinus/Curbstone

Nowlan, Alden—*I Might Not Tell Everybody This: Poems.* Clarke, Irwin

Noyes, Alfred—*The Highwayman.* Lothrop, Lee & Shepard Books

Nutting, Leslie—*Not Honesty.* Manoeuvres Press——*Theseus.* Manoeuvres Press

O

Oandasan, William—*A Branch Of California Redwood.* American Indian Study Center

Oates, Joyce Carol—*Invisible Woman: New & Selected Poems.* Ontario Review Press

Ochester, Ed—*Miracle Mile.* Carnegie-Mellon University Press

O'Gara, Gwynn—*Snake Women Poems.* Beatitude Press

Oles, Carole—*Quarry.* University of Utah Press

Oliver, Mary—*American Primitive: Poems.* Little, Brown

Olson, Charles—*The Maximus Poems* (edited by George F. Butterick). University of California Press

Oppenheimer, Joel—*At Fifty: A Poem.* St. Andrews Press

Orszag-Land, Thomas—*Anarctic Testimony.* Tern Press

Orth, Ghita—*The Music Of What Happens.* Saturday Press

Osborn, Marijane (translator)—*Beowulf: A Verse Translation With Treasures Of The Ancient North.* University of California Press

Ostergren, Jan—*Rainmaker* (translated by John Matthias and Goren Pritz-Pahlson). Ohio University Press

Ostriker, Alicia—*A Woman Under The Surface: Poems And Prose Poems.* Princeton University Press

Ovensen, Barney—*The Truth About Jesus.* Privately printed

Ovid—*The Erotic Poems* (translated by Peter Green). Penguin

P

Pacheco, Jose Emilio—*Signals From The Flames* (translated by Thomas Hoeksema). Latin American Literary Review Press

Page, William—*The Gatekeeper.* Raccoon Books

Panori, Michael—*Two Skies.* Glavin Press

Pasolini, Pier Paolo—*Poems* (selected and translated by Norman MacAfee with Luciano Martinengo). Vintage Books

Pastan, Linda—*PM/AM: New And Selected Poems.* W. W. Norton

Pasternak, Boris—*My Sister—Life; And, The Highest Sickness* (translated from the Russian by Mark Rudman and Bohdan Boychuk). Ardis

Pastorius, Francis—*Deliciae Hortenses, Or, Garden-Recreations; And Volpptates Apianae* (edited by Christoph E. Schweitzer). Camden House

Pau-Llosa, Ricardo—*Sorting Metaphors.* Anhinga Press

Paulin, Tom—*The Liberty Tree.* Faber and Faber

Pawlowski, Robert—*The Seven Sacraments And Other Poems.* Flower Mound Writing Co.

Paxston, Laura; Brunish, Corey—*Without Wings.* Privately printed

Pearson, Carol Lynn—*A Widening View.* Bookcraft

Perchik, Simon—*The Snowcat Poems, 1980-1981, To The Photographs Of Robert Frank.* Linwood Publishers

Percy, William Alexander—*Sewanee.* F. C. Beil

Perlman, Anne S.—*Sorting It Out.* Carnegie-Mellon University Press

Perry, Marion—*Establishing Intimacy.* Textile Bridge Press

Perse, Saint-John—*Selected Poems* (edited by Mary Ann Caws). New Directions Pub. Co.

Peters, Anne—*Rings Of Green.* Colin Smythe/Humanities Press

Peters, Robert—*What Dillinger Meant To Me.* Sea Horse Press

Petrie, Paul—*Strange Gravity.* Tidal Press

Petrosky, Tony—*Jurgis Petraskas: Poems.* Louisiana State University Press

Pfingston, Roger—*The Circus Of Unreasonable Acts.* Years Press

Pick, Michael Robert—*Childhood, Namhood, Manhood: The Writings Of Michael Robert Pick, A Vietnam Veteran.* Pizzuto

Pierce, David—*Ballads Of A Bench Warmer.* Caislan Press

Piercy, Marge—*Stone, Paper, Knife.* Alfred A. Knopf

Pinsky, Robert—*History Of My Heart.* Ecco Press

Plat, Hugh—*The Floures Of Phiosophie;* Whitney, Isabella—*A Sweet Nosgay* and *The Copy Of A Letter* (introduction by Richard J. Panofsky). Scholars' Facsimiles & Reprints

Plumly, Stanley—*Summer Celestial.* Ecco Press

Poe, Edgar Allan—*The Unabridged Edgar Allan Poe* (part poetry). Running Press

Ponge, Francis—*The Making Of Pre* (translated by Lee Fahnestock). University of Missouri Press

Porphyry—*The Cave Of The Nymphs* (translated by Robert Lamberton). Station Hill Press

Pound, Ezra—*Collected Early Poems Of Ezra Pound.* New Directions Pub. Co.

Powell, Neil—*A Season Of Calm Weather.* Carcanet New Press/Humanities Press

Prelutsky, Jack—*Zoo Doings And Other Animal Poems.* Greenwillow Books
—*It's Valentine's Day.* Greenwillow Books

Price, Bobby G.—*Strangulation.* St. Andrews Press

Price, Bren—*Inside The Wind.* Sunstone Press

Price, Larry—*Proof.* Tuumba Press

Price, Reynolds—*Vital Provisions.* Atheneum

Prince, Pamela—*The Secret World Of Teddy Bears.* Harmony Books

Prunty, Wyatt—*The Times Between.* Johns Hopkins University Press

P'u Ming—*Oxherding Pictures & Verses* (translated by Red Pine). Empty Bowl

Puri, Ishwar Kanwar—*Narcissus Wept.* Writers Workshop

Pushkin, Alexander—*Narrative Poems By Alexander Pushkin And By Mikhail Lermontov* (translated by Charles Johnston). Random House
—*The Bronze Horseman: Selected Poems Of Alexander Pushkin* (translated by D. M. Thomas). Viking

Q

Quinn, Bernetta— . . . *Dancing In Stillness.* St. Andrews Press

R

Ragosta, Ray—*Sherds.* Burning Deck

Rahman, Munibur—*Shahr-I Gumnam* (in Urdu). Urdu Publications (Canada)

Raine, B. N.—*The Crescent God And Other Poems.* Writers Workshop

Rando—*Most Recent Poems.* Dead Clam Press

Rao, K. R.—*Continents Of Silence.* Writers Workshop

Ratch, Jerry—*Hot Weather: Poems Selected And New.* Scarecrow Press

Rath, Sara—*Remembering The Wilderness: Poems.* Northword

Ratner, Rochelle—*Practicing To Be A Woman.* Scarecrow Press

Ray, David—*The Touched Life.* Scarecrow Press

Red, Jacques—*Recitatif/The Party Is Over* (translated by Dorothy Brown Aspinwall). International Book Publishers

Reed, John—*The Complete Poetry Of John Reed* (edited by Jack Alan Robbins). University Press of America

Reid, Christopher—*Pea Soup.* Oxford University Press

Reiss, James—*Express.* University of Pittsburgh Press

Rhodes, James R.—*James R. Rhodes' Poems.* E. Mellen Press

Richmond, Lee J.—*Diary Of A Winter Fly: Free-Metre Haiku.* HPC

Riley, James Whitcomb—*The Best Of James Whitcomb Riley* (edited by Donald C. Manlove). Indiana University Press
—*Little Orphan Annie.* Putnam

Rilke, Rainer Maria—*Orchards: A Sequence Of French Poems* (translated by A. Poulin, Jr.). Graywolf Press
—*Poems, 1912-1926* (translated by Michael Hamburger). Black Swan Books
—*The Selected Poems Of Rainer Maria Rilke* (edited and translated by Stephen Mitchell). Random House

Ritchie, Elisavietta—*Raking The Snow.* Washington Writers' Publishing House

Ritsos, Yannis—*Erotica* (translated by Kimon Friar). Sachem Press

Rivers, J. W.—*Proud And On My Feet.* University of Georgia Press

Roberts, George—*Scrut.* Holy Cow! Press

Roberts, Michele (see listing for Kazantzis, Judith)

Robinson, Kit—*Riddle Road.* Tuumba Press

Rodefer, Stephen—*Four Lectures.* The Figures

Rogow, Zack—*Make It Last.* Slow Motion Press

Roman de Renart—*Renard The Fox* (translated by Patricia Terry). Northeastern University Press

Romtvedt, David—*Moon: Poems.* Bieler Press

Ronan, Stephen—*Our Lady Of Fall River.* Ammunition Press

Ronsholdt, George A.—*Gastromancy: Plumbing The Psychostomatic Depths In 25 Fantastic Explorations Along The Alimentary Canal.* Sackbut Press

Rosen, Michael—*You Can't Catch Me.* Andre Deutsch

Rosenstein, Ira—*Left On The Field To Die: Yehudi Weissman.* Starlight Press

Rosini, Rosanna—*Hemispheric Transfer.* Writers Workshop

Rothenberg, Jerome—*That Dada Strain.* New Directions Pub. Co.

Rothman, Stewart N.—*A Window On Life.* Lens Unlimited

Ruark, Gibbons—*Keeping Company.* Johns Hopkins University Press

Rubin, Mendek—*Why Not Now?* Philosophical Library

Rudel, Jaufre—*Cercamon And Jaufre Rudel: Poems* (edited and translated by George Wolf and Roy Rosenstein). Garland

Rudnik, Raphael—*Frank 207.* Swallow Press

Ruffin, Paul—*Lighting The Furnace Pilot.* Spoon River Poetry Press

Rugo, Mariève—*Fields Of Vision.* University of Alabama Press

Russell, Peter—*Africa.* Privately printed
—*Elemental Discourse.* Humanities Press
—*Malice Aforethought.* Humanities Press

Ryan, David Stuart—*Love Poems And Love Words.* Kozmik Press Centre

Ryan, Kay—*Dragon Acts To Dragon Ends.* Taylor Street Press

S

Sagan, Miriam—*Aegean Doorway.* Zephyr Press

Sagstetter, Karen—*Half The Story.* Charles Street Press

St. John, Primus—*Love Is Not A Consolation: It Is A Light.* Carnegie-Mellon University Press

Sandburg, Carl—*Rainbows Are Made: Poems* (selected by Lee Bennett Hopkins). Harcourt Brace Jovanovich

Sandy, Stephen—*Riding To Greylock: Poems.* Alfred A. Knopf

Sanger, Peter—*The America Reel.* Pottersfield Press

Sassoon, Siegfried—*The War Poems Of Siegfried Sassoon.* Faber and Faber

Saunders, Sally Love—*Fresh Bread.* Golden Quill Press

Schechter, Ruth Lisa—*Speedway: Poems.* Chantry Press

Schevill, James—*The American Fantasies: Collected Poems, 1945-1981.* Swallow Press

Schneider, Franz—*The Roof Of Stone: Poems.* Temporal Acuity Press

Scully, James—*Santiago Poems.* Curbstone Press
—*Apollo Hamlet.* Curbstone Press

Sears, Donald A.—*The Magellan Heart.* Harian Creative Books

Seifert, Jaroslav—*The Casting Of Bells* (translated by Paul Jagasich and Tom O'Grady). The Spirit That Moves Us Press

Sen, Mihir K.—*Oh City City.* Writers Workshop

Sen, Ramprasad—*Grace And Mercy In Her Wild Hair: Selected Poems To The Mother Goddess* (translated by Leonard Nathan and Clinton Seeley). Great Eastern Book Co.

Service, Robert W.—*Best Tales Of The Yukon.* Running Press

Seth, Vikram—*Mappings.* Writers Workshop

Sexton, Anne—*The Complete Poems.* Houghton Mifflin

Shakespeare, William—*The Complete Poems Of William Shakespeare And Selected Verse From The Plays* (compiled by George Gesner). Avenel Books

Shange, Ntozake—*A Daughter's Geography.* St. Martin's Press

Shapiro, Alan—*The Courtesy.* University of Chicago Press

Shapiro, David—*To An Idea: A Book Of Poems.* Overlook Press

Shelnutt, Eve—*Air And Salt.* Carnegie-Mellon University Press

Shelton, Richard—*Selected Poems, 1969-1981.* University of Pittsburgh Press

Shomer, Enid—*The Startle Effect.* American Studies Press

Shurin, Aaron—*The Graces.* Four Seasons Foundation

Simic, Charles—*Weather Forecast For Utopia and Vicinity.* Station Hill Press

Simmerman, Jim—*Home: Poems.* Dragon Gate.

Simon, Leslie—*High Desire.* Wingbow Press

Simpson, Nancy—*Across Water.* State Street Press

Sinclair, Marjorie—*The Path Of The Ocean: Traditional Poetry Of Polynesia.* University of Hawaii Press

Singh, Shukdev (see listing for Hess, Linda)

Sinha, Subrata—*An Outline.* Writers Workshop

Sinisgalli, Leonardo—*The Ellipse: Selected Poems Of Leonardo Sinisgalli* (translated by W. S. Di Piero). Princeton University Press

Skelton, John—*John Skelton: The Complete English Poems* (edited by John Scattergood). Yale University Press

Skinner, Knute—*The Flame Room.* Folly Press

Skratz, G. P.—*The Gates Of Disappearance.* Konglomerati Press

Slatkin, Marcia—*Poems: 1973-1981.* Backstreet Editions

Slavitt, David R.—*Big Nose: Poems.* Louisiana State University Press

Sleigh, Tom—*After One.* Houghton Mifflin

Smart, Carolyn—*Power Sources.* Fiddlehead Poetry Books

Smith, Bruce—*The Common Wages: Poems.* Sheep Meadow Press

Smith, Dave—*In The House Of The Judge.* Harper & Row
—*Gray Soldiers.* Palaemon Press

Smith, Jared—*Song Of The Blood: An Epic.* The Smith

Smith, John—*Sucking-Stones.* Quadrant Editions

Smith, Jordan—*An Apology For Loving The Old Hymns.* Princeton University Press

Smith, R. T.—*Finding The Path.* Black Willow Press
—*From The High Dive.* Water Mark Press

Smith, Stevie—*Stevie Smith: A Selection* (edited by Hermione Lee). Faber and Faber

—The Collected Poems Of Stevie Smith. New Directions Pub. Co.
—Me Again: Uncollected Writings Of Stevie Smith (edited by Jack Barbera and William McBrien). Continuum

Smith, Tom—*Singing The Middle Ages: Poems.* Countryman Press

Snodgrass, W. D.—*Heart's Needle.* Alfred A. Knopf
—Six Minnesinger Songs. Burning Deck

Snotherly, Mary—*Four North Carolina Poets.* St. Andrews Press

Sobin, Anthony—*The Sunday Naturalist.* Swallow Press

Solle, Dorothee—*Of War And Love* (part poetry) (translated by Rita and Robert Kimber). Orbis Books

Sollov, Jacques—*Reborn Again In The Kingdom.* White Eagle Publisher

Sonders, Scott—*Razor Candy.* Caravan Press

Song, Cathy—*Picture Bride.* Yale University Press

Sonne, Jorgen—*Flights.* Curbstone Press

Sonnevi, Goran—*Goran Sonnevi: Poetry In Translation.* Swedish Books
—The Economy Spinning Faster And Faster (translated by Robert Bly). Sun

Sophocles—*Oedipus Rex* (in Greek) (edited and English commentary by R. D. Dawe). Cambridge University Press
—Trachiniae (edited by P. E. Easterling). Cambridge University Press

Spacks, Barry—*Spacks Street—New & Selected Poems.* Johns Hopkins University Press

Sparshott, Francis—*The Hanging Gardens Of Etobicoke.* Childe Thursday

Stafford, William—*A Glass Face In The Rain: New Poems.* Harper & Row
—Segues: A Correspondence In Poetry (with Marvin Bell). David R. Godine—*Roving Across Fields: A Conversation And Uncollected Poems 1942-1982* (edited by Thom Tammaro). Barnwood Press

Stanescu, Nichita—*Ask The Circle To Forgive You: Selected Poems, 1964-1979* (translated by Mark Irwin and Mariana Carpinisan). Globe Press

Steele, Timothy—*The Prudent Heart.* Symposium Press

Stefanile, Selma—*The Poem Beyond My Reach: A Book Of Haiku.* Sparrow Press
—In That Far Country. Sparrow Press

Stein, Charles—*Parts And Other Parts.* Station Hill Press

Stephens, Michael—*Circles End.* Spuyten Duyvil

Stephenson, Fairfax—*Lyrical Hystericals.* Gotuit Enterprises

Stevens, Wallace—*Opus Posthumous* (edited by Samuel French Morse). Vintage Books (reprint)
—The Collected Poems Of Wallace Stevens. Vintage Books

Stevenson, Anne—*Green Mountain Black Mountain.* Rowan Tree Press
—Minute By Glass Minute. Oxford University Press

Stoloff, Carolyn—*A Spool Of Blue: New And Selected Poems.* Scarecrow Press

Strausbaugh, John—*Prose Poems.* Dolphin-Moon Press

Strome, Celia Watson—*The Drum And The Melody.* The Smith/Horizon Press

Stroud, Joseph—*Signatures.* BOA Editions

Stryk, Lucien—*Cherries.* Ampersand Press

Stuart, Dabney—*Common Ground.* Louisiana State University Press

Sullivan, Elizabeth Hillery—*Louisiana Lullaby: Poems Of Old New Orleans.* Nightingale Press

Sund, Robert—*Ish River.* North Point Press

Sutter, Barton—*Sequoyah.* Ox Head Press

Swift, Jonathan—*The Complete Poems* (edited by Pat Rogers). Yale University Press

Swinburne, Algernon Charles—*Selected Poems* (edited by L. M. Findlay). Fyfield Books/Humanities Press

T

Tapscott, Stephen—*Penobscot.* Pym-Randall Press

Tardieu, Jean—*Formeries* (translated by Gail Graham and Sylvie Mathe). Ardis Publishers

Tate, James—*Constant Defender: Poems.* Ecco Press

Taylor, Andrew—*Selected Poems.* University of Queensland Press

Taylor, Bruce—*The Darling Poems: A Romance.* Red Weather Press

Taylor, James—*Tigerwolves.* Dolphin-Moon Press

Tennyson, Alfred—*In Memoriam* (edited by Susan Shatto and Marion Shaw). Oxford University Press
—Idylls Of The King (edited by J. M. Gray). Yale University Press

Theocritus—*Theocritus, Idylls And Epigrams* (translated by Daryl Hine). Atheneum

Thomas, D. M.—*Selected Poems.* Viking/Penguin

Thomas, John—*Abandoned Latitudes: New Writing By 3 Los Angeles Poets.* Red Hill Press

Thompson, Hilary—*Only So Far.* Fiddlehead Poetry Books

Tichy, Susan—*The Hands In Exile.* Random House

Tihanyi, Eva—*A Sequence Of The Blood.* Aya Press

Tobin, Juanita—*In Grape Time.* Publication Arts

Todd, Patrick—*A Fire By The Tracks.* Ohio State University Press

Traxler, Patricia—*The Glass Woman.* Hanging Loose Press

Triem, Eve—*Midsummer Rites.* Seal Press

Tsaloumas, Dimitris—*The Observatory: Selected Poems Of Dimitris Tsaloumas* (translated by Philip Grundy). University of Queensland Press

Tschacbasov, Nahum—*Machinery Of Flight.* Southampton College Press

Tsvetayeva, Marina—*Selected Poems* (translated by Elaine Feinstein). Oxford University Press
—Three Russian Women Poets: Anna Akhmatova, Marina Tsvetayeva And Bella Akhmdulina (edited and translated by Mary Maddock). Crossing Press

Tucker, Martin—*Homes Of Locks And Mysteries.* Dovetail Press

Turco, Lewis—*The Complete Melancholick.* Bieler Press

—*American Still Lives*. Mathom Publishing Co.
—*Seasons Of The Blood*. Mammoth Press
Turner, Alberta—*A Belfry Of Knees*. University of Alabama Press
Turner, Frederick—*The Return*. Countryman Press
Turner, Thomas Noel—*Hillbilly Night Before Christmas*. Pelican
Tyler, Cheever Pierce—*The Storefront Window*. Privately printed

U

Urdang, Constance—*Only The World*. University of Pittsburgh Press
Usher, Harlan—*The Grownups' Mother Goose*. Ell Ell Diversified

V

Van Duyn, Mona—*Letters From A Father, And Other Poems*. Atheneum
Vangelisti, Paul—*Abandoned Latitudes: New Writing By 3 Los Angeles Poets*. Red Hill Press
Vantuono, William (editor)—*The Pearl Poems: An Omnibus Edition*. Garland
Villon, Francois—*The Poems Of Francois Villon* (translated by Galway Kinnell). University Press of New England
Vince, Michael—*In The New District*. Carcanet New Press/Humanities Press
Vinz, Robert—*Climbing The Stairs*. Spoon River Poetry Press
Violi, Paul—*Splurge: Poems*. Sun
Virgil—*The Aeneid* (translated by Robert Fitzgerald). Random House
—*The Aeneid Of Virgil* (translated by Allen Mandelbaum). University of California Press
Vogelsang, Arthur—*A Planet: Poems*. Holt, Rinehart & Winston
Voigt, Ellen Bryant—*The Forces Of Plenty*. W. W. Norton

W

Wagner, Anneliese—*Hand Work*. Saturday Press
Wagner, D. R.—*Cruisin' At The Limit: Selected Poems, 1968-78*. Duck Down
Wagoner, David—*First Light: Poems*. Little, Brown
Wakoski, Diane—*The Lady Who Drove Me To The Airport*. Metacom Press
Walcott, Derek—*Midsummer*. Farrar, Straus, Giroux
—*Another Life*. Three Continents Press
Waldman, Anne—*Makeup On Empty Space: Poems*. Toothpaste Press
Waldrop, Keith—*The Space Of Half An Hour*. Burning Deck
Walker, Johnny—*The Poet*. Last Chance
Wallace, Ronald—*Plums, Stones, Kisses & Hooks*. University of Missouri Press
—*Tunes for Bears to Dance To*. University of Pittsburgh Press

Wallenstein, Barry—*Roller Coaster Kid, And Other Poems*. T. Y. Crowell
Waller, Gary—*Impossible Futures, Indelible Pasts*. Kallner/McCaffery Associates
Walsh, Chad—*The Psalm Of Christ: Forty Poems On The Twenty-Second Psalm*. Harold Shaw Publishers
Wandor, Michelene (see listing for Kazantzis)
Wann, David—*Log Rhythms*. North Atlantic Books
Warden, Marine Robert—*Love And The Bomb Don't Mix*. Grey Whale Press
—*The Illinois Suite*. Spoon River Poetry Press
—*Lullabies From Cochiti*. Seven Buffaloes Press
Warn, Emily—*The Leaf Path: Poems*. Copper Canyon Press
Warner, Sylvia Townsend—*Collected Poems* (edited by Claire Harman). Viking
Warren, Robert Penn—*Chief Joseph Of The Nez Perce, Who Called Themselves The Nimipu—"The Real People": A Poem*. Random House
Waterman, Andrew—*Out For The Elements*. Carcanet New Press/Humanities Press
Weekley, Richard J.—*Little Pianos And Other Poems From Europe 1982*. Star Garden Poets Cooperative
Weigl, Tom—*Little Heart*. Accent Editions
Werner, Warren—*The Structure Of Desire*. Riverstone Press
Westerfield, Nancy G.—*Welded Women* (edited by Helen Winter Stauffer). Kearney State College Press
Whalen, Philip—*Heavy Breathing: Poems 1967-1980*. Four Seasons Foundation
Wheelwright, John—*Collected Poems Of John Wheelwright*. New Directions Pub. Co.
Whitbread, Thomas—*Whomp And Moonshiver*. BOA Editions
White, James L.—*The Salt Ecstacies*. Graywolf Press
White, T. H.—*A Joy Proposed*. University of Georgia Press
Whitman, Cedric—*Chocorus And Other Poems*. W. L. Bauhan
Whitney, Isabella (see listing for Plat, Hugh)
Wikoff, Jack—*Adirondack Portfolio*. Open Book Publications
—*Penelope*. Open Book Publications
Wilbur, Richard—*The Whale And Other Uncollected Translations*. BOA Editions
Wild, Peter—*The Peaceable Kingdom*. Adler Press
Wildeman, June M. F.—*Colored Buttons*. Schori Press
Wilhelm, Fritz—*Next Step*. Alchemy Books
Wilkerson, Thomas—*Boaz*. American Studies Press
Willard, Nancy—*Household Tales Of Moon And Water*. Harcourt Brace Jovanovich
William VII—*The Poetry Of William VII, Count Of Poitiers, IX Duke Of Aquitaine* (edited and translated by Gerald A. Bond). Garland
Williams, C. K.—*The Lark, The Thrush, The Starling*. Burning Deck
—*Tar: Poems*. Vintage Books
Williams, Jonathan—*Get Hot Or Get Out: A Selec-

tion Of Poems, 1957-1981. Scarecrow Press
Williams, Miller—*The Boys On Their Bony Mules: Poems.* Louisiana State University Press
Williams, S. Bradford, Jr.—*Caress Softly Thy Love: Poems.* Copper Orchid Pub. Co.
—*Sunshine Grows The Day: Poems.* Copper Orchid Pub. Co.
Williamson, Alan—*Presence.* Alfred A. Knopf
Willitts, Martin, Jr. (see listing for Chang, Diana)
Wilmer, Clive—*Devotions.* Carcanet New Press/ Humanities Press
Wilson, Bill—*Fundamental Car.* Tamarisk Press
Wilson, Keith—*Stone Roses: Poems From Transylvania.* Utah State University Press
Winner, Robert—*Flogging The Czar: Poems.* Sheep Meadow Press
Winters, Bayla—*Mothers And Daughters, Daughters And Mothers.* Women Writers West
Witt, Harold—*The Snow Prince.* Blue Unicorn
Woessner, Warren—*No Hiding Place.* Spoon River Poetry Press
Wojtyla, Karol (see John Paul II, Pope)
Wolf, Jami—*Calling Back Our Lives.* Glavin Press
Woods, John—*The Valley Of Minor Animals.* Dragon Gate
Wordsworth, William—*Descriptive Sketches* (edited by Eric Birdsall). Cornell University Press
—*An Evening Walk* (edited by James Averill). Cornell University Press
—*Poems In Two Volumes, And Other Poems, 1800-1807* (edited by Jared Curtis). Cornell University Press
Wormser, Baron—*The White Words.* Houghton Mifflin
Wo'se, Shabaka—*In Praise Of African Women, African Queens, African Gods.* Black Star Publications

Wright, C. D.—*Translations Of The Gospel Back Into Tongues: Poems.* State University of New York Press
Wright, Carolyne—*Premonitions Of An Uneasy Guest.* Hardin-Simmons University Press
Wright, Charles—*Country Music: Selected Older Poems.* Wesleyan University Press
—*The Southern Cross.* Random House
Wright, Franz—*The One Whose Eyes Open When You Close Your Eyes.* Pym-Randall Press
Wroth, Lady Mary—*The Poems Of Lady Mary Wroth* (edited by Josephine A. Roberts). Louisiana State University Press

XYZ

Yau, John—*Corpse And Mirror.* Holt, Rinehart and Winston
Yeats, William Butler—*The Poems* (edited by Richard J. Finneran). Macmillan
—*Byzantium.* Black Swan Books
Yevtushenko, Yevgeny—*A Dove In Santiago: A Novella In Verse* (translated by D. M. Thomas). Viking
Young, Al—*The Blues Don't Change.* Louisiana State University Press
Zach, Natan—*The Static Element: Selected Poems Of Natan Zach* (translated by Peter Everwine and Shulamit Yasny-Starkman). Atheneum
Zimmer, Paul—*Family Reunion: Selected And New Poems.* University of Pittsburgh Press
Zolotow, Charlotte—*Some Things Go Together.* T. Y. Crowell
Zydek, Frederick—*Storm Warning.* Inchbird Press

(2) ANTHOLOGIES
(listed alphabetically by title)

An Anthology Of Alexandrian Poetry (compiled by Jerry Clack). Classical World
An Anthology Of New Belgian Poetry (edited by Werner Lambersy). Writers Workshop
Arizona Anthem (edited and compiled by Blair Morton Armstrong). Mnemosyne Press
The Batsford Book Of Religious Verse (edited by Elizabeth Jennings). Batsford
Bedtime Bear's Book Of Bedtime Poems (selected by Bobbi Katz). Random House
Birds, Beasts & Flowers, As Performed By Her Serene Highness Princess Grace Of Monaco (edited by John Carroll). William Morrow
Birthday Bear's Book Of Birthday Poems (selected by Bobbi Katz). Random House
Blues Lyric Poetry: An Anthology (by Michael Taft). Garland Publishing Co.
The Book Of Irish Verse: An Anthology Of Irish Poetry

From The Sixth Century To The Present (selected by John Montague). Macmillan
The Book Of Tears: Irish In Memoriam Poetry (compiled by Jordan O'Levenson). Levenson Press
A Chance To Live: Children's Poems For Peace In A Nuclear Age (edited by Gayle Peterson and Ying Kelley). Mindbody
The Charleston Book: A Miscellany In Prose And Verse (edited by William Gilmore Simms). Reprint Co. (reprint)
Chinese Folk Poetry (translated by Cecilia Liang). Beyond Baroque Foundation
Consolidation: The Second Paperback Poets Anthology (edited by Thomas Shapcott). University of Queensland Press (Australia)
Contemporary East European Poetry: An Anthology (edited by Emery George). Ardis

Contemporary Literature In Birmingham: An Anthology (part poetry) (edited by Steven Ford Brown). Thunder City Press

Cornwall In Verse (edited by Peter Redgrove). Secker & Warburg/David & Charles

Days Are Where We Live And Other Poems (compiled by Jill Bennett). Lothrop, Lee & Shepard

The Devil's Book Of Verse: Masters Of The Poison Pen From Ancient Times To The Present Day (compiled and edited by Richard Conniff). Dodd, Mead

The Dial: Arts And Letters In The 1920s (partly poetry) (edited by Gaye L. Brown). University of Massachusetts Press

The Emigrant Experience: Songs Of Highland Emigrants In North America (by Margaret MacDonell). University of Toronto Press

Everyman's Book Of Victorian Verse (edited by J. R. Watson). Dent (London)

Extended Outlooks: The Iowa Review Collection Of Contemporary Women Writers (edited by Jane Cooper, Gwen Head, Adalaide Morris and Marcia Southwick). Macmillan

Eye's Delight: Poems Of Art And Architecture (chosen by Helen Plotz). Greenwillow Books

The Faber Book Of Poems And Places (edited by Geoffrey Grigson). Faber and Faber

The Faber Book Of Useful Verse (edited by Simon Brett). Faber and Faber

Fables For Our Times And Famous Poems Illustrated (by James Thurber). Harper & Row

A Feast Of Creatures: Anglo-Saxon Riddle-Songs (translated by Craig Williamson). University of Pennsylvania Press

Fellow Mortals: An Anthology Of Animal Verse (chosen by Roy Fuller). Macdonald & Evans/International Ideas, Inc.

15 Contemporary New Zealand Poets (edited by Alistair Paterson). Grove Press (reprint)

Flights Of Imagination: An Illustrated Anthology Of Bird Poetry (compiled by Mike Mockler). Blandford Press/Sterling Publishing Co.

Four North Carolina Women Poets: Kate Blackburn, Agnes McDonald, Shirley Moody, Mary Snotherly. St. Andrews Press

Fourfront: Poems (by Valorie Breyfogle, et al.). Bearstone Publishing Co.

Gnosis Anthology Of Contemporary American And Russian Literature And Art, Volume I (part poetry) (edited by Arkady Rovner). Gnosis Press

Grass Hill: Poems And Prose By The Japanese Monk Gensei (translated by Burton Watson). Columbia University Press

Great Poems Of The English Language: An Anthology (compiled by Wallace Alvin Briggs). Granger Book Co.

Hard Lines: New Poetry And Prose (introduction by Ian Dury). Faber and Faber

Humps & Wings: A Selection Of Polish Poetry Since '68 (edited by Tadeusz Nyczek; translated by Bogus aw Rostworowski). Red Hill Press

I Will Always Stay Me: Writings Of Migrant Children (compiled by Sherry Kafka). Texas Monthly Press

In The Dreamlight: Twenty-Two Alaskan Writers (edited by Robert Hedin). Copper Canyon Press

In Praise Of Cats: An Anthology (compiled by Dorothy Foster). Beaufort Books

The Interior Landscape Of The Heart: Tamil Poetry From Malaysia And Singapore (edited by Anand Haridas and R. Dhandayudham). Writers Workshop

Jacobean And Caroline Poetry: An Anthology (edited by T. G. S. Cain). Methuen

Jiggery-Pokery: A Compendium Of Double Dactyls (edited by Anthony Hecht and John Hollander). Atheneum

Kicking Their Heels With Freedom: Poems From Pennsylvania Prisons (edited by John Paul Minarik). Academy of Prison Arts

Leaving The Bough: 50 American Poets Of The 80s (edited by Roger Gaess). International Press

The Longman Anthology Of Contemporary American Poetry 1950-1980 (edited by Stuart Friebert and David Young). Longman

Love Isn't Always Easy: A Collection Of Poems On Love And Making It Work, Because It's Worth It (edited by Susan Polis Schutz). Blue Mountain Press

Love Stories/Love Poems: An Anthology (edited by Joe David Bellamy and Roger Weingarten). Fiction International

Maori Poetry: An Introductory Anthology (by Margaret Orbell). Heinemann Educational Books

Michael Roberts' The Faber Book Of Modern Verse: A Reissue Of The Original Edition With An Account Of Its Making (by Janet Adam Smith). Faber and Faber

Modern Hebrew Poetry: A Bilingual Anthology (edited and translated by Ruth Finer Mintz). Greenwood Press (reprint)

Modern Metaphysical Lyrics (edited by J. Topham). American Poetry Press

Modern Poetry In Translation: 1983 (edited by Daniel Weissbort). Persea Books

Modern Scandinavian Poetry: The Panorama Of Poetry (edited by Martin Allwood). New Directions Books

My Song Is A Piece Of Jade: Poems Of Ancient Mexico In English And Spanish (adapted by Toni de Gerez). Little, Brown

New England Poetry Engagement Book 1983 (edited by Eric Linder and Paul Marion). Yellow Umbrella Press

New Poetry Of The American West (edited by Peter Wild and Frank Graziano). Longbridge-Rhodes

The Norton Anthology Of Poetry (edited by Alexander W. Allison). Norton

The Oxford Book Of Ballads (selected and edited by James Kinsley). Oxford University Press

The Oxford Book Of Contemporary New Zealand Poetry (chosen by F. Adcock). Oxford University Press

The Oxford Book Of Narrative Verse (chosen and edited by Iona and Peter Opie). Oxford University Press

The Penguin Book Of Homosexual Verse (edited by Stephen Coote). Penguin

Perspectives On A Grafted Tree: Thoughts For Those

Touched By Adoption (compiled by Patricia Irwin Johnston). Perspectives Press

Poems: A Celebration (edited by Carole Oles and Elinor Persky). Newton Free Library

The Poetry Of Childhood (edited by Samuel Carr). Batsford/David & Charles

The Poetry Of Geology (edited by Robert M. Hazen). Allen & Unwin

Poetry Project Three (edited by Joel Rudinger). Cambric Press

Poets Behind Barbed Wire: Tanka Poems (edited and translated by Jiro Nakano and Kay Nakano). Bamboo Ridge Press

Poets Of Nicaragua: A Bilingual Anthology, 1918-1979 (edited and translated by Steven F. White). Unicorn Press

Poetspeak: In Their Work, About Their Work: A Selection (by Paul B. Janeczko). Bradbury Press

Postwar Polish Poetry: An Anthology (selected and edited by Czeslaw Milosz). University of California Press

A Pumpkin Full Of Poems (illustrated by Sheila Beckett). Random House

The Random House Book Of Poetry For Children (selected by Jack Prelutsky). Random House

The Random House Book Of Twentieth-Century French Poetry (edited by Paul Auster). Vintage Books

Recent Poetry Of Spain: A Bilingual Anthology (edited and translated by Louis Hammer and Sara Schyfter). Sachem Press

Romantic Poetry On The European Continent: An English Language Anthology (edited by Miroslav John Hanak). University Press of America

Saturday's Women: Eileen W. Barnes Award Anthology (edited by Charlotte Mandel). Saturday Press

Scars Upon My Heart: Women's Poetry And Verse Of The First World War (edited by Catherine W. Reilly). Virago/Merrimack Book Service

The Seasons (poetry and prose) (selected by Louis Lawrence). Holt, Rinehart and Winston

Seventeenth-Century Prose And Poetry (selected and edited by Alexander M. Witherspoon and Frank J. Warnke). Harcourt Brace Jovanovich

The Sky Is Full Of Song (selected by Lee Bennett Hopkins). Harper & Row

A Song In Stone: City Poems (selected by Lee Bennett Hopkins). T. Y. Crowell

Story-Telling Ballads (selected by Frances Jenkins Olcott). Granger Book Co. (reprint)

Ten Jewish American Poets (edited by Isaac Mozeson). Downtown Poets

The Third Taboo: A Collection Of Items On Jealousy (edited by Heather Cadsby and Maria Jacobs). Wolsak & Wynn

1000 Years Of Irish Poetry: The Gaelic And Anglo-Irish Poets From Pagan Times To The Present (edited by Kathleen Hoagland). Devin-Adair

Toward An Image Of Latin American Poetry (edited by Octavio Armand). Logbridge-Rhodes

Translations (translated by Charles Tomlinson). Oxford University Press

Turmoil In Hungary: An Anthology Of Twentieth-Century Poetry (edited and translated by Nicholas Kolumban). New Rivers Press

Vietnam Heroes II, The Tears Of A Generation: An Anthology Of Poems And Prose (edited by J. Topham). American Poetry Press

The Vitalist Reader: A Selection Of The Poetry Of Anthony L. Johnson, William Oxley And Peter Russell (edited by James Hogg). University of Salzburg/Ember Press

Wetting Our Lines Together: An Anthology Of Recent North American Fishing Poems (edited by Allen Hoey, Cynthia Hoey and Daniel J. Moriarty). Tamarack Editions

When The Dark Comes Dancing: A Bedtime Poetry Book (edited by Nancy Larrick). Philomel Books

The Wings, By The Vines. McBooks Press

Women Poets Of The World (edited by Joanna Bankier and Deirdre Lashgari). Macmillan

The World's Best Poetry (edited by Bliss Carman). Granger Book Co. (reprint)

Why Am I Grown So Cold?: Poems Of The Unknowable (edited by Myra Cohn Livingston). Atheneum

(3) BIOGRAPHY AND COMMENT ON SPECIFIC POETS
(listed alphabetically by subject)

Aiken, Conrad— *Lorelei Two; My Life With Conrad Aiken* (by Clarissa M. Lorenz). University of Georgia Press

Alcaeus— *Three Archaic Poets: Archilochus, Alcaeus, Sappho* (by Anne Pippin Burnett). Harvard University Press

Archilochus— *Three Archaic Poets: Archilochus, Alcaeus, Sappho* (by Anne Pippin Burnett). Harvard University Press

Arlington, Edwin— *Revolution And Convention In Modern Poetry: Studies In Ezra Pound, T. S. Eliot, Wallace Stevens, Edwin Arlington And Yvor Winters* (by Donald E. Stanford). University of Delaware Press

Arnold, Matthew— *Arnold And God* (by Ruth Roberts). University of California Press

Auden, W. H.— *Auden: An American Friendship* (by Charles H. Miller). Scribner
—*Auden: A Carnival Of Intellect* (by Edward Callan). Oxford University Press
—*Early Auden* (by Edward Mendelson). Harvard University Press (reprint)

Baudelaire, Charles— *Baudelaire The Damned* (by F. W. J. Hemmings). Scribner
—*Romantic Weather: The Climate Of Coleridge And Baudelaire* (by Arden Reed). University Press of New England

—*Baudelaire, Mallarme, Valery: New Essays In Honor Of Lloyd Austin* (edited by Malcolm Bowie). Cambridge University Press
—*Intimate Journals* (translated by Christopher Isherwood). City Lights Books (reprint)
—*The Symbolic Method Of Coleridge, Baudelaire And Yeats* (by Anca Vlasopolis). Wayne State University Press

Bell, Julian— *Journey To The Frontier: Two Roads To The Spanish Civil War* (by Peter Stansky and William Abrahams). University of Chicago Press

Benn, Gottfried— *Consistency Of Phenotype: A Study Of Gottfried Benn's Views On Lyric Poetry* (by Angelika Manyoni). P. Lang

Bentley, E. Clerihew— *The First Clerihews* (by E. Clerihew Bentley). Oxford University Press

Bishop, Elizabeth— *Elizabeth Bishop and Her Art* (edited by Lloyd Schwartz and Sybil B. Estess). University of Michigan Press

Blake, William— *The Continuing City: William Blake's Jerusalem* (by Morton D. Paley). Oxford University Press
—*The Moment of Explosion: Blake And The Illustration Of Milton* (by Stephen C. Behrendt). University of Nebraska Press
—*Vision And Disenchantment: Blake's Songs And Words-Worth's Lyrical Ballads* (by Heather Glen). Cambridge University Press
—*Conversing In Paradise: Poetic Genius And Identity-As-Community In Blake's Los* (by Leonard W. Deen). University of Missouri Press
—*Literal Imagination: Blake's Vision Of Words* (by Nelson Hilton). University of California Press

Boccaccio, Giovanni— *Dante, Petrarch, Boccaccio: Studies In The Italian Trecento* (edited by Aldo S. Bernardo and Anthony L. Pellegrini). State University of New York at Binghamton Center for Medieval & Renaissance Studies

Booth, Philip— *Three Contemporary Poets Of New England* (by Guy Rotella). Twayne

Borges, Jorge Luis— *Simply A Man Of Letters: Panel Discussions And Papers From The Proceedings Of A Symposium On Jorge Luis Borges Held At The University Of Maine At Orono* (edited by Carlos Cortinez). University of Maine at Orono Press

Bradstreet, Anne— *Critical Essays On Anne Bradstreet* (edited by Pattie Cowell and Ann Stanford). G. K. Hall

Brecht, Bertolt— *Brecht: A Biography* (by Ronald Hayman). Oxford University Press

Bridges, Robert— *The Selected Letters Of Robert Bridges* (edited by Donald E. Stanford). University of Delaware Press

Browning, Elizabeth Barrett— *The Letters Of Elizabeth Barrett Browning To Mary Russell Mitford, 1836-1854* (edited by Meredith B. Raymond and Mary Rose Sullivan). Armstrong Browning Library of Baylor University

Browning, Robert— *The Elusive Self In The Poetry Of Robert Browning* (by Constance W. Hassett). Ohio University Press
—*Browning And Italy* (by Jacob Korg). Ohio University Press

—*Becoming Browning: The Poems And Plays Of Robert Browning* (by Clude de L. Ryals). Ohio State University Press

Burns, Robert— *The Letters Of Robert Burns* (edited by G. Ross Roy). Clarendon Press
—*The Art Of Robert Burns* (edited by R. D. S. Jack and Andrew Noble). Barnes & Noble

Byron, Lord— *Byron* (by Frederic Raphael). Thames and Hudson

Catullus— *Catullus, A Reader's Guide To The Poems* (by Stuart G. P. Small). University Press of America

Cavalcanti, Guido— *The Sonnets And Ballate Of Guido Cavalcanti* (translated by Ezra Pound). Hyperion Press (reprint)
—*Pound's Cavalcanti: An Edition Of The Translations, Notes And Essays* (by David Anderson). Princeton University Press

Chaucer, Geoffrey— *Chaucer: An Introduction* (by S. S. Hussey). Methuen
—*Chaucer And The Italian Trecento* (by Piero Boitani). Cambridge University Press
—*Chaucer's Lyrics And Anelida And Arcite: An Annotated Bibliography* (by Russell A. Peck). University of Toronto Press
—*Chaucer's Major Tales* (by Michael Hoy and Michael Stevens). Schocken Books
—*English Medieval Narrative In The Thirteenth And Fourteenth Centuries* (by Piero Boitani). Cambridge University Press
—*The Elements Of Chaucer's Troilus* (by Chauncey Wood). Duke University Press
—*Fourteenth-Century English Poetry* (by Elizabeth Salter). Oxford University Press
—*Telling Classical Tales: Chaucer And The Legend Of Good Women* (by Lisa J. Kiser). Cornell University Press
—*Chaucer's Mentality* (by Derek Brewer). Barnes & Noble Books
—*Dante, Chaucer, And The Currency Of The Word: Money, Images And Reference In Late Medieval Poetry* (by R. A. Shoaf). Pilgrim Books

Chekhov, Anton— *Chekhov's Poetics* (by A. P. Chudakov). Ardis Publishers

Chretien de Troyes— *Chretien De Troyes, The Man And His Work* (by Jean Frappier). Ohio University Press
—*The Sower And His Seed: Essays On Chretien De Troyes* (edited by Rupert T. Pickens). French Forum

Clare, John— *A Right To Song: The Life Of John Clare* (by Edward Storey). Methuen

Clarke, Austin— *The Poetry Of Austin Clarke* (by Gregory A. Schirmer). University of Notre Dame Press

Codrescu, Andrei— *In America's Shoes* (by Andrei Codrescu). City Lights Books

Coleridge, Samuel Taylor— *The Design Of Biographia Literaria* (by Catherine Miles Wallace). Allen & Unwin
—*Vision And Revision: Coleridge's Art Of Immanence* (by Jean-Pierre Mileur). University of California Press
—*Romantic Weather: The Climate Of Coleridge And*

Baudelaire (by Arden Reed). University Press of New England
—*The Symbolic Method Of Coleridge, Baudelaire And Yeats* (by Anca Vlasopolis). Wayne State University Press
—*What Coleridge Thought* (by Owen Barfield). Wesleyan University Press
Cornford, John— *Journey To The Frontier: Two Roads To The Spanish Civil War* (by Peter Stansky and William Abrahams). University of Chicago Press
Cowper, William— *Cowper's Task: Structure And Influence* (by Martin Priestman). Cambridge University Press
—*Cowper's Poetry: A Critical Study And Reassessment* (edited by Vincent Newey). Barnes & Noble
—*The Poetry Of William Cowper* (by Bill Hutchings). Croom Helm
Crane, Hart— *Hart Crane: A Reference Guide* (by Joseph Schwartz). G. K. Hall

Dante Alighieri— *Confessions Of Sin And Love In The Middle Ages: Dante's Commedia And St. Augustine's Confessions* (by Shirley J. Paolini). University Press of America
—*Dante In America: The First Two Centuries* (edited by A. Bartlett Giamatti). State University of New York at Binghamton Center for Medieval & Early Renaissance Studies
—*Dante, Petrarch, Boccaccio: Studies In The Italian Trecento* (edited by Aldo S. Bernardo and Anthony L. Pelligrini). State University of New York at Binghamton Center for Medieval & Early Renaissance Studies
—*On The Defense Of The Comedy Of Dante* (by Jacopo Mazzoni; translated by Robert L. Montgomery, Jr.). University Presses of Florida
—*Dante In The Twentieth Century* (edited by Adolph Caso). University of America Press
—*Dante's Italy And Other Essays* (by Charles T. Davis). University of Pennsylvania Press
—*Dante, Chaucer, And The Currency Of The Word: Money, Images And Reference In Late Medieval Poetry* (by R. A. Shoaf). Pilgrim Books
Dario, Ruben— *Ruben Dario And The Romantic Search For Unity* (by Cathy Logan Jrade). University of Texas Press
Davison, Peter— *Three Contemporary Poets Of New England* (by Guy Rotella). Twayne
Dickinson, Emily— *Emily Dickinson's Poetry: Stairway Of Surprise* (by Charles R. Anderson). Greenwood (reprint)
—*Feminist Critics Read Emily Dickinson* (edited by Suzanne Juhasz). Indiana University Press
—*The Marriage Of Emily Dickinson: A Study Of The Fascicles* (by William H. Shurr). University Press of Kentucky
Donne, John— *The Poetry Of John Donne: Literature And Culture In The Elizabethan And Jacobean Period* (by William Zunder). Harvester Press/Barnes & Noble
—*The "Inward" Language: Sonnets Of Wyatt, Sidney, Shakespeare, Donne* (by Anne Ferry).

University of Chicago Press
Duncan, Robert— *Robert Duncan: Portrait Of The Poet As Homosexual In Society* (by Ekbert Faas). Black Sparrow Press

Eliot, T. S.— *A Reading Of Eliot's Four Quartets* (by Julia Maniates Reibetanz). UMI Research Press
—*T. S. Eliot: The Critical Heritage, Volumes 1 And 2* (edited by Michael Grant). Routledge & Kegan Paul
—*The Waste Land* (by Grover Smith). Allen & Unwin
—*T. S. Eliot's Intellectual And Poetic Development, 1909-1922* (by Piers Gray). Humanities Press
—*Revolution And Convention In Modern Poetry: Studies In Ezra Pound, T. S. Eliot, Wallace Stevens, Edwin Arlington And Yvor Winters* (by Donald E. Stanford). University of Delaware Press
—*T. S. Eliot's Negative Way* (by Eloise Knapp Hay). Harvard University Press
—*T. S. Eliot And The Poetics Of Literary History* (by Gregory S. Jay). Louisiana State University Press
—*Hamlet And The New Poetic: James Joyce And T. S. Eliot* (by William H. Quillian). UMI Research Press
—*Conflicts In Consciousness: T. S. Eliot's Poetry And Criticism* (by David Spurr). University of Illinois Press
Emerson, Ralph Waldo— *Essays And Lectures* (of Ralph Waldo Emerson). Literary Classics of The United States
—*Emerson's Optics: Biographical Process And The Dawn Of Religious Leadership* (by Richard A. Hutch). University Press of America
—*Critical Essays On Ralph Waldo Emerson* (collected by Robert E. Burkholder and Joel Myerson). G. K. Hall
—*The Letters Of Ellen Tucker Emerson* (edited by Edith E. W. Gregg). Kent State University Press
Euripides— *The Textual Tradition Of Euripides' Phoinissai* (by Donald J. Mastronarde and Jan Maarten Bremer). University of California Press

Fergusson, Robert— *Robert Fergusson* (by David Daiches). Scottish Academic Press/Columbia University Press
Ferlinghetti, Lawrence— *Lawrence Ferlinghetti, Poet-At-Large* (by Larry Smith). Southern Illinois University Press
Frescobaldi, Dino— *The Poetry Of Dino Frescobaldi* (by Joseph Alessia). P. Lang
Frost, Robert— *Critical Essays On Robert Frost* (by Philip L. Gerber). G. K. Hall

Garcia Lorca, Federico— *Lorca's Romancero Gitano: A Ballad Translation And Critical Study* (by Carl W. Cobb). University Press of Mississippi
—*The Assassination Of Federico Garcia Lorca* (by Ian Gibson). Penguin Books
Giovanni, Niki— *A Poetic Education: Conversations Between Nikki Giovanni And Margaret Walker*. Howard University Press

Graves, Robert— *Robert Graves, His Life And Work* (by Martin Seymour-Smith). Holt, Rinehart & Winston

Hawes, Stephen— *Stephen Hawes* (by A. S. G. Edwards). Twayne Publishers

Heine, Heinrich— *Valiant Heart: A Biography* (by Philip Kossoff). Cornwall Books

Henryson, Robert— *Robert Henryson* (by Matthew P. McDiarmid). Scottish Academic Press/ Columbia University Press

Herbert, George— *Love Known: Theology And Experience In George Herbert's Poetry* (by Richard Strier). University of Chicago Press

Hesiod— *The Poems Of Hesiod: Translated With An Introduction And Comments* (by R. M. Frazer). University of Oklahoma Press

Homer— *Archery At The Dark Of The Moon: Poetic Problems In Homer's Odyssey* (by Norman Austin). University of California Press
—*Childlike Achilles: Ontogeny And Phylogeny In The Iliad* (by W. Thomas MacCary). Columbia University Press.
—*The Epithets In Homer: A Study In Poetic Values* (by Paolo Vivante). Yale University Press
—*The Homeric Imagination: A Study Of Homer's Poetic Perception Of Reality* (by Paolo Vivante). Indiana University Press
—*Pope's Iliad: Homer In The Age Of Reason* (by Steven Shankman). Princeton University Press

Hopkins, Gerard Manley— *The Great Sacrifice: Studies In Hopkins* (by David Anthony Downes). University Press of America

Housman, A. E.— *A. E. Housman: A Critical Biography* (by Norman Page). Schocken Books

Hughes, Ted— *The Achievement Of Ted Hughes* (edited by Keith Sagar). University of Georgia Press

Jarrell, Randall— *Critical Essays On Randall Jarrell* (edited by Suzanne Ferguson). G. K. Hall

Johnson, Ben— *Self-Crowned Laureates: Spenser, Johnson, Milton And The Literary System* (by Richard Helgerson). University of California Press

Keats, John— *Keats, The Myth Of The Hero* (by Dorothy Van Ghent; revised and edited by Jeffrey Cane Robinson). Princeton University Press

Kulish, Panteleimon— *Panteleimon Kulish: A Sketch Of His Life And Times* (by George Luckyj). East European Monographs

Langland, William— *Fourteenth-Century English Poetry* (by Elizabeth Salter). Oxford University Press
—*The Figure Of Piers Plowman: The Image On The Coin* (by Margaret E. Goldsmith). D. S. Brewer/Biblio Dist. Services

Larkin, Philip— *Philip Larkin* (by Andrew Motion). Methuin.
—*Larkin At Sixty* (edited by Anthony Thwaite). Faber and Faber

Lawrence, D. H.— *The Poetry Of D. H. Lawrence:* *Texts And Contexts* (by Ross C. Murfin). University of Nebraska Press

Lermontov, Mikhail— *Mikhail Lermontov* (by John Garrard). Twayne

Lowell, Robert— *Robert Lowell: An Introduction To The Poetry* (by Mark Rudman). Columbia University Press
—*Robert Lowell, Nihilist As Hero* (by Vereen M. Bell). Harvard University Press
—*Robert Lowell: A Biography* (by Ian Hamilton). Random House

MacLeish, Archibald— *Letters Of Archibald MacLeish, 1907 to 1982* (edited by R. H. Winnick). Houghton Mifflin

MacNeice, Louis— *The Cave Of Making: The Poetry Of Louis MacNeice* (by Robyn Marsack). Oxford University Press

Mallarme, Stephane— *Baudelaire, Mallarme, Valery: New Essays In Honor Of Lloyd Austin* (edited by Malcolm Bowie). Cambridge University Press
—*Desire Seeking Expression: Mallarme's Prose Pour Des Esseintes* (by Marshall C. Olds). French Forum

Mangan, Sherry— *The Revolutionary Imagination: The Poetry And Politics Of John Wheelwright And Sherry Mangan* (by Alan M. Wald). University of North Carolina Press

Marlowe, Christopher— *A Concordance To The Plays, Poems And Translations Of Christopher Marlowe* (edited by Robert J. Fehrenbach, Lea Ann Boone and Mario A. Di Cesare). Cornell University Press

Marvell, Andrew— *The Poet's Time: Politics And Religion In The Work Of Andrew Marvell* (by Warren L. Chernaik). Cambridge University Press

Meredith, George— *A Concordance To The Poetry Of George Meredith* (edited by Rebecca S. Hogan, Lewis Sawin and Lynn L. Merrill). Garland

Meredith, William— *Three Contemporary Poets Of New England* (by Guy Rotella). Twayne

Merrill, James— *James Merrill: Essays In Criticism* (edited by David Lehman and Charles Berger). Cornell University Press

Millay, Edna St. Vincent— *Edna St. Vincent Millay* (by Norman A. Brittin). Twayne Publishers

Milton, John— *Images Of Kingship In Milton's Paradise Lost* (by Stephanie Davies). University of Missouri Press
—*The Life Of John Milton* (by A. N. Wilson). Oxford University Press
—*The Sacred Complex: On The Psychogenesis Of Paradise Lost* (by William Kerrigan). Harvard University Press
—*John Milton: The Inner Life* (by James Thorpe). Huntington Library
—*The Moment Of Explosion: Blake And The Illustration Of Milton* (by Stephen C. Behrendt). University of Nebraska Press
—*Milton's Spenser: The Politics Of Reading* (by Maureen Quilligan). Cornell University Press
—*Milton's Lycidas: The Tradition And The Poem* (edited by C. A. Patrides). University of

Missouri Press
—*Milton's Eve* (by Diane Kelsey McColley). University of Illinois Press
—*Milton's Kinesthetic Vision In Paradise Lost* (by Elizabeth Ely Fuller). Bucknell University Press
—*Self-Crowned Laureates: Spenser, Johnson, Milton And The Literary System* (by Richard Helgerson). University of California Press
—*Things Unattempted: A Study Of Milton* (by M. V. Rama Sarma). Vikas/Humanities Press
—*Milton's Epic Voice: The Narrator In Paradise Lost* (by Anne Ferry). University of Chicago Press
—*Milton And The Postmodern* (by Herman Rapaport). University of Nebraska Press

Mistral, Gabriela— *Beauty And The Mission Of The Teacher: The Life Of Gabriela Mistral Of Chile, Teacher, Poetess, Friend Of The Helpless, Nobel Laureate* (by William J. Castleman). Exposition Press

Mokichi, Saito— *Fragments Of Rainbows: The Life And Poetry Of Saito Mokichi* (by Amy Vladeck Heinrich). Columbia University Press

Montale, Eugenio— *Eugenio Montale's Poetry: A Dream In Reason's Presence* (by Glauco Cambon). Princeton University Press
—*Montale And The Occasions Of Poetry* (by Claire de C. L. Huffman). Princeton University Press

Moore, Thomas— *The Journal of Thomas Moore* (edited by Wilfrid S. Dowden). Associated University Presses

Morris, William— *William Morris* (by Peter Stansky). Oxford University Press

Morse, Samuel French— *The Motive For Metaphor: Essays On Modern Poetry* (edited by Francis C. Blessington and Guy Rotella). Northeastern University Press.

Neihardt, John G.— *Dream Catcher* (by Marion Marsh Brown and Jane K. Leech). Little Brown

Neruda, Pablo— *Pablo Neruda, The Poetics Of Prophecy* (by Enrico Mario Santi). Cornell University Press

Olson, Charles— *The Poetry Of Charles Olson* (by Thomas F. Merrill). University of Delaware Press

Omar Khayyam— *Omar Khayyam, The Philosopher-Poet Of Medieval Islam* (by Irfan Shahid). Georgetown University Press

Ovid— *Publica Carmina: Ovid's Books From Exile* (by Harry B. Evans). University of Nebraska Press

Pasternak, Boris— *I Remember: Sketch For An Autobiography* (translated by David Magarshack). Harvard University Press
—*Pasternak: A Biography* (by Ronald Hingley). Alfred A. Knopf

Petrarch— *Dante, Petrarch, Boccaccio: Studies In The Italian Trecento* (edited by Aldo S. Bernardo and Anthony L. Pellegrini). State University of New York at Binghamton Center for Medieval & Renaissance Studies

Pindar— *Pindar's Olympian One: A Commentary* (by

Douglas E. Gerber). University of Toronto Press

Plath, Sylvia— *Plath's Incarnations: Women And The Creative Process* (by Lynda K. Bundtzen). University of Michigan Press

Pope, Alexander— *Vision And Re-vision In Alexander Pope* (by Wallace Jackson). Wayne State University Press
—*Pope On Classic Ground* (by G. F. C. Plowden). Ohio University Press
—*Pope's Iliad: Homer In The Age Of Reason* (by Steven Shankman). Princeton University Press
—*Old England's Genius* (by Brean S. Hammond). University of Missouri Press

Pound, Ezra— *Revolution And Convention In Modern Poetry: Studies In Ezra Pound, T. S. Eliot, Wallace Stevens, Edwin Arlington And Yvor Winters* (by Donald E. Stanford). University of Delaware Press
—*A Guide To Ezra Pound's Selected Poems* (by Christine Froula). New Directions
—*A Touch Of Rhetoric: Ezra Pound's Malatesta Cantos* (by Peter D'Epiro). UMI Research Press
—*Blossoms From The East: The China Cantos Of Ezra Pound* (by John J. Nolde). National Poetry Foundation, University of Maine
—*Ezra Pound: Tactics For Reading* (edited by Ian F. A. Bell). Barnes & Noble
—*Circe's Craft: Ezra Pound's Hugh Selwyn Mauberley* (by Jo Brantley Berryman). UMI Research Press
—*Pound's Cavalcanti: An Edition Of The Translations, Notes And Essays* (by David Anderson). Princeton University Press
—*Pound Revised* (by Paul Smith). Croom Helm/Biblio
—*Paradise & Ezra Pound: The Poet As Shaman* (by Scott Eastham). University Press of America

Pushkin, Alexander— *Alexander Pushkin: A Critical Study* (by A. D. P. Briggs). Barnes & Noble
—*Alexander Pushkin* (by Dmitrij Blagoi). Unipub

Quevedo, Francisco de— *The Love Poetry Of Francisco De Quevedo: An Aesthetic And Existential Study* (by Julian Olivares, Jr.). Cambridge University Press

Rilke, Rainer Maria— *The Sacred Threshold: A Life Of Rainer Maria Rilke* (by J. F. Hendry). Carcanet New Press/Humanities Press

Rimbaud, Arthur— *Rimbaud: Visions And Habitations* (by Edward J. Ahearn). University of California Press

Rochester, Earl of (John Wilmont)— *Spirit Of Wit: Reconsiderations Of Rochester* (edited by Jeremy Treglown). Archon Books

Roethke, Theodore— *Theodore Roethke: The Journey From I To Otherwise* (by Neal Bowers). University of Missouri Press

Rossetti, Dante G.— *Dante Gabriel Rossetti And The Limits Of Victorian Vision* (by David C. Riede). Cornell University Press

Sait o Mokichi— *Fragments Of Rainbows: The Life*

And Poetry Of Sait o Mokichi, 1882-1953 (by Amy Vladeck Heinrich). Columbia University Press

Sandburg, Carl— *Ever The Winds Of Chance* (by Carl Sandburg). University of Illinois Press

Sappho— *Three Archaic Poets: Archilochus, Alcaeus, Sappho* (by Anne Pippin Burnett). Harvard University Press

Sarton, May— *Plant Dreaming Deep* (by May Sarton). W. W. Norton

Sassoon, Siegfried— *Siegfried Sassoon Diaries* (edited by Rupert Hart-Davis). Faber and Faber

Sevcenko, Taras— *The Poet As Mythmaker: A Study Of Symbolic Meaning In Taras Sevcenko* (by George G. Grabowicz). Harvard University Press

Sewell, Elizabeth— *An Idea* (by Elizabeth Sewell). Mercer University Press

Shakespeare, William— *The Book Known As Q: A Consideration Of Shakespeare's Sonnets* (by Robert Giroux). Vintage Books
—*The "Inward" Language: Sonnets Of Wyatt, Sidney, Shakespeare, Donne* (by Anne Ferry). University of Chicago Press

Shelley, Percy Bysshe— *Shelley's Adonais: A Critical Edition* (by Anthony D. Knerr). Columbia University Press
—*The Inextinguishable Flame: Shelley's Poetic And Creative Practice* (by Dharni Dhar Baskiyar). University Press of America
—*Radical Shelley: The Philosophical Anarchism And Utopian Thought Of Percy Bysshe Shelley* (by Michael Henry Scrivener). Princeton University Press
—*Shelley Revalued: Essays From The Gregynog Conference* (edited by Kelvin Everest). Barnes & Noble

Sidney, Philip— *Faire Bitts: Sir Philip Sidney And Renaissance Political Theory* (by Martin N. Raitiere). Duquesne University Press
—*The Structures Of Sidney's Arcadia* (by Nancy Lindheim). University of Toronto Press
—*The "Inward" Language: Sonnets Of Wyatt, Sidney, Shakespeare, Donne* (by Anne Ferry). University of Chicago Press

Smith, Dave— *The Giver Of Morning: On The Poetry Of Dave Smith* (edited by Bruce Weigl). Thunder City Press

Snyder, Gary— *Gary Snyder's Vision: Poetry And The Real Work* (by Charles Molesworth). University of Missouri Press

Spenser, Edmund— *Self-Crowned Laureates: Spenser, Johnson, Milton And The Literary System* (by Richard Helgerson). University of California Press
—*Milton's Spenser: The Politics Of Reading* (by Maureen Quilligan). Cornell University Press
—*The Poetry Of The Faerie Queene* (by Paul J. Alpers). Princeton University Press.

Stevens, Wallace— *A Thought To Be Rehearsed: Aphorism In Wallace Stevens' Poetry* (by Beverly Coyle). UMI Research Press
—*Wallace Stevens And Company: The Harmonium Years, 1913-1923* (by Glen G. MacLeod). UMI Research Press

—*Images Of Wallace Stevens* (by Edward Kessler). Gordian Press
—*The Motive For Metaphor: Essays On Modern Poetry* (edited by Francis C. Blessington and Guy Rotella). Northeastern University Press
—*Revolution And Convention In Modern Poetry: Studies In Ezra Pound, T. S. Eliot, Wallace Stevens, Edwin Arlington And Yvor Winters* (by Donald E. Stanford). University of Delaware Press
—*Stanza My Stone: Wallace Stevens And The Hermetic Tradition* (by Leonora Woodman). Purdue University Press
—*Advance On Chaos: The Sanctifying Imagination Of Wallace Stevens* (by David M. La Guardia). University Press of New England
—*Wallace Stevens And The Idealist Tradition* (by Margaret Peterson). UMI Research Press

Swift, Jonathan— *Jonathan Swift: The Brave Desponder* (by Patrick Reilly). Southern Illinois University Press

Synge, J. M.— *Synge, The Medieval And The Grotesque* (by Toni O'Brien Johnson). Barnes and Noble Books

Tate, Allen— *Allen Tate And The Augustinian Imagination: A Study Of The Poetry* (by Robert S. Dupree). Louisiana State University Press

Tennyson, Alfred— *Tennyson And Madness* (by Ann C. Colley). University of Georgia Press

Thayer, Ernest Lawrence— *Mighty Casey, All-American* (by Eugene C. Murdock). Greenwood Press

Thomas, Dylan— *Letters To Vernon Watkins* (edited by Vernon Watkins). Greenwood Press (reprint)
—*Portrait Of Dylan: A Photographer's Memoir* (by Rollie McKenna). Stemmer House

Thomas, Edward— *The Poetry Of Edward Thomas* (by Andrew Motion). Routledge & Kegan Paul
—*The Childhood Of Edward Thomas: A Fragment Of Autobiography.* Faber & Faber

Trakl, George— *Georg Trakl, A Profile* (edited by Frank Graziano). Logbridge-Rhodes
—*Georg Trakl's Poetry: Toward A Union Of Opposites* (by Richard Detsch). Pennsylvania State University Press

Valery, Paul— *Baudelaire, Mallarme, Valery: New Essays In Honor Of Lloyd Austin* (edited by Malcolm Bowie). Cambridge University Press

Vaughan, Henry— *Henry Vaughan: The Unfolding Vision* (by Jonathan F. S. Post). Princeton University Press

Viau, Theophile de— *The Cabaret Poetry Of Theophile De Viau: Texts And Traditions* (by Claire Gaudiani). Narr/Benjamin's North America

Virgil— *Technique And Ideas In The Aeneid* (by Gordon Williams). Yale University Press
— *The Death Of Virgil* (by Hermann Broch; translated by Jean Starr Untermeyer). North Point Press

Warren, Robert Penn— *Then & Now: The Personal Past In The Poetry Of Robert Penn Warren* (by Floyd C. Watkins). University Press of Kentucky

—*Brother To Dragons: A Discussion* (edited by James A. Grimshaw, Jr.). Louisiana State University Press

Wheatley, Phillis— *Phillis Wheatley And Her Writings* (by William H. Robinson). Garland Pub. Co.

Wheelwright, John— *The Revolutionary Imagination: The Poetry And Politics Of John Wheelwright And Sherry Mangan* (by Alan M. Wald). University of North Carolina Press

Whitman, Walt— *Critical Essays On Walt Whitman* (edited by James Woodress). G. K. Hall
— *Language And Style In Leaves Of Grass* (by C. Carroll Hollis). Louisiana State University Press

Wilbur, Richard— *Richard Wilbur's Creation* (edited by Wendy Salinger). University of Michigan Press

Williams, William Carlos— *William Carlos Williams: A Poet In The American Theatre* (by David A. Fredo). UMI Research Press
—*William Carlos Williams' A Dream Of Love* (by Steven Ross Loevy). UMI Research Press
—*William Carlos Williams And The Painters, 1909-1923* (by William Marling). Swallow Press
—*The Prepoetics Of William Carlos Williams: Kora In Hell* (by Roy Miki). UMI Research Press
—*William Carlos Williams: A New World Naked* (by Paul Mariani). McGraw-Hill
—*The Visual Text Of William Carlos Williams* (by Henry M. Sayre). University of Illinois Press

Wilmot, John (see Rochester, Earl of)

Winters, Yvor— *Revolution And Convention In Modern Poetry: Studies In Ezra Pound, T. S. Eliot, Wallace Stevens, Edwin Arlington And Yvor Winters* (by Donald E. Stanford). University of Delaware Press

Wordsworth, William— *Wordsworth's Metaphysical Verse: Geometry, Nature And Form* (by Lee M. Johnson). University of Toronto Press
—*William Wordsworth: The Borders Of Vision* (by Jonathan Wordsworth). Oxford University Press
—*Wordsworth* (by Herbert Read). Greenwood Press (reprint)
—*Wordsworth And The Beginnings Of Modern Poetry* (by Robert Rehder). Barnes & Noble

—*Vision And Disenchantment: Blake's Songs And Wordsworth's Lyrical Ballads* (by Heather Glen). Cambridge University Press
—*William Wordsworth: The Poetry Of Grandeur And Tenderness* (by David B. Pirie). Methuen

Wyatt, Thomas— *The "Inward" Language: Sonnets Of Wyatt, Sidney, Shakespeare, Donne* (by Anne Ferry). University of Chicago Press

Wylie, Elinor— *The Life And Art Of Elinor Wylie* (by Judith Farr). Louisiana State University Press

Yeats, William Butler— *Yeats* (by Douglas Archibald). Syracuse University Press
—*A Guide To The Prose Fiction Of W. B. Yeats* (by William O'Donnell). UMI Research Press
—*A New Commentary On The Poems Of W. B. Yeats* (by A. Norman Jeffares). Humanities Press
—*Yeats: An Annual Of Critical And Textual Studies, 1983* (edited by Richard J. Finneran). Cornell University Press
—*The Last Courtly Lover: Yeats And The Idea Of Women* (by Gloria C. Kline). UMI Research Press
—*The Black Day: The Manuscripts Of Crazy Jane On The Day Of Judgment* (by David R. Clark). Humanities Press
—*Yeats & American Poetry: The Tradition Of The Self* (by Terence Diggory). Princeton University Press
—*Yeats At Songs & Choruses* (by David R. Clark). University of Massachusetts Press
—*Yeats On Yeats: The Last Introduction And The Dublin Edition* (by Edward Callan). Humanities Press
—*The Symbolic Method Of Coleridge, Baudelaire And Yeats* (by Anca Vlasopolis). Wayne State University Press
—*Yeats's Daimonic Renewal.* (by Herbert J. Levine). UMI Research Press
—*The Letters Of John Quinn To William Butler Yeats* (edited by Alan Himber). UMI Research Press

Zukofsky, Louis— *Zukofsky's "A": An Introduction* (by Barry Ahearn). University of California Press

(4) COMMENT AND CRITICISM
(listed alphabetically by author)

Ajuwon, Bade— *Funeral Dirges Of Yoruba Hunters.* NOK Publishers International

Allen, Judson Boyce— *The Ethical Poetic Of The Later Middle Ages: A Decorum Of Convenient Distinction.* University of Toronto Press

Amanuddin, Syed— *World Poetry In English: Essays & Interviews.* Sterling Publishers/Humanities Press

Anozie, Sunday O.— *Structural Models And African Poetics: Towards A Pragmatic Theory Of Literature.* Routledge & Kegan Paul

Armstrong, Isobel— *Language As Living Form In Nineteenth Century Poetry.* Harvester/Barnes & Noble

Attridge, Derek— *The Rhythms Of English Poetry.* Longman

Baker, Donald C. (see listing for Ogilvy, J. D. A.)

Baker, Sheridan (see listing for Frye, Northrop)

Bell, Marvin— *Old Snow Just Melting: Essays And Interviews.* University of Michigan Press

Berg, Stephen— *In Praise Of What Persists.* Harper & Row

Bergman, David; Epstein, Daniel Mark— *The Heath Guide To Poetry.* Heath and Co.

Blackstone, Bernard— *The Lost Travellers: A Romantic Theme With Variations.* Greenwood Press (reprint)

Bogdanos, Theodore— *Pearl, Image Of The Ineffable: A Study In Medieval Poetic Symbolism.* Pennsylvania State University Press

Boitani, Piero— *English Medieval Narrative In The Thirteenth And Fourteenth Centuries.* Cambridge University Press

Bourdette, Robert E., Jr.; Cohen, Michael— *The Poem In Question.* Harcourt Brace Jovanovich

Boyd, John D.— *A College Poetics.* University Press of America

Brooks-Davies, Douglas— *The Mercurian Monarch: Magical Politics From Spenser To Pope.* Manchester University Press

Brown, Ashley; Cheney, Frances Neel (editors)— *The Poetry Reviews Of Allen Tate, 1924-1944.* Louisiana State University Press

Brown, Frank Burch— *Transfiguration: Poetic Metaphor And The Languages Of Religious Belief.* University of North Carolina Press

Bruce-Novoa— *Chicano Poetry: A Response To Chaos.* University of Texas Press

Carpenter, Bogdana— *The Poetic Avant-Garde In Poland, 1918-1939.* University of Washington Press

Carruth, Hayden— *Effluences From The Sacred Caves: More Selected Essays And Reviews.* University of Michigan Press

Castro, Michael— *Interpreting The Indian: Twentieth-Century Poets And The Native American.* University of New Mexico Press

Caws, Mary Ann; Riffaterre, Hermine (editors)— *The Prose Poem In France: Theory And Practice.* Columbia University Press

Cheney, Frances Neel (see listing for Brown, Ashley)

Cheng, Francois— *Chinese Poetic Writing* (translated by Donald A. Riggs and Jerome P. Seaton), Indiana University Press

Cheyney, Arnold B.— *The Poetry Corner.* Scott, Foresman

Clausen, Jan— *A Movement Of Poets: Thoughts On Poetry And Feminism.* Long Haul Press

Clubbe, John; Lovell, Ernest J., Jr.— *English Romanticism: The Grounds Of Belief.* Northern Illinois University Press

Cohen, Michael (see listing for Bourdette, Robert E., Jr.)

Coleman, Antony; Hammond, Antony (editors)— *Poetry And Drama, 1570-1700: Essays In Honour Of Harold F. Brooks.* Methuen

Davis, Philip— *Memory And Writing From Wordsworth To Lawrence.* Barnes & Noble Books

Day, A. Grove— *The Sky Clears: Poetry Of The American Indians.* Greenwood Press (reprint)

Dow, Philip (editor)— *Golden Gate Watershed: Nineteen American Poets.* Harcourt Brace Jovanovich

Drake, Barbara— *Writing Poetry.* Harcourt Brace Jovanovich

Dryden, John— *An Essay Of Dramatic Poesy; A Defence Of An Essay Of Dramatic Posey; Preface To The Fables* (edited by John J. Mahoney). Irvington (reprint)

Duke, Charles R.; Jacobsen, Sally A.— *Reading And Writing Poetry: Successful Approaches For The Student And Teacher.* Oryx Press

Easthope, Antony— *Poetry As Discourse.* Methuen

Eekman, Thomas; Worth, Dean S. (editors)— *Russian Poetics: Proceedings Of The International Colloquium At U.C.L.A., September 22-26, 1975.* Slavica Publishers

Epstein, Daniel Mark (see listing for Bergman, David)

Everson, William— *Birth Of A Poet: The Santa Cruz Meditations* (edited by Lee Bartlett). Black Sparrow Press

Ferguson, Margaret W.— *Trials Of Desire: Renaissance Defenses Of Poetry.* Yale University Press

Fletcher, Pauline— *Gardens And Grim Ravines: The Language Of Landscape In Victorian Poetry.* Princeton University Press

France, Peter— *Poets Of Modern Russia.* Cambridge University Press

Frye, Northrop; Baker, Sheridan; Perkins, George— *The Practical Imagination: An Introduction To Poetry.* Harper & Row

Gall, Sally M. (see listing for Rosenthal, M. L.)

Ganim, John M.— *Style And Consciousness In Middle English Narrative.* Princeton University Press

Gefin, Laszlo K.— *Ideogram: History Of A Poetic Method.* University of Texas Press

Gingerich, Martin E.— *Contemporary Poetry In America And England 1950-1975: A Guide To Information Sources.* Gale Research Co.

Green, Martin (editor)— *The Old English Elegies: New Essays In Criticism And Research.* Fairleigh Dickinson University Press

Grigson, Geoffrey— *Blessings, Kicks And Curses: A Critical Collection.* Allison & Busby/Schocken Books
—*The Private Art: A Poetry Notebook.* Allison & Busby/Schocken Books

Hall, Donald— *To Read Literature, Fiction, Poetry, Drama.* Holt, Rinehart and Winston

Halsall, Maureen— *The Old English Rune Poem: A Critical Edition.* University of Toronto Press

Hamburger, Michael— *The Truth Of Poetry: Tensions In Modern Poetry From Baudelaire To The 1960s.* Methuen

Hammond, Antony (see listing for Coleman, Antony)

Hass, Robert— *Twentieth Century Pleasures: Essays On Poetry.* Ecco Press

Hayden, John O.— *Inside Poetry Out: An Introduction To Poetry.* Nelson-Hall

Hermans, Theo— *The Structure Of Modernist Poetry.* Croom Helm (London)

Hiroaki, Sato— *One Hundred Frogs: From Renga To Haiku To English.* Weatherhill

Hogg, James— *Poetic Drama And Poetic Theory.* Humanities Press

Hooker, Jeremy— *The Poetry Of Place.* Carcanet Press/Humanities Press

Houston, John Porter— *The Rhetoric Of Poetry In The Renaissance And Seventeenth Century.* Louisiana State University Press

Jackson, Richard— *Acts Of Mind: Conversations With Contemporary Poets.* University of Alabama Press

Jacobsen, Sally A. (see listing for Duke, Charles R.)

Jay, Paul— *Being In The Text; Self-Representation From Wordsworth To Roland Barthes.* Cornell University Press

Jimenez Fajardo, Salvador; Wilcox, John C. (editors)— *At Home And Beyond: New Essays On Spanish Poets Of The Twenties.* Society of Spanish and Spanish-American Studies

Kennedy, X. J. (compiler)— *Literature: An Introduction To Fiction, Poetry And Drama.* Little, Brown

Kintgen, Eugene R.— *The Perception Of Poetry.* Indiana University Press

Lawton, David A. (editor)— *Middle English Alliterative Poetry And Its Literary Background.* Byydell & Brewer/Biblio Distribution Center

Lesky, Albin— *Greek Tragic Poetry* (translated by Matthew Dillon). Yale University Press

Logan, John— *A Ballet For The Ear: Interviews, Essays And Reviews* (edited by A. Poulin, Jr.). University of Michigan Press

Lovell, Ernest J., Jr. (see listing for Clubbe, John)

MacQueen, John— *Progress And Poetry.* Scottish Academic Press/Columbia University Press

Magill, Frank N. (editor)— *Critical Survey Of Poetry.* Salem Press

McGann, Jerome J.— *The Romantic Ideology: A Critical Investigation.* University of Chicago Press

Mell, Donald C., Jr.— *English Poetry, 1660-1800: A Guide To Information Sources.* Gale Research Co.

Meredith, William— *Reasons For Poetry & The Reason For Criticism.* Library of Congress

Needham, J.— *The Completest Mode: I. A. Richards And The Continuity Of English Literary Criticism.* University Press, Edinburgh

Nims, John Frederick— *Western Wind: An Introduction To Poetry.* Random House

Ogilvy, J. D. A.; Baker, Donald C.— *Reading Beowulf: An Introduction To The Poem, Its Background And Its Style.* University of Oklahoma Press

Ostriker, Alicia— *Writing Like A Woman.* University of Michigan Press

Palmer, Michael (editor)— *Code Of Signals: Recent Writings In Poetics.* North Atlantic Books

Perkins, George (see listing for Frye, Northrop)

Perrine, Laurence— *Sound And Sense: An Introduction To Poetry.* Harcourt Brace Jovanovich

Peters, Robert— *The Black And Blue Guide To Current Poetry Journals.* Cherry Valley Editions

Piper, David— *The Image Of The Poet: British Poets And Their Portraits.* Clarendon Press

Prescott, Frederick Clark— *The Poetic Mind.* Greenwood Press (reprint)

Ramsey, Lee C.— *Chivalric Romances: Popular Literature In Medieval England.* Indiana University Press

Raspa, Anthony— *The Emotive Image: Jesuit Poetics In The English Renaissance* (by Anthony Raspa). Texas Christian University Press

Riffaterre, Hermine (see listing for Caws, Mary Ann)

Rodway, Allan— *The Craft Of Criticism.* Cambridge University Press

Rogers, William Elford— *The Three Genres And The Interpretation Of Lyric.* Princeton University Press

Rosenthal, M. L.; Gall, Sally M.— *The Modern Poetic Sequence: The Genius Of Modern Poetry.* Oxford University Press
—*Poetry And The Common Life.* Schocken Books

Rothenberg, Diane (see listing for Rothenberg, Jerome)

Rothenberg, Jerome; Rothenberg, Diane (editors)— *Symposium Of The Whole: A Range Of Discourse Toward An Ethnopoetics.* University of California Press

Salter, Elizabeth— *Fourteenth-Century English Poetry.* Oxford University Press

Saunders, J. W.— *A Biographical Dictionary Of Renaissance Poets And Dramatists.* Barnes & Noble

Sayce, Olive— *The Medieval German Lyric, 1150-1300: The Development Of Its Themes And Forms In Their European Context.* Oxford University Press

Schapiro, Barbara A.— *The Romantic Mother: Narcissistic Patterns In Romantic Poetry.* Johns Hopkins University Press

Segel, Harold B.— *The Baroque Poem: A Comparative Survey.* Irvington Publishers

Siegel, Lee— *Fires Of Love—Waters Of Peace: Passion And Renunciation In Indian Culture.* University of Hawaii Press

Simpson, Eileen B.— *Poets In Their Youth: A Memoir.* Vintage Books (reprint)

Sisson, C. H.— *English Poetry, 1900-1950, An Assessment.* Carcanet New Press/Humanities Press

Sleeth, Charles R.— *Studies In Christ And Satan.* University of Toronto Press

Smith, Colin— *The Making Of The Poema De Mio Cid.* Cambridge University Press

Smith, Stan— *Inviolable Voice: History And Twentieth-Century Poetry.* Humanities Press

Spitzer, Leo— *Essays On English And American Literature* (edited by Anna Hatcher). Gordian Press

Stanford, Donald E. (editor)— *British Poets, 1880-1914*. Gale Research Co.

Tate, Allen— *The Poety Reviews Of Allen Tate, 1924-1944* (edited by Ashley Brown and Frances Neel Cheney). Louisiana State University Press

Todorov, Tzvetan (editor)— *French Literary Theory Today: A Reader* (translated by R. Carter). Cambridge University Press

Tomlinson, Charles— *Poetry And Metamorphosis*. Cambridge University Press

Tripp, Raymond P., Jr.— *More About The Fight With The Dragon: Beowulf, 2208b-3182*. University Press of America

Vivas, Eliseo— *Vivas As Critic: Essays In Poetics And Criticism* (edited by Hugh Mercer Curtler). Whitson Publishing Co.

Waggoner, Wyatt H.— *American Visionary Poetry*. Louisiana State University Press

Weatherhead, A. Kingsley— *The British Dissonance: Essays On Ten Contemporary English Poets*. University of Missouri Press

West, M. L.— *The Orphic Poems*. Oxford University Press

Wilcox, John C. (see Jimenez Fajardo, Salvador)

Willson, A. Leslie (editor)— *German Romantic Criticism*. Continuum

Worth, Dean S. (see listing for Eekman, Thomas)

Zholkovsky, Alexander— *Themes And Texts: Toward A Poetics Of Expressiveness* (edited by Kathleen Parthe). Cornell University Press

Book Publishers Publishing Poetry

Following is a directory of U.S. and Canadian publishers who issued at least one book of current, original poetry during 1983; it is based on publishers represented in Section 1 of The Yearly Record *in this volume. Not included are foreign publishers or U.S./Canadian distributors of foreign-published books, or subsidy (vanity) publishers. The directory is for information purposes only; it does not indicate recommendation of any publisher listed.*

A

Abattoir Editions, University of Nebraska, Cleary House, P.O. Box 688, Omaha, NE 68101
Accent Editions, 446 E. 78th St., New York, NY 10021
Adams Press, 30 W. Washington St., Chicago, IL 60602
Adastra Press, 101 Strong St., Easthampton, MA 01027
Adinkra Press, 431 Coffield Ave., Napa, CA 94558
Adler Press, Box 9342, Rochester, NY 14604
Ahsahta Press, Boise State University, Dept. of English, Boise, ID 83725
Alchemy Press, 681 Market St., San Francisco, CA 94105
Alicejames Books, 138 Mt. Auburn St., Cambridge, MA 02138
American Indian Studies Center, University of California, 3220 Campbell Hall, Los Angeles, CA 90024
American Poetry Press, Box 2013, Upper Darby, PA 19082
American Studies Press, 13511 Palmwood Lane, Tampa, FL 33624
Ampersand Press, Roger Williams College, Bristol, RI 02809
Amphibian Publications, Box 5352, Athens, GA 30604
Anchor Press, c/o Doubleday & Co., Garden City, NY 11530
Anhinga Press, Florida State University, Dept. of English, Tallahassee FL 32306
Apple-wood Books, Box 2870, Cambridge, MA 02139
Applezaba Press, Box 4134, Long Beach, CA 90804
Ardis Publishers, 2901 Heatherway, Ann Arbor, MI 48104
Artefact Co., 5537 Germantown Ave., Philadelphia, PA 19144
Ashod Press, Box 1147, Madison Square Station, New York, NY 10159
Atheneum Publishers, 122 E. 42nd St., New York, NY 10017
Augustinus, c/o Curbstone Press, 321 Jackson St., Willimantic, CT 06226
Avant Books, 3719 Sixth Ave, San Diego, CA 92103
Aya Press, Box 303, Station A, Toronto, Ont. M5W 1C2, Canada

B

Backstreet Editions, Box 555, Port Jefferson, NY 11777
Barnwood Press Cooperative, R.R. 2, Box 11C, Daleville, IN 47334
Robert L. Barth, 14 Lucas St., Florence, KY 41042
W. L. Bauhan, Publisher, Old Country Rd., Dublin, NH 03444
Beatitude Press, 2940 Claremont Ave., #6, Berkeley, CA 94705
F. C. Beil, 321 E. 43rd St., New York, NY 10017
Belknap Press, c/o Harvard University Press, 79 Garden St., Cambridge, MA 02138
Berkeley Poets Workshop & Press, P.O. Box 459, Berkeley, CA 94701
Bieler Press, P.O. Box 3856, St. Paul, MN 55165
Bitterroot-West of Boston Press, 14 Bayfield Rd., Wayland, MA 01778
BkMk Press, University of Missouri, 5725 Wyandotte, Kansas City, MO 64113
Black Buzzard Press, 4705 S. 8th Rd., Arlington, VA 22204
Black Sparrow Press, Box 3993, Santa Barbara, CA 93105
Black Swan Books, Box 327, Redding Ridge, CT 06876

Black Willow, 3214 Sunset Ave., Norristown, PA 19403
Blue Cloud Press, Blue Cloud Abbey, Marvin, SD 57251
Blue Moon Press, University of Arizona, Dept. of English, Tucson, AZ 85720
Blue Spruce Press, Guildford, CT 06347
Blue Unicorn, 22 Avon Rd., Kensington, CA 94707
BOA Editions, 92 Park Ave., Brockport, NY 14420
Bookcraft, 1848 W. 2300 S., Salt Lake City, UT 84119
Boss Books, Box 370, Madison Square Station, New York, NY 10159
Bragdon Books, Pueblo, CO
Branden Press, 21 Station St., Boston, MA 02146
George Braziller, 1 Park Ave., New York, NY 10016
Breitenbush Books, Box 02137, Portland, OR 97202
Bruccoli-Clark Publishers, 2006 Sumter St., Columbia, SC 29201
Burning Deck, 71 Elmgrove Ave., Providence, RI 02906

C

Cadmus Editions, Box 687, Tiburon, CA 94920
Caislan Press, Box 28371, San Jose, CA 95159
California Street Editions, 723 Dwight Way, Berkeley, CA 94710
Calliope Press, 4122 E Cove Lane, Glenview, IL 60025
Cambium Press, Stone Ridge, NY 12484
Capra Press, Box 2068, Santa Barbara, CA 93120
Caravan Books, Box 344, Del Mar, NY 12054
Caravan Press, 343 S. Broadway, Los Angeles, CA 90013
Carnegie-Mellon University Press, Pittsburgh, PA 15213
Carpenter Press, Route 4, Pomeroy, OH 45769
Chantry Press, Box 144, Midland Park, NJ 07432
Charles Street Press, Box 4692, Baltimore, MD 21212
Cherry Valley Editions, 2314 Georgian Woods Place, Silver Spring, MD 20902
Childrens Press, 1224 W. Van Buren St., Chicago, IL 60607
Clarke, Irwin, Clarwin House, 791 St. Clair Ave., W., Toronto, Ont. M6C 1B8, Canada
Cleveland State University Poetry Center, Cleveland State University, Dept. of English,
    Cleveland, OH 44115
Coach House Press, 401 Huron St. (rear), Toronto, Ont. M5S 2G5, Canada
Colophon Books, 407 W. Cordova, Vancouver, B.C., Canada
Confluence Press, Lewis-Clark State College, Spalding Hall, Lewiston, ID 83501
Copper Beech Press, Box 1852, Brown University, Providence, RI 02912
Copper Canyon Press, Box 271, Port Townsend, WA 98368
Copper Orchid Publishing Co., 1966 Westbrook Dr., Jackson, MI 49021
Cordella Books, Station Hill Rd., Barrytown, NY 12507
Cornell Press, Santa Clara, CA
Cornwall Books, 4 Cornwall Dr., East Brunswick, NJ 08816
Countryman Press, Woodstock, VT 05091
Coyote Love Press, 27 Deering St., Portland, ME 04101
Crossing Press, 17 W. Main St., Box 640, Trumansburg, NY 14886
T. Y. Crowell, 10 E. 53rd St., New York, NY 10022
Crown Publishers, 1 Park Ave., New York, NY 10016
Curbstone Press, 321 Jackson St., Willimantic, CT 06226

D

Dawn Horse Press, Box 368, Clearlake Highlands, CA 95422
Dial Press, 2 Park Ave., New York, NY 10016
Doubleday & Co., Garden City, NY 11530
Dovetail Press, 250 W. 94th St., New York, NY 10025
Dragon Gate, 508 Lincoln St., Port Townsend, WA 98368
Dragon's Teeth Press, El Dorado National Forest, Georgetown, CA 95634
Druid Heights Books, 685 Camino Del Canyon, Muir Woods, Mill Valley, CA 94941
Dryad Press, Box 29161, Presidio, San Francisco, CA 94129
Duck Down, Box 1047, Fallon, NV 89406

Duke University Press, Box 6697, College Sta., Durham, NC 27706
E. P. Dutton & Co., 2 Park Ave., New York, NY 10016

E

Ecco Press, 18 W. 30th St., New York, NY 10001
Ell Ell Diversified, Box 1702, Santa Rosa, CA 94502
Elpenor Books, Box 3152, Merchandise Mart Plaza, Chicago, IL 60654
Faber and Faber, 39 Thompson St., Winchester, MA 01890
Farrar, Straus & Giroux, 19 Union Square W., New York, NY 10003
Fiddlehead Poetry Books, The Observatory, University of New Brunswick, Box 4400,
    Fredericton, N.B. E3B 5A3, Canada
Field, Oberlin College, Rice Hall, Oberlin, OH 44074
The Figures, 2016 Cedar, Berkeley, CA 94709
Flower Mound Writing Co., Box 22984, TWU Station, Denton, TX 76204
Fortress Press, 2900 Queen Lane, Philadelphia, PA 19129
Four Seasons Foundation, Box 31190, San Francisco, CA 94131
H. Frisch, 303 W. 10th St., New York, NY 10014
Full Count Press, 223 N. Broadway, Edmond, OK 73034
Full Court Press, 138-140 Watts St., New York, NY 10013

G

Garland Pub. Co., 136 Madison Ave., New York, NY 10016
Gavea-Brown, Box O, Brown University, Providence, RI 02912
Gay Sunshine Press, Box 40397, San Francisco, CA 94140
Gehry Press, 1319 Pine St., Iowa City, IA 52240
General Publishing Co., 30 Lesmill Rd., E., Don Mills, Ont., M3B 2T6, Canada
Geryon Press, Box 770, Tunnel, NY 13848
Glavin Press, Marblehead, MA 01945
David R. Godine, Publisher, 306 Dartmouth St., Boston, MA 02116
Golden Press, 850 Third Ave., New York, NY 10022
Golden Quill Press, Francestown, NH 03043
Gotuit Enterprises, 1300-9C Golden Rain Rd., Box 2568, Santa Barbara, CA 90740
Graywolf Press, Box 142, Port Townsend, WA 98368
Great Society Press, 451 Heckman St., Phillipsburg, NJ 08865
Greenfield Review Press, R.D. 1, Box 80, Greenfield Center, NY 12833
Greenwillow Books, 105 Madison Ave., New York, NY 10016
Grey Whale Press, 4820 S.E. Boise, Portland, OR 97206
Grove Press, 196 W. Houston St., New York, NY 10014
Guernica Editions, Box 633, Station N.D.G., Montreal, Que. H4A 3R1, Canada
Guild Press, Box 22583, Robbinsdale, MN 55422

H

Hanging Loose Press, 231 Wickoff St., Brooklyn, NY 11217
Harcourt Brace Jovanovich, 1250 Sixth Ave., San Diego, CA 92101
Hardin-Simmons University Press, Box 896, H.S.U., Abilene, TX 79698
Harian Creative Books, 47 Hyde Blvd., Ballston Spa, NY 12020
Harmony Books, 1 Park Ave., New York, NY 10016
Harper & Row, 10 E. 53rd St., New York, NY 10022
Harvard University Press, 79 Garden St., Cambridge, MA 02138
Hendricks Publishing, Box 724026, Atlanta, GA 30339
Holiday House, 18 E. 53rd St., New York, NY 10022
Holmgangers Press, 95 Carson Court, Shelter Cove, Whitehorn, CA 95489
Holt, Rinehart & Winston, 521 Fifth Ave., New York, NY 10175
Holy Cow! Press, Box 618, Minneapolis, MN 55440
Horizon Press, 156 5th Ave., New York, NY 10010
Houghton Mifflin Co., 1 Beacon St., Boston, MA 02108
Humana Press, Box 2148, Clifton, NJ 07015

I

Illuminati, 8812 W. Pico Blvd., Suite 204, Los Angeles, CA 90035
Indiana University Press, Tenth & Morton Sts., Bloomington, IN 47405
Iron Press, Box 176, Franklin, MI 48025
Ithaca House, 108 N. Plain St., Ithaca, NY 14850

J

Jawbone Press, Waldron Island, WA 98297
Jewish Publication Society of America, 1930 Chestnut St., Philadelphia, PA 19103
Johns Hopkins University Press, Baltimore, MD 21218
Juniper Press, 1310 Shorewood Dr., La Crosse, WI 54601

K

Kastrel 3, Whitehorn, CA 95489
Kearney State College Press, Kearney, NE 68847
Kesley Street Press, Box 9235, Berkeley, CA 94709
Alfred A. Knopf, Inc., 201 E. 50th St., New York, NY 10022
Konglomerati Press, Box 5001, Gulfport, FL 33737
Kosmos, 2580 Polk, San Francisco, CA 94109

L

La Morenita Publishers, 25-A Hill St., San Francisco, CA 94110
Landfall Press, 5171 Chapin St., Dayton, OH 45429
Larlin Corp., Box 1523, Marietta, GA 30061
Last Chance, Wilburton, OK 74578
Latin American Poetry Review Press, Box 8385, Pittsburgh, PA 15218
Lens Unlimited, Fairbanks, AK 99701
Lieb-Schott Publications, Box 229, Bourbonnais, IL 60914
Linwood Publishers, Box 70152, North Charleston, SC 29405
Literary Classics of the U.S., c/o Viking Press, 40 W. 23rd St., New York, NY 10010
Little, Brown & Co., 34 Beacon St., Boston, MA 02106
Liveright Publishing Corp., 500 Fifth Ave., New York, NY 10110
Logbridge-Rhodes, Box 3254, Durango, CO 81301
Lotus Press, Box 21607, Detroit, MI 48221
Louisiana State University Press, Baton Rouge, LA 70803
Lunchroom Press, Box 36027, Grosse Pointe Farms, MI 48236
Lynx House Press, Box 800, Amherst, MA 01004

M

Macmillan Publishing Co., 866 Third Ave., New York, NY 10022
Mammoth Press, 40-B Grecian Garden Dr., Rochester, NY 14626
Mathom Publishing Co., 68 E. Mohawk St., Box 362, Oswego, NY 13126
McClelland & Stewart, Ltd., 25 Hollinger Rd., Toronto, Ont, M4B 3G2, Canada
E. Mellen Press, Box 450, 460 Ridge St., Lewiston, NY 14092
Metacom Press, 31 Beaver St., Worcester, MA 01603
Middleburg Press, Box 166, Orange City, IA 51041
Momentum Press, 512 Hill St., #4, Santa Monica, CA 90405
Momo's Press, 45 Sheridan, San Francisco, CA 94103
William Morrow & Co., 105 Madison Ave., New York, NY 10016
Mosaic Press, 358 Oliver Rd., Cincinnati, OH 45215
Mosaic Press/Valley Editions, Box 1032, Oakville, Ont. L6J 5E9, Canada
Moving Parts Press, 419-A Maple St., Santa Cruz, CA 95060
Multnomah Press, 10209 S.E. Division St., Portland, OR 97266
Myriad Moods, 1530 Larkspur, Suite Z, San Antonio, TX 78213

N

National Poetry Foundation, University of Maine, 305 EM Bldg., Orono, ME 04469
National Writers Press, 1450 S. Havana, Suite 620, Aurora, CO 80012
New American Library, 1633 Broadway, New York, NY 10019
New Directions Publishing Corp., 80 Eighth Ave., New York, NY 10011
New Orleans Poetry Journal Press, 2131 General Pershing St., New Orleans, LA 70115
New Rivers Press, 1602 Selby Ave., St. Paul, MN 55104
Night Horn Books, 499 Ellis St., Box 1156, San Francisco, CA 94102
Nightingale Press, Box 6586, Gulfport, MS 39501
North Atlantic Books, 635 Amador St., Richmond, CA 94805
North Point Press, Box 6275, Berkeley, CA 94706
Northword, Box 5634, Madison, WI 53705
W. W. Norton & Co., 500 Fifth Ave., New York, NY 10110

O

Ohio State University Press, 1050 Carmack Rd., Columbus, OH 43210
Ohio University Press, Scott Hall 143, Athens, OH 45701
Oleander Press, 210 Fifth Ave., New York, NY 10010
Ontario Review Press, 9 Honey Brook Dr., Princeton, NJ 08540
Open Book, Station Hill Rd., Barrytown, NY 12507
Overlook Press, Rte, 212, Box 427, Woodstock, NY 12498
Ox Head Press, 414 N. 6th St., Marshall, MN 56258
Oxford University Press, 200 Madison Ave., New York, NY 10016; 70 Wynford Dr.,
    Don Mills, Ont. M3C 1J9, Canada

P

Panorama West, 8 E. Olive Ave., Fresno, CA 93728
Pelican Pub. Co., 1101 Monroe St., Gretna, LA 70053
Penguin, 40 W. 23rd St., New York, NY 10010
Pemnaen Press, R.D. 2, Box 145, Great Barrington, MA 01230
Penumbra Press, Box 340, Moonbeam, Ont. P0L 1V0, Canada
Perigee Books, 200 Madison Ave., New York, NY 10016
Perivale Press, 13830 Erwin St., Van Nuys, CA 91401
Persea Books, 225 Lafayette St., New York, NY 10012
Persephone Press, Box 7222, Watertown, MA 02172
Petronium Press, 1255 Nuuanu Ave., #1813, Honolulu, HI 96817
Philosophical Library, 200 W. 57th St., New York, NY 10019
Pisces Press, Box 4075, Lubbock, TX 79409
Pizzuto, 6979 Ferucroft Ave., San Gabriel, CA 91775
Porcupine's Quill, 68 Main St., Erin, Ont. N0B 1T0, Canada
Pottersfield Press, Halifax, N.S., Canada
Princeton University Press, Princeton, NJ 08540
Proscenium Press, 25 Music Square W., Nashville, TN 37203
Pryor-Pettingill, Box 7074, Ann Arbor, MI 48107
Publication Arts, 5 Schoon Ave., Hawthorne, NJ 07506
Puckerbrush Press, 76 Main St., Orono, ME 04473
Pulsar Publications, Box 714, Lafayette, CA 94549
G. P. Putnam's Sons, 200 Madison Ave., New York, NY 10016
Pym-Randall Press, 73 Cohasaset St., Roslindale, MA 02131

Q

Quadrant Editions, Dunvegan, Ont., Canada

R

Raccoon Books, 323 Hodges St., Memphis, TN 38111
Random House, Inc., 201 E. 50th St., New York, NY 10022
Raw Dog Press, 129 Worthington Ave., Doylestown, PA 18901

Read Weather Press, Box 1104, Eau Claire, WI 54701
Red Hill Press, Box 2853, San Francisco, CA 94126
Regal Books, 2300 Knoll Dr., Ventura, CA 93003
Riverstone Press, 809 15th St., Golden, CO 80401
Routledge & Kegan Paul, Ltd., 9 Park St., Boston, MA 02108
Running Press, 125 S. 22nd St., Philadelphia, PA 19103

S

Sachem Press, Box 9, Old Chatham, NY 12136
Sackbut Press, 2513 E. Webster Place, Milwaukee, WI 53211
St. Andrews Press, St. Andrews Presbyterian College, Laurinburg, NC 28352
St. Martin's Press, 175 5th Ave., New York, NY 10010
Saturday Press, Box 884, Upper Montclair, NJ 07043
Scarecrow Press, Box 656, Metuchen, NJ 08840
Schocken Books, 200 Madison Ave., New York, NY 10016
Schori Press, Evanston, IL
Sea Horse Press, 307 W. 11th St., New York, NY 10014
Seal Press, 310 S. Washington, Seattle, WA 98104
Seven Buffaloes Press, Box 249, Big Timber, MT 59011
Shadow Press, Box 8803, Minneapolis, MN 55408
Harold Shaw Publishers, Box 567, 388 Gundersen Dr., Wheaton, IL 60189
Sheep Meadow Press, 225 Lafayette St., New York, NY 10012
Signal Editions, c/o Vehicule Press, Montreal, Que., Canada
Signpost Press, 412 N. State St., Bellingham, WA 98225
Simon and Schuster, 1230 Ave. of the Americas, New York, NY 10020
The Smith, 5 Beekman St., New York, NY 10038
Sol Press, 2025 Dunn Place, Madison, WI 53713
Solaris Press, Box 1009, Rochester, MI 48063
Song Press, 808 Illinois, Stevens Point, WI 54481
Sono Nis Press, 1745 Blanshard St., Victoria, B.C. V8W 2J8, Canada
Sparrow Press, c/o Vagrom Publications, 103 Waldron St., West Lafayette, IN 47906
Spoon River Poetry Press, Box 1443, Peoria, IL 61655
Spuyten Duyvil, 520 Cathedral Pkwy., New York, NY 10025
Star Garden Poets Cooperative, Newhall, CA 91321
Starlight Press, Box 3102, Long Island City, NY 11103
State Street Press, 67 State St., Pittsford, NY 14534
State University of New York Press, State University Plaza, Albany, NY 12246
Station Hill Press, Station Hill Rd., Barrytown, NY 12507
Lyle Stuart, 120 Enterprise Ave., Secaucus, NJ 07094
Sultan of Swat Books, 1821 Kalorama Rd. NW., Washington, DC 20009
Sun, 347 W. 39th St., New York, NY 10018
Sun & Moon Press, 4330 Hartwick Rd., #418, College Park, MD 20740
Sunstone Press, Box 2321, Santa Fe, NM 87501
Swallow Press, c/o Ohio University Press, Scott Triangle, Athens, OH 45701
Sycamore Press, Box 825, Tucson, AZ 85702
Symposium Press, 1620 Greenfield, Los Angeles, CA 90025

T

Tamarack Editions, 128 Benedict Ave., Syracuse, NY 13210
Tamarisk Press, 319 S. Juniper St., Philadelphia, PA 19107
Taylor Street Press, 60 Taylor Dr., Fairfax, CA 94930
Temporal Acuity Press, 1535 121st Ave. S.E., Bellevue, WA 98005
Tern Press, 430 S.W. 206th St., Seattle, WA 98166
Textile Bridge Press, Box 157, Clarence Center, NY 14032
Three Continents Press, 1346 Connecticut Ave., N.W., Suite 1131, Washington, DC 20036
Thunder's Mouth Press, 242 W. 104th St., No. 5W., New York, NY 10025
Tidal Press, Cranberry Isles, ME 04625
Timberline Press, Box 327, Fulton, MO 65251
Tombouctou Books, Box 265, Bolinas, CA 94924
Toothpaste Press, Box 546, 626 E. Main, West Branch, IA 52358
Topgallant Pub. Co., Elizabeth Bldg., 845 Mission Lane, Honolulu, HI 96813
Turtle Island Foundation, 2845 Buena Vista Way, Berkeley, CA 94708
Tuumba Press, 2639 Russell St., Berkeley, CA 94705

U

F. Ungar, 250 Park Ave. S., New York, NY 10003
Unhinged Voice Press, Box 4388, Portsmouth, NH 03801
United Artists Books, 172 E. 4th St., New York, NY 10009
University of Alabama Press, Box 2877, University, AL 35486
University of Arkansas Press, McIlroy House, 201 Ozark St., Fayetteville, AR 72701
University of California Press, 2120 Berkeley Way, Berkeley, CA 94720
University of Chicago Press, 5801 Ellis Ave., Chicago, IL 60637
University of Delaware Press, 326 Hullihen Hall, Newark, DE 19711
University of Georgia Press, Waddell Hall, Athens, GA 30602
University of Illinois Press 54 E. Gregory Dr., Champaign, IL 61820
University Microfilms, 300 N. Zeeb Rd., Ann Arbor, MI 48106
University of Missouri Press, 200 Lewis Hall, Columbia, MO 65211
University of Nebraska Press, 901 N. 17th St., Lincoln, NE 68588
University of North Carolina Press, Box 2288, Chapel Hill, NC 27514
University of Notre Dame Press, Notre Dame, IN 46556
University of Pennsylvania Press, 3933 Walnut St., Philadelphia, PA 19104
University of Pittsburgh Press, 127 N. Bellefield Ave., Pittsburgh, PA 15260
University Press of America, 4720 Boston Way, Lanham, MD 20706
University Press of Hawaii, 2840 Kolowalu St., Honolulu, HI 96822
University Press of Kentucky, 102 Lafferty Hall, Lexington, KY 40506
University Press of Mississippi, 3825 Ridgewood Rd., Jackson, MS 39211
University Press of Virginia, Box 3608, University Station, Charlottesburg, VA 22903
University Presses of Florida, 15 N.W. 15th St., Gainesville, FL 32603
University of Queensland Press, Box 1365, New York, NY 10023
University of Toronto Press, St. George Campus, Toronto, Ont. M5S 1A6, Canada
University of Utah Press, 101 U.S.B., Salt Lake City, UT 84112

V

Viking Press, 40 W. 23rd St., New York. NY 10010
Vintage Books, Box 16182, Elway Station, St. Paul, MN. 55116

W

Wake Forest University Press, Box 7333, Winston-Salem, NC 27109
Wampeter Press, Box 512, Green Harbor, MA 02041
Washington Writers Publishing House, Box 50068, Washington, DC 20004
Water Mark Press, 175 E. Shore Rd., Huntington Bay, NY 11743
Wesleyan University Press, 110 Mt. Vernon St., Middletown, CT 06457
Wheat Forders, Box 6317, Washington, DC 20015
White Eagle Publisher, Box 1332, Lowell, MA 01853
White Ewe Press, Box 996, Adelphi, MD 20783
Wickwire Press, Cambridge, MA 02138
Wingbow Press, 2940 7th St., Berkeley, CA 94710
Wings Press, Rte. 2, Box 730, Belfast, ME 04915
M. & R. Wolfe, Box 1, Viola, ID 83872
Woodbridge Press, Box 6189, Santa Barbara, CA 93160

Y

Years Press, Michigan State University, Dept. of ATL, EBH, East Lansing, MI 48824
Yellow Press, 2394 Blue Island Ave., Chicago, IL 60608

Z

Zephyr Press, 13 Robinson St., Somerville, MA 02145
Zyga Multimedia Research, 642 El Dorado Ave., Oakland, CA 94611
Zygote Press, 1712 Mt. Curve Ave., Minneapolis, MN 55403

Magazines Publishing Poetry

The following is a select list of United States and Canadian periodicals that publish poetry on a regular basis.

A

Abraxas, 2518 Gregory St., Madison, WI 53711

Adventures In Poetry Magazine, 206 Patricia Dr., Junction, TX 76849

The Agni Review, Box 349, Cambridge, MA 02138

Alberta Poetry News, 6211-94 B Ave., Edmonton, Alta. T6B 0S5, Canada

The Alchemist, Box 123, LaSalle, Que. H8R 3T7, Canada

Alcoholism, Box C19051, Queen City Station, Seattle, WA 98109

America, 106 W. 56th St., New York, NY, 10019

The American Poetry Review, 1616 Walnut St., Room 405, Philadelphia, PA 19103

The American Scholar, 1811 Q St., N.W., Washington, DC 20009

Anima, 1053 Wilson Ave., Chambersburg, PA 17201

Ann Arbor Review, Washtenaw Community College, Ann Arbor, MI 48106

Antaeus, 18 W. 30th St., New York, NY 10001

The Antigonish Review, St. Francis Xavier University, Antigonish, N.S. B2G 1C0, Canada

The Antioch Review, Box 148, Yellow Springs, OH 45387

Ararat, 628 Second Ave., New York, NY 10016

Ariel, University of Calgary, Dept. of English, Calgary, Alta. T2N 1N4, Canada

The Arizona Quarterly, University of Arizona, Tucson, AZ 85721

Ascent, University of Illinois, Dept. of English, 608 S. Wright St., Urbana, IL 61801

The Atlantic Advocate, Gleaner Bldg., Phoenix Square, Fredericton, N.B. E3B 5A2, Canada

The Atlantic Monthly, 8 Arlington St., Boston, MA 02116

Atlantis, Acadia University, Box 294, Wolfville, N. S. B0P 1X0, Canada

B

Ball State University Forum, Ball State University, Muncie, IN 47306

The Bellingham Review, Signpost Press, 412 N. State, Bellingham, WA 98225

The Beloit Poetry Journal, Box 2, Beloit, WI 53511

Berkeley Poetry Review, Office of Student Activities, University of California, 103 Sproul Hall, Berkeley, CA 94720

Berkeley Poets Cooperative, Box 459, Berkeley, CA 94701

Bitterroot, Box 51, Brooklyn, NY 11219

Black American Literature Forum, Indiana State University, Parsons Hall 237, Terre Haute, IN 47809

Black Warrior Review, University of Alabama, Box 2936, University, AL 35486

Black Willow, 3214 Sunset Ave., Norristown, PA 19403

Blue Ridge Review, Box 1425, Charlottesville, VA 22902

Blue Unicorn, 22 Avon Rd., Kensington, CA 94707

Bogg Magazine, 422 N. Cleveland St., Arlington, VA 22201

The Boston Review, 991 Massachusetts Ave., #4, Cambridge, MA 02138

Boston University Journal, 704 Commonwealth Ave., Boston, MA 02215

Boundary 2, State University of New York, Binghamton, NY 13901

Broomstick Magazine, 3543 18th St., San Francisco, CA 94110

Buckle, State University College, Dept. of English, Buffalo, NY 14222

Buffalo Spree, 4511 Harlem Rd., Buffalo, NY 14226

C

California Quarterly, University of California, 100 Sproul Hall, Davis, CA 95616

Calliope, Roger Williams College, Creative Writing Program, Bristol, RI 02809

Calyx, Box B, Corvallis, OR 97331

Canadian Author & Bookman, 70 Champlain Ave., Welland, Ont. L3C 2L7, Canada

Canadian Forum, 20 The Esplanade, 3rd Floor, Toronto, Ont. M5E 9Z9, Canada

Canadian Literary Review, Box 278, Scarborough, Ont. M1N 1S6, Canada

Canadian Literature, University of British Columbia, 2075 Westbrook Mall, Vancouver, B.C. V6T 1W8, Canada

Canto Review of the Arts, 11 Bartlett St., Andover, MA 01810

The Cape Rock, Southeast Missouri State University, Dept. of English, Cape Girardeau, MA 63701

The Capilano Review, 2055 Purcell, North Vancouver, B.C. V7J 3H5, Canada

Carleton Miscellany, Carleton College, Northfield, MN 55057

Carolina Quarterly, University of North Carolina, Greenlaw Hall 066A, Chapel Hill, NC 27514

Cedar Rock, 1121 Madeline, New Braunfels, TX 78130

The Centennial Review, Michigan State University, Language and Literature Dept., 110 Morrill Hall, East Lansing, MI 48824

Centering, Michigan State University, East Lansing, MI 48824

The Chariton Review, Northeast Missouri State University, Language and Literature Dept., Kirksville, MO 63501

The Chattahoochee Review, De Kalb Community College, 2101 Womack Rd., Dunwoody, GA 30338

Chelsea, Box 5889, Grand Central Station, New York, NY 10017

Chiaroscuro, 108 N. Plain St., Ithaca, NY 14850

Chicago Review, University of Chicago, 5700 S. Ingleside, Box C, Chicago, IL 60637

The Chowder Review, Box 33, Wollaston, MA 02170

The Christian Century, 407 S. Dearborn St., Chicago, IL 60605

Christian Herald, 40 Overlook, Chappaqua, NY 10514

Christianity Today, 465 Gunderson Dr., Carol Stream, IL 60187

Chrysalis, 635 S. Westlake Ave., Los Angeles, CA 90057

Cimarron Review, Oklahoma State University, Stillwater, OK 74074

Cincinnati Review, University of Cincinnati, Cincinnati, OH 45202

Classical Outlook, Miami University, Oxford, OH 45056

Coe Review, Coe College, 1220 1st Ave., Cedar Rapids, IA 52402

College English, Indiana University, Dept. of English, Bloomington, IN 47405

Colorado-North Review, University Center, Greeley, CO 80639

Colorado Quarterly, University of Colorado, Hellems 134 E., Boulder, CO 80309

Columbia: A Magazine of Poetry And Prose, Columbia University, 404 Dodge, New York, NY 10027

Commonweal, 232 Madison Ave., New York, NY 10016

The Compass, University of Alberta, Box 632, Sub. Station 11, Edmonton, Alta. T6G 2E0, Canada.

Concerning Poetry, Western Washington University, Dept. of English, Bellingham, WA 98225.

The Congregationalist, 801 Bushness, Beloit, WI 53511

The Connecticut Quarterly, Box 65, Enfield, CT 06082

Cornfield Review, Ohio State University, 1465 Mt. Vernon Ave., Marion, OH 43302

Cream City Review, University of Wisconsin, Dept. of English, Curtin Hall, Box 413, Milwaukee, WI 53201

The Creative Woman, Governors State University, Park Forest South, IL 60466

Crosscurrents, 220 Glastonbury Rd., Westlake Village, CA 91361

Cumberlands, Pikeville College, Box 2, Pikeville, KY 41501

Cutbank, University of Montana, Dept. of English, Missoula, MT 59812

D

The Dalhousie Review, Dalhousie University, Halifax, N.S. B3H 4H8, Canada

Dandelion, The Alexandra Centre, 922 9th Ave., S.E., Calgary, Alta. T2G 0S4, Canada

Dark Horse, Box 9, Somerville, MA 02143

Day Tonight/Night Today, Box 353, Hull, MA 02045

Dakotah Territory, Box 775, Moorhead, MN 56560

The DeKalb Literary Arts Journal, 555 N. Indian Creek Dr., Clarkston, GA 30021

Delta Scene, Delta State University, Box B-3, Cleveland, MS 38733

Denver Quarterly, University of Denver, Denver, CO 80210

Descant, Texas Christian University, Dept. of English, TCU Station, Fort Worth, TX 76129

Descant (Canada), Box 314, Station P. Toronto, Ont. M5S 2S8, Canada

Dialogue, 202 West 300 North, Salt Lake City, UT 84103

The Dickinson Review, Dickinson State College, Div. of English, Dickinson, ND 58601

Dimension, Box 7939, Austin, TX 78712

Dreams, 76 Beaver St., Suite 400, New York, NY 10005

Dreamworks, Human Science Press, 72 Fifth Ave., New York, NY 10011

E

Earthwise, Box 680-536, Miami, FL 33168

Educational Studies, Illinois State University, 331 De Garmo Hall, Normal, IL 61761

The Emissary, 5569 N. Country Rd. 29, Loveland, CO 80537

En Passant/Poetry, 4612 Sylvanus Dr., Wilmington, DE 19803

Epoch, Cornell University, 251 Goldwin Smith Hall, Ithaca, NY 14853

Epos, Troy State University, Dept. of English, Troy, AL 36081

Etc.: A Review Of General Semantics, University of Wyoming, Laramie, WY 82070

Eureka Review, University of Cincinnati, Dept. of English, Cincinnati, OH 45221

event, Kwantien College, Box 9030, Surrey, B.C. V3T 5H8, Canada

F

The Falcon, Mansfield State College, Mansfield, PA 16933

The Fiddlehead, University of New Brunswick, The Observatory, Fredericton, N.B. E3B 5H5, Canada

Fiddler Gram, Eckerd College, Box 12560, St. Petersburg, FL 33733

Field, Oberlin College, Rice Hall, Oberlin, OH 44074

Firelands Arts Review, Firelands Campus, Huron, OH 44839

Focus/Midwest, 928a McKnight, St. Louis, MO 63132

Footwork Magazine, Passaic County Community College, Paterson, NJ 07509

Format, 405 S. 7th St., St. Charles, IL 60174

Four Quarters, La Salle College, Olney Ave., Philadelphia, PA 19141

Frontiers: A Journal of Women Studies, University of Colorado, c/o Women Studies, Boulder, CO 80309

Box 22412, Kansas City, MO 64113

Heresies: A Feminist Publication On Art And Politics, Box 766, Canal St. Station, New York, NY 10013

Higginson Journal of Poetry, 4508 38th St., Brentwood, MD 20722

The High Rock Review, Box 614, Saratoga Springs, NY 12866

The Hiram Poetry Review, Box 162, Hiram, OH 44234

The Hollins Critic, Hollins College, Hollins College, VA 24020

Hollow Springs Review Of Poetry, R.D. 1, Bancroft Rd., Chester, MA 01011

Hubris, Box 1543, Concord, NH 03301

The Hudson Review, 684 Park Ave., New York, NY 10021

G

Gargoyle, 40 St. John St., Jamaica Plain, MA 02130

Gargoyle, Box 3567, Washington, DC 20007

Geophysics, 3707 E. 51st St., Tulsa, OK 74135

The Georgia Review, University of Georgia, Athens, GA 30602

Good Housekeeping, 959 Eighth Ave., New York, NY 10019

Graffiti, Lenoir Rhyne College, Dept. of English, Box 418, Hickory, NC 28601

Graham House Review, Phillips Academy, Andover, MA 01810

The Great Lakes Review, Northeastern Illinois University, Chicago, IL 60625

Great River Review, 211 W. Wabasha, Winona, MN 55987

Green River Review, Saginaw Valley State College, University Center, MI 48710

Green's Magazine, Box 3236, Regina, Sask. S4P 3H1, Canada

The Greenfield Review, Box 80, Greenfield Center, NY 12833

Greensboro Review, University of North Carolina, Dept. of English, Greensboro, NC 27412

Grit, 208 W. Third St., Williamsport, PA 17701

Gryphon, University of South Florida, Dept. of Humanities-LE3 370, Tampa, FL 33620

I

Identity, 336 Queen St., E., Toronto, Ont. M5A 1S8, Canada

Illinois Quarterly, Illinois State University, Normal, IL 61761

Image Magazine, Box 28048, St. Louis, MO 63119

Images, Wright State University, Dept. of English, Dayton, OH 45435

Impressions, Box Station B, Toronto, Ont. M5T 2T2, Canada

Indiana Review, Indiana University, 316 N. Jordan Ave., Indianapolis, IN 46405

Inlet, Virginia Wesleyan College, Dept. of English, Norfolk, VA 23502

Inprint, 563 W. Westfield, Indianapolis, IN 46208

International Poetry Review, Box 2047, Greensboro, NC 27402

The International University Poetry Quarterly, 1301 S. Noland Rd., Independence, MO 64055

Intertext, Box 100014 DT, Anchorage, AK 99510

Iowa Review, University of Iowa, 308 EPB, Iowa City, IA 52242

Iowa Woman, Box 680, Iowa City, IA 52244

Israel Horizons, 150 Fifth Ave., Room 1002, New York, NY 10011

H

Hampden-Sydney Poetry Review, Box 126, Hampden-Sydney, VA 23943

Hanging Loose, 231 Wyckoff St., Brooklyn, NY 11217

Harbor Review, University of Massachusetts, Dept. of English, Boston, MA 02125

Harmony, University of New Hampshire, M.U.B., Room 151, Durham, NH 03824

The Harvard Advocate, 21 South St., Cambridge, MA 02138

Hawaii Literary Arts Council Newsletter, Box 11213, Moiliili Station, Honolulu, HI 96828

Hawaii Review, University of Hawaii, Dept. of English, Honolulu, HI 96822

Helicon Nine: The Journal Of Woman's Arts And Letters,

J

Jeopardy, Western Washington University, Humanities 350, WWU, Bellingham, WA 98225

Jewish Currents, 22 E. 17th St., Room 601, New York, NY 10003

The Jewish Spectator, Box 2016, Santa Monica, CA 90406

Journal of Irish Literature, Box 361, Newark, DE 19711

Journal Of New Jersey Poets, Fairleigh Dickinson University, Dept. of English, 285 Madison Ave., Madison, NJ 07940

Joycean Lively Arts Guild Review, Box 459, East Douglas, MA 01516

Jump River Review, 810 Oak St., Medina, OH 44256

K

Kaldron, Box 369, Grover City, CA 93433

Kalliope: A Journal of Women's Art, Florida Junior College, 3939 Roosevelt Blvd., Jacksonville, FL 32205

Kansas Quarterly, Kansas State University, Dept. of English, Denison Hall, Manhattan, KS 66506

Kayak, 325 Ocean View Ave., Santa Cruz, CA 95062

Kentucky Poetry Review, 1568 Cherokee Rd., Louisville, KY 40205

The Kenyon Review, Kenyon College, Gambier, OH 43022

The Kindred Spirit, 808 Maple, Great Bend, KS 67530

Kosmos, 381 Arlington St., San Francisco, CA 94131

L

Lake Street Review, Box 7188, Powderhorn Station, Minneapolis, MN 55407

The Lake Superior Review, Box 724, Ironwood, MI 49938

Latin American Literary Review, University of Pittsburgh, Dept. of Hispanic Language and Literature, 1309 Cathedral of Learning, Pittsburgh, PA 15260

Laurel Review, West Virginia Wesleyan College, Dept. of English, Buckhannon, WV 26201

The Limberlost Review, Box 1041, Pocatello, ID 83201

Lincoln Log, Rte. 2, Box 126-C, Raymond, IL 62560

The Literary Review, Fairleigh Dickinson University, 285 Madison Ave., Madison, NJ 07940

The Little Balkan Review, 601 Grandview Heights Terrace, Pittsburg, KS 66762

The Little Review, Marshall University, Box 205, Huntington, WV 25701

The Living Color, 417 Euclid Ave., Elmira, NY 14905

Lodestar, R.F.D. 5, Box 138, Gainesville, GA 30501

Long Pond Review, Suffolk Community College, Dept. of English, Selden, NY 11784

The Lookout, 15 State St., New York, NY 10004

The Louisville Review, University of Louisville, Dept. of English, 315 Bingham Humanities, Louisville, KY 40292

Lowlands Review, 6048 Perrier, New Orleans, IA 70118

The Lutheran Standard, 426 S. Fifth St., Minneapolis, MN 55415

The Lyric, 307 Dunton Dr., S.W., Blacksburg, VA 24060

M

Madamoiselle, 350 Madison Ave., New York, NY 10017

The Madison Review, University of Wisconsin, Dept. of English, H. C. White Hall, 600 N. Park St., Madison, WI 53706

Maelstrom Review, 8 Farm Hill Rd., Cape Elizabeth, ME 04107

Maenad: A Woman's Literary Journal, Box 738, 84 Main St., #3, Gloucester, MA 01930

Magazine, Pima College, 2202 W. Anklam Rd., Tucson, AZ 85709

Magic Changes, 553 W. Oakdale, #317, Chicago, IL 60657

Main Trend, Box 344, Cooper Station, New York, NY 10003

The Mainstreeter, University of Wisconsin, Dept. of English, Stevens Point, WI 54481

Maize, Box 8251, San Diego, CA 92102

The Malahat Review, University of Victoria, Box 1700, Victoria, B.C. V8W 2Y2, Canada

The Manhattan Review, 304 Third Ave., 4A, New York, NY 10010

Manna, Rte. 8, Box 368, Sanford, NC 27330

The Massachusetts Review, University of Massachusetts, Memorial Hall, Amherst, MA 01002

Matrix, Box 510, Lennoxville, Que. J1M 1Z6, Canada

Memphis State Review, Memphis State University, Dept. of English, Memphis, TN 38152

The Mennonite, 600 Shaftsbury Blvd., Winnipeg, Man. R3P 0M4, Canada

Michigan Quarterly Review, University of Michigan, 3032 Rackham Bldg., Ann Arbor, MI 48109

Mid-American Review, Bowling Green State University, Dept. of English, Bowling Green, OH 43403

Midstream, 515 Park Ave., New York, NY 10022

Midwest Arts & Literature, Box 1623, Jefferson City, MO 65102

The Midwest Quarterly, Pittsburg State University, Pittsburg, KS 66762

Milkweed Chronicle, Box 24303, Minneapolis, MN 55424

The Minnesota Review, Oregon State University, Dept. of English, Corvallis, OR 97331

Mississippi Mud, 1336 S.E. Marion St., Portland, OR 97202

Mississippi Poetry Journal, Box 875, Hazlehurst, MS 39083

Mississippi Review, University of Southern Mississippi, Center for Writers, Box 37, Southern Station, Hattiesburg, MS 39401

Mississippi Valley Review, Western Illinois University, Dept. of English, Macomb, IL 61455

The Missouri Review, University of Missouri, Dept. of English, 231 Arts and Science, Columbia, MO 65211

Mr. Cogito, Box 627, Pacific University, Forest Grove, OR 97116

Modern Haiku, Box 1752, Madison, WI 53701

Modern Images, Box 912, Mattoon, IL 61938

Modern Liturgy, Box 444, Saratoga, CA 95071

Modern Poetry Studies, 207 Delaware Ave., Buffalo, NY 14202

The Montana Review, 2220 Quail, Missoula, MT 59802

Moose Magazine, 1807 S.E. Stark St., Portland, OR 97214

The Moosehead Review, Box 169, Ayer's Cliff, Que., Canada

Moving Out: Feminist Literary & Arts Journal, Box 21879, Detroit, MI 48221

Ms. Magazine, 570 Lexington Ave., New York, NY 10017

MSS, State University of New York, Binghamton, NY 13901

Mundus Artium: A Journal Of International Literature & Art, University of Texas at Dallas, Box 688, Richardson, TX 75080

Muse-Pie: A Journal of Poetry, 73 Pennington Ave., Passaic, NJ 07055

N

The Nation, 72 Fifth Ave., New York, NY 10011

National Forum, East Tennessee University, Box 19420A, Johnson City, TN 37601

The Nantucket Review, Box 1444, Nantucket, MA 02554

Nebo: A Literary Journal, Arkansas Tech University, Dept. of English, Russellville, AR 72801

New America, University of New Mexico, Dept. of American Studies, Albuquerque, NM 87131

New Arts Review, Box 887, Athens, GA 30603

New Boston Review, 77 Sacramento St., Somerville, MA 02143

New Catholic World, 1865 Broadway, New York, NY 10023

New College Magazine, 5700 North Trail, Sarasota, FL 33580

New Directions, Howard University, Dept. of Human Relations and Publications, Washington, DC 20059

New England Review and Bread Loaf Quarterly, Box 170, Hanover, NH 03755

New England Sampler, R.F.D. 1, Box 2280, Brooks, ME 04921

New Jersey Poetry Journal, Monmouth College, Dept. of English, West Long Branch, NJ 07764

New Kauri, 2551 W. Mossman Rd., Tucson, AZ 85746

The New Kent Quarterly, Kent State University, 239 Student Center, Kent, OH 44240

The New Leader, 275 7th Ave., New York, NY 10001

New Letters, University of Missouri, 5346 Charlotte, Kansas City, MO 64110

New Literature & Ideology, Box 727, Adelaide Station, Toronto, Ont. M5C 2J8, Canada

New Mexico Humanities Review, New Mexico Tech, Box A, Socorro, NM 87801

New Moon, SF 3, Box 2056, Madison, WI 53701

New Oregon Review, 537 N.E. Lincoln St., Hillsboro, OR 97123

New Orleans Review, Loyola University, New Orleans, LA 70118

The New Renaissance, 9 Heath Rd., Arlington, MA 02174

The New Republic, 1220 19th St., N.W., Washington, DC 20036

The New Southern Literary Messenger, 302 S. Laurel St., Richmond, VA 23220

New Virginia Review, Box 12192, Richmond, VA 23241

The New Yorker, 25 W. 43rd St., New York, NY 10036

NeWest Review, Box 484, Sub. P.O. 6, Saskatoon, Sask. S7N 0N0, Canada

Neworld, 6331 Hollywood Blvd., Hollywood, CA 90028

Next Exit, Box 143, Tamworth, Ont. K0K 3G0, Canada

Nexus, Wright State University, Dayton, OH 45435

Night Light Magazine, 629 State St., #211, Santa Barbara, CA 93101

Nimrod, 2210 S. Main, Tulsa, OK 74114

North American Mentor Magazine, 1745 Madison St., Fennimore, WI 53809

The North American Review, University of Northern Iowa, 1222 W. 27th, Cedar Falls, IA 50614

The North Carolina Review, 3329 Granville Dr., Raleigh, NC 27609

North Country Anvil, Box 37, Millville, MN 55957

North County, University of North Dakota, Dept. of English, Grand Forks, ND 58201

North Dakota Quarterly, University of North Dakota, Box 8237, Grand Forks, ND 58202

Northeast Journal, Box 217, Kingston, RI 02881

Northern New England Review, Franklin Pierce College, Rindge, NH 03461

Northern Light, University of Manitoba, 605 Fletcher Argue Bldg., Winnipeg, Man. R3T 2N2, Canada

Northwest Review, University of Oregon, 369 P. L. C., Eugene, OR 97405

O

Obras (Beyond Baroque), Box 806, Venice, CA 90291

Occident, University of California, 103 Sproul Hall, Berkeley, CA 94720

The Ohio Journal, Ohio State University, Dept. of English, 164 W. 17th Ave., Columbus, OH 43210

The Ohio Review, Ellis Hall, Ohio University, Athens, OH 45701

Oikos: A Journal of Ecology and Community, c/o Arne Jorgensen, 130 Valley Rd., Montclair, NJ 07042

One World, Box 1351, State College, PA 16801

The Ontario Review, 9 Honey Brook Dr., Princeton, NJ 08540

Open Places, Stephens College, Box 2085, Columbia, MO 65215

Orpheus, c/o Illuminati, 8812 W. Pico Blvd., #204, Los Angeles, CA 90035

Orphic Lute, Box 2815, Newport News, VA 23602

Osiris, Box 297, Deerfield, MA 01342

Other Press Poetry Review, Douglas College, Box 2503, New Westminster, B.C. V3L 5B5, Canada

Outerbridge, College of Staten Island, English A323, 715 Ocean Terrace, Staten Island, NY 10301

Owlflight, 1025 55th St., Oakland, CA 94608

Oyez Review, Roosevelt University, 430 S. Michigan Ave., Chicago, IL 60614

P

Pacific Poetry And Fiction Review, San Diego State University, English Office, San Diego, CA 92182

Padan Aram, Harvard University, 52 Dunster St., Cambridge, MA 02138

Paintbrush: A Journal of Poetry, Translation & Letters, c/o Jelm Mountain Publications, 209 Park, Laramie, WY 82070

Paintbrush, Northeastern University, Dept. of English, Boston, MA 02115

The Pale Fire Review, 162 Academy Ave., Providence, RI 02908

Pan American Review, 1101 Tori Lane, Edinburg, TX 78530

The Panhandler, University of West Florida, Dept. of English, Pensacola, FL 32504

Parabola Magazine, 150 Fifth Ave., New York, NY 10011

The Paris Review, 45-39 171st Place, Flushing, NY 11358

Parnassus: Poetry In Review, 205 W. 89th St., New York, NY 10024

Partisan Review, 121 Bay State Rd., 3/F, Boston, MA 02215

Passages North, William Bonifas Fine Arts Center, 7th St. & 1st Ave., S., Escanaba, MI 49829

Passaic Review, 195 Gregory Ave., Passaic, NJ 07055

Pathways, Box 345, Middleton, ID 83644

The Pawn Review, 2903 Windsor Rd., Austin, TX 78703

Pembroke Magazine, Pembroke State University, Pembroke, NC 28372

The Pen Woman Magazine, 1300 17th St., N.W., Washington, DC 20036

Pendragon, 2969 Baseline Rd., Boulder, CO 80303

The Penny Dreadful, Bowling Green State University, Dept. of English, Bowling Green, OH 43403

Pequod, 536 Hill St., San Francisco, CA 94114

Periodical Of Art In Nebraska, University of Nebraska, Annex 21, Box 688, Omaha, NE 68101

Permafrost Magazine, University of Alaska, Fairbanks, AK 99701

Perspectives, West Virginia University, Dept. of English, Morgantown, WV 26506

Phantasm, 1116D Wendy Way, Chico, CA 95926

Philadelphia City Paper, 6381 Germantown Ave., Philadelphia, PA 19144

Philadelphia Poets, 21 Concord Rd., Darby, PA 19023

Phoebe, George Mason University, 4400 University Dr., Fairfax, VA 22030

Phoebus Magazine, Box 3085, Phoebus Station,

Hampton, VA 23663

Piedmont Literary Review, Box 3656, Danville, VA 24543

Pierian Spring, Brandon University, Brandon, Man. R7A 6A9, Canada

The Pikestaff Forum, Box 127, Normal, IL 61761

Pinchpenny, 4851 Q St., Sacramento, CA 95819

The Place In The Woods, 3900 Glenwood Ave., Golden Valley, MN 55422

Plains Poetry Journal, Box 2337, Bismarck, ND 58502

Plainsong, Box U245, College Heights, Bowling Green, KY 42101

Plainswoman, Box 8027, Grand Forks, ND 58202

Ploughshares, Box 529, Cambridge, MA 02139

Poem, Box 919, Huntsville, AL 35804

Poet & Critic, Iowa State University, Dept. of English, 203 Ross Hall, Ames, IA 50011

Poet Lore, 4000 Albemarle St., N.W., Washington, DC 20016

Poetic Justice, 8220 Rayford Dr., Los Angeles, CA 90045

Poetics Journal, 2639 Russell St., Berkeley, CA 94705

Poetry, Box 4348, Chicago, IL 60680

Poetry Canada Review, Box 1280, Station A, Toronto, Ont. M5W 1G7, Canada

Poetry East, Star Route 1, Box 50, Earlysville, VA 22936

Poetry/LA, Box 84271, Los Angeles, CA 90073

The Poetry Miscellany, University of Tennessee, Dept. of English, Chattanooga, TN 37402

Poetry 'N Prose, Box 456, Maxville, Ont. K0C 1T0, Canada

Poetry Newsletter, Temple University, Dept. of English, Philadelphia, PA 19122

Poetry North Review, 3809 Barbara Dr., Anchorage, AK 99503

Poetry Northwest, University of Washington, 4045 Brooklyn, N.E., Seattle, WA 98195

Poetry Now, 3118 K St., Eureka, CA 95501

Poetry Texas, College of the Mainland, Division of Humanities, Texas City, TX 77590

Poetry Today, Box 20822, Portland, OR 97220

Poets Corner, Calais, VT 05648

Poets On:, Box 255, Chaplin, CT 06235

Pontchartrain Review, Box 1065 Chalmette, LA 70044

Porch, Arizona State University, Dept. of English, Tempe, AZ 85281

Portland Review, Box 751, Portland, OR 97207

Portico, Sheridan College, Trafalgar Rd., Oakville, Ont. L6H 2L1, Canada

Prairie Fire, 304 Parkview St., Winnipeg, Man. R3J 1S3, Canada

Prairie Schooner, University of Nebraska, 201 Andrews Hall, Lincoln, NE 68588

Praxis: A Journal Of Cultural Criticism, Box 1280, Santa Monica, CA 90406

Presbyterian Record, 50 Wynford Dr., Don Mills, Ont. M3E 1J7, Canada

Primavera, University of Chicago, Ida Noyes Hall, 1212 E. 59th St., Chicago, IL 60637

Princeton Spectrum, Box 3005, Princeton, NJ 08540

Prism International, University of British Columbia, Dept. of Creative Writing, Vancouver, B.C. V6T 1W5, Canada

Pteranodon, Box 229, Bourbonnais, IL 60914

Pudding Magazine, 2384 Hardesty Dr., S., Columbus, OH 43204

Pulpsmith, 5 Beekman St., New York, NY 10038

Q

Quarry Magazine, Box 1061, Kingston Ont. K7L 4Y5, Canada

Quarry West, College V, University of California, Santa Cruz, CA 95064

Quarter Moon, Box 336, Warwick, NY 10990

Quarterly Review of Literature, 26 Haslet Ave., Princeton, NJ 08540

Quarterly West, University of Utah, 312 Olpin Union, Salt Lake City, UT 84112

Queen's Quarterly, Queen's University, Kingston, Ont, K7L 3N6, Canada

Quercus, 2791 24th St., Suite 8, Sacramento, CA 95818

Quilt, 2140 Shattuck Ave., Room 311, Berkeley, CA 94704

Quindaro, Box 5224, Kansas City, KS 66119

R

Raccoon, 323 Hodges St., Memphis, TN 38111

Radcliffe Quarterly, 10 Garden St., Cambridge, MA 02138

The Radical Reviewer, Box 24953, Station C, Vancouver, B.C. V5T 4G3, Canada

RE: Artes Liberales, Stephen F. Austin University, School of Liberal Arts, Box 13007, S.F.A. Station, Nacogdoches, TX 75962

The Reaper, 1710 E. Illinois, Evansville, IN 47711

Red Cedar Review, Michigan State University, Dept. of English, 325 Morrill Hall, East Lansing, MI 48824

Reflect, 3306 Argonne Ave., Norfolk, VA 23509

Review, 680 Park Ave., New York, NY 10021

Rhino, 77 Lakewood Place, Highland Park, IL 60035

Rhode Island Review, 85 Preston St., Providence, RI 02906

The Ridge Review, Box 90, Mendocino, CA 95460

Rikka, Box 6031, Sta. A, Toronto, Ont. M5W 1P4, Canada

River City Review, Box 34275, Louisville, KY 40232

River Styx, 7420 Cornell Ave., St. Louis, MO 63130

Riverfront, Box 3777, Omaha, NE 68103

Riverside Quarterly, Box 1763, Hartsville, SC 29550

The Rockford Review, Box 858, Rockford, IL 61105

Rocky Mountain Review, English Dept., Arizona State University, Tempe, AZ 85281

Russian Literature Triquarterly, 2901 Heatherway, Ann Arbor, MI 48104

S

Sackbut Review, 2513 E. Webster, Milwaukee, WI 53211

St. Andrews Review, St. Andrews Presbyterian College, Laurinburg, NC 28352

Salmagundi, Skidmore College, Saratoga Springs, NY 12866

Salome: A Literary Dance Magazine, 5548 N. Sawyer, Chicago, IL 60625

Sam Houston Literary Review, English Dept., Sam Houston State University, Huntsville, TX 77340

Samisdat, Box 231, Richford, VT 05476

San Fernando Poetry Journal, 18301 Halstead St., Northridge, CA 91325

San Jose Studies, San Jose State University, San Jose, CA 95192

Santa Fe/Poetry And The Arts, 115 Delgado, Santa Fe, NM 87501

Saturday Night, 70 Bond St., Suite 500, Toronto, Ont. M5B 2J3, Canada

Scandinavian Review, 127 E. 73rd St., New York, NY 10021

Scholia Satyrica, University of South Florida, Dept. of English, Tampa, FL 33620

Science, 1101 Vermont Ave., N.W., 10th Floor, Washington, DC 20005

The Seattle Review, University of Washington, Padelford Hall GN-30, Seattle, WA 98195

Second Coming, Box 31249, San Francisco, CA 94131

Second Growth, East Tennessee State University, Box 24, 292, Johnson City, TN 37619

Seems, University of Northern Iowa, Dept. of English, Cedar Falls, IA 50613

The Seneca Review, Hobart & William Smith Colleges, Geneva, NY 14456

Separate Doors, 911 W. T. Station, Canyon, TX 79016

Sequoia: Stanford Literary Magazine, Storke Publications Bldg., Stanford, CA 94305

Serpentine, College of Staten Island, P.C.A. Dept., 715 Ocean Terrace, Staten Island, NY 10301

Seventeen, 850 Third Ave., New York, NY 10022

Sewanee Review, University of the South, Sewanee, TN 37375

The Shakespeare Newsletter, 1217 Ashland Ave., Chicago Circle, Evanston, IL 60202

Shenandoah, Box 722, Lexington, VA 24450

Silverfish Review, Box 3541, Eugene, OR 97403

Sites-Architectural Magazine, 446 W. 20th St., New York, NY 10011

The Slackwater Review, Lewis-Clark Campus, Lewiston, ID 83501

The Small Pond Magazine, Box 664, Stratford, CT 06497

Smoke Signals, 1516 Beverly Rd., Brooklyn, NY 11226

Snapdragon, University of Idaho, Dept. of English, Moscow, ID 83843

Snowy Egret, 205 S. 9th St., Williamsburg, KY 40769

The Sojourner, 143 Albany St., Cambridge, MA 02139

Sonoma Mandala, Sonoma State University, Dept. of English, Rohnert Park, CA 94928

Sonora Review, University of Arizona, Dept. of English, Tucson, AZ 85721

Soundings/East, Salem State College, Dept. of English, Salem, MA 01970

Source, Queens Council on the Arts, 161-04 Jamaica Ave., New York, NY 11432

South Atlantic Quarterly, Box 6697, College Station, Durham, NC 27708

The South Carolina Review, Clemson University, Dept. of English, Clemson, SC 29631

South Dakota Review, Box 111, University Exchange, Vermillion, SD 57069

South Western Ontario Poetry, 396 Berkshire Dr., London, Ont. N6J 3S1, Canada

Southern Exposure, Box 230, Chapel Hill, NC 27514

Southern Humanities Review, Auburn University, 9090 Haley Center, Auburn, AL 36830

Southern Poetry Review, University of North Carolina, Dept. of English, U.N.C.C. Station, Charlotte, NC 28223

The Southern Review, Drawer D, University Station, Baton Rouge, LA 70893

Southwest Review, Southern Methodist University, Dallas, TX 75275

The Southwestern Review, Box 44691, Lafayette, LA 70504

Sou'wester, Southern Illinois University, Dept. of English, Edwardsville, IL 62025

The Spirit That Moves Us, Box 1585, Iowa City, IA 52244

The Spoon River Quarterly, Box 1443, Peoria, IL 61655

The Sproutletter, Box 62, Ashland, OR 97520

Star Line, 1722 N. Mariposa Ave., Los Angeles, CA 90027

Stone Country, 20 Lorraine Rd., Madison, NJ 07940

Street Magazine, Box 555, Port Jefferson, NY 11777

Studia Hispanica Editors, Box 7304, University Station, Austin, TX 78712

Studies In Poetry, Tex Tech University, Dept. of English, Lubbock, TX 79409

Studia Mystica, California State University, 6000 J St., Sacramento, CA 95819

Sulfur, California Institute of Technology, Box 228-77, Pasadena, CA 91125

Sulphur River, Box 3044, East Texas Station, Commerce, TX 75428

The Sun: A Magazine Of Ideas, 412 W. Rosemary St., Chapel Hill, NC 27514

Sun Tracks, University of Arizona, Dept. of English, Tucson, AZ 85721

Swallow's Tale Magazine, Box 4328, Tallahassee, FL 32315

T

Tamarack, 909 Westcott St., Syracuse, NY 13210

Tamarisk, 319 S. Juniper St., Philadelphia, PA 19107

Tar River Poetry, East Carolina University, Dept. of English, Austin Bldg., Greenville, NC 27834

Telescope, Box 16129, Baltimore, MD 21218

Tempest: Avant-Garde Poetry, Box 680-536, Miami, FL 33168

Tempo, 610 Mulberry St., Scranton, PA 18510

Tendril, Box 512, Green Harbor, MA 02041

The Texas Arts Journal, Box 7458, Dallas, TX 75209

The Texas Review, Sam Houston State University, Dept. of English, Huntsville, TX 77341

Theaterwork Magazine, 120 S. Broad, Mankato, MN 56001

Theology Today, Box 29, Princeton, NJ 08540

Third Coast Archives, Box 11204, Shorewood, WI 53211

Third Eye, 189 Kelvin Dr., Buffalo, NY 14223

Thirteen, Box 392, Portlandville, NY 13834

13th Moon, Drawer F, Inwood Station, New York, NY 10034

This Magazine, 70 The Esplanade, Third Floor, Toronto, Ont. M5E 1R2, Canada

Thoreau Journal Quarterly, University of Minnesota, 355 Ford Hall, 224 Church St., S.E. Minneapolis, MN 55455

Thought: The Quarterly Of Fordham University, Fordham University, Box L, Bronx, NY 10458

Three Rivers Poetry Journal, Carnegie-Mellon University, Box 21, Pittsburgh, PA 15213

The Threepenny Review, Box 9131, Berkeley, CA 94709

Thunder Mountain Review, Box 11126, Birmingham, AL 35202

Tightrope, 323 Pelham Rd., Amherst, MA 01002

Tiotis Poetry News, Rte. 24, Box 53c, Fort Myers, FL 33908

Touchstone, Kansas State University, Dept. of English, Manhattan, KS 66502

Towards, 3948 Bannister Rd., Fair Oaks, CA 95628

Tower Poetry Magazine, c/o Dundas Public Library, 18 Ogilvie St., Dundas, Ont. L9H 2S2, Canada

Translation, Columbia University, 307A Mathematics, New York, NY 10027

Triquarterly, Northwestern University, University Hall 101, Evanston, IL 60201

U

UT Review, University of Tampa, Tampa, FL 33606

Uncle: A Magazine For Those Who Have Given Up, Box 1075 CSS, Springfield, MO 65803

Universal Unitarian Christian, 5701 S. Woodlawn Ave., Chicago, IL 60637

The Universal Black Writer, Box 5, Radio City Station, New York, NY 10101

University of Portland Review, University of Portland, Portland, OR 97203

University of Windsor Review, University of Windsor, Windsor, Ont. N9B 3P4, Canada

Unknowns, 1900 Century Blvd., N.E., Suite 1, Atlanta, GA 30345

Uroboros, 111 N. 10th St., Olean, NY 14760

V

Vantage Point, Centre College, Danville, KY 40422

Velocities, 1509 Le Roy Ave., Berkeley, CA 94708

Veridian, Box 2324, Bloomington, IN 47402

Vernal, 522 E. Third Ave., Durango, CO 81301

The Villager, 135 Midland Ave., Bronxville, NY 10708

The Virginia Quarterly Review, 1 West Range, Charlottesville, VA 22903

Visions, 4705 S. 8th Rd., Arlington, VA 22204

Voices International, 1115 Gillette Dr., Little Rock, AR 72207

W

Wascana Review, University of Regina, Regina, Sask. S4S 0A2, Canada

Washington Review, Box 50132, Washington, DC 20004

Watchwords: A Monthly Review Of Poetry And Poetics, 8 Beecher St., London, Ont. N6C 1B4, Canada

Waves, 79 Denham Dr., Thornhill, Ont. L4J 1P2, Canada

Wayward Wind, 1340 19th St., #3, Boulder, CO 80302

Webster Review, Webster College, Webster Groves, MO 63119

West Branch, Bucknell University, Dept. of English, Lewisburg, PA 17837

West Coast Poetry Review, 1335 Dartmouth Dr., Reno, NV 89509

West Coast Review, Simon Fraser University, Burnaby, B.C. M5A 1S6, Canada

West End Magazine, c/o Kaliss, 31 Montague Place, Montclair, NJ 07042

West Hills Review: A Walt Whitman Journal, 246 Walt Whitman Rd., Huntington Station, NY 11746

Westerfield's Review, Box 246, Clinton, CT 06413

Western Humanities Review, University of Utah, Salt Lake City, UT 84112

Whetstone, R.R. 1, Box 221, St. David, AZ 85630

Whiskey Island Quarterly, Cleveland State University, University Center, Room 7, Cleveland, OH 44115

White Pine Journal, 73 Putnam St., Buffalo, NY 14213

White Walls: A Magazine Of Writings By Artists, Box 8204, Chicago, IL 60680

Willow Springs, Eastern Washington University, Box 1063, Cheney, WA 99004

Wind Magazine, R.F.D. 1, Box 809K, Pikesville, KY 41501

Wind Chimes, Box 601, Glen Burnie, MD 21061

The Windless Orchard, Indiana University, Dept. of English, Fort Wayne, IN 46805

Winewood Journal, Box 339, Black Hawk, CO 80422

Wip, Brown University, English Dept., Box 1852, Providence, RI 02912

Wisconsin Academy Review, 1922 University Ave., Madison, WI 53705

Wisconsin Review, University of Wisconsin, Dempsey Hall, Box 276, Oshkosh, WI 54901

The Wishing Well, Box 117, Novato, CA 94948

Womanspirit, 2000 King Mountain Trail, Wolf Creek, OR 97497

Women: A Journal Of Liberation, 3028 Greenmount Ave., Baltimore, MD 21218

Woodrose, 524 Larson St., Waupaca, WI 54981

Word Loom, Box 20, 242 Montrose, Winnipeg, Man., Canada

Working Classics, 298 9th Ave., San Francisco, CA 94118

World Literature Today, 630 Parrington Oval, Room 110, Norman, OK 73019

The Wormwood Review, Box 8840, Stockton, CA 95208

Writ, 2 Sussex Ave., Toronto, Ont., Canada

The Writ, 1827 N. Rampart St., New Orleans, LA 70116

Writer's Digest, 9933 Alliance Rd., Cincinnati, OH 45242

Writers Forum, University of Colorado, Colorado Springs, CO 80907

Writers News Manitoba, 304 Parkview St., Winnipeg, Man., Canada

X

X: A Journal of The Arts, Box 2648, Harrisburg, PA 17105

Xanadu, Box 773, Huntington, NY 11743

Y

The Yale Literary Magazine, Box 243-A, Yale Station, New Haven, CT 06520

The Yale Review, 1902-A, Yale Station, New Haven, CT 06520

Yankee, Dublin, NH 03444

Yarrow: A Journal of Poetry, Kutztown State College, Dept. of English, Lytle Hall, Kutztown, PA 19530

Yellow Silk: Journal of Erotic Arts, Box 6374, Albany, CA 94706

Z

Zahir, Box 715, Newburyport, MA 01950

Poetry Associations, Organizations and Clubs

This directory lists organizations in the United States and Canada devoted to poetry. An asterisk (*) denotes affiliation with the National Federation of State Poetry Societies.

ALABAMA
Alabama State Poetry Society*, c/o Dorothy Williamson Worth, 1399 Vista Leaf Dr., Decatur, GA 30033

ARIZONA
Arizona State Poetry Society*, c/o Edythe Bregnard, 10923 Meade Dr., Sun City, AZ 85351
First Friday Poets, c/o Changing Hands Bookstore, 411 Mill Ave., Tempe, AZ 85281
Phoenix Poetry Society, c/o Pauline Mounsey, 6511 W. Osborn, Phoenix, AZ 85033
University of Arizona Poetry Center, c/o Lois Shelton, 1086 N. Highland, Tuscon, AZ 85721

ARKANSAS
Poets Roundtable of Arkansas*, c/o Bonnie Lee Reynolds, 105 Euclid, Hot Springs, AR 71901

CALIFORNIA
Alchemedias Poets Circle, c/o Stephanie Buffington, 1005 Buena Vista St., South Pasadena, CA 91030
American Poetry Association, 1620 Seabright Ave., Santa Cruz, CA 95063
California Federation of Chapparal Poets, 1422 Ashland Ave., Claremont, CA 91711
California Poetry Reading Circuit, c/o James McMichael, University of California, Dept. of English, Irvine, CA 92664
California Poets-in-the-Schools, c/o J. O. Simon, San Francisco State University, 1600 Holloway (HLL Bldg.), San Francisco, CA 94132
California State Poetry Society*, c/o Jack Fulbeck, 2376 N. Cameron Ave., Covina, CA 91724
College of San Mateo Poetry Center, c/o Jean Pumphrey, 1700 W. Hillsdale Blvd., San Mateo, CA 94402
Grand Piano Poetry Readings, c/o Steve Benson and Carla Harryman, 1607 Haight St., San Francisco, CA 94117
Intersection Poets and Writers Series, c/o Jim Hartz, 756 Union St., San Francisco, CA 94133
Poetry Center, San Francisco State University, 1600 Holloway, San Francisco, CA 94132
Poetry Therapy Institute, P.O. Box 70244, Los Angeles, CA 90070
Poets Place, c/o Beverly Michaels-Cohn, Hyperion Theatre, 1835 Hyperion Ave., Los Angeles, CA 90027
Poets of the Vineyard, c/o Winnie E. Fitzpatrick, P.O. Box 77, Kenwood, CA 95452
Southern California Poets, c/o J. P. Watson, P.O. Box 85152, San Diego, CA 92138
World Order of Narrative Poets, P.O. Box 2085, Walnut Creek, CA 94596
World Poetry Society, c/o E. A. Falkowski, 208 W. Latimer Ave., Campbell, CA 95008
Yuki Teikei Haiku Society, c/o Haiku Journal, Kiyoshi Tokutomi, 1020 S. 8th St., San Jose, CA 95112

COLORADO
Columbine Poets, c/o Veda Steadman, 631 S. Grant Ave,, Fort Collins, CO 80521
Poetry Society of Colorado*, c/o Rosanna Webster, 2655 Eliot St., Denver, CO 80211
Poets of tbe Foothills Art Center, 809 15th St., Golden, CO 80401

CONNECTICUT
Connecticut Poetry Circuit, c/o Jean Maynard, The Honors College, Wesleyan University, Middletown, CT 06457
Connecticut Poetry Society*, c/o Mrs. Moraeg E. Wood, 2 Marina Point, Danbury, CT 06810
Golden Eagle Poetry Club, P.O. Box 1314, New Milford, CT 06776

DELAWARE
First State Writers*, c/o Francis R. Kesner, 400 W. 24th St., Wilmington, DE 19802

DISTRICT OF COLUMBIA
Federal Poets of Washington*, c/o Betty Wollaston, 5321 Willard Ave., Chevy Chase, MD 20015
Federation of International Poetry Associations, P.O. Box 39072, Washington, DC 20016

FLORIDA
Audio-Visual Poetry Foundation, 400 Fish Hatchery Rd., Marianna, FL 32446
Florida State Poetry Association, 1110 N. Venetian Dr., Miami, FL 33139
Florida State Poet's Association*, c/o Agnes Homan, 99 Spring Garden Rd., Sebring, FL 33870
Poetry Society of Jacksonville, c/o Carlota Fowler, 4411 Charles Bennett Dr., Jacksonville, FL 32225

GEORGIA
Atlanta Poetry Society, c/o Robert Manns, 1105-E N. Jamestown Rd., Decatur, GA 30033
Georgia State Poetry Society*, c/o Bettie M. Sellers, Box 274, Young Harris, GA 30582
Poetry at Callanwolde, c/o Gene Ellis, 980 Briarcliff Rd., N.E., Atlanta, GA 30306

IDAHO
Idaho Poets-in-the-Schools, c/o Keith Browning, Lewis & Clark State College, Dept. of English, Lewiston, ID 83501

ILLINOIS
Apocalypse Poetry Association, c/o Rose Lesniak, Creative Writing Center, 3307 Bryn Mawr, Chicago, IL 60625
Illinois State Poetry Society*, c/o Frank A. Lydic, Box 36, Joliet, IL 60434
Modern Poetry Association, P.O. Box 4348, Chicago, IL 60680
Poetry Center, c/o Paul Hoover, Museum of Contemporary Art, 237 E. Ontario, Chicago, IL 60611
Poets Club of Chicago, c/o Nolan Boiler Co., 8531 S. Vincennes Ave., Chicago, IL 60620
Poets and Patrons of Chicago, c/o Mary Mathison, 13924 Keeler Ave., Crestwood, IL 60445

INDIANA
Indiana State Federation of Poetry Clubs*, c/o Dena S. Adams. 1 Northview Dr., Valparaiso, IN 46383
Poets' Study Club of Terre Haute, 826 S. Center St., Terre Haute, IN 47807

IOWA
Ellsworth Poetry Project, c/o Daniel M. McGuiness, Ellsworth College, 1100 College Ave., Iowa Falls, IA 50126
Iowa Poetry Association*, c/o Pat King, 218 S. Main, Albia, IA 52531

KENTUCKY
Kentucky State Poetry Society*, c/o Alice Louise Frank, 159 Burnet Ridge, Fort Thomas, KY 41075

LOUISIANA
Louisiana State Poetry Society*, c/o Calvin A. Claudel, P.O. Box 1083, Chalmette, LA 70044
New Orleans Poetry Forum, c/o Garland Strother, 76 Marcia Dr., Luling, LA 70070

MAINE
Maine Poetry and Writers Guild*, c/o Warren L. Elder, 57 River Rd., Westbrook, ME 04092
National Poetry Foundation, University of Maine, Orono, ME 04469

MARYLAND
Howard County Poetry and Literature Society, c/o Ellen C. Kennedy, 10446 Waterfowl Terrace, Columbia, MD 21044
Maryland State Poetry Society*, c/o Leon L. Lerner, 3510 Kings Point Rd., Randallstown, MD 21133

MASSACHUSETTS
Blacksmith House Poetry Program, c/o Gail Mazur, 5 Walnut Ave., Cambridge, MA 02140
Longfellow Poetry Society, c/o Longfellow's Wayside Inn, Wayside Inn Rd., Sudbury, MA 01776
Massachusetts State Poetry Society*, c/o Jeanette Maes, 64 Harrison Ave., Lynn, MA 01095
New England Poetry Club, c/o Diana Der Hovanessian, 2 Farrar St., Cambridge, MA 02138

MICHIGAN
Miles Modern Poetry Committee, c/o Steve Tudor, Wayne State University, Dept. of English, Detroit, MI 48202
Poetry Resource Center, c/o Lori Eason, Thomas Jefferson College/Grand Valley State Colleges, Lake Huron Hall, Allendale, MI 49401
Poetry Society of Michigan*, c/o Joye G. Giroux, 825 Cherry Ave., Big Rapids, MI 49307
Rhyme Space and West Park Poetry Series, c/o Carolyn Holmes Gregory, 709 W. Huron, Ann Arbor, MI 48103

MINNESOTA
Hungry Mind Poetry Series, c/o Jim Sitter, Hungry Mind Bookstore, 1648 Grand Ave., St. Paul, MN 55105
League of Minnesota Poets*, c/o Elvira T. Johnson, 4425 W. 7th St., Duluth, MN 55807
University Poets' Exchange of Minnesota, c/o William Elliott, Bemidji State University, Dept. of English, Bemidji, MN 56601

MISSISSIPPI
Mississippi Poetry Society*, c/o Louise Wilkersow Conn, Box 875, Hazlehurst, MS 39083

MISSOURI
American Poets Series and Poetry Programs, c/o Gloria Goodfriend, Jewish Community Center of Kansas City, 8201 Holmes Rd., Kansas City, MO 64131
St. Louis Poetry Center, c/o Leslie Konnyu, 5410 Kerth Rd., St. Louis, MO 63128

NEBRASKA
Nebraska Poets' Association*, c/o Bonnie Stewart, Box 325, Dtn. Sta,, Omaha, NE 68101

NEVADA
Nevada Poetry Society*, c/o Sister Margaret McCarran, McCarran Ranch, via Sparks, NV 89431

NEW HAMPSHIRE
The Frost Place, c/o Donald Sheehan, Ridge Rd., Box 74, Franconia, NH 03580
Poetry Society of New Hampshire*, c/o Robert Pralle, Box 371, Wolfeboro Falls, NH 03896

NEW JERSEY
Kilmer House Poetry Center, c/o Robert Truscott, 88 Guilden St., New Brunswick, NJ 08901
New Jersey Poetry Society*, c/o James A. McMillan, 43 Beverly Rd., West Caldwell, NJ 07006
Poets & Writers of New Jersey, P.O. Box 852, Upper Montclair, NJ 07043
Walt Whitman International Poetry Center, c/o Frederick W. Missimer, 2nd and Cooper Sts., Camden, NJ 08102

NEW MEXICO
New Mexico State Poetry Society*, c/o Laverne Rison, 6616 San Bernardino, N.E., Albuquerque, NM 87109

NEW YORK
Academy of American Poets, 177 E. 87th St., New York, NY 10128
Bronx Poets and Writers Alliance, 5800 Arlington Ave., Bronx, NY 10471
Columbia Street Poets, c/o Emilie Glen, 77 Barrow St., New York, NY 10014
Committee for Spiritual Poetry, 86-16 Parsons Blvd., Jamaica, NY 11432
Haiku Society of America, Japan House, 333 E. 47th St., New York, NY 10017
Ithaca Community Poets, c/o Katharyn Machan Aal, 431-B E. Seneca St., Ithaca, NY 14850
National Association for Poetry Therapy, c/o Beverly Bussolati, 1029 Henhawk Rd., Baldwin, NY 11510
New York Poetry Forum*, c/o Dorothea Neale, 3064 Albany Crescent, Apt. 54, Bronx, NY 10463
New York State Poets-in-the-Schools, c/o Myra Klahr, 24 N. Greeley Ave., Chappaqua, NY 10514
Noho for the Arts Poetry Forum, c/o Palmer Hasty, 542 La Guardia Place, New York, NY 10012
Nuyorican Poet's Cafe, c/o Miguel Algarin, 524 E. 6th St., New York, NY 10003
Outriders Poetry Program, c/o Max A. Wickert, 182 Colvin Ave., Buffalo, NY 14216
Poetry Center, 92nd St. YM-YWHA, 1395 Lexington Ave., New York, NY 10028
Poetry Society of America, 15 Gramercy Park, New York, NY 10003
Poets Union, c/o Lester Von Losberg, Jr., 315 6th Ave., Brooklyn, NY 11215
Poets & Writers, Inc., 201 W. 54th St., New York, NY 10019
C. W. Post Poetry Center, Dept. of English, C. W. Post Center, Long Island University, Greenvale, NY 11548
Rochester Poetry Central, c/o Jim LaVilla-Havelin, 322 Brooks Ave,, Rochester, NY 14619
Rochester Poetry Society, c/o Dale Davis, 155 S. Main St., Fairport, NY 14450
St. Mark's Poetry Project, c/o Maureen Owen or Paul Violi, 2nd Ave. and 10th St., New York, NY 10003
Shelley Society of New York, c/o Annette B. Feldmann, 144-20 41st Ave., Apt. 322, Flushing, NY 11355
World Order of Narrative Poets, c/o Dr. Alfred Dorn, P.O. Box 174, Sta. A, Flushing, NY 11358

NORTH CAROLINA
North Carolina Poetry Society*, c/o Ellen Johnston-Hale, Route 7, Box 616-A, Chapel Hill, NC 27514

OHIO
Cleveland State University Poetry Center, Cleveland, OH 44115
George Elliston Poetry Foundation, University of Cincinnati, Cincinnati, OH 45221
Kenyon Poetry Society, c/o George C. Nelson, Kenyon College, Gambier, OH 43011
Ohio Poetry Day Association, c/o Evan Lodge, 1506 Prospect Rd., Hudson, OH 44236
Poetry Circuit of Ohio, c/o R. W. Daniel, P.O. Box 247, Gambier, OH 43022
Poets League of Greater Cleveland, P.O. Box 6055, Cleveland, OH 44101
Toledo Poets Center, c/o Joze Lipman, UH-507-C, University of Toledo, Toledo, OH 43606
Verse Writers Guild cf Ohio*, c/o Amy Jo Zook, 3520 State Route 56, Mechanicsburg, OH 43044
Yellow Pages Poets, c/o Jack Roth, P.O. Box 8041, Columbus, OH 43201

OKLAHOMA
Poetry Society of Oklahoma*, c/o Billie Menifee, 1605 Breadview Circle, Oklahoma City, OK 73127

OREGON
Oregon State Poetry Association*, c/o David Hedges, 20750 S. Sweetbriar Rd., West Lynn, OH 97068
Western World Haiku Society, 4102 N.E. 130th Place, Portland, OR 97230

PENNSYLVANIA
American Physicians Poetry Association, 230 Toll Dr., Southampton, PA 18966
Homewood Poetry Forum, Inner City Services, Homewood Branch, Carnegie Library, 7101 Hamilton
    Ave., Pittsburgh, PA 15206
International Poetry Forum, c/o Dr. Samuel Hazo, 4400 Forbes Ave., Pittsburgh, PA 15213
Pennsylvania Poetry Society*, c/o L. J. Reho, 235 E. Spruce St., Williamstown, PA 17098
Y Poetry Center/Workshop, YM-YWHA Branch of JYC, Broad & Pine Sts., Philadelphia, PA 19147

RHODE ISLAND
Rhode Island State Poetry Society*, c/o Lora Jean Gardiner, 870 Lafayette Rd., North Kingstown, RI 02852

SOUTH DAKOTA
Fireside Poetry Group, c/o Isabel Ackley, 416 S. Kline St., Aberdeen, SD 57401
South Dakota State Poetry Society, c/o Dr. Mary Weinkauf, 914 University Blvd., Mitchell, SD 57301

TENNESSEE
Poetry Society of Tennessee*, c/o Dr. Wanda Allender Rider, 254 Buena Vista, Memphis, TN 38112
Poets for Christ, c/o George Rickett, Rt. 6, Box 266, Tennessee Dr., Seymour, TN 37865

TEXAS
American Poetry League, 3915 S.W. Military Dr., San Antonio, TX 79601
Hyde Park Poets, c/o Albert Huffstickler, 609 E. 45th St., Austin, TX 78751
National Federation of State Poetry Societies, c/o Jack Murphy, 10436 Creekmere Dr., Dallas, TX 75218
Poetry Society of Texas*, c/o Dr. John D. Vaughan, 302 E. Travis, Marshall, TX 75670
Stella Woodall Poetry Society, P.O. Box 253, Junction, TX 76849

UTAH
Utah State Poetry Society*, c/o Barbara Latimer Catrow, 2988 Melbourne St., Salt Lake City, UT 84106

VIRGINIA
Pause for Poetry, c/o Margaret T. Rudd, 6925 Columbia Pike, Annandale, VA 22003

WASHINGTON
Poetry League of America, 5603 239th Place, S.W., Mountain Terrace, WA 98043

WEST VIRGINIA
Morgantown Poetry Society, 673 Bellaire Dr., Morgantown, WV 26505
West Virginia Poetry Society*, c/o Edith Howell Love, 501 Voorhis Rd., Morgantown, WV 26505

WISCONSIN
Wisconsin Fellowship of Poets*, c/o Gert H. Sennett, Rt. 2, Box 2534, Spooner, WI 54801

WYOMING
Poetry Programs of Wyoming, c/o David J. Fraher, P.O. Box 3033, Casper, WY 82602
Poets of Wyoming Writers*, c/o Janet Cravan, 716 Renshaw, Laramie, WY 82070

CANADA
League of Canadian Poets, 24 Ryerson Ave., Toronto, Ont. M5T 2P3

Poets Laureate

Numerous states recognize the excellence and stature of particular poets residing within their borders by officially designating a state poet laureate. Although the specifics of the appointment vary somewhat among the states, the title is usually bestowed by the Governor and is frequently for the life of the poet. The following list is correct for 1983.

ALABAMA: Carl P. Morton
ALASKA: Richard Dauenhauer
ARIZONA: None
ARKANSAS: Lily Peter
CALIFORNIA: Charles B. Garrigus
COLORADO: Thomas Hornsby Ferril
CONNECTICUT: None
DELAWARE: None
FLORIDA: Edmund Skellings
GEORGIA: John Ransom Lewis, Jr.
HAWAII: None
IDAHO: Sudie Stuart Hager
ILLINOIS: Gwendolyn Brooks
INDIANA: Arthur Franklin Mapes
IOWA: None
KANSAS: None
KENTUCKY: Lille Chaffin; Agnes O'Rear
LOUISIANA: Henry Thomas Voltz
MAINE: None
MARYLAND: Lucille Clifton
MASSACHUSETTS: None
MICHIGAN: None
MINNESOTA: None
MISSISSIPPI: Winifred Hamrick Farrar
MISSOURI: None
MONTANA: None
NEBRASKA: William C. Kloefkorn (Nebraska State Poet)
NEVADA: None
NEW HAMPSHIRE: Richard Eberhart
NEW JERSEY: None
NEW MEXICO: None
NEW YORK: None
NORTH CAROLINA: Sam Ragan
NORTH DAKOTA: Corbin Waldron (Lydia Jackson and Henry R. Martinson, associate poets laureate)
OHIO: None
OKLAHOMA: Maggie Culver Fry
OREGON: William E. Stafford
PENNSYLVANIA: None
RHODE ISLAND: None
SOUTH CAROLINA: Helen von Kolnitz Hyer

SOUTH DAKOTA: Audrae Visser
TENNESSEE: Richard M. "Pek" Gunn
TEXAS: None
UTAH: None
VERMONT: None
VIRGINIA: None
WASHINGTON: None
WEST VIRGINIA: Louise McNeill Pease
WISCONSIN: None
WYOMING: Peggy Simson Curry

Awards and Prizes for Poetry /
The 1983 Winners

For the purpose of this list, 1983 winners are those announced
during the calendar year 1983; they are arranged
alphabetically by name of sponsor.

Academy of American Poets
177 E. 87th St.
New York, NY 10128
Walt Whitman Award: Christopher Gilbert, for
"Across The Mutual Landscape."
Lamont Poetry Selection: Sharon Olds, for "The
Dead And The Living."
Fellowships: James Schuyler; Philip Booth.
Peter I. B. Lavan Younger Poets Award: Edward
Hirsch; Brad Leithauser; Gjertrud Schnack-
enberg.

Alabama State Poetry Society
c/o Ralph Hammond, President
Box 486
Arab, AL 35016
Annual Poetry Contest: First—June Owens, for
"Gentler Graces"; Second—Margaret Key
Biggs, for "Below Freezing"; Third—J. M.
Frank, for "A Quiet Place."

American Academy of Arts and Letters
633 W. 155th St.
New York, NY 10032
Witter Bynner Prize for Poetry: Douglas Crase.
Loines Award in Poetry: Geoffrey Hill.
Rome Fellowship in Literature (this year won by a
poet): Gjertrud Schnackenberg.
Awards in Literature (won by poets): Alfred
Corn, Robert Mezey, Mary Oliver and George
Starbuck.

American Poetry Association
1620 Seabright Ave.
Santa Cruz, CA 95063
Spring Poetry Contest
Grand Prize Category: Grand Prize—Bea Liu, for
"Kweiyang"; First—Ida Cruzkatz, for "The
Wish"; Second—Joanne Lowery, for "The
View From Space"; Third—Dan Olson, for
"The City Of Beautiful Churches."
Love: First—Ida Cruzkatz, for "Calling To My
Husband From The Lawn"; Second—Ida
Cruzkatz, for "To A Butterfly Hunter Who Is
Really A Magician"; Third—Jacqueline Arrow-
smith, for "Je Reviens."
Death: First—Jayne Harris, for "Untitled";
Second—Bea Liu, for "Bereavement"; Third—
Connie Copland, for "Memory Chest."
Humorous: First—Bill DeVoe, for "Foto-
Green"; Second—Sondra Arner, for "Puppy
Love"; Third—Dana Blumer, "Ham It Up."

Eclectic: First—Jean Musser, for "That Which
Issues From The Night's Dark Pelt"; Second—
Joan Stephen, for "The Photo, Enlarged, For
Posterity"; Third—Thalia Kitrilakis, for "First
Sail, First Line."
Haiku: First—Susan Love, for "Sea Mirror";
Second—John Fox (untitled); Third—Celeste
Harper-Hoverman, for "Watercolor."
Short Poetry (10 lines or less): First—R. M.
Davis, for "At Morning North Of Charleston";
Second—Marianne McFarland McNeil, for
"Silver Moire"; Third—J. M. Frank, for
"Faith."
Short Poetry (7 lines or less): First—Bill DeVoe,
for "Ruth In The Field"; Second—Jack
Bernier, for "The Carpet Weaver"; Third—
Josephine Liebhaber, for "Canopus."
Religion: First—Lorna Price, for "Magdalene";
Second—Pat Langford, for "Words"; Third—
Richard Bartholomew, for "On Chinese New
Year."
Nature: First—Jean Musser, for "Prepare To
Snow"; Second—Paul A. Allen, for "The
Maker Of Leviathan"; Third—Jean Musser, for
"Rondel."
Children: First—Glen Smith, for "Twins:
Cypress And Moon, Castor And Pollox";
Second—Tamara Francisco, for "Then";
Third—Neva Willhite, for "Aunt Rose,
Reading."

American Poetry Review
1616 Walnut St., Rm. 405
Philadelphia, PA 19103
A.P.R. Poetry Prizes: First—Jack Gilbert, for
"Threshing The Fire" and other poems;
Second—Jim Harrison, for "Not Writing My
Name" and other poems; Third—Gerald
Stern, for "Christmas Sticks" and "The Same
Moon Above Us."

Anhinga Press
English Dept.
Florida State University
Tallahassee, FL 32306
Anhinga Poetry Prize: Ricardo Pau-Llosa,
for "Sorting Metaphors."

Artists Foundation, Inc.
110 Broad St.
Boston, MA 02110
Massachusetts Artists Fellowship (poetry): Steven

675

Cramer; Joyce Peseroff; Diane Wald; Lindsay Knowlton; John Kapsalis. (Finalists) Teresa Cader; Stuart Dischell; John Hodgen; Cynthia Huntington; George E. Murphy, Jr.

Associated Writing Programs
Old Dominion University
Norfolk, VA 23508
Anniversary Awards (poetry): Grand Prize— Michael Blumenthal, for "Night Baseball"; Winning Finalists—Dorothy Barresi for "Bombay Hook Wildlife Refuge," David Ray for "Croquet In Sussex," Stephen Tapscott for "A Travelling Scroll," Marcia Aldrich for "Victorian Manners," Nina Payne for "Summertime Waltz," Geraldine Little for "Diptych: In The House Of Special Purpose," Sandra Agricola for "The Wanderer," BH Fairchild for "Swimming At Menninger's," Rochelle Nameroff for "Runaway," and Sarah Brown Weitzman for "Forbidden."
Award Series in Poetry: Lisa Ress, for "Flight Patterns."

Association of American Publishers
1 Park Ave.
New York, NY 10016
American Book Award for Poetry: Not awarded in 1983.

Bitterroot Magazine
P.O. Box 51
Blythebourne Sta.
Brooklyn, NY 11219
William Kushner Award: First—David A. Ellis, for "On A Park Bench"; Second—Steven C. Levi, for "That Generation"; Third—Alice Mackenzie Swaim, for "Signposts On The Safari."
Heershe Dovid-Badonneh Award: First—David Oates, for "Trout"; Second—Martha Campbell, for "A Woman's Gift"; Third— Lynne Cheney-Rose, for "When Leaves Thin."

Black Warrior Review
P.O. Box 2936
University, AL 35486
Literary Award (poetry): Daniel Mark Epstein, for "Schoolhouses"; Irene McKinney, for "Deep Mining."

Blue Unicorn
22 Avon Rd.
Kensington, CA 94707
Poetry Contest: First—Don Welch, for "Carved By Obadiah Verity"; Second—Beth Bentley, for "The Pastry Maker"; Third—Judith Skillman, for "Blue Stone."

Caddo
Writing Society
P.O. Box 37679
Shreveport, LA 71133
Haiku: First—Mary Thomas Eulberg; Second—Nelle Fertig; Third—Helen V. Johnson.
Rhymed Verse: First—Karin C. Warren; Second—Mary Webster Griffin; Third—Janet McCann.
Free Verse: First—Linda Beth Toth; Second—

Jill King; Third—Ione Kolim Pence.
Sonnet: First—Ernestine Gravley; Second— Margaret Bland Sewell.

California State Poetry Society
c/o Helen Shanley
6601 Eucalyptus Dr., #97
Bakersfield, CA 93306
Chapbook Award: Nancy King, for "Under This Roof."
Monthly Contests: (Dec. '82) Pat. J. Holloway, for "Turtle Beach"; (Jan.) Esther M. Leiper, for "Guns For Christmas"; (Feb.) Evelyn Amuedo Wade, for "Insomnia"; (Mar.) Phil Eisenberg, for "First Encounter"; (Apr.) Nancy King, for "Psychiatrie—Cinq Centimes"; (May) Patricia S. Grimm, for "Anasazi, 'Basketmaker,' In The Lost City Museum, Overton, Nevada"; (June) Harry B. Sheftel, for "Legalities"; (July) Gus Pelletier, for "In Late Autumn At The Rathskeller"; (Aug.) Charles B. Dickson, for "Unfinished Business"; (Sept.) Elizabeth House, for "Supermarket Dilemma"; (Oct.) Roy Benjamin Moore, for "Small Claims Court."

Canada Council
255 Albert St.
P.O. Box 1047
Ottawa, Ont. K1P 5V8
Canada
Governor General's Literary Awards (poetry): English language—Phyllis Webb, for "The Vision Tree: Selected Poems"; French language—Michel Savard, for "Forages."

Canadian Author & Bookman
70 Champlain Ave.
Welland, Ont. L3C 2L7
Poetry Award: Ian Sutherland, for "For Bijou."

Canadian Authors Association
131 Bloor St., W., Suite 412
Toronto, Ont. M5S 1R1
Canada
Literary Award (poetry): George Amabile, for "The Presence of Fire."

Canadian Authors Association
Edmonton Branch
c/o Cora Taylor
R.R. #1
Winterburn, Alta. TOE 2NO
Canada
Alberta Poetry Yearbook Competition
June Fritch Memorial Award: Sandra L. Stewart, for "Barewater."
Alberta Scouten Memorial Award: John G. Trehas, for "Cavafy: The Last Silences."
Sonnet: First—Hazel Firth Goddard, for "Tag Ends"; Second—Frances Johnson, for "Winter Song"; Third—Susan Ioannou, for "Sonnet V."
Georgia May Cook Sonnet Award: Luetta Trehas, for "Renewal."
Short Poem: First—Dorothy Howe Brown, for "Plaza De Toros"; Second—Linda Jeays, for "A Matter Of Principles"; Third—William H. Rice, for "In Discotheques."
Humorous Verse: First—Mary Chryssoulakis, for

"Reunion"; Second—Eilene Burnett, for "Reckoning"; Third—Gladys Nolan, for "Sad Tale."

Haiku (adult): Gudrun Wight for "In The Cherry Tree," and Hazel Firth Goddard for "Grey Wings Swing Softly."

Jessie Drummond Boyd Prize: Jannis Allan Hare, for "The Trail To San Josef Bay."

Youth Class: First—Tammie Aubin, for "Pommes"; Second—Stacy L. Landers, for "Exterior Facade"; Third—Gwen Foss, for "Carnival Sky."

Haiku (youth): Tanya Burrant for "Haiku," and Tracy Leeks for "Haiku."

Henry Vermeulen Memorial Award: Ted Stefan, for "Artificial Snow."

Canadian Broadcasting Corporation
Attn: Robert Weaver
P.O. Box 500, Sta. A
Toronto, Ont. M5W 1E3
Canada

CBC Radio Literary Competition (poetry): First—David Helwig, for "Catchpenny Poems"; Second—Diana Hartog, for "Free Box"; Third—Richard Lemm for "Guide To The Perplexed," and John V. Hicks for "Group of poems."

Columbia University
Advisory Board on Pulitzer Prizes
New York, NY 10027

Pulitzer Prize in Poetry: Galway Kinnell, for "Selected Poems."

Committee for Spiritual Poetry
86-16 Parsons Blvd.
Jamaica, NY 11432

Sri Chinmoy Poetry Awards: First—Kirpal Gordon, for "Music Heard While Passing A Park Avenue Water Garden"; Second—Rayne MacKinnon, for "Elegy (2nd Series)—Peace"; Third—Cynthia Dwyer, for "Dry-Lipped."

Coordinating Council of Literary Magazines
2 Park Ave.
New York, NY 10016

General Electric Foundation Awards for Younger Writers (poetry): August Kleinzahler; Alice Notley; Luis Omar Salinas.

Cross-Canada Writers' Quarterly
P.O. Box 277, Sta. F
Toronto, Ont. M4Y 2L7
Canada

Editors' Prize (poetry): First—Jill Adamson, for "Guatemalen Morning"; Second—Carol Malyon, for "My Daughter Asks The Burning Question About God And Immortality."

Delaware State Arts Council
State Office Bldg.
Wilmington, DE 19801

Individual Artist Fellowship (poetry): Vanessa Haley, for "Home," "The Housesitter," "The Swimmer," "Anna And The Pigeon," "Letters From My Mother" and "They Used To Live In Kansas."

Earthwise
P.O. Box 680536
Miami, FL 33168

Song of Spring Competition: (Traditional Poetry) First—Mary Ann Napoleone, for "Underground"; Second—Jenni Douglas, for "A Poem's Pentameter In Living"; Third—Esther M. Leiper, for "A Prescription For Learning." (Modern/Free Verse Poetry) First—Esther Leiper, for "Elopement By Water"; Second—Malcolm Scott Mackenzie, for "Mood Of A Teen Age Boy On Behalf Of A Cat"; Third—Beverly Metso Hubbs, for "In My Aging Years."

T. S. Eliot Chapbook Competition: Dawna Maydak Andrejcak, for "Because The Death Of A Rose."

Eckerd College
P.O. Box 12560
St. Petersburg, FL 33733

A. Howard Carter Memorial Poetry Contest: Fred. W. Wright, Jr., for "My Dead Pelican," "Party Boy" and "The Daredevil."

Edmonton Journal
Community Relations Dept.
Box 2421
Edmonton, Alta. T5J 2S6
Canada

Literary Awards (poetry): (Short Poetry) First—Peggy Morgan, for "Journey"; Second—Melanie S. Isaac, for "Flight Into Egypt"; Third—Bonnie Bishop, for "Harmony." (Long Poetry) First—Aaron Bushkowsky, for "Prairie Perceptions"; Norman Sacuta, for "Miss Wintamute"; Third—Rebecca (Jean) Luce-Kapler, for "The Real Thing."

Encore Magazine
1121 Major Ave., N.W.
Albuquerque, NM 87107

Jeanne Bonnette Memorial Contest: First—Emma Crobaugh, for "Winter Icicles Reflect Eternity"; Second—Anne Marx, for "A Rushing Of Her Seasons"; Third—Marie F. Petroceli, for "Lapidaries Of The Past."

Wendell P. Long Memorial Contest: First—Robert Finley, for "Sundown"; Second—Alice Mackenzie Swaim, for "In Forests Of My Mind"; Third—Anne L. Zoller, for "The White Dead On The Pond."

Alice Moser Claudel Memorial Contest: First—Maya Sinha, for "What Susie Said And What Became Of It"; Second—Robin Wamsher, for "Great Grandma."

Catharine A. Waldraff Award: Alice Mackenzie Swaim, for "Lapsang Souchong Tea."

Mara Youth Award: Alicia Keith, for "Under The Sun."

The Federal Poets of Washington
5321 Willard Ave.
Chevy Chase, MD 20815

No awards given this year.

Fireside Poetry Group/Aberdeen Area Arts Council
c/o Isabel Ackley

416 S. Kline St.
Aberdeen, SD 57401

Clifford Poetry Contest: First—Susan L. Williams, for "Motherweave"; Second—Richard Solly, for "The Closed Door"; Third—Paula Schulz, for "China Dream."

First State Writers
c/o Frances Kesner
400 W. 24th St.
Wilmington, DE 19802

Doris Inscho Memorial Award: First—Elizabeth Corey, for "Starlight, Starbright"; Second—Jaye Giammarino, for "Just Desserts"; Third—Wanda B. Blaisdell, for "Ear-reversible."

Women & Women's Concerns: First—Edythe Q. Caro, for "Who Will Teach"; Second—Janice Hays, for "The Clerk-typist's Prayer On A Wednesday Night In May"; Third—Ginny Foster, for "Anguish On A Sunday Morning."

Florida State Poetry Society
1110 N. Venetian Dr.
Miami Beach, FL 33139

Monthly Contests (July) Alice Mackenzie Swaim; (August) Blanche Landers; (September) Blanche Landers, Louise Pink, Mickey Huffstutler; (October) Blanche Landers; (November) Louise Pink, Blanche Landers; (December) Louise Pink, Blanche Landers.

Florida State Poets Association
c/o Madleyn Eastlund
Box 387
Beverly Hills, FL 32665

Florida State Poets Award: First—Donna Thomas; Second—Alice Lee; Third—Leigh Hunt.

Walter H. Flaig Memorial Award: First—Opie Houston; Second—Donna Thomas; Third—Donna Thomas.

Theodore Lindgren Memorial Award: First—Alice Morrey Bailey; Second—Randall Cadman; Third—Magi Schwartz.

Russell Leavit Memorial Award: First—Margaret Key Biggs; Second—R. R. Rothechilde; Third—Nancy E. Swenson.

Tanka Award: First—Robert "Amigo" DeWitt; Second—Alice Morrey Bailey; Third—Katherine Newman Krebs.

Gilbert Maxwell Memorial Award: First—Randall Cadman; Second—Helen Mar Cook; Third—Ruth Shaver Means.

Sylvia Alkoff Memorial Award: First—Randall Cadman; Second—Donna Thomas; Third—Wanda B. Blaisdell.

Katherine F. Gordy Award: First—Margaret Key Biggs; Second—Elaine Dallman; Third—Robert "Amigo" DeWitt.

Berneice McConahay Memorial Award: Donna Thomas; Beverly Fine; Edna Parrish; Robert "Amigo" DeWitt; Marie Spears.

Jeanne Burns Memorial Award: First—Alice Lee; Second—Robert "Amigo" DeWitt; Third—Katherine Newman Krebs.

Margaretta Curtin Memorial Award: First—Gladys Kennard; Second—Alice Morrey Bailey; Third—Randall Cadman.

Student Award: First—Christy Angerer; Second—James Campbell.

A Galaxy of Verse Literary Foundation
200 S. Chandler Dr.
Fort Worth, TX 76111

Galaxy International Poet Laureate Award: First—Lynetta W. Ryan, for "Runaway Child"; Second—Louise Branson Pollard, for "To Dylan Thomas"; Third—D. G. Augustyn, for "Morning Exercise."

John Williams Andrews Memorial Narrative Award: First—Sibyl N. Gutkowski, for "The Purging"; Second—Violette Newton, for "Family Fuss"; Third—Emma Crobaugh, for "This Man Of Old Canoes."

James Tedwell Spencer Award: First—William Pollard, for "The Value Of Words"; Second—Amy Jo Schoonover, for "Confessions"; Third—Catherine Case Lubbe, for "Euthanasia For A Wasp."

Henrietta Ford Award: First—Vera L. Eckert, for "A Bit Of Stardust"; Second—Ruth W. Shively, for "Signature Southwest"; Third—Teresa Burleson, for "Reflections By A Rosebud."

Planetary Press/David Andrews Award: First—Mary B. Wall, for "Out Dated Wall"; Second—Emma Crobaugh, for "The Color Of Tears"; Third—Golda E. Walker, for "Precepts For Brotherhood."

Vito P. Sasso Award: (Spring & Summer) First—Catherine Case Lubbe, for "Urban Renewal"; Second—Robert Brown, for "Void On An Asteroid"; Third—Beatrice Branch, for "Springtime In Florida." (Fall & Winter) First—William Barney, for "Fundambulist"; Second—Goldie Capers Smith, for "Stoic"; Third—S. J. Vivier, for "Signs."

Georgia State Poetry Society
c/o Edward Davin Vickers
1421 Peachtree St., N.E.
Suite 111
Atlanta, GA 30309

Daniel Whitehead Hicky National Awards: First—Jeanne Lebow, for "Whirling"; Second—Bettie Sellers, for "And All The Princes Are Gone"; Third—James Brennan, for "Fast Break"; Sonnet: Mareen Cannon, for "Visit To An Old Friend."

Traditional Award: First—Betty Maine, for "Time Heals."

Contemporary Award: First—Alice B. Howard, for "Arthur Rubinstein."

Youth Competition: (Elementary) First—Mary Katherine Defoor, for "Balloons"; Second—Earl Gaskin, for "Magic"; Third—Aleta Angelina Mills, for "The Sun Shines." (Middle School) First—Laurie McConnell, for "Communion"; Second—Alice Bailey, for "The World"; Third—Shawn Copeland, for "Smile." (High School) First—Kimberly Dow Flint for "Wassau"; Second—Mary Taormina, for "1983 And Beyond"; Third—Laura Faussone, for "Music."

Evelyn Wallace Byington Memorial Awards (spring): First—Thelma R. Hall, for "Jonathan Eaves"; Second—Glenna Holloway, for "The Answering"; Third—Jacquelyn Spratlin, for "The Rendezvous."

Paths to Peace Prizes (spring): First—Leigh Hunt, for "The Falcon"; Second—Glenna Holloway, for "Afternoon Among The Artifacts"; Third—Dorothy Williamson Worth, for "And They Shall Have Dominion"; Fourth—William L. Davenport for "Stirrings Of The People," and David McCowen for "Maybe Next Time."

Great Lakes Colleges Association
220 Collingwood, Suite 240
Ann Arbor, MI 48103
New Writers Award (poetry): Maria Flook, for "Reckless Wedding."

Grolier Book Shop
6 Plympton St.
Cambridge, MA 02138
Grolier Poetry Prize: Lucie Brock-Broido; Linda McCarriston.

Houghton Mifflin Company
2 Park St.
Boston, MA 02108
New Poetry Series: Tom Sleigh, for "After One."

Hudson Review
684 Park Ave.
New York, NY 10021
Bennett Award: Seamus Heaney.

Illinois Arts Council
111 N. Wabash Ave.
Chicago, IL 60602
Literary Awards (poetry): Ralph J. Mills, Jr., for "Two Poems"; Helen Degen Cohen, for "The Trains"; Kazys Bradunas, for "Prierasa: Prie Genezes"; Helen Valenta, for "Sometimes In The Grey Of Mirrors"; Paul Carroll, for "Ode To Ed Pashke"; Elaine Equi, for "Hairi-Kari"; Molly McQuade, for "Apple-Bearers"; Lisel Mueller, for "Letting Go Of Summer"; Elaine Tuennerman, for "A Visit With My Sister"; Lucien Stryk, for "November"; Barbara Kynett, for "The Roads Taken."

Artists Grant (to poets): Duane Taylor; Bruce Guernsey; Paul Carroll; Maxine Chernoff; Paul Hoover; Carla Kaplan; Lucien Stryk; Dave Etter; Nance Van Winckel; Robin Metz; Margie Hurst; Richard Holinger; Mary Kinzie; Susan Mitchell.

Illinois State Poetry Society
c/o Prentice Douglas
Route 2, Box 126-C
Raymond, IL 62560
Annual Poetry Contest: First—Mildred Rowan Henderson, for "Nude"; Second—Ann L. Zoller, for "The White Dead On The Pond"; Third—Marguerite A. Brewster, for "A Flight Of Swallows."

Indiana State Federation of Poetry Clubs
c/o Dena S. Adams
1 Northview Dr.
Valparaiso, IN 46383

Grand Prize: First—Edith Hite McElfresh, for "The Storm"; Second—Sophia E. McElhaney, for "Creature Of The Crutch"; Third—Esther Leiper, for "Marks Of An Old Fire."

Goldie Souris Memorial Award: First—Pauline Shortridge, for "Sycorax, C. 1870"; Second—Verna Lee Hinegardner, for "Second-Hand Joy"; Third—Ida Crane Walker, for "Intangible Chain."

Glenna Glee Award: First—Susan Zivich, for "Heaven's Canopy"; Second—Vonnie Thomas, for "White-Tailed Unicorn"; Third—Esther Leiper, for "Evening At Waterstock." ·

Margaret Hiner Hight Award: First—Vonnie Thomas, for "A Taste Of The Past"; Second—Ida E. Sprague, for "The Stone Mermaid"; Third—Ida Crane Walker, for "Rider Of The Wind."

Geneva Muster Award: First—June Shipley, for "The Undefeated"; Second—Ainsley Jo Phillips, for "A Question Of Brotherhood"; Third—Judith M. Frank, for "In Our Speaking."

Emma C. Archibald Memorial Award: First—Aileen R. Jaffa, for "Ivory Dogwood"; Second—Barbara Stevens, for "New Ferns Uncurl Green"; Third—Ida Crane Walker, for "Thorn Piercing Brown Wing."

Tomorrow's Treasures Award: First—Charles Isley, for "Antique Chest"; Second—Verna Lee Hinegardner, for "Quest Of The Restless"; Third—Ben Sweeney, for "Grandma."

Historic Award: First—Margaret Key Biggs, for "Three Moons Before The Trail Of Tears"; Second—Helen Marr Cook, for "Prairie Fire 1847"; Third—David Spencer, for "The Horse-Bowmen."

Poets' Pathfinder Award: First—Esther Leiper, for "A Raw Deal"; Second—Beverly Topa, for "Cricket Philosophics."

Indiana University
Bloomington, IN 47405
American Academy of Poets Prize: Robyn Wiegman.
Keisler Undergraduate Poetry Prize: Hilary Sideris.

International Peace Poetry Contest
c/o Claire J. Baker
2451 Church Lane, #47
San Pablo, CA 94806
International Peace Poetry Contest: Knute Skinner, for "An Old Lady Watching TV"; Dorinda Moreno, for "The Best Of Silences"; Carol O'Toole, for "Even Though"; Paris Flammonde, for "Overture."

International Platform Association
2564 Berkshire Rd.
Cleveland Heights, OH 44106
Carl Sandburg Award: Not awarded in 1983.

Johns Hopkins University Press
Baltimore, MD 21218
Galileo Press Ha'Penny Book Contest (poetry): John Engman, for "Keeping Still, Mountain."

Chester H. Jones Foundation
P.O. Box 43033
Cleveland, OH 44143

National Poetry Competition: First—Tim Hunt, for "Lake County Elegy"; Second—Donald Lawder, for "In The Sweet Briar Library"; Third—Hadassah Stein, for "The Ladder"; Fourth—Katherine Soniat for "The Poetry Teacher Watches Metaphor Extend," and Jill Young for "Mentor."

Kansas Poetry Contest
c/o Ossie E. Tranbarger
619 W. Main St.
Independence, KS 67301
Category One: First—Alice Morrey Bailey, for "Fleeting Hour"; Second—Margaret Stavely, for "Of Change And Swift Glimpses"; Third—Ida Crane Walker, for "Chansonettes And Violettes."
Category Two: First—Charles Ross West; Second—Lenard D. Moore; Third—Jeanne Esch.

Kansas Quarterly
Dept. of English, Denison Hall
Kansas State University
Manhattan, KS 66506
KQ/Kansas Arts Commission Awards (poetry): First—David Kirby, for "Unnatural Acts" and "Conversations With The Dead"; Second—David Wagoner for "The Author Says Goodbye To His Hero," Laurence Lieberman for "Death," and Nancy Lee Couto for "Metemphychosis, For Aunt Susanna."
Seaton Awards (Poetry): First—Carol Miles Petersen, for "Untitled"; Second—Richard F. Gillum, for "Cottonwood Country"; Third—Philip M. Royster, for "Grandma's House."

Kentucky Dept. of Libraries and Archives/Kentucky Arts Council
Box 537
Frankfort, KY 40602
Chapbook Competition: Millard Dunn, for "Engraved On Air."

League of Canadian Poets
24 Ryerson Ave.
Toronto, Ont. M5T 2P3
Canada
Pat Lowther Memorial Award: Rhea Tregebov, for "Remembering History."

League of Canadian Poets/Writers' Union of Canada
24 Ryerson Ave.
Toronto, Ont. M5T 2P3
Canada
Gerald Lampert Memorial Award: Diana Hartog, for "Matinee Light."

Lincoln College
Lincoln, IL 62656
Billee Murray Denny Poetry Award: First—Sibbie O'Sullivan, for "Listening For Trains"; Second—Susan Donnelly, for "The Rooms"; Third—Laura Kasischke, for "The Poem The Poet Tells Me."

Los Angeles Times
Times Mirror Square
Los Angeles, CA 90053

Book Prize (poetry): James Merrill, for "The Changing Light At Sandover."

The Lyric
307 Dunton Dr., S.W.
Blacksburg, VA 24060
Lyric Memorial Prize: Rhina P. Espaillat, for "Falling."
Nathan Haskell Dole Prize: Donna Dickey Guyer, for "Old Cemeteries."
Roberts Memorial Prize: Larry Michaels, for "Barking After Trains."
Leitch Memorial Prize: C. Sand Childs, for "The Poet And Her Cat."
Virginia Prize: Violette Newton, for "A Train In The Night."
New England Prize: Hans Brockerhoff, for "Apples."
Panola Prize: Kurt J. Fickert, for "Those Who Lie Awake In Darkness."
Fluvanna Prize: Robert N. Feinstein, for "Wrong Turnings."
College Poetry Contest: First—Carla Wood, for "Heart's Treasure"; Second—James Nawrocki, for "Main Street"; Third—Gabriella Mirollo, for "Midas."
Quarterly Prizes: Winter—C. Sand Childs, for "The Poet And Her Cat"; Spring—Maureen Cannon, for "Letter To Dylan"; Summer—Donna Dickey Guyer, for "Old Cemeteries"; Fall—Harold McCurdy, for Vine Leaves."

Maine State Commission on the Arts and the Humanities
55 Capitol St.
State House Sta. 25
Augusta, ME 04333
Chapbook Competition: Ruth Mendelsohn, for "Sixteen Pastorals."

Mid-South Poetry Festival
c/o Lola Mae Adams
24 Ballehaven Rd.
Memphis, TN 38109
First President of the Poetry Society of Tennessee Award: First—Kitty Yeager, for "The Elf That Was Myself"; Second—Gloria Okes Perkins, for "The Hunter"; Third—Frieda B. Dorris, for "Broken Glass."
Past President of the Poetry Society of Tennessee Award: First—Tom Whiteside, for "In The Spirit Of Socrates"; Second—Esther M. Leiper, for "Socrates Addresses The Generations"; Third—Lanita Moses, for "Water Stone Of The Wise."
B. J. Long Memorial Award: First—Robert Lee Simonton, for "His Gentle Hand"; Second—Vonnie Thomas, for "Let Me Sell You Life"; Third—Vivian Smallwood, for "Ghost Story."
Inez Elliott Andersen, First Lady of Poetry, Honorary Award: First—Robert Lee Simonton, for "Something Special"; Second—Frieda B. Dorris, for "Rebel Dignity"; Third—Margaret Kerr, for "Woman Attired In Her Cape Of Dignity."
Inez Elliott Andersen Honorary Award: First—Bee Bacherig Long, for "What A Lady"; Second—

Eve Braden Hatchett, for "Poem For The Sunshine Lady"; Third—James W. Proctor, for "Voluntary."

Lealer G. Brown Memorial Award: First—Claudia Watson Stewart, for "Surviving All These"; Second—Frieda B. Dorris, for "A Time Of Grace"; Third—Catherine T. Jordan, for "The Harvest Years."

Nostalgia Award: First—Robert Lee Simonton, for "Going Back"; Second—Marianne McNeil, for "Middle-Age Wade"; Third—Orville Hancock, for "Song And Dance."

Chosen Children Award: First—Eve Braden Hatchett, for "Sliding Past Go"; Second—Burnette B. Benedict, for "In Between"; Third—Tom Whiteside, for "Decisions."

Astrological Poetry Award: First—Raymond McCarty, for "Leo Born"; Second—Kitty Yeager, for "Libra Man"; Third—Eve Braden Hatchett, for "Pull In Your Claws."

Edith Brown Thomas Honorary Award: First—Esther M. Leiper, for "Portrait Of My Thirteenth Summer"; Second—Dawn Fraser, for "Fantaisie Impromptu"; Third—Frances Sydnor Tehie, for "The Homecoming Of Robin."

Dorsimbra Award: Frieda B. Dorris, for "From Blood To Honey"; Second—Ruth Peal Harrell, for "A Sea Of Boats—A Sea Of People"; Third—Eve Braden Hatchett, for "Like The Morning Star."

Beaudoin Gemstone Award: Elaine D. Hardt for "Will You Step Inside My Poetry," Lanita Moses for "Many Gifts In One," and Kitty Yeager for "Homesick In Trolley Town."

Elliott Gemstone Pendant Award: First—Leonard Helie, for "Villanelle Of The Java Sea"; Second—Frieda B. Dorris, for "Almost Midnight"; Third—Carol Sowell, for "Orphans Of Camelot."

Student Award: First—John Worth, for "The Old Ones"; Second—Dawn Baldwin, for "Child's Play"; Third—Gretchen Schwarz, for "A Guitar."

Poetry Society of Tennessee Award: First—Ann Henning, for "Rain"; Second—Harry B. Sheftel, for "Prescience"; Third—Inez Elliott Andersen, for "State Bird Of Tennessee."

Alabama State Poetry Society Award: First—Henry Tim Chambers, for "Somewhere Among The Andes"; Second—Eve Braden Hatchett, for "Under The Silk Blue Wonder"; Third—Ann Carolyn Cates, for "No Medals For Me."

Mississippi State Poetry Society Award: First—Alice Mackenzie Swaim, for "Mississippi Flood."

Henry Tim Chambers, Dean of Poets, Award: First—Frances Tehie, for "Aria Mit Verschiedenen Veranderungen"; Second—James W. Proctor, for "Exit"; Third—Tom Whiteside, for "The Great Moment."

Midwest Poetry Review
Box 776
Rock Island, IL 61201
Annual Grand Award: First—Patricia Hladik, for "Pro Tempore"; Second—Sara Wilbridge, for

"Shrinking"; Third—Linda Ulmer, for "Springhouse Retreat."

Sonnet Contest: Kay Harvey, for "First Frost."

Haunting Memory Contest: A. Byrne Knudsen, for "1933."

Love Poem Contest: Lethe Hunter Bishop, for "Love Song."

Mississippi Poetry Society
P.O. Box 875
Hazlehurst, MS 39083
Octoberfest Contest—

Mississippi Poetry Society Award: First—Cecile Brown Clement, for "Star Repair"; Second—Brenda Brown Finnegan, for "Requiem For A Young Priest"; Third—Robert Simonton, for "Natchez."

Traditional Award: First—Dorothy Rogers, for "As Setting Sun Peers"; Second—Charles E. Treas, for "At Table"; Third—Patricia G. Kersey, for "New Orleans Song."

Humor Award: First—Mildred Rowan Henderson, for "May We Substitute Something Of Equal Or Greater Value?"; Second—Ken Alvey, for "The Fly And I"; Third—Louise Rogers, for "The Full, Rich Life Of A Lady Writer."

Spiritual Award: First—Monette M. Young, for "Eve's Lament"; Second—Jo M. Shaw, for "Sparrow's Fall"; Third—Jo M. Shaw, for "Carpenter."

Fantasy and Romance Award: First—Cecile Brown Clement, for "Absolution"; Second—Steve Walkinshaw, for "At Four A.M."; Third—Carroll Case, for "Daylilies."

Open Award: First—Steve Walkinshaw, for "Dance"; Second—Cecile Brown Clement, for "Service Station Window"; Third—Jo M. Shaw, for "Flight Of Birds."

Recitations, Songs and Ballads: First—Goldie Jane Feldman, for "If Goneril Repented: 1937"; Second—Charles E. Treas, for "The Church Where The Organ Played"; Third—June Shanahan, for "This Is A New Game."

Student Award: First—Matt McGlone for "A Record Of The Saturday Night Her Parents Weren't Home (As I Remember It)," and Michelle Jones for "Baby-Sitting"; Second—Mary Lee Harper, for "The Other Side Of Life"; Third—David Williams, for "God's Wrath."

National Book Critics Circle
c/o Robert Harris
4000 Tunlaw Rd., N.W., #1019
Washington, DC 20007
Poetry Award: Katha Pollitt, for "Antarctic Traveler."

National Federation of State Poetry Societies
c/o Amy Jo Zook, Contest Chairman
3520 State Route 56
Mechanicsburg, OH 43044
NFSPS Prize: First—Sallie Anderson, for "Have You Noticed How Dark It Is Getting Outside"; Second—Glenda Frank, for "Plum For Bob"; Third—Mary Oler, for "Once There

Was A Man Named Jeso."

Jerry Rose Memorial Award: First—J. A. Totts, for "At Winter Solstice"; Second—Jack Fenwick, for "Charon's Landing"; Third—Ruth Shiller Flanger, for "Paxton's Pond."

NFSPS Past Presidents Award: First—Donna Thomas, for "The Caretaker"; Laverne Rison, for "What The Boy Scouts Said"; Third—Alfred Dorn, for "In The Doorway."

John A. Lubbe Memorial Award: First—Mary Logan Sweet, for "Inheritance"; Second—J. A. Totts, for "Sylvia"; Third—Donna Thomas, for "Tuesday With Janet."

Patriotism Award: First—Glenna Holloway, for "Continuing Education Series"; Second—Mrs. R. E. Gatlin, for "We Stood Together"; Third—Renee L. Oelschlaeger, for "The Execution Of David O. Dodd."

Poetry Society of Texas Award: First—Lois Beebe Hayna, for "Living With Fear"; Second—Nelle Fertig, for "Familiar Intruder"; Third—Ruth Shiller Flanger, for "Never Measuring Love."

Music Award: First—Katherine Larsen, for "His Indescribable, Incomparable Music"; Second—Margauerite Arthur Brewster, for "These Chords Ascend"; Third—Alice Briley, for "Midsummer Night's Dream."

Beymorlin Sonnet Award: First—Marilyn Eynon Scott, for "Echo Of Emptyness"; Second—Nancy Tucker Wilson, for "Bacchanalian Cup"; Third—Kitty Yeager, for "Grandpa's Blessing."

Nan Fitz-Patrick Memorial Award: First—Juavanta Walker, for "Four-Letter Words Like Food, Fuel, Fear"; Second—Alice Mackenzie Swaim, for "Lost Innocence"; Third—Red Hawk, for "The Neighbors Come And Go."

Alabama State Poetry Society Award: First—Margaret Key Biggs, for "A Ritual Of Spring"; Second—Gretelle Suzanne LeGron, for "Family Album"; Third—Lucille Morgan Wilson, for "Footlights On Monday."

Indiana Award: First—Willis A. Kropp, for "Ode To A Little Girl With A Wild Flower In Her Hand"; Second—Marion Brimm Rewey, for "Talisman"; Third—Ida Crane Walker, for "Nothing Is Forever."

Random Rhyme Award: First—Marion Brimm Rewey, for "A Few Lines For Betty And Birds"; Second—Kathryn Kay, for "Sidewalk World"; Third—Helen Stallcup, for "Libraries Breed On Need."

Amelia Reynolds Long Memorial Award: First—Minnie Bowden, for "Woman And Car, 1928"; Second—Louis Watt Seger, for "Barnyard Critic"; Third—Maureen Cannon, for "Sorry!"

Mary Ellen Riddell No. 85 Award: First—Anne Barlow, for "Sonnet From The Hearth"; Second—Daniel Fernandez, for "Lean Time"; Third—Mary B. Finn, for "Widow's Way."

Vivian Laramore Rader Memorial Award: First—Mabel Juliar Nisbet, for "Edna St. Vincent Millay"; Second—Doris R. Goldberg, for "A Letter To My Son"; Third—Donna Thomas,

for "Half Past Time To Go."

Arkansas Award: First—Marion Brimm Rewey, for "On Waking A Hundred Years Older"; Second—Ruth Shiller Flanger, for "Combing"; Third—Margaret Kay Biggs, for "Confession Of A Seductress."

Florida State Poets Award: First—Sy Swann, for "Shunted"; Second—Linda Zeis Segars, for "Anniversary Number Twelve"; Third—Margaret Parker, for "Tantalus."

Oklahoma State Poetry Society Award: First—Ruth E. Reuther, for "The Mystery Of Mesquite"; Second—Violette Newton, for "The Gypsy Wind"; Third—Georgene Collins, for "Huge Bloodcolored Rock."

Our American Indian Heritage Award: First—Lael W. Hill, for "For A Passing Redman"; Second—Aileen R. Jaffa, for "In Navajo Country"; Third—Dorothy Logan, for "Grandmother Sleeps In A Red Earth Meadow."

South Dakota Poetry Society Award: First—Ida Crane Walker, for "Hopi Girl"; Second—Geneva I. Crook, for "Broken Treaties"; Third—Marguerite Arthur Brewster, for "Return To Taste The Apples."

Manningham Award: First—Renee L. Oelschlaeger, for "Stocking Stuffers"; Second—Maxine R. Jennings, for "Stoppin' Shoppin'"; Third—Dolores E. Teufel, for "Opportune!"

Humorous Poetry Award: First—Gwen Casilli, for "Bovine Ruminations"; Second—Anne McClaughery for "Why Waxing's On The Wane"; Third—Hannah Fox, for "Inferior Decoration."

Modern Award: First—Verna Lee Hinegardner, for "Death Of A Child"; Second—Jack Fenwick, for "Legion's Wife And Child"; Third—Alfred Dorn, for "Wrestling Night."

Traditional Award: First—Vivian Ricker, for "The Belle Of Lakenhagen"; Second—Margaret C. Blaker, for "The Watchers"; Third—Donna Thomas, for "Reminiscence Of A Brief Understanding."

Mabel Meadows Staats Award: First—Margaret Ricks, for "Earth-Dirge"; Second—Kitty Yeager, for "Melissa In Mourning"; Third—Eve Braden Hatchett, for "For Carol."

Olive H. McHugh Memorial Award: First—Barbara Latimer Catrow, for "An Intended Link"; Second—Kitty Yeager, for "Taming A Gringo"; Third—Joyce A. Chandler, for "Free Spirit."

Bible Award: First—Alfred Dorn, for "Offerings"; Second—Anne Barlow, for "Barabbas"; Third—Carlee Swann, for "And Fell Among Thieves."

Evans Spencer Wall Memorial Award: First—Jack E. Murphy, for "The Surprise Of Poetry"; Second—Nancy W. Basham, for "Artist And Subject"; Third—Cecilia Parsons Miller, for "My Problem With Picasso."

Arizona State Poetry Society Award: First—Bernita Coffey, for "Graceful Flyers"; Second—Florence Wahl Otter, for "Ever-Widening Circles"; Third—William Schroll, for "The Adventurer."

Spoon River Award: First—Ora Pate Stewart, for "From A Civil Engineer—To A Pioneer Child"; Second—Emma S. McLaughlin, for "Mozart's Taste Of Brine"; Third—Joanne M. Riley, for "Emily Dickinson."

Louisiana State Poetry Society Award: First—Jean Humphrey Chaillie, for "On The Way To The Post Office"; Second—Pat King, for "Macho Melon"; Third—Kitty Yeager, for "Last Moments."

Utah State Award: First—Linda Beth Toth, for "The Summer Puppies"; Second—Ann L. Zoller, for "Instincts In Slow Motion"; Third—Julia Hurd Strong, for "Special Event."

Wisconsin Poetry Award: First—Joy Gresham Hagstrom, for "Miracle Of The Monarchs"; Second—Wauneta Hackleman, for "No Place To Plant Acorns"; Third—Isobel Routly Stewart, for "Northland Revisited."

Verse Writers' Guild of Ohio Award: First—Lael W. Hill, for "Burnings, I & II"; Second—Shirley Handley, for "Trail Of The Completed Circle"; Third—Anne Barlow, for "The Garden At His Rising."

Poet Laureate of Texas Award: First—Vivian Ricker, for "For A Poet Long Dead"; Second—Nelle Fertig, for "Desert Cloudburst"; Third—Alice Mackenzie Swaim, for "Step Softly, Traveller."

Leona Lloyd Memorial Award: First—Hollis A. Schmitt, for "Half Blue"; Second—Nancy Jo Rinehart, for "Office Rose"; Third—Vivian Beck Rosetti, for "Nostalgia?"

Pteranodon Award: First—Jack Fenwick, for "A Still Life With Wind"; Second—Patricia S. Grimm, for "To A Difficult Poet"; Third—Carl P. Morton, for "The Gentleness Of Change."

Poetry Society of Tennessee Award: First—Vesta P. Crawford, for "Consider The Wind"; Second—Agnes Wathall Tatera, for "The Gift"; Third—Percival R. Roberts, for "A Few Lines For F. T."

West Virginia Poetry Society Award: First—Betsy Kennedy, for "The Midwife"; Second—Kitty Yeager, for "Land Of Blue Wind"; Third—Margaret Ricks, for "Taking Up Serpents."

Perryman Visser Award: First—Julia Hurd Strong, for "At A Watch Party"; Second—Dorman John Grace, for "To Answer Yes Or No"; Third—Anne Lambert Cowley, for "Plane Geometry."

Massachusetts State Poetry Society Award: First—Jean Humphrey Chaillie, for "Scenes From An Uncolored Day"; Second—Richard Allen Barnes, for "Elegy"; Third—Gretelle Suzanne LeGron, for "Neptune's Daughter."

Arlena Robbins Honorary Award: First—Marion Brimm Rewey, for "An Absent Minded Hero"; Second—Althea Andelin Roberts, for "Coulter, Discoverer Of The Yellowstone"; Third—Diane Glancy, for "Anny Tarpley."

New York Poetry Forum Award: First—Randall Cadman, for "Sunbelt Sonnetiers"; Second—

Esther Robinson, for "The Treatise Of Leonardo"; Third—Alfred Dorn, for "Slum Poet."

Carl I. Nelson Award: First—June Owens, for "Dear Girl, There Are No Nightingales On Staten Island"; Second—Grace Haynes Smith, for "Teacher Of Botany And More"; Third—Catherine Eckrich, for "This Day Is Memory."

Leona Jones Smith Award: First—Kitty Yeager, for "Looking For Camelot"; Second—Marion Brimm Rewey, for "Eagle Man, Running For His Life"; Third—Kay Huerta, for "The Children Go Easy To Star Kissed Sleep."

Rhode Island State Poetry Society Award: First—Dorothy Williamson Worth, for "To Paradise, Sadat"; Second—Maxine R. Jennings, for "The Memoirs Of Richard Nixon—Thirty-Seventh President"; Third—Gretelle Suzanne LeGron, for "Vanished World."

Poetry Organization for Women Award: First—Alfred Dorn, for "Thena"; Second—Mary Kenney Rumm, for "The Communion"; Third—Wauneta Hackleman, for "A Prayer For Stephen."

PSNH Larry Wiggin Award: First—Helen Fountain, for "Claire Clairmont To Her Confessor"; Second—Marion Brimm Rewey, for "The Farmer As Artist"; Third—Clarence P. Socwell, for "Prayer for Aluminum Cans."

Student Award: First—Karen Frayne, for "Shepherd To Shepherd"; Second—Arden Davidson, for "Crystal Lake"; Third—Chris Thomas, for "Assassination."

National League of American Pen Women
New Mexico State Board
c/o Alice Briley, Contest Chairman
1121 Major Ave., NW
Albuquerque, NM 87107
National Poetry Contest: First—Christie Cochrell Parker, for "Waking From Disturbing Dreams"; Second—Agnes Wathall Tatera, for "The Wintered Boat"; Third—Dawn Fraser, for "To A Black Widow"; Fourth—Mickey Huffstutler, for "Haunted Land"; Fifth—Jane E. Logan, for "Hear The Beauty"; Sixth—Sandra Lake Miller, for "St. Anne's—Moscow."

National Magazine Awards Foundation
44 Eglinton Ave. W., Suite 501
Toronto, Ont. M4R 1A1
Canada
du Maurier Award for Poetry: Erin Moure, for "Tricks."

National Poetry Day Committee
1110 N. Venetian Dr.
Miami Beach, FL 33139
Annual Contest: Blanche Landers; Mickey Huffstutler.

National Poetry Foundation
University of Maine at Orono
Orono, ME 04469
National Poetry Foundation Award: Desmond Egan, for "The Collected Poems."

National Poetry Series
18 W. 30th St.
New York, NY 10001

National Poetry Series: Mary Fell, for "The Persistence Of Memory"; Wendy Battin, for "In The Solar Wind"; Stephen Dobyns for "Black Dog, Red Dog"; James Galvin, for "God's Mistress,"; Ronald Johnson, for "Ark 50."

Nevada Poetry Society
McCarran Ranch
via Sparks, NV 89431
Mary Win Summerfield Memorial Contest: First—Dorothy Walter Powell, for "The Witch"; Second—Sherri Hanover, for "My Onery Ways"; Third—Joy Ripson, for "The Clown."

New England Poetry Club
2 Farrar St.
Cambridge, MA 02138
Golden Rose Award: Galway Kinnell.
Daniel Varoujan Award: Peter Viereck, for "Portrait Of The Artist."

New England Review and Bread Loaf Quarterly
Box 170
Hanover, NH 03755
Narrative Poetry Competition: John Engels, for "Winter Flight" and "After The Stroke."

New Hope Foundation
Lenore Marshall/The Nation Poetry Prize: George Starbuck, for "The Argot Merchant Disaster: Poems New And Selected."

New Letters Magazine
University of Missouri-Kansas City
5346 Charlotte
Kansas City, MO 64110
William Carlos Williams Prize for Poetry: Mbembe Milton Smith, for fourteen poems in Vol. 50, No. 1 of New Letters.
Barbara Storck Award (poetry): Janet Lowe, for "The Power Of Small Circles"; (poem/short story combination) Mark Dion.

New Mexico State Poetry Society
c/o Laverne Rison
6616 San Bernardino, NE
Albuquerque, NM 87109
Rhymed Verse: First—Prentice Douglas, for "Exit"; Second—Richard M. Berthold, for "Security"; Third—Alice Briley, for "Take A Letter."
Free Verse: Mildred Yeager Murray, for "Night Court"; Second—Lois Beebe Hayna, for "January Moon"; Third—Helena Dominian, for "If You Are There."
Traditional: First—Prentice Douglas, for "Winter Trees"; Second—Helena Dominian, for "Lost Memories"; Third—Alice Briley, for "Autumn Flower Show."
General: First—Amy Jo Schoonover, for "Or By Act Of God"; Second—Pamela Y. Henry, for "Brown July"; Third—Helena Dominian, for "To Mind My Going."

New York Contemporary Press
P.O. Box 670
New York, NY 10021
Poetry Award: George Murphy.

New York University
Dept. of English
19 University Pl., Room 200
New York, NY 10003

Thomas Wolfe Memorial Prize: Frank Menchaka, for "Selected Poems."

Nimrod Magazine
2210 S. Main St.
Tulsa, OK 74114
Pablo Neruda Prize for Poetry: First—Alison Deming, for "Letter To Nathaniel Hawthorne"; Second—Phyllis Collier, for "Continuing."

North American Mentor Magazine
Fennimore, WI 53809
Annual Poetry Contest: First—James Richard Hurst, for "Silence"; Second—Mary B. Finn, for "Beethoven Pathetique"; Third—Haywood Jackson, for "The Mind Machine."

North Carolina Literary & Historical Society
109 E. Jones St.
Raleigh, NC 27611
Roanoke-Chowan Poetry Award: Reynolds Price, for "Vital Provisions."

Ohio Poetry Day Association
c/o Evan Lodge
1506 Prospect Rd.
Hudson, OH 44236
Ohio Poetry Day Special Award: First—Marilee Pallant, for "Another Harvest Poem For Scott"; Second—Amy Jo Schoonover; Third—Betsy Greiner.
Tessa Sweazy Webb Memorial: First—J. Louise Pink, for "So Passeth The Passing Day"; Second—Amy Jo Schoonover; Third—Margaret E. Fox.
Upward Bound Award: First—Michelle Kimball, for "Tomorrow's Tears"; Second—Doris Hinderson; Third—Tina Foster.
Verse Writers' Guild Student Award: First—Tara Lynn Pallant, for "The Savage"; Second—Debbie Dewald; Third—Kelly Bradshaw.
Student Haiku Awards: Leanne Prater; Adam Ramseyer; Michelle Flowers.
Workshop Awards: Dorotha Bradford; Yvonne Hardenbrook; Joanne Niswander; Barbara North; Marilyn R. Wiesen; J. R. Wilson.
Greater Cincinnati Writers' League Award: First—J. A. Totts, for "Spring Storm"; Second—Sally McGriff; Third—Alma Graham Jenks.
Leesburg Wednesday Club Award: First—Loretta Bird Metzger, for "When War Is Done"; Second—Ruth Binkley; Third—Harriet McFerren.
Akron Area Poetry Society Award: First—Deborah S. Glaefke, for "The Collector"; Second—Vera Whitmer; Third—Sandra Basner Shrigley.
Henry Chapin Memorial: First—Cecil Hale Hartzell, for "The Ballad Of Time And The River"; Second—Catherine A. Callaghan; Third—Edward S. Chamberlain.
Carl G. Goeller Memorial: First—Jeanette Haas, for "Spring"; Second—Margaret Ricks; Third—Erica Stux.
National League Of American Pen Women, Cincinnati Branch Award: First—Novella Humphrey Davis, for "Letter To My Son Who

Sits All Day At A Desk"; Second—J. A. Totts.
Wells of Salvation Award: First—Diana Kendig; Second—Martha P. Evans; Third—Delma Dwyer Fairley.
Three Cheers for Dad Award: First—Doris R. Goldberg, for "Sonnet For My Father"; Second—Kaye Coller; Third—Maria Angelos; Fourth—Lonnie Hi Higgins, Jr.
Louis & Anna Ryman Memorial: First—Sharon Cusick, for "Repercussion"; Second—Deborah S. Glaefke; Third—Edwin S. Chamberlain.
In Praise of Our Foremothers Award: First—Marcia L. Hurlow, for "Making a Dictionary"; Second—Rita D. Haban and J. R. Totts; Third—Sharon Cusick.
Toledo Poetry Society Award: First—Dalene Workman Stull, for "Newly Blind"; Second—E. Cole Ingle.
Writers' Roundtable Award: First—Vera Whitmer for "Until Death Do Us Part," and Novella Humphrey Davis for "The Neighbor"; Second—Laura Hilton; Third—Rose Ann Spaith.
Mt. Vernon Poetry Group Award: First—Charlotte Mann, for "Marriage Portrait"; Second—Doris R. Goldberg; Third—Cathryn Essinger.
Verse Writers' Guild Award: First—Patricia Shullick, for "Strawberry Nights"; Second—Cathryn Essinger; Third—Karen Handwork.
Bobbi & Amy Rosenbloom Memorial: First—J. A. Totts, for "Requiem"; Second—J. R. Wilson.
Lyric Free Verse Award: First—Michael Lepp, for "To Randy Who Attempted Suicide Last Night"; Second—J. R. Wilson.
June Margeson—Daffodils Award: First—J. A. Totts, for "April Earth"; Second—Dalene Workman Stull.
David R. Goldberg Memorial Award: First—Carol Moburg, for "Sunset Memory"; Second—Yvonne Hardenbrook.
Marion Area Writers Association Award: First—Margaret Ricks, for "Love Scene—Mexico City"; Second—Joan E. Jenny; Third—Yvonne Hardenbrook.
Great Expectations Award: First—Kathryn J. Burt, for "Without Body"; Second—Janeen Lepp; Third—Maria Angelos.
Ohioana Library Association Award: First—Virginia N. Nelson, for "Ohio's Jewels"; Second—J. A. Totts.
To Please a Child Award: First—Jeanette Barnes Thomin, for "Spring Colt"; Second—Vera Whitmer; Third—Rita D. Haban.
Wooster Poetry Society Award: First—Margaret Ricks, for "The Night Before The Sale"; Second—Ann McIntire Baldwin.
Modern Sonnet Award: First—J. R. Wilson, for "While Mowing"; Second—Yvonne Hardenbrook; Third—J. A. Totts and Betty Dodge Bennington.
"Sunny" Memorial: First—Margaret Ricks, for "Song Of A Mayan Flute"; Second—Kaye Coller.
A Matter of Meter Award: First—J. Louise Pink,

for "Ohio Autumn"; Second—Doris R. Goldberg; Third—Dalene Workman Stull.
Ida Wade Hank Award: First—Rodney M. Best, for "Spiderlife"; Second—J. A. Totts; Third—Vincent J. Tersigni.
National League of American Pen Women, Central Ohio Branch Award: First—Dalene Workman Stull, for "Rose Garden"; Second—Yvonne Hardenbrook.
Woman's Press Club, Cincinnati, Award: First—Ruth Binkley, for "Star Song"; Second—Mary Ann Lowry.

Olivet College
Olivet, MI 49076
Abbie M. Copps Poetry Contest: First—Evelyn Pohl, for "Love Poem."

Ozark Writers & Artists Guild
Crowder College
Neosho, MO 64850
Verna's Lyric: First—Doryes Daves, for "When You Cross The Great Missouri"; Second—Marnelle Robertson, for "Never Throw Away A Glove"; Third—Colleen Dahlman, for "A Little Seed Of Faith."
Lucy Babcock Free Verse: First—Virginia Bridges Smith, for "Reciprocation"; Second—Lois Snelling, for "Disciplinarian"; Third—Ellen Anderson, for "Pieces Of Eight."
Clara Willis' Shakespearean Sonnet: First—Dorothy Winslow Wright, for "Last Lap"; Second—Isabel D. Howard, for "Frustration"; Third—Kitty Yeager, for "The Munchkin."
Zenita's Juvenile Verse: First—Marnelle Robertson, for "My News Came Straight"; Second—Jan Stone, for "A Twilight Tale"; Third—Edna S. Browne, for "Repetition."
Dr. Nichols Bible Based Poetry: First—Kitty Yeager, for "Adopted Heir"; Second—Lois Snelling, for "Joy Through Humility"; Third—Bonnie Lee Reynolds, for "Wisdom."
Linda's Limerick: First (5)—Anna Nash Yarbrough, for "Who Gets What"; Edna S. Browne, for "You May Think"; G. Bryan Morton, for "I Once Knew"; Lois Snelling, for "Next Stop"; Lillian Barone, for "Home Cookin'."
Diane's Ballad: First—Kitty Yeager, for "Ballad Of Shatoca And The Silver Wolf"; Second—Louise Hajek, for "Bayou Ballad"; Third—Marcia Camp, for "Old Miss Jessie."
Ossie's Haiku: First (5)—Elizabeth House, for "A Cardboard Coffin"; Nida Jones Ingram, for "Autumn Moon Rises"; Virginia Bridges Smith, for "Hunting The Right Spot"; Lenard D. Moore, for "Through The Graveyard Pines"; Mary B. Wall, for "Petals Fallen From."
Marjorie's Tanka: First (5)—Earl J. Westcott, for "The Comet"; Rose Melody, for "Baby Girl"; Fern Ward, for "Roses By The Door"; Gladys Lawler, for "The Wind And The Lake"; Edwin A. Falkowski, for "Curve Of The Rainbow."
Elizabeth Lamb's Senryu: First (5)—Winona Kernan Champagne, for "Summer Afternoon"; Virginia Golden, for "My Nagging

Neighbor"; Ossie Tranbarger, for "The Three Little Pigs"; Pauline Carl Prince, for "Dashes To Class Late"; Lenard D. Moore, for "Cutting The Hedges."

Blanche Lander's Mason Sonnet: First—June Owens, for "Poems My Father Read To Me"; Second—Louise Hajek, for "Like Fingers On A Lyre"; Third—Lois Snelling, for "Beyond The Hilltop."

Aileen's All American Patriotic Poem: First—Edna S. Browne, for "Patriotism, American Style"; Second—Christina Pace, for "Did Betsy Dream Of This?"; Third—Jesse L. Green, for "America Is My Legacy."

Peggy's Triolet: First—Marnelle Robertson, for "Answer To An Unwanted Letter"; Second—Virginia Golden, for "Sunday Painter"; Third—Verna Lee Hinegardner, for "Granny Sue."

Pacific Northwest Writers Conference
1811 N.E. 199th
Seattle, WA 98155

Poetry Contest: First—Mildred Irmscher, for "Memories Of Kentucky Springs"; Second—Sallie Tierney, for "Disposition Of The Body"; Third—Diane Westergaard, for "Desert Woman."

P.E.N. American Center
47 Fifth Ave.
New York, NY 10003

P.E.N. Translation Prize: Richard Wilbur, for his translation of "Four Comedies," by Jean Baptiste Moliere.

P.E.N. Writing Awards for Prisoners (poetry): First—W. M. Aberg; Second—Henry Johnson; Third—Becky D. Brown.

Pennsylvania Poetry Society
c/o Bill Medland, Contest Chairman
2399 W. Market St.
York, PA 17404

Grand Prize: Ruth Schiller Flanger, for "White."

Katherine Lyons Clark Memorial Award: First—Amy Jo Schoonover, for "White Horses"; Second—Elaine Mason Lazzeroni, for "The Searcher"; Third—Alice Mackenzie Swaim, for " 'By The Pricking Of The Thumbs'."

Edna Shoemaker Memorial Award: First—Maureen Cannon, for "A Sudden Silence"; Second—Kathleen M. Cullen, for "Thoughts On A Snowy Sunday"; Third—Edward R. Brandt, for "Belief And Knowledge."

Edna Groff Diehl Memorial Award: First—Esther M. Leiper, for "The Wood Child's Song"; Second—Lois Beebe Hayna, for "The Glaciers Are Coming! The Glaciers Are Coming!"

Contemporary Idiom Award: First—Conne Reese, for "High"; Second—Catherine G. McCord, for "Look Out Below."

Estella Mayer MacBride Memorial Award: First—Dorman J. Grace, for "In Universal Clef Of La Boheme"; Second—Ana Barton, for "Kisses Worth The Price."

Amelia Reynolds Long Memorial Award: First—Agnes Homan, for "Prairie Woman";

Second—Lois Beebe Hayna, for "To Lie Down Lean."

Richard E. Gardner Memorial Award: First—Evelyn Ritchie, for "Ordered Pair, Graphed"; Second—Gwen Casilli, for "Bellweather."

Sans Souci Award: Andrew T. Roy, for "The Mosquito."

Marjorie Thompson Cheyney Memorial Award: First—Gordon LeClaire, for "Requiem For A Starless Night"; Second—Evelyn Ritchie, for "The Downtrodden."

Haiku Award: Gwen Glassberg, for "Fountains Overflow."

Lottie Kent Ruhl Memorial Award: First—Rose Rosberg, for "TV Relatives"; Second—Gwen Casilli, for "Pizza Maker At Casa Blanca"; Third—Frances Sydnor Tehie, for "After The Piano Lesson."

Col. Henry W. Shoemaker Memorial Award: First—Alice Mackenzie Swaim, for "Carroll Township"; Second—Margaret Ricks, for "Ole Bull's Violin"; Third—Andrew T. Roy, for "Philadelphia."

Blanche Whiting Keysner Memorial Award: First—Alice Mackenzie Swaim, for "Greenwich Village Artist"; Second—Mariam C. Malloy, for "Your Wordless Pledge"; Third—James W. Proctor, for "From A Prison Window."

C. Sterling Clifton Memorial Award: First—Anne Marx, for "Tante Marie: Her Sheltered Existence"; Second—Emma S. McLaughlin, for "Mellie Coleman"; Third—Ana Barton, for "Reflections On A Listener."

Piedmont Literary Review
c/o Evelyn Miles, Contest Chairman
Route 1, Box 512
Forest, VA 24551

Free Verse: First—Patrick Lawler, for "Hunger"; Second—Frederick A. Raborg, Jr., for "Sidewalk Preacher Man"; Third—Thomas De Conna, for "Before Seeds."

Light Verse: First—Debbie Hughes Gunia, for "Ideal Meal"; Second—Jack Bernier, for "A Clock In Danville, Va."; Third—Claire Mira Kentz, for "Computer-Crazed."

Traditional Verse: First—Frederick A. Raborg, Jr., for "To Her Important Face"; Second—Kay Harvey, for "Night Music"; Third—Thelma Monger Preble, for "I May Not Leave."

Haiku: First—Lewis Sanders; Second—Ruby P. Shackleford; Third—Lenard D. Moore.

Poetry Canada Review
P.O. Box 1280, Sta. A
Toronto, Ont. M5W 1G7
Canada

Mainstream Prize: Don Polson, for "What's In A Name."

Experimental Prize: Al Purdy, for "In Cabbagetown."

New Voices Prize: Sandy Bell, for "Let Me Say All I Have To Say."

The Poetry Center of the 92nd Street YM-YWHA
1395 Lexington Ave.
New York, NY 10028

Discovery/The Nation Poetry Contest: Karen Chamberlain, for "Point Conception: Sailing South"; Lee Edelman, for "The Inside View"; Paul Genega, for "Memorial To Labor Day"; Mary Jo Salter, for "Rocky Harbour, Newfoundland."

The Poetry Center
C. W. Post Center
Long Island University
Greenvale, NY 11548
Post Library Association Community Awards: First—Carol Miller, for "We All Lose Everything"; Second—Lynn Kozma, for "The Slug."
Winthrop Palmer Prize: L. J. Cunningham, for "For Grayson."
Post Poetry Center Awards: (Undergraduate) First—(see *Winthrop Palmer Prize,* above); Second—John Sergio, for "Sun God." (Graduate) Ralph McGinnis, for "Same Old Gang." (Alumni) First—Peg Wanser, for "First Love I See Tonight"; Second—Paulette Strachman, for "Gall's Children"; (Staff) First—David Petteys, for "Venetian Permutations"; Second—Margaret Seymour, for "The Beach In Winter."
Young Poets of Long Island Awards: Floyd and Dorothy Lyon Award—Richard Thau, for "An Electrical Separation For A Nuclear Family's Kids"; Second—Nancy Freilicher, for "Another Glimpse"; Third—Richelle Baugh, for "Lincoln Street House"; Honorable Mention, Peter Spagnuolo, for "Diners"; Social Issues Poetry—Bernadette Passade, for "Faces Without Features."

The Poetry Center
San Francisco State University
1600 Holloway Ave.
San Francisco, CA 94132
Poetry Center Book Award: Gloria Frym, for "Back To Forth"; Stephen Rodefer, for "Four Lectures."

Poetry Magazine
P.O. Box 4348
Chicago, IL 60680
Levinson Prize: Frederick Turner and Ernest Poppel, for "The Neural Lyre: Poetic Meter, The Brain, And Time."
Oscar Blumenthal Prize: William Matthews, for "Poems From Right" and "Poems From Wrong."
Eunice Tietjens Memorial Prize: Robert Pinsky, for "History Of My Heart."
Bess Hokin Prize: Lawrence Raab, for "Other Children."
Frederick Bock Prize: Richard Kenney, for "The Encantadas."

Poetry Northwest Magazine
University of Washington
4045 Brooklyn Ave., N.E.
Seattle, WA 98105
Helen Bullis Prize: Stephen Dunn, for five poems in summer and autumn 1982 issues.
Theodore Roethke Prize: Rodney Jones, for four poems in winter 1982-83 issue.
Young Poet's Prize: Suzanne Matson, for six poems in summer 1982 and winter 1982-83 issues.

Poetry Society of America
15 Gramercy Park
New York, NY 10003
Melville Cane Book Award: Ian Hamilton, for "Robert Lowell: A Biography."
William Carlos Williams Award: John Logan, for "Only The Dreamer Can Change The Dream."
Alice Fay Di Castagnola Award: Thomas Lux, for "Fireplace Full Of Crutches."
Shelley Memorial Award: Jon Anderson; Leo Connellan.
Gustav Davidson Award: Geraldine C. Little, for "Atropus Who Carried 'The Abhorred Shears' "; Sarah Lockwood, for "Late Voices From: 'The Merchant Of Venice.' "
Lucille Medwick Award: Willis Barnstone, for "The Boys Who Climb The Marble Squares On The Soldiers And Sailors Monument."
Gertrude B. Claytor Award: Virginia R. Terris, for "The Bridge: Clark Fork, Missoula, Montana."
Mary Carolyn Davies Award: Stanley Moss, for "For James Wright."
Consuelo Ford Award: Kathleen Spivack, for "The Water-Skaters."
Gordon Barber Award: Robert J. Levy, for "Kuli Loach."
Alfred Kreymborg Award: David McAleavey, for "While Holding Obsidion From M ____"
Celia B. Wagner Award: Carolyne Wright, for "Message To Cesar Vallejo."
John Masefield Award: Carolyne Wright, for "Josie Bliss, October 1971"; John Menfi, for "Dogwood Trees."
Elias Lieberman Student Poetry Award: Ann Chois, for "Dust Plates."

Poetry Society of Jacksonville
c/o Carlota Fowler
4411 Charles Bennett Dr.
Jacksonville, FL 32225
Fixed Forms of European Origin: First—Shirley Vatz, for "October Holding II"; Second—Patricia Johnson, for "Victims Of Vesuvius"; Charles Dickson, for "Considering The Emminence Of Three-Score Years & Ten."
Continuous Form (Free Verse): First—Ann Zoller, for "The Black Angel In Iowa City"; Second—Mildred Harding, for "Return"; Third—Elizabeth Friedmann, for "Christmas Rain."
Stanzaic Form: First—Alfhid Wallen, for "Gushers—& Some That Don't"; Second—Elizabeth Friedmann, for "Dominion"; Third—Mildred Harding, for "Sea Journey."

Poetry Society of Texas
c/o Don Stodghill, Awards Chairman
1424 Highland Rd.
Dallas, TX 75218
Nortex Press Award: Daisy Elmore Tennant, for "Now The Trumpet."
Voertman Award: Doris K. Ferguson, for "First Link In Chain Of Beginning."
Jess L. Gerding Memorial Award: Mary Stallard McGaughy, for "Symmetry."
Poetry Society of Texas Award: Gene Shuford, for

"Sleeping With Lions."
Lilith Lorraine Memorial Award: Mary Oler, for "Small Publishing Company."
Old South Prize: Gene Shuford, for "The News."
John A. Lubbe Memorial Award: Helen M. Rilenge, for "The Poet's Instrument."
Panhandle Penwomen Award: Violette Newton, for "A Bell Rang."
President's Award: Marcella Siegel, for "Walking His Slender Moment."
Abbie Frank Smith Memorial Award: Martha Freeman France, for "The Rest Is Up To Man."
Catherine Brooks Shuford Memorial Award: Evelyn Corry Appelbee, for "A Shorter Distance."
Appreciation Prize: Mrs. Clark Gresham, for "The Wild Gulls Call."
Eloise Kelley Adamson Memorial Award: Julia Hurd Strong, for "After The Razing."
Earl Bonine Memorial Award: Lois V. Thomas, for "Boone's Lick Ferry."
Mahan Award: Nelle Fertig, for "Not You At All."
Montgomery Award: Maurene McDonald, for "In Requiem."
Wheeler Sonnet Award: Julia Hurd Strong, for "Holy Days."
Aguinaldo A. LeNoir Memorial Award: Opie R. Houston, for "Paternalism."
Olivia Lewelling Cobb Memorial Award: Mildred Vorpahl Baass, for "Tribute To 'Livy.' "
David Atamian Memorial Award: Betty Brown Hicks, for "Other Men, Other Nations."
Narrative Prize: Susan Daubenspeck, for "The Journey Of Travis Henry."
Odessa Prize: Julia Hurd Strong, for "Huisache."
Joy Award: Mary Stallard McGaughy, for "The Reading."
Rabbi Arthur Bluhm Memorial Award: Buz Craft, for "Concert."
Experimental Poetry Award: Peggy Zuleika Lynch, for "Fountain Of Life."
Lyndon Baines Johnson Award: Marjorie Burney Willis, for "A Piece Of Texas."
Austin Poetry Society Memorial Award: Letty G. Moon, for "Alaska Fisherman."
Inez Puckett McEwen Award: Mickey Huffstutler, for "A Seed For Thought."
Moody Nelson Nichols Memorial Award: Julia Hurd Strong, for "2:55 A.M."
Vivian Page Wheeler Memorial Award: Bernice Chenault Howard, for "To Each Of You."
Odessa Award: Vivian Ricker, for "Pastured."
Country Trader Wood Burning Stove Award: Ida Fasel, for "Those Evenings."
Dedication Award: Mrs. Clark Gresham, for "A Taste Of Salt."
San Antonio Poetry Forum Award: James M. Thomas, for "Texas Hill Man."
William Arthur Bair Memorial Award: Carlyse Bliss, for "Planting Rice In Texas."
David and Hallie Harner Preece Award: Ida Fasel, for "Newcomers."
Dr. Henry Wallis Ewing Memorial Award: Pauline Durrett Robertson, for "Counting On Dad."

Anne Pence Davis Award: Vivian Ricker, for "Hymn Of Praise."
Dorothy Coker Memorial Award: Fay Duncan, for "Flea Market Photo."
Protest Prize: Ovon Ross, for "Such Love?"
Heritage Award: Violette Newton, for "The Gift Of Song."
Reverence Award: Sibyl Nichols Gutkowski, for "I Will Build A New Mountain."
Friendship Award: Mildred Vorpahl Baass, for "The Golden Threads Of Friendship."
Barron Award: N. W. Ogle, for "Through The Glass Darkly."
Carl and Evie Stripling Memorial Award: Maurene McDonald, for "Lament For A Deserted House."
F. G. Jeffers Memorial Award: Mary Coker Anderson, for "Goddess Of The Gulf."
Anne Pence Davis Memorial Award: Daisy Elmore Tennant, for "Slow Rain."
High Plains Chapter Memorial Award: Nelle Fertig, for "Prayer For A Space Traveler."
Palestine Poetry Society Award: Violette Newton, for "The Knock Upon The Door."
Ida Bassett Botts Memorial Award: Violette Newton, for "Notes For A Novel."
Maj. Donald J. Crocker Purple Heart Award: Bernice Chenault Howard, for "No Greater Love."
Harry Kovner Memorial Award: Gladyse Bryan Carrico, for "We Are Our Brother's Keeper."
Ernest Bobys Memorial Award: Alice Glenn, for "Recompense."
Bruce Bobys Lyric Award: Nelle Fertig, for "The Open Hand."
Helen Claire Mueller Memorial Award: Julia Hurd Strong, for "Miss Hattie Stern."
Alamo Prize: Hugh Pendexter III, for "Suburban Aubade."
Globe Peace Award: Alice Glenn, for "Christmas Eve."
Horse in Poetry Prize: Marcella Siegel, for "Central Park Carriage Horse."
Julia H. Ricker Memorial Award: Maurene McDonald, for "Stale Bread."
Bible Award: Vivian Ricker, for "The Samaritan."
Grace and Jerry Huffaker Memorial Award: Margarete Schuette, for "Amen—With Enthusiasm."
San Angelo Chapter Award: Maurene McDonald, for "Courage Incarnate."
Light Verse Award: Maurene McDonald, for "Retribution."
Galaxy of Verse Award: Violette Newton, for "Lucy."
Paul and Margaret Graham Award: Virginia Gravley, for "Field Trip."
Byliners of Corpus Christi Award: Ida Fasel, for "With A Comma."
Ada Elliot Award: Zinita Fowler, for "Poetic Surgery."
John A. Lubbe Memorial Award II: Joy Gresham Hagstrom, for "I Saw A Stallion."
Garland Chapter Award: Roberta Pipes Bowman,

for "Treasures Of Laughter."
Houston Chapter Award: Nelle Fertig, for "Oliver Hannis."
Patriotism Award: Darlene Bowden, for "A Candle Glows."
Katherine Schutze Haiku Memorial Award: Marianne McFarland McNiel, for "Lonely North Winds Wail."
San Antonio Poets Association Award: Reba Baker, for "The Tumbleweed And The Tree."
Mockingbird Chapter Award: Ann Matthews Moorhead, for "The Making Of Gardens."
Charles Day Windell Award: Roberta Pipes Bowman, for "Flight Of A Minor Poet."
Cibola Award: Pauline Crittenden, for "Green Grow The Willows."
Cat Award: Ida Fasel, for "My Lady."
Anne Parks Memorial Award: Velma Ashton Millican, for "Poet's Song."
Libby Stopple Lyric Award: Julia Hurd Strong, for "Wind Song."
Dream Award: Carlyse Bliss, for "Aurovision."
W. A. Stephenson R.F.D. Memorial Award: Budd Powell Mahan, for "The Mail Carrier."
Poetry Society of Texas Annual Awards Banquet Award: Julia Hurd Strong, for "Codicil."
Annual Critic's Award: Mary E. Petty, for "Enchantment."

Poetry Toronto
217 Northwood Dr.
Willowdale, Ont. M2M 2K5
Canada
Valentine Contest: First—Michael Warren, for "Valentine From Exile"; Second—Ben Phillips, for "The Love Faded."

Poets of the Foothills Art Center
809 15th St.
Golden, CO 80401
Riverstone International Poetry Chapbook Competition: Lynne McMahon, for "White Tablecloths."

Poets of the Vineyard
c/o Winnie E. Fitzpatrick, President
P.O. Box 77
Kenwood, CA 95452
Grand Prize: Eileen Lofthouse Sweet, for "The Fish Are Dying."
Traditional Form: First—John McCoy Parsons/Daniel, for "Resignation Ode"; Second—Donna Thomas, for "The Alchemist"; Third—John P. Caffey, Jr., for "Composite Confusion."
Short Free Verse: First—Margaret Hays, for "The Morning After Shrove Tuesday"; Second—Esther M. Leiper, for "At North Gate Pub"; Third—J. B. Grant, for "When You Multiply."
Long Free Verse: First—Maureen Hurley, for "The Architecture Of Bones"; Second—Daniel Williams, for "Trout/Man"; Third—Diane Glancy, for "Demosthenes."
Light/Humorous: First—Elna Forsell Pawson, for "Plain English"; Second—Roberta Stimmel, for "Wine: What Would We Do Without It?"; Third—Roses McReynolds, for "Two Minute Earthquake."

Short Verse: First—Mary R. Killian, for "If You Knew"; Second—Ellen Anderson, for "Random Roll"; Third—John P. Caffey, Jr., for "Preposterous Plots."
Haiku/Senryu: First—Stella Worley, for "Unseasonal Snow" and "I Find Hidden Wealth"; Second—Louise Hajek, for "Haiku"; Third—Winnie E. Fitzpatrick, for "Haiku."
Tanka: First—Mary B. Wall, for "Old Eyes"; Second—Nida E. Jones Ingram, for "Song At Midnight"; Third—Esther M. Leiper, for "March Inbetween."
Theme Poem: First—Stephen J. Wersan, for "Take Us To Your Liter"; Second—Eileen Lofthouse Sweet, for "Easter, California Style"; Third—Elizabeth Pizer, for "To Gaze Into Worlds Of Ferment Unspent."

Prairie Schooner Magazine
201 Andrews Hall
University of Nebraska
Lincoln, NE 68588
Strousse Memorial Award: Steven Bauer, for poems in fall 1982 issue.

Primapara Magazine
P.O. Box 371
Oconto, WI 54154
Linda Jensen Memorial Award: Bonnie Rehliner, for "The Last Debutante."
Marie Dolan Memorial Award: Sandra Lindow, for "Some Things Do Last: Neilsville, Wisconsin, 1958."
Lydia Kamke Memorial Award: Nancy Ellrodt, for "The Stripper."

Pudding Magazine
2384 Hardesty Dr. S.
Columbus, OH 43204
National Looking Glass Chapbook Competition: Fred Waage, for "Minestrone."

Pulitzer Prize (see Columbia University)

Pulpsmith Magazine/New York Quarterly
5 Beekman St.
New York, NY 10038
Madeline Sadin Award: J. R. Solonche, for "On Being Asked By A Child To Teach Her How To Tell Time."
Edna St. Vincent Millay Award: Carol Henrie, for "A Childless Woman Speaks."

Quarterly Review of Literature
26 Haslet Ave.
Princeton, NJ 08540
Contemporary Poetry Series: Jane Hirschfield, for "Alaya"; Christopher Bursk, for "Little Harbor"; Marguerite Guzman Bouvard, for "Journeys Over Water"; and translations from Polish poet Wislawa Szymborska and Swedish poet Lars Gustafsson.

Religious Arts Guild
25 Beacon St.
Boston, MA 02108
Dorothy Rosenberg Annual Poetry Award: First—Michael J. Kiefel, for "Sign"; Second—Robert S. Lehman, for "Constancy."

Rhode Island State Poetry Society
c/o Muriel Hanna
28 Oakhill Ave.
Warwick, RI 02886
Chapbook Award: Gail Ghai, for "Woman Above The Water."
Rhymed Verse: First—Thelma Lantz; Second—Dorothy Wilder Halleran.
Free Verse: First—Brian Ellerbeck; Second—Naomi Cherkofsky.

Rhyme Time Magazine
P.O. Box 2377
Coeur d'Alene, ID 83814
Dreams Contest: First—Betty Mitchell; Second—Beulah Strobel; Third—M. Rosser Lunsford.
Open Title Contest: First—Winnie E. Ftizpatrick, for "Love's Lament"; Second—Alice Mackenzie Swaim, for "Sighs For Lost Seas And Summers"; Third—Helen E. Rilling, for "An Old Barn."
My First Love Contest: First—Richard Franklin; Second—Ben Sweeney; Third—Madolyn Jamieson.

San Francisco Foundation
500 Washington St.
San Francisco, CA 94111
James D. Phelan Literary Award (this year awarded to a poet): Gary Young, for "The Dream Of A Moral Life."

Saskatchewan Writers Guild
Box 3986
Regina, Sask. S4P 3R9
Canada
Poetry Awards: Kim Dales, for "Sanctuary"; Thelma Poirier, for "She Gathers Feathers"; Bruce Rice, for "Chased By Horses."
Poetry Manuscript: Mick Burrs, for "The Blue Pools Of Paradise"; Lorna Crozier, for "The Weather"; E. F. Dyck, for "Pisscat Songs And Other Failed Poems."

Saxifrage Prize
36C Stratford Hills
Chapel Hill, NC 27514
Saxifrage Prize: David Brendan Hopes, for "The Glacier's Daughter."

Seven Magazine
3630 N.W. 22nd St.
Oklahoma City, OK 73107
Jesse Stuart Contest: First—G. Bruce Bunao, for "Night Visit"; Second—Serena Fusek for "Escape," and Rachel Adams for "A Remembrance Of Lemons"; Third—Regina Murray Brault, for "Precious Possession"; Fourth—Betsey Kennedy, for "Forewarning Of Autumn."

Signpost Press
412 N. State St.
Bellingham, WA 93225
Signpost Press Poetry Chapbook Competition: Linda Mizejewski, for "The Other Woman."

South Dakota State Poetry Society
c/o Dr. Mary Weinkauf
914 University Blvd.
Mitchell, SD 57301

Sonnet: First—Jessie Ruhl Miller, for "Gift Enclosed"; Second—Anna Marie Weinress, for "Goodbye Caboose"; Third—Betty Jane Simpson, for "Ernest Hemingway: In Memorium."
Humorous: First—Elizabeth House, for "A Patient's Lament"; Second—Mary B. Wall, for "Ask Eve"; Third—Jessie Ruhl Miller, for "Apply The Rod Equally, Equitably."
Free Verse: First—Emma Dimit, for "I, Arachne"; Second—Alice Mackenzie Swaim, for "Last Splendid Leaf"; Third—Carlee Swann, for "Trophy, One Feather."
Midwest: First—Lois Bogue, for "The Land Of Dakota"; Second—Dorothy W. Worth, for "On The Flyway"; Third—Thelma Ireland, for "Surprise."
Poet's Choice: First—Audrae Visser, for "Hurry, Hurry, Hurry"; Second—Jane Hoyt Lamb, for "Conflagration"; Third—Margaret Stallkamp, for "Haiku."
Storm: First—Lois Bogue, for "Christmas Snowstorm"; Second—Ferne Ramsdell, for "Sinister, The Silence"; Third—Jane Hoyt Lamb, for "The Storm."
Poetry for Children: First—Ferne Ramsdell, for "Horses, Horses"; Second—Robert C. Vessey, for "Cuddly Puppies"; Third—Lois Bogue, for "Cloud Pictures."
The Family: First—Margaret Brekke, for "Growing Pains"; Second—Robert C. Vessy, for "Unwed Mother"; Third—Ferne Ramsdell, for "A Pastor For Patsy."
Badger Clark: First—Carlee Swann, for "Still Revising"; Second—Margaret Brekke, for "Return Of Badger"; Third—Audrae Visser, for "Badger Clark's Soliloquy."

Southern California Poet's Pen
c/o J. P. Watson
P.O. Box 85152, MB 187
San Diego, CA 92138
Poetry Contest: First—Judith M. Frank, for "Song Across The Space"; Second—June Owens, for "Spin Poems"; Third—Grettelle Suzanne LeGron, for "Yesterday's Window."

Southern Poetry Review
Dept. of English
University of North Carolina
Charlotte, NC 28223
Guy Owen Poetry Prize: Coleman Barks, for "The Great Blue Heron."

Southwest Review
Southern Methodist University
Dallas, TX 75275
Elizabeth Matchett Stover Memorial Award: William Stafford, for "Beyond Appearance."

Spitball Magazine
231 E. 7th St.
Covington, KY 41011
Spitball Poetry Contest: First—Nancy Breen, for "Devotion"; Second—Robert Rinehart, for "Candlestick Park"; Third—Gene Fehler for "If Robert Frost Were Billy Martin, 'Stopping By Woods On A Snowy Evening' Might Be

'Grabbing An Illegal Bat At Yankee Stadium',"
and Jim Palana for "Recalling Vic Wertz";
Fifth—Terry O'Toole, for "Trivia Hotline";
Sixth—Timothy Peeler, for "Touching All
The Bases."

The Spoon River Quarterly
P.O. Box 1443
Peoria, IL 61655
Editor's Award: Walter McDonald, for "Witching On Dry Ground."

Stanford University
Creative Writing Center
Dept. of English
Stanford, CA
Wallace E. Stegner Fellowships (in poetry):
Andrew Hudgins; Ruth Olson.

Stone Country Magazine
P.O. Box 132
Menemsha, MA 02552
Phillips Poetry Award: Haywood Jackson, for
"Holidays," and Philip Bartram for "The
Messenger" (for fall/winter); Judith Steinbergh, for "On Planting Holland Bulbs In
November" (spring/summer).

Walter F. Stromer
410 7th Ave., S.
Mt. Vernon, IA 52314
Hephaestes Poetry Contest: First—Irene Payan,
for "Nursing Home"; Second—Carrie Takamatsu, for "The Tides Of Depression";
Third—Gary W. Plourde, Sr., for "A Light
Tragedy."

Syracuse University
Dept. of English
Syracuse, NY 13210
Allan Birk Prize: George Honecker, for "By
The Influence And Risk Of Knowing Only
Ghosts."
Loring Williams Memorial Prize: John Kandl, for
group of poems including "Another Zebra"
and "Morning Off Key West."
Wiffin Prize: Sherry E. Fairchok, for "Behind A
Lit Window In Upstate New York."
Delmore Schwartz Prize: David Lazar, for "In
Sumatra."

Texas Institute of Letters
Box 8594
Waco, TX 76714
Voertman Poetry Award: Naomi Shihab Nye,
for "Hugging The Jukebox"; Thomas Whitbread, for "Whomp And Moonshiver."

Triton College
2000 Fifth Ave.
River Grove, IL 60171
Salute to the Arts Poetry Contest: Freedom—Tom
Benediktsson for "Manumission," Daniel Daly
for "In Between Times He Played," Alfreda de
Silva for "Night Walk," Bernhard Frank for
"Blue Jay," Connie J. Green for "Chimney
Swifts," Norman Leer for "Choices," Jan
Rejzek for "A Pilgrim," Nicholas Rinaldi for
"The Road," Franklin D. Romero for "Bag
Full Of Blues Travels," and Ruth Zimmerman

for "Becky." Triumph—John D. Briggs for
"Talk To Me," Soraya Erian for "Flying Mermaid," Gary Fincke for "Where We Used To
Be," Marvin Gerstein for "Untitled," Mykl
Herdklotz for "Pursuit Of Happiness," Myron
S. Hoyt for "Bright Girl Running," Richard
Nilsen for "Around The Campfire," Drew
Shaw for "Icarus Returned," John A. Sours for
"The Flying Miguel Vasquez," and Margaret
Watts for "To The Stow Ferry On Its Last
Trip." Dilemmas—William B. Cannon for
"Diffraction," Alfreda de Silva for "Going
Back," Gary Fincke for "Selling Paper," Bernhard Frank for "Woman Between Sandwich
Boards," Connie J. Green for "February-July
Love," Nata Robinson for "Wedding
Women," Sarah Roller for "The Science Of
Forgetting," Ron Whitehead for "From
Marduk To Urantia," R. N. Wijnants for "Like
Last Year," and Marcia Youngman for "And
To The Republic For Which It Stands." Local
winners—Samuel Blechman for "Euphony,"
Ruth El Saffer for "Downstream Deliberating" and "Beginnings," Agnes Tatera for
"Declaration Of Independence" and "Act
Three Rewrite," Dolores Tully for "Dream
Weaver," Tina Valentino for "On Winchester," and Sharon Wydra for "My Next
Duchess." Grade school winners—Kelly
Conner for "Timmy," Wendy Schaedel for
"The Moment Before Triumph," and Tammy
Thomas for "Freedom."

University of Massachusetts Press
Box 429
Amherst, MA 01004
Juniper Prize: Marc Hudson, for "Afterlight."

University of Missouri Press
P.O. Box 7088
Columbia, MO 65205
Devins Award for Poetry: Wesley McNair, for
"The Faces Of Americans In 1853."

University of Pittsburgh Press
127 N. Bellefield Ave.
Pittsburgh, PA 15260
Agnes Starrett Poetry Prize: Katherine Anne
Daniels, for "The White Wave."

University of Toronto
Toronto, Ont. M5S 1A1
Canada
Pratt Medal for Poetry: Lyn King, for "A Terrible
Open-endedness"; Runner-up—Jeffery Donaldson, for "With Heidegger In A Clearing."

University of Toronto
Victoria College
Toronto, Ont. M5S 1K7
Canada
Alta Lind Cook Prize: Jeffery Donaldson, for
"With Heidegger In A Clearing."

University of Toronto
University College
Toronto, Ont. M5S 1A1
Canada
Norma Epstein Award (poetry): First—Greg
Scully, for Talks By The Clock"; Second—

Karen S. Pieper, for "Messages"; (Third through Sixth not for poetry); Seventh—Rita Furgiuele, for "Retirement"; Eighth—Robert Lindsey, for "Eight Tongues Say No Hands."
National Norma Epstein Award: Richard Stevenson, for "Driving Offensively."

Utah Arts Council
617 East South Temple
Salt Lake City, UT 84102
Utah Original Writing Competition—
Book-Length Collection of Poems: First—C. L. Rawlins, for "A Ceremony On Bare Ground: Great Basin Poems"; Second—Stephen Ruffus for "Borderline," and Joseph H. Bottom IV for "On The Unity Of The Intellect Against The Averroists."
Serious Poetry: First—Janene S. Bowen, for "Traveling Southern Utah And Other Poems"; Second—Kathy Fagan, for "Migration And Other Poems."
Serious Poetry Related To A Single Theme: First—David Lee, for "The Muffler And The Law"; Second—Edward Byrne, for "Words Spoken, Words Unspoken."
Light Verse: First—Lael W. Hill, for "Rube Barbs"; Second—Jean B. Boyce, for "They Say . . . And Other Poems."

Virginia Quarterly Review
One West Range
Charlottesville, VA 22903
Emily Clark Balch Prize (poetry): Conrad Hilberry, for "Mexico: Explosions At 4 A.M."

Washington State Library
AJ-11
Olympia, WA 98504
Governor's Writers Award (poetry): William Matthews, for "Flood."

West Virginia Poetry Society
c/o Edith H. Love
501 Voorhis Rd.
Morgantown, WV 26505
West Virginia Poetry Society Award (category 1): First—Mary C. Hertz, for "The Third Voice."
West Virginia Poetry Society Award (category 2): First—William Paulk, for "Matthew."
Limerick Award: First—Thomas Lynn, for No Title.
Haiku Award: First—Karen Maceira, for No Title.
Student Award: First—Kim Tate, for "My Walk With You"; Second—Tracie Wood, for "The Dark Mask"; Third—Denise Danford, for "William Stevens."
Parkersburg Chapter Award: First—Mary C. Ferris, for "All Cows Eat Grass"; Second—Esther M. Leiper, for "Lines Composed Upon Compost."
Parkersburg Chapter Youth Category: First—Ravindra Rajmane, for "Persistent Remorse."
Lee Mays Chapter Award: First—Mary Elizabeth Ward, for "Alpha"; Second—D. M. Anton, for "Moving South"; Third—Amy Jo Schoonover, for "Spring Fashion Show."

Charleston Chapter Award: First—Gary P. Adkins, for "Up That West Virginia Hollow."
Wheeling Chapter Award: First—Louise Marsh Gabriel, for "Fountain Of Youth."
Harold C. Jacobs Memorial Award: First—Alice Mackenzie Swaim, for "At The Wood's Green Heart"; Second—Edna M. Vogel, for "Another World Created."
Morgantown Chapter Award: First—Elaine Rowley, for "Christmas In A One Room Schoolhouse."
Edith Hite McElfresh Award: First—Edith H. Love, for "Liz"; Second—Gary P. Adkins, for "You Can Never Come Back Home Again."
Anne Clendenning Award: First—Jaye Giammarino, for "Summer Happening"; Second—Margarette Parker, for "Lady In Waiting"; Third—Anthony Mendenhall, for "North Pole Parole."
O'Connor-Parker Award: First—Patricia A. Lawrence, for "Nocturne"; Second—June Owens, for "Fantasia On June Night Timepieces"; Third—Helen A. Wolfe, for "My Days."
Vance W. McKee Memorial Award: First—Pauline Shortridge, for "Spring Freeze"; Book Prize—June Owens, for "Love"s Constancy."
George M. Nolte Award: First—Mary Holmes Jones, for "Mountain Paradise."
Osa Mays Memorial Award: First—Alice Mackenzie Swaim, for "No Longer Limited"; Second—Richard Heinemann, for "Lines On The Death Of A Leader": Third—Peggy Flanders, for "Preoccupation."

World of Poetry
2431 Stockton Blvd.
Sacramento, CA 95817
Special Poetry Contest: Grand Prize—Ruth Newton Mattos, for "Winter Solstice"; First—Bobbie Joe White, for "The God Of Guts."

World Poetry Day Committee
1110 N. Venetian Dr.
Miami Beach, FL 33139
Annual Contest: Blanche Landers; Mickey Huffstutler.

Writer's Digest
9933 Alliance Rd.
Cincinnati, OH 45242
Writer's Digest Writing Competition (poetry): First—John G. Hammond, for "Fish Story"; Second—Michael Spence, for "The Factory"; Third—Glenna Holloway, for "Falling Weather."

Writers Unlimited
c/o Mildred Henderson
907 Canal St.
Pascagoula, MS 39567
Writers Unlimited Award: First—Vivian Smallwood, for "The Midwife And The Dwarfs"; Second—Winona Kernan Champagne, for "The Tale Of Tante Titine"; Third—Laverne Rison, for "La Llorona."
Mark Hicks Memorial Award: First—Grace Haynes Smith, for "Pompeii Revisited"; Second—Betsy Kennedy, for "When 'Billy

The Kid' Played 'The Ritz' ''; Third—Esther M. Leiper, for "Fall Of A Bull Rider."
Rowan Memorial Award: First—Alice Glenn, for "Requiem For Old Pie"; Second—Grace Holliday Scott, for "Beauty Descending"; Third—Madolyn Jamieson, for "The Storm."
Wilma Harper Memorial Award: First—Helen Thomas Allison, for "In The Shadow Of A Rainbow"; Second—June P. Gergeron, for "Adella"; Third—Betty Maine, for "Banquets And Beans."
Patriotic Award: First—James W. Proctor, for "The Medic"; Second—Day Lander, for "Them Cold Dam' Yankees"; Third—Douglas Elmore, for "Peach Blossoms."
Traditional Award: First—Dorothy Winslow Wright, for "A Secret Laughing Place"; Second—Esther M. Leiper, for "Before Childbirth"; Third—Charles B. Dickson, for "Musing While Watching My Wife Engrossed In A Novel."
Limerick Award: First—Mary C. Ferris, for "There, There"; Second—Laverne Rison, for "There Was A Young Lady Named Lee"; Third—Ben Sweeney, for "Good Shough."
Lyric Poetry Award: First—Roberta Graham Powalski, for "False Face"; Second—Maurine McDonald, for "Faith's Advocate"; Third—Helen Thomas Allison, for "My Autumn Poem."
Sea Award: First—Carolan S. Norwood, for "Seagulls"; Second—Memye Curtis Tucker, for "First Sail"; Third—Vivian Smallwood, for "The Request."
Touch of Earth Award: First—Winona Kernan Champagne, for "Shadows"; Second—Sheryl L. Nelms, for "Country Cream"; Third—Ann L. Zoller, for "A Birthing."

Pascagoula Civic Guild Award: First—Lenard D. Moore, for "Rain Mile After Mile"; Second—Dorothy Winslow Wright, for "In That Empty House"; Third—Grace Holliday Scott, for "The Sorrowing Doe."
Open Mind Award: First—Dorothy Winslow Wright, for "Night Walkers"; Second—Margaret Baker McKinnon, for "Word Wallowing"; Third—Ruth S. Perot, for "Time's Chariot."
Pascagoula Evening Civic League Award: First—Maurine McDonald, for "Harvest Yield"; Second—Lois Snelling, for "Woodland Meditation"; Third—Ruth S. Perot, for "The Stream."
Magnolia Award: First—Roberta Graham Powalski, for "Legacy Of A Legend"; Second—Mary Frances Langford, for "The Haunted Mansion"; Third—Alice Glenn, for "Mississippi Blues."

Yale University Library
Box 1603A, Yale Sta.
New Haven, CT 06520
Bollingen Prize in Poetry: Anthony Hecht; John Hollander.

Yale University Press
92A, Yale Sta.
New Haven, CT 06520
Yale Series of Younger Poets: Richard Kenney, for "The Evolution Of The Flightless Bird."

Yankee Magazine
Dublin, NH 03444
Yankee Poetry Awards: First—Ann Stanford, for "The Woman On The Island"; Second (tie)—Raymond Roseliep for "Low Tide," and John Hodgen for "Old Men Know The Sound That The Earth Makes Is Sad"; Third—Martin Robbins, for "River Piece."

Acknowledgments

The publisher expresses appreciation to the authors represented in this anthology for graciously permitting the inclusion of their poetry.

In addition, credit has been given to all magazines where material in this volume originally appeared, with their names stated after each respective poem.

In individual instances where certain authors, magazines or book publishers required special acknowledgments or credit lines for copyrights they control, such recognition is hereby given as follows:

"Gotterdammerung," by Bonnie L. Alexander, first appeared in the *Southern Humanities Review,* Vol. XV, No. 1, Winter, 1981. Copyright © 1981 by Auburn University, Auburn, AL.

"Grand Central Station," by Asa Paschal Ashanti, first appeared in *Black American Literature Forum,* Summer, 1982. Copyright © 1982 by Asa Paschal Ashanti and *Black American Literature Forum.*

"From Vietnam Letters," by R. L. Barth, first appeared in the *Southern Humanities Review,* Vol. XV, No. 1, Winter, 1981. Copyright © 1981 by Auburn University, Auburn, AL.

"Jane Was With Me," by Marvin Bell, first appeared in *The Atlantic Monthly* and is reprinted with permission of Marvin Bell. Copyright © 1982 by Marvin Bell.

"My Old Friend," by S. Ben-Tov, first appeared in *Sojourner,* the New England Women's Journal of News, Opinions and the Arts (143 Albany St., Cambridge, MA 02139) Vol. 6, September, 1980. Reprinted with permission of Sojourner, Inc.

"Voyeur," by P. C. Bowman, first appeared in the *Southern Humanities Review,* Vol. XV, No. 4, Winter, 1981. Copyright © by Auburn University, Auburn, AL.

"What Makes Things Tick," by Marion D. Cohen, first appeared in *Sojourner,* the New England Women's Journal of News, Opinions and the Arts (143 Albany St., Cambridge, MA 02139) Vol. 7, No. 1, September, 1981. Reprinted with permission of Sojourner, Inc.

"Struggling and Surviving," by Schavi Mali Diara, first appeared in *Black American Literature Forum,* Summer, 1982. Copyright © 1982 by Schavi Mali Diara and *Black American Literature Forum.*

"Tantrik X-ray," by Clayton Eshleman, is copyright (c) 1983 by Clayton Eshleman and published in FRACTURE (Black Sparrow Press).

"Wishes and Needs," by Sybil P. Estess, first appeared in the *Southern Humanities Review,* Vol. XVII, No. 4, Fall, 1983. Copyright © by Auburn University, Auburn, AL.

"Letters from Jerusalem," by Amy Clampitt, first appeared in *The Yale Review* and is published in her book, THE KINGFISHER (Alfred A. Knopf, Inc.). Copyright © 1983 by Alfred A. Knopf, and reprinted with permission.

"On Nudity," by Jorge de Sena, translated from the Portuguese by Alexis Levitin, is copyright © 1982 by Alexis Levitin and reprinted with permission.

"Jewish Wife," by Marcia Falk, is copyright © by Marcia Falk and reprinted with permission.

"Flame," by Brewster Ghiselin, first appeared in *Poetry.* Copyright © 1983 by The Modern Poetry Association and reprinted with permission of the Editor of *Poetry* and of the author, Brewster Ghiselin.

"Home," by James W. Hood, first appeared in the *Southern Humanities Review,* Vol. XVII, No. 2, Spring, 1983, p. 132. Copyright © 1983 by Auburn University, Auburn, AL.

"To Mark, My Retarded Brother, Who Lived 20 Years and Learned to Speak 300 Words," first appeared in the *Southern Humanities Review,* Vol. XV, No. 4, Fall, 1981. Copyright © 1981 by Auburn University, Auburn, AL.

"A Chant for Michael S. Harper," by Kenneth S. McClane, first appeared in *Black American Literature Forum,* Spring, 1981. Copyright © 1981 by Kenneth S. McClane and *Black American Literature Forum.*

"Against the Odds," by Harold G. McCurdy, first appeared in *Theology Today* (January, 1982) and is reprinted with permission of the author and publisher.

"Veni Creator," by Czeslaw Milosz, first appeared in *Antaeus.* Copyright © 1983 by Czeslaw Milosz. From the book, THE SEPARATE NOTEBOOKS, by Czeslaw Milosz, published by the Ecco Press, Inc., 1983. Reprinted by permission.

"Two In Twilight," by Eugenio Montale, translated by William Arrowsmith and copyright © by William Arrowsmith in the United States, is reprinted with permission of the translator. The poem also was published in the book, EUGENIO MONTALE: SELECTED POEMS (Arnoldo Mondador Editore) and copyright © 1957 in Italy by Arnoldo Mondador Editore.

"Winter Sermon: Northside Chicago," by G. E. Murray, first appeared in the *Southern Humanities Review,* Vol. XV, No. 1, Winter, 1981. Copyright © 1981 by Auburn University, Auburn, AL.

"A Touch of Impatience," by Peter of Blois, translated by Fleur Adcock, is included in her book, THE VIRGIN AND THE NIGHTINGALE, published by Bloodaxe Books, 1983.

"Skin-Game," by Elisavietta Ritchie, first appeared in *Poet Lore* and is included in her book, RAKING THE SNOW (Washington Writers Publishing House, 1982).

"A Farewell," by May Sarton, first appeared in *The Paris Review* and is reprinted with permission of May Sarton and *The Paris Review.*

"Seeing Wind," by Floyd Skloot, first appeared in the *Southwest Review;* reprinted with permission of the *Southwest Review.* Copyright © 1983 by Southern Methodist University Press.

The English translation of the poem, "Life," by Edith Södergran (translated by Christer I. Mossberg), first appeared in *Calyx,* A Journal of Art and Literature by Women, Vol. 5, Nos. 2 and 3.

"Accusations 4," by Jane Somerville, first appeared in *Sojourner,* the New England Women's Journal of News, Opinions and the Arts (143 Albany St., Cambridge, MA 02139) Vol. 6, No. 11, July, 1981. Reprinted with permission of Sojourner, Inc.

"Necessity," by Rhea Tregebov, first appeared in *The Canadian Forum,* Toronto, Ont., Canada.

"Birthday," by Ellen Wittlinger, first appeared in *The Antioch Review,* Vol. 41, No. 3, Summer, 1983. Copyright © 1983 by The Antioch Review, Inc.; reprinted with permission of the Editors.

"Jozepha," by Ree Young, first appeared in the *Southern Humanities Review,* Vol. XVII, No. 4, Fall, 1983, p. 325. Copyright © 1983 by Auburn University, Auburn, AL.

The following poems first appeared in *America* and are reprinted with permission of America Press, Inc., 106 West 56th St., New York, NY 10019. Copyright © 1983 by America Press, Inc.: "The Small Brown Bat," by Dorothy Donnelly; "In Memory of Eight Firemen," by Lawrence Dugan; "The Young Skater," by Peter Krok; "Climbing Out," by Warren Leamon; "A Middle-Aged Dream," by Larry Coe Prater; "Canoe at Evening," by Robert Siegel; " Transparencies," by Robert Joe Stout.

The following poems first appeared in *The Atlantic Monthly* and are reprinted with permission of the authors and of *The Atlantic Monthly.* Copyright © 1983 by The Atlantic Monthly Company, Boston, Mass.: "Viewing The Body," by Sharon Bryan; "The Image Maker," by Stanley Kunitz; "Mark's Used Parts," by Rennie McQuilkin; "Ibis," by Harvey Oxenhorn; "Relativity," by Charles Pratt.

The Ball State University Forum holds the international copyright on the following poems which first appeared in that publication: "Orleans Revisited," by Vincent Canizaro, and "Rhythm of Dishes," by Karen Steiner.

The following poems first appeared in *The Classical Outlook,* copyright by American Classical League: "Horace Carmina," by Georgia C. Atwood; "Reflections at Delphi," by Martha Dreadin Davis; "Ode's Bodkins," by Tony M. Lentz; "Slowly the Evening: Athens," by Sarah Litsey; "Nevertheless" and "Erase Tape," by Robert J. M. Lindsay; "Narcissus In Death," by David E. Middleton; "Greece," by Christina Rainsford; "Euripides: Iphigenia Among the Taurians (1138-51)," by Diana Robin; "Live Life Now," by Susan K. Weiler; "A Curious Fancy," by Rose Williams.

The following poems first appeared in *The Hudson Review:* "For Us To Lose Freshness," by Anna Akhmatova, translated by Judith Hemschemeyer and Anne Wilkinson. Reprinted by permission from *The Hudson Review,* Vol. XXXIV, No. 4 (Winter, 1981-1982). Copyright © 1981 by Judith Hemschemeyer and Anne Wilkinson; "Procession," by Philip Booth. Reprinted by permission from *The Hudson Review,* Vol. XXXV, No. 2 (Summer, 1982). Copyright © 1982 by Philip Booth; "A Christian Childhood," by Prescott Evarts, Jr. Reprinted by permission from *The Hudson Review,* Vol. XXXV, No. 4 (Winter, 1982-1983). Copyright © 1983 by Prescott Evarts, Jr.; "Observations of the Tower Block," by Ruth Fainlight. Reprinted by permission from *The Hudson Review,* Vol. XXXV, No. 2 (Summer, 1982). Copyright © 1982 by Ruth Fainlight; "Photograph of My Mother as a Young Girl," by Dana Gioia. Reprinted by permission from *The Hudson Review,* Vol. XXXIV, No. 3 (Autumn, 1981). Copyright © 1981 by Dana Gioia; "In the Light of October," by Emily Grosholz. Reprinted by permission from *The Hudson Review,* Vol. XXXV, No. 1 (Spring, 1982). Copyright © 1982 by Emily Grosholz; "The Cricket," by Krassin Himmirsky, translated by Denise Levertov. Reprinted by permission from *The Hudson Review,* Vol. XXXV, No. 4 (Winter, 1982-1983). Copyright © 1983 by Krassin Himmirsky and Denise Levertov; "Venetian Blinds," by Martha Hollander. Reprinted by permission from *The Hudson Review,* Vol. XXXV, No. 1 (Spring, 1982). Copyright © 1982 by Martha Hollander; "Fall," by Kate Jennings. Reprinted by permission from *The Hudson Review,* Vol. XXXV, No. 2 (Summer, 1982). Copyright © 1982 by Kate Jennings; "The Same," by Robert Louthan. Reprinted by permission from *The Hudson Review,* Vol. XXXV, No. 1 (Spring, 1982). Copyright © 1982 by Robert Louthan; "The Hour Before Dawn," by Jayanta Mahapatra. Reprinted by permission from *The Hudson Review,* Vol. XXXV, No. 2 (Summer, 1982). Copyright © 1982 by Jayanta Mahapatra; "On Burnett Avenue," by Jane Mayhall. Reprinted by permission from *The Hudson Review,* Vol. XXXIV, No. 2 (Summer, 1981). Copyright © 1981 by Jane Mayhall; "Poppies," by Robert McDowell. Reprinted by permission from *The Hudson Review,* Vol. XXXIV, No. 2 (Summer, 1981). Copyright © 1981 by Robert McDowell; "Winter Approaches," by Boris Pasternak, translated by Jon Stallworthy and Peter France. Reprinted by permission from *The Hudson Review,* Vol. XXXIV, No. 4 (Winter, 1981-1982). Copyright © 1981 by Jon Stallworthy and Peter France; "Schilfgraben," by James Reiss. Reprinted by permission from *The Hudson Review,* Vol. XXXV, No. 4 (Winter, 1982-1983). Copyright © 1983 by James Reiss; "In the Garden at Midnight," by Barry Spacks. Reprinted by permission from *The Hudson Review,* Vol. XXXV, No.4 (Winter, 1982-1983). Copyright © 1983 by Barry Spacks; "Little Rooms," by William Stafford. Reprinted by permission from *The Hudson Review,* Vol. XXXV, No. 3 (Autumn, 1982). Copyright © 1982 by William Stafford; "Looking at a Painting of Constantinople by Paul Signac," by Robert Swanson. Reprinted by permission from *The Hudson Review,* Vol. XXXV, No. 4 (Winter, 1982-1983). Copyright © 1983 by Robert Swanson; "Jewelweed," by Gail Mazur. Reprinted by permission from *The Hudson Review,* Vol. XXXVI, No. 2 (Summer, 1983). Copyright © 1983 by Gail Mazur; "They Used to Have a Homecoming Day," by Richmond Lattimore. Reprinted by permission from *The Hudson Review,* Vol. XXXIV, No. 1 (Spring, 1981). Copyright © 1981 by Richmond Lattimore; "The Epilogue," by Charles Tomlinson. Reprinted by permission from *The Hudson Review,* Vol. XXXIV, No. 1 (Spring, 1981). Copyright © 1981 by Charles Tomlinson.

The following poems first appeared in *The Literary Review,* published by Fairleigh Dickinson University, Madison, NJ 07940, reprinted with permission of the Editors: "God," by Willis Barnstone, Spring, 1981, Vol. 24, No. 3; "Hands," by Marguerite C. Bouvard, Spring, 1981, Vol. 24, No. 3; "Winter Apples," by Deborah Burnham, Spring, 1982, Vol. 25, No. 3; "Telling the Bees," by David Citino, Spring, 1981, Vol. 24, No. 3; "The Ideal and The Real" and "New Marriage," by Richard Eberhart, Summer, 1982, Vol. 25, No. 4; "I, Too, Look Into the Fire," by Israel Eliraz, translated by Beate Hein Bennett, Spring, 1983, Vol. 26, No. 3; "After the Gleaning," by Stefan George, translated by Peter Viereck, Fall, 1982, Vol. 26, No. 1; "The Demons of the Cities," by Georg Heym, translated by Peter Viereck, Fall, 1982, Vol. 26, No. 1; "Alchemy," by Marjorie Deiter Keyishian, Spring, 1982, Vol. 25, No. 3; "To Himself," by Giacomo Leopardi, translated by Burton Raffel, Spring, 1981, Vol. 24, No. 3; "Yesterday's Children," by Jerome Mazzaro, Summer, 1982, Vol. 25, No. 4; "Gifts from Gamberaia," by Philip Raisor, Spring, 1982, Vol. 25, No. 3; "Dear Neighbor God," by Rainer Maria Rilke, translated by Steven Lautermilch, Summer, 1981, Vol. 24, No. 4; "For Eve On Her Seventieth Birthday," by Chad Walsh, Summer, 1982, Vol. 25, No. 4; "In The Green Stream," by Wang Wei, translated by Joseph Lisowski, Spring, 1983, Vol. 26, No. 3; "If I Forget Thee," by David Zeiger, Spring, 1981, Vol. 24, No. 3.

The following poems first appeared in *The Massachusetts Review* and are reprinted with permission; copyright © 1981 and 1982 by The Massachusetts Review, Inc.: "Marconi Station, South Wellfleet," by Steven Bauer, Vol. 22, No. 2; "The Portrait," by Jane Flanders, Vol. 22, No. 2; "Paris," by Renee G. Hartman, Vol. 23, No. 2; "For the Sin," by Shirley Kaufman, Vol. 23, No. 2; "On Growth and Form," by Howard Nemerov, Vol. 22, No. 1; "Salamander, Severed in Spring Plowing," by David Lyon, Vol. 22, No. 1; "Away," by Andrew Salkey, Vol. 22, No. 1; "Paper White Narcissus," by Chase Twichell, Vol. 23, No. 2.

The following poems first appeared in *The New Orleans Review,* copyright © 1982 by Loyola University, reprinted with permission of *The New Orleans Review:* "Braille for Left Hand," by Octavio Armand, translated by Carol Maier; "In a Suburb of the Spirit," by Paul

Hoover; "How Many Times," by Eric Trethewey.

The following poems first appeared in *The New Yorker* and are reprinted with permission of the authors and of *The New Yorker:* "Finale," by Dick Allen. Copyright © 1983 by Dick Allen; "Freeze," by George Amabile. Copyright © 1983 by George Amabile; "A Short History of the Middle West," by Robert Dana. Copyright © 1983 by Robert Dana; "Dear George Eliot," by Peter Kane Dufault. Copyright © 1983 by Peter Kane Dufault; "Chelsea," by Robert Long. Copyright © 1983 by Robert Long.

The following poems first appeared in *Poetry,* copyright © 1983 by The Modern Poetry Association, and are reprinted with permission of the Editor of *Poetry:* "Red Light," by Richard Barnes; "The Wild Horses of Asseateague Island," by John Bensko; "Calling My Grandmother From New York," by John Brehm; "The Other," by Becke Broughton; "Eros," by Frederick Buell; "Of Ellipses and Deviations," by Jerald Bullis; "A Picture of the Reverend's Family With the Child of One," by Thomas Carper; "Room 9639," by Florence Elon; "Plumbline," by Alice Fulton; "Simplicity," by Sandra M. Gilbert; "The Sunday News," by Dana Gioia; "Teeth," by Barbara Goldberg; "Heart," by William Greenway; "Looking Out on Africa," by Susan Hahn; "Home," by Vanessa Haley; "Between Flights," by William Heyen; "Scraping the House," by Jonathan Holden; "For My Children," by Mary Karr; "The Act of Letting Go," by Elizabeth Libby; "The Sunday Drunk," by Suzanne Matson; "Inverse Proportions," by Jack Matthews; "Territories," by Riikka Melartin; "The Way of the World," by Askold Melnyczuk; "The Initial Tree," by Michael Milburn; "Source of Lake Ochrid," by Mark O'Connor; "Taking the Shuttle with Franz," by Alicia Ostriker; "Jogging on the Beach," by Kevin Pilkington; "Oxford, On an Ancient Crossroads Beside the Thames," by Susan Prospere; "7:00 A. M. Lakefront," by Paulette Roeske; "The National Anthem," by Robin Seyfried; "The Going-Part," by Susie Shulman; "Getting Serious," by Gary Soto; "Before the Harvest," by James Ulmer.

The following poems first appeared in *The Yale Review* and are copyright © by Yale University; reprinted with permission: "Frog Hunting," by Peter Cooley; "Opossum Spring," by Mark DeFoe; "Tangier," by Stephen Dunn; "In the Album," by John N. Morris; "Blues Remembered," by Robert B. Shaw; "After a Disappointing Visit with Old Friends, I Try in Vain to Recover the Joys of Childhood," by Ira Sadoff; "Crazy Quilt," by Elizabeth Spires.

The following poems first appeared in *Yankee* Magazine: "On Commonwealth Avenue and Beacon Hill," by Diana Der Hovanessian. Reprinted with permission from the May, 1981, issue of *Yankee* Magazine, published by Yankee Publishing, Inc., Dublin, NH 03444, copyright © 1981; "Sleepless Nights," by Hildegarde Flanner. Reprinted with permission from the November, 1983, issue of *Yankee* Magazine, copyright © 1983; "Signs," by J. B. Goodenough. Reprinted with permission from the May, 1983, issue of *Yankee* Magazine, copyright © 1983; "For My Wife, Cutting My Hair," by Bruce Guernsey. Reprinted with permission from the April, 1983, issue of *Yankee* Magazine, copyright © 1983; "The Dealer," by Madeleine Hennessey. Reprinted with permission from the May, 1983, issue of *Yankee* Magazine, copyright © 1983; "The Book of Moonlight," by Gary Kerley. Reprinted with permission from the November, 1983, issue of *Yankee* Magazine, copyright © 1983; "The Thin Edge," by Joan La Bombard. Reprinted with permission from the November, 1983, issue of *Yankee* Magazine, copyright © 1983; "Iron," by Diana O'Hehir. Reprinted with permission from the July, 1983, issue of *Yankee* Magazine, copyright © 1983; "The Woman on the Island," by Ann Stanford. Reprinted with permission from the September, 1982, issue of *Yankee* Magazine, copyright © 1982; "Connecting," by Larkin Warren. Reprinted with permission from the October, 1983, issue of *Yankee* Magazine, copyright © 1983.